Pearson
BTEC National
Children's Play, Learning and Development

Student Book

Penny Tassoni
Brenda Baker
Louise Burnham
Karen Hucker

Published by Pearson Education Limited, 80 Strand, London, WC2R 0RL.

www.pearsonschoolsandfecolleges.co.uk

Copies of official specifications for all Edexcel qualifications may be found on the website: www.edexcel.com

Text © Pearson Education Limited 2016

Edited by Tracey Cowell

Page design by Andy Magee

Typeset by Tech-Set Ltd

Original illustrations © Pearson Education Ltd

Illustrated by Tech-Set Ltd

Cover design by Vince Haig

Picture research by Caitlin Swain

Cover photo/illustration © Shutterstock/Artulina

The rights of Penny Tassoni, Brenda Baker, Louise Burnham and Karen Hucker to be identified as authors of this work have been asserted by them in accordance with the Copyright, Designs and Patents Act 1988.

First published 2016

19

10 9 8 7 6 5 4

British Library Cataloguing in Publication Data

A catalogue record for this book is available from the British Library

ISBN 978 1 292 13362 1

Printed and bound in Great Britain by Bell and Bain Ltd, Glasgow

Acknowledgements

We would like to thank Gill Squire for her invaluable help in reviewing the content of this student book.

The publisher would like to thank the following for their kind permission to reproduce their photographs:

(Key: b-bottom; c-centre; l-left; r-right; t-top)

Alamy Images: Blue Jean Images 360, BSIP SA 316 /1, Bubbles Photolibrary 6, FogStock 307, INSADCO Photography 264, Jason Smalley Photography 164, Mark Richardson 131, Maskot 268, MediaWorldImages 239, Paul Doyle 42, PBWPIX 245, PhotoAlto 506, Picture Partners 416, 418, Profimedia.CZ a.s 180, RGB Ventures / SuperStock 370, Shotshop GmbH 487, SJA Photo 57, UpperCut Images 329; **BananaStock:** 79; **Corbis:** Celia Peterson. Arabian Eye. 300; **DK Images:** Howard Shooter 406; **Fotolia.com:** Daxiao Productions 398, marilook 444, micromonkey 445, Monkey Business 88, 111, 399, 490, 513, 316 /7, Philip Date 316 /6, shsphotography 18, Tomsickova 187, WavebreakMediaMicro 139, 234; **Getty Images:** acilo 85, Alija 25, Blend Images 69, Blend Images - Ariel Skelley 87, Blend Images - Jose Luis Pelaez Inc 430, Carol Yepes 1, Christopher Futcher 491, Image Source 351, 541, Itziar Aio 17r, JGI / Jamie Grill 143, KidsStock 108, Peter Hendrie 127, s0ulsurfing - Jason Swain 99, Tetra Images - Jamie Grill 381, Tim Platt 461; **Imagestate Media:** BananaStock 17l, 151; **Pearson Education Ltd:** Anna Marlow 244, Lord and Leverett 123, 357, 426, MindStudio 439, Lisa Payne Photography 385, Jules Selmes 16-a, 16-d, 16-c, 16-b, 90, 102, 152, 183, 278, 295, 503, 524, 527, 548, 316 /2, 316 /3, 316 /4, 316 /5, Studio 8 56b, 148, 168, 199, 202, 274, 359, 364, 372, 414, 452, 469, 498, Susie Williams 92, Tudor Photography 157, Ian Wedgewood 396; **Science Photo Library Ltd:** DR P. MARAZZI 347; **Shutterstock.com:** Ana Bokan 186, Faiz Zaki 554, Felix Mizioznikov 350, ISchmidt 301, kondrytskyi 56t, leungchopan 516, matka_Wariatka 261, Monkey Business Images 429, oliveromg 248, Robert Kneschke 533, Suslik1983 318, Syda Productions 105, vitmark 118; **www.imagesource.com:** 517

All other images © Pearson Education

The authors and publisher would like to thank the following individuals and organisations for permission to reproduce their materials:

p.201: Hospital Episode Statistics (HES) Copyright © 2014. Re-used with the permission of The Health and Social Care Information Centre. All rights reserved. **p.236:** Link to an article from the National Literacy Trust, Copyright © National Literacy Trust is used by kind permission of the National Literacy Trust. **p.405:** Quote from The Effective Pre-School and Primary Education 3–11 Project: Final Report from the Primary Phase: Pre-school, School and Family Influences on Children's Development during Key Stage 2, by Kathy Sylva, Edward Melhuish, Pam Sammons, Iram Siraj-Blatchford and Brenda Taggart, published in 2008 by The Department of Children, Schools and Families, is used with permission.

Websites

Pearson Education Limited is not responsible for the content of any external internet sites. It is essential for tutors to preview each website before using it in class so as to ensure that the URL is still accurate, relevant and appropriate. We suggest that tutors bookmark useful websites and consider enabling learners to access them through the school/college intranet.

Contents

iii

How to use this book

Welcome to your BTEC National Children's Play, Learning and Development course.

You are joining a course that has a 30-year track record of learner success, with the BTEC National widely recognised within the industry and in higher education as the signature vocational qualification. Over 62 per cent of large companies recruit employees with BTEC qualifications and 100,000 BTEC learners apply to UK universities every year.

Your BTEC National Children's Play, Learning and Development qualification will give you the opportunity to gain specific knowledge, understanding and skills that are relevant to your chosen subject or area of work. This new BTEC is a great foundation for you to build the skills you need for employment or further study.

Choosing to study for a BTEC National Children's Play, Learning and Development qualification is a great decision to make for lots of reasons. In recent years, there has been a growing understanding that children's earliest experiences shape their life changes and it is vital that children receive the best possible early education and care. As a future early years professional, you can play a significant part in making sure that the provision children receive is of the highest quality.

How your BTEC is structured

Your BTEC National is divided into **mandatory units** (the ones you must do) and **optional units** (the ones you can choose to do). The number of units you need to do and the units you can cover will depend on the type and size of qualification you are doing.

This book covers all the mandatory units – **units 1 to 11**. The table below shows how each unit in this book maps to the BTEC National Children's Play, Learning and Development qualifications.

Unit title	Mandatory
Unit 1 Children's Development	All sizes
Unit 2 Development of Children's Communication, Literacy and Numeracy Skills	All sizes
Unit 3 Play and Learning	All sizes
Unit 4 Enquiries into Current Research in Early Years Practice	Extended Diploma only
Unit 5 Keeping Children Safe	All sizes except Extended Certificate
Unit 6 Children's Physical Development, Care and Health Needs	Diploma and Extended Diploma only
Unit 7 Children's Personal, Social and Emotional Development	Diploma and Extended Diploma only
Unit 8 Working with Parents and Others in Early Years	Diploma and Extended Diploma only
Unit 9 Observation, Assessment and Planning	Diploma and Extended Diploma only
Unit 10 Reflective Practice	Diploma and Extended Diploma only
Unit 11 The Early Years Foundation Stage	Diploma and Extended Diploma only

Your learning experience

You may not realise it but you are always learning. Your educational and life experiences are constantly shaping you, your ideas, your thinking, and how you view and engage with the world around you.

You are the person most responsible for your own learning experience so it is really important you understand what you are learning, why you are learning it and why it is important both to your course and to your personal development.

Your learning can be seen as a journey with four phases.

Phase 1	Phase 2	Phase 3	Phase 4
You are introduced to a topic or concept and you start to develop an awareness of what learning is required.	You explore the topic or concept through different methods (e.g. research, questioning, analysis, deep thinking, critical evaluation) and form your own understanding.	You apply your knowledge and skills to a task designed to test your understanding.	You reflect on your learning, evaluate your efforts, identify gaps in your knowledge and look for ways to improve.

During each phase, you will use different learning strategies to secure the core knowledge and skills you need. This student book has been written using similar learning principles, strategies and tools. It has been designed to support your learning journey, to give you control over your own learning, and to equip you with the knowledge, understanding and tools you need to be successful in your future studies or career.

> **Important note**
> The authors of this book have followed the qualification specification to ensure that all the points you will need to know and understand have been covered. In order to enhance your learning experience, to provide greater clarity, or to further support your understanding of a topic, they have occasionally included details that are not in the specification and that will not be assessed or examined. Your tutor will advise you on what is likely to be covered in an assessment or external examination.

Features of this book

In this student book there are lots of different features. They are there to help you learn about the topics in your course in different ways and understand them from multiple perspectives. Together these features:

▶ explain what your learning is about
▶ help you to build your knowledge
▶ help you understand how to succeed in your assessment
▶ help you to reflect on and evaluate your learning
▶ help you to link your learning to the workplace.

In addition, each individual feature has a specific purpose, designed to support important learning strategies. For example, some features will:

▶ get you to question assumptions around what you are learning
▶ make you think beyond what you are reading about
▶ help you make connections across your learning and across units
▶ draw comparisons between your own learning and real-world workplace environments
▶ help you to develop some of the important skills you will need for the workplace, including team work, effective communication and problem solving.

Features that explain what your learning is about

Features that help you to build your knowledge

Step-by-step

1 This practical feature gives step-by-step descriptions of particular processes or tasks in the unit, including a photo or artwork for each step. This will help you to understand the key stages in the process and help you to carry out the process yourself.

Further reading and resources

This feature lists other resources – such as books, journals, articles or websites – you can use to expand your knowledge of the unit content. This is a good opportunity for you to take responsibility for your own learning and prepare for research tasks you may need to complete academically or professionally.

Features connected to your assessment

Your course is made up of mandatory and optional units. There are two different types of mandatory unit:

▶ externally assessed
▶ internally assessed.

The features that support you in preparing for assessment are below. But first, what is the difference between these two different types of unit?

Externally assessed units

These units will give you the opportunity to demonstrate your knowledge and understanding, or your skills, in a direct way. For these units, you will complete a task, set directly by Pearson, in controlled conditions. This could take the form of an exam or it could be another type of task. You may have the opportunity to prepare in advance, to research and make notes about a topic which can be used when completing the assessment.

Internally assessed units

Internally assessed units will involve you completing a series of assignments, set and marked by your tutor. The assignments you complete will allow you to demonstrate your learning in a number of different ways, from a written report to a presentation to a video recording and observation statements of you completing a practical task. Whatever the method, you will need to make sure you have clear evidence of what you achieved and how you did it.

Assessment practice

These features give you the opportunity to practise some of the skills you will need during the unit assessment. They do not fully reflect the actual assessment tasks but will help you to prepare for them.

Plan – Do – Review

You will also find handy advice on how to plan, complete and evaluate your work. This is designed to get you thinking about the best way to complete your work and to build your skills and experience before doing the actual assessment. These questions will prompt you to think about the way you work and why particular tasks are relevant.

Getting ready for assessment

This section will help you to prepare for external assessment. It gives practical advice on preparing for and sitting exams or a set task. It provides a series of sample answers for the types of question you will need to answer in your external assessment, including guidance on the good points of these answers and ways in which they could be improved.

Features to help you reflect on and evaluate your learning

PAUSE POINT   Pause Points appear regularly throughout the book and provide opportunities to review and reflect on your learning. The ability to reflect on your own performance is a key skill you will need to develop and use throughout your life, and will be essential whatever your future plans are.

Hint
Extend   These sections give you suggestions to help cement your knowledge and indicate other areas you can look at to expand it.

Reflect

These features allow you to reflect on how the knowledge gained in the unit may affect your behaviour in a workplace situation. This will help to place the topic in a professional context, and also help you to review your own conduct and develop your employability skills.

Features which link your learning with the workplace

Case study

Case studies throughout the book will allow you to apply the learning and knowledge from each unit to a scenario from the workplace or industry. Case studies include questions to help you consider the wider context of a topic. They show how the course content is reflected in the real world and help you to build familiarity with issues you may find in a real-world workplace.

THINK ▶FUTURE

This is a special case study where someone working in the industry talks about the job role they do and the skills they need. This comes with a *Focusing your skills* section, which gives suggestions for how you can begin to develop the employability skills and experiences you will need to be successful in a career in your chosen sector. This is an excellent opportunity to help you identify what you could do, inside and outside your BTEC National studies, to build up your employability skills.

Children's Development 1

Getting to know your unit

Child development is a large area of study with many facets. It covers the way in which children gain skills and abilities and how they learn. It also covers processes such as the development of language and thinking. As a professional working with young children, you will need a good understanding of children's development and of the different theories about children's learning and development. This is because child development underpins every aspect of working with children, from health and safety through to providing play opportunities. The knowledge you gain from this unit will support many other units within the qualification.

How you will be assessed

This unit will be assessed through a written exam. You will be given various scenarios based on children in an early years setting and asked to answer a series of questions about these scenarios. Questions will cover all the knowledge requirements of the unit and will assess your understanding of how the principles, theories and models of development apply to individual children.

Throughout this unit you will find assessment practice opportunities that will help you develop the skills and knowledge you will need for the assessment.

As the guidelines for assessment can change, you should refer to the official assessment guidance on the Pearson Qualifications website for the latest definitive guidance.

You will be assessed on your ability to achieve the following outcomes.

▶ **AO1** Demonstrate knowledge of the principles and patterns, theories and models that inform children's growth and development from birth to 7 years 11 months

▶ **AO2** Demonstrate understanding of the principles and patterns, theories and models that inform children's growth and development from birth to 7 years 11 months

▶ **AO3** Apply knowledge and understanding of children's growth and development to real-life scenarios from birth to 7 years 11 months

▶ **AO4** Analyse and evaluate information related to children's holistic growth and development in context, through demonstrating the ability to interpret theory and predict the potential impact on early years practice

Getting started

Read the following list of skills: can eat skilfully with a spoon and fork; no longer puts toys in mouth; can turn pages in a book; does not understand the need to share.
Can you work out how old each child is likely to be?

A   The principles of growth and development and how they are applied from birth up to 7 years 11 months

A1   Principles and patterns of growth and development

'Hasn't he grown?' is a comment that most adults make when they meet a child they have not seen for a while. Indeed, growth and development are closely linked. This section begins by looking at some of the issues and debates in child development. We then consider the principles and patterns of growth and development, and how they can help us to understand how a child develops and learns.

Issues when looking at growth and development

A good starting point for this first unit is to consider some of the issues that psychologists have found when looking at theories of child development.

Nature or nurture?

Is children's development tied closely to human instincts and genetics, or could it be that what happens to children shapes their learning and development? These are fundamental questions in psychology. Many of the early theories of development were influenced by the idea that we inherit skills, abilities and behaviours. Subsequent research has shown that our behaviour can also be shaped. The issue for many psychologists is to define how much of our skills and personalities is inherited and how much is influenced by our environment. Increasingly, the view being taken is that both cases apply, although we may be born with certain **predispositions**. This is sometimes called the nature versus nurture debate. Theories that come down in favour of nature can be described as **nativist**, and theories that come down in favour of environment can be thought of as **behaviourist**.

Is development continuous or does it occur in stages?

Some of the theories you will look at later in this unit are 'stage' theories, such as Erikson's stages of personality or Piaget's stages of cognitive development. These theories are based on the idea that development passes through defined and separate stages, and that each stage has recognisable features. For example, in language development children babble before they speak words, so babbling is seen as a stage in itself.

Other psychologists feel that development is more gradual and that it is a continuous process. This means that development in stages versus continuous development is another area of debate for psychologists.

> **Key terms**
>
> **Behaviourist** – behaviourist theories state that development is shaped by the environment.
>
> **Nativist** – nativist theories state that children's skills and personalities are predetermined and not affected by the environment.
>
> **Predisposition** – an increased likelihood of showing a particular skill, trait or developing a condition as a result of genetic inheritance.

Theory into practice

Many early years professionals feel that children do not jump from stage to stage, but that development is gradual. It can be hard to see sudden jumps on a day-to-day basis, although over a few weeks they can see that children's development has progressed.

What are the views of the staff in your placement? Do they think that children's progress fits into stages or do they feel that their development is continual?

You may like to ask if there are any areas of development that seem particularly stage-like.

Limitations of research

Unlike theories in some 'hard' sciences such as physics, it can be difficult to prove beyond doubt how children learn and develop. This is because there are many **variables** such as culture, parenting style, environment and genetic influences. Even research studies on identical twins do not give a consistent picture. Add to this the difficulty of communicating with babies and very young children, and it becomes clear why theories of development are constantly being revised and adapted. Having said this, such research does help practitioners to work in ways that are likely to be advantageous to children.

Key principles of growth and development

Let us now focus on the principles and patterns of growth and development. A good starting point is to define the terms **growth** and **development**.

Growth

Growth refers to an increase in physical size and is responsible for a long list of things that we may take for granted such as height and weight gain. It begins with development of muscles and structures within the brain.

There are some key principles that relate to the way that children grow.
1 **The rate of growth is variable** – growth is not smooth and continuous. In terms of height and weight, the first 2 years are marked by significant growth, after which children grow more steadily until the onset of **adolescence**.
2 **Different parts of the body can grow at different rates** – growth across the body is not simultaneous. Different parts of the body grow at different rates. This is one reason why children's body shape changes over time. In terms of **neural growth**, there are clear **spurts**. We consider physical and neural growth in more detail in Section A3.

PAUSE POINT Explain the difference between growth and development.

> Hint Think about size and skills.
> Extend What is meant by the term 'spurt', which is often used in relation to growth?

Development

There is a well-known phrase, 'don't run before you can walk'. This neatly ties up the idea that physical development and the acquisition of certain skills happen in a sequence.

Three principles of physical development have been identified.

Key terms

Adolescence – a period of time over which children's bodies develop into sexually mature adult bodies.

Development – the acquisition of skills, knowledge, or physical or mental abilities, in a set order (or sequence).

Growth – an increase in physical size, beginning with muscular control and development of coordination and balance.

Neural growth – when neuron cells increase in size and complexity.

Spurt – a short period of intense growth.

Variables – factors that may be involved in development.

1 **Development follows a definite, orderly sequence** – as you watch children growing and developing, you see a pattern emerging that certain movements have to be in place before others can follow. For example, the child has to be able to walk before he or she can skip.

2 **Development begins with the control of head movements and continues down the body** – babies gain control of their head and top of the spine before other parts of their body. This is thought to be a survival mechanism as it is important for babies to be able to turn their head to feed.

3 **Development begins with uncontrolled large (gross motor) movements before movements become precise and refined** – at first, a young baby's arm and leg movements are uncontrolled. However, some control is quickly gained – first, control of the arms and then of the wrists. By 6 months, most babies are usually able to take an offered toy reasonably easily. An adult may have had a similar learning experience if they have learned to use a computer with a mouse. Most people find that at first it is hard to keep the cursor visible on the screen, before gradually learning more refined movements that allow them to move the mouse and position the cursor more accurately.

> **Theory into practice**
>
> The principles of physical development must be applied in practice to make sure that activities you provide for children are appropriate. For example, there is little point in providing a sit-and-ride toy to a child who is not yet sitting independently, or giving a pair of scissors to a child who cannot control their hand movements.

Rates of growth and development vary between children

Two children from different families who are born at the same time are likely to be different heights and weights. This is because the rate of growth varies between individual children. The difference in growth is linked to a multitude of factors including genetics, diet, environment and illness.

As well as physical growth varying between children, the rate at which children develop skills is also variable. This again is thought to be linked to a range of factors including genetics and environment. Rates of development can also vary between children if there is a delay in one area of development. As you will see in Section A2, in order to study children's development, it is often split into five defined areas: physical, cognitive, language, emotional and social, although they are interrelated. Delay in some children's development can be caused because different areas of development impact on each other. For example, a child who is slower to talk than is typical may find it harder to play with other children as communication is a key part of social skills.

⏸ **PAUSE POINT**   What are the three principles of development in children?

| Hint | Think about babies' early movements and how development happens. |

| Extend | Explain the importance of recognising a child's stage of development when you are planning activities. |

Measuring development

To measure children's development, professionals look at the skills that children have acquired. These skills are sometimes referred to as milestones, or 'norms', and are linked to children's ages. These milestones have been determined by looking at development within large groups of children and considering what is typical or the

Link

Go to Section A3 for more information about monitoring delays in development.

▶ This child is able to pull himself up into a standing position using the chair for support

norm for each age. This means that there will always be some variation, with some children showing development that is in advance of the milestones. Significant delays in development based on these milestones are likely to be monitored and investigated.

The relationship between growth and development

Growth and development are both vital and work together in supporting children's overall development.

Growth provides the background for development

Physical growth is essential to helping children's development as it makes certain movements possible. One example is that once a child can walk they see their environment from a new height. Another example is that children's hand movements are linked to the growth of the bones in their wrists. This in turn means that new opportunities for stimulation are available to the child.

Growth supports speech

The production of sounds and words is partly linked to the arrival of teeth and the building of muscles in the tongue. The easier it is for children to be understood, the more likely they are to keep on talking.

Growth can affect social and emotional development

As children begin to grow, they often start to feel more capable. Children who are taller than other children the same age, for example, usually have higher self-esteem. The shape of a child's body can also affect how they feel about themselves.

Growth affects adults' responses

The size and shape of a child affects the way adults respond to them. For example, a tall child may be given more responsibility. Development as a result of growth also affects adults' responses. Adults may, for example, start to expect more of a child once they are able to dress themselves.

Bowel and bladder control

As well as the general ways in which we can see that growth and development are interlinked, there are some more specific ways. One example is bowel and bladder control. For children to move out of nappies, they need to understand what is happening when they wet or soil themselves. They also need the skills to move themselves to a potty and undress. These are developmental skills but growth also plays a significant part. The bladder has to be able to retain urine and expel it on demand. Interestingly, there is huge variation in when children are ready to move out of nappies.

❚❚ PAUSE POINT   Outline three ways in which growth impacts on children's development.

> **Hint**   Think about the impact of physical growth and appearance on different types of development.

> **Extend**   Consider the impact on a child who might not be growing typically.

A2 Areas of development

Children's development is often subdivided into five broad areas: physical, cognitive, language, emotional and social. Within each area, there are often further subdivisions.

Physical development

Physical development (also known as motor development) concerns the way that children learn to move and coordinate their bodies. It is often divided into three areas, as shown in Figure 1.1. Fine motor skills, large (or gross) motor skills and locomotive skills will be looked at in detail in Section B.

In addition to these areas, children need to develop coordination (including **hand–eye coordination**), balance and **visual perceptual skills**. These skills allow children to move smoothly and eventually to combine skills so that they can take part in activities such as catching a ball.

Key terms

Hand–eye coordination – the ability to use the eyes to direct the muscles towards completing a task.

Visual perceptual skills – the ability to understand and interpret what you see, for instance, being able to recognise an object when seen from different angles.

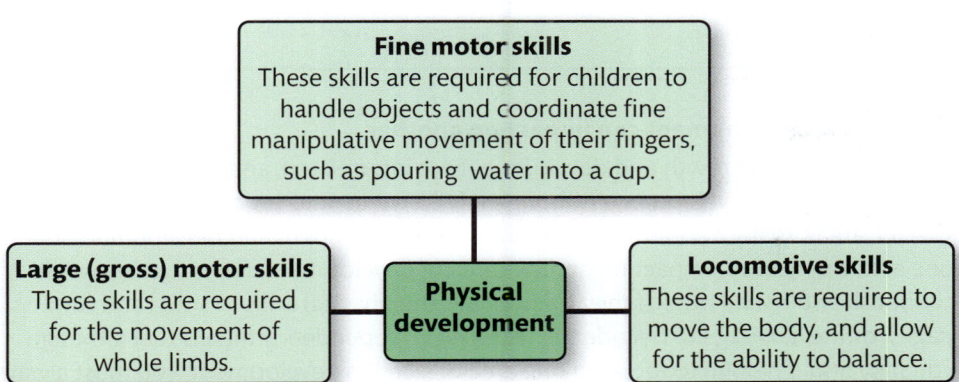

▶ **Figure 1.1:** The three areas of physical development

Cognitive development

Cognitive development is sometimes referred to as intellectual development. It relates to the way that children learn to think and to understand and process information. Cognitive development includes being able to remember and make connections between new information and previous experiences. It is also about the way children can learn to predict, reason, make sense of their experiences and solve problems.

Language development

Language development is about our ability to talk, understand what others are saying and interpret facial expressions and body gestures. It includes verbal and non-verbal forms of communication. It also encompasses the skills of literacy (reading and writing). Communication and language development are linked to cognitive and emotional development because more sophisticated communication involves thinking about what others are trying to convey as well as thinking about what you are trying to express.

Emotional development

Emotional development is about the way children develop awareness of their feelings and learn to express and control them appropriately. Emotional development is linked closely to social development and it includes the development of self-esteem, confidence and our own sense of self (known as self-concept). It also includes the development of feelings towards others. Children's behaviour is complex, but it is often linked to their emotional and social development.

Social development

Social development refers to the ability to make relationships and attachments with other people. Children need to develop their knowledge and skills in order to do this, such as being able to adapt their behaviours in line with the values of others and understanding other people's thoughts and intentions. Emotional and social development are often codependent, so you may find that they are written about together.

One area of development can impact on another

We have seen that growth and development are interrelated, and so too are the different areas of development. Although it is convenient to break them down into specific areas, many developmental skills are interdependent and development in one area can have an impact on another area of development. For instance, a child cannot sit and read a book if they do not have the physical skills to sit up and turn pages, or the language to decode the text. This codependency means that although you may find it helpful to focus on one area of a child's development, you must always remember that children are 'whole' people.

A3 Patterns of development

Measuring growth

During children's early years, and especially the first year, health professionals measure children's growth. Height, weight and head circumference are all noted.

Measurements are plotted onto a growth chart, which some professionals refer to as a centile chart. There are separate charts for boys and girls, which reflects the fact that boys are usually heavier and taller than girls. Health professionals also have to take into account a child's ethnic background, as some races are lighter or shorter than others.

> **Reflect**
>
> Did you know that children triple their birth weight by the end of their first year and usually gain 30 cm in height? By 2 years old, children may have reached half their adult height.

As you saw earlier, physical development begins with basic reflexes, progresses to control of head movement and continues down the body. While it is easy to see how babies and children are gaining control of their bodies, what is of equal interest is what is happening inside their brains.

The importance of brain development

Over the past few years, **neuroscience** has helped us understand more about children's development. Neuroscience is a relatively new area of study and, over the next few years, it is likely that much more will be learned and revisions to current thinking will be made. What is known, however, is that brain development in babies and children underpins their overall development. Brain development is also referred to as **neurological development**.

> **Key terms**
>
> **Neurological development** – the growth and development of the brain, including the formation of new neurological connections.
>
> **Neuroscience** – the study of how the brain grows and works.

Neurons

A good starting point when looking at the brain is to know a little bit about **neurons** and how they work. Neurons are the brain cells. A single neuron is of no use because what makes the brain work is the way that neurons connect together to transmit and receive electrical signals. It is these signals that operate and reflect our feelings, thoughts and actions.

Figure 1.2 shows a single neuron connecting to another. The connection is not a physical one as there is a tiny gap between the **axon terminals** and the **dendrites** of the other neuron. This gap is known as a **synapse**. Electricity seems to jump across this gap, almost like lightning. Although the diagram shows a single neuron, the reality is that there are billions of neurons and, at any given time, there will be millions of signals sent across the brain. Every new experience we have creates new connections between neurons within the brain.

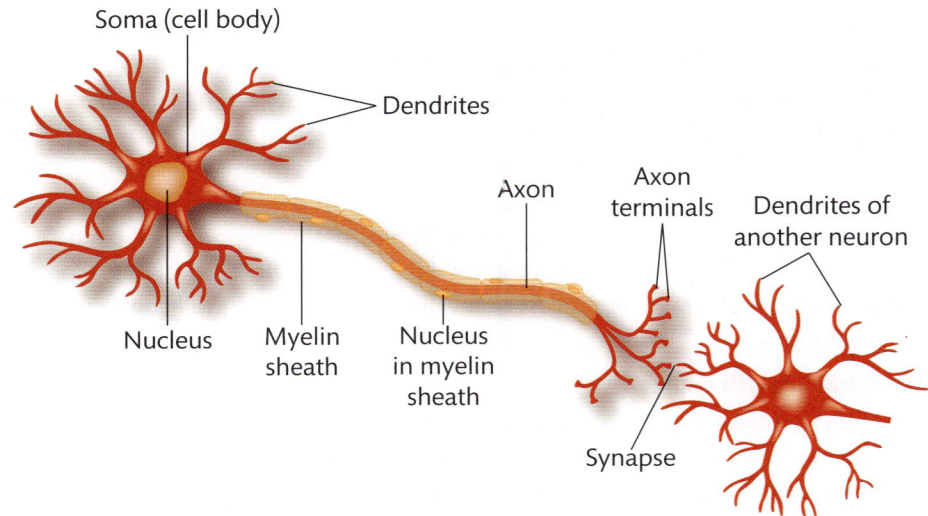

▶ **Figure 1.2:** A neuron

At any time, there are millions of neurons firing off electrical signals, so the brain has ways of making sure that these signals can travel quickly.

Neural pathways

Repeated experiences and stimulation create stronger and longer-lasting connections between different neurons. These are known as **neural pathways** and have been likened to motorways because they allow the signals to move faster through the brain. Some neural pathways seem to be present at birth, but many others are formed as a result of repeated experiences.

Myelination

To prevent electrical pulses from straying, the **axons** of the neurons need to be coated with a substance called **myelin**. This process – **myelination** – begins at birth but is not complete until early adulthood. Myelination has the effect of improving the speed of connections within the brain and so allows for smoother physical movements but also faster thinking.

Neural pruning

Many synapses or connections will not often be used or needed. A process of pruning regularly takes place in the brain to remove these unused synapses. The first round of pruning takes place when children are 18 months old. Pruning sounds disastrous, but removing unused connections allows the brain to be more efficient.

Key terms

Axon – the part of the neuron through which electricity travels.

Axon terminal – a part of the neuron involved in making a connection with another neuron.

Dendrite – a part of the neuron involved in making a connection with another neuron.

Myelin – the substance that coats the axon of a neuron.

Myelination – the process by which the myelin coating of an axon is formed.

Neural pathway – an established route for signals within the brain.

Neuron – a brain cell.

Synapse – the gap between two neurons; electrical impulses pass across this gap from the dendrite of one neuron to the axon terminal of the other neuron.

PAUSE POINT   Explain how neural pathways are formed.

Hint   What creates the connections between different neurons? What kinds of connection are created?

Extend   Why is myelination important?

Early brain development

Brain development begins well before birth. Although we are born with approximately 100 billion neurons, most of these are formed between the tenth and twentieth weeks of pregnancy. This is one reason why it is important for pregnant women to take care of themselves during pregnancy. In the final 2 months before birth, the dendrites and axons of the neurons develop and begin to make some connections.

From birth

There is a huge amount of growth and many processes taking place in a child's development from birth onwards. The brain triples in weight in the first 2 years. This is as a result of the axons and dendrites increasing in size, allowing an increasing number of synapses to be formed. Interestingly, the process of growth within the brain does not occur uniformly. Synapses that enable visual processes form earlier than synapses for language. It is not clear whether synapses follow a predetermined pattern, but the role of stimulation is definitely important. Babies' brains respond well to an environment that includes positive emotions, language and new sensations. Alongside the formation of synapses, the process of myelination begins and will continue until early adulthood.

Additional growth spurts

In addition to the growth that takes place in a child's first couple of years, neurons also grow at other times. These growth spurts are thought to account for some astounding progress in children's development. Figure 1.3 shows the effects neural growth has on children's development.

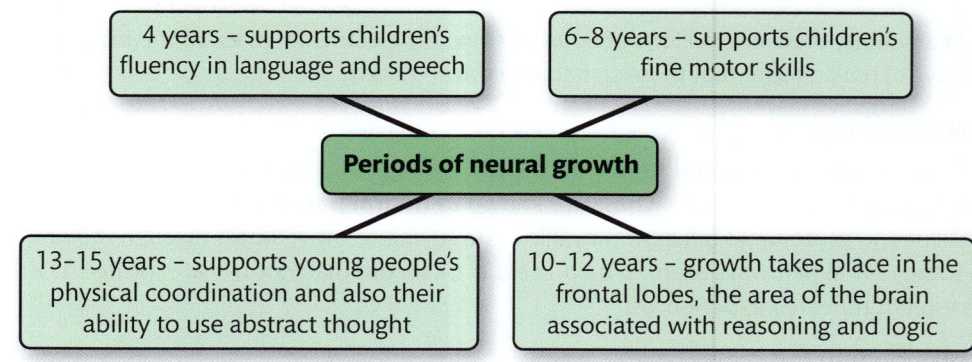

▶ **Figure 1.3:** Periods of neural growth and their effects on children's development

The effects of early experiences on children's brains

Neuroscience is in its infancy but there is some speculation that children's developing brains can be affected by stress. When babies and young children are distressed, neglected or are in stressful situations, such as being in a chaotic or unpredictable environment, a hormone called cortisol is released in large quantities. If the stress is short lived, and especially if the child is reassured, the production of cortisol is not thought to pose a problem and there is an argument that it actually helps the child to develop resilience.

On the other hand, there is some evidence that suggests babies' and young children's brain development is affected if they are exposed to long-term stress. It is believed that this exposure may affect their memory, ability to learn and level of resilience. In addition, there is also speculation that maternal stress during pregnancy may have an impact on an unborn child's developing brain.

The brain, as we have seen, is also shaped through being stimulated. Talking to children, showing them interesting things and giving them new experiences are all ways which seem to influence early brain development. This means that children who are in rich environments with caring adults and have opportunities to explore, play and, crucially, to interact are likely to have a good start.

Theory into practice

The first four years of a child's life are thought to be important in terms of brain development.

This understanding has meant that frameworks such as the Early Years Foundation Stage (EYFS) now encourage early years professionals to spend time playing with and talking to babies and toddlers to ensure that they have sufficient stimulation.

1   Make a list of the ways that babies and toddlers might be stimulated during the day.
2   Why is it important that babies and toddlers spend time outdoors and in changing environments?

How does an understanding of patterns of development help practitioners?

There are four key reasons why it is important to understand the usual patterns of development that children show at different ages.

1   **To recognise a child's stage of development** – it is always helpful to recognise a child's stage of development as we can then tailor our practice accordingly. For example, a child whose speech is still in the early stages will need us to point to things that we are talking about. Similarly, a child who is not yet able to travel up and down stairs unaided will need a helping hand. Recognising a child's stage of development also affects our practice in terms of keeping them safe. Children whose stage of development means that they are still impulsive will need more supervision than children who are more aware of risks and dangers in their environment.

2   **To support development** – another important reason why practitioners need to have a good knowledge of child development is so that babies and children can be given the support they need. This is done in several ways by tailoring activities and resources to meet the interests and stage of development of the child. For example, a child who is able to play cooperatively with other children may enjoy short structured games such as 'What's the time, Mr Wolf?' as they understand the importance of rules.

3   **To anticipate the next stages of development** – by understanding a child's stage of development and the sequences of development, we can also plan for their next steps appropriately. This is an important part of a practitioner's role with children. There are a number of ways in which we can anticipate a child's next stage of development including using activities and resources, and providing children with a range of different experiences. By anticipating the next stages of development, we can also think about how best to prepare the environment. This may include the provision of appropriate equipment.

4 **To recognise delays in development** – although children do have variable rates of growth and development, practitioners need to recognise when children are not making progress or their development is atypical. Early recognition is linked to better outcomes for children as more support can be given.

The following section looks at the definition of atypical development, the impact it can have and why it is important to recognise it in children.

⏸ **PAUSE POINT**   Give four reasons why it is important for you to have a good understanding of patterns of development.

    Hint   Think of the difficulties you would have if you did not know anything about a child's stage of development.

    Extend   Explain the importance of anticipating the next stages of children's development.

What is atypical development?

Key terms

Atypical development – where the pattern and rate of a child's development falls outside the expected range for the child's age group.

Delayed global development – where a child's rate of progress across all areas of development is lower than the expected range for their age group.

Gifted – with the potential to develop cognitive abilities significantly ahead of other children in the same age group.

Talented – demonstrating higher than average skills in a practical area, such as creative, musical or sporting achievements.

While no two children of the same age will show exactly the same rate of development, the term **atypical development** is used to refer to children whose patterns and rates of normative development are unusual and are significantly different from those expected within their age range.

Delayed global development

There are some children whose rate of progress across all areas of development is significantly lower than that associated with normative development for their age range. The term often used to describe this type of atypical development is **delayed global development**. Thus, if a child aged 4 years has the overall development profile of a 2 year old, their development may be described as being 'globally delayed'.

Specific delay

Some children may have delay across several areas, but it is more common to find that children have a specific delay within one area of development. A good example of this would be a child who cannot pronounce certain speech sounds, but who is otherwise communicating and understanding well.

Gifted

It is important not to assume that all atypical development is related to children who have a delay or specific need. Some children's development is atypical because their development, especially in relation to cognition and language, is significantly advanced and thus very different from the normative development within their age range. Over the past few years, there has been some debate about defining **gifted**, especially in view of a government initiative that encouraged schools to identify the highest ten per cent within a cohort. Many organisations that support gifted children and their families argue that this is an inflated number.

Research

Find out more about giftedness by visiting the websites for the National Association for Gifted Children (www.nagc.org), the National Association for Able Children in Education (www.nace.co.uk) and Potential Plus UK (www.potentialplusuk.org).

Talented

Some atypical development may relate to a specific skill that a child has acquired within or across an area of development. The term often used is **talented**. For example, if a 3-year-old child can play tennis, his or her development in relation to this skill could be described as talented.

The impact of delay in one area of development

A key reason in favour of early recognition of atypical development is that areas of development are interrelated (as we saw earlier). A significant delay or unrecognised need in one area of development is likely to impact on other areas of development.

The potential impact of a delay within social development

Children who have a delay within their social development may not be able to socialise and play with other children. As young children's play often requires physical movement, there can be a knock-on effect on physical development as the child may not be practising physical movements. Children whose social skills are limited may also not seek or respond to opportunities for interaction both with adults and other children and may, therefore, be excluded from play or bullied. This can have an impact on their acquisition of communication skills, their self-esteem and the development of speech and language. In addition, children who are not developing social skills and engaging in play may also find it hard to meet the behaviour expectations within settings.

Ⅱ PAUSE POINT   Explain the impact on a child's overall development if their social development is delayed.

> Hint   Think about what children are learning and doing when they are with other children.

> Extend   Consider ways in which your setting supports children to gain social skills.

The potential impact of a delay within cognitive development

Children's cognition and speech is closely linked. This means that some children who have a delay with cognition may struggle to cope with the abstract use of language and so may only understand what is said when there are visual cues and props. Cognition is also an element in learning to read and write, as print is an abstract concept. Shapes of letters correlate with sounds and so a child who has difficulty in processing in the abstract is more likely to have difficulty in understanding the link. In addition, children with cognition difficulties may not play in the same way as their peers and this can affect their social development. It can lead to feelings of low self-esteem and may impact on their behaviour if they are excluded from play.

The potential impact of a delay within language development

Being able to talk and communicate is essential for children to express their feelings and also respond appropriately to those of others. Some children with a delay in their language development may find that it has a knock-on effect on their emotional and social development, as they will experience fewer opportunities to interact and play with other children. In addition, children's behaviour can be affected by language delay as they may become frustrated by being unable to join in other children's play, or get upset as they are not being understood.

Language is closely associated with cognition as words are a tool for information processing. Children with lower levels of language development are likely to find it harder to talk about what has happened and also to use language to organise and express their thoughts.

The impact of language delay for Karl

Karl is 4 years old. His language is delayed and he communicates mainly through pointing and touching. He is learning to use **Makaton** and this is helping him to communicate his needs.

Makaton helps Karl to make sense of what is being said, although he struggles to understand the concept of time. He is very much in the 'here and now' and copes better when conversations are about what is happening and what he can see. He finds it easier to play with much younger children as they do not use so much language in their play and also do not use language to plan and talk about things that are not actually happening.

1 What is the impact of Karl's atypical language development on other areas of his development?

2 Explain why Karl may find it hard to play with children of a similar age to him.

3 Identify the importance of early identification and support for Karl's overall development.

Makaton – a language programme used to help children with specific difficulties understand the spoken word.

For more information about language and communication, refer to Unit 2.

The potential impact of a delay within emotional development

Emotional development includes the skills of being able to recognise feelings in others and create relationships with them. Children who show atypical development in this respect may miss out on opportunities to play with other children and to develop a whole range of social and physical skills as a result. Children's emotional development is also linked to their ability to manage their behaviour appropriately. This in turn may mean that other children are less likely to want to interact with them. In addition, emotional development is linked to concentration and attitudes towards learning. Children who are emotionally secure, confident and happy will find it easier to concentrate and thus learn.

The potential impact of a delay within physical development

Children who have a delay in physical development may find it hard to explore new materials and their environment. This may mean that they have fewer opportunities for interaction with adults and other children as they may not talk about what they are doing and seeing. This can impact on speech and cognitive development. In addition, most play has an element of physical movement. Depending on the type of delay, children may have restricted opportunities to join others in play and this may result in social isolation and bullying. Children may also become aware of their limitations in respect of self-care and mobility, and this in turn can impact on their behaviour, self-esteem and self-concept.

Children who show atypical advanced development in cognition and language

Genuinely gifted young children may need additional support because their advanced cognition and linguistic development makes it harder for them to form relationships with their peers. They may not be able to sustain interest in the play of their peers. As a result of increased cognition, some children are also self-aware and so are able to realise that they are in some way 'different' from other children of a similar age. This can result in a lowered self-esteem. In addition, some children may show unwanted behaviours as a result of a lack of stimulation or frustration.

The impact on children's outcomes where atypical development is not recognised

You have seen how development that is in some way atypical may have a knock-on effect in other areas of a child's development. This may result in a child not being able to access all areas of learning at the level of need. A major implication of unrecognised delay that is reported by children and their families is the effect on their self-esteem. This may be because of bullying, their recognition of being 'different' and their difficulties in making strong and equal friendships with other children. In addition, for children with communication and language and/or cognition difficulties, there is a likely impact on their literacy.

Reasons for early recognition of atypical development

In order to meet children's needs, it is important that we recognise them first of all. Children whose development is atypical are likely to need additional support or resources. In some cases, early recognition followed by professional support can lessen the impact of any delay or disability. Early recognition will also help adults and parents to respond in ways that support the child. This is particularly important where atypical development creates unwanted behaviours either through frustration or, in the case of gifted children, boredom. In addition, early recognition can sometimes lead to the diagnosis of medical conditions, which if left unchecked could further impact on a child's development.

Influence of heredity and genes

There are many factors that affect children's development. Interestingly, as well as environmental factors such as how much attention and stimulation they are given, children's development is also affected as a result of their genes. Children will inherit two sets of genes: one from each of their parents. This genetic information will determine many of the physical characteristics of a child and in some cases will be responsible for certain diseases, such as cystic fibrosis. Alongside things that we clearly inherit, research also seems to show that our complex genetic make-up will give us some predispositions that might affect all areas of our development, including personality, cognitive abilities and also illness. This is the point at which nature and nurture come together. A child who has a predisposition towards asthma may only go on to develop it when living in an area where the air quality is poor, or in damp housing. In the same way, it is thought that a child who has a predisposition towards music may only go on to develop a talent fully if given sufficient opportunity to do so.

Assessment practice 1.1   AO1 AO2 AO3 AO4

You have been asked by a children's centre to provide information for parents about typical patterns of development in young children. Your information should:

- identify the general principles of growth and development
- describe the broad areas of development and how these are interrelated
- explain neurological and brain development
- discuss the influence of heredity and genes on children's development.

Plan

- What aspects of this section do I need to revise further?
- Am I able to give examples in relation to children's development?

Do

- Can I find all the information I need?
- Are my explanations clear and have I used examples to support my work?

Review

- Am I confident that I have learned and understood the content of this section?
- Have I presented the information in a concise and accurate way?

Physical development from birth up to 7 years 11 months

Physical development plays an important role in children's overall development. When children can move, hold objects and carry things, they are able to learn more about the world and increasingly become independent. In this section we look at typical milestones for physical development and also some of the ways in which adults may support this aspect of children's development.

B1 Physical development

Normative ages and stages of children's gross and fine motor skills

In Section A, you saw that children's growth impacts hugely on their development. As children grow in height, for example, they are able to see more and this can encourage them to develop the coordination skills needed to reach out and grab objects of interest. In this section we look in detail at how children are likely to develop physically in their first 8 years.

Babies at birth

Most babies are born at around 40 weeks' **gestation**, although very few arrive on their due date! Growth and development have been ongoing since conception and by the time babies are born, they are already able to recognise their mother's voice.

It is always interesting to see just how much babies manage to achieve in the first few months of life. Newborns have many survival reflexes that can be clearly seen. First, babies instinctively breathe, cry and suckle. They also have a 'rooting' reflex that allows them to search for a nipple or teat. Other **reflexes** that newborns show will disappear over time and be replaced by conscious movements.

Well-known newborn reflexes include the Moro reflex, where the baby flings out their arms if they sense a sudden downward movement, the palmar grasp reflex, where babies cling onto fingers tightly, and the stepping reflex, where a newborn moves their legs as if walking when held vertically.

For the first few weeks, babies will develop a pattern of sleeping and feeding and, over time, they will increase the amount of time they spend awake.

> **Key terms**
>
> **Gestation** – the period of time between conception and birth.
>
> **Reflexes** – automatic movements that occur without conscious thought.

(a) 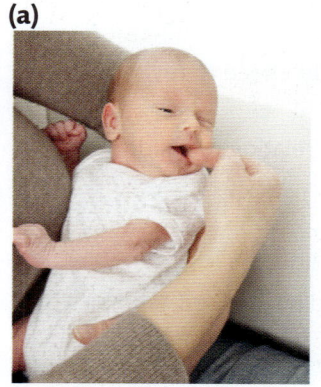 **(b)** 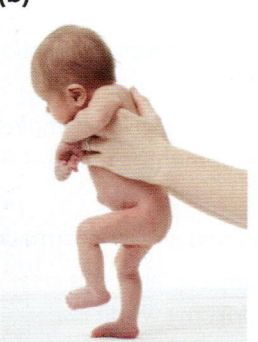 **(c)** 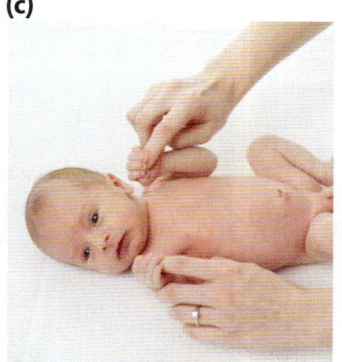 **(d)**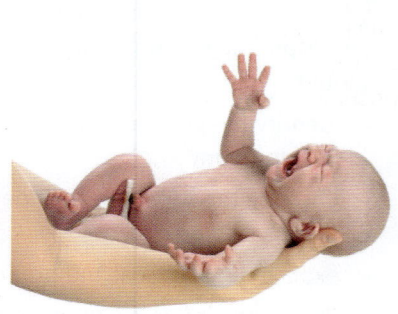

▶ The reflexes seen in a newborn baby: (a) the rooting reflex, (b) the stepping reflex, (c) the palmar grasp reflex and (d) the Moro reflex

3 months

The first few months will hail the gradual disappearance of the newborn reflexes, which will be replaced over time with controlled movements. At 3 months, babies can hold a rattle, but cannot yet control it, and they are less easily startled.

6 months

At 6 months, babies are becoming increasingly strong and may, for example, be able to roll over. In the next 3 months, they will learn to become mobile, usually by crawling, although some will bottom shuffle or develop a rolling technique. Most babies will also be close to sitting up, at first supported but, by around 9 months, without support.

This gives babies new opportunities as they can sit and use their hands to play or touch things. Over the next few weeks, babies will be weaned and will be introduced to some new tastes. Weaning is a vital step in babies' development as their bodies now need a wider range of nutrients, especially iron. Some babies are quick to accept foods from a spoon but others will be slower; patience will be required as foods may be spat out.

9 months

Many babies will now be crawling or otherwise mobile and they will be extremely active. This opens up new opportunities as they can now move towards what they can see and thus begin the journey to independence. Babies are usually also able to sit unsupported and this means that they can now see something, get to it, and sit and play with it. They are able to play independently with toys, but will particularly enjoy being played with, especially where games are repetitive. They can now hold and manipulate objects easily and will start to pick up small things with a pincer grasp.

By 9 months, babies should be weaned and may be starting to feed themselves with simple finger foods such as soft bread. Routines such as feeding time and bathing time are now recognised, although some babies will try to roll away during a nappy change.

❚❚ PAUSE POINT   State three physical skills that a 9-month-old baby has acquired.

> (Hint)   Think about gross and fine motor skills.
>
> (Extend)   Describe the key developmental differences between a baby at 3 months and a baby at 9 months.

12 months

A baby's first birthday reminds us just how many skills they have developed. Most babies will be mobile and some may now be walking. Others will be able to walk by holding onto furniture in a movement that is sometimes called 'cruising'.

At birth babies are passive but by now they are truly active and trying to be independent. They point to things they want and will try to grab at things they see. Their physical coordination means that they can now hold things and pass them between their hands, although they will still have difficulty in, for example, using a posting toy or getting a spoon into their mouths.

▶ This baby is cruising – he is holding onto the sofa for help

▶ These children are feeding themselves using their fingers

15 months

At 15 months, many babies are walking, although they may be very unsteady on their feet. They often enjoy exploring from this new position and as a result they can be very restless. They may fall down and bump into things. At 15 months, babies are starting to explore items through touch and sight, rather than **mouthing**.

> **Theory into practice**
>
> Assessing whether children are still mouthing is important. If children are still exploring using their mouth, resources have to be carefully chosen in a setting. They will need to be large enough so that they cannot be swallowed, but also interesting enough for the child to learn from mouthing. Useful resources could include those with an interesting texture or taste.

▶ This child is exploring his surroundings

Table 1.1 shows a summary of children's typical gross (large) and fine motor skills development from birth to 15 months.

▶ **Table 1.1:** Summary of children's typical physical development up to 15 months old

Age	Fine motor development	Gross (large) motor and locomotive development
0–3 months	• Reflexes including sucking, rooting, 'Moro'	
3 months	• Watches hands and plays with fingers • Clasps and unclasps hands • Can hold a rattle for a moment	• Lifts head and chest up • Waves arms and brings hands together over body
6 months	• Can reach for a toy • Can move a toy from one hand to another • Puts objects into mouth	• Moves arms to indicate that they want to be lifted • Can roll over from back to front
9 months	• Can grasp an object with index finger and thumb • Can deliberately release objects by dropping them	• Can sit unsupported • Is likely to be mobile – crawling or rolling
12 months	• Uses index finger and thumb (pincer grasp) to pick up small objects • Can point to things with the index finger	• May stand alone briefly • May walk holding onto furniture (cruising) • Some children may walk unaided
15 months	• Can make precise movements with pincer grasp to pick up crumbs or small objects • Grasps crayons with palmar grip	• May be walking with hesitation • May fall and also bump into furniture • Crawls up stairs

18 months

There is a significant shift in development at this age. Most babies have now become toddlers and are walking. Their style of walking may be unsteady, with a certain characteristic gait, but being mobile now provides them with new opportunities.

They are able to see their world from a new angle and also to see things that were previously out of sight. As well as being able to walk, toddlers learn to climb and increase control over their hands.

2 years

The physical skills of a 2-year-old child are relatively advanced, so they can climb on furniture and run. However, they will not be aware of the associated dangers. This often leads to adults stopping them doing things, which can cause frustration.

In terms of fine hand movements, they may know what they want to achieve but struggle to get their hands to manage the task. They may, for example, want to do a jigsaw puzzle, but can't quite get the pieces to fit together.

$2\frac{1}{2}$ to 3 years

At this age, hand preference is usually established and children begin to enjoy mark making on a large scale with paints and crayons.

At around this time, many children will be toilet trained, but some children will be three before they are out of nappies. This development gives children great independence and enormous confidence.

Table 1.2 shows a summary of children's typical gross (large) and fine motor skills development from 18 months to 3 years.

▶ **Table 1.2:** Summary of children's typical physical development from 18 months to 3 years

Age	Fine motor development	Gross (large) motor and locomotive development
18 months	• Can use a spoon to feed with • Can scribble • Can build a tower of three bricks • Uses palmar grasp to hold crayons and other long-handled objects	• Can walk unaided • Can walk upstairs with help (two feet to a stair) • Is restless • Can climb up onto a toy • Can squat to pick up a toy
2 years	• Can draw circles and dots • Can use a spoon effectively to feed with • Can put on straightforward items of clothing such as shoes (may be on wrong feet)	• Can run • Climbs onto furniture • Can use sit-and-ride toys
2 ½ years	• Has a hand preference • Can do simple jigsaw puzzles • Can pour sand and water into cups • Is starting to develop a tripod grasp • Can pull down items of clothing such as trousers	• Runs quickly and confidently • Can kick a large ball • May begin to use a tricycle • Walks upstairs confidently, but may still use two feet to each step • Can jump with two feet together off a low step
3 years	• Washes and dries hands with help • Holds a crayon and can draw a circle • Has established hand preference for most tasks • Tripod grasp is developing, using two fingers and thumb	• Can steer and pedal a tricycle • Can run forwards and backwards • Can throw large ball • Can walk upstairs on alternate feet • Can throw and kick with approximate aim

Unlike the younger age group, the milestones for expected development for older children become broader. This is because there can be wide differences between children on account of the many factors that affect children's development.

3 to 4 years

At 3 years old, children have again increased their physical skills. They can now pedal and steer a tricycle, and enjoy the sensation of speed and control.

4 to 5 years

Children are now able to manage many tasks that give them increasing pleasure and independence. They can, for example, eat with a knife and fork and dress themselves, and they are able to catch and throw a large ball. Their hand-eye coordination means that they can draw more representational pictures and make items such as a simple necklace by threading beads onto a string.

Ⅱ PAUSE POINT   List five physical skills that a typical 4 year old will have acquired.

Hint   Think about what you have seen 4 year olds doing on your placement.

Extend   Explain the importance of a child having opportunities to use resources, including toys, in gaining physical skills.

5 to 8 years

In previous years, development in all areas has been rapid. From this point through until puberty, development might be described as steady. The key changes that take place are the refinements of existing skills. A good example of this is using scissors. Previously, children were able to cut out shapes roughly, but in these years, children should refine this skill so they are able to cut along a line. In the same way, children show increasing coordination of the larger movements so that they can run, swerve and dodge more easily than before, such as during chasing games.

Table 1.3 shows a summary of children's typical gross (large) and fine motor skills development from 3 to 8 years.

▶ **Table 1.3:** Summary of children's typical physical development from 3 to 8 years

Age	Fine motor development	Gross (large) motor and locomotive development
3–4 years	• Buttons and unbuttons own clothing • Cuts out simple shapes • Draws a person with head, trunk and legs	• Walks along a line • Aims and throws a ball • Hops on one foot
4–5 years	• Forms letters and writes own name • Colours in pictures • Completes 20-piece jigsaw	• Skips with a rope • Runs quickly and is able to avoid obstacles • Throws a large ball to a partner and catches it
5–8 years	• Cuts out shapes accurately • Produces detailed drawings • Ties and unties shoelaces • Can colour in shapes	• Hops, skips and jumps confidently • Can balance on a beam • Chases and dodges others • Can use a bicycle and other wheeled toys such as roller skates

Factors affecting healthy growth and development

Many different factors, positive and negative, can shape children's development. These factors can contribute to children's uniqueness.

Positive and negative factors

There are many factors that can influence a child's pattern of development. It is important to note that delayed development in one or more area can impact on a child's overall development. Often, when people think about factors affecting a child's development, they focus on negatives such as abuse and poverty. Though these can certainly influence a child's development, it is also important to be aware of positive factors, such as having caring parents or good schooling.

Children are unique

Children's development often follows a similar pattern but children are in themselves unique and special. We know that all of our experiences affect the shaping of the brain but that we also seem to have some innate dispositions. A combination of positive and negative factors and experiences is, therefore, likely to provide a good explanation for why each child is unique even when following typical patterns of development. It also explains why some children in disadvantaged circumstances can still do well, as the effects of positive factors can outweigh the disadvantages of the negative factors.

Maslow's hierarchy of needs

It is often easy in a relatively affluent society to forget the importance of having our physical needs met. One theorist, Abraham Maslow (1908–1970), considered physical needs in relation to the ability of humans to achieve other things. While his theory was linked to motivation and to the business world, it is widely quoted.

Maslow suggested that until our physical needs – food and drink, shelter, sleep and warmth – were met, we would not be able to fulfil our personal potential. Maslow's model also looked at other human needs, which he divided into different levels. His model is often represented as a pyramid in which the needs are put into a hierarchy, starting with physical needs at the bottom and then moving up the pyramid, as follows:

▶ safety and security needs – feeling physically secure, protected and out of danger

▶ social needs – friendship, love and affection

▶ self-esteem – the opportunity to be independent, gain approval and to achieve.

Once these needs have been met, then growth and fulfilment can begin to take place. Maslow divided this next self-actualisation level further into:

▶ cognitive – exploring, thinking and being stimulated

▶ aesthetic – enjoying beauty, creating patterns.

When these growth needs have been fulfilled, Maslow argued that we are able to realise our potential.

> **Link**
>
> For more information about Maslow's hierarchy of needs, see Section A1 of Unit 6.

Case study

The importance of meeting a child's physical needs

Emily is 3 years old. Her welfare is currently being monitored by social services as her mother has depression in addition to being a substance user. Emily's mother finds it hard to organise mealtimes or even to remember to top up the electric meter. Emily is often cold and hungry. In addition, Emily's mother does not always show her love and affection and sometimes she can become very angry. Emily does not always feel secure.

Emily attends a nursery five times a week but staff have noticed that she does not play or take up the opportunities in the same way as other children of her age. She often takes food and hides it in her clothing.

1   Give three reasons why Emily's needs are not being met.

2   Using Maslow's hierarchy of needs, analyse how Emily's home life might be affecting her potential development.

3   Evaluate the importance of the nursery meeting Emily's physical needs as a priority.

The link between Maslow's hierarchy of needs and children's development

We have seen that Maslow identified a hierarchy of needs. While his theory was not designed to be linked specifically to child development, we can see how the needs that he identified might impact on children's growth and development.

Love, affection and friendships

While love and affection are not at the bottom of Maslow's pyramid, they are needs that Maslow identified. Feeling emotionally secure, having friends and a sense of belonging is essential for young children's development. You saw in Section A that early stress can have an impact on children's brains.

Diet and nutrition

Food and water is one of the basic needs that Maslow identified. A healthy diet is important during childhood. A diet lacking in sufficient nutrients is likely to affect children's growth and development. A good example of this is where children are lacking in iron and become anaemic. Anaemia can cause children to become listless and lacking in energy. We look in detail at the nutrients children need in Unit 6. Children who are overweight (note that it is possible to be both overweight and malnourished) are more likely to have atypical physical development. Their emotional and social development might also be affected in later childhood.

Rest and exercise

Rest and exercise are also basic physiological needs. Lack of sleep can create significant problems in children's development. It is thought that most children under 5 years old should be sleeping between 10 and 12 hours per night, with babies sleeping significantly more. Figure 1.4 shows how ongoing insufficient sleep may affect a child.

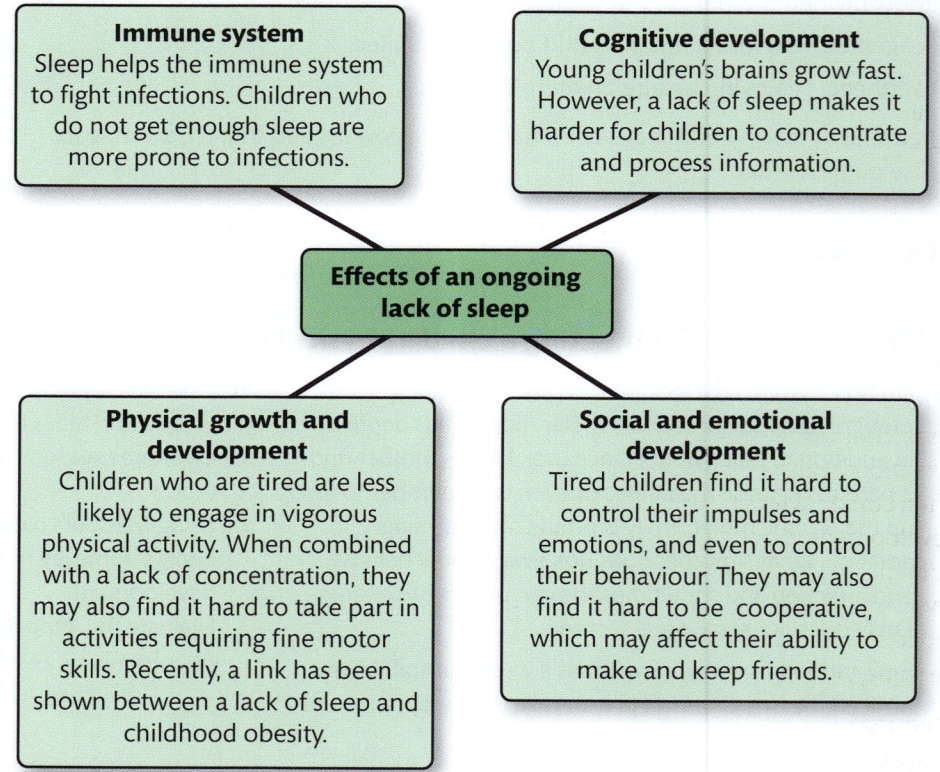

▶ **Figure 1.4:** The effects of insufficient sleep on children

Children also need to exercise. We have seen that in order to develop, children need to use their muscles. Physical activity, for example, running around, riding a tricycle or playing on a climbing frame provides a range of benefits for children, including strengthening their heart and lungs, increasing their energy levels and improving their sense of emotional well-being.

Security and protection

Feeling physically safe is another important need identified by Maslow. In terms of children's growth and development it is important, as children who are experiencing fear are likely to become stressed. We have already seen that high levels of stress have an impact on children's neural growth.

Stimulation and interaction

We know that stimulation and interaction are important, as it is through these that children can develop language and cognition skills. In terms of Maslow's hierarchy of needs, they are part of the human need to explore and have opportunities to think.

Independence

Children need to develop opportunities to do things for themselves. This helps them develop a sense of self-efficacy, which in turn leads to self-esteem. We look at this in more detail in Section D. The importance of having opportunities to develop self-esteem is one of the higher needs recognised by Maslow.

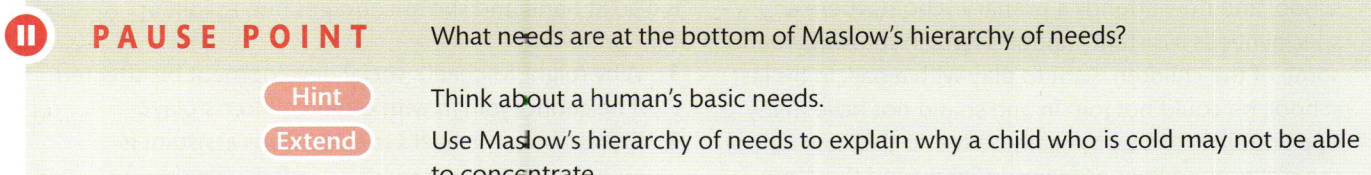

❚❚ PAUSE POINT   What needs are at the bottom of Maslow's hierarchy of needs?

Hint   Think about a human's basic needs.

Extend   Use Maslow's hierarchy of needs to explain why a child who is cold may not be able to concentrate.

Biological and environmental factors

A range of biological and environmental factors can affect children's physical development.

Nature versus nurture

We started to look at nature versus nature in Section A1. One of the interesting features of physical development, indeed many aspects of child development, is the link between both nature and nurture in shaping development. When the subject of how children developed was first studied by biologists, theorists and philosophers, there was significant debate about whether children's development was a product of nurture (their upbringing) or nature (genetics and human instincts). Today, most researchers agree that there is interplay between individual genetic dispositions, evolutionary instincts and where and how a child is raised. Thus, nature and nurture often come together to support positively (or in some cases, negatively) a child's development. A good example of this is the way that children who may be genetically primed to be tall (nature) may not reach a good height if they are significantly undernourished (nurture). In some ways scientists are still trying to work out which aspects of development are more influenced by nature as opposed to nurture. It will be some time before we can be sure.

Medical factors

Some long-term medical conditions have the potential to affect children's overall development, including their physical development. There are several reasons for this.

▸ Some illnesses (or the drugs that a child takes to treat an illness) may reduce the child's energy level and so affect their capacity to exercise and develop their coordination and muscles.

▸ Some long-term medical conditions require time away from nursery or school settings. This can affect the child's learning as they may not have the opportunities to use a range of equipment that would promote physical development.

▶ As with disability, a medical condition that affects a specific developmental area might impact on other areas if practitioners are not sensitive. For example, a child with asthma might not be able to run around and so will miss out on playing with other children.

Disability

In Section A2, you saw that each area of development is codependent on others – for example, a 6-year-old child who is playing skittles is using both cognitive and physical skills. This codependency can mean that a child who has specific difficulties may be disadvantaged in other areas of development. Disadvantage is not inevitable if the child is properly supported, as the case study shows.

Case study

Joining-in activities

Michael was born without sight. He has just changed school and now attends a primary school where a special needs assistant supports him. In the playground some of the children want to play with a ball. In his last school, he could not join in and so did not have many opportunities to be physically active. In this new school, the playground lines are raised slightly and there are balls that have bells in them. His special needs assistant is also at hand and she encourages him to join in.

1 Why might Michael's social development be affected if he cannot join in with other children's play?
2 Explain how Michael's special needs assistant is making a difference to his overall development.

Genetic disorders

Some children's physical development can be linked to faulty genes that have been inherited. These can result in medical conditions, an example of which is sickle-cell anaemia. Sickle-cell anaemia is a blood condition and causes, among other things, a lack of energy. This can mean that children cannot engage in as much physical activity as their peers, which can impact on development. Genetic disorders can sometimes cause disability. When working with children with genetic disorders, it is always important to find out more about their needs.

Prenatal factors

A number of factors can influence a child's development before they are born.

Preconceptual care

Parents' health before a baby's conception is now recognised as playing a part in a child's later development. Smoking, drugs and alcohol can all affect the eventual health of a baby.

Lifestyle choices during pregnancy

It is well known that expectant mothers should take care during pregnancy. This is because the baby's overall health and later development can be affected by the following factors.

▶ **Poor diet** – ideally, expectant mothers should eat a balanced diet throughout the pregnancy. In the first 12 weeks, it is important for mothers to take folic acid supplements and eat plenty of green vegetables. This can help to prevent a baby being born with spina bifida.

▶ **Smoking** – when a pregnant woman smokes, the amount of oxygen available to the unborn baby is reduced. This seems to have significant and possibly long-term effects on the health of children. As with many areas of child development, research is still ongoing, but a clear link between cot death (sudden infant death syndrome) and smoking while pregnant has been established. Babies are also likely to be born preterm and lighter in weight.

▸ **Alcohol** – over the past few years, women have been advised not to drink while pregnant, especially in the first 3 months of pregnancy. This is because alcohol can cause a condition known as fetal alcohol syndrome. Babies born with this syndrome are likely to develop learning and behavioural difficulties. Alcohol interferes with the development of healthy brain cells and so affects brain functioning.

▸ **Drugs** – if you read the packaging of most prescribed and over-the-counter drugs, there will be a warning for pregnant women. This is because the chemicals in drugs can interfere with the healthy development of an unborn baby.

▸ **Stress** – there is ongoing research looking at the effects of stress on pregnant women and on their children's later development. There is some speculation that high levels of stress during pregnancy may have an impact on children's cognitive and motor development.

▸ **Infection** – some infections, such as rubella (German measles), chickenpox and influenza can affect an unborn baby's development and, in some cases, cause a miscarriage.

Antenatal checks

Women who are pregnant are advised to attend antenatal checks. As part of an antenatal visit, the baby's development and the mother's health will be checked. This is important because pregnancy can cause problems for women's health, including diabetes and high blood pressure. Antenatal visits are also opportunities for women to gain information, support and advice.

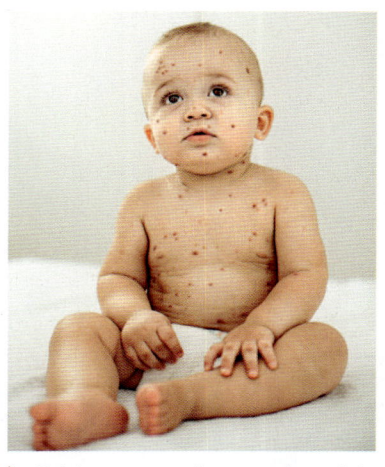

▸ Chickenpox can be more harmful to unborn babies than to young children

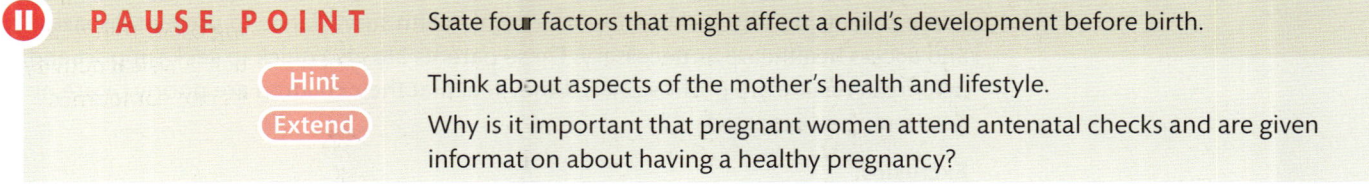

❚❚ PAUSE POINT   State four factors that might affect a child's development before birth.

        Hint   Think about aspects of the mother's health and lifestyle.

       Extend   Why is it important that pregnant women attend antenatal checks and are given information about having a healthy pregnancy?

Birth

Children's development can be influenced by what happens during birth. Birth itself can be tricky for a few babies. A baby may not breathe straight away or may be injured during the birth. Lack of oxygen (hypoxia) or oxygen starvation (anoxia) can affect brain function and may result in learning difficulties.

Premature or preterm births

Most pregnancies last around 40 weeks, but a few babies are born too early and this can play a part in their later development. A baby that is born before 37 weeks is usually considered to be preterm or premature. Today, with medical advances, babies born at 25 weeks are often able to survive, but early births can cause many complications, as the breathing and other systems within the body are not sufficiently mature. This is one reason for the higher incidence of hearing, sight and learning difficulties in babies born before the final 12 weeks of a pregnancy.

When babies are born preterm, their progress is usually measured according to the date they were due rather than their actual birth date. It can take some babies born preterm several years to reach their 'birth' age norms.

Illness, accidents and injuries

While children may miss out on play and learning if they have a long-term medical condition, the same can be true of some short-term illnesses or injuries. This is particularly true if children have repeated episodes of illness. This may result in several absences, with the same effects that you saw previously. In addition, medical conditions such as conductive hearing loss or glue ear can cause problems for children.

Conductive hearing loss

Conductive hearing loss, sometimes known as glue ear, is a common childhood condition, but its effect on development can be significant. Children with conductive hearing loss have a build-up of fluid in their Eustachian tubes. This results in fluctuating and partial hearing loss, with children's hearing being better at some times than at others. This type of hearing loss affects children's speech, social development and also their ability to learn.

> **Research**
>
> Find out about the signs of hearing loss due to glue ear by visiting the NHS website: **www.nhs.uk/Conditions/glue-ear/Pages/symptoms.aspx**

Lifestyles

Families have different lifestyles. Some parents are more affluent than others; they may have a range of contacts that will be helpful for children and they may be better informed about how to promote children's development. This means that some children grow up in well-heated and safe homes with parents who have sufficient income to meet their basic needs.

Some parents understand the importance of health surveillance to prevent diseases and access healthcare as necessary. These parents are also quick to seek support and help from healthcare professionals if they feel that their children are poorly or are not developing as expected.

Exclusion

Although in the UK there is universal access to a healthcare system and to education services, some families are not able to take advantage of this support. This exclusion may occur because they are not receiving information about health care and education opportunities for a variety of reasons. Exclusion and poverty are often linked. Families may not have access to the internet or be able to afford transport costs to go to a clinic or to a drop-in play session. In some cases, exclusion may also be caused through language and literacy barriers. A parent who does not read very well may not see that there is a poster or leaflet about free swimming sessions in the local pool. Similarly, parents who do not speak English may find it hard to learn about what local services are available. Exclusion can also occur where families do not feel that services or opportunities are 'for them'. They may fear being different from other families or that professionals will judge them. Exclusion can result in children not having the same opportunities as other children. This can impact on their physical as well as overall development.

Poverty

Poverty affects children and their families in a variety of ways. Poverty in the UK is categorised as relative rather than absolute – children are not starving, but the effects of growing up in poverty are still very marked in terms of many children's life chances.

This plays out in many respects, including children's health outcomes. Health statistics indicate that there is a higher incidence of **infant mortality** as well as a higher rate of **morbidity**. This is the incidence of ill health. In addition, a child growing up in poverty is likely to have a lower life expectancy.

Children growing up in poverty are also statistically less likely to perform well in terms of educational attainment and so may leave school with few qualifications. This in turn can affect their prospects of finding work. Figure 1.5 shows how poverty can affect children's development.

> **Key terms**
>
> **Infant mortality** – the rate of death in the first year of life.
>
> **Morbidity** – the rate of incidence of ill health within a population.

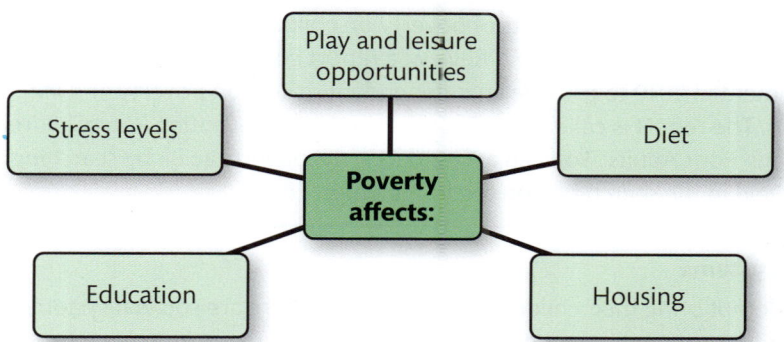

▶ **Figure 1.5:** How poverty can affect children's development

Diet

Families on low incomes may buy cheaper foods, and often foods that are manufactured, which have lower nutritional value. This may be a contributing factor in terms of later life expectancy and also in the rate of morbidity, as poor nutrition is linked to a weaker immune system. Poor nutrition can also mean that children lack energy.

Housing

Families on lower incomes may live in poorer quality housing and may not have sufficient money to heat their homes adequately. Damp, crowded housing is more likely to affect children's health and also limits their opportunities to play freely. Poor housing is thought to be a factor in the higher incidence of morbidity.

Stress

Parents managing on low budgets are more likely to show signs of depression and develop stress-related illnesses. This in turn can affect how much energy they have to parent effectively.

Education

Children from low-income households are less likely to do well academically because they may not attend the best schools or have the same access to educational tools and resources such as books or the internet. This is considered to be a factor in lower levels of academic attainment and qualifications.

Play and leisure opportunities

Stimulation is important for children's cognitive development and other areas of their development. Play is one of the ways in which this takes place, but as children become older it also occurs through leisure activities such as swimming, playing an instrument or joining clubs. Low-income families may not have transport or the financial resources to allow their children to access play and leisure opportunities. Lack of opportunities for stimulation is also thought to be a factor in lower attainment in schools.

Explain three ways in which a child living in poverty may be disadvantaged in their development.

Think about the resources and opportunities that 'lucky' children may have.

Why is it important that early years settings understand the impact on children who are living in poverty?

> **Research**
>
> Find out more about the effects of poverty on children's well-being. A good starting point is to read the Field Review, a report commissioned by the government in 2010 to provide an independent review on poverty and life chances. The report is called 'The Foundation Years: Preventing Poor Children Becoming Poor Adults'. You can access it at www.poverty.ac.uk by searching for Frank Field in the search box on the home page.

Societal systems

Families do not bring their children up in isolation. There are societal systems in place that can impact on children's development. These systems include family and friends, teachers and educational opportunities, as well as the wider society.

Wider family and friends

Children's interactions with others beyond their immediate family can influence development. This can be both positive and negative. For instance, if family and friends of children living in poverty have high expectations and, using their contacts, provide children with opportunities for learning and stimulation, some of the effects of poverty may well be counterbalanced. If, on the other hand, there is little support for the child, there is a likelihood that the effects of poverty may be compounded.

Carers and teachers/tutors

Carers and teachers/tutors can have a significant impact on children's self-belief, both positively and negatively. If carers, including early years professionals and teachers/tutors, have low expectations of children, they are less likely to provide them with stimulation and opportunities to learn. On the other hand, carers, practitioners and teachers/tutors who have high expectations of children, regardless of their family background, are more likely to support children's achievement.

'Pygmalion in the classroom'

The effects of raising expectations were studied by researchers Robert Rosenthal and Lenore Jacobson in the 1960s in an experiment that was later dubbed 'Pygmalion in the classroom'. The researchers randomly picked some children's names from a class register at the start of the academic year, but told the class teacher that these children had been identified as having potential and this would show itself during the year. At the end of the school year, those children whose names had been given to the teacher had indeed made significant improvements.

Wider society

Societies that are materialistic and in which the differences between rich and poor are significant may reinforce the negative effects of poverty. Where this is the case, there are likely to be negative and even prejudiced attitudes towards those who are not wealthy. This in turn can affect services for families as well as individuals' sense of self-worth. On the other hand, in societies that provide more equal opportunities and where there is more social mobility, a child living in relative poverty is less likely to be disadvantaged.

How the family experience of education can affect the child's development

There is some statistical evidence that the level of parental education can have a determining effect on children's educational attainment. This was reaffirmed by the Effective Provision of Pre-School Education (EPPE) project. The EPPE project, which began in 1997 and tracked a group of children from the age of 3 years, suggests that the level of education of a child's mother influences academic outcomes. This is interesting and research is ongoing to explain why this should have such an effect. There is some thinking that a more educated mother may interact more with her child and may also engage in activities such as reading.

On the other hand, it may be that if parental levels of qualification are high, this gives them access to higher-paid employment. This in turn may allow for better housing and choice of schools. Interestingly, there is a link yet again to poverty and social mobility, as education is claimed by some researchers to be the key to improving outcomes for children.

In addition, a family's experience of education and its benefits may also affect the parents' attitudes and interest in their own child's education. Parents who have had positive experiences of education and correlate this with their employment prospects are more likely to value it and thus become involved. On the other hand, parents whose own experience of education has not been positive, and where they feel that they have not derived any direct benefit, are less likely to be actively involved in their child's education, and this can lead to underachievement.

Social class

Defining 'social class' is increasingly difficult. It is related to levels of education, employment status and also levels of income. As you have seen, children from more affluent backgrounds or those whose own parents have higher levels of education are statistically more likely to have positive outcomes in terms of child development.

B2 Promoting children's physical development

There are many ways of promoting children's physical development. In Unit 3 and Unit 6 we consider a range of activities and play opportunities that adults can use to promote physical development.

Promoting physical development through exercise and play activities

There are a number of ways in which you can support children's physical development through exercise and play activities. Ideally, children need a wide range of activities in order to exercise muscles and develop skills. Most of the activities that provide exercise will be gained by children playing outdoors as well as indoors. It is very rare in early years settings that exercise is planned for its own sake, as children are naturally able to exercise while engaged in play.

There are many play activities that can support physical development at all ages. These include baby gym, treasure basket and heuristic play for babies and toddlers, through to climbing and balancing on obstacle courses for older children. You will look in detail at how play can support physical development in Units 3 and 6.

Early years settings also provide opportunities for children to engage in activities such as dance and movement. Adults may put on music for children to move to, or may organise activities involving movement and music such as musical statues. Such activities are usually planned for children who are over 3 years old, but younger children may join in musical games and rhymes such as 'Ring A Ring O'Roses'. Planning activities that encourage movement supports children's physical development as well as other skills including language and social development.

> **Link**
>
> For more information about the EPPE project, see Section A1 of Unit 8.

> **Link**
>
> Look at Unit 3 to find more information about treasure basket play and heuristic play.
>
> Refer to Unit 6 (particularly Section A2) for more information about supporting physical development in babies and toddlers.

Encouraging children to explore and experiment

Most children are naturally curious and interested in learning new skills and trying out new resources. Most early years settings provide a range of wide opportunities including tools such as malleable materials, paint, but also scissors, hole punchers and glue sticks so that children can explore and make things. Such opportunities encourage children's fine motor development, but also imagination and creativity.

It is common for most early years settings to have an 'arts and craft' area. This might be a place where children can collage, paint or do junk modelling. The term 'arts and craft' is not always used and you might find that your setting talks about a 'creative play area'. In some early years settings children are also encouraged to use tools, such as hammers and screwdrivers, and to become engaged in small projects. This is normally led and supervised by an adult who will help children learn to use tools.

Supporting children's creativity and imagination through physical activity

A range of physical movements can be practised when adults provide opportunities to support children's creativity and imagination. A good example of this is the way that often when playing outdoors, children over 2 years will start to use resources to pretend to be doing something, for example, pushing a pram or chasing 'baddies'. This is one reason why physical activity and play go hand in hand. In addition, many early years settings find that during role play, children are using their imagination as well as physical activity. Common role play opportunities that are great at supporting creativity and imagination through physical activity include: 'At the car wash', 'Bear hunt' or 'Train stations'.

Children's creativity and imagination can also be supported during physical activity when they are encouraged to create an obstacle course or build dens.

Finally, children's creativity and imagination can be supported when children are engaged in activities that require small hand movements. 'Arts and craft' (or the equivalent term used in early years settings) is a good example of how physical activity links to creativity and imagination as children explore media and materials.

Assessment practice 1.2   AO1   AO2   AO3   AO4

A nursery owner is keen to focus on children's physical development. She has asked you to prepare information that will help staff understand this area of development in more depth. Your information should:

- identify typical stages and patterns of development from birth to 7 years 11 months
- explain how adults can support children's physical development
- discuss the relevance of Maslow's hierarchy of needs
- evaluate the factors that can influence physical development.

Plan
- What aspects of physical development require further revision or research?
- Do I fully understand all of the information within this section?

Do
- Have I read the relevant parts of Units 3 and 6 to find out more about ways of promoting physical development?
- Have I used relevant examples to support my work?

Review
- What areas do I still need to revise?
- Do I need to practise writing under exam conditions again?

 C Cognition, language and communication development

C1 Theoretical approaches

Normative ages and stages of children's cognitive, language and communication development

When adults are working with children, it is important that they understand what is typical in terms of children's cognitive, language and communication development. This helps them to ensure that they are working effectively and can pick up on any child with atypical development. As with all areas of development, there are variances between individual children and so the milestones given over the next few pages can only be used as a guide. For additional information about language development, you may like to read parts of Unit 2.

Birth to 3 months

At around 3 months, babies' temperaments are beginning to show. Some babies will be easy-going and smiley, others will require more careful treatment as they may find it hard to settle or relax. Babies will show that they enjoy being with others by smiling, making eye contact and even protesting if they are not being given enough attention!

6 months

By the age of 6 months, the amount of crying should have decreased, with babies now using their voices to attract attention. They are likely to laugh, coo and also make some early babbling sounds and show that they enjoy being with adults.

9 months

From 9 months, babies will start to look for an object if it is hidden in front of them. This concept is known as **object permanence**. Before this age, babies appear to accept something being taken out of their sight. The development of object permanence means that babies begin to enjoy games such as peek-a-boo.

Babies at this stage will also be trying to communicate and over the next few weeks they will start to point to things to draw adults' attention. They now understand a few words and will enjoy looking at books.

12 months

Over the next couple of months, the baby's main carers should notice that, among the tuneful babbling, some words appear. First words are easily produced sounds, such as 'baba' or 'dada', and they will refer to a person or important object.

> **Key term**
>
> **Object permanence** – recognition that when objects are out of sight, they have not disappeared.

> **Link**
>
> Later in this section, the concept of object permanence is explained in more detail (the theories of Jean Piaget).

 PAUSE POINT   Identify the language and communication milestones in the first year of a child's life.

> **Hint**   Babies are learning about language rather than saying any words.
>
> **Extend**   Consider the effect of developing communication and language on a baby's social and emotional development.

15 months

At 15 months, strong communication skills are in place, with most babies knowing how to draw an adult's attention by either pointing or making loud noises. Many children at this age will also be starting to use just a few words. Even though they cannot say much, they will understand quite a lot of what is being said. Children are also remembering routines and where things belong, although they can be easily distracted.

18 months

At 18 months most toddlers are using around 15 words or more and are able to understand many more. They are also able to communicate their needs through facial expressions, pointing and using single words. Toddlers are able, with support, to post simple shapes and use toys such as pop-up toys.

2 years

Life can be very frustrating for 2-year-old children as they are at a crossroads in their development. This often shows in temper tantrums. The source of their anger and frustration is often that they can see what they want, understand what is said, but have not yet developed the skills required to express their needs. Language is a key factor in resolving this and fortunately, over the next year, children's language continues to develop. At the beginning of this year, toddlers will have many words. By the end of it, they should be able to put together a simple sentence and use it to express their feelings and desires.

$2\frac{1}{2}$ to 3 years

At $2\frac{1}{2}$ years, children are still pushing for independence. They are extremely active and restless and may want frequent changes of activities. Tantrums may still be a feature for some children, but if language is developing well and adults are thoughtful, these will decrease during the next few months.

3 to 4 years

At 3 years old, children can express themselves fairly well. They can use questions and have a large vocabulary, although they are not yet fluent. They usually enjoy songs and rhymes and may well sing to themselves. Most of what a 3-year-old child says should be intelligible to someone who does not know the child.

4 to 5 years

Most 4-year-old children are able to use language well and fairly grammatically, although there will be some speech immaturity and mispronunciations.

By the age of 4 they have also usually developed what is known as **theory of mind** – the ability to work out what other people might be thinking in a given situation. At around 4 years old, most children are able to recognise that other people may not have the same thoughts or knowledge as them and that this in turn might influence their behaviour. A good example of this is the way that a 4-year-old child may offer a banana to an adult even though the child does not like bananas. He does this because he knows that the adult does like bananas.

> **Key term**
>
> **Theory of mind** – children recognising their own conscious mind and understanding that other people will have different thoughts to them.

5 to 8 years

Most children will be established in school and, as part of their schooling, will be developing their literacy skills including reading and writing. This is a long process and most children will need to put considerable effort into decoding simple words. As well as learning to read and write, children will also be exposed to new concepts such as learning about numbers.

Table 1.4 shows a summary of children's typical language development from birth to 8 years.

▶ **Table 1.4:** Summary of children's typical cognitive and language development up to 8 years

Age	Cognitive and language development
0–3 months	• At 1 month, turns head and may stop crying on hearing an adult and a familiar voice • Begins to coo at 6 weeks
3 months	• Recognises familiar routines such as bath time • Enjoys playing in water
6 months	• Blends vowels and consonants together to make babbling sounds, e.g. 'ba', 'ma', 'da'
9 months	• Begins to string syllables together to create tuneful babbling, e.g. 'dadada' • Understands some simple words such as 'no' and 'bye bye'
12 months	• First words begin to appear alongside tuneful babbling • Understands simple instructions such as 'where's your hat?' • Knows own name
15 months	• Communicates by pointing and vocalising • May have four to six words • Understands and responds to simple instructions
18 months	• Is keen to explore and is very curious • Has around 15 words • Communicates wishes and understands simple requests • No longer mouths to explore objects and toys • Remembers where things belong
2 years	• May have 50 words • Is likely to be combining words, e.g. 'dada gone' • Is extremely curious • Remembers where things belong and can remember past experiences • Enjoys looking at books • Recognises self in mirror
$2\frac{1}{2}$ years	• Has 200 words or so • Is making simple sentences • Enjoys asking questions • Is using personal pronouns such as 'I' instead of name • Enjoys looking at books and may have favourites
3 years	• Speech is clear enough for someone unfamiliar with the child to understand • Uses simple sentences • Asks many questions and may use questions as a way of getting attention • Enjoys books and turns pages • Understands difference between past and present
3–4 years	• Recognises and names a few colours • Knows names of numbers and can count aloud up to ten • Talks in sentences and by 4 years old is fluent although there are some speech immaturities in certain sounds such as 'th'
4–5 years	• Can count objects accurately up to ten • Can make simple patterns • Sentences are well constructed but some speech immaturities remain • Speech is used to argue with others
5–8 years	• Is able to understand and enjoy jokes and riddles • Can use language to reason and explain ideas • Is able to do simple calculations although may need to use fingers or counters • By 7 years old, has mastered early reading and writing skills

Table 1.7, later in this section, has more detail about children's language development.

The impact of cognitive, language and communication development on children's overall growth and development

As children develop language and, alongside this, cognitive skills, they are increasingly able to participate with others around them. Language and communication skills enable them to express their feelings and needs. This supports their social development as they can increasingly play with other children, but also understand the adults around them. Being inquisitive and also remembering previous experiences is motivating for children's physical development as they often want to reach, walk or climb to get at an object or toy that they have seen before. We know that as children learn from and increasingly explore opportunities, their brain grows and shapes in response.

Case study

Jodie's overall development

Read the following details about 4-year-old Jodie.

Jodie enjoys playing with other children. Her favourite activity is playing in the home corner. She washes her hands and face, but she is in nappies. She talks in full sentences and loves listening to stories. She enjoys simple jigsaw puzzles with six or so pieces. Jodie insists that her mother stays at playgroup with her and cries when she leaves.

1 Write down the parts of Jodie's development that are typical for her age group.
2 Explain the parts of Jodie's development that are atypical for her age group.

Key terms

Constructivist approach – a model to explain children's cognitive development, which considers that children develop their own ideas based on experiences and interactions.

Social constructivist – a model that explains children's cognitive development by suggesting that their logic and reasoning is developed through experiences, but also by interactions with, and questions from, adults and older children.

Link

Later in this section we discuss Piaget's theory of cognitive development, another **constructivist approach** to learning theory.

Theories that consider the development of cognition and language

For years, parents/carers and teachers/tutors have been fascinated by the questions that children ask and the peculiar comments they make. Most people who have worked with children of different ages can clearly see that the way in which children think and understand changes as time goes by. There are several models that try to explain how children's logic and reasoning is developed. Later on in this section, we will also consider theories that attempt to explain the development of language.

Lev Vygotsky

Lev Vygotsky (1896–1934) was a Russian psychologist who developed a theory of learning. His theory is described as a **social constructivist** model as it focuses on the role that adults and other children play in a child's learning. Vygotsky focused on how children might learn when others engaged and extended their thinking.

Vygotsky's work was not published in English until the early 1960s, although it was known in Russia in the 1920s and 1930s. He believed that children's social environment and experiences are very important. He considered that children were born to be sociable and that they acquired skills and concepts by being with their parents and then with their friends. Vygotsky saw children as 'apprentices', learning and gaining understanding through being with others. He suggested that younger children's thinking could be extended by adults and older children engaging with them. In support of Vygotsky's work, researchers looked at the ways mothers worked with their children on a construction task. They saw that although techniques varied, mothers were able to encourage their children either by demonstrating or by praising movements that would help the children to complete the task.

Vygotsky also suggested that maturation was an important element in children's development and that we need to extend children's learning so that they can use their emerging skills and concepts. He used the term 'zone of proximal development' to define this idea.

Zone of actual/proximal development (ZAD/ZPD)

The zone of proximal development is the gap between what a child is currently able to do (their zone of actual development) and what they might just be able to achieve if an adult provides some support.

For example, a child's current zone of actual development might mean that they have the fine motor skills that allow them to untie a shoelace and make a simple knot. If an adult takes time to guide the child in tying their shoelaces, the child might, with practice, be able to tie a bow. It is highly unlikely that without the adult's input, the child would be able to master tying shoelaces. For the child to be able to achieve tying their shoelaces it is essential that the adult initially judges the child's skill level accurately. If the child's fine motor skills are not sufficiently developed, they will not be able to cope with the task.

Vygotsky and language

Vygotsky saw that language was key to cognition. He suggested that there were two functions of language:

▶ social language or external speech used in front of others

▶ inner speech, which we use for thinking.

Vygotsky suggested that children began by using external speech but over time developed inner speech. Interestingly, in the development of inner speech, you may notice that children under 6 years old often talk aloud to themselves. This is because the process of fully internalising inner speech is not complete. Next time you talk aloud to yourself, think about how you are using this talk. It is likely that you are using inner speech to clarify your ideas, organise yourself or get to grips with a problem!

Ⅱ **PAUSE POINT** Explain the role of adults or older children in supporting learning as a central aspect of Vygotsky's theory.

> Hint Think about how adults support children's learning in your work placement.

> Extend Using Vygotsky's zone of actual and proximal development, explain the importance of adults observing and reflecting on a child's stage of development.

Supporting sustained shared thinking

One of the key ways in which early years settings are encouraged to work with children follows on from Vygotsky's theory of learning, and also Jerome Bruner's – see 'Scaffolding' section below. Early years settings now encourage adults and children to talk during play and also during activities in ways which support children to explore ideas, problem solve and work collaboratively with the adult. This style of working has been dubbed 'sustained shared thinking' as adults and children come together to share and develop ideas.

A good example of this is the way that an adult and a child might cook together. At times the child will learn by being an 'apprentice' and watching the adult, but the adult and the child can also work together on the task of cooking. A sensitive adult working in this way will be more of a partner in style, and will follow and respond to the child's interest.

Link

For more information about sustained shared thinking, see Section A2 of Unit 3.

Research

In England, when inspecting early years settings, Ofsted look carefully to see whether adults are working in ways that will support sustained shared thinking.

Find out the criteria for 'Outstanding' by downloading the early years inspection handbook from the UK Government website: www.gov.uk

Apprenticeship learning and guided participation

Vygotsky's theory of learning has led to the use of the term **apprenticeship learning** to describe the way in which a child can learn a new skill by observing an adult carrying out a task. When the adult works more collaboratively with the child to complete a task or solve a problem, this is known as **guided participation**. Rather than simply showing the child how something is done, the adult helps with the task and encourages the child to think about what they are learning.

Scaffolding

Jerome Bruner (1915–2016) was an American psychologist whose work has been influenced by Vygotsky. Bruner suggested that children gradually acquire cognitive skills, which he referred to as 'modes of cognitive representation', or modes of thinking.

Bruner believed that children are born with a biological structure, which means that thinking and cognitive development are linked to maturation. He also believed that children are naturally curious and that they learn at first through being active. Abstract thought develops from action.

Bruner coined the term **scaffolding** to explain the role that adults could play in developing children's thinking. The idea is that adults can find ways to support children's thinking by, for example, simplifying a task/action or asking questions, so that little by little, children can understand a concept.

How theories of learning explain thought, language and communication

There are many different theories that consider the way that children learn, think and develop language and communication. Many of these theories were developed before the advent of neuroscience but are still considered to be influential. Over the next few pages, we consider the theories of Jean Piaget, Noam Chomsky, Jerome Bruner and B. F. Skinner. We also consider the information processing approach to learning. At this point in time, no single theory completely explains the complexity of how children learn and think. This is partly because development is extremely complex and is linked to both nature and nurture.

The theories of Jean Piaget

Jean Piaget (1896–1980) was a zoologist who became interested in children's cognitive development as a result of working on intelligence tests. He noticed that children consistently gave similar 'wrong' answers to some questions and began to consider why this was. Piaget used his own children to make detailed observations and gradually developed a theory that has been influential in education in many countries. It has also acted as a starting point for other theories and research.

Although Piaget's theory is based on children's cognitive development, he also used it to explain the way that children play and their moral development.

As with Vygotsky, his theory of learning is sometimes referred to as a constructivist approach, as he suggested that children construct or build up their thoughts according to their experiences of the world around them. Piaget used the term **schema** to mean a child's conclusions or thoughts. Piaget felt that the development of thoughts was an ongoing process, with children needing to adapt their original ideas if a new piece of information seemed to contradict their conclusions – to describe this, he coined the term 'adaption'. For example, a toddler may come to believe that milk is served in blue beakers, because their experience of having milk is linked with it being served in a blue beaker. If one day the toddler is given juice in the blue beaker instead of milk, they will need to consider their theory, so coming to the conclusion that milk and other drinks come in blue beakers. Piaget used specific vocabulary to describe the process of children learning in this way.

Figure 1.6 outlines Piaget's theory.

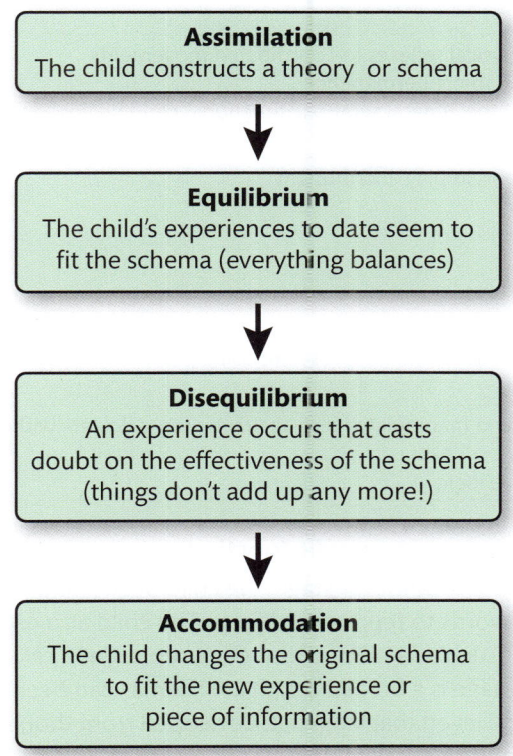

Assimilation
The child constructs a theory or schema

↓

Equilibrium
The child's experiences to date seem to fit the schema (everything balances)

↓

Disequilibrium
An experience occurs that casts doubt on the effectiveness of the schema (things don't add up any more!)

↓

Accommodation
The child changes the original schema to fit the new experience or piece of information

▶ **Figure 1.6:** Piaget's theory of learning

Why children think differently from adults

Piaget's belief that children develop schemas based on their direct experiences can help us to understand why young children's thinking is sometimes so different from ours. A child who has a father with a beard may come to the logical conclusion that all fathers must have beards. Piaget also suggested that, as children develop, so does their thinking.

Piaget's universal stages of cognitive development

Piaget grouped children's cognitive development into four broad stages. Table 1.5 outlines these four stages and they are described in more detail in the following paragraphs.

Sensorimotor stage (birth to 2 years)

This is the first stage of children's lives. It begins at birth with babies using their reflexes to survive. Babies are also very reliant on using their senses in the first 2 years, especially taste and touch. Babies' first schemas are physical ones, as they learn to repeat and then control their movements.

Development of object permanence

One of the tests that Piaget used to show the development of thought in babies was object permanence. In the first few months, a baby will appear to accept the disappearance of an object. Piaget suggested that this is because babies have not learned the idea that an object is still in existence somewhere, even if it is not visible. At around 8 or 9 months, babies seem to understand this concept and we can test it by taking an object from a baby and hiding it under a cushion near them. The baby should lift up the cushion to find it.

Stage	Ages (approximately)	Features
Sensorimotor	0–2 years	• Moving from physical reflexes to coordinated movements • Development of object permanence • Development of the general symbolic function – child begins to use symbols, e.g. language
Pre-operational	2–7 years	• Child uses symbols in play and thought • Egocentrism • Centration • Animism • Inability to conserve
Concrete operations	7–11 years	• Ability to conserve • Children begin to solve mental problems using practical supports such as counters and objects
Formal operations	11–15 years	• Ability to think and manipulate ideas abstractly, e.g. calculate without the need for counters • Start of deductive logic

Development of the general symbolic function

Towards the end of the sensorimotor stage, the child begins to use symbols. Language is symbolic as we use words to represent objects. The child also uses objects to stand for things in their play, such as a piece of dough to represent a cake. Piaget felt that being able to use language is a breakthrough as schemas can become internal rather than physical. Piaget believed that language developed from thought. Others, such as Vygotsky, believed that thought developed from language.

Pre-operational stage (2 to 7 years)

During this stage, children develop their skills in using symbols, i.e. language. Many early years professionals will find that children in this stage are using a lot of imaginative play, for example, using objects in a representational way: sticks may become guns or cardboard boxes may become cars. Piaget did divide this stage into two further sub-stages – preconceptual and intuitive – but there are four main features that run through both of these sub-stages:

▶ egocentrism

▶ difficulty with conservation

▶ centration

▶ animism.

These sub-stages are particularly helpful in explaining children's thought processes and approach to problem-solving.

Egocentrism

According to Piaget, children in the pre-operational stage tend to see things from their own perspective and thus their logic is different from that of adults. Piaget called this egocentrism and this is a strong feature of the whole of the intuitive stage. Piaget designed several tests that showed the way in which children were seeing problems – one of the most famous being the Swiss mountain scene test (see Figure 1.7). In this test children were shown a model of a mountain range. A doll was put in the scene and the children were shown a series of photos and asked which of the views the doll would be able to see. Children under 7 years consistently chose a photo that corresponded to the view they were seeing themselves. Piaget argued that this was because they could not 'decentre', i.e. take themselves out of their bodies and see something from another perspective.

Egocentrism explains why children may not always take an overview when solving problems and instead focus on the detail. For example, they might be interested in finding their favourite parts in a construction set rather than thinking about what might be needed to build a tower.

Egocentrism in practice

Jason is 4 years old. At lunchtime, his friend pushes away the carrots on his plate explaining that he doesn't like them. Jason is surprised. He says to his friend that he likes carrots. He goes on to say that 'you must like carrots – everybody loves carrots.'

1 Explain how Jason has reached this conclusion.
2 How does Jason's reaction link to Piaget's cognitive theory?
3 At what age might Jason start to understand that not all children will like the same things as him?

▶ **Figure 1.7:** The Swiss mountain scene made famous by Piaget

Difficulty with conservation

In the pre-operational stage, children find it difficult to understand that things can remain the same, even though their appearance may change. Piaget suggested that the inability to 'conserve' was an important feature of the pre-operational stage. He designed many tests to show whether children could conserve in different ways.

Table 1.6 shows some of the tests that are commonly used with children. You might like to try these with children on your placement.

Difficulty with conservation explains why children may say things such as 'you've become a girl' when a boy puts on a dress in the role play area. This may seem illogical to adults, but it is logical to a young child.

Centration

In this stage, children are beginning to classify objects and make associations. However, they are often doing this by looking at only one attribute at a time, such as sorting objects according to size, but not size and colour. Piaget called this centration. This may be why children are unable to conserve, i.e. in the mass conservation test described in Table 1.6, they concentrate on the shape of the clay rather than its quantity.

▶ **Table 1.6:** Tests commonly used with children to show whether they can conserve

Name of test	Method used
Number	• Two parallel rows with equal numbers of counters are shown to the child • The counters in one of the rows are then put closer together so that one row appears longer than the other • Children are asked, 'Are there the same number of counters in each row?'
Length	• Two pencils of identical length are put side by side • One pencil is then moved diagonally so that its point is no longer alongside the other pencil • The child is asked, 'Are they the same length?'
Volume	• Two identical beakers are filled with the same amount of water • The contents of one beaker are poured into a narrower but taller beaker • The children are asked, 'Is there still the same amount of water?'
Mass	• Two balls of clay or dough are rolled out to exactly the same size • The child is asked to pick them up to check that they are the same • One of the balls is rolled into a sausage shape • The children are asked, 'Is there the same amount of clay in each ball?'

Animism

Many children show signs of animism: believing that because they have feelings, other objects must also have feelings. Many early years professionals see this when children say things such as 'that dog's mummy will be cross with her' or 'that wall is bad, it hurt me'.

> **Reflect**
>
> We can see animism in children's drawings. Many children, even after the preconceptual stage, will draw animals and objects that smile, such as a sun with a smiling face.
> • Look at several drawings done by children between the ages of 4 and 8 years.
> • Can you see any signs of animism in the drawings?

Concrete operations stage (7 to 11 years)

The concrete operations stage marks a great leap in children's logical abilities. They begin to use rules and strategies to help their thinking. Piaget called this the concrete operations stage because children's understanding is aided by the use of practical tools, for example, using counters to find the answer to 15 minus 9.

Children in the concrete operations stage are also able to conserve and decentre – they see things from the point of view of others – for example, they understand that the view the doll sees in the Swiss mountain scene test will be different from their own view. Piaget also suggested that these children would understand the concept of reversibility. An example of reversibility is when clay is rolled into a ball, then into a sausage and back into a ball, it will still have the same mass. In mathematical terms, it means that children are able to understand that there is a link between division and multiplication. For example, they will understand that $7 \times 5 = 35$ and $35 \div 7 = 5$.

Formal operations stage (11 to 15 years)

The main difference between the formal operations stage and the concrete operations stage is that children are now able to manipulate thoughts and ideas to solve problems without needing practical props. This means that in theory, tasks such as map reading can be done without having to turn the map around to work out whether a turning is on the right or left. This is an interesting example of a formal operations task, as many adults may have difficulty reading maps!

Piaget suggested that thinking at the formal operations level would not be an automatic step and that in some areas of learning we would not all achieve this level all of the time; and in some areas this would depend on the training and experiences that we were given. In the case of map reading, we might be able to manage to read a map without turning it around given enough experience and training.

Another feature of the formal operations stage is that children are able to **hypothesise** about situations in a realistic way, for example, what would you do if someone broke into your home? The ability to hypothesise means that children can speculate on outcomes. Piaget described this feature of thinking as hypothetico-deductive reasoning.

Summary of Piaget's theory

Piaget's work on the theory of cognitive development was so influential that it is perhaps useful to summarise some of its main features.

▸ Children develop their thoughts according to their experiences.

▸ Children's learning passes through distinct stages, although attaining formal operations seems to depend on training and experiences.

▸ Children's language is used to support their cognitive development.

> **Key terms**
>
> **Hypothesise** – to speculate or propose an idea or theory.
>
> **Qualitative** – relating to opinions or feelings rather than facts, for instance, how someone feels about something.

Ⅱ PAUSE POINT   Name the stages of cognitive development according to Piaget.

> Hint   There are four and the last stage is 'formal operations'.
>
> Extend   Explain how Piaget's theory is based on the idea that children's direct experiences affect their logic and thoughts.

Criticism and further developments of Piaget's theory

Though Piaget developed a comprehensive theory about how children might learn, his work also acted as a springboard for other theorists, many of whom have found flaws in his theory.

Piaget's research methods may have been biased

Piaget used clinical interviews as the major research method with children. This method is open to bias. Piaget carried out hundreds of interviews and the type of data that was collected is **qualitative**. Despite this, the data is very informative. Piaget also used experiments, but the tests he constructed have also been criticised.

Does cognitive development really happen in stages?

This is one of the criticisms of Piaget's early work. However, from the 1970s Piaget suggested that cognitive development was a spiralling process and considered that at times children will show features of more than one stage at once. This he referred to as décalage. Despite this, he maintained that children would not be able to skip whole elements of the stages and progress to another stage.

Piaget and early years practice

Although Piaget had no particular recommendations about how his theory should be used to teach children, his work did have an effect on educational practice. There are two main strands: readiness and learning by discovery. Both of these strands were used to suggest that an individual approach to children's learning should be taken.

Readiness

Children's thought processes cannot be fast tracked, so we can only work at the child's pace. For example, if a child does not have the concept of conservation of number, there is no point in teaching that child addition or multiplication.

Learning by discovery

Children develop their thinking by reviewing their schemas and adapting their ideas (accommodation) to new information. In order to do this, children will need a wide range of experiences.

> **Theory into practice**
>
> Think about your work placement setting.
>
> 1 Is there an assumption that children need to work at their own pace?
> 2 Are children grouped according to their stages of development or according to their ages?
> 3 What types of activities are chosen that encourage learning through discovery? For example, children using containers and water to find out about the properties of water.

Piaget underestimated children

One of the most widely accepted criticisms of Piaget's work is that the ages he gave for children's thinking are inaccurate. He underestimated children's level of thinking. One of the reasons given for his inaccuracies is the type of tasks that he used with children. Margaret Donaldson, who worked with Piaget at one point, was a particular critic. With a colleague, she showed that results could be very different if the task made sense to children and linked with their experiences. Their use of a 'naughty teddy' to manipulate counters showed that children as young as 4 years old could 'conserve'. In a famous book called *Children's Minds*, Donaldson outlined that children could be logical thinkers when they were able to make 'human sense' of the situation.

Babies' abilities

More recent research studies are now showing that Piaget underestimated babies' abilities, particularly in reference to object permanence. Several researchers, including Elizabeth Spelke at Harvard University, have carried out tests showing that babies express surprise if a number of items are shown, disappear and then a different (either decreased or increased) number of objects reappear.

Piaget underestimated how training and practice can help children

Piaget suggested that the cognitive development of children was heavily linked to maturation and, therefore, children could not be fast tracked through the stages. There has, however, been some research suggesting that children can achieve tasks if they are given experiences to help them.

Information processing theories of cognitive development

Information processing theories of cognitive development consider the mental processes that allow us to learn. There are several different researchers associated with this approach to cognitive development including Robert Kail (born 1950), Robert Siegler (born 1949) and David Klahr (born 1939). This is very much an area of ongoing research with some suggesting a stage-like model of development, but others suggesting that development is continuous. Information processing theorists also draw on the language and concepts used in computing to help talk about cognitive development.

Attention and memory

In order for children to learn, they have to have a memory. Memory is an important component in our ability to process information and so is at the heart of information processing theory.

At its simplest, there are three processes involved in memory.

1 **Encoding** – the starting point for memory is that children have to notice something or 'attend' to it. Once there is attention, the encoding process can begin. Encoding is about organising information so that it can be stored. Poorly encoded information sometimes results in us not quite remembering something, for example, recognising the tune but not knowing the words of a song. Sometimes poorly encoded information is a result of partial attention or a child not being able to attend to all aspects of what is happening. This can result in difficulties in recalling information. Complex information seems to be harder for children to encode than simple information.

2 **Storage** – this is about keeping the information and not losing it.

3 **Retrieval** – this is about being able to recall information.

Multi-store model of memory

The most influential work carried out on memory was done by Richard Atkinson (born 1929) and Richard Shiffrin (born 1942). They proposed a multi-store model that has formed the basis for further work on memory. You can see an outline of their model in Figure 1.8. Today, most work on memory suggests that it is made up of different components through which information can be transferred. A filtering process is also in place, which explains why we do not remember every detail of every experience we have had.

Sensory memory

This is at the start of the process. Information received from the five senses can be stored temporarily, rather like a pause button. The information will either be transferred to the short-term memory – in which case it needs to be interpreted or encoded very quickly – or it will be lost.

Short-term memory

Information moving to the short-term memory will be held temporarily. The short-term memory is extremely short – this is why you may forget a phone number unless you keep repeating it or write it down. Work done on memory suggests that only about seven or so items can be held in the short-term memory at any time. You can try this out by seeing how many random numbers or names your friends can remember. As children get older, they seem to be able to use strategies to hold onto information in the short-term memory. The development of these strategies mean that as a child grows and develops they are likely to be able to use their memories more effectively, although this development takes place over many years.

Long-term memory

Unlike the short-term memory, the long-term memory can hold information for a few minutes or even a lifetime. The long-term memory is seen as having unlimited capacity. This may come as a surprise if you are someone who has difficulty remembering things, but storage capacity is completely different from the process of retrieving information.

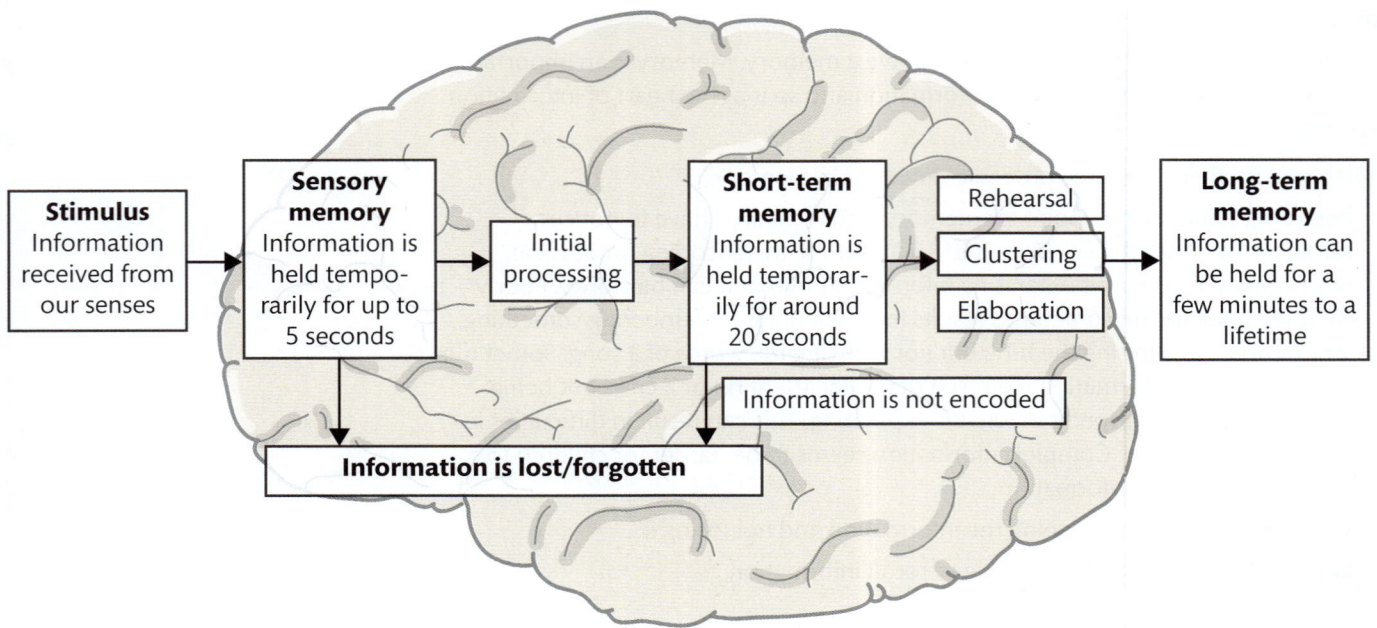

▶ **Figure 1.8:** Atkinson and Shiffrin's multi-store model of memory

Language, making connections and memory

There are strong links between language and children's ability to process information. A good example of this is the way that when we talk to a child about something they have seen, they may then be able to recall the object. The 'words' help to unlock the memory. In the same way, it is good practice to help children process information by accurately naming what they are doing or seeing, as afterwards these words will help them with recall. In the same way, it is thought to be helpful for adults to assist children to make connections between past and present, for example what they are doing or seeing and what they have done before. By helping children to use recall to make connections between past and present, and talking through these connections, children's cognitive growth can be supported. From such conversations, children can often reach further conclusions.

Where children's language is still developing or is atypical, they will find it harder to encode information that is presented to them as speech. This is one of the reasons why we have to show and do things for young children. It is also one of the reasons why children who seem to have listened to a story may not afterwards be able to tell us anything about it.

Case study

The importance of making connections

Isaac is 4 years old. He is cooking with his key person, Anna. The recipe requires that an egg is used. Isaac wants to crack the egg open. His key person reminds him that he saw an egg when they visited a city farm. Isaac replies that there were a lot of eggs and that it was the hens that had laid them. Isaac thinks for a moment and then exclaims, 'but those eggs were not broken!'

1 Why was it important for Isaac's key person to help him find the connections between past and present experiences?

2 Describe how Isaac's key person was using 'scaffolding' to support children's learning.

3 Analyse how Isaac is using the connection between past and present experiences to learn more.

Key points from information processing theorists that explain how children's problem-solving and thinking develops

1 **Information processing appears to improve with age** – there have been quite a few experiments showing that children's ability to process information improves with age. One experiment asked children of different ages to name familiar objects as they appeared out of a bag. Younger children, although they knew the names of the objects, were consistently slower. Children also seem to acquire more strategies as they become older.

2 **Experience enhances information processing** – information processing theorists suggest that part of the reason that children think differently from adults is that they are processing the information in different ways. At the heart of this processing is our ability to use our memories As we get older we use our past experiences to help us solve new problems; when presented with several pieces of information, we also become more skilled at holding them until we need to use them.

3 **Information processing may be at the heart of intelligence** – there has been some thought that the speed at which information is processed is at the heart of intelligence, with some children of the same age seeming to be faster at solving problems. Children with high IQs seem to be good at remembering things and solving problems by applying existing knowledge to a new situation.

Language development

Language helps children to communicate and understand more about the world around them. It is also the basis for developing literacy skills. Language is an important developmental topic and we will be looking at it again in the next unit.

Understanding the structure of language

It is important to have some understanding of the structure of language. All languages have rules, which are understood and used by both the speaker and listener. These rules are often referred to as grammar. By following the rules of grammar, speakers and listeners can understand each other. Linguists who study the structure of language use the term grammar to describe the package of a language. This consists of three key elements: phonology, semantics and syntax.

Phonology

Languages have a sound system, known as phonology. When we hear someone speaking, we may recognise the language that they are using, even if we cannot speak it. This recognition may be based on listening to the sounds that are being used. The sounds that are used in a language are called **phonemes**. Some languages use fewer phonemes than others. There are 44 phonemes used in English, as opposed to 11 in Rotokas, an East Papuan language.

Semantics

Languages are composed of words, or units of meaning. When we learn a language we also have to learn what these units are and how they can be changed. An example of a unit is adding '-less' onto the end of a word, which changes the meaning of the original word.

Syntax

Finally, we have to learn the rules for using the words and how their place in a sentence can change their meaning. For example, 'the cat ate the mouse' has a different meaning from 'the mouse ate the cat' even though the same words have been used.

> **Link**
>
> Unit 2 has more information about language development.

> **Key term**
>
> **Phonemes** – the smallest units of sound in a language that help to distinguish one word from another. In the English language, for example, 'p' and 'b' are separate phonemes because they distinguish words such as 'pit' and 'bit'.

PAUSE POINT Identify the three elements of spoken language and their importance.

Hint Think about what you need to know and do in order to take part in a conversation.

Extend Consider how the three elements of spoken language are interrelated.

The sequence of language development

A good starting point when considering language development is to look at the pattern of how children learn to speak. It is interesting to note that babies and children, in whichever country they are born, all follow a similar pattern. The first year of a baby's life is spent trying to tune in to the language that they are hearing and learning the skills of communication, i.e. making eye contact and responding to other people's facial expressions and words. This first year is often known as the prelinguistic phase and is now considered to be vital in children's overall language development.

Table 1.7 outlines the major stages in language development.

▶ **Table 1.7:** Stages in language development

Stage	Age	Features	Comments
Prelinguistic			
Cooing	6 weeks	Cooing	Babies make cooing sounds to show pleasure. These early sounds are different to sounds made later on, mainly because the mouth is still developing
Babbling (phonemic expansion)	6–9 months	Babies blend vowels and consonants together to make tuneful sounds, e.g. 'ba', 'ma', 'da'	Babbling has been described as learning the tune before the words. The baby seems to be practising sounds. Babies increase the number of sounds or phonemes. This is sometimes called phonemic expansion. All babies, even deaf babies, produce a wide range of sounds during this period. During these months babies also learn some essential communication skills. These include making eye contact, recognising some emotions in others and responding to them
Babbling (phonemic contraction)	9–10 months 11–12 months	• Babies babble, but the range of sounds is limited • Babies seem to repeat the same sounds in long strings, e.g. 'babababababa' (echolalia)	The range of sounds or phonemes that babies produce becomes more limited and reflects the phonemes used in the language that they are hearing. At this stage, it would in theory be possible to distinguish between babies who are in different language environments. At 10 months babies understand 17 or more words. Babies' communication skills have also developed further. They now know how to attract an adult's attention by pointing and raising their voice. They can also understand a lot of what is being said to them either through word recognition, but also by reading faces
Linguistic			
First words	Around 12 months	Babies repeatedly use one or more sounds, which have meaning for them	The first words are often unclear and emerge gradually. They are often one sound, but are used regularly in similar situations, e.g. 'baga' to mean drink and cuddle. Babbling continues
Holophrases	12–18 months	Toddlers start to use one word in a variety of ways	Toddlers use holophrases to make their limited vocabulary more useful for them. One word is used in several situations, but the tone of voice and the context helps the adult understand what the toddler means. Most toddlers have between 10 and 15 words by 18 months. By this time toddlers have often learned how to get an adult's attention and how to make them laugh
Two-word utterances (telegraphic speech)	18–24 months	Two words are put together to make a mini sentence	Toddlers begin to combine words to make sentences. They seem to have grasped which are the key words in a sentence, e.g. 'dada gone' or 'dada come'

▶ **Table 1.7:** Stages in language development – *continued*

Stage	Age	Features	Comments
Language explosion	24–36 months	• A large increase in children's vocabulary combined with increasing use of sentences	• This is a period in which children's language seems to evolve rapidly. Children learn words so rapidly that it becomes hard for parents to count them! At the same time the child uses more complicated structures in their speech. Plurals and negatives begin to be used, e.g. 'no dogs here'
	3–4 years	• Sentences become longer and vocabulary continues to increase	• Children are using language in a more complete way. Mistakes in grammar show that they are still absorbing the rules and sometimes misapplying them! Mistakes such as 'I wented' show that they have learned that '-ed' makes a past tense. These types of mistakes are known as 'virtuous' errors • By this time, children are able to use their communication skills in order to socialise with others in simple ways, e.g. they may repeat a question if they think that they have not been understood
Fluency	4–6 years	Mastering the basic skills of the language	Children have mastered the basic rules of English grammar and are fluent, although will still be making some 'virtuous' errors
Speech maturity	6–8 years	Mastering the reproduction of most sounds	During this period, children's speech becomes clearer as their tongue, teeth and jaw develop. Children begin to use language to get their point of view across to others, although some do this by simply raising their voice! In this period, children's level of language is key to acquiring the skills of reading and writing

Theories of how children acquire language

The nature versus nurture debate appears once more when we look at the theories of how children learn language.

Noam Chomsky's Language Acquisition Device

Noam Chomsky's (born 1928) work on language is based on the idea that our ability to learn language is instinctive. Another way of saying this is that it is innate: we are born with it. This is a nature, or nativist, theory. His theory has been widely accepted as it is comprehensive and explains why all babies' language development follows a pattern. He is famous for suggesting that humans have a Language Acquisition Device (LAD). This is not an actual physical part of the brain, but a structure within our brains that allows babies to absorb and understand the rules of the language they are being exposed to. The brain is able to analyse the language and work out the system that the language uses. This is a complex process, but explains why children can quickly understand and then use their language creatively and correctly without ever being formally taught or knowing the rules.

The LAD would explain why all babies can learn any language they are exposed to and why all babies follow the same pattern of development even though their abilities may be very different.

Reflect

The idea of there being a critical period for learning language is an attractive one. It has been suggested that if children are not exposed to language in the first 10 years of their lives, they would not be able to learn to speak. There is some evidence both for and against this idea.

Teenagers and adults who have been brain damaged as a result of an accident find it harder to regain language they have lost, whereas children with similar injuries find it much easier. This would support the idea of a critical period.

Children who have suffered severe deprivation have still managed to acquire some language. One of the most famous of these children is Genie. Genie was 13 years old when she was rescued in 1970. She had spent her childhood in appalling conditions. She was punished for making any sounds and was strapped down. When she was found she could understand a few words, but essentially had no speech. Although she made progress in learning to speak, she struggled with the rules of speech. This would cast doubt on the idea of a 'critical period' because speech was still gained. Having said this, cases such as this are complicated because of the abuse that the children have suffered. It could be argued that the effects of physical and emotional abuse play a part in any difficulty that children have with learning.

Jerome Bruner's modes of cognitive representation

Jerome Bruner's work was influenced by Piaget, but more particularly by the work of Vygotsky. Bruner does not have a stage theory as such but he suggested that children gradually acquire cognitive skills, which he referred to as '**modes of cognitive representation**'. Bruner viewed the acquisition of language as important in children's learning and cognition.

Bruner particularly stressed the social aspect of learning and the link between thought and language. As you saw earlier in this unit, Bruner also suggested that the role of the adult is important in helping the child to develop as a thinker.

Table 1.8 shows Bruner's three modes of thinking in children's development and skill acquisition.

▶ **Table 1.8:** Bruner's three modes of cognitive representation

Mode	Description and use	
Enactive	Learning and thought take place because of physical movements	
Iconic	Thoughts are developed as mental images	
Symbolic	Symbols including language are used in thinking	

Enactive mode

Through repeating physical movements we often learn a skill such as tying our shoelaces or learning to drive a car. The enactive mode is the first type of cognitive skill that Bruner suggested babies are able to use. This fits in with Piaget's sensorimotor stage where children repeat movements and learn about their world through their physical movements.

Iconic mode

An icon is something that is visual and Bruner suggests that the iconic mode involves building up a picture of things we have experienced in our minds. We may, for example, be able to shut our eyes and imagine the room that we are in. The iconic stage does relate to Piaget's pre-operational stage as children concentrate more on appearances than adults and this is what often confuses them during Piaget's tests of conservation.

Symbolic mode

Like Piaget, Bruner believes that children's thinking drastically changes at around 7 years. Bruner links this change to the child's ability to use symbols but particularly to the use of language. In symbolic mode, thinking can take place without us having direct experience. For example, we may listen to the news on the radio and retain this information, even though we have not directly witnessed the events mentioned.

Skinner's operant conditioning theory

Skinner's **operant conditioning** theory is a nurture theory. Skinner suggests that we learn language mainly because our first efforts at communicating as a baby are rewarded or reinforced in some way. For example, a baby may get a smile from a parent if they gurgle. A toddler saying 'more' and pointing at food will learn that by using language they can get what they want. Skinner used this idea of reinforcement to explain why babies stop making some sounds. He reasoned that when babies made sounds that parents did not recognise they would not receive any attention, whereas sounds that were recognisable were noticed and reinforced. He called this process selective reinforcement.

This approach would explain why children often speak in similar ways to their parents, using familiar phrases and intonation.

Later in this unit we will look in detail at B. F. Skinner's operant conditioning theory in relation to how children learn behaviours.

Criticisms of Skinner's theory

Skinner's theory does not explain why all babies and children follow the same pattern of learning language. If Skinner's theory was correct, you would expect to see that children's language developed very differently depending on the amount and type of reinforcement that adults and others gave. This is not the case, however, as most children seem to pass through the same stages.

The theory does not explain why young children speak in different ways from the adults around them, for example, 'dada gone'. If children learn by imitating what they hear and by incorrect sounds or sentences not being reinforced, why do they say things such as 'wented' or 'swimmed'?

Nor does the theory explain how children learn the rules of a language in such a way that they are quickly able to make up their own sentences. Learning through imitation and reinforcement would mean that children would only be repeating what they have heard, rather than being able to invent their own sentences.

> **Key term**
>
> **Operant conditioning** – a theory that suggests that the environment 'operates' on and thus influences a child's learning. Skinner's theory of operant conditioning suggests that learning occurs through behaviour being rewarded or punished.

> **Link**
>
> Go to Section D1 to read more about Skinner's operant conditioning theory.

> **Theory into practice**
>
> Although Skinner's model of how language develops has many limitations, we do know that it is important for children to be encouraged so that their language develops. Children who are acknowledged learn that adults are pleased when they talk and so are more likely to interact.
>
> Watch an experienced member of staff in your setting. How are they giving babies positive reinforcement when they try to communicate?

C2 How applying theories of cognition, language and communication helps practitioners understand their practice

One of the reasons for considering the theories and models of child development is that they can help us to understand what is happening to a child in relation to normative development. In addition, we can use some of the theories and models of development to influence our own practice, where this is appropriate.

There are several theories that have been influential in early years practice relating to the development of cognition and language. Interestingly, many of them complement each other, as Table 1.9 shows.

▶ **Table 1.9:** How theories that consider how children develop cognition and language can influence practice within settings

Description	How the theory could influence practice	How to apply the theory to practice
Piaget's theory of cognitive development		
Jean Piaget suggested a stage-like approach to cognitive development. He focused on the child as an 'active learner', believing that children construct their own ideas and logic about their immediate world based on the experiences they have had	• To recognise that children learn at their own pace • To provide plenty of opportunities for exploration and play so that children can develop their own thinking	• Provide opportunities for children to explore a range of materials, particularly those that lend themselves to concepts, e.g. sand, water and dough • Provide opportunities for children to take part in a wide range of practical skills so that they can develop schemas • Provide opportunities for role play as children use this to play out their experiences with other children, using their own 'rules' • Do not mock children who say things such as, 'Where is your mummy?', as this is a logical statement to them • Be aware of a child's stage of development in respect to their ability to conserve, as this is a requirement before children can explore some areas of number work
Vygotsky's zone of proximal development		
Lev Vygotsky suggested that interaction with adults and older children plays an important part in children's development. He suggested a model known as the zone of proximal development, whereby a child can develop a new skill or level of complex thinking, extending them beyond their current level, with the support of an adult	• To help children develop new skills, knowledge or level of reasoning	• You need to accurately identify a child's current level of skill, knowledge and reasoning. This is done through careful and sensitive observation • Plan for the next steps for individual children • Work closely with children, using sensitive interaction and questioning so that children can be supported to acquire a new skill, level of reasoning or piece of knowledge
Bruner's theoretical framework		
Jerome Bruner suggested that children process information in different ways according to their age. He also suggested that children learn through play and exploration, especially when adults play an active role in questioning or engaging with the child. He used the term 'scaffolding' to explain this process	• To help children learn concepts and develop their reasoning and logic	• Provide plenty of opportunities for meaningful interaction with children that follow the format of a 'discussion' rather than instruction • Refer children back to their previous experiences so that they can make the connection between them and their new thoughts, experiences and ideas • Revisit topics and activities with children every few months so that they can experience them again and gain new insights • Plan challenging but enjoyable activities so that children gain new experiences – learning through play • Talk to parents about the importance of active learning that is supported by adults in helping their child's cognitive development

▶ **Table 1.9:** How theories that consider how children develop cognition and language can influence practice within settings – *continued*

Description	How the theory could influence practice	How to apply the theory to practice
Information processing theory		
This theory considers the role of memory and language in the way that children interpret, store and retrieve memories. Theorists who looked at this include Kail, Siegler and Klahr	• To help adults and parents support young children's learning and understand why children may not always process information in the way we might have expected • To provide activities that are sensory, active or visual to make processing easier for young children	• Recognise that young children process information when there is a visual or active component • Use props and puppets, and make sure that children can see pictures when reading stories • Show children what you want them to do rather than just telling them • Allow children plenty of time to respond to you when asking a question. They need time to process what has been said • Use photographs to help children remember things they have experienced in the past • Use play and sensory opportunities as a way to support learning • Expect that children of the same age may have different 'processing speeds' • Keep instructions short • Use visual timetables so that children can understand what is going to happen next • Expect to give children reminders as 'words' are easily forgotten
Chomsky's Language Acquisition Device Theory		
Noam Chomsky proposed that humans have an innate sense of language and a device that allows babies and young children to acquire language if they are sufficiently exposed to it	• To ensure that there are sufficient opportunities for meaningful and age-/stage- appropriate interaction • To support the language development of children who have an additional home language	• Think about whether children have sufficient opportunities to interact with you • Make sure the length of interactions with children allow them to acquire language • Speak in a way that is grammatically correct and clear • Do not correct children's language, but instead repeat it back to them in a corrected format • Reduce the level of background noise that may be acting as a distractor • Encourage parents to use their home language while their children are young so that it can be acquired. Learning a language later in life can be more difficult

How understanding theories can help practitioners to support children's literacy skills

Through understanding cognitive and language theories, practitioners can support the development of literacy skills. In order to read and write, children need to be fluent in their language and also have the ability to use abstract concepts. Letters and words are symbols representing sounds and so are abstract in their nature. According to the theories of Piaget and also Bruner, very young children will find it hard to learn to read and so practitioners will need to observe whether or not they are ready to use abstract symbols. In terms of the style in which adults might work with children, both Vygotsky's and Bruner's work suggest that a collaborative approach, where adults work alongside children, might be useful. In many early years settings and reception classes, adults share books with children and encourage them to decode words with them.

Link

There is more information about how children develop cognition and literacy skills in Unit 2, Section B1.

The impact on children's learning if atypical development is not recognised

Language is key to other areas of development, so children with any delay or atypical development need to be assessed and supported. Atypical language development may affect children's learning in a variety of ways.

▸ **Social development** – children learn by being with others. Not being able to understand what others are saying, or struggling to communicate using language, will affect children's opportunities to play with others. This is more noticeable among older children, who use language to organise games. Children with unidentified language needs are more likely to become socially isolated or show inappropriate behaviours due to frustration.

▸ **Cognition** – learning becomes increasingly sophisticated as children grow older, because language allows children to process information, store memories, reason and problem solve. Children with atypical language development may find it harder to learn and need longer to think through ideas and problems.

▸ **Mathematics** – mathematics requires children to think in the abstract. While they may cope with simple problems where physical counters and objects are used, children with atypical language development are likely to find mathematics increasingly difficult as they move on to more advanced ideas.

▸ **Literacy** – fluent language is needed so that children can start to read and write, so it is essential to identify any atypical language early on. Chomsky, for example, suggested that there is a critical period in which language is learned, although this is hotly debated by other researchers. If there is a critical period, a child whose language is significantly atypical may not be able to access the skills needed for literacy. There is also a cognitive aspect to literacy that is often overlooked, in that children need to use symbols. This means that children with an unrecognised learning difficulty might find it harder to learn to read and write.

How theories of learning can help to explain development of children's drawing and writing skills

In the very early stages of children's development, drawing and writing are blended. This stage is often called mark making. Later, after children have been introduced to letter shapes, drawing and writing diverge; this usually happens from around 3 years.

Children's mark making is often linked to their physical development, as well as their language and cognitive development. At first children are very exploratory in the way that they mark make, which links to Bruner's enactive mode.

Mark making is abstract but, from around 4 years old, children's drawings become more representative. As we saw in Section C1, children's drawings may also show animism. If practitioners understand that children's drawings are linked to cognitive aspects of development, they can use them as a way of noting children's stage of development. Children need plenty of opportunities to make marks and to watch adults engage in drawing. In order to support writing, adults need to model writing and spend time with children helping them to understand the connection between letter shapes and words. This can be done through a process of scaffolding, with adult and child taking a collaborative approach. This links to Vygotsky's and Bruner's theories.

Using verbal and non-verbal communication to support children's interaction

It takes time for children to learn language and, as you saw in Section C1, an important component of language is semantics (the understanding of what words mean). One of the key ways that we can support children's language is to communicate meanings of words by using both verbal and non-verbal methods of communication. For example, early years settings may use pictures and also Makaton to help children understand the meaning of what is being said. Visual timetables use pictures to support children in understanding what will happen next in a routine or activity. They can be helpful for very young children, children with literacy difficulties or children who are anxious about going somewhere or doing something new.

Using non-verbal communication, including facial expressions, can help children to process information more effectively. Gestures such as pointing at objects are very important in helping babies to see 'concrete' objects and learn their names. Later on, children are able to talk about and understand comments about objects that are not present. At this point, children are using abstract symbols effectively. We look in more detail about how to support children's interaction in Unit 2.

For children who are unable to use phonology – the sound system of a language – because, for example, they cannot hear sounds, sign language may be used as an alternative to spoken language. Sign language is a complete language, as whole sentences involving grammar are used, so it is rarely used with children other than those who are hearing or vocally disabled.

Understanding how children develop numeracy skills

Both Bruner's and Piaget's theories of cognition suggest that children need to be active learners in order to acquire basic mathematical skills. These include the concept of number, how to place numbers in order and the understanding of basic mathematical language. This is why objects are used to help children count before written numerals are introduced. Piaget and Bruner also suggested that young children find it hard to think in the abstract until they are around 7 years old. This is interesting, as many nurseries and schools introduce numerals (essentially, abstract symbols to represent a quantity) well before children are 7 years old. This is not the approach taken in other countries in the world.

While Piaget focused on the importance of practical experiences, research from the information processing theories suggests that children's interest in activities is also important. This is because attention is a key step in laying down memories. If children are not interested in a mathematical activity, they may not pay sufficient attention and so will not be able to process information. In terms of early years practice, this means that numeracy needs to be taught in ways that are enjoyable and fun for children so that they can concentrate.

Early years settings plan carefully to ensure that numeracy and mathematical activities are developmentally appropriate to the stage and capabilities of individual children. This takes place in a continual cycle of observing children, then planning next steps for them. This is at the heart of Vygotsky's suggestion that adults can support children to make progress from their 'zone of actual development'.

Language also plays a part in developing mathematical concepts; both Vygotsky and Bruner stress the role of language in children's learning. This is one reason why early years settings often begin to teach children about numeracy and mathematics by drawing their attention to what they are doing through conversations.

Understanding how children develop mathematical concepts, problem-solve, construct hypotheses and make decisions

The theories of language and cognition help us to understand the way in which children develop more advanced skills in numeracy. Piaget, Bruner and Vygotsky all believed that language, learning and cognition were interrelated. This means that the starting point for early years practice is to ensure that children have plenty of opportunities for interaction with adults in ways that will help them to acquire language. A grasp of mathematical concepts – such as the understanding of conservation, size, weight, capacity, position, distance, time, and comparison of quantities – usually develops during the concrete or formal operational stages of development.

> **Link**
>
> Look back at Section C1 for more detail about Piaget's operational stages.

The ability to problem-solve requires children first to have an understanding of logic, rules and patterns, while hypothesising requires selecting relevant information. A child who sees a caterpillar moving may not focus on the movement but instead may suggest that it is looking for its mummy. Piaget's theory of cognition focuses on the way that children's logic will be different from adults, as their hypotheses will be influenced by their stage of development, but also their experiences. The difficulty that children have decentring and conserving, which we looked at earlier, means that constructing hypotheses and problem-solving in a mathematical way is often hard for them. Practitioners need to understand that they cannot 'fast track' children, but instead, they can provide opportunities and an environment that will support development. Vygotsky and Bruner also recognised that cognition develops over time, but stressed the role of adults in guiding children's thinking, and using questions and conversations to help children problem-solve.

Understanding how children observe, investigate, and explore objects and environments

Piaget's theory of cognitive development suggests that one of the ways that children learn is by playing and exploring materials. Early years settings often plan opportunities for children to use a wide range of materials and objects, both indoors and outdoors. From such experiences, young children start to come to conclusions about change, patterns, similarities and differences. While Piaget's theory suggests that children may be able to draw conclusions for themselves, most early years settings take the approach that adults need to draw children's attention to what is happening and then discuss with them what they are observing, touching or doing.

This links to both Bruner's and Vygotsky's belief that adults are instrumental in developing children's thinking. Vygotsky, Piaget and Bruner all concluded that language was key to children's developing thoughts, so it is good practice to encourage children to ask questions about what they are observing and exploring. In children whose language is developing typically, this can be seen quite early on, as from around 2 years children start to use simple questions such as 'What's dat?' Later, from around 3 years, children usually begin to use 'how' or 'why' when they are with adults. Babies from around 9 months also use pointing to draw adults' attention to what they can see, in order to interact with them.

Skinner's theory of operant conditioning in relation to children's language suggests that where children gain immediate and positive responses from adults to their gestures, questions and comments, they will be more likely to use language in this way.

How children's understanding becomes more sophisticated and they begin to represent thoughts and ideas

One of the key features of children's cognitive development is the way that they can use language to support higher level thinking. Vygotsky and Bruner suggest that through adults using language with children in ways that help them to make connections, children's understanding can become more sophisticated. This is one reason why early years settings encourage adults to interact with children during activities. The style of interaction is important and it is good practice for adults to use sustained shared thinking where adults and children talk together. This helps children to develop new knowledge as they make connections between past and new experiences.

The development of language also helps children to control their behaviours and actions. While 2 year olds are very impulsive, because their language has not yet developed, older children can use their language to think through the consequences of their actions and to guide themselves. As mentioned in Section C1, we often hear young children 'talk aloud' as they attempt to use language. This links to Vygotsky's observation that language can be social, but also 'inner', and that it is our inner language that is our 'thinking' voice. Interestingly, Vygotsky noted that it was not until children reached 6 or 7 years old that they were able to keep their 'inner speech' to themselves.

In some early years settings, children from 3 or 4 years old are encouraged at the end of sessions to talk about what they have done, discovered and learned. This works well in small groups when children's language is fairly fluent. Being able to explain and report what they have been doing is empowering for children, and helps them to use words to clarify their thoughts and ideas. Adults can help children do this by allowing them to take their time, using the odd prompt and helping children to make connections.

As we saw earlier in this section, early years settings encourage children to represent their thoughts in more abstract ways as they develop, for instance, drawings and writing. While many children use mark making to record their thoughts and ideas, most will not be able to master this as a recording technique until they are at least 7 years old.

Assessment practice 1.3 | AO1 | AO2 | AO3 | AO4

A group of parents has asked you to provide information about children's cognitive and language development. Your information should:

- identify the typical stages of language and cognitive development
- discuss the key theories that explain cognitive and language development
- evaluate the impact of theories of language and cognitive development on early years practice.

The parents have also submitted some individual questions for you to answer.

- One parent wants to know why her 4-year-old child talks to her toys as if they are really alive.
- Another parent wants to know if it is normal for his 3-year-old child to talk to himself.

Make sure your work includes answers to these questions.

Plan
- Can I identify the key stages of cognitive and language development?
- Do I understand the theories of language and cognitive development?
- Am I able to evaluate how theories have influenced early years practice?

Do
- Have I read Unit 2 to gain more information about communication, literacy and numeracy?
- Have I written confidently about the theories of cognitive and language development?

Review
- Have I applied theories of cognitive and language development to early years practice?
- Have I used relevant examples to support my evaluation?

D Theories of social and emotional development

D1 The self, others and place in the world

Children are not born into the world knowing who they are and about the society in which they are growing up in. This is something that they learn through interactions with others, including their family, early years practitioners and also their friends. In this section we look at some of the theories that are important in understanding children's social and emotional development.

Normative ages and stages of social and emotional development from birth to 7 years 11 months

Early years practitioners need to have a good understanding of the usual stages and sequences of social and emotional development. This helps them to understand children's behaviours, and also how to support transitions and work effectively with them.

Birth to 3 months

By 3 months, many babies have already started to recognise key elements in their routine by, for example, showing excitement when they see the bath water. Babies are also showing that they like to play and need adults or older children to play with them. Although they recognise their main carers' voices, they are still happy to be held by people that they don't know. This phase, when babies form **indiscriminate attachments**, is likely to last until babies reach around 7 months, when they will develop **specific attachments**.

6 months

At 6 months, few babies cling to their main carers but over the next 2 months they will begin to have distinct preferences for being with familiar people. From 7 to 8 months, these specific attachments will be very obvious.

9 months

With object permanence comes babies' unhappiness if their parents or key carers go out of sight. Babies will now have strong specific attachments to their parents and key people in their lives, and they will develop other attachments too. This is known as the **multiple attachment** phase and is important in the socialisation process. Babies will be happy to be with the people they have formed attachments to, but they are likely to become very distressed when strangers approach and will try to hold onto their parents or key carers.

12 months

Babies definitely have personalities at this stage and their families will know their strong likes and dislikes. They will also have favourite toys and people. Strangers and unfamiliar faces are likely to be a source of upset and the baby will immediately seek reassurance from people they know.

15 months

At this age the need to be near a familiar adult, especially a parent, is strong. These older babies will follow an adult or cry if 'their' adult is out of sight.

18 months

Newly developed physical skills such as walking or climbing mean that toddlers at this age may be quite determined and may show the first signs of becoming frustrated.

Emotionally, toddlers need to be with their main carers and will often check that they are still present even when busy playing.

> **Key terms**
>
> **Indiscriminate attachments** – when babies and children respond equally to anyone who interacts with them, and do not seem to have formed special relationships with anyone in particular.
>
> **Multiple attachments** – when babies and children have many specific attachments to other people.
>
> **Specific attachments** – when babies and children show a particular preference for a single person, or a few people.

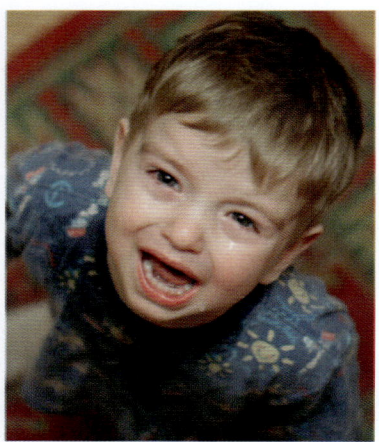

▶ Two-year-old children may throw tantrums when they are frustrated or angry

▶ This child is having fun engaging in role play

2 years

As we saw earlier, 2-year-old children are at a crossroads in their development and this can be a source of frustration and anger. This shows in their behaviour as they may bite others and have strong temper tantrums. As children's language continues to develop, their frustration usually diminishes.

Many 2-year-old children are extremely loving, as they now have strong bonds with their main carers and will want to spend time with them. They show positive emotions such as laughter and try to amuse adults, for example, by pulling faces. They are also keen to be independent and will want to dress or feed themselves. Play is developing and can provide a good channel for their energies as well as a way in which they can practise skills and independence. They are not ready to **play cooperatively**, but they will at times play alongside other children. This is called **parallel play**. The beginnings of imaginative play can be seen, and many 2-year-old children will take out their frustrations on a hapless teddy, for example.

2½ to 3 years

Children at this age still need reassurance from their main carer and will want to spend time being with them. Being afraid of strangers and being left with unfamiliar faces will still cause distress and anxiety. As children move closer towards 3 years, they will be increasingly interested in role play.

At this age, children may start to be interested in other children of their age, although may not necessarily have the social skills to cope with waiting for their turn or the language for cooperative play. This means that children are still playing side by side or standing and watching older children play – **onlooker play**. Once children are near 3 years old, play will become more cooperative.

Table 1.10 summarises children's social and emotional development from birth to 3 years.

▶ **Table 1.10:** Summary of children's typical social and emotional development from birth to 3 years

Age	Social and emotional development
0–3 months	• At 1 month, focuses on human faces with interest • Smiles from 6 weeks
3 months	• Cries when alone • Enjoys being held and spoken to • Indiscriminate attachments – is happy to be held by anyone
6 months	• Recognises emotions in others and responds • Likes being held and played with – indiscriminate attachments
9 months	• Wary of strangers • Prefers being with parents/key carers – specific and multiple attachments • Imitates others' actions such as clapping or peek-a-boo
12 months	• Enjoys simple games with adults such as pat-a-cake or roll-a-ball • Stays close to familiar adults • Enjoys the company of familiar adults and siblings
15 months	• Emotionally dependent on parents and key carers • Dislikes parents or key carers being out of sight • May follow adults out of rooms • Enjoys being played with
18 months	• Is emotionally dependent on parents and key carers • Imitates actions of adults • Plays alone, but enjoys being with adults and siblings • Wants immediate attention

▶ **Table 1.10:** Summary of children's typical social and emotional development from birth to 3 years – *continued*

Age	Social and emotional development
2 years	• Can be distracted from some early tantrums • Has no understanding of waiting for needs to be met • Plays in parallel with others, but cannot share toys
2 ½ years	• Is highly dependent on adults • Can be jealous of other children gaining adult attention • Has tantrums when frustrated • Is impulsive and restless • Enjoys adult attention and praise
3 years	• Is starting to take turns and share for short periods • Enjoys being with other children and may have some friendship preferences • Finds it easier to wait and understand why it might not be possible for wishes to be granted • Will comfort another child

3 to 4 years

After the storm of being 2 years old, the development of most 3-year-old children allows them to be calmer and more sociable. They begin to play well with other children of the same age and gradually start to share and learn to take turns. One reason for this is that their language is more developed.

They are able to play independently, although they still enjoy being with adults. Another significant shift is the way in which 3-year-old children begin to cope when separated from their main carer. Though they are still wary of strangers, most 3-year-old children will happily leave their main carer for someone they know, such as their key worker.

4 to 5 years

During this year, most children will begin school. This is a huge change and means that they will be with many more children than before. For most children, this is not a problem as their social skills have developed and they enjoy playing with others, particularly of the same sex. Most children will also have developed one or two close friendships and although the odd squabble may break out, they have usually learned how to do some simple negotiating.

Most 4-year-old children's behaviour is cooperative, although they do need plenty of reassurance and praise from adults and, as with the younger age group, they need play activities that interest them.

▶ These children have just started school. Can you see how their development of social skills has helped the transition?

5 to 8 years

Socially, most children in this age group have developed some strong friendships. These are based mainly on shared interests, although it is interesting to note that most children will choose same-sex playmates. Children are starting to ascribe reasons to the behaviours of others as they have a developing understanding of theory of mind. For example, a child may say, 'I think he did that because he was missing his mummy.'

Table 1.11 summarises children's social and emotional development from 3 to 8 years.

▶ **Table 1.11:** Summary of children's typical social and emotional development from 3 to 8 years

Age	Social and emotional development
3–4 years	• Comforts children who are in distress • Will now have clear friendship preferences, many of which will be same sex
4–5 years	• Understands the need for rules • Is starting to develop theory of mind • Begins to enjoy sharing with others • Enjoys having friends and is upset if friends are not available • Is able to separate more easily from parents/carers
5–8 years	• Enjoys having rules and reminding others of rules • Is starting to understand the difference between behaviours that are accidental rather than done on purpose • Is protective towards young children • Has strong friendships that are likely to be same sex • Is able to stay overnight with relatives and friends

The impact of social and emotional development on children's overall growth and development

As children's social and emotional development changes over time, it can have a huge impact on other areas of development. As children learn social skills, for example, they are able to play with other children and so develop a range of other skills, including physical ones. As we saw from Vygotsky's theory, children who can develop relationships with others are also likely to be able to learn and develop new ideas as a result. Similarly, as children learn to regulate their emotions and control their frustrations, they are able to persevere for longer and this in turn helps them to concentrate and learn more.

Theories that relate to children's development

For many years, psychologists have been considering the processes by which young children learn and develop. In this part of the unit, we are going to consider some of the classical theories of child development and how they have influenced practitioners' understanding of children. The classical theories of child development provide a starting point, but much research has been carried out since these theories were developed, so some more modern perspectives are also covered.

How children develop self-concept, self-esteem and self-identity

Who are we? What are we like? These are fundamental questions for children, almost like being able to place oneself on a map. In some ways, the development of self-concept is the process by which we gather information about ourselves. It is important because it is closely linked with self-esteem. It is useful to understand the differences between the terms used when talking about self-concept.

▶ Self-concept – this is our vision of our whole selves. It includes our self-esteem, our self-image and our ideal self.

▶ Self-image or self-identity – this is the way that we define ourselves, for example, who we are, where we live, our gender, etc.

▶ Ideal self – this is our view of what we would like to be.

▶ Self-esteem – this is also referred to as self-confidence. Self-esteem is a global evaluation of how we feel about ourselves.

Susan Harter's model of self-esteem

A widely recognised theory of how children develop self-esteem has been put forward by Susan Harter. Her model suggests that our self-esteem is related to how close our self-image and ideal self are. The closer our self-image and ideal self are to each other, the higher our self-esteem. This is shown in Figure 1.9. It is worth noting that it is considered normal for there to be some difference between an individual's self-image and their ideal self.

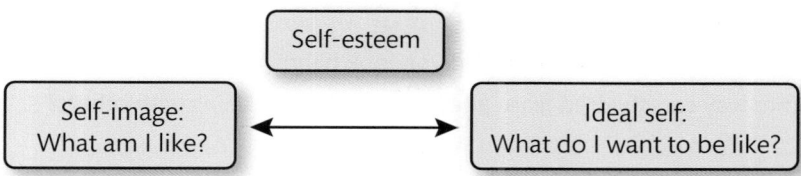

▶ **Figure 1.9:** Susan Harter's model of self-esteem

How children develop self-image

Children gradually develop self-image. The first step for children is to be able to recognise themselves. A well-known test for this is to put a touch of red lipstick on a baby's nose and then put the baby in front of a mirror. A child who is beginning to recognise themselves will touch their nose, rather than the nose in the reflection. Many babies are doing this by the time they are 18 months old and nearly all by the age of 2 years.

The reaction of others

Children also develop self-image as a result of how others react to them. Children may listen to what their parents say about them or notice how carers talk to and treat them. This is sometimes known as the 'looking-glass self' theory. It was first described by Charles Cooley (1864–1929) and has been widely adopted as a popular theory of how self-image is formed. It is thought that this process begins as babies.

If children perceive that they are wanted, liked and loved they will have positive self-regard. If they are constantly criticised they will come to the conclusion that they are not good enough or naughty. Children may also link performance to praise – believing that they must always achieve if they are going to be liked or loved by their parents and carers. This means we must be careful to make sure that we give children 'unconditional praise' to show them that we like them for themselves, as well as praise for their achievements and efforts.

Learning about yourself from others is also thought to contribute to children learning gender expectations. A famous study showed that adults reacted differently towards baby boys than they did towards baby girls.

We also notice the reaction of others to our achievements. If we are good at a skill that is valued, we are likely to feel positive, but if we are good at a skill that others do not value, it does not become a positive part of our self-image. This becomes an issue particularly when children reach school age. For example, a boy who is an excellent dancer will not necessarily have a high self-esteem if dancing is not valued by his friends and peers.

Comparison to others

From around 5 or 6 years, children begin to compare themselves to others. They may notice that they are not running as fast as others in their class or that they are not able to read as fluently. The process of comparison helps children to work out 'their place' but it can also lead them to feel that they are not as good as others. Increasingly, children also look at some children whom they perceive as being popular and make comparisons. It is interesting to note that sometimes children who are doing well at school may still have low self-esteem, simply because they are comparing themselves to their friends whom they may perceive as doing better.

⏸ PAUSE POINT   Explain the concept of 'looking-glass self' in the development of self-identity.

Hint   What do you feel when people around you look happy to see you?

Extend   What other way can children learn about themselves by being with others?

The development of the ideal self

The development of the ideal self is complex. Children will start to pick up messages from teachers, parents, carers and other children about what is valued. We also know that as they grow older children pick up messages from media such as the television. These sources and experiences start to give children ideas of what the 'perfect' child is like.

Case study

'Girls do not play football'

Anna is 7 years old. She has three older brothers, and her family is football mad – her father takes them to support the local football team. Anna loves playing football, and she is quite good at it. However, her parents have noticed that since she went to school, she seems less interested in football. She has even started to refuse to go to football matches, saying that she cannot be a princess if she plays football.

1   What factors may have made Anna change her attitude towards football?

2   How could the school help to make Anna feel that football can be a girl's game?

How a sense of self influences children's confidence, self-image, and understanding of the feelings and emotions of others

Children who have a positive view of themselves are more likely to perceive and relate to others more positively. They are also more likely to become confident and persevere when things are difficult as they are more likely to feel that eventually they can achieve a task. On the other hand, children who have reached the conclusion that they are not liked or that they are not capable are more likely to find it harder to understand others' feelings and actions, and may interpret these incorrectly. Children who have low self-esteem are more likely to ascribe actions and words of others as being hostile and this can affect their responses.

Case study

Jaden's sense of self

Four-year-old Jaden has had a difficult year. His new stepfather has not bonded with him and is often either aggressive or ignores him. Jaden is constantly criticised and his home circumstances are beginning to affect him. At preschool, he is playing with a train set. Another child picks up a train as he wants to join Jaden. Jaden hits out at the other child violently. The preschool supervisor reprimands Jaden.

1 Explain Jaden's behaviour towards the other child.

2 Analyse how Jaden's stepfather's reactions towards him affect his self-image.

3 Why is it important for the early years setting to support Jaden in developing a positive self-image?

Theories that consider moral development

Moral development is about developing values that in turn help you to do the 'right' thing. As part of moral development, children need to learn to show behaviours that help others. This is sometimes called pro-social behaviour. Moral development is a hot topic because the media often suggest that children are not as well behaved as in previous generations.

Pro-social behaviour

Pro-social behaviour is the type of behaviour that we tend to encourage in young children, such as comforting another child or sharing equipment. Psychologists have studied this behaviour to consider whether pro-social behaviour is instinctive or learned. The conclusions reached by some of their studies are interesting, though at times also uncomfortable.

Universal egoism

It is debated among psychologists and social scientists whether pure altruistic behaviour (helping others for no obvious gain) exists. Many believe that all acts of pro-social behaviour are in some way selfish – hence the term 'universal egoism'. If we consider this idea carefully, we may be able to see the logic. Do we stop and give someone a hand when they drop their bag because if we don't we may feel guilty later? Do we sympathise when our friends have problems so that one day they will do the same for us?

If we think about these sorts of questions, it is possible to see the logic of universal egoism. It is suggested that universal egoism is actually one way that the human race ensures its survival and continued existence. For example, a mother might starve herself in order to be able to feed her children.

Reflect

- How do you feel about the concept of universal egoism?
- Can you think of any acts of goodwill, kindness or self-sacrifice that show this theory to be false?

Social learning theory

Later in this section we will look at Bandura's social learning theory, which supports the idea that children learn pro-social behaviour from their parents. Children who grow up seeing adults sharing and helping are more likely to show this type of behaviour themselves.

The social learning theory approach to pro-social behaviour would suggest that we can help children to show caring behaviour by being good role models. We can also take a behaviourist approach and make sure that caring behaviour is reinforced by praising or rewarding 'wanted behaviour'.

1 Give some examples of how you might model pro-social behaviour in your setting.
2 Does your setting have a code of conduct about how adults must behave in the presence of children?

Moral development

At what age are children able to tell right from wrong? In England and Wales the age of legal responsibility – 10 years old – is one of the lowest in Europe.

The development of moral reasoning in children is complex because it involves children's own experiences of being treated fairly, their ability to understand a situation and their ability to empathise with others. One of the most famous approaches to understanding moral development is through a cognitive, i.e. stage, model. This cognitive approach was put forward by Jean Piaget.

Piaget's theory of moral development

In line with his view that cognitive development followed a stage process, Piaget suggested that moral development did the same. Piaget used a clinical interview approach with children, asking them to explain how they were playing games and also by telling them stories. He suggested that children's moral development was a three-stage process. Table 1.12 outlines these three stages.

Piaget felt that during the three stages, children gradually move away from the concept of morality and fairness being imposed by others (heteronomous morality) to a state of understanding that we can be in control of our moral reasoning (autonomous morality).

▶ **Table 1.12:** Piaget's stages of moral development

Stage	Age	Comments
Pre-moral	0–4 years	Children in this stage are learning about right and wrong through their own actions and by considering the effects on adults around them
Moral realism	4–7 years	• In this period children's moral development is greatly influenced by the adults in their lives. Their judgements very much depend on what they think the adults' expectations would be
	7–11 years	• Children are preoccupied with justice and following rules. This means that children have developed a concept of fairness
Moral relativism	11+ years	In this stage children understand the concept of equity, i.e. that treating people in exactly the same way may not result in fairness. For instance, a child who does not understand their homework may need more of a teacher's time than a child who does. The motive for people's actions is also considered by children

Case study

Paint on clothes

Daniel is 4 years old. He loves painting at nursery. Children are encouraged to put on aprons before they start painting, but these aprons do not have any sleeves. One day Daniel did not put an apron on and his mother was angry with him because the new shirt he was wearing got paint on it. Today Daniel is busy painting, but accidentally gets paint on the cuffs of his jumper although he is wearing an apron. He tries to wipe off the paint, but his hands have paint on them as well. More paint gets on the jumper. Daniel starts to cry. He tells the supervisor that he has been naughty.

1   Why might Daniel think that he has been naughty?

2   Is Daniel likely to know the difference between an accident and a deliberate act?

3   Why is it important for adults to consider their reactions to such situations?

Reflect

If Piaget is correct, young children are essentially amoral. They are learning about morality from the actions and reactions of the adults that they are with. They are, therefore, not making judgements for themselves. If children are with adults who have very different moral codes from the setting, this might create difficulties for the child, for example believing it is acceptable to hit another child.

1   How does your setting communicate its values to parents?

2   Why might it be difficult for a child where the setting and parents have very different codes?

Behaviourist theories of social development

Skinner's theory of operant conditioning

In Section C1, we looked at Skinner's theory in terms of how children acquire language. Skinner (1904–1990) also believed that all learning could be shaped by controlling the environment. His theory is therefore used to explain how children may learn aspects of social development, particularly in relation to wanted and unwanted behaviours.

His work was based originally on that of Edward Thorndike (1874–1949). He had shown that when cats were put in a maze they could learn the skills to escape and gain a reward. If they were put in a similar box again, they could then use the skills they had developed to escape once more.

Skinner's research developed Thorndike's work further. His behaviourist theory is known as operant conditioning. The basis of the operant conditioning theory is that learning occurs through behaviour being rewarded or punished. In other words, an association is made between a behaviour and a consequence of that behaviour. Consequences – known as **reinforcers** – can be either negative or positive, and primary or secondary. A reinforcer is anything that strengthens the behaviour it follows.

Positive reinforcers reinforce behaviours because they are pleasurable or meet a need of the child in a positive way. Positive reinforcers commonly used in early years include praise, stickers and attention.

Negative reinforcers are likely to make us repeat behaviour, but this is in order to stop something negative from happening to us. For example, we may continue to wear oven gloves to stop us from being burnt or a child might tidy up to avoid being nagged by their parent.

Key term

Reinforcers – positive or negative experiences that strengthen children's behavioural responses.

63

Punishers are often confused with negative reinforcement. They are another type of reinforcer but are likely to stop us from repeating behaviour. For example, we may learn to stay away from an electric fence after receiving a shock.

PAUSE POINT   Give an example of a positive reinforcer used by adults in early years settings.

Hint   Think about how adults encourage children to show positive behaviour in your work placement.

Extend   What is the difference between a negative reinforcer and a positive reinforcer?

Unexpected positive reinforcers

Skinner found during his experiments that it was often hard to predict what would act as a primary reinforcer, and that it was sometimes only after the event that this became clear. An example of this is when children sometimes deliberately behave badly in order to attract their carer's attention. If they manage to attract attention they are more likely to show the behaviour again, although they might be told off. Gaining the carer's attention in this case is the positive reinforcer even if the child is being reprimanded.

Primary and secondary reinforcers

There are some reinforcers that give us instant pleasure, satisfaction or meet a need. These are referred to as primary reinforcers. Chocolate is a primary reinforcer because most people find that once they put it into their mouth, they enjoy the taste.

Secondary reinforcers are different because they do not give us satisfaction in themselves, but we learn that they symbolise getting primary reinforcement. A good example of secondary reinforcement in our daily lives is money. Coins and notes in themselves do not reward us, but we learn that they can be used to buy things that will give us primary reinforcement, such as food. The learning used when making the association between money and being able to get something in return is classical conditioning.

> **Theory into practice**
>
> Young children do not understand the value of money because they have not made the association between money and pleasure. Toddlers, for example, are often more interested in the size, colour and shape of coins than in their value. This means that offering money as a reward to young children is not very effective.

Schedules of reinforcement

Skinner looked at the effect that giving positive reinforcement at different intervals would have on behaviour. How long would behaviour continue to be shown without a positive reward before extinction takes place?

Interestingly, he found that unpredictable reinforcement works better than continual reinforcement. This would seem to work because it teaches the learner not to expect a reward or reinforcement every time – so they keep on showing the behaviour just in case a reward is given!

In everyday life, this is one of the reasons why gamblers find it so hard to stop playing. They know that they will not win every time, but carry on just in case they get lucky.

Delaying reinforcement

Delaying positive reinforcement, such as saying to a child that they can have a sticker at the end of the week, weakens the effect of the reinforcement. Immediate positive reinforcements are the most effective, partly because the behaviour is then more strongly linked to the reinforcement.

Applying conditioning theory to practice

Conditioning is a very powerful form of learning. It means that children can be encouraged to show wanted behaviour through positive reinforcement, i.e. through giving praise, attention and stickers. However, it also means that if you give positive reinforcement in response to unwanted behaviour, for example, giving a child a packet of sweets to stop them from whining – you may encourage the unwanted behaviour.

In some cases it might be better to ignore a child's behaviour if it is not dangerous. Giving children attention may lead to them being positively reinforced and in doing so help them to learn the unwanted behaviour.

Summary of Skinner's theory

Conditioning, especially operant conditioning, seems to explain in part why, in certain situations, children may learn and demonstrate certain behaviours. As such, operant conditioning is involved in some popular behaviour modification strategies such as star charts or ignoring behaviours, as we have seen. It is also used commercially by retailers. For instance, a reward card is effectively a star chart for adults!

Criticisms of the theories of conditioning

The model of conditioning, especially when applied to child rearing and development, has many limitations. It does not properly address the issues of free will, creativity and temperament. Skinner's work in particular attracted many critics, including Chomsky, who disagreed with Skinner's argument that a controlled environment could totally shape human behaviour for the better.

> **Research**
>
> Read Noam Chomsky's article 'The Case against B. F. Skinner', which appeared in the *New York Review of Books* in 1971. You will be able to find this article online.

Bandura's social learning theory

The social learning theory is a widely accepted theory that originated in America in the 1940s. The key figure among social learning theorists is Albert Bandura (born 1925). The social learning theory is sometimes called 'observational learning'. More recently it has been renamed the social cognitive theory. Social learning theorists are particularly interested in looking at the moral and social behaviour that humans display.

Learning by watching others

Social learning theorists suggest that children learn through **conditioning** and by observing others. This is sometimes referred to as observational learning. It is an interesting theory and many early years professionals will have seen children learn from the behaviour of other children or the behaviour of adults around them.

One of the features of observational learning is that it is spontaneous – children will learn through watching others rather than being shown or taught to do something. For early years professionals and parents/carers, this means that children may copy some aspects of our behaviour that we are unaware of! Though some children will directly copy behaviours, observational learning also means that some children learn not to do something by watching others' experiences.

> **Key term**
>
> **Conditioning** – learning to act in a certain way because past experiences have taught us to do, or not do, certain things.

Terms used in social learning theory

It is useful to understand two terms that are used in observational learning:

▶ model – the person whose behaviour is being imitated/learned from

▶ modelling – the process by which learning takes place.

Bandura's bobo doll experiment

The bobo doll experiment is a famous experiment carried out by Bandura, which showed that children can learn behaviour by watching adults. In the experiment, Bandura showed a film to three groups of children. The film showed an adult in a room with a bobo doll (a large inflatable doll). The three groups of children each saw a different variation of the behaviour of the adult.

▶ Group A saw the adult acting aggressively towards the doll.

▶ Group B saw the adult being aggressive towards the doll but at the end of the film, the adult was rewarded with sweets and lemonade by another adult.

▶ Group C saw the adult being aggressive towards the doll but at the end of the film, a second adult appeared and told off the adult.

After the film, each child was taken in turn into a playroom that had a variety of toys, including the bobo doll. The reactions of the children were recorded. Group C children were the least aggressive towards the doll but there was little difference between groups A and B. This suggested that the children were less influenced by the reward that had been offered to the adult than they were by the behaviour of the adult that they observed.

As a follow up to the experiment, the children were asked if they could demonstrate how the doll had been attacked and they were rewarded for doing so. There was little difference between the three groups of children. This showed that they could all imitate the behaviour they had seen.

Research

Search on video-sharing websites such as YouTube for freely available videos showing Albert Bandura talking about the bobo doll experiment.

The social cognitive theory

Since his original work on social learning theory, Bandura has further explored the elements that are required in order for observational learning to take place. Children do not seem to learn everything that is modelled so it is clear that certain elements must be present. Indeed, Bandura suggests that there are several conditions that are required in order for children to be able to learn from watching others. We will now look at these in some detail.

Attention

First, children need to be interested enough to pay attention and to notice what the adult or other child is doing. In addition, they have to focus on the right elements and avoid distractions or anything irrelevant. For example, an adult might stop and blow their nose while logging on to the computer, but the blowing of the nose is irrelevant to the process. Being able to filter out the irrelevant and focus attention is a skill that develops over time.

Encoding and retrieving information

As we discussed in Section C1, in order for us to learn, information has to be encoded into the long-term memory so that it can be retrieved. The processes that allow **encoding** and **retrieval** of memories are still developing during childhood. Situations that are very complex to understand are, therefore, more difficult for children to learn from.

Key terms

Attachment – a special relationship or bond between a child and people who are emotionally involved with them.

Encoding – the process by which ideas or experiences are converted to memories by the brain.

Retrieval – the process by which memories are 'activated' or recalled, i.e. remembering.

Opportunity to reproduce actions

Children also need to be in the position where they can replicate what they have seen. For instance, a child sees an adult tidying away toys – but they need an opportunity to join in.

Physical skill

A sufficient level of physical skill might also be necessary. For example, a 2-year-old child may see an adult cut a piece of paper along a line, but the child's fine motor skills may not have developed sufficiently to allow them to learn from this.

Motivation

Children need to be interested and motivated to try out what they have learned. They may also have seen that an action results in a reinforcer, such as admiration from others. For example, a 6-year-old child may notice during a PE lesson that other children laugh at a boy who makes silly sounds and be motivated to try this out in order to provoke a similar response.

Self-efficacy and empowerment

As well as looking at how children learn, Bandura has also suggested that as early as the first year of life, babies are learning about self-efficacy. Self-efficacy is the belief that you are able to be successful. Children who have a strong sense of self-efficacy when trying out a new skill believe that eventually they will be able to master it. This means that instead of giving up, a child with self-efficacy will persevere. As self-efficacy is linked to internal beliefs, it is therefore linked to self-esteem.

Bandura suggests that adults have a role in developing self-efficacy. Children who are empowered by adults are more likely to develop a strong sense of self-efficacy. Empowering babies and young children includes providing them with choices, respecting what they are trying to communicate and positively encouraging them to do things for themselves. This includes self-feeding, dressing and exploring their environment.

Theories that consider attachment

The study of children's early relationships and their importance in overall development did not really start until the 1950s when John Bowlby (1907–1990) published *Maternal Care and Mental Health*. The results of this and subsequent research have had noticeable and continuing effects on childcare practice. This means that adults working with babies and children need to have a good understanding of the stages of **attachment** and attachment theory, as well as the effects of separation.

What is meant by attachment?

The term 'attachment' is widely used by psychologists studying children's early relationships. An attachment can be thought of as a unique emotional tie between a child and another person, usually an adult. Research has repeatedly shown that the quality of these ties or attachments will shape a child's ability to form other relationships later in life.

Psychologists have also studied the effects on children when attachments are not made in infancy or when they have been broken, for example, through separation.

Attachment as a process

Psychologists have studied the ways in which babies form early attachments. It is generally accepted that unlike geese, which immediately start to follow the first creature they see after hatching, babies form attachments gradually. There seems to be a general pattern to the way children develop attachments and Table 1.13 summarises these stages.

▶ **Table 1.13:** The stages of forming attachments

Age	Stage	Features
6 weeks–3 months	Pre-attachment	• Babies begin to be attracted to human faces and voices • First smiles begin at around 6 weeks
3 months–7/8 months	Indiscriminate attachments	• Babies are learning to distinguish between faces, showing obvious pleasure when they recognise familiar faces • They are happy to be handled by strangers and prefer to be in human company rather than left alone, hence the term 'indiscriminate attachments'
7–8 months	Specific attachments	• Babies begin to miss key people in their lives and show signs of distress such as crying when a carer leaves the room • Most babies also seem to have developed one particularly strong attachment, often to the mother • Babies show a wariness of strangers even when in the presence of their key people; this may quickly develop into fear, if the stranger makes some form of direct contact with the baby, e.g. by touching them
From 8 months	Multiple attachments	• After making specific attachments, babies go on to form multiple attachments – this is an important part of their socialisation process

Bowlby's theory of attachment

The work of John Bowlby has greatly influenced social care policy, childcare practices and research into early relationships. After the Second World War he was asked to investigate the effects on children who were being brought up in orphanages or other institutions. In 1951 his findings were published. Bowlby showed that meeting children's physical needs alone was not sufficient: children were being psychologically damaged because of the absence of their mothers. He reached this conclusion by looking at the life histories of children who had been referred to his clinic. He noticed an overwhelming trend: most of these children had suffered early separation from their mothers and families.

Features of Bowlby's theory of attachment

1 **Monotropy** – Bowlby believed that babies need to form one main attachment that would be special and of more importance to the child than any other. Bowlby suggested that in most cases this relationship would be formed with the mother, but that it could be formed with the father or another person.

2 **Critical period** – Bowlby was greatly influenced by **ethologists** such as Konrad Lorenz (1903–1989) and therefore he believed that babies need to have developed their main attachment by the age of 1 year. Bowlby also believed that during a child's first four years, prolonged separation from this person would cause long-term psychological damage.

Key term

Ethologist – a person who studies patterns of animal behaviour.

3 **Children need 'parenting'** – Bowlby showed through his findings that simply meeting a child's physical and care needs is not enough for healthy growth and development. Children need to have a main attachment in their early lives to give them consistent support. His early papers suggested that the mother should play this role, although his position changed in later years.

4 **Children show distress when separated from their main attachment** – Bowlby outlined a pattern of distress that babies and children show when separated from their carers. He made links to show that when adults had been separated from their mothers in infancy, they would not form deep and lasting relationships. He called this effect 'maternal deprivation'.

5 **Internal working models** – Bowlby suggested that one of the reasons that strong attachments were so important was because they helped children to develop a view of themselves in relation to others. He called this an 'internal working model' (IWM). The IWM provides children with expectations about themselves, how others behave and how others might behave in relation to them. A child who has positive, loving and consistent responses from their primary carer may develop an internal working model based on these experiences. The child may reach the conclusion that they are loved, worth loving and that others can be trusted to be available and interested. The IWM will therefore influence the child's own responses towards others. The internal working model is not fixed as such, as children's later experiences will continue to inform their model.

Separating babies and children from their main attachments

Most early years professionals will notice that as children become older, they find it easier to separate from their parents. This is because they have formed other attachments to staff and, as they get older, to other children. They have also learned that although their parent is absent, they will return. However, babies and toddlers find it difficult to cope with the absence of their main attachments and will show signs of distress.

Bowlby noted that there seemed to be a pattern to the way children reacted if they were separated from their main attachments. This pattern is often referred to as **separation anxiety**.

Separation anxiety is clearly seen in babies from around 7 months and seems to reach a peak at around 12 to 15 months. Older children will show separation anxiety if they are separated for long periods, for example, if a parent dies or goes away for a period of time.

There seem to be three distinct stages of separation anxiety. These stages are described in Table 1.14.

▶ **Table 1.14:** The stages of separation anxiety

Stage	Features
Protest	Children may cry, struggle to escape, kick and show anger
Despair	• Children show calmer behaviour, almost as though they have accepted the separation • They may be withdrawn and sad • Comfort behaviour such as thumb sucking or rocking may be shown
Detachment	• Children may appear to be over the separation and start to join in activities • The child is actually coping by trying to forget the relationship, hence the term 'detachment' • The effects of detachment may be longer-lasting, as the child may have learned not to trust people they care for

Key term

Separation anxiety – a set of behaviours and actions that occur when a child is distressed as a result of being separated from the person or people to whom they are attached.

Criticisms of Bowlby's work

There are many criticisms of Bowlby's work and it has been superseded by other pieces of research. When looking at the criticisms of his work it is, however, important to remember the political, economic and social climate of the time.

The role of the mother was overemphasised

This has been a major criticism of Bowlby's early work. At the time of writing, women were the traditional caregivers. For economic reasons, after the Second World War, the government was keen for women to return to their traditional roles within the home. Bowlby's later work did emphasise that babies could form an attachment with someone other than the mother.

Attachments to more than one person were not explored

Bowlby placed a lot of emphasis on the importance of one single attachment. Subsequent research has shown that as children get older, they can develop equally strong attachments to other figures such as their fathers and siblings. These are known as multiple attachments, which were defined at the start of this section.

The quality of the substitute care was not taken into consideration

Bowlby did not take into consideration the effect of being in poor-quality care. This means that it is hard to be absolutely sure that the psychological damage done to the children was the result of only maternal deprivation.

Later studies have suggested that children's development may not be affected if there is a substitute person acting as an attachment figure. This is the concept behind the key person system that is used in early years settings today.

Attachment behaviour

It is important for adults working with children to be able to identify when babies and children have made attachments. This can generally be observed through looking at their behaviour. There are four broad indicators that babies and children might show. What is interesting about attachment behaviours of young children is that they are active. Babies and young children show clear responses to a person they have made an attachment to, as follows.

1 They actively seek to be near the other person.
2 They cry or show visible distress when that person leaves or, for babies, is no longer visible.
3 They show joy or relief when that person appears.
4 They show an acute awareness of that person's presence, such as looking up at them from time to time, responding to their voice or following their movements.

▶ Why might a child become upset when their parent or carer leaves them at nursery?

The quality of attachments

There has been some research that has looked at the quality of babies' early attachments. It would seem that, where babies and children are 'securely' attached, they are able to explore and develop their independence. Babies and children whose attachment is less secure seem to show either indifference or clingy types of behaviour.

Mary Ainsworth and the 'strange situation'

The quality of attachments was looked at by Mary Ainsworth (1913–1999) who is considered, alongside Bowlby, to be a key figure in this area of psychology. Mary Ainsworth created a scenario that she used to measure babies' reactions to being left with a stranger and then reunited with their mothers (or fathers). This scenario is now widely used to study attachment behaviour.

The scenario is known as the 'strange situation' and it is divided into eight parts with each part lasting about three minutes. During the experiment, the baby (a 1-year-old) has some time by itself as well as with a stranger, as follows.

1 Parent and baby enter room.
2 Parent remains inactive, baby is free to explore room.
3 Stranger joins parent and infant.
4 Parent leaves room.
5 Parent returns, settles baby and stranger leaves.
6 Parent leaves and baby is alone in the room.
7 Stranger returns and interacts with baby.
8 Parent returns again and stranger leaves.

Ainsworth and her colleagues were particularly interested in the reactions of the baby to the parent when they left or returned and the way in which the parent interacted with the baby.

They categorised the behaviour into three types.

- **Type A: insecure anxious/avoidant** – baby largely ignores parent and shows little sign of distress when parent leaves, continuing to play. Baby ignores or avoids parent on their return. Baby dislikes being alone, but can be comforted by stranger.

- **Type B: secure** – baby plays while parent is present, but shows visible distress when parent leaves, and play is reduced. Baby is easily comforted on return of parent and carries on playing. Cries when alone because the parent is not there but can be partly comforted by the stranger. Reactions towards stranger and parent are markedly different.

- **Type C: insecure ambivalent/resistant** – baby is wary and explores less than other types. Very distressed when parent leaves and actively resists stranger's attempts to comfort. Wants immediate contact with parent on return but is ambivalent, showing frustration and anger alongside clinginess, for example, wanting to be held but then immediately struggling to get down.

Later, an additional category of attachment (disorganised/disoriented) was added to Ainsworth's work by Mary Main, which Ainsworth accepted. The additional category was added because it was noticed that while some children were in theory showing 'secure attachments' there were some aspects of their responses which indicated that they were under stress in the presence of their caregiver. This included looking towards their parent for reassurance, but not making eye contact. Children might also show uncertainty or fear, although these responses were noted to be momentary in their nature.

Why are some children more securely attached than others?

Ainsworth came to the conclusion that the quality of attachment depended on the parenting that the baby received. Where parents were able to sense and predict their babies' needs and frustrations, the babies showed type B behaviour, i.e. securely attached. This meant that they were able to explore and play, knowing that their parent was a safe base. Parents who have received poor parenting themselves, or have been depressed or misusing substances, are less likely to have securely attached children as they are unable to consistently respond to their children in a positive way.

> **Research**
>
> Search on video-sharing websites such as YouTube for freely available videos showing Mary Ainsworth's 'strange situation' experiment.

⏸ PAUSE POINT What attachment style does a child have who is distressed when their parent leaves, but after immediate contact with the parent on return shows frustration and anger?

Hint Choose from secure, insecure anxious/avoidant, disorganised/disoriented or insecure ambivalent/resistant.

Extend Explain why a child might not have a secure attachment to their parent.

> **Theory into practice**
>
> Research findings on the need for babies and young children to have surrogate attachments in order to cope with separation from their parents or key carers has changed practice in early years settings. It is now good practice for settings to have a key person or key worker system in place. This is a member of staff who will take special responsibility for developing a strong relationship with a particular child.
>
> 1 How does your placement setting help children to settle in?
>
> 2 Why is it important that children have a strong bond with their key person?

Theory that considers children's development in relation to their environment

We saw earlier in this unit that there is an interplay between 'nature' and 'nurture' in terms of children's development. We also looked at the role of societal systems in relation to their development. An interesting theory that looks at children's development in terms of their social environment has been proposed by Urie Bronfenbrenner.

Urie Bronfenbrenner's ecological systems theory

Urie Bronfenbrenner (1917–2005) proposed that children's development has to be seen in the context of the overall environment that the child experiences, or the 'ecological system'. He proposed five systems that are usually represented in concentric circles to demonstrate how they interrelate.

▶ **Microsystem** – refers to all the settings with which children have strong direct connections. Children are likely to have several microsystems. One microsystem will be the child's home and family, but a child may also attend a nursery (another microsystem) or go to a swimming club.

▶ **Mesosystems** – situations and times when two or more of the child's microsystems come together in some way. For example, the child's parent may volunteer at the child's school or the child's swimming club might organise a family picnic.

▶ **Exosystems** – these are one step beyond the child's immediate experiences, but have an impact on what happens in the mesosystems and microsystem. The example commonly given is the parent's workplace. The threat of redundancy is likely to impact on the child's home, even though the child is not directly linked to the workplace.

▶ **Macrosystem** – this is a further layer outwards and something that is out of the control of the child and their family, but it still has an influence on the other systems. It is about the economic and cultural situation of the community and society in which the child and their family is living – for example, a new government decides to cut the funding for preschool places. This in turn affects whether the parent can work and also whether the child can spend time in education.

▶ **Chronosystem** – this is the final layer and provides the context in terms of the 'history' of both the society and the child's life. A family feud may have influenced generations of attitudes towards trusting others with money or, taking a larger view, the development of telecommunications has influenced how some work is carried out. For example, some parents may now be able to work from home.

The influence of Bronfenbrenner's theory

Since Bronfenbrenner's theory has emerged, greater consideration has been given to seeing child development as interrelated to the cultural and social context in which the child is raised. It has also influenced policies with a view to supporting children and their families. It means that early years settings need to think about experiences that the child and their family have had which might impact on development.

Ⅱ **PAUSE POINT**   Name each of the systems of Bronfenbrenner's ecological systems model.

Hint   There are five, ending with chronosystem.

Extend   Why is it important for early years settings to understand the impact of children's immediate and wider networks?

D2 Applying theories of social and emotional development to early years practice

In the previous section we looked at the theories and models that discuss how children learn behaviours, and their social and emotional development. The following tables show how these theories can be applied to work in early years.

First, Table 1.15 shows how Piaget's theory of moral development can impact your practice.

▶ **Table 1.15:** How Piaget's theory of moral development can influence practice within settings

Description	How the theory could influence practice	How to apply the theory to practice
Piaget came to the conclusion that children are essentially amoral. He did, however, recognise that children are influenced by adult reactions	• To make sure that expectations of children's moral behaviour are age/stage appropriate • To make sure that adults understand that children's early learning about pro-social and moral behaviour is dependent on their reactions	• Recognise that children are likely to follow the examples set by the adult • Make sure that your reactions to incidents and unwanted behaviour are proportional and provide explanations of why it is good to behave in certain ways, e.g. if a child has forgotten something, do not react as if aggressive behaviour has been shown • Expect that although children may be able to tell you the setting's rules, they will not necessarily be able to resist temptation!

The behavioural theories we discussed can also influence early years practice, as Table 1.16 shows.

▶ **Table 1.16:** How theories that consider how children learn behaviours can influence practice within settings

Theory of social learning (e.g. Bandura)	
Description: Suggests that children learn skills and attitudes, but that they also learn behaviours from watching adults	
How the theory could influence practice	**How to apply the theory to practice**
• To help children learn manners, thoughtfulness and turn taking • To help inspire children to try out a new activity or skill • To help children learn a new skill from observing an adult (if the skill is developmentally within their grasp)	• Make sure that you are role modelling the attitudes and behaviours you wish children to repeat • Recognise that children can pick up unwanted behaviours after observing adults • Set up role play activities following a visit or outing • Remember: the later version of this theory also considered the factors that are required for this to take place. We looked at these factors in Section D1. When developing practice based on this theory, remember that the age of the child will affect the skills they are able to learn

Theory of operant conditioning (e.g. Skinner)	
Description: Suggests that adults can reinforce children's wanted behaviour	
How the theory could influence practice	**How to apply the theory to practice**
• To help children learn wanted behaviours such as manners, tidying up after an activity and turn taking • To encourage children to persist at an activity • To consider whether some behaviours have been learned because young children have had reinforcement for showing unwanted behaviours, e.g. children may tip out toys onto the floor because an adult always reacts	• Remember that positive reinforcements work better when they are provided at the time of the wanted behaviour or very shortly afterwards • When providing positive reinforcements, explain to a child why the reinforcement is given so that the child understands the link • Use intermittent schedules of reinforcement, e.g. reinforcements that are not regular • Recognise that the strongest positive reinforcement is usually adult attention and that if a child is showing an unwanted behaviour it is sometime best to ignore it • Make sure that you do not use secondary reinforcers, such as star charts, with children whose cognitive development means that they do not understand the concept • Make sure that expectations of wanted behaviour are age/stage appropriate • Understand that some unwanted behaviours are not linked to getting adults' attention but because the behaviour itself is pleasurable, e.g. children run rather than walk because it is more fun to run • Remember: in the long term, children's internal motivation is key to their later success, e.g. children who learn to feel pride in their own efforts will enjoy an activity for its own sake. Another example is a child who chooses to help another child because they wish to, rather than because they want praise from adults. Both of these examples demonstrate internal motivation

John Bowlby's attachment theory has been influential on the key person system that operates in settings today. It has also been useful for improving our practice in other ways. Table 1.17 outlines these ways.

▶ **Table 1.17:** How theories that consider attachment can influence practice within settings

Bowlby's attachment theory and Ainsworth's research into the security of attachment	
Description: The work of John Bowlby and Mary Ainsworth suggests that children need strong attachments to their parents, but also to the adults who are with them when their parents are not available. This has resulted in the introduction of the key person system to settings	
How the theory could influence practice	**How to apply the theory to practice**
<ul><li>To ensure children are not distressed when separation from their parents takes place</li><li>To ensure the smooth transition between home and the setting</li><li>The provision of a key person system within settings</li></ul>	<ul><li>Make sure that each child in the setting has a key person and has time to become settled – settling-in procedures must be flexible</li><li>Find out about the child's previous experiences of separation, recognising that children who have previously been distressed may take longer to settle in and build a relationship with you</li><li>Build a relationship with children before their parents leave them for the first time</li><li>Consider the routines of the day and whether there are enough opportunities for key children to spend time with you</li><li>Work closely with parents to provide continuity of care and act to reunite the child with their parent if there are signs of separation anxiety</li><li>Make sure that you show unconditional care for the child</li></ul>

We also discussed Urie Bronfenbrenner's ecological systems theory in Section D1. Table 1.18 shows how his theory can be applied to our practice.

▶ **Table 1.18:** How a theory that considers children's development in relation to their environment can influence practice within settings

Bronfenbrenner's ecological systems theory	
Description: This theory suggests that the child's immediate environment, community and wider society can influence their development	
How the theory could influence practice	**How to apply the theory to practice**
<ul><li>To understand the importance of working in partnership with parents</li><li>To find ways of working closely within and with the local community</li></ul>	<ul><li>Aim to build strong relationships with parents</li><li>Provide plenty of information about what the child is doing within the setting</li><li>Talk to parents about their child and what they feel their child's strengths and weaknesses are</li><li>Involve parents in the planning for their child and, if appropriate, provide advice about activities they could do at home</li><li>Create opportunities for parents to participate within the setting</li><li>Look for ways of lending resources and materials to parents</li><li>Take an interest in what children enjoy doing at home and with their family and friends</li><li>Create links with the local community, e.g. the allotment society, local faith groups and health services</li><li>Organise visits to the local community</li></ul>

Developing and maintaining friendships

We have seen that over time, children develop friendships with others. We look at the stages of this in more detail in Unit 7. Attachment theory would suggest that the ease with which children make relationships and friendships will depend on their experience of attachments with their parents and primary carers. We saw earlier that Bowlby suggested that one aspect of attachment is the way that children develop an 'internal working model' about what they can expect of others and this in turn can impact on their own responses. Children, for example, who have insecure attachments may not have developed the underlying skills to cope with reciprocal relationships from around 3 years and so may act aggressively, not be interested or show very inconsistent behaviours.

The behaviourist model that Skinner put forward can in theory be used to explain how some children may learn skills that will help them develop friendships and the trust of other children. A child who is encouraged and praised for sharing toys or waiting for a turn may repeat this behaviour. The question is, of course, whether in the long term the child is able to maintain this behaviour when the adult is not there. If, on the other hand, the child spontaneously shares a toy and then is thanked with a smile by another child, the child may learn to associate sharing with feeling good.

Children may also learn about friendships and making relationships by seeing the behaviours that are valued by others modelled by adults. This links to the social learning theory, as explained by Bandura. It has implications, as we will see later, for the practical ways in which adults may work in early years settings.

Developing an understanding of self

We have seen several theories that explain how children develop an understanding of self and others, as well as their own place in the world. As mentioned above, Bowlby suggests that children develop an 'internal working model' which later influences how they relate to others. In terms of early years practice, this would suggest that we should seek to ensure that children have secure attachments with their key person and that the key person needs to show consistent love and care.

In terms of developing self-esteem, we have seen that children learn from seeing how they are responded to by others. This is the 'looking-glass self' theory and means that how we and other children respond to a child will impact on their self-identity. We have also seen that Bandura proposes that self-efficacy is gained through empowerment. Brought together, this means that adults working with children need to provide positive encouragement and plenty of opportunities for children to be able to explore independently.

Many early years settings look for ways of making children feel positive about themselves. They may, for example, put up photographs of children or ensure that a child has a named peg on which to put their coat to encourage a sense of belonging. It is also common for early years settings to provide opportunities for role play so that children can try out 'powerful' roles and also explore their own place in the world. This often involves modelling actions and words that adults use in their lives. Having opportunities for role play can support self-efficacy as it can help children to feel competent and powerful.

Theory into practice

Does your work placement have the following?
- displays of photographs of children
- mirrors in baby and toddler rooms
- personalised pegs in the cloakroom
- named trays for personal possessions.

Do children seem positive about these ways of making them feel special?

Influences on social and emotional development

We have seen that the context in which a child grows up can affect their social and emotional development. This is the basis of Bronfenbrenner's theory. The influence of the immediate family and network around very young children needs to be taken into consideration by practitioners in early years settings. Each child's experiences will be different and will depend on a range of factors, including:
- the social and economic class into which they were born
- whether their immediate family members are in work or unemployed
- what level of education the child's parents or main carers have had.

It is important that we do not make assumptions about the experiences that a child has had. For example, a child who is used to being cared for by a childminder, because his parents go to work, may settle in very differently from a child who has never been left with anyone other than family members.

The influence of family systems is complex, as to an extent every child and every family is unique and will have its own values, customs and behaviours. These may be the result of social class, environment or attachment styles. In some families, for example, children will always sleep with their parents and so a baby may become distressed at nap time, if put alone in a cot. Co-sleeping might be a result of a family being housed in a one-bedroom flat or it might be as a result of parents' attachment style.

The many variables in the way that children will experience their earliest years means that adults working with children need to work in partnership with parents. This will help them think about how best to support children's social and emotional development appropriately.

The wider network surrounding a child's family, including the local community, can affect a child's social and emotional development. A **cohesive society** is likely to provide a supportive and healthy environment, which may help positive parenting. Children may also benefit from the protection of the wider community. Children from communities that lack this cohesion may find it more difficult to develop social relationships.

Cohesive society – a society or group whose members identify with the same values and beliefs and who work together to ensure the well-being of all members.

Case study

The impact of family system on a child's social development

Jamie is 4 years old and has just started at the nursery. He comes from a family that uses swear words as part of their communication style. In nursery, he has sworn at a member of staff. Jamie is taken to one side and reprimanded. Jamie looks confused.

1 Using a theory, explain the technique by which Jamie has learned this behaviour.
2 How is Jamie's social development being affected by family systems?
3 Consider why it is important for the nursery to consider the context in which Jamie is growing up when working with him.

How children form attachments

We have seen that attachment begins in the first year of life and that, according to theorists such as Bowlby, the quality of a child's attachment can play an important role in the way that children interact with others. In Unit 7, we consider the stages of friendship and also how adults play an important role in supporting children's relationships and attachments to others.

In practice, the starting point in early years settings to support attachments and relationships with others is to ensure that babies and young children have a secure relationship with their key person. While this relationship will not replace their attachment to their parents or primary carers, it will prevent children from showing separation anxiety.

Using the key person as their base, children can then develop relationships and, from around 3 years old, reciprocal friendships with other children. The key person can play an important part in this by providing an environment that allows children's social skills to develop. This might include using mealtimes as social occasions where children can pass things to each other or work collaboratively to lay a table or prepare food. It might also mean thinking about the resources on offer and providing

opportunities for the youngest children to play side by side (parallel play) without actually having to share materials. Sand, water and other sensory materials often work well in this respect.

Adults can also provide opportunities for supervised activities such as cooking, going to feed a pet or sharing a book to help children come together and share a focus. With children from 3 years who are normally starting to play cooperatively, it is usual for early years settings to provide plenty of opportunities to use role play. This type of play helps children to explore their role in relation to others in a safe way. This can be helpful in relation to self-identity, but also to help children learn about the rules and boundaries within friendship.

Supporting positive relationships

Over time, children need to learn how to interact with other children and develop positive relationships. As we have seen, social development is linked to other developmental areas including cognition, language and particularly to emotional development. Most children start to show cooperation with other children from around 3 years. Adults working with children need to support them through the many aspects of being with others. This includes being able to collaborate, resolve potential conflicts and also helping children to follow codes and rules. We have seen that Bandura's social learning theory suggests that many of these skills can be developed through adults' role modelling behaviours. For example, an adult may join children in play and ask whether or not they can take some of the construction bricks, thus showing children how to be cooperative in play. The adult may also role model collaborative behaviour by demonstrating skills such as listening to others' ideas and helping out as a team member.

It is also thought that children can learn some skills by watching and repeating adults' responses to conflict. This means that when adults intervene if there are squabbles, children will be learning the skills of negotiation and also problem-solving. If adults talk calmly and listen to each child's point of view, it is more likely that children will repeat this behaviour later. Similarly, if the adult introduces a strategy such as the use of an egg timer so that children can take 'fair' turns with, for example, a wheeled toy, children are more likely to repeat this strategy.

Adults working with children may also find it helpful to consider Piaget's work about children's understanding of rules, and how very young children may find it hard to follow rules, especially during play with others. This might result in adults understanding that very young children will need additional support and supervision in order to cope in situations when rules and boundaries are important.

PAUSE POINT   Explain the role of modelling in supporting children to make positive relationships.

Hint   Think about how adults might intervene when children have squabbles.

Extend   Which theorist put forward the view that children can learn by copying the actions of adults?

Effects of transitions

The term 'transition' is used when children move from one setting or carer to another. Bowlby suggested that where children did not have an attachment available to them, they would show signs of separation anxiety. When a child's attachment needs are not being fully met, a transition between home and school, or even between different family members, can impact negatively on their social and emotional development. Even a securely attached child, if put in a situation where an attachment is not available, may start to show some separation responses including withdrawal, distress or anger. We looked at the role of stress and cortisol in Section A3 and researchers now believe that when children are showing separation anxiety, high levels of cortisol are being produced.

This means that transitions have to be carefully managed in order for children to remain secure and so maintain positive social and emotional development. This is why early years settings have a key person system whereby an adult spends time creating a bond with a child, so that the child will always have an attachment. It is also good practice for early years settings and schools to have a settling-in system.

Where a child already has a strong attachment with their parent or primary carer, it is often easier for them to develop a new attachment as they have developed a positive 'internal working model'. This means they are more likely to respond positively to a transition, provided that time is given for a new attachment to be formed. On the other hand, where a child has an insecure attachment to their parent or primary carer, or where the family dynamics are such that children have inconsistent responses, they may find transitions harder.

Case study

Harry's response to separation

Harry is 2 years old. He lives with his mother and 6-year-old sister. As a family, they keep to themselves, although Harry's sister is at school and has many friends. While his sister is at school, his mother starts to feel unwell. She calls 999 and an ambulance comes to the house. A neighbour offers to keep an eye on Harry. Harry does not know the neighbour at all. Harry is distraught and the neighbour cannot comfort him. For 3 hours, Harry screams and cries on and off. The neighbour tries to distract him and tells him that everything will be all right. When his sister arrives, Harry's response is immediately different.

1   Using a theory, explain Harry's initial responses when he is alone with the neighbour.

2   Explain why Harry's behaviour changed after his sister arrived.

3   Consider whether this incident might affect Harry when he starts nursery next year.

Link

Go to Unit 7, Section B to find more information about managing transitions.

Supporting children to understand and express feelings

Learning to understand and express feelings appropriately is linked to many aspects of children's development including cognition and language. Having said this, children are also influenced by their own experiences of watching what others do. Bandura's theory of social learning suggests that children learn by copying the reactions and responses of adults. This theory could therefore be applied to help children learn how to express their feelings appropriately. It would mean that practitioners need to talk about how they are feeling and also show appropriate strategies to deal with their feelings. Through the process of modelling combined with an explanation, children are more likely to understand their own and others' feelings.

As well as dealing with feelings appropriately, adults can also help children to learn about sympathy and, eventually, empathy if they role model sympathetic and empathetic responses to children. Sympathy is about recognising others' feelings and very young children are often able to show this. Empathy is often harder for young children to demonstrate as it requires imagining what it might feel like to be the other person and then to respond appropriately. In some ways, the skill of empathy is similar to 'decentring', which Piaget considered in his theory of cognitive development (see Section C1).

The theory put forward by Skinner would also suggest that if children were positively reinforced for expressing their feelings appropriately, showing empathy or sympathy towards others, they would be more likely to learn and repeat strategies. In early years settings, this means, for example, that we might positively acknowledge a child who offers a crying child a toy.

Assessment practice 1.4   AO1   AO2   AO3   AO4

A childminder is keen to understand more about children's social and emotional development and has asked you to share your learning. She wants to be able to apply theories of development to her practice.

Your information should:

- identify the typical stages of social and emotional development

- explain relevant theories of social and emotional development

- evaluate the importance of attachment theory on current early years practice

- analyse, using theories of social and emotional development, how children can be supported to develop friendships.

Plan
- Can I identify ages and stages of children's social and emotional development?

- Do I understand the theories of social and emotional development?

- Do I understand the links between practice and theory?

Do
- Have I read Unit 7 about social and emotional development?

- Are my explanations relevant to a childminder?

Review
- Am I confident that I understand the key theories of social and emotional development?

- Am I able to relate these theories to practice?

Further reading and resources

Books

Donaldson, M. (1986) *Children's Minds*, London: HarperCollins.

Gerhardt, S. (2004) *Why Love Matters: How Affection Shapes a Baby's Brain*, Hove: Routledge.

Lindon, J. (2012) *What Does It Mean To Be Two?* 3rd edition, London: Practical Pre-School Books.

Lindon, J. and Brodie, K. (2016) *Understanding Child Development 0–8 Years: Linking Theory and Practice*, 4th edition, London: Hodder Education.

Smith, P. K., Cowie, H. and Blades, M. (2015) *Understanding Children's Development*, 6th edition, Chichester: John Wiley & Sons.

Thornton, S. (2008) *Understanding Human Development: Biological, Social and Psychological Processes from Conception to Adult Life*, Basingstoke: Palgrave Macmillan.

Websites

www.gov.uk – UK Government: access to the *Early Years Inspection Handbook*.

www.nace.co.uk – National Association for Able Children in Education: support and resources for teachers working with able, gifted and talented children.

www.nagc.org – National Association for Gifted Children: information and resources to support teachers and parents of gifted learners.

www.potentialplusuk.org – Potential Plus UK: support and information for parents and carers of gifted and talented children.

www.poverty.ac.uk – Poverty and Social Exclusion: access to *The Foundation Years: Preventing Poor Children becoming Poor Adults.*.

THINK ▶ FUTURE

Debra Collinson Nursery manager

Debra has been the manager of Little Angels nursery for 6 years. She cannot emphasise strongly enough how important it is to have a good knowledge of child development when working with children. A lot of parents want to know what normal behaviour is and whether their child is doing well. Being able to reassure parents, especially when it comes to the behaviour of their 2-year-old, is very important.

An understanding of child development and theories also helps the nursery to plan. Understanding that children learn from copying, for example, means that staff often sit and do an activity, knowing that children will come over, watch them and then join in.

Having a good knowledge of child development also helps staff to identify children who are not making the type of progress that is expected for their age. Sometimes, there are short-term factors that explain this, such as a change in the family, but at other times, the team work with parents and may suggest a referral. The good news is that, in this area, children who need some additional help are well supported, and early intervention seems to make quite a lot of difference.

Focusing your skills

Sustained shared conversations

One of the ways that practitioners can affect children's cognitive and language development is by talking to them and interacting with them. Here are some tips.

- Look carefully at what a child is doing. What seems to be of interest to them?
- Go down to the child's level and spend some time doing the activity they are engaged in.
- Allow a little time to pass and then make a statement about the activity, for example 'The spider is very busy.'
- Be aware of the child's reaction and allow time for a response.
- If the child makes a response, follow their conversational direction.
- If appropriate, ask for their thoughts about what is happening, e.g. 'Do you think the spider gets tired?'

Supporting self-efficacy

Bandura suggests that developing positive beliefs about one's own competence begins early in life. The way that adults support children can make a difference to whether or not they come to the conclusion that they can be active and competent, or that they are essentially helpless. With children under 2 years old, it is particularly important not to intervene too early when a child has a set goal. For example, if a baby is trying to reach something it might be tempting just to pass it to him, but this will not support self-efficacy. A better approach would be to wait a moment and observe. If the child is not frustrated, perhaps with a little more effort he will be able to achieve his goal. If this is not possible, perhaps you can discreetly nudge the object a little closer so that the child is still able to accomplish what he set out to reach.

Getting ready for assessment

This section has been written to help you to do your best when you take the external test. Read through it carefully and ask your tutor if there is anything you are not sure about.

About the test

The externally assessed test for Unit 1 will consist of a written paper set and marked by Pearson. All questions are designed to assess your understanding of how the principles, theories and models of development apply to individual children.

The assessment is in two parts. Section A will consist of scenario-based questions which assess how well you can apply theory to practical real-life situations. Section B will contain long-answer questions that will assess your ability to analyse and interpret theories, how they relate to other domains of development and their impact on early years practice.

There are two test dates every year and your tutor will decide when to enter you for the test. It is possible to resit the exam.

As the guidelines for assessment can change, you should refer to the official assessment guidance on the Pearson Qualifications website for the latest definitive guidance.

Preparing for your written assessment

You will need to have a good knowledge of children's normative development in each of the developmental areas. This often requires repeated practice and revision.

By the test date you should be able to recall what children at each age/stage of development should be able to do.

In order to help you revise, you could set true or false quizzes for yourself and your peers, or play games where someone describes what a child is doing and you have to say what age the child is.

You also need to be able to identify when a child is portraying atypical behaviour. This might be a 3-year-old child who is not able to talk at all, or even a 3-year-old child who is able to read a book fluently.

Some of the questions test whether you can apply the information given in the case study to theories of, and approaches towards, development.

The specification that you may be given, or that you can download from the Pearson website, lists theorists and models of child development that you may be tested on. It is important that you familiarise yourself with the specification well before the test, and make sure that you revise all aspects of it.

To help you revise theories of development

- Make a series of cards that give you brief information about the main points of each theory and how they relate to what children do. Then, test your peers on the name of a theorist and the main points of their theory.

- Look at what children are doing while you are on placement. Think about their actions and how these actions relate to a theorist.

In the test you will need to read the case study scenario carefully and think about what might relate to children's development. Remember that factors can either have a positive or negative effect on children's development.

Think about the children in your setting. What positive factors are influencing their development? In what way is their development being negatively affected?

Look for opportunities for doing case study type activities – there are some in this unit.

Worked Example

Here is a sample case study. Although the case study is shorter than the ones given in the test, it will help you to get a feel for this type of task.

Case study

Kyle is 3 years old. He came to our nursery when he was just 2 years old. He found it very difficult to separate from his mother but we have a strong settling-in system and he soon made a good attachment with his key person. He mostly prefers to play alone or with his key person and does not seem to be interested in role play. He enjoys being outdoors and last week his key person spotted that he was copying other children who were playing on tricycles. Kyle soon enjoyed going round and round on a tricycle and manoeuvring it skilfully. Kyle is beginning to talk and communicates mainly through a combination of signs and single words. Tests have shown that he has a conductive hearing loss.

Question 1

Describe how **one** aspect of Kyle's physical development meets the expected pattern of development.

Tip: Always look at the 'descriptor' verb in a question (e.g. 'describe' or 'explain'). This question asks you to describe one aspect of Kyle's physical development. Just writing a couple of words is not likely to get you full marks as you have to say what Kyle is doing and how this relates to the usual pattern of development. Ask your tutor for more information about these 'descriptor' verbs so that you can familiarise yourself with them before the test.

Question 2

Explain how a social learning theory can be applied to Kyle's play.

Tip: To answer this kind of question, you will need to know your theorists well. Begin by working out how Kyle's behaviours or actions link to a theory you have studied. Then, tie these behaviours in with the theory. Do not just write everything you know about the theorist, as this will waste words and time.

Question 3

Describe **one** factor in the scenario that may have affected Kyle's development.

Tip: This question is asking you to write about one factor and how it might have affected Kyle's development. Do not write about more than one factor as you will waste time. You should, however, read the question carefully and make sure that you give the number of examples the question is asking for. Hint: in this case study there is one factor that is likely to be affecting two areas of Kyle's development.

Sample answers

Answer to Question 1

Kyle is showing typical physical development in relation to gross motor movements. He has used the skills of steering, pedalling and balance at the same time, thus showing a good level of coordination. As most children aged 3 years can manoeuvre a tricycle skilfully and avoid obstacles, Kyle is showing typical physical development in this area.

Examiner's comment

This learner has accurately assessed this child's physical development and has demonstrated that they understand the physical skills involved. The answer could have been more concise as there is some repetition, but overall it is a good answer.

Answer to Question 2

Kyle was motivated to use the tricycles after seeing other children use them. This is an example of Bandura's social learning theory as Kyle has observed the other children and is now following their actions. The older children have 'modelled' this behaviour.

Examiner's comment

The learner has mentioned Bandura's theory, but has not fully explained the theory in relation to what has happened. The answer implies that the reader will know about the theory. This is therefore not quite a full answer.

Answer to Question 3

Kyle is not playing with the other children because his conductive hearing loss is preventing him from hearing them properly. It is also likely to affect the clarity of his speech, so the other children may not understand what he is saying. This will affect his social development because he is spending time alone and not practising social skills.

Examiner's comment

This is a comprehensive answer and shows that the learner understands the impact of conductive hearing loss on this child's social development. Alternative answers could have looked at Kyle's emotional development as a result of his conductive hearing loss and also his language development.

Here is another example of a case study.

Case study

Ben is 2 years old and has just started at nursery. He lives with his sister who is 5 years old and his mother. Before Ben was born, his mother had depression and also misused alcohol. Money is very tight and Ben's mother finds it hard to manage the budget. Some days, the children are given a packet of crisps for dinner rather than a meal.

When at nursery, Ben tends to like to be in sight of his key person. His key person has noted that he barely misses his mother and at the end of the session often ignores her. The nursery has also noticed that Ben does not want to play outdoors and seems constantly tired. He always asks for additional food at snack time. His mother said that he only started walking at 20 months. When Ben is encouraged to play, he often plays alongside other children of his age, although he does not cooperate or share his things with them. He sometimes snatches toys from other children rather than asking first.

Question 1

Identify Ben's stage of social development.

Tip: This question uses the descriptor 'identify' which means that the answer you provide can be quite concise. To answer this question, you need to know what the typical stage of development is for Ben's age range.

Question 2

Explain Ben's responses to his key person and mother in relation to attachment theory.

Tip: To answer this question you need to show that you understand the theories of attachment and that you can apply them to this case study.

Question 3

Analyse how Ben's physical development might be affected by his diet.

Tip: This question is about Ben's physical development and so marks will not be awarded for answers that deal with other aspects of development. The descriptor is 'analyse' and so your answer should show that you can apply your knowledge of factors and theories affecting physical development to the case study.

Sample answers

Answer to Question 1

> Ben's social development is delayed because he is not playing with other children and also because he snatches things from them.

Examiner's comment

This answer is incorrect. The learner has not accurately identified the stage of development of this child.

Ben's stage of development is typical for a 2-year-old. The milestone for sharing and cooperative play is 3 years, so Ben is within the normal range of expected development.

Answer to Question 2

> Ben is not securely attached. Most children would respond positively when their parents come to pick them up at the end of the session while Ben ignores his mother. He seems to like his key person though.

Examiner's comment

This answer is not complete and so cannot be awarded full marks. The learner has not fully answered the question as no links to attachment theory are given. The learner has identified that Ben is not securely attached but has not given a sufficiently detailed analysis of his attachment. The learner has shown knowledge of what responses children would typically give if they were securely attached.

Answer to Question 3

> From the information given, it would appear that Ben may not be eating a healthy diet. According to Maslow's hierarchy of needs theory, food is a basic need and so if Ben is not eating a nutritional diet, he will not be able to engage in other activities such as going outdoors that will further other aspects of his physical development. Ben's lack of energy is unusual for his age. Most children are very active at this age. He was also slow to walk as most children are walking by 18 months. The lack of energy and late walking might be caused by a diet lacking in nutrition. If he is constantly tired, he will not be able to develop both gross and fine motor skills, which in turn will affect his development in these. The nursery will need to ensure that Ben's needs for food are met and they should ensure that the food that they are serving is nutritious.

Examiner's comment

This is a good answer. The learner has shown that they can apply theory correctly to the case study. The learner has also compared Ben's development to typical development and shown the impact of poor nutrition on future development. The recommendation that the nursery should focus on serving nutritious food also shows that the learner can apply theory to early years practice.

Development of Children's Communication, Literacy and Numeracy Skills

2

Getting to know your unit

Do you remember learning to talk? The chances are that you have no particular memory of it. This is because most children have mastered talking by around the age of 4 years. Being able to communicate and talk with others is an important skill as it leads to children being able to read, write and learn about mathematical concepts. This unit looks at children's development of communication, early literacy and numeracy skills. You will see how children acquire these important skills and how adults can support children at all stages of their journey.

How you will be assessed

This unit will be assessed through a task set and marked by Pearson and taken under supervised conditions.

You will be provided with a task brief and related task activities, based around a scenario involving an early years setting. You will be able to spend time preparing and planning before writing your answers to the task activities. You will also be able to some A4 notes into the supervised assessment. Your tutor will tell you the amount and format of these notes. A task book will be provided, which you will use to answer questions related to the task activities.

Throughout this unit you will find assessment practice opportunities that will help you develop the skills and understanding you will need for the assessment.

As the guidelines for assessment can change, you should refer to the official assessment guidance on the Pearson Qualifications website for the latest definitive guidance.

You will be assessed on your ability to achieve the following outcomes.

▸ **AO1** Demonstrate knowledge and understanding of the concepts, activities, processes and theories that support the development of communication, language, literacy and numeracy.

▸ **AO2** Apply knowledge and understanding of the concepts, key activities, processes and theories that promote development of communication, language, literacy and numeracy.

▸ **AO3** Analyse and evaluate information about children and early years demonstrating the ability to interpret the potential impact and influence of activities and approaches on communication, language, literacy and numeracy development.

▸ **AO4** Be able to recommend activities and approaches to support development of communication, language, literacy and numeracy in context with appropriate justification, using theory to support arguments.

Table 2.1 shows key terms that will be used consistently by Pearson in its assessments. These terms will not necessarily be used in every paper, and are provided for guidance only.

▸ **Table 2.1:** Key terms used in this unit

Command or term	Definition
Activity	A planned play and learning experience to develop a child's skills and abilities
Activity plan	A structured breakdown of an experience to develop a child's skills and abilities
Early years theory	Ideas that underpin early years teaching practices
Resources	Pieces of equipment needed to support children's activities

Getting started

Before you start this unit, write a list of practical ways in which learning to communicate and the use of language will support children in the development of their reading, writing and mathematical skills. At the end of the unit, see if you can add to your list.

 **A** # Stages of speech, communication and language development and its link to overall domains of development

A1 The role of speech, communication and language in children's development

Verbal and non-verbal communication

Learning to communicate with others is an important part of young children's development. Both verbal and non-verbal skills are important in communication.

Non-verbal communication

▶ Eye contact is one of the earliest skills to develop in babies

▶ **Eye contact** – eye contact is one of the earliest skills to develop in babies as it is fundamental to most communication. Babies are quickly able to gaze into the eyes of an adult. Eye contact is needed to show that you are listening, to be able to register others' feelings and to assess the impact of communication.

▶ **Contact** – babies and young children often use physical contact as a tool to aid communication. They may tap our back to get our attention or hug us to show that they are happy.

▶ **Gesture** – one of many skills that babies learn is to use gestures. From around 9 months, babies will often start to point to things in order to draw our attention to them. Babies and children will also clap their hands to show that they are pleased and will learn some early gestures, such as waving to indicate goodbye.

▶ **Body language** – babies and children use body language as a key way of expressing how they feel. They may clench their fists when angry, quiver when excited and show us that they want to be picked up by opening their arms.

❚❚ PAUSE POINT   Explain the different ways in which children use non-verbal communication.

      (Hint)   You have looked at four ways.

      (Extend) For each way, give a practical example.

Verbal communication

Very early on, babies start to use their voices to communicate. They use crying, cooing and babbling to help gain attention, but also as a way of communicating with adults. Being able to talk and use verbal communication increasingly helps children express their feelings and develop strong relationships with others.

▶ **Active listening** – children are active when they listen. Up to 6 or 7 years old, they are likely to ask questions and blurt out ideas and thoughts when they are listening. This means that listening is quite a 'loud' activity, as children seem to need to talk

Link

Revisit *Unit 1 Children's Development* to remind yourself of Vygotsky's sociocultural approach to language and communication development.

in order to process information and make new connections with it. This links to Vygotsky's suggestion that up to 6 or 7 years old, children still talk aloud their private thoughts.

Theory into practice

Observe a group of children aged 3–5 years who are having a story read to them.
- Do any of the children seem to need to talk as they are listening?
- See how many of their comments are related in some way to what they have just heard.
- Why might talking aloud be a positive sign that children are listening?.

▶ Talking aloud can be a positive sign that young children are listening

How adults use non-verbal and verbal communication to support children's development

You have seen the importance of non-verbal and verbal communication in children's acquisition of communication and language. Interestingly, it is these skills that adults use to motivate, bond with and support children's communication and language development.

▶ **Eye contact** – from the moment a baby is born, their parents will seek to make eye contact with them. Eye contact is a powerful communication device that adults use with children in a variety of ways. It can be used to show a child attention and love, and as a way of showing that they are listening to a child. It can also be used to reprimand a child!

▶ **Contact** – physical contact including cuddling or sitting on a lap helps babies and young children to feel secure and is often a natural prompt to encourage communication and language.

▶ **Gesture** – gestures often help babies and young children understand what is being said to them. One of the most important early gestures that adults use is to point to objects.

▶ **Body language** – our body language and particularly our facial expressions are an important way of communicating with children. Raised eyebrows and mock surprise are particular features of how adults use body language to support communication and language (see Section A2).

Link

You will look at non-verbal and verbal communication skills again in Section A2.

▸ **Verbal tools** – as you will see in Section A2, the tone of voice, interest and how adults simplify and expand young children's statements all play an important part in helping babies and young children acquire language.

▸ **Active listening** – responding to babies and young children by carefully listening and thinking about what they are trying to express is an important part of supporting communication and language.

Stages of language acquisition

For children to be competent language users they pass through two stages of learning: pre-linguistic and linguistic phases.

Pre-linguistic phase

The first phase of language learning is known as the **pre-linguistic phase**. This phase begins from birth and continues until children begin to use their first words. For most children this will be at around 12–15 months. In this phase babies are learning the rules of communication, which include turn taking, eye contact and also responding to others. Babies also tune into the sounds of the language that they are hearing. Their babbling increasingly sounds similar to the language or languages that they hear and they also start to work out the meanings of specific words.

Linguistic phase

The **linguistic phase** starts when children begin to use words that have meaning. Single words are gradually replaced – first by two-word utterances and then simple sentences. Most children will be fairly fluent language users at around 4 years old and be able to hold conversations easily.

Development of higher order language skills

There are several components of speech that children need to acquire. Once they have mastered these components, they will, in theory, be able to use language to think, predict and explain. These are known as higher order language skills.

Phonology

Phonology is the study of speech sounds used in a language. Speech sounds are often known as **phonemes**. Some languages have more sounds than others. English has around 44 (this number does vary depending on the way that the language is being analysed). Note that speech sounds can be written in a variety of ways. For example, 'ee' as in feed is the same sound as 'ea' as in bead!

Children have to 'tune in' to the phonemes and then make the phonemes of the language that they are exposed to. Babies begin this process before they are born. From around the 26th week of pregnancy, they are already recognising the speech patterns of their mother. However, producing the sounds is a gradual process and is dependent on the growth and development of teeth and muscles in the mouth, including muscles in the tongue. It is, therefore, normal for many children at 3 years old to say 'dat' rather than 'that'.

Semantics

Semantics is about understanding the meaning of words. At first babies learn the meaning of words by associating sounds with objects or actions. A parent or carer may say, 'Where's your hat?' and touch the child's hat. After a while the child will associate the sound of the word 'h-a-t' with the object.

Key terms

Linguistic phase – the second stage of language acquisition when children begin to use words that have meaning.

Phonemes – the smallest units of sound in a language that help to distinguish one word from another. In the English language, for example, 'p' and 'b' are separate phonemes because they distinguish words such as 'pit' and 'bit'.

Pre-linguistic phase – the early stage of language learning when babies start to understand words and babble, but are not producing intelligible words.

Syntax

Syntax is about the grammar of a language, or the way that words are put together to make sentences. Children seem to be primed to work out the structure of a language and, although they may simplify a sentence, they rarely get the word order of a sentence wrong.

Putting it all together – receptive and expressive language

Once children begin to master the components of speech, they are able to understand what others are saying. This is called **receptive language** and it is the first step in learning to use language. Once further progress is made in mastering the components of speech, children can start to express themselves using talk. This is known as **expressive language**.

II PAUSE POINT   Can you explain what the term 'semantics' means?

Hint   You are using semantics to answer this question!

Extend   Explain the link between receptive language and semantics.

Key terms

Expressive language – the ability of a child to communicate actively using sounds and, over time, words.

Key person – an early years professional designated to take responsibility for a child's emotional well-being by having a strong attachment with them and a good relationship with their parents/carers.

Receptive language – the ability to listen to, and understand, what is being communicated.

Links with emotional and social development

Communication and language are interlinked with children's emotional and social development, and their behaviour.

Emotional development

Children who have strong attachments to their parents and to their **key person** in a setting are likely to develop language more easily. This is because there is a strong link between attachment and language. Babies who are held and cuddled start to 'read' their parents and other carers, and this in turn helps them to understand body language in others. Babies and young children who have strong attachments are also motivated to babble and communicate with their parents as they have learned that they will gain a positive response.

When you look at theories of language development, you will see later in the section the link between emotional and communication and language development and the danger of overcorrecting children.

▶ Early experience of communication will help this baby learn how to read others' body language

Positive reinforcement

Children are more likely to communicate when they feel happy and comfortable with the adult. They also need to feel that they are listened to and that their communications are valued. Smiling, responding to a child and showing interest are all ways that children's attempts at communication can be positively reinforced.

In Unit 1 you looked at Skinner's theory of operant conditioning and language development in relation to how children learn. Skinner extended this theory to the development of children's language. He suggested that children are encouraged to talk when they are positively reinforced by adults who may praise or make eye contact with them. His theory of language is controversial as he also suggested that parents tended to ignore children's ungrammatical talk. This, he said, encouraged a child to focus on speaking correctly. Research, however, from other theorists would suggest that this is not the case.

Social development

There is a strong link between language and social development. Children who can read other people's body language and communicate with them are more likely to be accepted by others and engage in playful situations. The acquisition of language also makes a difference to the way that children play together, as language seems to help children interact.

Behaviour

There is a significant link between children's behaviour and language. This is very noticeable in children between the ages of 2 and 3 years whose speech is developing well. At 2 years, children are likely to be impulsive, have difficulties in waiting and sharing, and become frustrated. Once children are able to talk in simple sentences, their behaviour changes. They start to become less impulsive, more aware of the needs of others and more cooperative. However, when children's language does not follow the typical pattern of development, they may show behaviour that would not usually be expected for their age.

Links with cognitive development

Speech, communication and language play an important part in children's cognitive development in a variety of ways.

Information processing

Language helps children to process information and is linked to recall and memory. As children's language develops, they are more likely to use it to explore new ideas, explain their thinking and solve problems.

Making the link between spoken sounds and the written symbols

Before children can read and write, they need to become fluent speakers.

In the case of children learning to read, speech is needed in order for them to make the connection between the sounds they hear or make and the written symbols on a page. Children also need to make sense of what they are reading.

Good language skills are also needed in order for children to write. This is because writing is about putting words down on paper or screen. If children do not have words or cannot form sentences, they will have nothing to write.

Understanding the meaning of words

The vocabulary level of children also helps with their cognitive development. When children have good vocabulary and understand the meanings of words, they perceive things in more detail and can think about them differently. A child who knows the word for 'pigeon' as well as 'cockerel' – rather than simply knowing 'bird' – is able to think about the differences between them.

Link

Look back at *Unit 1 Children's Development* to remind yourself of other theorists' research about positive reinforcement and language development.

▶ These children are talking well; this will help them learn to read later on

Key terms

Behaviourist theory – a theory of learning that states development and behaviour can be conditioned and shaped by the environment.

Innate – inborn. An innate characteristic is one a child is born with.

Innate theory – a theory of learning that states children are able to complete certain behaviours or actions instinctively.

Social interactionist theory – a theory of learning that states children learn behaviour/actions as a result of gaining information and feedback during interaction with adults and other children.

Link

Revisit *Unit 1 Children's Development* to look at the key points that the following theorists make in the context of children's communication and language development: Bruner, Chomsky, Vygotsky and Piaget.

How theories help us to understand speech, communication and language development

There are several theories of how children acquire language. These theories are useful in understanding how best to support children's communication and language development. They can be divided into three categories: **innate theory**, **behaviourist theory** and **social interactionist theory**.

Bruner's theory of development

In Unit 1, you looked at Bruner's approach to explaining how children learn and think. He suggested that there were three stages (also known as modes) of representation. One of these was the symbolic stage where children began to use language to represent objects and ideas.

Bruner also focused on the role of adults, particularly parents, in supporting young children to learn language. He is famous for using the term Language Acquisition Support System (LASS) to describe the way that a parent or key carer works sensitively with the child to help them understand and break into speech. The baby or child is like an apprentice and the adult helps the child to join in by interacting with them.

Impact on early years practice

The importance of relationships in language development and also in other areas of development is seen as key in early years practice. It is helpful if children and adults have good relationships, but also if adults modify and use their language to help the child.

Chomsky's concept of the Language Acquisition Device (LAD)

In Unit 1, you learned that Noam Chomsky thought that children's language development is **innate**. He suggested that a specific structure in the brain, known as the Language Acquisition Device (LAD), allows children to break into a language code and use it. His concept suggests that children can pick up more than one language at an early age without being formally taught, although he does speculate that there may be a 'critical period' for language learning. Chomsky's theory is sometimes criticised for not addressing factors in language development such as the role of the parent or key person interacting with the child.

Chomsky's work has helped to explain why all children learn language, regardless of the particular language they are exposed to.

Impact on early years practice

Many linguists, including Chomsky, wonder whether there might be a period in which babies and children are primed to learn language. Beyond this period, learning a language without studying it becomes difficult. The idea that there is a critical period for language learning means that young children in the early years need a lot of opportunities for interaction with adults.

> **❚❚ PAUSE POINT**   In what category does Chomsky's theory of language acquisition fall?
>
> > **Hint**   The three options are: innate, biological and constructivist.
> >
> > **Extend**   What are the key differences between Chomsky's and Bruner's approach to language acquisition?

Vygotsky's constructivist learning theory

In Unit 1 you looked at Vygotsky's learning theory. One of the main aspects of his theory was the role of adults and social interactions in supporting children's learning. Vygotsky believed that through the adult talking, questioning and directing conversations, children's learning could be developed.

Vygotsky also made an important observation about differences in the ways that we use language. He recognised that there was external speech (where we talk outwardly to others) and internal speech (our private thoughts and ideas). He observed that while children from around 3 years old were able to use speech to talk to themselves, they were doing this aloud. It was only from around 6 or 7 years old that children's private speech became internal.

Impact on early years practice

Vygotsky's work suggests that the quality and style of adult interaction with children will make a difference to children's progress, both in terms of language acquisition and in how they use language to predict, analyse and develop high-level thinking. His observation that children use private speech from 3 years old, but it is not until later that it becomes internal, also means that we would expect children to make comments aloud that adults would keep private.

Roger Brown's stages of language development

Through his research, Roger Brown (1925–97) outlined five stages of language development in young children (see Table 2.2). He is known for the term 'telegraphic speech'. This is when children use sentences that are stripped back but still grammatically correct, for example, 'Daddy gone'.

Brown used **longitudinal observations** to record children's emerging speech and to classify different types of telegraphic speech. He noted that children often made **virtuous errors** as their language was emerging, for example, 'goed' or 'wented', but that the word order they used was correct. He also noted that the length of children's sentences (**mean length of utterance** or **MLU**) increased as their language developed.

> **Key terms**
>
> **Longitudinal observations** – observations of individual children that take place over a number of months or years.
>
> **Mean length of utterance (MLU)** – the average length of children's sentences.
>
> **Virtuous errors** – mistakes in children's expressive language that are logical.

Table 2.2 summarises the five stages that Brown identified.

▶ **Table 2.2:** A summary of Roger Brown's five stages

Stage	Mean length of utterance	Age	Examples
1	1.75	15–30 months	Two-word sentences, e.g.: 'No want' 'Go car' 'Teddy sleep'
2	2.25	28–36 months	Use of: • 'ing': 'Daddy going' • 'on': 'Hat on now' • 'in': 'Duck in water' • regular plurals using 's', e.g. 'sheeps there'
3	2.75	36–42 months	Use of: • some irregular past tenses, e.g. 'Me fell down' • possessives, e.g. 'Mummy's hat'
4	3.5	40–46 months	Use of: • 'a' and 'the': 'I want the book' • 'ed' on regular verbs, e.g. 'Charlie chased the squirrel' • third-person present tense, e.g. 'He works', 'Daddy likes books'
5	4.0	42–52+ months	Use of: • third person (he, she) irregular, e.g. 'he has' (rather than 'he have')

Impact on early years practice

Brown's work has been helpful to those studying children's language as he outlined a clear sequence for children learning to use grammar in their speech. Although researchers have questioned whether his model can be applied to all languages, the five stages have helped early years professionals understand the sequence by which children learn English. His work has also helped adults to realise that children are quite logical in their speech from an early age and that they often keep the correct word order.

Piaget's stages of learning and the importance of observing children's language development

In Unit 1 you looked at Piaget's stages of learning. One of the key features of his theory was the way that children's learning was reflected in their logic and the way that they play. His theory suggests that one of the roles of adults is to observe children's language and its use. By doing this in early years settings, adults are able to plan more effectively for children and provide them with learning experiences that will support their learning.

The importance of not overcorrecting

There is an important practical point to take away from the different theories of language, which you can apply to your practice with babies and young children.

Assuming that Chomsky's and Brown's work provides an accurate account of how children learn language, there are dangers associated with overcorrecting children. Many of children's 'mistakes' will be because they are attempting to detect underlying grammar.

As English has grown out of many languages, there are several different rules that children will only acquire over time. A good example of this is the different rules that applies to pluralising common words: 'dog' becomes 'dogs' but 'sheep' do not become 'sheeps'. Instead of overtly correcting children, which may reduce their motivation to communicate, the suggested approach is to repeat the sentence back to the child using the correct form. For example, 'so you saw sheep in the field'.

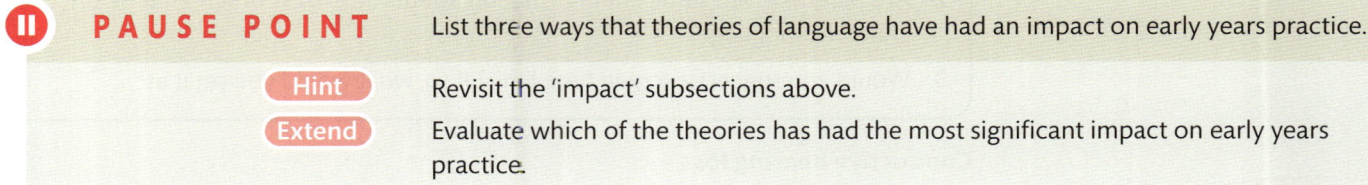

❚❚ PAUSE POINT   List three ways that theories of language have had an impact on early years practice.

> **Hint**   Revisit the 'impact' subsections above.
> **Extend**   Evaluate which of the theories has had the most significant impact on early years practice.

Factors that may affect speech, communication and language development

A range of factors can affect children's acquisition of language (see Figure 2.1). It is important to be aware of these factors when working with children.

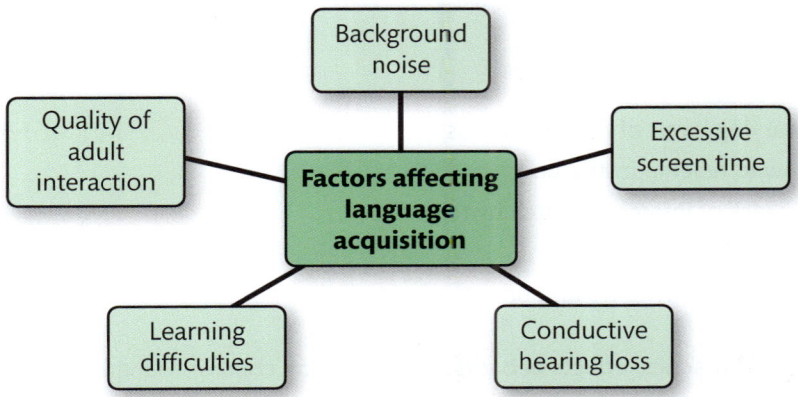

▶ **Figure 2.1:** Factors affecting language acquisition

Background noise

Background noise affects children's speech. Babies have to 'tune in' during their first year. This process can be disrupted if there is a lot of background noise, especially from the radio and television. This is thought to be because other human voices make it harder for the baby to focus on their parent or key person.

Background noise does not just affect babies. Toddlers and older children are less likely to talk when it is noisy and this includes times when music is being played. When there is noise, there is a reduction in the amount of **vocalisations** that take place.

Excessive screen time

Watching television and DVDs, or using computers for a number of hours each day, can have an impact on children's speech and language. Some screen time is fine but children who spend too much time looking at a screen, particularly by themselves, are more likely to have a delay in speech and language development. This is because learning language is an active process and requires face-to-face interactions. When children are spending time in front of the screen, they are not getting the same level of interaction.

> **Link**
>
> Look at Section A2 for ideas for reducing background noise. These should help to provide an environment that encourages communication and language development.

> **Key term**
>
> **Vocalisations** – sounds that are made by babies either for communication or as a way of exploring. Sounds may include words.

Conductive hearing loss

Conductive hearing loss is very common, particularly between the ages of 2 and 6 years. Conductive hearing loss is usually caused by **glue ear**, which is a build-up of a sticky fluid within the ear, preventing sound from travelling into the inner ear.

Conductive hearing loss affects children's ability to hear sounds clearly. This in turn makes it hard for them to speak clearly or to understand what others are saying. How badly children are affected depends on the severity of the condition. A child might have a conductive hearing loss if they:

▶   have muffled speech

▶   stare intently at adults' lips

▶   have varying levels of responsiveness

▶   are slow to react to instructions

▶   show a lack of interest in watching television

▶   appear withdrawn

▶   are aggressive due to frustration.

Learning difficulties

Some children have difficulty learning and using language because they have particular learning difficulties. Language is abstract and this means that some children with learning difficulties struggle to understand that sounds can have meanings. Other children may find it hard to understand the 'rules' of the language they are being exposed to. Some children who have learning difficulties are supported by systems such as **Makaton**. Makaton uses visual signs to help children make the link between words and their meaning.

Quality of adult interaction

Language development is closely linked to how much interaction a child has with adults, particularly parents and key carers. Babies and young children who have plenty of opportunities to talk are likely to acquire language quickly. It is also important that adults are good at listening to children and allowing them to respond. As children develop, they need increasing opportunities to talk and also to hear specific words in order to improve their vocabulary, for example, 'sandals' rather than 'shoes'.

The importance of observation and assessment

One of the key roles of adults working with young children is to observe and assess their speech, communication and language development. This is important because children who are not showing typical language patterns may need additional help or the support of a specialist such as a speech and language therapist.

Early detection of difficulties is important because children with the right support can make significant progress. If you have concerns about a child's communication and language, you should first check their progress against normative development for their age group. You should also talk to parents so that you can find out about the child's language use at home and how they feel about their child's progress.

The importance of early detection is why many local areas have drop-in sessions for parents, as well as online referral processes. Some speech and language teams also produce referral guidelines, which can be helpful if you are not sure whether a referral is needed. Referrals can only be made with parents' consent or by parents themselves directly. Although many referrals are to speech and language teams, some children need to be referred for an **audiology test** to check whether they are fully hearing. This referral is usually done via a health visitor or GP.

> **Link**
>
> Look ahead to *Unit 9 Observation, Assessment and Planning* to read more about these processes.

> **Key term**
>
> **Audiology test** – a hearing test carried out with a machine called an audiometer.

Assessment practice 2.1 — A01 A02 A03

A children's centre is applying for additional funding to run communication and language groups with parents. They have asked you to prepare information that they can use in support of their application.

1 Describe the impact of communication and language on children's development.

2 Analyse the factors that might affect children's language acquisition. Which ones would be relevant for parents to know, and why?

3 Evaluate which theories of language acquisition could be used as a basis for helping parents to understand how they might support their children's language development.

Plan
- Where can I find information relevant to this task?
- How long will I need to collate and analyse the information I find?

Do
- Is the information I have found accurate and concise?
- Am I managing my time effectively?

Review
- Can I justify why I have decided to approach the task this way?
- Have I evaluated my work and am I confident that it fulfils the task?

A2 Developing children's speech, communication and language

One of the key roles for adults working with young children is to promote their speech, communication and language. This section looks at ways in which this can happen in early years settings.

The sequence of language development

It is important for adults working with children to understand that language develops in a certain sequence. By recognising where children are in the sequence of language learning, adults can adapt their language style to support children. Table 2.3 shows the usual pattern in which children develop expressive language.

▶ **Table 2.3:** The sequence of language development

Stage	Features
Babbling	• Associated with babies • Changes over time – babbling becomes longer and more tuneful
Single words	• Single words often begin at around 12–15 months • By 18 months, most children have 15–18 single words • Single words may have more than one meaning, i.e. 'dog' might refer to any animal
Two words	• Joining of two words to make mini sentences begins from 18 months to 2 years • Words often contain a verb and a noun, e.g. 'Daddy go'
Multi-word sentences	• From 2½ years, most children form simple sentences of three or more words • Longer and more complex sentences are seen at 4 years

Supporting early verbal interactions with babies

In order for babies to 'tune in' to the language or languages that they are meant to be learning, it is essential that they spend time with adults who are directly interacting with them. This is because in the pre-linguistic phase babies learn about the sounds and tune of the language, as well as communication techniques such as making eye contact and recognising others' emotions. There are some important ways that adults can help babies break into what is otherwise a code made from sounds.

Holding babies

The starting point and the motivation for babies to break into the 'code' is often linked to their need for love and attention. Simply holding a baby and talking to them makes a significant difference. Babies who spend long periods on the floor away from adults or in forward-facing pushchairs will find it hard to connect what they are hearing with any meaning.

Eye contact

Making eye contact is a key communication skill. Babies seem to want to make eye contact very early on, as they will often gaze into the adult's eyes when they are being fed. Making eye contact with a baby when you are with them is key to helping them feel included in the conversation – albeit a one-sided conversation at first.

Using gesture

Often, and without realising it, adults who communicate well with babies point things out to them. This is important as it helps babies to focus on an object, person or action. This in turn means that babies are more likely to understand what the accompanying words are about.

Using facial expression

Babies can also have their attention drawn to language through our facial expressions. Babies need strong facial expressions to help them to be interested in what is happening. Eyebrows and mouths are of particular interest to babies as they help them 'read' the human face more easily. If you have a fringe, think about clipping it back so that babies can see your whole face.

Running commentary

As well as directly pointing things out to babies, adults need to keep chatting to them, even when they are busy doing other things. This means, for example, that while an adult is setting the table, the baby should still be spoken to. This style is sometimes called 'running commentary'. Some adults find it difficult to do this as the baby does not reply, but it is essential because it allows the baby to hear direct communication.

▶ Strong facial expressions seem to encourage young children to communicate more

Acknowledging babies' vocalisations

Babies are not silent! They cry, moan and also make babbling sounds. It is important to respond to babies' sounds by talking to them, picking them up, or, if necessary, comforting them. This helps babies to practise vocalisations and to help them feel that they are understood.

> **Reflect**
>
> Babies need high-quality adult interaction to acquire communication and language.
> - Evaluate your interaction style with babies.
> - Consider whether you are using sufficient gestures and facial expressions. Are you working in ways that prompt babies to vocalise?
> - Ask an experienced adult to provide you with feedback so that you can improve your interactions further.

The importance of appropriate adult support

There are simple things that adults can do to help children's language development.

Time to respond

One of the most important things to remember when working with babies and children is that they need time to respond to what you say. This is because they have to process the information or, in other words, they require thinking time. In recordings of adults talking to children, not giving children time to respond is one of the most common mistakes.

Acknowledging attempts to communicate

You have seen that acknowledging vocalisations is important with babies; this remains important throughout early childhood. You can show that you are acknowledging attempts to communicate by making eye contact and getting down to the child's level.

Reflecting back

When children start to talk, they are likely to make mistakes. You should not correct children; instead, repeat the word or phrase back correctly, as in the following example.

▶ Child: 'Look. I'm a mermelaid.'
▶ Adult: 'A mermaid. How exciting!'

Sensitively expanding statements

Babies and children need adults to acknowledge what they are saying but also to expand their statements. Expanding a child's statement in a sensitive way helps them make connections to things that they have already experienced. Here are some examples.

▶ Baby at 11 months: 'Dadada.'
  Adult: 'Can you hear Daddy coming down the stairs?'

▶ 2-year-old child: 'All gone now.'
  Adult: 'Have you finished everything? You were very hungry, weren't you?'

▶ 4-year-old child: 'I've got new shoes.'
  Adult: 'They're lovely new shoes. And they've got very smart buckles too.'

▶ 6-year-old child: 'We're going on holiday and I am going on a plane!'
  Adult: 'That's exciting. I wonder if you'll fly over France where Josh now lives.'

Features of child-directed speech (motherese)

The term **motherese** was originally used in the 1970s to describe a style of language that was used when mothers spoke to their babies. As fathers and other carers also play a part in children's language development, the terms **parentese** or **child-directed speech** (CDS) are now often used.

There are several features of child-directed speech that adults can use when they are talking to babies and young children (see Figure 2.2). These features seem to help babies and young children understand what is being said and will eventually help them to talk.

Key terms

Child-directed speech (CDS) – speech patterns used by parents speaking to their children, usually involving slow and simplified vocabulary, a high-pitched voice and the use of repetition and questions.

Parentese (originally motherese) – the language patterns of parents speaking to their children, which are often simplified and repetitive. The term was originally used to refer to mothers.

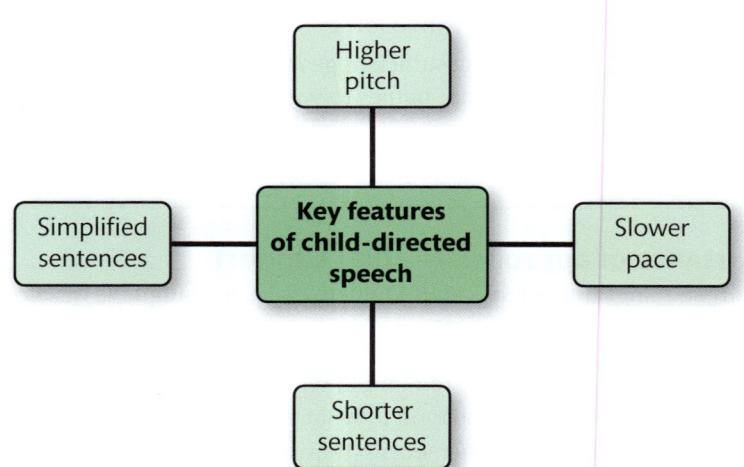

▶ **Figure 2.2:** Key features of child-directed speech

▶ **Higher-pitched voice** – adults use a higher pitch of voice than usual. This is thought to appeal more to babies and young children, and draw their attention to what is being said.

▶ **Slower pace** – adults use a slower pace than usual. This helps babies and young children 'tune in' and distinguish between words.

▶ **Shorter sentences** – adults use shorter sentences with fewer words than usual. This helps babies and young children work out what is being said.

▶ **Simplified sentences** – adults use simple grammar and vocabulary, such as 'look at the ball'. This helps babies and young children to pick up grammatical constructions.

Theory into practice

In your work placement, ask if you can spend ten minutes observing an experienced adult working with a baby or toddler. Make a list of the different features of child-directed speech (parentese) that you notice.

Consider to what extent the adult uses these features when interacting with the baby or toddler.

Environments that encourage speech, communication and language development

Babies, children and adults need things to talk about. This means that the environment we create, including the development of routines and activities, becomes very important. New things seem to attract babies' and children's attention. Although at some level routine is important, the environment needs to be of sufficient interest to encourage communication and speech.

Here are some ideas for creating an environment that promotes language.

Small spaces

Many children enjoy being in small spaces such as tents, dens or role play areas. Small spaces are often places where children sit and enjoy talking. In settings with children aged over one, it is good practice to create small spaces. Older children might talk to each other but adults working with younger children need to use these small spaces to interact with children or tell a story.

Reducing background noise

Children interact and vocalise less in noisy environments. Noisy environments can also be very distracting for young children who may find it hard to concentrate. In group-care settings, where there might be a large number of children, strategies to cut down background noise are important. They include:

▶ changing the layout of the setting to create smaller areas

▶ making sure that adults do not call out across the room to children

▶ using all available space at all times, including outdoors

▶ avoiding the use of continual background music

▶ using sound-absorbing materials such as carpets in some areas

▶ moving games and activities that might be noisy to other areas

▶ modelling quiet talking to children.

Activities and objects that excite children's interest

Here are examples of activities and objects that promote children's language development.

Story sacks

Story sacks have been very popular in the UK over the past few years. They are usually used with children from around 3 years old. The idea behind a story sack is that children and adults talk and read a story book that is accompanied by props and objects. Most story sacks comprise a well-known story, puppets or objects, and some suggestions for follow-up activities. In many settings parents are encouraged to take story sacks home with their child.

▶ Story sacks can contribute to a child's lifelong love of books and reading

Rhyme

Babies and young children benefit from all types of rhyme. The rhythm and **alliteration** in rhymes seem to help children with **auditory discrimination** and this helps them become aware of different sounds. Rhymes also help children with speech production, as they will often be repeating the same sounds during a rhyme.

Reflect

Nursery rhymes support children's auditory discrimination.
- Think about how many rhymes you know by heart.
- Consider how confident you are at singing or saying nursery rhymes with children.
- Could this be an area of practice that you need to develop further?

Group size

As you have seen, the amount of interaction a child has with an adult is closely linked to their speech, communication and language development. This means that when children are in group care, you need to think carefully about group size and composition. When children are talking well, they are likely to dominate conversations. This is not their fault and they should not be reprimanded, but it means that a younger child in a group, or a child with delayed speech may not have as many opportunities for interaction. In some situations, a small group may give quieter children more opportunities to speak and might also help children to hear more of what is being said.

How to promote speech, language and communication development

There are other ways that adults can promote children's language development and also support their cognitive development.

Attention to detail

To develop children's language, it is important that adults encourage attention to detail. This helps build children's knowledge of the world around them and gives them descriptive vocabulary. Examples include pointing out the bark or the buds on a tree, or telling a child that their jumper has stripes on it.

Accurate naming

Once children have understood and are using general words such as 'shoe' or 'dog', it is important to give them more accurate words such as 'sandal' or 'terrier'. This helps them to develop a more sophisticated vocabulary, which in turn helps them to see and think about the world in more detail. Children who have detailed vocabularies are more likely to remember what they have done and seen with greater accuracy. Later on, they can draw on their vocabulary to help them write descriptively.

❚❚ PAUSE POINT What are the benefits of attention to detail and accurate naming for children's cognitive development?

Hint   How does knowing the name of something help you remember it?

Extend   Name the theorist who stressed the importance of adults in supporting children's cognitive development.

Active listening

As you saw earlier in this chapter, it is essential to listen carefully to children and use active listening skills. These skills include making good eye contact, showing interest and acknowledging what a child is saying. When interacting with children, the active listening skills you use need to be more exaggerated, for example, your facial expression.

Helping children to sequence

When children first start talking, they can find it hard to remember the sequence of things they have done. Adults can help children talk about things that they have done by asking prompting questions such as, 'and what happened next?'

Children can also be helped to sequence through the use of visual prompts such as photographs. A series of photographs taken while out shopping can help the child remember what happened first. Learning how to sequence their talk is an important skill for children to learn, as it is something that links to their later literacy skills.

Talking about new and interesting things

Children need things to talk about. When children go on outings they often have plenty to say because they are seeing new and interesting things.

As there is a link between the development of communication and language and stimulation, it is important to provide new and exciting things for children to look at. This might mean bringing in new objects that children may not have seen before, such as a star fruit or a small suitcase full of different-sized and coloured socks.

Regular routines for children can become a source of stimulation if small changes are made, for example, by using place mats on one day and tablecloths on another.

Link

To find out more about active listening with adults, look at *Unit 8 Working with Parents and Others in Early Years*.

Assessment practice 2.2   AO1 AO2 AO3

A local nursery has asked you to plan a training session for new staff about how adults can support children's speech, communication and language development.

1 Describe strategies that adults might use to support a baby's language development.

2 Analyse ways in which adults might promote children's language development (for children aged 2–5 years).

3 Evaluate the impact of the adult's role in supporting children's communication and language development.

Plan
- What information do I have about ways in which adults support children's speech, communication and language development?
- Where can I go to gain additional information?

Do
- Have I presented the information in a way that will be accessible to the nursery staff?

Review
- Can I justify why I have decided to approach the task this way?
- Have I evaluated my work and am I confident that it fulfils the task?

B Supporting children's literacy and numeracy skills through speech, communication and language development

B1 Development of literacy skills

In order for children to develop skills in reading and writing, they need to have developed a sufficient level of language skills. This means that they need to have experience of using language in context through:

▶ speaking and listening to others

▶ the development of an appropriate level of vocabulary.

Children are then able to recognise the meanings of words and components of language.

How children develop reading skills

Young children are naturally curious. In a suitable environment they will want to pick up books and look at them with adults. It is important to harness this curiosity and encourage them to develop their interest through valuing books and enjoying reading in a supportive environment.

To be ready to learn to read, children need to have had different experiences so that books and reading have a context, or there is some understanding of where reading fits into their world.

Many young children will have been given or shown books from a very early age; this means they will have started to build up their pre-reading skills. They may also have had experience of nursery rhymes and songs, so they will begin to be able to hear patterns in words and start to be able to predict what comes next.

Children should be read to as much as possible. They should be given plenty of opportunities for speaking and listening through talking about books. Often, young children will be able to recite whole pieces of text from books long before being able to read, and will 'correct' adults if they get anything wrong.

> **Discussion**
>
> In two minutes, make a list of all the 'text' you might read in a typical day. Remember to include **all** types of text, including books, signs, text messages, emails, instructions, road signs, etc. Then, with a partner, see if you can come up with your own definition of reading.
>
> Share your findings with the rest of the group.

By being read to, children start to learn that print carries meaning. It is important that they look at books with adults and learn how to handle them. They will start to learn how to hold a book and turn pages. They will also begin to understand the way we look at print, both from left to right and top to bottom.

Giving children access to interactive computer programs also helps to encourage and reinforce **phonic awareness** by looking at print in another medium.

> **Key term**
>
> **Phonic awareness** – being aware of different sounds within words.

How adults support children's skills in reading and writing

To develop children's abilities in reading and writing, they need to practise a number of different skills regularly and in close succession. They should do this through both adult-supported and independent activities so that these skills gradually build up over time. As children like to mimic adults, taught activities will often spill over into their play so that their learning is reinforced.

Links between spoken sounds, letters and symbols

Children need to be taught that letters represent sounds through focused work on **phonics**. They need to spend some time regularly looking at the shapes of letters with an adult to recognise the different sounds these letters represent. Often, early years settings will follow a scheme that outlines the way in which the sounds are taught. This can be helpful for planning and also where different adults work with the children, as it ensures consistency. Children then start to build words with the sounds they know, at first with simple c–v–c (consonant–vowel–consonant) words so that they can learn to blend the sounds together by saying them slowly.

Recognising simple words

At the same time as they develop other literacy skills, children will start to recognise simple, common words without needing to sound out and blend each letter. For example, you may notice when children are reading to adults they will be able to say the word straight away. This often happens quite rapidly as children's skills become more proficient. You may point out these words to children as they occur, particularly those that are frequent or more challenging and need to be learned without sounding out, such as 'said' or 'the'.

Understanding simple sentence structures

As well as learning to decode when reading, it is important that children are able to understand what they have read in context. You should, at all stages, ask them questions about the text and its context to ensure they are not just going through the motions of sounding out each word. Children should show that they are using all cues available to them, for example, pictures and other clues in the text, to help them make sense of what they are reading.

When it comes to writing, provide children with encouragement from the earliest stage of development so that they develop confidence in what they are doing. Many children seek reassurance from adults but they should not be afraid of 'getting it wrong'.

> **Link**
>
> To find out about early mark making and writing development, see the start of Section B4.

For children to develop writing and reading skills they need to be provided with a supportive environment. This means that they should have stimulation and resources available when their skills are developing. These may include:

- environmental print – for example, displays with captions and information, key words, clearly labelled areas within and outside the setting in all areas of the learning environment
- dictionaries and topic-based word banks
- adult role models so that children can see the purpose of writing
- a variety of clearly labelled materials and writing areas so that children can use them to write for their own purposes.

▶ Looking at print in different media can support phonic awareness

> **Key term**
>
> **Phonics** – a method used to teach reading that breaks down different letter patterns into their individual sounds.

Providing a supportive environment

Ava and Khavarn are 4 years old and are in the reception class. They have just taken part in a large group activity where they have been practising sounds with an adult. After the two children go off to play, they sit in the corner and Ava tells Khavarn that she is going to test him. She then finds some letter sound cards and holds them up so that he can identify the sounds. As she does this, more children join in and soon there is a large group working together.

Check your knowledge

1   Why is this kind of play valuable in developing reading skills?

2   What skills is this kind of play developing, as well as sound recognition?

PAUSE POINT   How can adults support the development of children's reading and writing skills?

Hint   Look at the different methods used in your setting.

Extend   What could you do to support children further?

Building a language-rich environment

As well as exposing young children to books and language as much as possible to promote their literacy development, you also need to build a language-rich learning environment.

Always label displays so that children's work can be identified and put into context. There should also be other examples of environmental print in the setting. This may be for information, for example, to tell children where to hang their coats or put book bags, or for reference, for example, alphabet or word banks.

You will probably have seen a dedicated reading and/or writing area in your setting, and print used in displays and texts at children's eye level. This is very important so that children are able to read and refer to them, and adults are able to point them out. Children should be encouraged to use writing areas to create their own labels, for example, to use in the role play area, or to label a display such as a model they have made.

Although young children may not always be able to read environmental print, they will be starting to learn that it carries information. It is important that adults build language-rich environments and that they are used as much as possible, so that children are able to develop their literacy skills.

Figure 2.3 summarises how a setting can promote a language-rich environment.

Reflect

Look for the different places in your setting that encourage children to:
- be aware of print or develop their mark making or writing skills
- use interactive computer programs that develop their phonic awareness.

What kinds of message are children encouraged to look at in the environment? How does the setting give them opportunities to try out reading and writing?

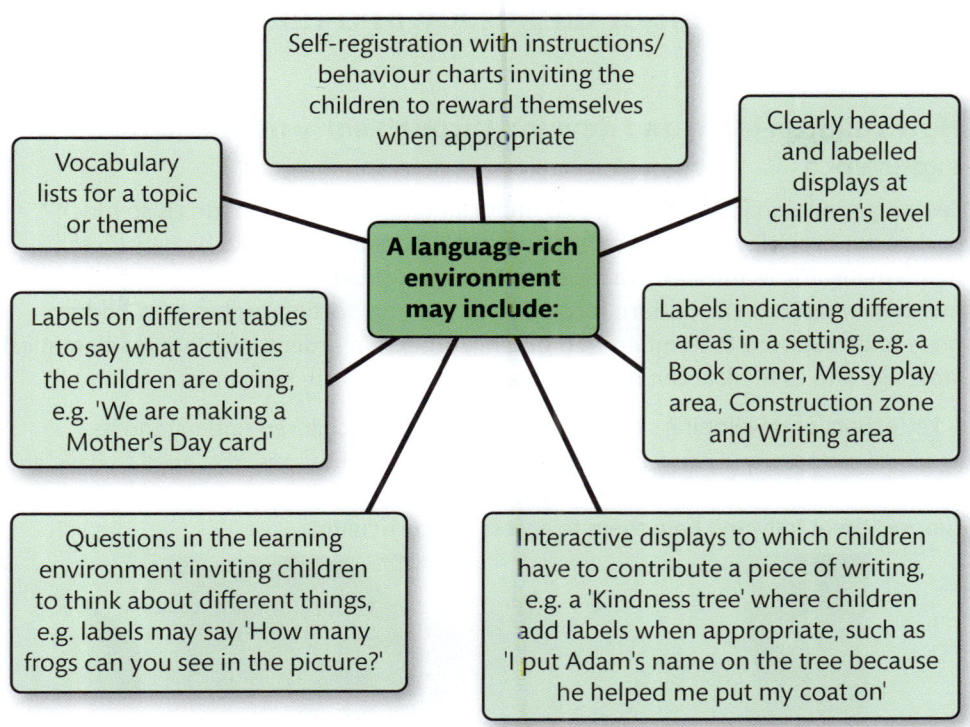

▶ **Figure 2.3:** Examples of how a setting can promote a language-rich environment

Phonemic awareness in learning to read

As well as looking at books and starting to pick up on different cues, it is important that young children begin to develop **phonemic awareness** as they look at and listen to words. This will happen if adults start to point at words and relate the print on the page to the sounds and words that they are saying.

Children should also be taught to listen for sounds within words as they begin to tune into speech sounds, for example, through being able to hear alliteration (words starting with the same sound). In this way, they start to understand that what they are looking at relates to what they are hearing. This will make it easier for them to relate **graphemes**, or written representations of sounds, to what they are hearing.

> **Key terms**
>
> **Graphemes** – individual written symbols.
>
> **Phonemic awareness** – the ability to hear individual sounds (phonemes) in words.

Assessment practice 2.3   AO1   AO2   AO3   AO4

You have been asked to write a description for preschool parents of some of the different experiences that support the development of young children's reading and writing skills.

1 Outline some of the experiences offered in your setting.

2 Discuss and evaluate the role of early reading and writing experiences in children's literacy development.

3 Recommend activities that parents could undertake at home to support their child.

Plan
- What information do I have in my setting about ways in which adults support children's speech, communication and language development?
- Where can I go to gain additional information?

Do
- Can I question my own learning environment?
- Can I seek others' opinions?

Review
- Can I justify why I have decided to approach the task this way?
- Can I make informed choices based on reflection?

B2 Development of numeracy and mathematical skills

How children learn and develop through early mathematical experiences

Learning provision for mathematics is important for children, as maths is so much part of our everyday lives. From the earliest stages, children should be developing mathematical skills through practical work that introduces them to shape, space, number, measurement, pattern recognition, counting, sorting, and so on. Children need to be exposed to numbers in different contexts in order to explore mathematical language and to think about different ways in which we use measures.

A key aspect of developing skills in mathematics is that children understand its practical purpose and can learn to apply it to real-life situations. You need to have an awareness of the skills that children in your setting are working towards in order to support them fully and help them to access the curriculum.

▶ Opportunities should be provided for children to develop through hands-on and practical experiences

Reflect

In your setting, see what evidence you can find of mathematics in action over the course of one day. This could be displays and information, activities, or adults talking to children using mathematical language.

Why do you think this is useful for children's future mathematical understanding?

Supporting children's early mathematical skills

The development of early mathematical skills gives children a basis from which to develop their mathematical understanding as they become more familiar with different concepts. Practical exploration is important from the earliest stages of developing mathematical skills because it enables children to have a secure grounding in different aspects of mathematics. Table 2.4 shows basic practical skills that will support children's development of different areas of mathematics.

▶ **Table 2.4:** Practical skills that will support children's development of different mathematical areas

Skill	Purpose
Matching	Matching numbers and shapes encourages children to look at similarities and differences so that they can start to identify things that go together, or sets
Pattern making	Pattern making is important as it enables children to identify simple repeated ideas. This is a good basis for finding patterns in numbers later on
Sorting	Early sorting activities help children's understanding of numbers. They should have opportunities to sort as many different materials as possible and in as many different ways as they can. This will also support the development of language – why should these items be put together? Which ones do not belong with the others?
Comparing objects	Comparing different objects or groups of objects helps to develop children's language skills
Counting and ordering	Children need to become familiar with the number system. They do this through counting and ordering numbers and groups of numbers with the same criteria. They should also begin to count in 2s, 5s and 10s
Recording	Children will start to record numbers, patterns and what they have found out in simple ways through pictures and simple charts and tallies. This will lead on to being able to express their ideas through symbols
Sharing	Children start to learn how to share items between groups of two and more. This will enable them to gain practical experience of division

❚❚ PAUSE POINT What strategies have you used to support children's mathematical skills?

Hint Use examples from your current topic.

Extend Share your ideas with others in your school/college group.

Strategies for developing early mathematical skills

You need to be able to use different strategies in order to develop mathematical skills in young children. You can do this through focused activities as well as using the learning environment. Here are some examples.

Counting from 1 to 20 and placing numbers in order

Count with young children as much as possible in different contexts so they are used to hearing numbers in order. Display numbers both indoors and outdoors so that children see them being used. Numbers should also be part of children's play activities or included in class routines. For example, create a 'car park' in the outside play area that contains numbered spaces. Ask children to park numbered toys or bicycles in the correctly numbered spaces.

Adding and subtracting single digit numbers

As well as working on very simple addition and subtraction activities, use day-to-day problems to develop the concepts of adding and taking away. For example, there are enough skipping ropes for six children – how many more would we need for eight children?

Describing the shape and size of 2D and 3D shapes

Use a feely bag and ask children to describe what they can feel. Encourage them to think about whether the object (e.g. cube, cuboid, square) has edges and corners, whether it is curved or has straight lines, and whether it is flat (2D) or solid (3D), large or small. The focus in this activity should be on mathematical language.

Understanding mathematical language

When teaching young children mathematical concepts, remember the importance of language. There are different ways in which failing to understand mathematical vocabulary may come to light, including if children:

▶ do not understand instructions – for example, language such as 'find the difference', 'arrange in order' or 'read the table below'

▶ are not familiar with the vocabulary – for example, 'pattern', 'in between', 'more/less than', 'greater or larger/smaller than', 'in front of', 'inside' or 'heavier/lighter'

▶ do not understand a mathematical term – for example, 'subtract', 'double', 'match' or 'circle'.

It is easy to make assumptions about what children understand, particularly in maths. If you focus on the concept rather than the language, some young children, or those who speak English as an additional language, may have difficulties. Tutors should introduce a new topic, general activity or assessment task by going through mathematical vocabulary to check children's understanding.

Mathematical vocabulary and language should be displayed in the learning environment, particularly any new words that are being used as part of a topic. As children work on practical activities, these displays should be discussed with adults so that children can build up their knowledge of the kind of vocabulary used in mathematics.

Reflect

The *Mathematical Vocabulary Book* supports the development of children's mathematical vocabulary by identifying words and phrases that they need to understand and use to help them make good progress in mathematics. This publication is available as a PDF online; simply search for 'Mathematical Vocabulary Book'.

Assessment practice 2.4 | A01 | A02 | A03 | A04

Consider the mathematical skills below:
- counting from 1 to 20
- placing numbers in order
- adding and subtracting single-digit numbers
- shape and size of 2D and 3D shapes.

Outline different activities that you could do with children to support these skills. Explain why you have chosen them and how you would support children in understanding mathematical language.

Plan
- What existing knowledge do I have about these mathematical skills?
- What aspects of the task will take the most/least time? How will I balance these?

Do
- Am I presenting the information accurately and concisely?
- Do I understand my thought process and why I have decided to approach the task in a particular way?

Review
- Can I use this experience in future learning experiences to improve my planning and to monitor my own progress?

B3 Supporting literacy development

Supporting early reading

When you are working with children in an early years setting, you need to know how to support their early reading development and encourage them to have a love of books. This is one of the most important things that early years professionals can do. Children respond to an adult's enthusiasm, so provide as many opportunities as possible to engage and support children.

Two ways in which you can do this are:

▶ using stories and rhymes

▶ linking pictures and words to actions that carry meaning.

Using stories and rhymes that include rhyme recognition and repetition

Many books for young children have text that is repeated. Action or nursery rhymes and stories that include rhythm and repetition support children's early auditory discrimination – that is, they encourage children to start hearing patterns, rhyming and alliteration in words. They also develop children's confidence when using language as they will start to be able to predict what happens next. This involves children in the process, as well as helping them to develop an understanding of how language works because they are able to find patterns in words.

Linking pictures and words to actions that carry meaning

Looking at pictures at the same time as the text helps children to develop their vocabulary. Making the link to actions will help to engage them in the act of reading.

Use of activities to support development of literacy skills

Children should have access to a wide range of activities so that they have different opportunities to develop their literacy skills. Although they often do this through play, children are very imaginative and will use these skills to develop further. Engaging the imagination of children is an excellent way to encourage them to learn. The kinds of activities you might use include the following.

▶ **Story sacks** – as we saw in Section A2, children enjoy using story sacks that contain different elements of a familiar story. For example, a 'Little Red Riding Hood' story sack might include a red cloak, a small stuffed wolf, a basket of fruit, or a granny's hat. Story sacks encourage discussion and develop children's vocabularies as they talk about the text.

▶ **Role play** – all early years settings should have a role play area that changes regularly. This gives children opportunities to develop their speaking and listening skills in different contexts, as well as their confidence and imagination.

▶ **Puppets** – puppets are a good opportunity for children to 'decentre' and think about things from another point of view. They can also help to develop the confidence of children who are more reticent in some situations.

▶ **Circle time** – circle time in small groups with young children encourages them to discuss different topics and listen to one another.

▶ Circle time encourages young children to discuss different topics and listen to one another

- **Storytelling** – young children love stories and they should start to be able to retell their favourite stories in their own words. This will help them to sequence ideas.
- **Recorded stories and music** – early years settings will usually have a listening corner where children can sit quietly and listen to stories, rhymes and music.
- **Small-world play** – when children play with small-world toys, such as building blocks, toy towns and other small figures or animals, they are encouraged to use spoken language and their imagination as they 'act' stories out.
- **Imaginative play** – this supports the development of literacy skills through speaking and listening with others and developing different scenarios based on children's own experiences.

PAUSE POINT	List four activities that support children's literacy development. How are they supportive?
Hint	Think about activities that include speaking and listening, or encourage children to use their imagination.
Extend	Use your setting to note other activities that support children's literacy development. How are they supportive?

Theoretical approaches to helping children learn to read

Children usually begin to learn to read when they start school, between the ages of 4 and 5 years. Different theoretical approaches have emerged relating to how children learn to read, and you should have some understanding of these in order to support children effectively. We already know that before learning to read, it is important that children have been exposed to a language-rich environment and have been able to look at books and share them with adults regularly, as well as taking part in pre-reading activities. This will form a solid basis on which to build their reading skills.

Phonics and phonemes

The phonics approach is based on the link between graphemes or letters so that children learn to link them with individual sounds or phonemes. The sound system is more complex and inconsistent in English than in other languages as there can be a number of different phonemes to represent the same sound (for example, 'f' and 'ph'). Phonics is, therefore, used as a method of teaching sounds as it helps to look at the different letter patterns together, along with their sounds. As we saw in Section A1, there are around 44 different phonemes in spoken English.

There are two main different phonics methods – synthetic phonics and analytical phonics.

Synthetic phonics

Synthetic phonics requires the reader to learn individual sounds and blends in a particular order, then put them together to form words. The sounds are taught in a particular way, not to sound like the letters. For example, the sound for 't' would be taught as a short sound and not as 'tee' or 'tuh'. The simpler and most commonly used sounds are the first to be taught, as these are also straightforward (s, a, t, l, p and n). These can then be put together to form many simple three-letter words, which can be sounded out by children from a relatively early stage.

Link

Look back at Section B1 to find more information about phonics.

Link

To find out more on the teaching of synthetic phonics, please refer to the end of this section: 'Understanding systematic synthetic phonics in the teaching of reading'.

Development of Children's Communication, Literacy and Numeracy Skills

Analytical phonics

In analytical phonics, blends are taught rather than individual letter sounds, for example, 'sh', 'th' and 'ch'. Children are encouraged to learn sets of whole words that have a similar spelling, such as 'cat', 'hat', 'mat', 'fat' and 'bat'. A disadvantage of this system is that many words in English are not written phonetically (for example, 'said', 'know' or 'was') and children still need to learn these words separately.

Whole language/apprenticeship

Another approach to phonics is the whole-language/apprenticeship approach. This grew from Noam Chomsky's ideas about language acquisition. Chomsky theorised that we all have an innate ability to learn any language and do not learn it by imitating others.

In 1967, Ken Goodman had an idea about reading that he thought was similar to Chomsky's theory. He described a system for reading by which learners have to use four different cues in order to decipher the words.

▶ **Graphophonemic** – the shapes of the letters, and their corresponding sounds.
▶ **Semantic** – what you would expect the word to be, based on the meaning of the sentence so far.
▶ **Syntactic** – what word or phrase would make the most sense, based on the context and grammatical structure of the language – word order, tense and gender.
▶ **Pragmatic** – the function of the text.

The whole-language approach is also sometimes called the 'look and say' approach. It encourages the learner to look at, and recognise, whole words when learning to read, rather than breaking them down into sounds. In this way, the child will be introduced to high-frequency words such as 'said', 'because', 'they', 'were' and 'who', which do not fit into regular phonic patterns. Although the child may take longer to learn this way, they are less likely to make errors than a child who has learned synthetic phonics.

Theory into practice

Read the text below. Can you answer the questions?

'A frotterpat was losping a ticklepup. A binker wootled. The binker wisped "Frimto" to the frotterpat. The frotterpat mantered bentistly.'
- What was the frotterpat doing?
- What wootled?
- What did the binker wisp?
- How did the frotterpat manter?

This exercise is based on Chomsky's idea that sentences can be grammatical without making sense and that we can produce new sentences without ever having heard them before.

What do you think the implications of this exercise are for supporting children's reading?

Using phonics and whole language

Most educationalists agree that a combination of phonics and the whole-language approach works best, as different children will approach reading in different ways.

It is likely that in most settings, although there will be a structured environment for the teaching of reading, you will also find that children are, for example, encouraged to learn high-frequency words as well as learning to sound them out using phonics.

Role-model reading books and writing

It is important for young children to make sense of why they are learning to read and write, and be able to put this into context. They should have opportunities to see that adults read books for pleasure and to find out information, and that they write things down to refer to or pass information to others. They are also likely to see adults engaging with print through technology. For this reason, children should have role models who read and write and refer to books and print as a matter of course.

In the setting, there may be limited opportunities for this, but they can still be found, for example, when referring to recipes for cooking activities, or when using books or the internet to find out information for a particular topic. Early years professionals should draw attention to the fact that they need to look at a book to find things out, or make a list so that they remember to do things. They may also refer to books that they are reading at home so that children can relate their own reading to adult experiences.

Remember, children learn all the time from their environment and the adults around them. Praise and encouragement are very strong motivators, as they support the child in gaining confidence. Children should be exposed to good adult role models so they can see reading skills used and the pleasure that can be derived from reading.

Understanding the usual sequence by which children learn to read

Even allowing for the different methods used to teach reading, the sequence by which children learn to read will follow a similar pattern. If children have had a positive experience at the earliest pre-reading stages, they will have learned that print is significant and will be more aware of the conventions of how to handle and use books. They will have started to make a link between the verbal and visual word and be aware that text reads from left to right. They may also have learned to recognise their own name written down, or a few basic letters and sounds. At this stage they will start to develop their use of phonics, which will support their reading skills and enable them to use the letters in context.

There are different schemes and resources available to support the teaching of phonics. Usually these require the child to learn all the letters and sounds quite quickly so that they are able to start to use them. They will then be revised and extended to form blends and whole words, and children will start to build a visual vocabulary of high-frequency words.

As we mentioned at the start of this section, it is important at this stage for children to have as many different cues as possible when reading, for example, pictures that tell the story and word repetition within the text.

When listening to children read, ask them about the text and discuss what they are reading. This may take the form of talking about how a character might be feeling, retelling the story or discussing a point that might be ambiguous within the text. This is vital because decoding the writing, although important, is only part of reading. As they learn to read, children also need to develop comprehension skills and be able to relate the text to their own experience to make sense of it.

Figure 2.4 summarises some of the different ways in which you can support children with reading, while also promoting their independence.

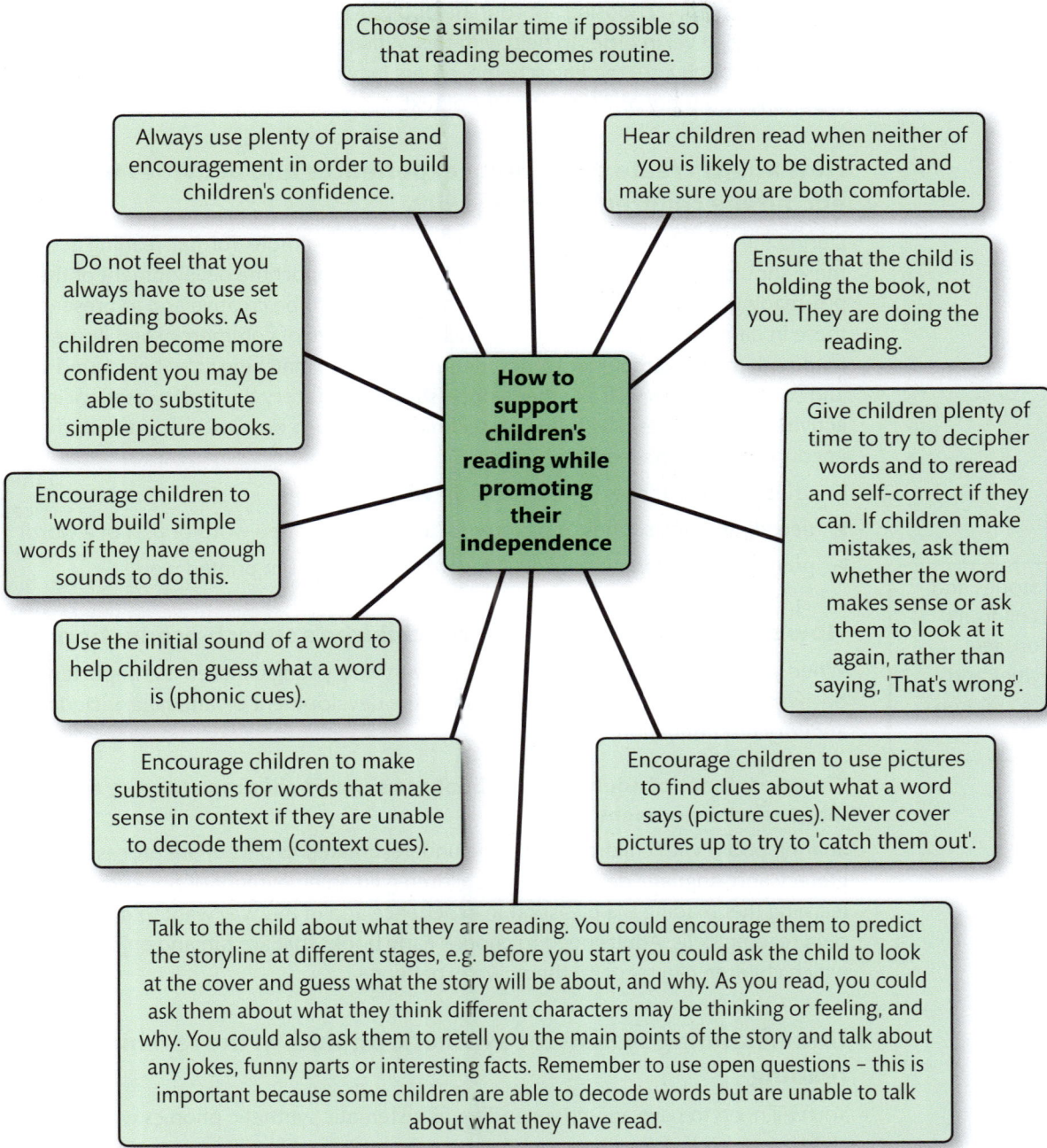

Choose a similar time if possible so that reading becomes routine.

Always use plenty of praise and encouragement in order to build children's confidence.

Hear children read when neither of you is likely to be distracted and make sure you are both comfortable.

Do not feel that you always have to use set reading books. As children become more confident you may be able to substitute simple picture books.

Ensure that the child is holding the book, not you. They are doing the reading.

Encourage children to 'word build' simple words if they have enough sounds to do this.

How to support children's reading while promoting their independence

Give children plenty of time to try to decipher words and to reread and self-correct if they can. If children make mistakes, ask them whether the word makes sense or ask them to look at it again, rather than saying, 'That's wrong'.

Use the initial sound of a word to help children guess what a word is (phonic cues).

Encourage children to make substitutions for words that make sense in context if they are unable to decode them (context cues).

Encourage children to use pictures to find clues about what a word says (picture cues). Never cover pictures up to try to 'catch them out'.

Talk to the child about what they are reading. You could encourage them to predict the storyline at different stages, e.g. before you start you could ask the child to look at the cover and guess what the story will be about, and why. As you read, you could ask them about what they think different characters may be thinking or feeling, and why. You could also ask them to retell you the main points of the story and talk about any jokes, funny parts or interesting facts. Remember to use open questions – this is important because some children are able to decode words but are unable to talk about what they have read.

▶ **Figure 2.4:** Ways to support children's reading while also promoting their independence

How to choose appropriate books for children

All settings should have a wide variety of books available to children so that different interests and abilities are catered for when learning to read. At the very early stages, books should have simple storylines and vocabulary, and contain some repetition. Some early pre-reading books will simply consist of pictures in a sequence so that the adult and child can discuss what is happening. Many early reading books also contain rhymes, which make it easier for children to predict words as they come up.

Some children will be particularly interested in fictional texts such as picture books and stories, while others may prefer non-fiction and information books. It is important as you get to know children and find out about what interests them that you are able to support them in choosing appropriate books. Many books will display the suitable age or ability level in order to help with this. While some settings will insist on children working through a set reading scheme, others may mix books up so that children experience a variety of different types of text.

How adults create stimulating experiences and activities to encourage children's reading skills

During the Foundation Stage, and before children start more 'formal' reading activities, there should be a range of activities available that support the development of their pre-reading and reading skills. There is room for you to be creative and to present these in different ways, but they may include a mixture of commercial and home-made activities. Examples are letter identification and matching activities, sound snap and sound bingo, as well as other games, small-group story time, story sequencing activities and puzzles. The following techniques can also be used to support and encourage children's reading:

- using pictures as cues or reminders for word meanings
- decoding (using sounds or pictures to 'translate' a printed word or part of a word)
- pointing out common or irregular words and patterns in printed words.

How stories and rhymes support children's speech production

When you are reading stories and rhymes with very young children it is important to be aware of their significance in relation to the development of language, including auditory discrimination.

The importance of adults sharing books to support children's literacy and language development

Sharing books with children cannot be underestimated as part of the process of literacy and language development. Children gain an enjoyment of books through learning that reading is a pleasurable experience and in this way want to develop their own reading skills. Adults need to choose early books that are fun and enjoyable and which children can relate to their own experience.

Understanding systematic synthetic phonics in the teaching of reading

You will need to have an understanding of systematic synthetic phonics when teaching children to read.

This is a method through which children are taught the sounds or phonemes associated with the letters or graphemes quite rapidly. As we touched on in Section B1, children then learn to segment and blend the phonemes together, firstly through the use of c–v–c (consonant–vowel–consonant) words such as 'hen', 'dog', 'bat', and later more complex sound variations. Children are not taught the alphabet, letter names or high-frequency words until they have a thorough knowledge of the phonemes and have started to learn how to segment and blend them together.

Settings may use different phonics programs to teach children to read but all are likely to teach the phonemes using a similar approach.

Link

To find out how stories and rhymes support children's speech production, see Section A2: 'Activities and objects that excite children's interest'.

The government website (www.gov.uk) has a useful page entitled 'Phonics: choosing a programme'. This provides helpful evaluation sheets for the various phonics programmes.

Ⅱ PAUSE POINT There are a number of commercial programmes for teaching synthetic phonics. How much do you know about your school's method?

Hint Speak to your literacy coordinator or early years manager about the teaching of phonics.

Extend Investigate some other teaching methods for phonics, such as Jolly Phonics, Sounds-Write, Read Write Inc. and Letterland. How do they vary and how are they the same?

Assessment practice 2.5   AO1 AO2 AO3 AO4

You have been asked to write a report for someone preparing a reading course for children.

1 Outline two different theoretical approaches to helping children learn to read. Discuss the extent to which they may help children.

2 What further information can you find out about the different methods?

3 How does synthetic phonics help children to read and write?

4 Evaluate the role of the early years professional in planning provision to support literacy development in the early years.

Plan
- What do I already know about the different theoretical approaches?
- Where can I go to gain additional information about them?
- How long will I need to collate and analyse the information required for the task?

Do
- Am I presenting the information accurately and concisely?
- Can I make connections between what I am researching and the task, and identify important information?

Review
- Can I describe my thought processes?
- Have I evaluated my work and am I confident that it fulfils the task?

B4 Supporting writing development

Early mark making and writing development

When supporting children's early writing, provide them with encouragement from the earliest stage of development so that they develop strength and confidence in what they are doing. As we mentioned earlier, many children seek reassurance from adults. They should not be afraid of making mistakes and lose confidence as a result.

The kinds of activities that support the development of writing skills will be familiar to you from nurseries and preschools, even if they do not immediately appear to be linked to this process. These activities will, among other things, support the development of children's upper body **gross motor skills**. They are very important as they will strengthen the muscles in a child's upper body and arms so that they will have more control when they start mark making and writing. The activities will also support the development of a child's **fine motor skills** as they start to develop hand–eye coordination, as well as control over their arms and hands.

Key terms

Fine motor skills – control of the smaller muscles, such as those in the fingers, to carry out activities such as threading beads onto a necklace, using a knife and fork, or holding a pencil.

Gross motor skills – control of the larger muscles, such as those in the arms and legs, to carry out activities such as running, throwing or kicking a ball.

As children develop physically, they will start to become stronger and more skilled in both their fine and gross motor movements, all of which will support the development of their writing skills.

Encourage children when they start to make marks as symbolic representations of their thoughts and experiences. They will begin to understand that words convey meaning and that they are able to communicate not just through speech but through the medium of writing. They may at first use either hand (it can take some time for them to decide on a preferred hand), create marks in any direction and use a number of different materials, such as brushes, large markers, crayons, paint, or make marks in materials such as sand. However they choose to express themselves, encourage children to develop their control as much as possible. Adults should praise them and ask questions about what they are writing so that children learn that they are communicating.

Be aware of the handwriting policy in your setting so that you use the agreed method for the formation of letters and numbers. This means that you and other adults should consistently form letters and numbers in the same way so that children will not be confused by different methods. You should also make this method clear to parents and carers so they are able to work with children in the same way at home, for example, using lower case rather than capital letters.

During the Foundation Stage, provide children with stimulating opportunities to develop their pre-writing and writing skills through activities that encourage them to strengthen their muscle control. Give them a variety of media with which to make marks as they start to experiment. Talk to children about what marks mean so they can start to make links between speech and writing. Experiences may include:

▶ making marks in shaving foam, sand, dried rice, or cornflour and water

▶ practising using different media such as pens, brushes and water

▶ using sponges or playdough to strengthen hand muscles

▶ threading, sewing and using tweezers to develop fine motor control.

▶ You can use a wide range of activities to help children develop the skills they will need to learn to write

As their control develops, children at this stage should be given opportunities to write for a purpose through play activities – for example, writing appointments in a diary in a role play area that is a doctor's surgery, or making shopping lists. Although they may still be mark making, their writing will have a clear purpose and they will be able to tell you about it. They may also start to practise writing their own name.

How activities support the links between learning to write and learning to read

Children need to be provided with a wide range of literacy experiences in order to support their development of both reading and writing skills. These experiences could include the following.

▶ **Sand play** – children can use sand to play and experiment with letter sounds in a different context. For example, adults can hide letter shapes in the sand and ask children to find simple words, or put them in different containers and ask children to match up the same sounds.

▶ **Role play** – role play areas are ideal for encouraging children's communication and imaginative skills. These can be developed through storytelling if the home corner is themed, for example as 'Goldilocks's house'.

▶ **Painting** – painting is a good way of encouraging the development of children's fine motor skills and their hand–eye coordination. For example, you could use different thicknesses of brushes.

▶ **Story sacks** – as we have already seen in this unit, story sacks encourage children to think about how a story is constructed through the use of different prompts.

▶ **Print making** – print making supports children's handwriting development and coordination.

▶ **Patterns** – pattern recognition in rhymes and stories helps children to develop their prediction skills when learning to read.

▶ **Storytelling and poetry** – children need a wide repertoire of stories and poetry read to them so that they can identify the key features and themes that run through them, as well as helping them to look at patterns in language.

▶ **Music and drama** – as with storytelling and poetry, children are able to recognise patterns and rhythms in music, and develop their confidence when acting out different situations, for example, in the role play area and predicting lyrics in songs and nursery rhymes.

▶ **Cutting and sticking** – cutting and sticking activities develop children's fine motor skills and control, which helps them when developing the skills that are necessary to write.

The development of handwriting and the usual sequence of learning to write

The development of handwriting

As we discussed at the start of this section, from the earliest stages children begin to develop their handwriting skills through activities that promote hand–eye coordination and strengthen their hand muscles through fine motor movements. Children should also be developing gross motor movements in their upper body so that they have the strength needed in their shoulders to be able to write.

At this stage, see whether the child has developed a preference for using a particular hand to write. Support their development of an efficient pencil grip, although children aged 2–3 years may still be using a **palmar grip**. Chunky pencils and other writing media are available to help with this, as well as pencil grips that fit normal-sized pencils. Although a **tripod grip** is best, with three fingers on the pencil, there may be variations on this, and left-handed children in particular may find different grips easier.

The sequence by which children learn to write

When learning to write, children usually pass through different stages as they become more skilled at forming letters and developing ideas. In the earliest stages, they may focus on mark making and forming letters. This will develop into being able to talk about what they have written as they ascribe meaning to marks. Then they should gradually word-build through their phoneme and grapheme knowledge, and write longer sentences.

Here is a summary of the sequence by which children usually learn to write.

1   In the earliest stages, children start to form strings of letters to represent words.
2   Children start to be able to hear and write individual letter sounds within words – this is usually the first and last letter of the word.
3   Children start to be able to hear and write several sounds within a word, although letters may not all be correctly formed and spaced out.
4   Words become spaced out and letters correctly formed with some punctuation. Children may start to use joins if they have not done so from the start.
5   As well as continuing to work on punctuation and presentation, the content of children's work becomes more involved as they start to use more adventurous and descriptive language.

Key terms

Cursive script – form of writing in which the letters are joined together in a flowing manner.

Palmar grip – holding an object with the palm of the hand.

Tripod grip – a way of holding a pencil or pen. The pencil is gripped between the thumb and first (index) finger, and rests against the side of the middle finger.

PAUSE POINT   Can you remember the stages of handwriting development?

Hint   Draw a flow chart to help you memorise the stages in the correct order.

Extend   Research different ways of teaching handwriting. Do you think **cursive script** should be taught from the start or that children should learn simple lower case first?

Theory into practice

Choose two different children in your setting and identify the stage that they have reached with their writing. Using samples of their work, justify the reasons for your answer.

Supporting left-handed children

Children who are left-handed may need more support than their right-handed peers. Make sure you are aware of left-handed children and give them additional attention when they start mark making, developing their writing skills or using scissors. When left-handed children write, they may have a more 'awkward' pencil grip – so when they are starting to write and make marks, encourage them to find a grip that is comfortable, but make sure you support them.

It can be difficult for left-handed children on a practical level, particularly if they are sitting next to a right-handed child who is also trying to write, as they may knock into one another. Resources such as scissors and easy-grip pens are available to support left-handed individuals, and, for older children, rulers that read from right to left.

> **Research**
>
> Look at the different ways in which your setting supports children who have an awkward pencil grip, whether they are left-handed or just find holding a pencil difficult. Find out how you can help them and give examples of some of the resources that are available.
>
> You may find LeftHandedChildren.org (www.lefthandedchildren.org) useful for suggestions and resources.

Encouraging enjoyment of literacy

Your setting will need to work closely with parents and carers at all stages of the Early Years Foundation Stage (EYFS). The Statutory Guidance stresses the importance of partnership working between practitioners and parents/carers so that the child is supported in all areas of development.

Parents should feel that they can approach the setting with any questions or queries, but there should also be a range of activities and events that they can be involved in so that they can encourage enjoyment of literacy. These may range from formal meetings so that the school can outline how reading and writing are taught and how they can support their child, to book days where children dress up as characters from their favourite book.

Figure 2.5 shows some of the different ways that your setting and parents/carers can support children's enjoyment of literacy.

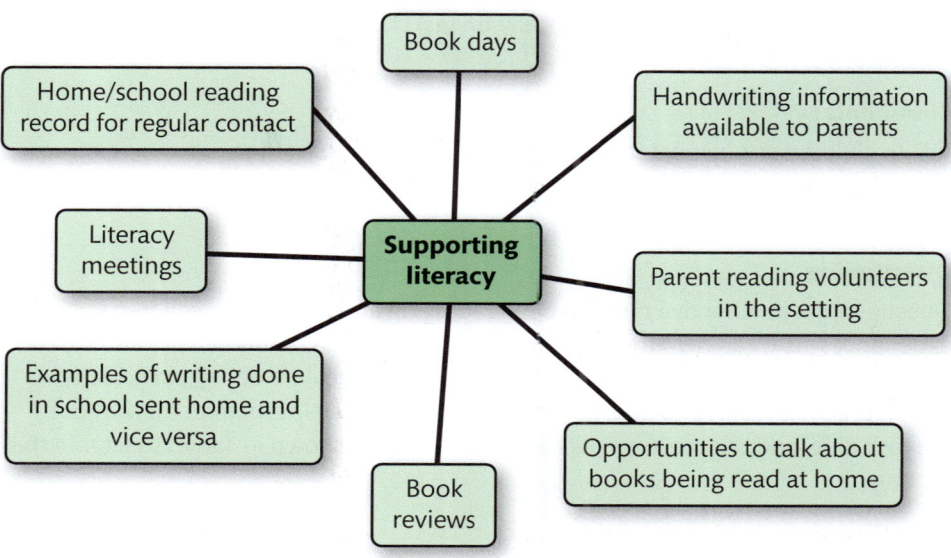

▶ **Figure 2.5:** Ways to support literacy

Write a case study about a child you are supporting in learning to read and write.

- What experiences and activities have you provided in order to encourage the child to read and write? Why is it important to understand the links between the two?
- Using examples of the child's writing from the earliest stages, describe the usual sequence of writing development and show how the child has passed through the relevant stages.
- How do you see your own role in providing appropriate experiences and activities to support reading and writing?

Plan

- I can think about which child I will choose to write about and how I have encouraged them. What aspects of the task do I think will take the most/least time? How will I balance these?
- Do I need to work with anyone else? If so, how will we support each other?

Do

- Have I spent time planning how I am going to structure the task?
- Am I using all the support available to me?

Review

- Can I explain what skills I employed and which new ones I have developed?
- Do I know where I have learning gaps and can I resolve them?

B5 Supporting numeracy development

Supporting children's early experiences of numeracy

The EYFS emphasises the importance of play during learning activities. As mathematics is sometimes an abstract subject, it is very important that early years professionals support children's early experiences through play, by linking mathematical concepts such as number, measurement, shape, space and pattern recognition to practical activities as much as possible to make them meaningful for children. Ensure that mathematics makes sense to young children so that their experiences provide the basis for understanding these mathematical concepts.

When working with children on mathematical activities, you may need to act as a facilitator for their learning. You may need to support them through talking to them in different ways to encourage them to stay on task. Key methods for doing this include the following.

Commentary

Talk to children about what they are doing as they are doing it, in order to reinforce the task. For example, you may say, 'Oh, I see, you are making a pattern with the different coloured pegs'.

Questioning

Questioning is an effective method of encouraging and developing children's experiences, as it can help them to think about the task in different ways and extend their learning. Encourage children to talk about what they are doing, particularly during practical tasks, and question them in a way that helps them to think about the task differently. Some examples of questioning are shown in Table 2.5 later in this section.

Repetition

Going over or repeating concepts is important with young children, as they need opportunities to practise what they have learned.

Praise

Use praise wherever possible. It is an excellent motivator and gives children confidence. Praise can be verbal, but you can also give stickers or rewards, or ask the child to show another adult what they have done or describe it to other children.

▶ Can you see how this practical activity is helping to deliver the mathematics curriculum to a group of reception children?

Understand how to plan and organise numeracy provision

In the early years, mathematics is usually taught through topic work. This means mathematics is part of wider study around a subject, such as 'Myself' or 'Toys'.

Topics can last from between 2 weeks to half a term. In nurseries and reception classes, the curriculum requires the delivery of mathematics mainly through practical activities and discussion. Children carry out a range of activities, including those based on prediction and problem-solving. Activities should be meaningful and purposeful, and in the context of the topic they are exploring.

Maths should also be brought into children's routines and should be spoken about, for example, by asking questions such as 'How many children are here today?', 'Do we have enough pieces of fruit for everyone?', 'Who is taller?' By hearing mathematical language, children start to develop their own mathematical thinking skills.

The process of supporting children to link concepts to experience and why this is important

As we mentioned at the start of this section, mathematics is sometimes an abstract subject, so early years professionals need to link concepts to practical activities to make them meaningful for children. This means, for the youngest children, their introduction to the subject will be mainly through play and exploration.

Encourage children to recognise numbers and patterns in their environment and use them when they can. Examples include selecting coins and counting aloud when making purchases in the role play area, and looking at numbers in different situations such as on number plates or till receipts.

Figure 2.6 shows the kinds of activities that support numeracy development in the early years. As you can see, many of them are examples of how we use mathematics in our day-to-day life. It is important that we are able to show children why mathematics is useful through everyday activities and talk to them about what they are doing.

Children may enjoy being taken on a 'maths walk' in small groups to look at numbers and shapes around the school and outdoor area, or in the local environment. Depending on the amount of adult support available, you may like to give them a series of questions to answer, or simply allow them to find out what they can and report back to others.

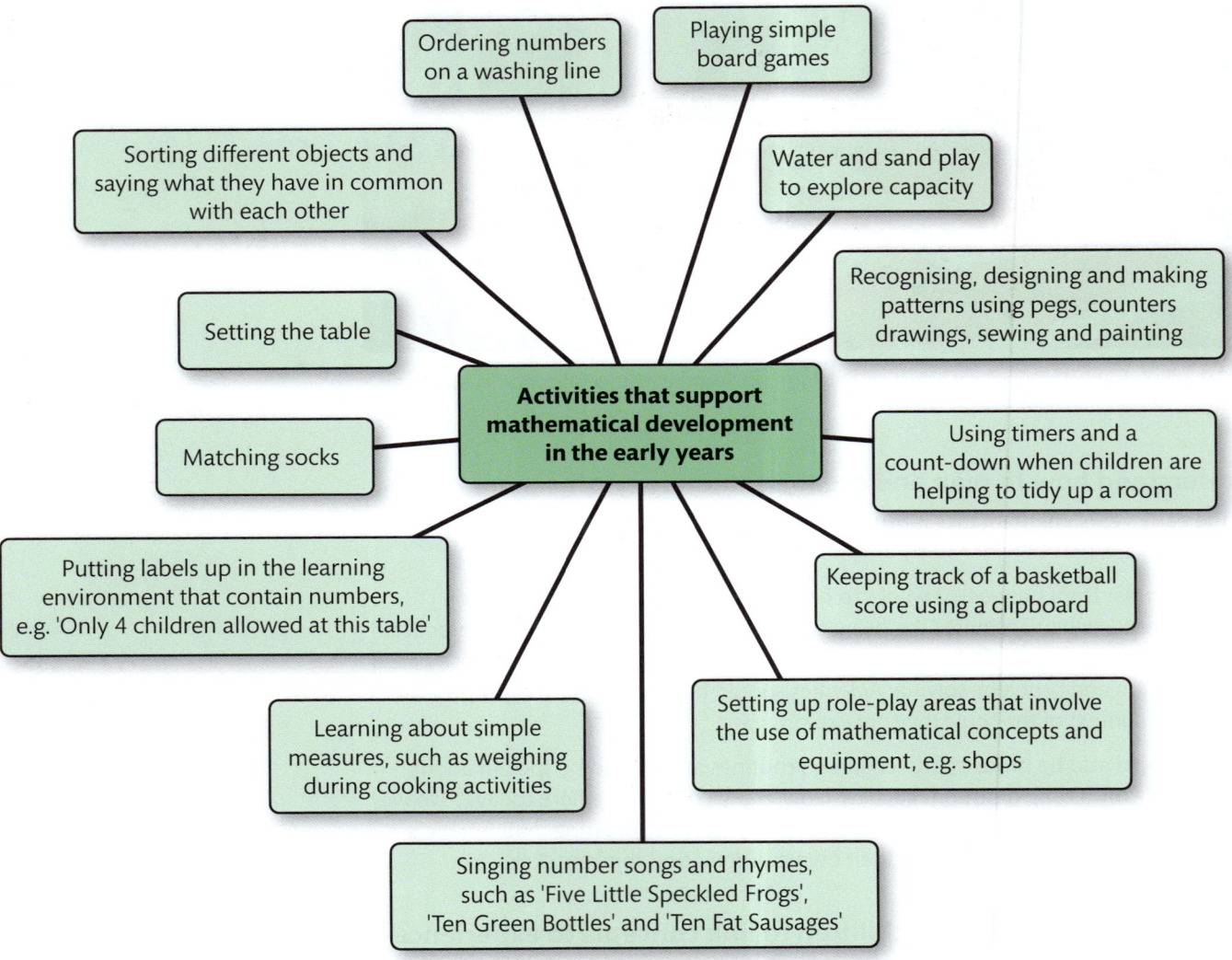

▶ **Figure 2.6:** Activities that support mathematical development in the early years

Assessing a child's understanding of numeracy

You need to constantly observe children's reactions in mathematical situations, so make sure you direct your questions accordingly. This is because it is easy for children to misunderstand mathematical concepts. It is likely that you will use observation, modelling and questioning regularly as children will need to be refocused or asked specific questions to redirect their thinking.

As we have noted above, it is important that early years professionals model to children how mathematics is used in everyday life and discuss it with them. For example, when:

▶ solving problems – are there enough chocolate coins for everyone here to have two each?

▶ using money – how many pennies would I need for everyone to have one penny each?

▶ thinking about capacity – is there enough orange juice in the jug to fill six cups?

▶ counting – count slowly alongside children.

When questioning children, make sure that you ask them in a way that does not 'lead' them to the answer. Questions should be open where possible. For example, 'The answer is 5. What could the question be?' Some further examples are shown in Table 2.5.

▶ **Table 2.5:** Examples of closed and open questions

Closed questions	Open questions
What is the next number?	How do you know what number comes next?
What is 6 add 2?	Can you add different numbers together to make 8?
Is 6 an even number?	Can you tell me some even numbers between 0 and 10?
What is this shape?	How do you know what shape this is?

❚❚ PAUSE POINT

Outline a **new** mathematical concept that you could present to a group of children. This may relate to number, shape, space or measures. How will you make sure you build children's confidence and encourage them to develop their ideas?

Hint   Speak to your manager and use something that is in your current planning to give you guidance.

Extend   Give examples of the kinds of questions you will ask.

Supporting and reinforcing use of mathematical language

Always reinforce vocabulary that is being used in the setting, extend children's vocabulary and check their understanding of any terms used. Young children, or children who speak English as an additional language, may need you to explain mathematical terms to them.

Commentary, or talking through with children what they are doing as they are doing it, enables them to become more familiar with the mathematical language they are using and also encourages them to think through the process as they are working.

Discussion

How do these nursery rhymes and songs relate to mathematical language and/or the development of number?
- One, two, three, four, five, once I caught a fish alive...
- Five currant buns in a baker's shop...
- The grand old Duke of York...
- Five little ducks went swimming one day...
- The wheels on the bus...

Work in a group – can you think of any others?

Using interactive computer programs to encourage and reinforce mathematical concepts

There are a number of interactive computer programs and websites that encourage and reinforce mathematical concepts – these can be used on different devices such as interactive whiteboards, tablets and PCs. Most children are used to working with computers and these programs can be useful in engaging them.

Encouraging enjoyment of mathematics

It is very important for schools and early years settings to work alongside parents to encourage their child's enjoyment of mathematics. However, many parents may have had poor experiences while they were at school and find these hard to overcome. The setting can help in different ways: running information evenings, giving talks and providing guidelines or booklets for parents on how to support their child when learning mathematics.

Here are some specific ideas that might help parents and carers support children.

- Look for shapes and numbers in the environment. Move on to finding odd/even numbers, or numbers higher/lower than.
- Play card and board games, and complete puzzles with children.
- Count up small change with children after going 'shopping'.
- Cook with children to give them experience of weighing ingredients and reading scales. Talk about ingredients being heavier/lighter than others.
- Try not to put too much emphasis on formal 'sums', particularly with very young children. It is more important that they have plenty of practical experience of mathematics.

> **Research**
>
> Many schools now use Mathletics (uk.mathletics.com) to encourage children to enjoy mathematics.
>
> The website provides interactive maths activities for schools, and it encourages children to carry out activities at home too. Take a look at the website and the service it offers.

Parents should be encouraged to come into the setting if possible to see maths in action and to carry out games and activities with children. In this way, they will be able to develop their own confidence, as well as gain ideas. There are also plenty of excellent books for parents to support mathematical development.

> **Case study**
>
> ### Supporting children at home
>
> Andy is the father of twins who are in Year 2. Although both the children are at an age-equivalent level in mathematics, he would like to support them at home and has approached the school for advice. Apart from working on times tables with them, he says that maths is so different from when he was at school, he is worried about 'getting it wrong'.
>
> **Check your knowledge**
>
> 1 What kinds of suggestions could you give Andy?
> 2 Why is it important to work with Andy and other parents?

Assessment practice 2.7

AO1 | AO2 | AO3 | AO4

Your supervisor has asked you to write a description of three practical activities that you have carried out with children aged 2–5 to support the development of their mathematical skills.

- Explain why you chose the activities and how they support children's mathematical development.
- Evaluate how early years professionals contribute to the mathematical development of children from birth to 5 years.

Plan
- Which activities should I use? Do I need clarification on anything?
- Should the activities all be very different? Where can I go to gain additional information?

Do
- Am I recording my own observations and thoughts?
- Do I understand my thought process and why I have decided to approach the task in a particular way?

Review
- Can I explain how I approached the task and why I chose the activities?
- Can I identify how this learning experience relates to future experiences?

C Approaches to the varied needs of individual children

C1 Supporting the concept of multilingualism

Today in the UK, many children are learning English alongside another language, or even languages. Many people think this is a recent development, but that is not true. For many centuries, parts of the UK have spoken other languages alongside English, such as Celtic and Welsh. Indeed, English itself is a mixture of several languages! This section looks at the importance of supporting children to acquire another language alongside English, although the principles apply to the support of any combination of languages.

Supporting children who are multilingual

There are many ways in which adults can support children who are multilingual. A good starting point is to understand the cognitive benefits and impact on children's self-concept when they have two or more languages.

Information processing

As we saw earlier in this unit, in Section A1, language and cognition are linked. Children who are multilingual are able to process information differently as they have access to more than one code. This flexibility is often associated with creativity and problem-solving. It is also thought to help children to acquire further languages more easily. Later on in life, research suggests that speaking more than one language has protective effects on the brain, with fewer bilingual adults having dementia.

Self-concept

Most children who are learning more than one language are doing so because they are with one or more family members who speak the language. The languages spoken will have a strong association, either with a religion or another culture. Being able to communicate in these languages allows children to be part of their family's culture or religion. This in turn gives children a strong sense of cultural or religious identity and self-concept. In many cases, having access to their family's language will also mean that children can communicate with their extended family, who in some cases may be living in other countries.

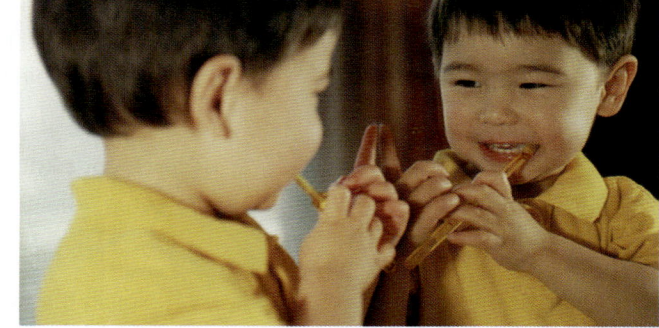

▶ Languages spoken at home are part of children's identity and self-concept

Simultaneous or sequential learning

There are two ways in which children may learn more than one language: simultaneously or sequentially. A simultaneous language learner is exposed to two or three languages from a very young age. A sequential language learner will have an established home language and then go on to pick up another language.

Children who come into a setting and need to learn English sequentially will need significant support. It is therefore helpful to understand that these children will go through four broad stages in the process of picking up English.

1 **Continued use of home language** – in this stage, children will continue to use their home language. It may take a while for them to realise that this language does not elicit responses from other children and adults. This can be a frustrating time for children because they want to communicate but may not understand why, when they use their home language, it does not seem to 'work'. In this phase, adults need to acknowledge that the child is trying to communicate, and use non-verbal methods including pictures, photographs, gestures and facial expression.

2 **Non-verbal or silent period** – in this stage, children stop using their home language and begin the process of 'tuning in' to the sounds and words being used in the setting. Adults can help children in this phase by simplifying their language, pointing to objects and naming them, and also creating familiar routines. It is essential that no pressure is put on children to talk in this phase and that every communication that a child attempts to make, such as pointing, is acknowledged. It is important for adults to observe children in this phase to note progress in children's receptive language. For instance, a child might start to respond to phrases such as 'snack time' by going over to a table. Children are likely to need plenty of emotional support during this period and also opportunities to demonstrate their competency in other areas, e.g. putting on their own coat, helping an adult to lay a table.

3 **Telegraphic and formulaic speech** – in this phase, children start to talk. They are likely to use 'formulaic' phrases such as 'Thank you' or 'That's mine!', which they have picked up and find useful. It is important for adults to recognise though that a child using 'formulaic' phrases has not yet mastered English.

Case study

Learning two languages

Regina is 4 years old. She has been at Cherry Tree nursery for 3 months. Before coming to the nursery she had not heard much English as her parents had moved from Germany.

At first, she tried to talk in German to the other children but quickly gave up. She is now joining in with rhymes and songs, and has several phrases that she uses.

Check your knowledge

1 What is Regina's stage of language learning in English?

2 Why is it important for her to have plenty of adult interaction?

3 Explain the strategies that adults need to use to support her English learning.

Alongside formulaic phrases, children are also likely to start making their own mini sentences in a similar way that toddlers do, e.g. 'car down'. In this period, adults need to acknowledge their communications, expand and recast sentences, and involve the child in routines so that they regularly hear the same phrases and expressions.

4 **Productive language** – during this final phase, children increasingly start to make up their own sentences before eventually becoming fluent. During this stage, children will need additional time to respond and also plenty of adult interaction. They will benefit from sharing simple books and also having opportunities to play simple language games such as picture lotto.

Understanding the context in which languages are being learned

When you are working with children who may have more than one language, it is important to begin by finding out which languages are spoken and by whom.

The following questions can be used to understand children's language use.

▶ What language or languages does your child hear at home?

▶ Who speaks these languages?

▶ Which language or languages are spoken to your child directly?

▶ If you speak more than one language to your child, how do you do this? For example, you might speak one language in the house, another language outside the house.

▶ Has your child heard English before? If so, how much?

▶ Does your child speak any English?

These questions should help you to establish whether children are learning English alongside another language or whether they are learning English 'from scratch'. It will also help you to know whether children are hearing the languages in a consistent way, which, as you will see, can make a difference to the acquisition of them.

The impact on a child of being introduced to English with an established home language

When children come into the setting with an established home language, they may feel unsettled at first. This can be quite daunting for them.

When children join the setting, it is important that parents realise the impact that learning English may have on the child's home language or languages. The impact will very much depend on how much time the child spends being exposed to English, and at what age.

A baby in day care, for example, may spend ten hours a day being exposed to English. The same baby may only hear 1–2 hours a day of the parents' language. This lack of exposure to the parents' language may lead to the baby growing up able to understand the parents' language, but not being able to speak it.

On the other hand, a child who is 3 years old and has been immersed in the parents' language for 3 years, with minimum exposure to English, is likely to pick up English quickly but still retain their home language, providing that parents continue to use it.

Recognising the emotional impact on a child

When children are able to communicate easily in their home language, it is a great shock for them to come to a setting and find that other children and adults do not understand them when they talk. It is also hard for children to understand why, all of a sudden, they no longer understand what is being said to them by other children and adults in that setting.

For some children, this can be very distressing and can cause **regression**. It is, therefore, important to make sure that the settling-in process is managed carefully and that children have a strong relationship with a key person before being separated from their parents.

There are positive benefits too for children who become bilingual, provided that they are supported. Firstly, having more than one language allows children to maintain contact with their parents' culture. This in turn can enhance a child's self-concept and self-esteem. Children may also take pride in being able to move from one language to another as they grow up.

Recognising the cognitive impact on a child

If children are emotionally supported during the process of learning more than one language, there are positive cognitive benefits. Children who are able to use more than one language have been shown to be stronger at particular cognitive tasks. This is thought to be due to the need for the brain to remain flexible as it uses more than one code at a time.

More recent research suggests that later on in life there are also cognitive benefits of knowing more than one language. Bilingualism seems to have a protective effect against brain disease such as dementia.

The importance of a key person

Whether children arrive in a setting with some or no English, the key person has an essential role in settling children in and also establishing a relationship with the child and their parents. Many children will want to stay near the key person at all times to make them feel safe. This relationship will be an important factor in helping the child to acquire language.

The principles of helping children to acquire English when they join a setting at 2 or 3 years old is similar to helping babies to talk. The key person needs to build up a good bond with the child and then use the simplified language that characterises adult speech with babies. This includes facial expressions, gestures and plenty of pointing.

Language routines

The key person should help children by creating language routines with them. For example, they may go with a child to set beakers out on a snack table. If these tasks are done every day with the same child it means that the child will start to 'break in' to some key words that are used each time. In this example, the key words may include 'beaker' and 'table'.

The importance of allowing children to tune into the sounds of the setting's language

As we mentioned earlier, when children come into the setting without any English they are likely to spend time 'tuning in'. In some ways this could be compared to a baby's pre-linguistic phase. Although it might take a baby several months to tune in, young children who have already begun to talk in another language will tune in much quicker. As you have seen, when tuning in it is helpful for children if similar phrases are used each time a routine event happens – this way the child begins to tune in more quickly.

As many children need 'tuning in' time before they are ready to talk, it is important not to pressurise them into speaking. Interestingly, children will often be able to join in with songs and rhymes before they start to talk. This is because songs and rhymes are processed differently in the brain.

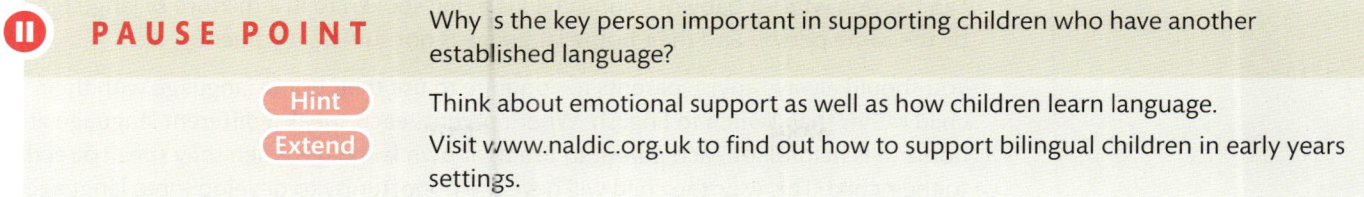

⏸ **PAUSE POINT**

Why is the key person important in supporting children who have another established language?

Hint   Think about emotional support as well as how children learn language.

Extend   Visit www.naldic.org.uk to find out how to support bilingual children in early years settings.

Working with parents and carers to support the development of language

It is important to work closely with parents and carers to support children who have more than one language. Many parents may have concerns about how well their child will settle in and whether or not they will make sufficient progress before starting school. As we have mentioned, it is therefore vital that the child's key person builds a strong relationship with both the child and the parents/carers. This way, parents can see that their child is happy and settled, and that through quality interactions with the key person, their child is making good progress.

Valuing the home language

You saw earlier that multilingualism can have some important benefits to children's emotional, social and cognitive development. Sadly, these benefits can be negated when adults working with children and the wider community do not value the home language. Children who feel they are different because they use more than one language, or that there is disapproval of them using a home language, can develop lower levels of confidence and self-esteem, and this in turn can affect their overall development.

As well as being important for children's development, showing parents that you value the language they use with their child will help your relationship with them. It can be hard for parents to feel confident and relaxed in your company if they feel that you disapprove of them using a different language.

▶ Early years settings need to find ways of valuing children's home languages

Ensuring consistency in the way languages are used

All children learn language by being exposed to its sounds and structures. Children with more than one language should not necessarily develop a speech delay, but this can happen when a baby or young child is being spoken to in a mixture of languages by the same person and their home language is not sufficiently fluent.

You should always advise parents to continue to use their home language with their child rather than switch to English. Where parents each speak a different language at home, it is helpful for each parent to use their own language when they speak directly to their child. This way, the child will have the opportunity to develop three languages.

Case study

Supporting children who have more than one language

Baran's family have moved from Turkey. He is 4 years old and a confident child, although he has never attended an early years setting. Today his mother is visiting a nursery to start the process of settling him in. Baran is quite excited as he has found out that there are some pets at the nursery and he loves animals. His mother is a little worried because he does not know any English, although she is thinking about teaching him some English words.

Check your knowledge

1 Why will it be important for the key person to establish a good relationship with Baran and his family?

2 What advice should the nursery give his mother about supporting his language at home?

3 Explain how Baran's love of animals might help his key person to support Baran's acquisition of English.

Assessment practice 2.8 | AO1 | AO2 | AO3 | AO4 |

A preschool has noticed that there has been an increase in the number of children who have an established home language. They are keen to find out more about multilingualism and have come to you for information.

1 Describe the stages in which children may acquire English sequentially.

2 Explain the range of strategies that can be used to support children who have more than one language.

3 Analyse the impact of the key person in supporting bilingual children.

4 Evaluate the importance of working closely with parents and carers.

Plan
- What information do I have about multilingualism?
- Where can I go to gain additional information?

Do
- Am I presenting the information accurately and concisely?
- Am I managing my time effectively?

Review
- Have I evaluated my work and am I confident that it fulfils the task?

C2 Understand how adults support children who have additional language needs

Some children need additional support in order to be able to communicate and use language. There are a variety of reasons why a child might need additional support, including if they have hearing loss, learning difficulties or speech delay. This section looks at some of the principles involved in supporting children with additional communication and language needs.

Resources for children with hearing loss, language delay or additional language needs

There are a variety of resources that can support children who have additional language needs including hearing loss or language delay.

Visual cues and props

Many children who have language and communication needs are helped when visual cues and props are provided in settings. The visual information helps them to understand or process the spoken language more easily. All babies and children benefit from having visual cues and props, but they are particularly helpful for children who find it hard to convert spoken words into meaning.

There are many different ways for you to incorporate a visual element to support children's communication and language.

▸ Puppets can help to motivate children to communicate. They can be used to act out actions alongside the words being spoken by adults, so they can help children to understand the meanings of words. They also help children to enjoy communicating.

▸ Facial expressions and gestures help children to understand the meaning of what is being said by adults. Children can copy gestures to help them to be understood by others.

▸ Pointing to objects or people at the start of a conversation helps children know what is being talked about. Pointing is usually accompanied by a facial expression and also the word 'look!' to help draw children's attention to the object.

▸ Photographs and pictures are used in many early years settings. These are key to helping children remember what they have been doing or to help them understand what is being spoken about.

▸ Visual timetables are usually photographs or pictures arranged in a way that helps a child to know what is going to be happening throughout a session. This helps them to feel secure.

▸ As we mentioned in Section A1, Makaton is used to support children's communication skills. It is not a language and is very different from British Sign Language. Makaton is generally introduced on the advice of a speech and language therapist.

Quality interaction

All children benefit from quality interaction with adults, but it is particularly important when working with children who have a speech delay or additional needs.

Here are some key areas that are essential to get right when interacting with children.

The environment

▸ Avoid distracting environments with a lot of background noise.

▸ Make sure that there is something to trigger children's interest and allow you to communicate together.

▸ Think about where the child seems to communicate most and where they like spending time.

Your relationship

▶ Make sure that your relationship with children is good and positive.

▶ Consider whether you are fun to be with.

▶ Observe the child's body language when you are with them – is the child relaxed and pleased to be with you?

Your communication skills

▶ Speak clearly and moderate your style according to the age/needs of the child.

▶ Use high levels of facial expression, gesture and note children's reactions.

▶ Give children sufficient time to answer or respond to you. Be patient!

▶ Acknowledge their communication positively – smile, show interest and, if appropriate, ask further questions.

▶ Expand what they are trying to communicate to you.

▶ Use props, photographs or pictures if needed.

▶ Do not overtly correct children's speech – rephrase correctly instead.

Case study

The importance of quality interaction

Chara, a practitioner, is meant to be supporting Jonas's communication and language.

Jonas is happily playing with some building blocks in the corner of the room. Chara goes up to him and tells him to come with her. Jonas is not happy.

Chara takes Jonas to a table in the centre of the busy room and gets out some cards with pictures on them. Jonas does not seem interested. Chara becomes irritated, partly because Jonas is not interested and also because she is frequently interrupted by other children. She is also frustrated because when she asks Jonas a question, he does not seem to respond. After five minutes, she tells Jonas that he can go.

Check your knowledge

1 Where should the interaction have taken place?

2 Why might Jonas's responses have been influenced by Chara's style?

3 What suggestions could you give to Chara for the future?

Professionals who support children's speech, communication and language

There are a range of professionals who may be involved in supporting children's speech, communication and language. The first port of call is normally the speech and language therapist, but where children have complex needs other professionals may also support the child.

Speech and language therapist (SLT)

Many children who have additional communication and language needs will be referred to speech and language therapists. Depending on the age and also a child's need, speech and language therapists may work with the child directly and/or they may suggest activities that need to be carried out at home by parents and also in settings.

The type of activities will very much depend on the nature of the child's difficulty. For children who are not producing certain sounds, a therapist may suggest games and rhymes that strengthen the muscles in the mouth and teach the child new mouth movements. If you know that a child is working with a speech and language team, it may be worth asking the parent for permission to contact the team so that you can find out more about the child's programme. Following the advice and programmes suggested by the speech and language therapist is essential because otherwise children are not likely to make progress. In addition, inconsistent or incorrect use of methods such as Makaton can create more problems for the child.

Educational psychologist

Some children may have difficulties in communication and language because of emotional or other difficulties, including learning difficulties. To understand the full nature of the child's difficulties, an educational psychologist and speech and language therapist may jointly assess a child in order to construct a programme of support.

Physiotherapist and occupational therapist

Where children have physical difficulties alongside communication and language needs, a physiotherapist or occupational therapist may work together with a speech and language therapist to support the child. A good example of this is where it is thought that a child may benefit from using Makaton, but the child is finding it hard to make the hand signs.

> **Link**
>
> Revisit Section A1 to remind yourself about conductive hearing loss.

Hearing support services

Many young children are likely to have some hearing loss at one time or another. There are different types of hearing loss but the most common type in children is known as conductive hearing loss or 'glue ear'.

The other type of hearing loss is usually permanent and is, fortunately, relatively rare. This type of permanent loss is known as sensorineural loss and is likely to be picked up in the few months after birth. Children with sensorineural loss require hearing aids or, in some cases, a cochlear transplant. It is useful to gain professional advice about how best to support a child with a sensorineural loss. While parents may be able to provide you with some information, it is likely that the child will also be supported by a local team of hearing support professionals. Contacting and following the advice of these professionals, as well as the parents, will help you to work effectively with a child.

Portage worker

Portage is a home support system for young children who have complex additional needs. A portage worker works alongside parents to help a child maximise their development at home. Parents decide on small goals or steps for their child and the portage worker helps create a programme of activities that will support a skill.

For children with complex needs who also attend a setting, it is worth finding out from parents what activities they are focusing on at home.

⏸ PAUSE POINT   Name two professionals who may support a child with communication and language needs.

Hint   One is often abbreviated as SLT.

Extend   Find out more about speech and language therapy by visiting www.rcslt.org.

The importance of working closely with parents and carers to support the development of language

It is always good practice to work closely with parents, but it is essential when you are supporting children who have additional needs with their language development. Some parents may have found particular ways of communicating with their children that are useful for you to know about. You can also share your knowledge with parents about particular ways you may work with their children.

Gaining information for assessment

As children can behave and communicate differently at home, it can be useful for parents to share information and, if possible, recordings of their child at home. Recordings can be taken on a mobile phone or on a recording device such as an MP3 player. If recordings are kept, of course with parents' permission, you can go back to them at a later date and see if children have made progress.

Activities that promote language development

When working with children who have additional language needs, it is important to recognise activities that might promote language development. These include imaginative play, puppets and story sacks. It is also vital to use the skills covered in Section A2.

> **Link**
>
> Revisit Sections A2, B3 and C2 to remind yourself about imaginative play, puppets and story sacks.

Table 2.6 shows examples of activities that might support language development. Remember, though, that activities always need to be carefully planned according to children's language needs. In some cases, this may mean asking for advice or following the programme that has been put in place by the child's speech and language therapist.

▶ **Table 2.6:** Activities you could use to support language development

Activity – how it promotes language development	What the task involves
'What's in the bag?' Speaking	The child takes an object from the bag and says what it is
'What's happening?' Speaking	The child is shown a picture of a scene, e.g. a person in the kitchen making cakes, but things are going wrong. The child explains what is happening
'Animals in the tube' Understanding and following instructions	A selection of toy animals are on display. The adult describes an animal and the child drops it down the tube, e.g. the big lion, the small dog
'Can you find Teddy?' Listening	The adult hides a teddy bear. The child has to follow the adult's instructions to find it
'Stop and go' Listening	Children run around (go!) and stop when they hear a shaker
'Follow my leader' Listening	The adult plays a simple rhythm using a shaker. The children play it back

Understanding children's body language

It is important to find out from parents how their child communicates their feelings if they are not talking. Parents may be able to tell you about their child's body language in certain situations. For example, if a child is nervous they might touch their ear. Being able to interpret a child's body language is particularly important when settling children in.

Assessment practice 2.9

AO1 AO2 AO3 AO4

An opportunity playgroup is running a training session for new volunteers. The playgroup is noted for its outstanding work with children with additional communication and language needs. They have asked you to collate information that might form the basis of the initial training session.

They would like you to:

- identify professionals who may work alongside children and their families with communication needs
- evaluate the range of resources that adults might use to support children's communication and language
- evaluate the importance of information sharing and close working with parents.

Plan
- What information do I have about supporting children with additional needs?
- Where can I find additional information?

Do
- Is the information I have found accurate and concise?
- Am I managing my time effectively?

Review
- Have I evaluated my work and am I confident that it fulfils the task?

Further reading and resources

Communication, language and literacy

Books

Brock, A. and Rankin, C. (2008) *Communication, Language and Literacy from Birth to Five*, London: Sage Publications.

Callander, N. and Nahmad-Williams, L. (2010) *Communication, Language and Literacy*, London: Continuum.

Fisher, J. (2009) *Puppets, Language and Learning*, London: Featherstone Education.

Jolliffe, W., Waugh, D. and Carss, A. (2015) *Teaching Systematic Synthetic Phonics in Primary Schools*, 2nd edition, London: Learning Matters.

Lee, W. (2008) *The Communication Cookbook*, London: I Can.

Tassoni, P. (2012) *Penny Tassoni's Practical EYFS Handbook,* 2nd edition, Harlow: Pearson.

The Communication Trust (2011) *Misunderstood: Supporting Children and Young People with Speech, Language and Communication Needs*, 2nd edition, London: The Communication Trust, Early Support.

Websites

www.mrthorne.com – Mr Thorne Does Phonics: this website has useful ideas and clips for supporting the teaching of synthetic phonics. Many of these are also available on YouTube.

www.literacytrust.org.uk – National Literacy Trust: the National Literacy Trust supports the development of early language and communication skills, and provides advice, resources and case studies.

www.phonicsplay.co.uk – Phonics Play: this is a useful website for teaching phonics but you need to subscribe to use the resources.

www.talkingpoint.org.uk – Talking point: this website gives the milestones in ages and stages for the development of children's communication. It also provides ideas for supporting children's communication and language development.

Apps

The apps below all have ideas and activities for children who are learning phonics. You need to purchase Pocket Phonics. Twinkl Basic is free although there is a platinum service that you need to subscribe to and you do have to pay for the Phonics Suite.

Twinkl Phonics Suite: **www.twinkl.co.uk/store/product/twinkl-phonics-suite**

Nessy Hairy Letters: **www.nessy.com/hairyletters**

Blending Dragon: **www.ictgames.com/blendingDragon**

Pocket Phonics: **https://itunes.apple.com/gb/app/abc-pocketphonics-letter-sounds/id299342927?mt=8**

Mathematics

Books

Boaler, J. (2010) *The Elephant in the Classroom: Helping Children Learn and Love Maths*, London: Souvenir Press Ltd.

Deboys, M. and Pitt, E. (1980) *Lines of Development in Primary Mathematics*, Belfast: Blackstaff Press Ltd.

Donaldson, M. (1986) *Children's Minds*, London: HarperCollins.

Eastaway, R. and Askew, M. (2010) *Maths for Mums and Dads*, London: Square Peg.

Sani, N. (2010) *How to Do Maths So Your Children Can Too: The Essential Parents' Guide*, London: Vermilion.

Websites

http://nrich.maths.org – NRICH: this useful website gives suggestions for a large number of mathematical activities, including problem-solving.

www.teachfind.com – Teachfind: this website provides lots of ideas and resources to support children's mathematical development.

uk.mathletics.com – Mathletics: the Mathletics website has a large number of resources for tutors and exciting activities for children. Your setting will need to subscribe to access the full site.

Apps

www.apps4primaryschools.co.uk/apps/maths – Apps 4 Primary Schools: this is a paid-for app with a range of activities from early years upwards.

www.cowlyowl.com/apps/little-digits – Little Digits: this paid-for app teaches children about numbers.

THINK ▶FUTURE

Gina Paulsen

Nursery worker

Gina has been working in a nursery attached to a school for 4 years. The nursery takes children from 3 years old and many families are bilingual.

One of the main features of her work with the youngest children is to develop their language. She plans the environment and routines to encourage this. Quite often you will find her in the role play area pretending to be a shopkeeper. Gina also spends time helping children who are learning English alongside a home language.

Another focus for Gina's work is to introduce children to the early skills they will need for literacy and numeracy. She does this mainly through play. She encourages the children to sing nursery rhymes, play sound games and to look out for opportunities to count and play games involving numbers. Gina also plans a range of mark-making activities so that children can enjoy the process of early writing.

Focusing your skills

The best way to develop your own skills in supporting children's speech, language, literacy and numeracy is to plan and carry out some simple activities with children. Try some of these practical ideas.

Supporting speech, communication and language
- Remember to speak clearly.
- Avoid asking question after question.
- Expand children's statements so they have the opportunity to hear a wide range of vocabulary.
- Do not correct children's speech; instead, respond using phrases correctly.

Using puppets
- Bring the puppet close to you and cross your wrists so that children do not see that you are using your hand. Try to choose a puppet that fits your hand well.
- Make eye contact with your puppet as if it were real.

Supporting literacy
- When you share books with children, talk to them and develop your relationship.
- Remember that rhymes and songs also support literacy.
- Use props to bring books to life.
- Create writing areas and encourage children to write by giving them specific topics to write about.

Supporting mathematics and numeracy skills
- Use a range of opportunities to develop children's counting skills and assess their understanding of maths.
- Counting songs, puzzles, noting down scores in sports and talking about shapes are all forms of mathematics.
- Look for mathematics in the environment, for example, patterns in tiles and shapes. Devise activities that encourage children to think about numbers in the environment, for example, 'maths walks'.

Getting ready for assessment

This section has been written to help you to do your best when you take the external test. Read through it carefully and ask your tutor if there is anything you are not sure about.

About the test

The externally assessed task for Unit 2 will consist of a paper set and marked by Edexcel. You will have to complete activities based on fictional case studies.

Your tutor will give you a task booklet containing the case studies and you should spend time planning and preparing on your own before you write up the final task. You will then have time during the assement period to complete the write-up of your activities under supervised conditions. You can take notes from your planning work into the supervised sessions. Your tutor will tell you the amount of notes you can take in.

As the guidelines for assessment can change, you should refer to the official assessment guidance on the Pearson Qualifications website for the latest definitive guidance.

Preparing for your written assessment

The activities are designed to assess your knowledge and understanding of the concepts and theories supporting the development of children's communication, language, literacy and numeracy. You will be assessed on your ability to apply that knowledge to fictional scenarios involving early years settings and one or more children. Your answers should show that you can analyse and evaluate information about children, with reference to the impact of certain activities and theoretical approaches on their communication, language, literacy and numeracy development. You should also show that you can recommend appropriate activities and approaches to support children's development.

Make sure you arrive in good time for the supervised sessions and leave yourself enough time at the end to check through your work. Listen to, and read carefully, any instructions you are given, including the information in the task booklet. Many people lose marks because they do not read instructions properly or misunderstand what they are being asked to do.

The following key terms may appear in your assessment. Understanding these terms will help you to understand what you are being asked to do.

Term	Definition
Activity	A planned play and learning experience to develop a child's skills and abilities
Activity plan	A structured breakdown of an experience to develop a child's skills and abilities
Early years theory	Ideas that underpin early years teaching practice
Resources	Pieces of equipment needed to support children's activities

▶ Always plan your answer before you begin writing. Include an introduction and a conclusion and think about the key points you want to mention in your answer. In your plan, think about how much time you have: make sure you have time to cover everything you want to and to write a conclusion.

Make sure your answer focuses on the key points you want to make. If you find your answer drifting away from those main points, refer back to your plan!

▶ Make sure you understand what the activity instructions are asking you to do. It might help you to underline or highlight the key terms in the instructions so you can be sure your answer is focused on exactly what you have been asked to do.

Remember, you can take up to four sides of A4 notes from your research into the supervised assessment, so make sure your notes are clear and concise.

Sample answers

Set task brief

St Andrew's Nursery

St Andrew's pre-school is a nursery of 25 children, attached to a small, one-form entry village primary school. A new housing development has recently been built near the school and St Andrew's is starting to welcome more children who are speakers of other languages and from a variety of ethnic backgrounds. It is likely that the school will grow and the local authority is currently discussing extending both the school and nursery with a view to becoming two-form entry.

The headteacher is aware that the school and nursery will need to review the communication and language aspect of the early years policy as well as the EAL (English as Another Language) policy, and has included this in the school development plan.

Activity 1

As nursery manager, you have been asked to work with the literacy coordinator to write a report for the headteacher, recommending ways to support the development of children's language skills in the setting. She has asked you to highlight the impact of language skills on the teaching and learning of mathematics.

You must:

1. make recommendations to the headteacher for the early years curriculum

> Underline the key words in the text to check you fully understand what you are being asked to do.

2. describe what will be needed to implement your recommendations

> Find some examples of similar schools or nurseries and research how they developed their policies in this area.

3. link your suggestions to early years theory.

> Research theories about communication, language and literacy.

Answer guidance:

To answer this question, you will need to consider:

- priorities for the nursery and reception classes in communication, language and literacy
- the impact of language skills on the mathematics curriculum
- how you will work with parents and the wider community
- resources you may need
- how you will research other schools and nurseries which have developed their policies.

Look at a range of early years policies to see how much is included on the prime area of communication and language, as well as literacy and mathematics. Look for ideas about how you can present information for speakers of other languages.

Give examples of opportunities and activities which will help children to develop their communication and language in all areas, but focus particularly on literacy and mathematics.

Think about how you can support parents as part of the wider community, particularly those who are speakers of other languages. You might wish to organise welcome events and include bilingual speakers or have leaflets available in other languages. You must also make sure the school and nursery websites are accessible to all.

You may begin your answer with an introduction such as:

> Communication and language is one of the prime areas of the early years curriculum. As such, it is a crucial aspect of each child's development. Through language and communication with others, young children develop not only language skills, but also social, emotional and cognitive skills. Strong levels of communication and language also support children's progress in other areas of the early years curriculum including mathematics and literacy. In order to highlight what is needed as our school grows and welcomes children from different cultures and backgrounds, it is very important that we recognise some of the theory behind language development. We will also need to look at additional resources we will need to be able to support the children.

When discussing theories of language development, make sure you write about any difficulties to look out for when supporting bilingual children.

Activity 2

Ricky is three years old and has recently started at St Andrew's pre-school. He is brought to the setting by his mother on her way to work and collected by his childminder. Staff at the setting have noticed that he has very limited vocabulary and does not speak to the other children, tending to gesture to them or try to pull them towards him in order to communicate.

Ricky has been observed as part of the assessment process and is seen to be playing alongside rather than with the other children. He does not try to initiate conversation and is often seen on his own engaging in solitary play.

As you are Ricky's key worker, produce a plan which you can share with other nursery staff and with Ricky's parents and childminder to support his communication development.

1. Suggest an action plan based on what you have observed and discussed with others.

2. Describe the types of resources you may need, including the role of adults and any outside help you may need.

3. Justify your actions with reference to early years theory.

Answer guidance:

You might begin your answer along these lines:

My action plan is based on observations and assessments which I have carried out as Ricky's key worker, and that others have carried out since Ricky came to the nursery six weeks ago. Ricky seems to have limited communication skills and needs to develop these as a priority.

First, before implementing any action plan, I would ask Ricky's parents about his hearing in case there is an underlying cause to his communication difficulties. If his hearing has been checked and is normal, and if he does not have any kind of infection which could be affecting his hearing, I would start to think about activities that would interest him and stimulate his desire to communicate. We might then start to implement the following recommendations...

Your answer should then outline a detailed action plan. Remember to include the names of everyone who will be involved in the implementation of the plan, and include a date for review.

When suggesting activities that can be carried out with children to develop their skills, you do not need to give a lot of examples. Instead, give examples of several different types of activity and explain why they may help Ricky.

Jot down some of the activities you might want to carry out with Ricky and underline the ones that his parents could do at home. You could also have a discussion with Ricky's childminder about activities she could try with him.

Play and Learning 3

Getting to know your unit

Play is a major part of childhood. Children can be seen playing all over the world – either in groups, by themselves or alongside adults.

In this unit you will look at the benefits for children as they play, different approaches to organising play and the role of adults in play. You will also consider a range of theoretical and philosophical perspectives that underpin the way that play is organised and provided for in early years settings.

The knowledge that you gain in this unit will support your work while you are on placement.

How you will be assessed

This unit will be assessed by a series of internally assessed tasks set by your tutor. Throughout this unit, assessment activities will help you work towards your assessment. Completing these activities will not mean that you have achieved a particular grade, but you will have carried out useful research or preparation that will be relevant when it comes to your final assignment.

To achieve the tasks in your assignment, it is important to check that you have met all of the Pass grading criteria. You can do this as you work your way through the assignment.

If you are hoping to gain a Merit or Distinction, also make sure that you present the information in your assignment in the style that is required by the relevant assessment criterion. For example, Merit criteria require you to analyse and discuss, and Distinction criteria require you to assess and evaluate.

The assignment set by your tutor will consist of a number of tasks designed to meet the criteria in the table. This is likely to consist of written assignments but may also include activities such as:

▶ producing a report that examines the benefits of different play types and how play impacts on children's development

▶ producing a report that considers different philosophies and approaches to play and their benefits to children's development

▶ providing a reflective account in relation to your skills with working with children to support play and learning activities.

Assessment criteria

This table shows what you must do in order to achieve a **Pass**, **Merit** or **Distinction** grade, and where you can find activities to help you.

Pass	Merit	Distinction
Learning aim **A** Examine types of play and learning activities and the benefits for children's learning and development		**AB.D1** Evaluate the extent to which play and learning provision in a selected early years setting has been influenced by theoretical perspectives and curriculum approaches and the benefits for children's learning and development. **Assessment practice 3.3**
A.P1 Explain play types for children at different ages and stages of development. **Assessment practice 3.1**	**A.M1** Assess the benefits of different types of play and learning activities for children's learning and development. **Assessment practice 3.2**	
A.P2 Explain how play and learning activities support the physical, cognitive, language, social and emotional development of young children. **Assessment practice 3.2**		
Learning aim **B** Investigate theoretical perspectives to learning and development, curriculum approaches to play and their influence on current early years practice		
B.P3 Explain theoretical perspectives to learning and development. **Assessment practice 3.3**	**B.M2** Assess the extent to which play and learning provision in a selected early years setting has been influenced by theoretical perspectives and curriculum approaches. **Assessment practice 3.3**	
B.P4 Compare two curriculum approaches to play and learning and their influence on a selected early years setting. **Assessment practice 3.3**		
Learning aim **C** Demonstrate skills required by early years professionals to support children's purposeful play and learning opportunities		
C.P5 Explain skills that are required by early years professionals to support purposeful play and learning activities. **Assessment practice 3.4**	**C.M3** Justify strategies used to support children engaged in purposeful play and learning activities. **Assessment practice 3.4**	**C.D2** Evaluate the impact of purposeful play and learning activities for children's learning and development. **Assessment practice 3.4**
C.P6 Support children in adult-initiated and child-initiated purposeful play and learning activities in an early years setting. **Assessment practice 3.4**		**C.D3** Evaluate own skills and their application to supporting purposeful play and learning activities. **Assessment practice 3.4**

Getting started

Make a list of toys and resources that you might find in a preschool or nursery. When you have finished this unit, see if you can add to this list and group them into play types.

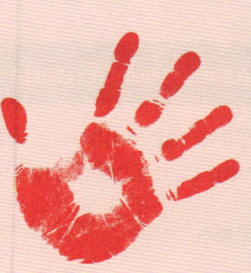

A Examine types of play and learning activities and the benefits for children's learning and development

A1 Play types and opportunities

Play types

Play and resources are often grouped into five different types to make them easier to talk about. Each type of play has particular benefits to children's development and an understanding of these benefits is necessary in order to plan for play. These play types often best describe the play of children aged between 2 and 8 years old, rather than babies and very young children.

> **Link**
>
> Later in this section you will look at play for babies and children under 2 years old.

Physical play

Physical play refers to any type of play where the main focus is some sort of physical activity. This might be play where children are running, climbing, kicking or throwing. It supports the development of physical skills, confidence and social skills.

Imaginative play

Imaginative play involves children pretending in some way and is sometimes referred to as 'pretend play'. It helps support the development of children's communication and language skills, their social skills and helps them understand identity as they take on different roles.

There are many forms and levels of imaginative play. Here are a few examples.

▶ **Role play** – where children take on a role, often an adult one, and incorporate props to make it more lifelike.

▶ **Superhero play** – where children enjoy dressing up and acting out a hero role. This can be influenced by what children have seen on screen. Spiderman, Batman and various Disney characters are often popular.

▶ **Small-world play** – where children create their own small worlds and direct the action. Popular resources include farm animals, dinosaurs, play people and trains.

Sensory play

Sensory play involves children playing with tactile materials such as dough, sand and water to help them develop their fine motor skills and hand–eye coordination, become familiar with concepts of volume and shape, and explore the textures and properties of different materials. Over recent years, many settings have started to use a wide range of materials, including cornflour and water (**gloop**), mashed potato, cold cooked spaghetti and gravel.

> **Key terms**
>
> **Gloop** – a mixture of cornflour and water used as a resource for sensory play.
>
> **Small-world play** – a type of imaginative play that involves children using toys to re-create scenarios on a small scale, e.g. a farm, a railway track.

Creative arts and design play

Creative arts and design, more commonly referred to as 'creative play', involves children using resources freely in a creative way. Resources may include collage materials, junk for modelling, paints, crayons and also musical instruments. This type of play is only genuinely creative for children when they have freedom to explore the resources rather than being directed to make something that the adult has in mind. It helps children develop their fine motor skills and hand–eye coordination, and allows them to express and release their emotions.

Construction play

Construction play involves children using resources to build things or join things together in some way. This may include jigsaws and train tracks as well as bricks, both large and small. This type of play helps children develop spatial awareness and improve their hand–eye coordination. They are also able to explore how things work.

❚❚   PAUSE POINT   List the main play types for children aged 2–8 years old.

Hint   There are five!

Extend   Can you explain the benefits of each play type?

Social stages of play

In the 1930s, Mildred Parten looked at young children's play. She noticed that as children become older, they tend to play more cooperatively. Her work has been widely accepted as it showed that children's social development was reflected in the way they played. Her work has since been built on and ages have been added alongside the different stages (see Table 3.1). This can be helpful as a guide to planning play and provision for groups of children.

▶ **Table 3.1:** The social stages of play

Age	Stage of play	Characteristics
0–2 years	Onlooker	Babies are fascinated by what others are doing but may not be engaged in play. Onlooker behaviours are also found in older children when they are new to a group or unsure
0–2 years	Solitary	Babies may be aware of others but will engage in their own play
2–3 years	Parallel	Children will be aware of other children. They play side by side. At times they may notice what each other are doing and copy each other's actions (or try to take what the other child is using)
3–4 years	Associative	Children will be very interested in others. They may be engaged in the same play and share materials but not actually coordinating their actions, e.g. if a child is dancing, another child may copy the actions, smile and make eye contact
4 years and onwards	Cooperative	Children are playing with each other without the support of an adult. They interact and engage in the same play, e.g. pretending to be a family in the home corner

It is important to note that the ages listed in the table are only a guide. Repeated and careful observation of children in different situations is always the best way to assess the changes in children's play.

▶ These children are engaged in parallel play – they are aware of each other but they are not interacting

Definitions of play

It may seem hard to believe, but defining what is and is not play is quite controversial and potentially difficult. Most people would agree that two children digging enthusiastically in the sand on a beach were playing, but not everyone would describe it as play if there was an adult telling the children how best to do it.

Tina Bruce's features of play

Professor Tina Bruce has been very influential in the field of early years education, with particular reference to play and learning. Bruce looked at play and considered the features that it might have. She came up with the following 12 features of play.

1 Play is an active process without a product.
2 Play is **intrinsically motivated**.
3 Play exerts no pressure to conform to rules, goals or tasks or to take definite directions.
4 Play is about possible, alternative worlds that involve the concepts of 'supporting' and 'as if' and that lift the player to the highest levels of functioning. This involves being imaginative, creative, original and innovative.
5 Play is about wallowing in ideas, feelings and relationships, and becoming aware of what we know (metacognition).
6 It actively uses first-hand experiences.
7 It is sustained and, when in full flow, helps us to function in advance of what we can actually do in our real lives.
8 In play we use technical prowess, mastery and competence that we have previously developed. We are in control.
9 Children or adults can initiate play but each must be sensitive to each other's personal agenda.
10 Play can be solitary.
11 It can be with others, who are sensitive to other players.
12 Play integrates everything we learn, know, feel, relate to and understand.

Key term

Intrinsically motivated – if an activity is intrinsically motivated, the interest or the drive towards action comes from within the child.

Free-flow play

The term free-flow play is used by Tina Bruce to consider the way that children bring together their experiences, skills and relationships to create play. Famously, Bruce talks about children 'wallowing' in play.

Interestingly, although acknowledging their value in feeding into free-flow play, Bruce does not believe that experiences such as exploring gloop or being shown a game by an adult can be counted as play.

Recent use of the term

Bruce is known for using the term free-flow play to describe children playing freely and combining the 12 features of play. This term has now been absorbed into the general vocabulary of early years education and has a much broader sense.

At the time of writing, it is taken to mean that children can move freely from one play opportunity to another, both indoors and outdoors. Free-flow play also means that children can help themselves to resources and also choose to mix resources if they wish. The idea is that they are free to explore and take play in the direction that they choose. Most preschool group settings are likely to have some periods of free-flow time built into their routine, although whether this allows for what Bruce originally described is questionable in some settings.

❚❚ PAUSE POINT   Explain Tina Bruce's definition of the term free-flow play.

> **Hint**   Her definition links to features of children's play.
>
> **Extend**   Explain the difference between Tina Bruce's definition of free-flow play and current uses of this term in some early year settings.

Structured play

Structured play is also referred to as **adult-directed play** or **adult-initiated play**. Structured play puts emphasis on helping children to learn while they are playing and so it is sometimes called 'purposeful play'. When you are on your placements in different settings that care for children of similar ages, you may find that their approach to structured play varies. This is because play can be structured at many different levels. Many would question whether very structured play is indeed play at all.

Structured play is the opposite of **child-initiated play**, where children are able to decide what to play with and also the way in which they use the resources or toys.

> **Key terms**
>
> **Adult-directed play** – where an adult takes a role in planning, organising or leading play.
>
> **Adult-initiated play** – play in which an adult provides resources or sets up an activity with a specific learning intention in mind.
>
> **Child-initiated play** – where children choose the resources, the location and how to play.

Table 3.2 shows the different ways in which play can be structured, along with their advantages and disadvantages.

▶ **Table 3.2:** Different ways that play can be structured

Level of structured play	Examples	Advantages and disadvantages
Highly structured – adult-directed Children are told what they will be doing. The adult explains how to play and use the resources. The adult joins in or supervises the play. The adult discourages children from using the resources in ways different from the planned objective Note: this level of structure is unlikely to work well with younger children	• Drama productions and plays • Board games such as snakes and ladders • Games of cards • Structured cooking	Advantages • Children may learn new skills • Parents may be reassured that their child is 'learning' Disadvantages • If play is not of interest to children, there will be few benefits • Reduces options for creativity and independence and is not empowering
Structured – adult-directed Children are asked if they are interested in taking part. Play is based on children's interests or something that the children are likely to enjoy. Children are free to leave at any time. Other children may come and join in. Adult takes the role of a play partner rather than director	• Building dens • Collecting leaves • Making a conveyor belt for the home corner shop • Seeing who can make the largest sand castle • Going on a 'sound' walk	Advantages • Children are given opportunities to learn new skills or to do something that is different from their usual play or experiences • Interaction levels are high • Concentration levels are high • Children feel part of process Disadvantages • Children are not leading the play
Structured play opportunities where children are directed to play in certain ways The environment is set up ready for play. Children are encouraged to play with different materials and may be given specific tasks, e.g. 'You two, go to the jigsaws.' Children are not encouraged to deviate from the 'adult' purpose of the play	• Play is set up in different areas, e.g. mark making, jigsaws, cars, dough table	Advantages • Children experience different types of play • Adult can make sure that the curriculum is covered Disadvantages • Children cannot be creative or explore materials • Concentration levels can be low
Structured play opportunities that children can choose to use and deviate from – adult-initiated Resources are put out by adults in ways that may prompt children to play in certain ways or take their play interests forward. Children are free to ignore the prompts or use them in other ways as part of their play	• Play is set up in different areas but in ways that might encourage children to learn or experience something new, e.g. coins are hidden in the sand tray, blocks of ice are put in the water tray	Advantages • Children may gain new experiences from the resources provided and this may support the curriculum objectives • Children are more likely to concentrate Disadvantages • Children may be diverted from their original play interests

▶ Where do you think this structured activity would fit in Table 3.2?

Play and learning opportunities for babies and children from birth up to 2 years

Babies and very young children need play opportunities that are different from those needed by older children. This is partly because they need more adult interaction, but also because they are likely to be mouthing until they are 18 months or so. Playing with an adult is essential for babies and very young children as, through play, they learn the skills of interacting with others.

As an adult, playing with babies and toddlers requires great sensitivity. Adults have to be ready to stop a game if a child becomes bored but equally need to seize the moment if the child shows that they want to play. You will now look at some popular play opportunities for children under 24 months.

Treasure-basket play

This type of play is easy to prepare and very beneficial to babies. Thirty or so objects made from natural materials (not toys) are placed in a low basket. The baby is then free to explore the items as they choose. The role of the adult is to supervise for safety and to be close by as a reassuring presence. The aim is not to direct the play. This is a form of child-initiated play for babies who can sit up and so are able to select their own resources, but who may not be mobile.

Heuristic play

Heuristic play has many similarities to treasure-basket play. It is used with older babies and toddlers. Children play with an assortment of objects that they can explore. The key difference is that items made of plastic can be introduced – although not toys.

Everyday items work the best and, because toddlers enjoy repetitive movements, it is usual to put out collections of small items, for example, several shells or several wooden rings. As with treasure-basket play, children need a wide range of objects in sufficient quantity to provide a multitude of combinations.

When providing for heuristic play, make sure that none of the items included are toys. The child should be in front of a pile of materials, which can include tins of different sizes (e.g. biscuit tins, cake tins, cylindrical tins), wine corks, shells, hair curlers, chains, plugs, wooden dolly pegs, pompoms or cardboard tubes. Make sure that an adult is not engaged with the child and that the child is able to explore freely.

> **Key term**
>
> **Heuristic play** – provision of natural and man-made everyday objects that give babies and children opportunities for exploration and open-ended play.

PAUSE POINT   What are the main features of treasure-basket play?

Hint	Think about the type of materials used in this play and the age of the child.
Extend	What are the key differences between treasure-basket and heuristic play?

▶ This child is engaging in heuristic play

Adult-initiated games

Children under 2 years rely heavily on adults to be their play partners. Through adult-initiated games, babies and toddlers develop strong communication and language skills, but also social skills such as turn taking and reading other's emotions. Many different adult-initiated games can be played with children. Table 3.3 describes some of them.

▶ **Table 3.3:** Examples of adult-initiated games for babies and children under 2 years old

Adult-initiated game	Description
Building and knock-down play	Babies and toddlers love knocking down towers of bricks and stacking beakers. With young babies, the adult has to build up the tower but, by around 8 months, most babies are trying to help too
Peek-a-boo and hide and seek	From around 6 months, babies begin to enjoy simple games of peek-a-boo. At first they are interested in watching as adults hide behind their hands and then reappear, but by 8 months they join in. Toys and puppets can also be used to support this type of play, e.g. Jack-in-the-box or pop-up puppets
	Once babies and toddlers are moving, try creating small spaces where they can go and hide. Part of the fun for older babies and toddlers is to hear the adult saying in a pretend voice that they cannot see the child. Although these games can be planned, it is also important for this type of play to be spontaneous. For example, when putting on a jumper over a baby's head, you might say 'peek-a-boo'
Roll a ball	From around 6 months or so, most babies enjoy having a ball rolled over to them. As they develop, they begin to be able to roll it back. With toddlers, expect to find that they sometimes hog the ball or tease you
Action rhymes	Action rhymes such as 'Humpty Dumpty' and 'Row, row, row your boat' are play opportunities for babies and toddlers
Water play	Whether it is part of a bathing routine or put out as an activity, babies and toddlers love playing with water. Water play can be provided in paddling pools or baby baths, but also with toddlers in buckets. Look out for scoops and buckets as well as fabric. Always supervise water play

Play and learning opportunities for children from 2 up to 7 years 11 months

Most early years settings provide a range of play opportunities, as they are thought to be helpful in supporting children's learning.

Role play

There are different forms of imaginative play, as you saw at the start of the unit. Most early years settings provide a range of role play opportunities so that children can play out different experiences. For role play to work well, it is important that children have some knowledge of the scenario, e.g. going to a garden centre or to a shop. Figure 3.1 shows some common role play themes.

As children become older, they often choose more imaginative and adventurous themes. These are sometimes based around a book, e.g. *Goldilocks and the Three Bears*.

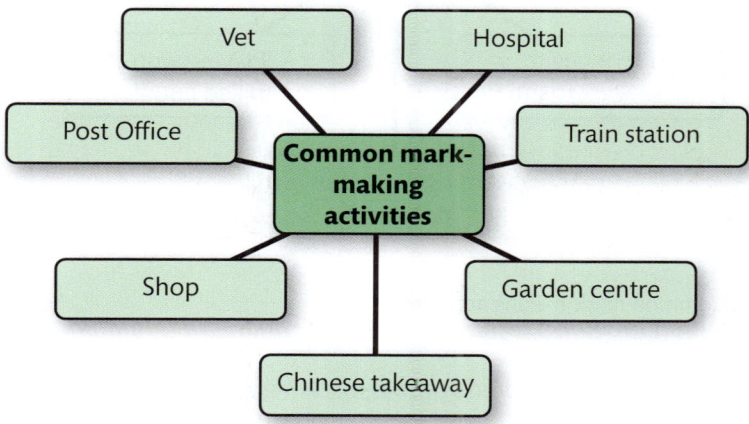

▶ **Figure 3.1:** Common role play themes

Theory into practice

1   Find out from your placement setting how they choose role play themes.

2   Observe children engaged in role play.

3   How much language do they use during their play?

Small-world play

As you saw at the start of the unit, small-world play is a form of imaginative play where children create a miniature world using specific resources such as cars, farm animals, play people or dinosaurs. This type of play gives children opportunities to build their own world and have influence over it. This is thought to develop children's confidence and understanding of the real world. While some children choose to play alone, others enjoy the company of one or two other children. As well as supporting children's emotional development, small-world play is an important language and cognitive learning opportunity as children tend to use talk to self-direct and organise their thoughts.

Painting and mark making

Painting is a form of creative play but it is also a way in which children can start to learn to make marks. Eventually, from making marks with pens, chalks, paint and other materials such as sand or dry rice, children learn the handwriting movements that are needed in early writing. Mark making also helps motivate children to write – through mark making they start to 'pretend' to write.

Link

Unit 2 provides more information about the importance of mark making for children's early literacy.

Painting and other mark-making activities also help children to express themselves in a visual way. Figure 3.2 shows some popular mark-making activities that many early years settings provide.

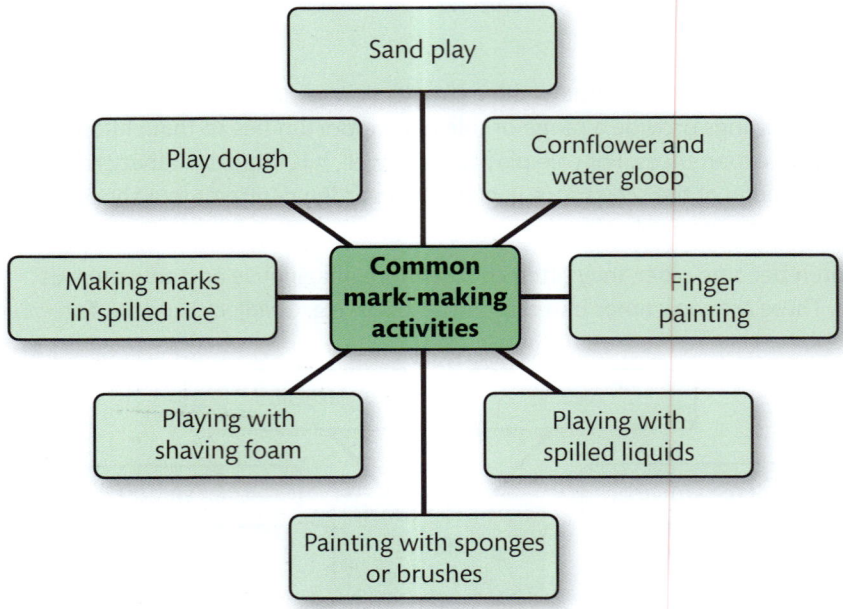

▶ **Figure 3.2:** Common mark-making activities

Puzzles and games

Puzzles and games support children's problem-solving skills. Jigsaws are particularly good at helping children recognise and rotate shapes, and they promote fine motor skills. Children can also learn matching skills as they link the individual pieces to the picture. It is good practice for children to have access to a variety of different jigsaw puzzles so that there is sufficient ongoing challenge.

In addition, as children develop, it can be helpful for them to play a range of games such as picture lotto, snap and board games that involve counting. As well as learning problem-solving and logic, children also develop the social skills of turn taking and learning to cope when they do not win.

Natural and malleable materials

Key term

Malleable – soft and able to be moulded and shaped.

As you saw at the start of the unit, tactile materials such as water, sand and playdough are used in sensory play. This type of play helps children to develop their fine motor skills and hand–eye coordination. It also allows them to explore concepts about shape and volume, and to experiment with different materials.

The importance of suitable resources

When planning, it is important to think about the resources that support each of the different types of play. It is usual to provide children with slightly different resources according to their age and stage of development, and as their interests and skills develop.

Types of play indoors and outdoors

There has been concern that many children no longer spend time outdoors. To reverse this trend, early years settings have been encouraged to use resources and equipment both inside and outdoors. Most things that can be done indoors can also be done outdoors. This means that some resources are taken outdoors or duplicated, or similar materials are provided and kept outdoors.

There are many advantages for children playing outdoors – these include greater freedom, the possibility of having larger quantities of things such as sand and water, and the opportunity to combine play types. This means that it is usual now to find role play areas outdoors, as well as resources for mark making and painting.

Table 3.4 gives some examples of popular resources that can be used indoors and outdoors for the five different types of play.

▶ **Table 3.4:** Resources that can be used indoors and outdoors for the different types of play

Type of play	0–24 months	24 months–4 years	4 years–7 years 11 months
Physical play	• Swings • Sit-and-ride toys • Balls • Low climbing frame	• Tricycles • Balls (different sizes) • Stilts • Tree stumps • Climbing frames • Scooters • Hoops • Slides	As for younger ages, but also: • bicycles • skateboards • roller skates • skipping ropes
Imaginative play	• Puppets • Toy telephones • Dolls • Cuddly toys	As for 0–24 months, but also: • small-world toys such as farm animals, dinosaurs, play people, cars and garage • dressing-up clothes • props for dressing up: hats, belts, shoes, notepads • home corner props, e.g. kitchen, bed, cot	As for younger ages, but also: • a puppet theatre • a dolls' house
Expressive arts and design (creative play)	• Treasure-basket play • Heuristic play	• Dough: rolling pin, shape cutters, plates • Paint: rollers, sponges, brushes • Mark making and drawing: felt-tips, crayons, stampers, charcoal • Collage materials: glue sticks, sequins, ribbons, feathers • Junk modelling materials: masking tape, boxes, tubes, double-sided tape	As for younger ages, but also: • staplers • kits and more intricate materials
Sensory play	• Cold cooked spaghetti • Jelly • Water play: baby baths, paddling pool • Gloop	As for 0–24 months, but also: • sand, gravel • pasta, rice • tea leaves • materials that can be used with: bottles, scoops, sieves, tubes • digging (outdoors)	As for younger ages, but combined with small-world play
Construction play	• Pop-up toys • Stacking beakers • Post-it toys • Lift-up puzzles • Heuristic play	• DUPLO® • Wooden blocks • Jigsaw puzzles • Interlocking tubes and guttering	As for younger ages, but also: • construction kits with more intricate components, such as LEGO® and MECCANO®

Ⅱ PAUSE POINT   Name five resources that could be used indoors with children aged 2–4 years.

Hint   Think about each of the play types.

Extend   Explain the reasons why toys and resources need to change as children develop.

Different ages/stages of development

Resources have to be matched to children's stages of development, otherwise they may be unsafe. This means, for example, that small items are unlikely to be suitable for children under 2 years. Thinking carefully about a child's stage of development also means that the toys you choose are likely to meet their play needs and interests. Table 3.5 shows how children's play interests and resources change according to their age/stage of development.

▶ **Table 3.5:** How resources and play interests change according to children's age/stage of development

Age	Characteristics	Examples of play interests and resources
0–18 months	• Babies enjoy playful activities with adults • Play with adults is closely linked to communication and relationship building • Repetitive simple movements combined with adults' facial expressions seem to be important, e.g. peek-a-boo and shake-a-rattle • Babies can spend time playing and exploring objects independently • Everyday routines can become playful opportunities for babies, e.g. dropping a spoon for the adult to pick up, and bath time • A key feature of babies' play is mouthing. They will often explore objects by taking them into their mouth. At around 18 months this usually reduces or disappears	• Treasure-basket play • Heuristic play with older babies • Water and sensory play • Games with adults such as roll a ball, building and knocking down beakers • Pop-up toys and musical games • Swings for babies who are starting to sit up
18 months–3 years	• Children needing to play near or with adults. This seems to be for reassurance. Children may break off their activity if they cannot see 'their' adult • May have moments watching or copying other children, but are likely to need an adult to support play with others • Sensory play enjoyed and is likely to engage children without adult involvement for long periods, i.e. 30 minutes. • Play is often exploratory, repetitive and involves gross motor movements, e.g. opening and closing doors • Small-world play is of interest, particularly cars, trains and play characters from around 2 years • Interest in role play from around $2\frac{1}{2}$ years • Adult supervision required for safety reasons but adult involvement required to support children's engagement in play	• Transporting – moving items from one place to another, e.g. filling up a pushchair with items • Dropping and posting activities, e.g. pushing a ball down a tube, dropping a puzzle onto the floor • Sensory materials, especially water • Simple puzzles and construction toys, with adult encouragement
3–4 years	• Beginning to show cooperation during play, but adult involvement is required to sort out sharing of equipment between different groups of children • Children enjoy opportunities to play with each other independently of adults and may seek to be out of sight • Simple games enjoyed when played in a small group with an adult • Sensory materials tend to be particularly popular and played with independently of adults • Small-world and role play starting to reflect children's ability to pretend and be imaginative	• Wheeled toys • Paint • Sensory activities such as dough, water and sand • Small-world play • Dressing up and home corner play • Construction sets and opportunities to make things such as dens and houses
4 years– 7 years 11 months	• Generally cooperative, with children being able to sustain play without an adult's involvement • Children often able to sustain play that is of interest to them for more than an hour • Wide play interests including activities that require fine motor skills and patience • Same-sex play becomes more common • Increased complexity in role playing, with characters being assigned • Board games and games with specific rules enjoyed • Children may enjoy completing activities or kits by themselves	• Bicycles • Ball games • Dressing up • Small-world play • Construction play – often intricate play such as using LEGO®, as well as block play • Sensory play combined with small-world play • Games such as snap, pairs and snakes and ladders

Safe play and resources

It is important to consider the safety of any resources used during play. For example, you will need to consider the following points.

▶ **Buying and finding resources** – most practitioners are given opportunities to add to their existing resources. It is important to choose new resources carefully. Figure 3.3 shows some of the important points to consider when choosing new equipment.

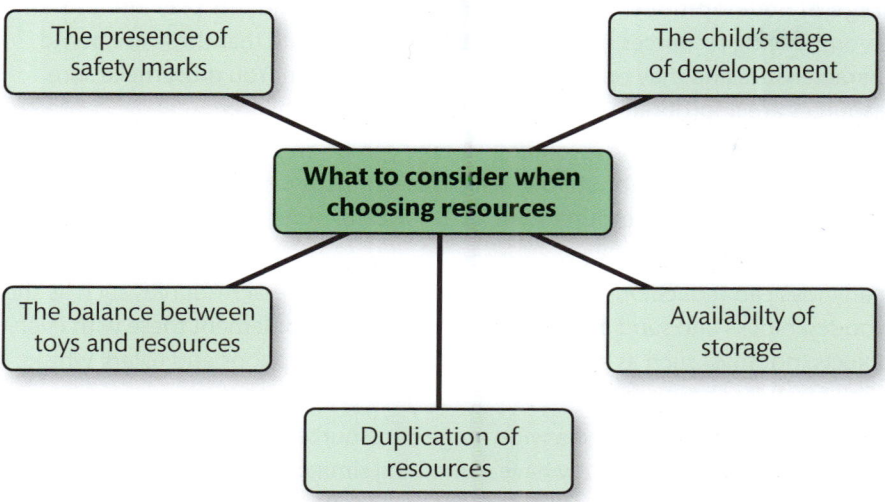

▶ **Figure 3.3:** What to consider when choosing resources

▶ **Safety marks** – all toys and resources provided for children must be safe for them to play with and handle. Look out for marks that indicate toys conform to certain standards. There are three marks that you should look out for: the CE mark, the Lion Mark and the Kitemark. The CE mark is a declaration by toy manufacturers that their products are safe; the Lion Mark indicates that toys have been tested; and the Kitemark indicates that safety requirements have been met.

▶ This fabric book shows the CE mark and Lion Mark

- **Stage of development** – Table 3.5 summarises how children's play interests and accompanying resources may change and develop. Note that these are broad characteristics and may not apply to individual children. You must make sure resources are appropriate to the age and stage of the children.
- **Storage** – when choosing resources, storage can be an issue. Early years settings have to think carefully about how easily the resources can be stored; it may not be safe to have too many resources out all at the same time.
- **Balance between toys and resources** – toys have their place, but sometimes too many toys can reduce opportunities for challenge. General resources such as shells, wooden blocks and sand are often what is needed. Supplement these with everyday objects (not toys) such as saucepans with lids, serving spoons and rotary whisks, but think carefully about any risks that these objects may present.
- **Duplication** – children need a wide range of resources. Early years settings should consider whether they already have something similar.

Assessment practice 3.1   A.P1

The shadow minister for childcare and the early years has asked for more information about how play is used in early years settings. You need to:
- describe the main types of play
- explain how play can be structured differently according to the role that adults take
- state how play opportunities vary according to the age and stage of children
- describe how different types of play may be provided with different ages of children.

Plan
- How is play used in the settings I am familiar with?
- Where can I go to gain additional information?

Do
- Am I presenting the information accurately and concisely?
- Am I managing my time effectively?

Review
- Can I justify why I have decided to approach this task in the way that I have?
- How can I apply this information in my future work with children?

A2 The benefits of play for children

The importance of different types of play to children's holistic development

Play can form a significant part of children's holistic development. It naturally prompts children to practise and develop skills and knowledge. This is why in recent years it has become the foundation of all the early years curricula in the UK.

How play can support children's physical development

One of the challenges that babies and young children face is to be able to control their movements. This is linked partly to the process of maturation but also to practice. As well as physical control of the body, children also need to develop strength and stamina. From early on, play provides the motivation for this to take place effortlessly. Babies, for example, will try to move cot toys or grab a rattle, while toddlers will push a brick trolley around a room.

Table 3.6 gives examples of how common toys and play activities support physical development.

▶ **Table 3.6:** How play activities support physical development

Toy or activity	What physical development it supports
Treasure-basket play	• Fine motor skills, as objects are handled • Hand–eye coordination, as objects are taken to the mouth for exploring • Gross motor movements, as whole-arm movements are needed to reach out and select an object
Swing	• Balance, as the child has to maintain an upright position • Fine motor movements, as the child grabs the sides
Wheeled toys such as sit-and-ride items or tricycles	• Gross motor movements, as legs are strengthened • Spatial awareness and general coordination, to avoid obstacles • Stamina, as children keep moving
Water and sand play	• Fine motor skills, as children scoop, pour and use their hands to play • Hand–eye coordination, as children scoop and pour, splash and dig • Muscle tone, as children are standing

How play can support children's cognitive development

Play gives children first-hand experiences of touching and doing things, and so supports their understanding of the world through a process that is often referred to as 'active learning'. A baby, for example, learns that a spoon falls, and a 4-year-old child learns that a torch may have batteries.

Although children can gain a lot of knowledge from play, adults have an important role while children are playing. They may point out to a child that their favourite train is blue, and in this way the child learns about colour. As well as learning about specific concepts such as colour and shape, children will gain other skills such as concentration and memory skills. There are several play activities that seem to be particularly useful when it comes to developing skills linked to cognition, including problem-solving and creativity. These include jigsaw puzzles, logic games and construction play. As children become older, role play can provide them with opportunities to develop problem-solving skills as well as creativity if they decide to make props for themselves, e.g. deciding to make cakes out of dough to go into their cake shop.

In addition, through play – especially when an adult is involved – children may have the opportunity to develop their thoughts about a skill or concept further. This is sometimes known as **sustained shared thinking** and is important because, through interactions with adults, children are able to explore a concept or skill in more depth. An example of this would be when an adult helps children to build a den and together they talk through the types of materials they could use and the advantages of each material. During the play, with the adult's support, the children would keep thinking about how best to construct the den. This type of adult interaction helps children to progress their thinking as well as their language. For sustained shared thinking to work well, adults have to spend sufficient time with children, hence the term 'sustained'.

How play can help children's communication and language development

Play is a great vehicle for children to learn to communicate and also to use language. Children are able to hear the structure of language as they play with each other and also with adults.

They can also join in conversations, especially during role play where dialogue between children is a key way of interacting. Interestingly, children also use language to organise their play and so it is not uncommon to hear 2-year-old children talk to themselves as they play. Children cannot learn language without having interaction with adults or older children, and play provides opportunities for this to happen. An adult may play 'Humpty Dumpty' with a baby and the baby will learn to recognise new vocabulary (key words) such as 'fall down'. The interaction during play also stimulates the baby so that later on they are likely to babble and vocalise more.

Key term

Sustained shared thinking – opportunities for children to interact with adults in ways that will extend their thinking and develop their thoughts about a topic or concept.

Link

Unit 2 has more detail about the role of play in learning language.

Rich play opportunities give children a reason for learning words and extending their vocabulary – a new item in the home corner is likely to prompt a 'what's that?' question from a child. Once children are starting to talk, they tend to vocalise as they are playing. A 2-year-old child playing alone is likely to be talking and older children tend to talk to each other. Table 3.7 lists some examples of how certain activities support children's language development.

▶ **Table 3.7:** How play activities support language development

Toy or activity	What language development it supports
Toy telephone	Babies and toddlers talking aloud
Home corner and small-world play	Children talking to each other and aloud
'I spy' and other language games	Older children thinking about sounds in words

How play can support children's social development

Most children begin to play in their first year of life when an adult is with them. The early skills of play begin as babies learn to respond positively and to take turns; for example, when an adult plays peek-a-boo or roll-a-ball games. It is interesting that from quite early on, babies will prompt an adult to play with them. They may pull a hat over the face as a signal that they want to play peek-a-boo or crawl with a ball that they put in the adult's lap. These early experiences of play help children's social development and pave the way for playing with other children. By the time most children are 3 years old, they want to play with other children. They therefore learn to build relationships by sharing, taking turns, responding to others' reactions and negotiating.

Adults can support older children to learn skills such as playing fairly and playing games with rules by introducing games such as snap or physical games such as hide and seek. Once children have learned these games and the social skills, they can go on to use them independently.

How play can support emotional development

Play is a pleasurable experience for children and so it has immediate effects on their sense of well-being. It also supports other aspects of their emotional development. First, play is important in helping to form **attachments**. When adults and babies play together, they are likely to be spending time together that is pleasurable and intense for both of them. This helps create, but also sustain, bonds. This is one reason why encouraging parents to play with their children is so important. It is also a reason why early years professionals should play with children in their settings, especially during settling-in periods, to support children's transitions when they need to develop bonds with their **key person**.

Play can also help foster children's independence, particularly during child-initiated activity when they choose what and who to play with. By collecting materials and organising how they are going to play with them, children can develop the skills of making choices and taking responsibility for themselves. This in turn builds their self-confidence as they learn that they can take control and become competent.

In addition, imaginative play can support children's self-awareness as they take on a variety of roles and explore different aspects of their emotions and personalities. Through dressing up and taking on specific roles, children can also learn from the reactions of others about aspects of themselves. As you will see in Unit 7, the exploration of identity is one of the steps towards children developing self-esteem.

Key terms

Attachment – a special relationship or bond between a child and someone who is emotionally involved with them.

Key person – an early years professional designated to take responsibility for a child's emotional well-being by having a strong attachment with them and a good relationship with their parents/carers.

Through play, children learn that we are all different. They may learn this by seeing other children choosing to play with resources that are different from the ones they normally choose to play with. For example, a child may see children playing with items in the home corner that they would not normally play with. This would help the child to understand that people use different objects to cook with than the ones used in their own home. Learning that other people are different is a significant step for children and one that is important as they learn to respect others. Through play, children also learn more about their own identity.

Ⅱ   PAUSE POINT   How does play support children's emotional and social development?

> **Hint**   Think about what children might learn as they play with an adult or with other children.

> **Extend**   Read the EYFS statutory framework to find out how play is used to promote children's development in the different curriculum areas.

The importance of play for making sense of the world

Play helps children understand their role and that of others in the world; it can enable them to make sense of their experiences. This often comes through role play opportunities. A young child will often imitate what they have experienced and put themselves into different roles; for example, 'I'm the mummy today and you have to do what I tell you'. This benefit of play is one reason why it is used to support children who have been in traumatic situations: quite often children will play out what has happened to them in a safe environment.

How play gives children freedom to make mistakes

Play is often liberating for children because they can make mistakes. For example, a sandcastle may disintegrate because the sand was not damp enough, but this may not matter to the child.

Play also gives children a sense of control and freedom. This in itself is empowering for them, especially where young children have little real control over their lives. Babies handling objects in the treasure basket are able to choose for themselves what to touch, what to drop and what to bang together.

> **Discussion**
>
> There have been concerns that schoolchildren are under more pressure than before.
> - Do you think this is true?
> - How might more opportunities for children to play make a difference to their stress levels?
>
> In small groups, discuss these questions. Then share your feedback with the rest of the group.

How play helps children to cope with transition and significant events

Play can be a useful way of children exploring their emotions in relation to transitions and significant events. A role play of moving home might be planned to help a child who is due to move, or a hospital role play may be set up to help a child who is due to go into hospital or whose relative was recently ill.

Through play, children can act out different roles safely and older children may be able to use it to talk about their feelings. This is one reason why play is often used as part of therapy for children who have experienced trauma.

How play supports children's early mathematical concepts of volume and shape

As part of cognitive development, play can help children acquire some early mathematical concepts. For children to fully benefit, they need an adult to draw their attention to what is happening during play and to label the concepts being explored. Table 3.8 shows examples of how play can support early mathematical concepts.

▶ **Table 3.8:** Examples of how toys and play activities support early mathematical concepts

Toy or activity	The mathematical concepts it supports
Shape sorter	Shape recognition, although an adult or older child will need to name the shapes so that a child can acquire the language
Jigsaw puzzle	Problem-solving, through sorting pieces
Water play	Learning about volume, although an adult will have to give children the language of 'full' or 'empty'
Games such as snap, noughts and crosses or picture lotto	Matching, sorting and recognising numbers, as well as developing strategies for winning

Theory into practice

List the ways in which your work setting helps children learn about mathematical concepts through play.

Assessment practice 3.2   A.P2   A.M1

A few parents have recently queried why most of the activities in the local preschool are play-based. You have been asked by the preschool to help parents understand the importance of play.

The information that you provide should:
- explain how play supports the physical, cognitive, language, social and emotional development of children at different ages, using examples
- assess how different types of play support children's learning at different ages
- evaluate the importance of play to children's overall development.

Plan
- What information is most relevant for this task?
- How long will I need to collate and analyse the information required for the task?

Do
- Am I presenting the information in a way that will be accessible to parents?
- Am I managing my time effectively?

Review
- Can I justify why I have decided to approach this task in the way that I have?
- Have I evaluated my work and am I confident that it fulfils the set task?

B Investigate theoretical perspectives to learning and development, curriculum approaches to play and their influence on current early years practice

B1 Theoretical perspectives to learning and development

Play in early years settings has been shaped by a range of approaches and theorists. In this section you look at some of the key theorists and curriculum approaches that have influenced the way in which play is provided in many settings.

Jean Piaget

Jean Piaget believed that children learn by doing and that their cognitive development was reflected in their play. He described children's development in a series of stages of play. Table 3.9 outlines these stages. Piaget spent time watching children play and noted that as children developed, their play became more complex and they started to create rules. He felt this was connected to their ability to deal with abstract concepts – rules being something that you cannot see. He believed this showed a high level of cognitive development.

▶ **Table 3.9:** Piaget's stages of play

Age	Type of play	Common features
0–2 years	Mastery play	Children are gaining control of their bodies. Play allows them to explore their environment. Play in this age group tends to be repetitive – as if the child is trying to master their movements and understand the world
2–7 years	Symbolic play	Children are using language as a means of communicating and this is reflected in their play. Children are using symbols in their play, e.g. a stick becomes a spoon
7–11 years	Play with rules	Children are developing an understanding of rules and find them fascinating and fulfilling. Children may make rules, but then break them

Lev Vygotsky

In Unit 1, you looked at Vygotsky's view of cognitive development, but here the focus is on his thoughts about play. He was particularly interested in imaginative play, which he suggested began when children were 3 years old. In 1933 he gave a lecture entitled 'Play and its role in the mental development of the child' in which he examined the nature and purpose of play in children. He suggested that play was essential to the development of preschool children rather than just a characteristic that young children shared.

He also suggested that imaginative play allowed children to explore thoughts, rules and roles beyond their current level of competence and so was effectively the child's **zone of proximal development**. In the lecture, Vygotsky also looked at the way in which imaginative play develops and, in turn, how this develops the child. He noted that at first, imaginative play starts with a re-creation of what children have seen first-hand, but that children quickly begin to explore beyond this. This, he suggested, helps children to make the move into abstract thought – and so higher mental function.

Vygotsky, like Piaget, was interested in the way that children develop rules in their play and how these allow play to become more challenging and enjoyable. Vygotsky was clear that it was not just children's cognitive development that was developed through play, but also their emotional and social development.

> **Key term**
>
> **Zone of proximal development** – the gap between what a child is currently able to do and what they may be able to achieve if an adult provides some support.

▶ These children have devised a game where one has to follow the other along the lines – whoever 'falls' off the line is out

Jerome Bruner

Jerome Bruner has been very influential in early years practice. He is famous for coining the term **scaffolding** to explain the way in which adults can support children's learning by asking questions, guiding or breaking information down into small steps.

For Bruner, like Vygotsky, play is essential for development. In the 1970s, with other researchers, he investigated play in preschools. The results proved interesting, as it was noted that children's play was richer and more sustained in the presence of sensitive adults who engaged with them. It was also noted that children played for longer periods and more richly when they were engaged in construction-type activities rather than those with no 'end', such as sand and water.

Research

Use the internet to find out more about Jerome Bruner's ideas. How do these theories relate to the practice that you have seen in nurseries or preschools?

Chris Athey

Chris Athey developed Piaget's theory in relation to schemas and you may encounter her schema theory in action in early years settings. In her work Athey identified several schemas that seem to occur in children's play and suggested that these were linked to the child's cognitive exploration. Since her original work, the idea of using schemas to make sense of children's play and also to use them as a way of planning for individual children has become popular. Table 3.10 shows Athey's schemas and others that have since been added, as well as examples of resources that might be used to support a child's interest.

▶ **Table 3.10:** Chris Athey's play schemas

Schema	What you may observe	Opportunities/resources that can be put out to support play
Transporting	Children who are interested in moving things from one place to another, e.g. putting objects in a pushchair and taking them across the room or pouring water from the water tray into a bucket	• Pushchairs • Wheeled toys • Brick trolleys • Bags • Buckets
Enveloping	Children who enjoy covering things or themselves, e.g. putting a blanket over the whole of a dolly	• Blankets and fabrics • Wrapping paper
Enclosing/containing	Children who enjoy putting things in and out of containers or spaces, e.g. sitting in a tent	• Russian dolls • Boxes with lids • Stacking boxes • Tents
Trajectory	Children who are interested in the way things move through the air, e.g. throwing and dropping	• Balls • Beanbags • Sticks
Rotation	Children who are interested in circles and things that spin round, such as washing machines	• Salad spinner • Spinning tops • Rotary clothes line • Chair that swivels
Transforming	Children who enjoy watching things change, e.g. mixing paint, dropping food colouring into water	• Opportunities to mix things, e.g. sand and water
Connecting	Children who are interested in putting things together, e.g. lines of cars or tying string from a chair leg to a table leg	• Construction materials • Opportunities to tie things together
Positioning	Children who take time to place objects and themselves in a particular order or position, e.g. enjoying laying a table with accuracy	• Ice cube trays and small objects that can be put inside • Peg boards • Opportunities for children to group objects and not be disturbed by others
Orientating	Children who are interested in seeing things from different positions and viewpoints, e.g. trying to climb to be up high	• Climbing equipment • Balancing equipment, e.g. see-saws • Looking through binoculars

Ⅱ PAUSE POINT What type of schema would children be exploring if they enjoy running back and forth in a play area while carrying a bag?

Hint Think of the actions that children show.

Extend Give an example of how each play schema in Table 3.10 could be provided for within an early years setting.

Friedrich Froebel

Friedrich Froebel was born in Germany towards the end of the eighteenth century. Through his own schooling, he learned about the natural world and this influenced his later thoughts about the importance of children spending time playing outdoors. In Germany at that time, there was much philosophical interest in the nature of childhood. Froebel believed that children were essentially born good, but that adults needed to provide the right care and environment to protect them from evil.

Froebel recognised that play was essential for learning, but that adults might support it by giving children objects for them to explore. These 'gifts' would help children to learn concepts, for example, learning about texture by giving them a hard ball and a soft ball. In addition, Froebel gave children wooden blocks to use so that they could build and make structures with them. Froebel also used rhymes and music as a way of helping children learn about concepts. He is thought to be responsible for rhymes such as 'Round and round the garden, like a teddy bear'.

Froebel's belief that children should learn through nature and the outdoors is still of major importance. His use of blocks to help children learn through play is also reflected today in the **block play** that is used in many early years settings. Rhymes are also a major feature of early years practice with babies and older children.

Key term

Block play – play using wooden bricks of different shapes and sizes.

> **Theory into practice**
>
> Does your work placement setting have block play? If so, how is it used to support children's play and development?

B2 Curriculum approaches to play

Current play practice in early years settings is based on some of the theories discussed in Section B1. It is also influenced by a range of influential approaches, all of which have their roots in other countries and cultures.

Reggio Emilia

Reggio Emilia is a province in Northern Italy. It has become famous for its approach to preschool education, which began with collaboration between parents and practitioners after World War II. This collaboration is very much at the heart of practice in the Reggio preschools and is one of the many features that have influenced practitioners from other countries who have visited them. Unlike many early years programmes, there is no curriculum to follow – children and adults follow their interests and the role of the adult is to be a supporter for the children, but also a learner.

Adults also take the role of being the recorder of children's work and play. Photographs and notes are displayed so that children can refer to them and reflect on their projects. Another feature of Reggio Emilia's preschools is that they see children as being competent learners and individuals. A well-known phrase is 'the hundred languages of children', which refers to the idea that children will have many different ways of expressing their ideas and learning, and that practitioners have to be ready to recognise and provide for them. Music, drawing and sculpture are genuinely valued forms of expression.

Benefits of Reggio Emilia's approach

This approach has the following benefits.

- Children are seen as competent learners.
- Parents and early years educators work closely together.
- Adults and children explore ideas, problems and play together.
- Children are able to reflect back on their play, experiences and learning as photographs, and recordings are made by adults.

HighScope

HighScope, an approach to early years education, has grown out of a project in America that ran in the 1960s. It started life as a small research project that was trying to improve the life chances of young children from vulnerable families. The project quickly showed through its research that children who attended were benefiting from its approach compared to children in the control group, who were in other settings. Several features of HighScope are famous.

▸ **Plan–do–review** – HighScope is perhaps best known for its 'plan–do–review' approach to play. The idea is that children spend time talking about what they want to do before getting out the materials and resources. Afterwards in small groups they talk about what they have done or how their plan changed.

▸ **Daily routine** – HighScope is a structured approach and a daily routine is followed. The routine consists of small and large group times and also times for transition. The aim of this routine is to give children a sense of order and security. This perhaps reflects the origins of Highscope's work with disadvantaged children.

▸ **Role of the adult** – Again, perhaps reflecting the needs of vulnerable children who may not have opportunities to interact, HighScope has a clear vision of the role of adults. Adults are seen as key to children's learning and support children through sensitive interactions, which in turn are based on a careful assessment of children's development. This role links to the work of Vygotsky.

Benefits of the HighScope approach

This approach has the following benefits.

▸ Children are seen as competent.

▸ Adults work in partnership with children.

▸ Children are given opportunities to reflect on what they have been doing and have learned.

▸ Adults are thoughtful about children's development and needs.

▸ Children who may be from homes where there is little predictability can gain a sense of security through the daily routine.

In addition, HighScope has shown the benefits of research-based practice and set a trend in measuring outcomes for children.

Ⅱ PAUSE POINT Describe two benefits of the HighScope approach.

Hint Think about what children may gain if they are decision makers and if there is some predictable structure.

Extend What similarities are there between the HighScope approach and that of Reggio Emilia?

Forest Schools

Forest Schools have their origins in Scandinavian countries, which have vast woodlands. The idea of integrating playing outdoors with early education has long been part of the Danish education system and it is this model that has been adapted by some early years settings in the UK. The idea behind Forest Schools is that by playing out in the woodlands, and also learning skills such as building a campfire, children's all-round development is enhanced. Children seem to develop more confidence and social skills while also benefiting physically. The ideal, as seen in Denmark, is that an early years setting is based in or within walking distance of a forest, but for many settings in the UK this is not possible. This means that many settings will take children out for sessions in a local woodland or will build some of the principles, such as children having opportunities for risk and challenge, into their outdoor play.

▶ These children are enjoying playing in the woods

Benefits of the Forest School approach

This approach has the following benefits.

▶ Children have feelings of freedom.

▶ There are opportunities for children to express themselves.

▶ Children gain confidence and independence.

▶ Children gain practical skills and knowledge.

▶ Social skills improve as children make and do things with others.

▶ Children learn awareness of, and respect for, nature including temperature, seasons and wildlife.

▶ Children gain physical skills including balance, coordination and fitness.

▶ There are genuine opportunities to explore risk and challenge.

▶ Access to a rich environment with plenty of spontaneous learning opportunities.

The New Zealand Te Whāriki

Te Whāriki is the early years curriculum framework of New Zealand. The term means 'woven mat' and comes from the idea that many strands are important in the education and nurture of children including their parents, the community and children's interests. It covers ages 0–6 years and is based on four key principles.

▶ **Empowerment** – children need to be empowered in order to grow and learn.

▶ **Holistic development** – children's development is seen as holistic (and includes spiritual development) and so is key to all of their experiences.

▶ **Family and community** – children's family and community are seen as central to their development.

▶ **Relationships** – children learn through relationships.

As well as these principles there are five strands or areas of development that are seen as being crucial to children's learning and development. Each strand has goals. It is worth noting that these goals are focused on what practitioners might try to achieve for the child. The strands are:

1 wellbeing – Mana Atua

2 belonging – Mana Whenua

3 contribution – Mana Tangata

4 communication – Mana Reo

5 exploration – Mana Aotūroa.

There is a strong emphasis on **reflective practice**. This has also become a feature of recent early years practice in the UK. As a way of creating partnerships with parents and involving them in their child's education, practitioners create **learning journeys** or **learning stories** that they can share with parents. These include photographs and comments from parents and children. 'Learning journeys' have been adopted/adapted in many UK settings as a way of observing and assessing children's development.

Benefits of the New Zealand Te Whāriki approach

This approach has the following benefits.

▶ Parents, family and community are seen as vital in children's education.

▶ Families' cultures and languages are genuinely respected.

▶ Practitioners are expected to reflect on practice.

Key terms

Learning journey/learning story – a way of assessing and planning for children's development using a narrative approach that can easily be constructed and shared with parents and children.

Reflective practice – thinking about the way you work in order to make changes, build on strengths and stay up to date with developments.

- Daily observations of children are used as a tool for planning and reflection.
- Children are seen as competent, individual learners.
- Play and exploration led by children is seen as important.

Maria Montessori

Maria Montessori (1870–1952) was a doctor who worked in a psychiatric clinic with children who had learning difficulties. In 1899 she was appointed director of an institute where she was able to explore her ideas about how to help children with learning difficulties. A structured approach that was based on the children's own pace of learning had notable success and this formed the basis of her later work with young children in a school called the Casa dei Bambini (Children's House).

Montessori believed that up until the age of 6 years, children had the capacity to learn easily and quickly. She called this phase the 'absorbent mind' and believed that their ability to learn should be capitalised on rather than wasted. This belief meant that Montessori saw that the role of the adult was to guide children in their play or 'work' and provide them with the equipment and an environment from which they would be ready to learn. This means that although she saw children as active learners, she also felt that play without a clear purpose would be wasting valuable time. Figure 3.4 shows some examples of Montessori equipment made from natural materials.

Montessori had great confidence in children's abilities and felt that they could concentrate for long periods and be independent in their learning. This means that the role of the adult is to be there as a guide for the child, but to allow children to learn for themselves. Montessori also believed that children's independence and skills could be fostered by mastering everyday skills such as dressing, cooking and even gardening. Montessori's philosophy is still in use today and there are many Montessori nursery schools in the UK and throughout the world.

(a)

(b)

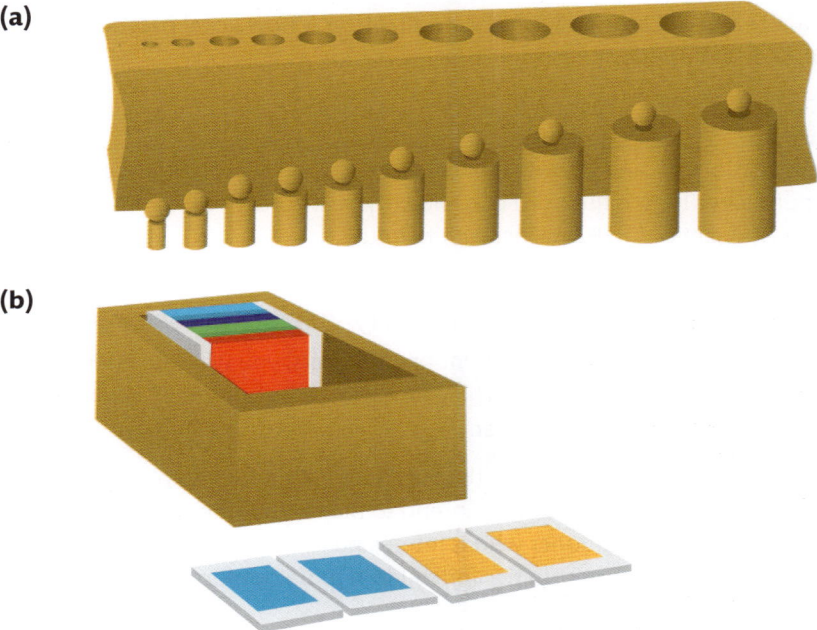

▶ **Figure 3.4:** Montessori settings still use the equipment that Maria Montessori designed to help children learn concepts: (a) cylinder blocks help children to learn about size and dimensions and (b) colour tablets teach children to recognise and match different colours

Benefits of the Montessori approach

This approach has several benefits.

▸ Children have opportunities to be supported by adults.

▸ Children are encouraged to be independent.

▸ There is a structured approach to the development of skills and learning new skills.

▸ Children learn to become organised and to care for their environment.

▸ Children's play is planned with a clear purpose.

> **Research**
>
> Find out more about Montessori education at the Montessori UK website: www.montessori.org.uk.

B3 Influences on current early years practice

Theoretical perspectives to learning and development, and approaches to play

There are many ways in which current early years practice has been influenced by both theoretical perspectives and other approaches to play, as you saw in Sections B1 and B2.

Today, the early years are considered to be an important stage in children's lives and play is seen as fundamental in supporting children's learning and development. This is one reason why, in the UK, all early years curricula, including the Early Years Foundation Stage (EYFS), have play at the centre of their delivery.

As you saw in Section B1, theorists such as Vygotsky and Bruner emphasised the role of adults in promoting children's cognitive development through play and through conversations with children. This means that talking with children is a key part of early years practice. Even during child-initiated activity, it is now good practice for adults to play alongside children or to engage in conversation as they play.

> **Link**
>
> Re-read Sections B1 and B2 with a particular focus on how the different theorists and approaches have influenced current early years practice. You may find the 'Benefits of...' sections in B2 particularly helpful.

How views of play can affect the early years professional's role

If you work alongside a range of different practitioners, you will see differences in their approaches towards providing play. This is likely to be because they favour, or were trained in, one approach over another.

For example, a practitioner who uses the HighScope approach to play may encourage children to talk more about what they intend to play with rather than set out specific play opportunities. A practitioner who is interested in the Forest School approach to play may plan frequent opportunities for children to be outdoors and in wooded areas.

Influences on child-initiated play

One of the many decisions that practitioners have to consider is the role of the adult in children's play. The balance between child-initiated play and adult-directed play and activities is often what differentiates the different perspectives.

A good example of this is the way that Montessori settings provide more adult-directed activity than, say, a setting that uses the Reggio Emilia approach, where children's interests are often the starting point for activities.

Influences on hands-on/exploratory play

Most approaches stress the importance of children being active in their play and learning. For instance, settings that use a Forest School approach are keen for children to have plenty of first-hand experiences of being outdoors. Interestingly, the Montessori approach, which is often considered to be more adult-directed, still stresses the importance of children doing things first-hand, e.g. practical life activities.

Influences on outdoor play

As a result of the work of pioneers such as Froebel, the McMillan sisters and, more recently, the Forest School movement, it is now an established principle within early years that children need to spend some time outdoors. It is also a legal requirement of the EYFS for children to be outdoors at least once in the day. Many early year settings go beyond this as outdoor play is now seen as being hugely beneficial for young children.

PAUSE POINT   Give an example of how the Forest School approach has influenced current early years practice.

Hint   Think about where the Forest School approach may take place.

Extend   What other theorists stressed the importance of children exploring outdoors?

The use of natural materials and sensory play

Toys, especially plastic ones, were not universally available in the first part of the last century when many of the leading theorists and pioneers of play were working. This means that many of the resources advocated by theorists such as Froebel (e.g. wooden blocks for block play) are made of natural materials. Montessori's teaching equipment (see Figure 3.4) is also made of natural materials as she favoured the use of the senses for teaching skills and concepts. Today, in most early years settings, there is often a mixture of natural and man-made materials, but there is an increasing focus on the importance of natural materials.

In terms of sensory materials, sand, water and malleable materials are an important part of most early years settings. The use of these materials has been influenced by the approaches of Froebel and HighScope but also from the early years curricula used by Te Whāriki and Reggio Emilia.

Influences on observing and planning play appropriate to age/stage of development

If you look back at the key theoretical perspectives and curriculum approaches to play, you will see that a good understanding of the child's development and interests is at the centre of what is being advocated.

A good example of this is Montessori's approach of ensuring that the equipment provided for children is tailored to their specific development stage. Another example is Vygotsky's approach of considering children's current level of abilities and planning something that will help them to develop further. This is embedded into the EYFS as it is expected that all settings will observe and then plan for individual children.

Placing the child at the centre of learning

Piaget, Vygotsky, Bruner, Athey and Froebel all looked at child-centred approaches to learning. While there are differences within these theoretical approaches about how the adult needs to work to maximise learning, they all focus on carefully observing children and thinking about their developmental stages and needs.

Children as competent learners

The term 'competent learners' is in the guiding principles of the EYFS. Many of the pioneers and theorists saw children as being capable of constructing their own thoughts. While the theme of competent learners is associated more recently with the approaches of Te Whāriki and Reggio Emilia, it is interesting to see that Piaget believed that children constructed their own thoughts through play and experiences.

Assessment practice 3.3　　　　　B.P3　B.P4　B.M2　AB.D1

An early years nursery chain is due to open a series of early years centres. Their management team wants to develop a clear pedagogical model and is interested in exploring different approaches to play in the early years. With examples, you have been asked to:
- explain different theoretical and curriculum perspectives to play in the early years
- compare and contrast a range of different theoretical and curriculum perspectives and assess how they have influenced current practice
- evaluate the impact and benefits of a range of different early years perspectives on current practice.

Plan
- What information is most relevant for this task?
- Can I use examples from my own experience?

Do
- Am I presenting the information accurately and concisely?
- Am I managing my time effectively?

Review
- Can I justify why I have decided to approach this task in the way that I have?
- Have I evaluated my work and am I confident that it fulfils the set task?

 **C**

Demonstrate skills required by early years professionals to support children's purposeful play and learning opportunities

C1 Professional skills for supporting purposeful play and learning

There are different ways in which adults can work with children to support children's learning during play. The role of the adult during play can make a significant difference to the extent to which children gain from their activity. In this section you look at the range of skills that all early years professionals need to develop.

Skills that early years professionals need

It takes time and experience to acquire all of the skills needed to support children in both adult-directed and child-initiated play. There are, however, some key strategies for developing professional skills.

Building on children's play interests

Adults working with children need to plan and provide resources that build on children's existing play interests. You may, for example, observe that a toddler is walking around with a shopping bag, picking up bits and pieces, moving them to the other side of the room and then tipping them out. Your conclusion might be that the child is exploring the transporting schema. To support the child further you may decide to put out a pushchair.

Modelling new skills

During play, children can become interested and learn new skills if adults model them. An adult may, for example, write a shopping list as part of pretend play in the home corner. A child may then choose to have a go for themselves at writing a shopping list. Similarly, a toddler may watch an adult roll dough into a ball and then try to do the same. When modelling skills for children to pick up during their play, adults have to make sure that the skill is attainable for the child and also that the resources to copy the actions are on hand. Children often have to see an adult repeat an action several times before they decide to have a go themselves.

Discussion

What is the difference between modelling a skill for a child and teaching a skill?

Discuss this in pairs and share your responses with the rest of the group.

Sensitive interactions

During play, adults need to be very sensitive. They have to decide when, how and whether questions are appropriate. They also have to match their language level to that of the child and follow the child's lead.

Where adults are able to sensitively interact with children during play, children's communication and language skills can be supported. On the other hand, if adults ask too many questions or interrupt children's thoughts or play, there is a danger that children may talk and communicate less.

Link

Look back at Unit 2, Section A2, to see how many of the skills in play are also needed to develop children's communication and language.

Engaging children and encouraging participation

In order to benefit from play activities, children need to join in. Many factors can either engage children to participate or put them off. In terms of adult-directed activities, children are more likely to participate if they have a strong relationship with the adult, the activity looks engaging and it matches their development level. This is one reason why there is a significant focus in the early years on observing children, to ensure that play and activities are developmentally appropriate for individual children as well as groups of children. Children under 3 years are also likely to be put off if the activity is passive or if they have to listen to a long explanation of the activity.

It is important that child-initiated activities build on children's known interests or on resources that you know are likely to be of interest to the age and stage of the child. When using materials and resources that children have already explored and played with, it may also be important to enrich them with other resources or lay them out differently. In addition, some children may need an adult to stay and play with them. This is particularly the case with babies and children under 3 years old.

Playfulness

Children love playful adults. Being playful and also knowing how to play alongside children is a key skill for all adults. Being playful is not the same as being childish and this is important to remember. Playfulness is hard to define, but it is often about an adult showing enthusiasm, smiling and being ready to follow children's responses carefully.

PAUSE POINT   Identify three skills that adults need to show as they support children during play.

Hint   Think about how you have seen an experienced adult work with children in your placement setting.

Extend   Explain how each chosen skill will support children's learning and development.

How to recognise children's individual needs

You can learn a lot about children while they are engaged in play. You can see what interests them and recognise their needs. You can also see whether the current opportunities are sufficiently challenging for children.

Tips for watching babies and children at play

Think about the following questions when you are observing a child at play.

▶ How interested is the child in the play?

▶ How long does the child stay engaged with the play?

▶ How is the child using the resources and toys?

▶ Are they interacting with adults or other children?

▶ Are there any other resources that might be more suitable for the child?

▶ Does the child need more/less adult support to be able to use the resources/toys or to access the play?

▶ Is the play sufficiently challenging for the child?

▶ Is the play sufficiently pleasurable for the child?

See the case study for an example of how to recognise a child's individual needs.

Case study

The use of play to meet children's individual needs

Jasmine is 3 years old and is new to the playgroup. She is settling in but looks anxious at times. Her dad has dropped her off today and mentioned that at home she loves playing with her brother's train set. Her key person decides to put out a train set so that she and Jasmine can play with it together.

Check your knowledge

1 Identify Jasmine's current needs.

2 Explain the rationale behind putting out a train set.

3 Why is it important for the key person to spend time playing with Jasmine?

How to scaffold children's learning and development

As you saw in Section B1, scaffolding is a way of working with children so that they can acquire skills and concepts. In terms of children's play, this might mean asking questions that help children to think about new possibilities, but it also might mean putting out additional equipment or resources that help enrich the child's play.

Adults can scaffold children's learning and development by:

▶ putting out new materials or different combinations for babies and children to explore and play with

▶ using naturally occurring opportunities to draw babies' and children's attention to things

▶ drawing babies' and children's attention to different features while joining in with their play.

How to use play and learning activities to meet the requirements of the early years curriculum framework

Early years settings follow the early years curriculum for their country. In England, early years settings have to follow the EYFS. This is a statutory framework and so there are legal requirements that all early years settings have to meet.

While there are differences between the early years curricula for the different home countries, there are many common themes. These include the requirement for young children to carry out the majority of their learning through play and play-based activities. Every early years setting looks at the curriculum requirements of the early years framework when planning play and learning activities. They may, for example, link what learning the children may gain from an activity to the different areas of the curriculum. A good example of this is the way that a setting may put out bottles and jugs in the water tray and then link this to the curriculum area of mathematics by using these materials to highlight the concepts of 'full', 'empty' or 'half full'.

How to balance adult-led and child-initiated activities

Both child-initiated and adult-directed activities are vital to children's development and learning. It is, therefore, important to check that there is a balance of each type of activity during a session. The balance between adult-directed and child-initiated play also needs to reflect children's age and stage of development. Children who have particular developmental needs are likely to need more adult-directed activities. There is also an expectation in the English early years curriculum framework that older children will benefit from more adult-directed activities that focus on literacy and numeracy.

Skills for adult-directed play

There are many skills needed for adult-directed play and activities. The starting point is always to plan play and activities that are carefully linked to children's age and stage of development. This is important to prevent children from becoming frustrated.

While sometimes the role of the adult is to introduce children to new toys, resources and activities, there must also be times when you build on children's interests. During adult-directed play and activities, you should also be observing children's reactions and assessing whether they are finding the play interesting and enjoyable. This is essential otherwise children are unlikely to benefit and learn from the activity. Table 3.11 outlines the role of the adult in adult-directed play.

> **Research**
>
> Download the early years framework for your home country. Find out the requirements of the curriculum in relation to play and learning.

▶ **Table 3.11:** The role of the adult in adult-directed play

Area of development	Role of the adult in adult-directed play
Physical	• Put out suitable equipment based on children's interests and developmental stage • Encourage and reassure babies and children so that they attempt movements • Model or join in with children to help them learn or practise a skill, e.g. holding a toddler's hand as they walk on a low wall • Plan play activities to develop specific movements or skills
Cognitive	• Put out interesting objects that may excite children's interest • Combine toys and resources to maintain interest and encourage new learning opportunities • Draw children's attention to any concepts that occur during play
Language	• Put out new materials or different materials so that babies and children have something new to talk about • For children from around 2 years onwards, put out small-world and role play props for children to play with and encourage use of language • Take an interest in what babies and children are doing and spend time questioning, chatting and listening to them

Area of development	Role of the adult in adult-directed play
Emotional	• Plan play activities that will allow children to express their feelings using resources such as musical instruments, puppets or paint • Join in with babies and children as they play. This can help develop closer bonds between you • Observe children as they play to help you understand how they may be feeling • Encourage babies and children as they are playing to help develop their self-esteem
Social	• Plan play activities that will prompt children to play alongside or with other children • Join in with children to model how to take turns or how to support an individual child • Help babies and toddlers develop social skills by playing with them

Skills for supporting child-directed play

The key to engaging with children during child-initiated play is that ownership and direction of the play stays with the children. For example, if children are happily creating a boat using wooden blocks, the adult should not come along and suggest that they build a tower.

Here are some tips that might support child-directed play.

▶ Observe what children are doing – stand near them or sit with them. Do not interfere but show that you are interested.

▶ Make interested comments about what children are doing such as: 'Wow, you are busy' or 'I used to love doing that when I was your age.'

▶ Monitor children's reactions to your presence. Do they want an adult present? Do they turn or move away? Do they respond and want you to be involved?

C2 Support children's purposeful play and learning activities

How to organise a play environment indoors and outdoors

There is no single way in which an early years setting will organise their play environment indoors and outdoors. Many factors need to be taken into consideration. This means that during your course, you are likely to see many different ways in which settings organise and provide for play indoors and outdoors. When you first join a setting, it is important to quickly learn what and how items are put out. Consider the factors below, which influence how the play environment is set up.

Number of children

The number of children who attend each session will influence the play environment. In large group settings, there are likely to be a wider range of play opportunities at any one time. A good example of this is physical equipment such as wheeled toys where, unlike in home-based settings, there may be five, six or more tricycles and wheeled toys available. Similarly, indoors, in larger group settings, there is likely to be a wider choice of small-world play resources and more than one role play area available.

Staffing levels

The number of staff available to supervise, maintain the environment and directly work with children is likely to be a factor in how the play environment is organised. While the early years framework specifies a minimum level of staffing, the adult–child ratios can vary according to the type of early years setting.

A good example of this is the way that childminders in England usually have three children under 5 years old in their settings, while in a school nursery the adult–

child ratio for 3-year-olds is often 1:13. Where adult–child ratios are less favourable, resources that require a lot of adult supervision (for safety reasons or because children cannot access them independently) may be kept to a minimum or available only at certain times.

Organisation of age ranges

In some group-care settings, children are divided according to their age ranges. This is very common in day care but also in some nurseries. This means that babies and toddlers are likely to be in separate environments that have dedicated resources for them. In Section A1 of this unit, you saw the type of play activities and resources that you are likely to find in baby and toddler environments.

In other early years settings, children may be spending a lot of time in mixed age groups. This is likely to be the case in childminding settings and also in nurseries and preschools taking children from 2 to 5 years.

Pedagogical principles

In Section B, you saw that early years settings are influenced by theoretical or philosophical pedagogies. A good example of this is the way that in many Montessori settings, resources are carefully chosen and put onto shelves for children to be guided towards, with equipment and resources having specific purposes. This is very different from other early years settings, which may put out a mixture of toys for water or sand play so that children can decide on their own purpose.

Storage

Many early years settings take place in a shared space, such as a community hall. This is common in the playgroup sector. Settings where everything has to be put away at the end of the session are often referred to as 'pack away settings'. Pack away settings have to plan carefully to ensure that there are sufficient play types and opportunities.

Access to outdoor space

Many early years settings share their outdoor space with different ages of children, for example, in a school provision or with the community. The access to outdoor space affects what and how items are put out. In addition, local factors such as vandalism, theft, weather or animals can play a part in setting up the provision.

Some settings have very small outdoor spaces. When this is the case, they may choose to rotate toys and provision during the session or the course of the week.

❚❚ PAUSE POINT

Identify three factors that influence how a play environment is organised indoors and outdoors.

Hint   Think about what your work placement setting has to consider when organising their indoor and outdoor space.

Extend   In your workplace setting, how do theoretical or pedagogical approaches influence the provision of toys and resources, and the role of adults?

Discussion

Discuss with other learners how their work placement organises the play environment both indoors and outdoors. What differences are there between settings? What have been their responsibilities when they have been on placement?

How to recognise and build on children's interests

As you saw in Section C1, it is helpful to recognise and build on children's interests when planning for their play. Even very small children can let you know what it is that they would like to be able to do or play with. They may point to a toy or resource or lead you to it. Older children, if asked, will talk about what they would like to do or what they enjoy doing at home. You can also ask parents what their children enjoy doing.

There are many ways of building on children's interests. Here are a few examples.

▶ Put out the toys that babies are interested in and add in other similar toys.

▶ Model how to use a new toy and resource that is linked to an interest that the child has already shown.

▶ Develop a role play area based on the child's interest, e.g. a garage for a child who is interested in cars.

How to select resources appropriate for play type

In Section A1 (Table 3.4), you looked at a range of play types and how they might be used indoors and outdoors. For children to benefit from learning through play, it is important that they access the different play types. There are a wide range of toys and resources available to support each type.

Most early years settings create a layout that allows for the range of play types to be supported. Table 3.12 shows examples of resources and play opportunities for the different play types.

▶ **Table 3.12:** Examples of play opportunities and resources for different play types

Play opportunity	What to do	Play types
Delivering 'shopping'	• Outdoors, children can use wheeled toys to deliver shopping • Put out boxes or shopping bags and create an outdoor home	Imaginative play Physical play
Farm animals in the leaves and straw	• Using a large container such as a builder's tray, put out farm animals with leaves and some straw	Imaginative play Sensory play
Painting with brushes and water	• Put out buckets of water and grown-up paintbrushes • Children can practise mark making by pretending to paint	Imaginative play Expressive arts and design (creative play) Sensory play
Making 'cakes' in the home corner	• Put out dough, muffin cases and baking trays in the home corner • Children can pretend to cook	Sensory play Imaginative play
Hiding jigsaw pieces in dry sand	• Hide jigsaw pieces in dry sand • See if the children can find all the pieces and make up the puzzle • You could also do the same with construction blocks	Sensory play Construction play

Reflect

Observe how your early years work placement ensures that a range of play types is available for children. How are resources set up for each of the play types?

Does your placement setting have a plan each day or week as to the toys and resources that will be used? Find out how the adults decide what to put out.

How to select age- and stage-appropriate resources

As children develop, so does the way in which they play. It is important to be aware of how children's play changes so that you can plan appropriately. If you work with children of very different ages, it is also important to make sure that you are providing for their varying needs.

Link

Look back at Section A1 (the section entitled 'The importance of suitable resources', in particular 'Different ages/stages of development' and Table 3.5) to remind yourself of the way that children's play changes according to their age and stage.

One of the key issues when selecting resources is to think about children's safety. How children use resources depends on their age and stage of development. A good example of this is the way that toddlers often cast things to the ground, unaware of the safety of others. In the same way, while most children over 18 months no longer routinely explore objects by bringing them to their mouths, it may be that a 3-year-old child with a developmental delay will continue to do this. So objects need to be carefully selected to prevent a choking incident.

How to support purposeful play

You have looked at some of the key skills needed to support both child-initiated and adult-initiated play. You will now look at other factors that are important to ensure that play is purposeful.

Building supportive relationships

Remember that for play to be pleasurable for children, they need to have a strong relationship with the adult they are with. You have seen already that this requires the adult to act as a strong play partner and also to be playful.

Supportive relationships also mean that adults have to observe children's reactions carefully and be responsive. This might mean offering a word of advice or practical support if a child is disappointed because they cannot join in with other children or because they are having difficulties achieving what they have set out to do in their play, e.g. they cannot find a piece of the jigsaw puzzle or a ball has rolled out of reach.

Extending children's physical, communication and social skills

As you have already seen in Sections A2 (Tables 3.6 and 3.7) and C1 (Table 3.11), adults need to look for opportunities to extend the different areas of children's development, including their physical, communication and social skills.

> **❚❚ PAUSE POINT**   Identify five ways in which adults might support children's development during adult-directed play.
>
> **Hint**   Think about the five areas of development.
>
> **Extend**   For each area of development, can you think of an adult-directed activity that would support a 3-year-old child's learning?

Encouraging higher-level thinking skills

One role of the early years professional during play is to develop and extend children's thinking and learning. This can happen during both child-initiated and adult-directed activities. Professionals often do this by drawing children's attention to features of what they are doing. An adult might comment, for example, that 'the sand is dry today' and so 'it is hard to make sandcastles'. From this comment, a conversation might develop about how much water should be added in order to make the perfect sandcastle, or about the difference between dry and wet sand.

Through carefully chosen resources and the location of play, adults can create opportunities that may prompt interesting conversations. These in turn can help children to think, explain and reason. The skill of the adult is to engage children in this thinking and learning without spoiling the children's enjoyment of their play. This can be done by carefully monitoring children's responses to your comments or questions to check that they are still interested.

Being a play partner

A play partner is able to respond to and follow a child's lead. This means that the child is able to remain in control of the play but enjoy the company of the adult. While the adult might make suggestions or bring additional resources to the play activity, the adult follows what the child is interested in and plays a supportive role.

Being a play partner is particularly important when working with very young children as it can encourage the development of a child's communication and language skills. Learning to be a play partner does require patience. The key is to be interested in the child and what the child is trying to achieve in the activity.

The case study shows how challenging being a play partner can be, particularly if you are new to working with children.

▶ This child wanted a practitioner to pretend to be a customer at her grocery shop

Case study

Being a play partner requires skill

Jamie is new to working with children – he is at his first placement in a day care setting. He has been asked by the manager to play in the construction area with a couple of children who have started to make a boat.

When Jamie joins them, he tells them that it would be more fun to make a rocket. He asks the children to pass him some of the larger bricks and then tells them how to stack them together to begin to create the rocket.

The children look at each other briefly before going to play outdoors.

Check your knowledge

1   Why do you think the children left the activity?

2   Analyse why Jamie's approach was not that of a play partner.

3   Consider ways in which Jamie could have helped to extend and support the children's learning.

How to support children's group learning and socialisation

Play is one way for children to develop social skills including turn taking, and learning to follow instructions and rules. These are important skills for children as they learn to be a part of a group and learn to socialise. Adult-directed play can be a good starting point.

One of the most important things when planning for children's group learning is to make sure that the activity is developmentally appropriate. In particular, children's level of language needs to be taken into consideration; if children are not able to understand or process spoken information well, they will find it hard to remain engaged in a group activity.

Most early years professionals find that it is best to work with small groups of children because it is easier to ensure that an activity is interactive. Many professionals plan activities that will allow children to interact or participate in some way. Games such as parachute play and 'What's the time, Mr Wolf?' which have simple rules, can be used before introducing games where children need to be able to sit or stay still for longer periods.

Recognising the learning potential of spontaneous or unplanned events

One of the wonderful things about working with children is the way that unplanned learning can take place in a spontaneous way. This is more likely to happen outdoors and also during open-ended play activities such as building a den or playing with sensory materials. For example, children might lift up a tarpaulin and notice some earwigs under it.

Spontaneous and unplanned learning can take place during adult-directed play activities too. For instance, during a cooking activity, a child may crack an egg open and find it has two yolks, or that the colour of the yolk is particularly yellow.

It is important not to waste unplanned learning opportunities as they can open the door to interesting conversations with children. They can also be used as a springboard for sharing books, doing internet research or to plan further activities.

How to respond to children's individual needs

You have seen in this unit that play can contribute to children's development. For this to take place, you need to ensure that play meets children's individual needs. This may mean that activities or how play is set up is adapted to suit the child. In order to ensure that activities meet children's individual needs, the role of the adult is to gain as much information as possible and to understand what is appropriate for each child's age and stage of development. There are many ways of doing this.

Parents

Parents often know what their children enjoy playing with and also what support they may need. Talking to parents may also help you understand children's culture and ensure that this is reflected in the materials and props that you provide. In the case of children with additional needs, parents can give you advice about how they adapt resources at home.

Other professionals

To ensure that provision for play and learning is inclusive, you may also need to work with other professionals. Some children with a learning difficulty or a physical or sensory impairment will need particular support. To support these children, you will need to talk to their parents, but may also find it useful to seek advice from professionals such as a physiotherapist or a professional from the sensory impairment team. In addition, there are organisations that lend out specialist equipment.

How to balance safety with purposeful and challenging play

For play to be interesting and challenging, children need to enjoy it. One of the things that makes play enjoyable for children is excitement. Children gain excitement in many ways, but key among these are exploration and challenge. Where adults can be overly concerned with safety, there is a real danger that the environments that children find themselves in will be dull, predictable and lacking in stimulation. Having said this, adults working with children do have a legal duty to provide a reasonable standard of care, which includes keeping children safe.

> **Link**
>
> For more information on health and safety and risk assessments, see Unit 5.

Identifying potential hazards

A key way to keep children safe is to carry out ongoing risk assessments. You should be aware of how resources and materials might be used in potentially hazardous ways. Ropes, for example, can find their way around children's necks, and a heavy item such as a rock might fall on a child's toe. A swing can easily catch a child in the face.

Once you have thought about what might happen, the next step is to think about ways of preventing or reducing the impact of an accident. You might talk to children about how they should use the resources, supervise the area more closely or join in with play. You might move some items, such as swings, to a particular spot where children can still access them but there is less likelihood of another child passing by being injured.

In settings where children are of different ages, items might be fine to use with certain age groups but become risky with younger children. Marbles are a good example of this – they can be great resources for 6 and 7-year-old children but dangerous for babies and toddlers.

▶ Although this outdoor area is probably safe, what might you need to think about?

Supervision

Good supervision is a fantastic way of allowing children to explore and try out challenging activities. Adults can provide children with reassurance, practical advice and also words of caution where necessary. Good supervision does not just mean standing like a prison guard watching children – it should be about taking a genuine interest in what the children are doing, by chatting or being an unobtrusive presence.

Knowing and understanding the children

If you get to know individual children well, it becomes easier to manage potential risks and find a good balance between safety and exciting play.

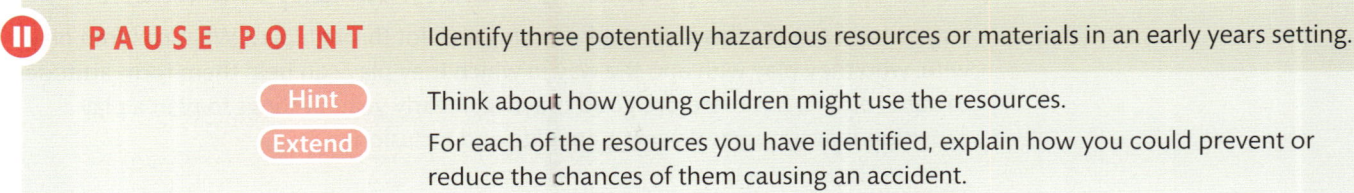

Ⅱ PAUSE POINT Identify three potentially hazardous resources or materials in an early years setting.

Hint Think about how young children might use the resources.

Extend For each of the resources you have identified, explain how you could prevent or reduce the chances of them causing an accident.

Strategies to extend children's learning

One of the key ways in which adults can support children to learn through play is to help them think about what they are doing and draw their attention to possibilities. You have looked at some of the skills involved in sustained shared thinking earlier in the unit. They include asking children open questions such as 'I wonder what would happen if the sand was wetter?' or 'Do you think that it would make a difference to the car's speed if the ramp was longer?'

Link

See Section A2 to remind yourself about sustained shared thinking.

You can extend children's learning by drawing their attention to details and accurately naming objects and actions. This develops their vocabulary but also helps them notice concepts. An example of this is the way that adults might say to a child who is pouring water onto a water wheel, 'Look at the way that the water makes the wheel **rotate**'.

> **Theory into practice**
>
> Observe an experienced adult working with children at a sand or water tray. Make a note of the skills that are used to support and extend children's learning as the adult engages in sustained shared thinking.
>
> Consider the impact of these skills on children's mathematical development.

How to support children to develop positive attitudes through play

During play there are often opportunities for early years professionals to help children develop positive attitudes towards others and learn to value and respect other people. Below are a few examples of how you might do this.

Role modelling

Adults can role model caring and thoughtful behaviours. For example, they can show children how to take turns, share resources and help others.

Better understanding

Where a range of culturally rich resources are on offer, especially in the home corner, adults can model their use and talk to children about how and why they are used. This can help children to learn about differences and similarities, and develop respect.

Direct intervention

Sometimes, adults might intervene in play to help children respect others or help them understand that there are differences between people.

The importance of promoting diversity, equality and inclusion

As you have seen in this unit, children can gain a lot through play. What children play with, who they play with and the way in which they play can help them form attitudes towards others. It is therefore good practice in early years settings to plan a play provision that supports diversity, equality and inclusion.

Diversity

Early years settings should recognise children's diverse backgrounds by choosing play types, resources and equipment that link to their culture and home experiences. This means that most home corners will be equipped with cooking utensils that replicate children's different home backgrounds and there will be dolls that have different skin tones. This allows children to play with resources that they can identify with, but it also enables other children to learn about differences between people in a positive way.

Equality

Early years settings also have to promote equality during play. This may happen by challenging children if they make discriminatory comments, but also by ensuring that children have equal access to toys and resources during their play.

Inclusion

Some children may need additional support so that they can actively participate in play. Early years settings therefore look for practical ways in which children, some of whom may have disabilities, can join in.

As you saw earlier in this section, you may need to ask advice from parents or other professionals, such as occupational therapists, in order to support some children.

Case study

The importance of inclusion

Kai, aged 1, has a visual impairment. Staff have spoken to Kai's parents and also taken advice from the sensory impairment team. They have made sure that toys and resources are put on light-reflecting surfaces so that Kai is able to find them more easily. They have also looked for toys that make sounds and are tactile so that Kai can enjoy using them.

Check your knowledge

1 Why is it important for staff to find out as much as possible about Kai's individual needs?

2 Explain the impact on Kai's development if toys and resources are not chosen specifically to meet his needs.

Assessment practice 3.4 | C.P5 | C.P6 | C.M3 | C.D2 | C.D3 |

The Rainbow preschool is due to have an Ofsted inspection. After their last inspection they were given a 'good' grading. This time they are hoping to get 'outstanding'.

Following the comments in the last inspection report, they are trying to extend children's learning during play. You have been asked to provide information about the skills that are needed to support and extend children's play, and to give practical examples from your own experience. The information should:

- explain the range of skills that adults need in order to support purposeful play and learning activities
- give examples of ways in which you have used these skills and evaluate why you felt they were effective
- evaluate the impact on children's learning and development when adults use a range of skills to support play and learning
- assess and evaluate the development of your own skills in supporting purposeful play and children's learning, giving examples.

Plan
- What experiences can I draw on for this task?
- Where can I go to gain additional information?
- How long do I need to collate and analyse the information required for the task?

Do
- Am I presenting the information accurately and concisely?
- Am I managing my time effectively?

Review
- Have I included a range of skills and given examples of how they might be used in practice?
- Have I evaluated my work and am I confident that it fulfils the set task?

Further reading and resources

Bruce, T. (1991) *Time to Play in Early Childhood Education*, London: Hodder Arnold.

Moyles, J. (2014) *The Excellence of Play*, 4th edition, Maidenhead: Open University Press.

Tassoni, P. and Hucker, K. (2005) *Planning Play and the Early Years*, 2nd edition, Oxford: Heinemann.

Tassoni, P. (2012) *Penny Tassoni's Practical EYFS Handbook*, 2nd edition, Oxford: Heinemann.

Tassoni, P. (2014) *Getting It Right For Two Year Olds*, London: Hodder Education.

THINK ▶FUTURE

Molly Stones

Reception teacher

Molly has been working as an early years teacher for three years. In the school where she works, the reception class and nursery work closely together and children spend a lot of time engaged in play. The staff plan the play environment and specific play activities. They pride themselves on creating a stimulating play environment that is inclusive but also supports the development of every child.

Molly often takes time to observe children during play so she can see how they are benefitting and also how to challenge them further. The team recognises that it is important to look out for and listen to the things that interest children. In the past few months, for example, there has been a nail bar, a mechanic's yard and a dinosaur garden. Children have made props, written signs and explained to others the rules for each area.

It takes time and experience to learn how to use play to support children's learning, especially when it comes to joining them in play. But Molly would not change her job for the world.

Focusing your skills

Setting out and maintaining role play

- Create a cosy area so that children think they cannot be seen.
- Look out for as many real-life props as possible.
- Make sure the necessary props are ready.
- If a role play situation is new to children, be ready to join in and model what happens.
- Be ready to discreetly tidy up.

Maintaining sand and water

- Keep a dustpan and brush ready, and a cloth to wipe up water spills.
- Make sure aprons are clean and easy for children to put on.
- Water needs to be changed daily or in some settings at the end of each session.
- Toys and objects for water and sand should be washed thoroughly and dried.

- Many settings have separate sand and water toys because sand scratches the surfaces.
- Sand and water activities need some supervision. Look out for children who are throwing sand and immediately intervene to prevent eye injuries. Wipe up spillages from both promptly.
- Be ready to do some discreet tidying away as too many objects in the sand and water trays can make them unattractive.
- If sand is outdoors, cover it when the outdoor area is not being used. Always check the sand for animal mess.

Creating a treasure basket

- Items have to be sufficiently large and robust so that a baby can mouth them safely.
- Avoid items that may break into smaller pieces or are small enough to swallow.
- Look out for items that are straightforward to wash afterwards.

Enquiries into Current Research in Early Years Practice

4

Getting to know your unit

Assessment

You will be assessed through an external task set and marked by Pearson.

Research into early years practice is seen as an important part of the development of effective practice within early years provision. Early years professionals need to understand the purposes of research, how it is carried out and how it is used to improve the well-being and development of those using early years provision. In this unit you will study the importance of research in developing early years practice by looking at current research and how it impacts on early years practice. You will also explore the importance of ethics in research and how this can affect how research is carried out. Understanding how to carry out research as well as reviewing the effectiveness of other people's research will help you develop essential research skills which will also help you progress within your chosen field.

How you will be assessed

This unit will be assessed through a task set and marked by Pearson and taken under supervised conditions. The task is worth 65 marks.

You will be provided with an article related to current research in early years. First you will need to undertake your own secondary research into the topic. To do this, you will have to apply your understanding of research methodologies and your knowledge of current issues within early years settings.

You will be given 18 hours to carry out this research over a period of 6 weeks. This time should be used for planning, making your own enquiries and preparation before the supervised write-up of the task. You will be able to take a maximum of six sides of A4 notes into the supervised assessment.

For the write-up you will have three hours and you will be supervised during this time. A task book will be provided, which you will use to answer questions related to the article and write up your findings.

Throughout this unit you will find assessment practice opportunities that will help you develop the skills and understanding you will need for the assessment.

You will be assessed on your ability to achieve the following outcomes.

▶ **AO1** Demonstrate knowledge and understanding of methods, skills and ethical issues related to carrying out research in the early years sector

▶ **AO2** Apply knowledge and understanding of methods, skills and ethical issues to current research in the early years sector

▶ **AO3** Analyse information and data related to current research on early years, demonstrating the ability to interpret the potential impact and influence of the research on early years practice

▶ **AO4** Evaluate current early years research to make informed judgements about the validity of the research methods used, further areas for research and the potential impact of the research on early years practice

To achieve maximum marks, you must demonstrate achievement of all of these assessment outcomes. You need to show you understand research methods and appreciate the impact of different methods, skills and ethical issues on the effectiveness of the research. In addition, you need to show you are able to analyse research data effectively to draw relevant conclusions. You will need to analyse the information you are presented with and discuss this using extended writing skills.

Table 4.1 shows key terms that will be used consistently by Pearson in its assessments. These terms will not necessarily be used in every paper, and are provided for guidance only.

▷ **Table 4.1:** Key terms used in this unit

Term	Definition
Article	The pre-released account of a piece of recent research relating to an aspect of children's play, learning and development; could be based on a longer report
Ethical issue	Ethically related aspect that may have affected how the research was carried out
Issue	The subject of the research that the article is describing
Literature review	An assessment of existing research around a particular issue or area of study
Primary research	Research compiled directly from the original source (e.g. by speaking to parents), which may not have been compiled before. You will not have to carry out primary research but you should understand the advantages and disadvantages of different primary research methods
Qualitative research	Descriptive data, for example, data from open-ended questions in questionnaires, interviews or focus groups
Quantitative research	Data in numerical form which can be categorised and used to construct graphs or tables of raw data, such as data drawn from results of experiments, hospital data showing admissions of individuals with certain health conditions, or closed questions in questionnaires
Research methods	How the research was carried out, for example, through quantitative methods (such as analysis of figures from hospitals or GP surgeries) or qualitative methods (based on focus groups or questionnaires)
Secondary sources/ research	Published research reports and data, usually based on analysis of primary research

Getting started

Think about how research might be used in the following situations.

- Observing a child who is kicking other children.
- Asking parents about their experiences of the setting.
- Researching a medical condition that a new child who is joining a nursery may have.

Explain why you think research might be useful.

A | Types of issues where research is carried out in the early years sector

Whatever childcare setting you work in, you will use research and research skills as part of your everyday routine. You may not realise it, but you will be drawing on information gained through other people's research to inform your practice. While working with children and other early years professionals, you will also be gathering information, analysing it, drawing conclusions from it and taking action as a result. This is research. However, it is important not to draw conclusions without well-researched and analysed evidence as this can lead to mistakes. Therefore, understanding how the research process works is essential.

A1 Purpose of research in the early years sector

The purpose of research

Research is an activity where we aim to find out information and/or gain knowledge about something. It is carried out in an organised way. Research can range from observations about how a child interacts with others in a setting to a nursery carrying out a questionnaire with parents and/or carers to see how its service might be improved.

Sometimes people draw conclusions but may not have any evidence to back them up. When statements or assumptions are made about things that happen with children, research can provide the evidence to support or disprove those statements. The results of research can make people change their minds about something they may have seen, or help them decide what action to take to improve or change something, or to help a child progress.

Research within the early years field can be used to:

- ▶ inform policy or practice
- ▶ identify and highlight gaps in provision
- ▶ extend individual practitioners' knowledge and understanding
- ▶ improve outcomes for children, parents and carers by improving practice
- ▶ help professionals reflect on their work.

Research activities could cover several of these purposes. For example, a piece of research on how children use outdoor play areas could extend your knowledge and understanding of children's play habits and how they use outdoor play equipment, depending on their age and stage of development. As a result, it could inform policy on how outdoor areas are used in the curriculum and might also highlight gaps in terms of the facilities available for outdoor play provision. Changes that may happen as a result of these findings would lead to improving practice and, in turn, outcomes for children.

Improving practice and policy

Research can encourage a practitioner to reflect on the work they are currently doing and identify areas of change which might result in improvements in practice. Here are some examples of research that have led to an improvement in reflection, practice and policy within the early years sector.

▶ Research by early years educators such as Piaget and Montessori has helped us to understand and reflect on how children learn, and how we can use play to build on this and effectively enable children to develop.

▶ Research into the impact of praise and punishment on behaviour, such as research carried out by B. F. Skinner, is used as the basis for supporting children's social development.

▶ Research into children's language and thinking skills development, such as research carried out by Jerome Bruner and Chomsky.

▶ Research into the development of literacy and numeracy has influenced recommendations on how these skills should be developed with young children.

Case study

Developing writing skills

Vanessa, a key worker in a nursery, noticed that one of her children, George, was struggling with a construction task. He kept trying to build a tower but it was too tall and thin and kept falling down. He was becoming more and more frustrated.

Vanessa had been reading about Vygotsky's Zone of Proximal Development Theory. This explained that, with appropriate support from an adult, a child can develop skills beyond their current level. Vanessa decided to help George complete the construction by showing him

how to create a more stable base for the tower. Then she encouraged him to try again for himself, gradually giving him less support on each attempt.

Check your knowledge

1 Why is this an effective use of research?

2 Why is it important to draw on research to support the development of children?

3 How else could Vygotsky's theories be used to support development?

Link

Look back over Unit 1 and Unit 2 to remind yourself of the main theories and models of learning that inform our work in supporting all areas of children's development and learning.

Ⅱ PAUSE POINT   Why is research important in the early years sector?

     Hint   Think broadly, including how research might impact on the work of the early years practitioner, on parents and carers, and on policy development.

     Extend   Find an example of where research has had a significant impact on early years provision.

A2 Issues in early years

Early years provision

Research has a key role to play in influencing current thinking about early years provision.

Current legislation and guidance

Current early years legislation is based on the belief that providing children with high quality education and care in their earliest years can help them succeed at school and in later life. This has resulted in a government agenda that aims to provide a range of opportunities within society, which everyone can access regardless of their background. The government also believes that good, affordable childcare is essential as it can provide the infrastructure for more families to be in work while raising children. More working families means a healthier economy.

In September 2013 the state introduced the provision of 15 hours per week of free childcare during term time for all children from the age of 3. It also provides 15 hours of free childcare for the most vulnerable 2-year-olds whose families meet the criteria for free school meals. From September 2016, the government will introduce a pilot scheme in some areas of England. This scheme will increase the entitlement to 30 hours per week in term time for families where parents work more than 16 hours (or 2 days) per week and have an annual income less than £100,000 per year. In addition, more flexibility has been allowed in terms of who is permitted to look after children – up to three hours a day of care can be provided by a neighbour or relative not registered with Ofsted. As part of this policy, the government also recognises the need to create an early years workforce that is better qualified.

The effectiveness of types of provision

Early years provision is made up of a range of different private, voluntary and maintained providers who offer a range of services.

Research is commonly used to evaluate the effectiveness of different types of provision. There are many more working parents nowadays and therefore more children have to be in childcare provision to allow their parents to work. In addition, current government policy of providing free childcare for all children from the age of 3 years highlights the importance placed by the government on access to early years education and its role in helping children develop and learn. Therefore, it is essential that research is used to ensure this area of provision is developed to provide the best service it can to children and their parents.

Benefits and information from statutory, voluntary and private services

Research is often carried out to find out how different types of provision benefit families and what kind of information is available for parents and children from statutory, voluntary and private services. Each type of service has different challenges for children and parents including accessibility and costs. Therefore, it is useful to research into how each type of provision contributes to supporting the sector.

Multi-agency working

There have been a number of high-profile cases involving neglect or abuse at the hands of a parent or carer, where the lack of effective multi-agency working was considered to be a factor that led to the death of a child. Working closely with other professionals is essential in early years services and therefore is often the subject of detailed research. The purpose of this research can be to ensure improved services and outcomes for children and their families or to study different models of information sharing or safeguarding procedures.

Research

Find out about the government-funded Multi-Agency Working and Information Sharing Project. The final report, published in 2014, can be found at www.gov.uk.

1 What was the main purpose of the research?

2 The report identifies a number of key barriers to multi-agency working. Identify three of these barriers.

Provision of integrated support

Research is often used to examine how agencies work together to provide effective integrated support for children and to pass on key findings to those in the sector who can use the information to improve early years provision. This kind of research might be into specific areas, such as provision for children with disabilities, or for those who have English as a second or other language or for children living in poverty.

The Early Years Foundation Stage

Principles and themes

The Early Years Foundation Stage (EYFS) is covered in detail in Unit 11 but, in brief, contains four overarching principles which all early years providers must adhere to. It also outlines the areas of learning that children must cover through the activities planned for them in the different settings. There are seven areas of learning.

1 Communication and language

2 Physical development

3 Personal, social and emotional development

4 Literacy

5 Mathematics

6 Understanding the world

7 Expressive arts and design

(Source: Statutory Framework for the Early Years Foundation Stage (2014) p7 © Crown copyright 2014)

The EYFS sets out learning goals that a child will be reviewed against at ages 2–3 years and then at the end of the school year in which they turn 5 years old. Assessment of a child's progress is via observation rather than testing and this is an important area where we can see how research is used every day in childcare settings to inform practice. Each child has an 'EYFS profile', which is intended to provide an accurate assessment of attainment against the 17 learning goals at the end of the EYFS.

In many early years settings, children are allocated a key worker (key person) who will review their progress against the EYFS profile.

Aims and objectives of the EYFS

The EYFS is the statutory framework (meaning that it is mandatory in England) that sets out the standards for the learning, development and care of children from birth to 5 years of age in England. All schools and Ofsted registered providers must follow this framework. This includes nurseries, preschools and childminders.

The aim of the EYFS is to provide quality, consistency and equality of opportunity in all early years settings. It focuses on providing a secure foundation for all children to make good progress through school and life. It also promotes partnerships between different early years practitioners and with other agencies, as well as between parents or carers, and practitioners.

Link

For more information about the principles and themes of the EYFS, as well as the areas of learning and the learning goals, go to Unit 11.

The EYFS also aims to provide practical ideas for how practitioners might approach the progress check against the EYFS profile. This is a useful area for research as researchers can explore how effectively the objectives are met from the perspective of a provider or a child.

Play and education programmes which support areas of children's development

Research can be used to look at how effectively play and education programmes support children's development. This might include how different elements of the EYFS are implemented and their success in helping children to develop.

Safeguarding and welfare requirements

Research might be used to explore safeguarding and welfare requirements and how effectively these are met. Findings of government-funded research can be used to ensure that there is wider awareness of the importance of early recognition of child abuse or neglect, as well as to improve the ability of various children's services to respond and intervene appropriately.

Equality and inclusion

Research is often used to look at equality and inclusion issues. Research can be used to identify the most effective methods of promoting inclusion as well as the impact of different approaches to equality on individual development.

> **Reflect**
>
> Think about the role of the key person in early years settings. (You can find out more about this in Unit 11.) Reflect on how they can effectively support a child's learning and development. How would good research skills help them with this role?

❚❚ PAUSE POINT

Why do you think it is important to have a statutory early years curriculum (one that is laid down by law)?

Hint Think about how the EYFS framework supports children.

Extend Why might researching the EYFS be important in terms of improving learning outcomes for children? Give examples linked to the early years curriculum.

Assessment practice 4.1   AO1

Choose one of the early years educators you are familiar with and explain how their research has been used in early years settings to influence practice and improve learning outcomes for children.

Plan
- Which early years educators could I choose and where could I find out more about them?
- Do I know where to find information about the EYFS?

Do
- Can I explain in detail the research carried out by my chosen early years educator?
- Can I explain how this research improves learning outcomes for children, using specific examples?

Review
- How effective was my approach to my research? Did I find enough detailed information to be able to complete the task?
- Does my answer show how research is used to improve children's learning?

 **B** Research methods in early years

A range of different people and organisations carry out research for different reasons. This can influence both the approach and the way in which the findings are reported and used.

B1 Research methodologies

Organisations involved in research

Table 4.2 includes some of the many organisations that are involved in research into the early years sector as part of their work.

▶ **Table 4.2:** Organisations involved in research

Organisation	What it does	Involvement in research
Department for Education (DfE) www.gov.uk/government/organisations/department-for-education	Responsible for education and children's services in England	Undertakes a range of research that informs policy and practice
British Educational Research Association (BERA) www.bera.ac.uk	A charity that encourages educational research and its application to improve practice	Publishes policy advice based on findings from research with the aim of influencing policy
Association for Professional Development in Early Years (TACTYC) www.tactyc.org.uk	Focuses on promoting high quality professional development for early years practitioners; aims to ensure this enhances the well-being of children	Publishes regular papers on early years issues; some are free to access – others have to be purchased
National Institute of Economic and Social Research (NIESR) www.niesr.ac.uk	Focuses on producing independent economic research that influences decision makers	Publishes its own reports but also flags up related projects
The Early Childhood Research Centre (ECRC) www.roehampton.ac.uk/Research-Centres/Early-Childhood-Research-Centre	The ECRC is based at the University of Roehampton and investigates practices, pedagogies, policies and histories of early childhood	Publishes articles of interest that influence the development of early years practice
Department of Education Northern Ireland www.deni.gov.uk	Responsible for education and children's services in Northern Ireland	Undertakes a range of research that informs policy and practice
Children in Wales www.childreninwales.org.uk	Works with policy makers, along with practitioners and managers, to promote the importance of supporting children's development and to support improvement in children's services	Promotes research into various aspects of child development and early years issues; offers events that disseminate research and allow good practice to be shared, and influence policy locally and nationally
Centre for Research in Early Childhood (CREC) www.crec.co.uk	A charity whose purpose is to promote and carry out research into issues relevant to early childhood provision	Involved in theoretical and empirical research, including research into new methods of working that can be applied to current practice

Another good source of research in early years is the Education Endowment Foundation, which is a charity focused on breaking the link between family income and educational achievement. Their website contains a lot of information on current and past research into this area.

Research methods

Research can be classified as either primary or secondary. **Primary research** involves collecting your own original data using research techniques such as interviews, questionnaires or surveys. **Secondary research** involves the use of previously published material as a source of information.

As well as being primary or secondary, research can be **qualitative** or **quantitative**. See page 202 for more information about qualitative and quantitative research methods.

Questionnaires

A questionnaire is a list of questions that are given to potential respondents in a written format. Questions might be open or closed. Questionnaires are not usually completed with a researcher present and therefore can be a cost-effective way to gather a lot of information.

▸ A closed question gives the respondent a selection of answers to choose from or asks for a yes or no answer with no opportunity for expanding on the response. For example, a closed question might ask: 'How long have you been using this nursery?' and give the answer options 'Under 1 year', '1–2 years', '2–3 years' and '3 years or more'.

▸ An open question is one which allows the respondent a free answer. For example: 'Tell me why you chose this nursery.' Open questions can elicit a lot more information but can be more difficult for a researcher to analyse.

A questionnaire can provide lots of responses relatively easily and responses can be directly compared, collated and analysed. It is a good way of asking straightforward questions of a large number of people. Questionnaires are often carried out online and can be fairly quick to complete. However, it can take time to collate and analyse all the responses.

Interviews

An interview is an example of qualitative research. It can take place face to face with the respondent, using electronic connections such as Skype or FaceTime or over the phone. It provides more detailed information than a questionnaire. Interviews often take longer to carry out than questionnaires but they make it possible to explore issues in more depth. This is particularly useful when researching beliefs, attitudes and feelings, as these cannot be fully explored through observations or questionnaires.

The structured nature of an interview allows you to draw out reasons and explanations for answers given. It also allows people to speak to you directly and at length, in a way that questionnaires cannot.

Interviews can follow a semi-structured format, which allows for greater flexibility, as it is possible to change the questions in response to the answers the interviewee gives. This means that an interviewer can get more information than might otherwise be possible. However, because interviews are generally one-to-one they are quite time-consuming, so they are generally used for relatively small samples.

Interviews can also be recorded. This means that the researcher can replay an interview as many times as needed to collect the information accurately.

Interviews rely on effective communication between two people. For an interview to be successful, the interaction between the interviewer and the participant is very important, as this can affect the responses. Factors such as the interviewer's appearance, gender, age and even accent can affect the answers given, as the interviewee may form an opinion about them. Interviewers can also influence responses without knowing they are doing so, through mannerisms such as nodding or smiling. Uttering 'mmm' or even 'yes' when someone speaks can influence the relationship. Leading questions such as, 'Don't you think the new government has introduced some poor policies?' can also affect the answers that are given. You must remain non-judgemental when interviewing to get the best outcome. A good rapport may allow you to ask questions of a sensitive or more personal nature, but it is worth remembering that interviewees may sometimes respond to questions with what they feel the interviewer wants to hear rather than stating their true feelings or behaviour.

Finally, the nature of the data collected during interviews makes it difficult to draw overall conclusions or generalisations. Such qualitative data is not generally used to produce detailed statistics.

Case studies

A case study is an in-depth study of a person, group or community. You might use a case study within a research project to investigate a particular aspect that is based on an individual or organisation. For example, if a research project was looking into the support the voluntary sector provides for children in a particular town, a case study of a voluntary organisation would be extremely relevant. If you were looking at a topic where you wanted to see how something applied to an individual child, you might also use a case study. For example, you might research why some parents do not have their children vaccinated, and a case study of a child who was not vaccinated would be a useful research method for that topic. Bristol Early Years Research provides good examples of using case studies in practice. Their work can be found at www.bristolearlyyearsresearch.org.uk.

When using a case study for research purposes, an in-depth investigation is required and you will need to consider historical evidence. Case studies look at the impact of past and present events on the topic being studied. Most case studies will draw on a range of research methods. You might start a case study with some secondary research and then use interviews, questionnaires or observations to investigate further.

Scientific experiments

Scientific experiments might be used in the early years environment to understand **causal relationships**. This approach is often used in psychology to look at behaviour. The plan for the experiment will involve identifying a dependent **variable** and an independent variable. A variable is anything that can change or be changed (for example, the amount of time taken to complete a task, or the score on a test). The dependent variable is what is being measured in the experiment, and the independent variable is what is introduced in order to see the effect it has on the dependent variable. Keeping all the other variables the same will allow researchers to measure accurately the impact of the change they have made. Within any experiment there is always a control group where none of the variables are changed.

In an early years setting, a researcher might want to research the age at which children understand the concept of conservation (as explained by Piaget). In this experiment the test (the dependent variable) would stay the same but the independent variable would be the children, as the researcher would have to carry out the test with children of different ages.

> **Key terms**
>
> **Causal relationships** – relationships where something happens (the cause) and produces a reaction (the effect). Casual relationships may occur between events, properties, behaviours or other variables.
>
> **Variable** – an element, feature or factor in an experiment or research project.

In order to ensure that the results of an experiment are valid, it is important that it is set up accurately and carried out with precision. An experiment is reliable if, when repeated by another person at a later date, using the same variables, they get similar results.

> **Reflect**
>
> Jean Piaget was the first psychologist to study cognitive development in children in a systematic way. You will have covered his work in Unit 1. He used experiments and tests to assess how children's thinking developed. How might you use the same experiments that Jean Piaget carried out to look at the stages of cognitive development in children?

Checklists

A checklist is a list of specific things being looked for or assessed during an observation. In the case of research into children's development, the list could include skills, **attributes** or behavioural signs. You can use a checklist to assess the observed subject against norms or expectations.

> **Key term**
>
> **Attribute** – a particular quality that is characteristic of an individual.

This kind of methodology is very quick to carry out and produces clear results, which are easily interpreted. However, to be really effective, the checklist needs to be well prepared and thought through. It is important that the observer only records what they see. There may be a risk of not getting true results if the person being observed feels under pressure to perform.

Checklists can be used effectively:

▶ to compare skill levels across different groups, such as groups of the same gender, age or developmental stage

▶ to assess physical development, gross and fine motor skills, social skills, levels of ability (such as reading levels) or key health indicators (such as blood pressure and heart rate).

Participant and non-participant observations

There are two different types of observation: participant and non-participant. The main difference is whether or not the observer chooses to get involved with what they are observing.

Participant observation

This is where the observer becomes part of the group they are observing. Being part of a group and observing at the same time can make recording details difficult. The observer may also influence the outcome by being involved. However, this type of observation can result in a more reflective picture, as the observer is part of the group and can therefore draw on their own experiences of what actually went on.

Non-participant observation

In this type of observation, the observer is an onlooker who is not involved in the action in any way. They record only what they see and have no interaction with the person or people being observed. This means that the observer can record a lot of detail as they can concentrate on this, rather than getting involved. They can also see things that are not immediately obvious when part of a group. The main disadvantage with this type of observation is that the observer may have an effect on what happens, as those involved know they are being watched. This may make them feel intimidated or self-conscious.

Overt or covert

In both participant and non-participant observations, the observer can be overt or covert.

▶ Overt observation is where the observer is open about their intention to carry out an observation and the people being observed are aware of this.

▶ In covert observation, on the other hand, the observer does not inform those being observed of what they are doing or why they are doing it. This type of observation is useful when observing children who are likely to behave differently when surroundings or people change. However, in some circumstances, covert observation may raise ethical issues if those being observed feel they have been misinformed (or not informed at all) when they find out what has happened.

▶ This practitioner is observing a child. What method of observation could she be using?

Advantages and disadvantages of participant and non-participant observations

Observation as a method of research in childcare settings can have limitations that affect the quality of the results gained. We have seen that the objectivity of observation can be affected by the actions of the observer. Other factors can also affect the situation and the child or children being observed so that they behave in a way that is out of the ordinary. It is worth being aware of some of these factors and thinking about ways in which you can conduct observations to get the best possible results.

▶ **Knowing the environment** – if the environment in which the observation is taking place is familiar, those being observed will be more relaxed and feel more comfortable. This situation is likely to result in a more accurate impression than one that takes place in unfamiliar surroundings.

▶ **Changes in the immediate environment** – changes in noise levels, the organisation of the immediate environment and the people who are in an area (for example, a new practitioner) can all trigger changes in behaviour that will be reflected in any observation that is carried out.

▶ **The timing of the observation** – if a child is tired they may have a lower concentration span and, therefore, an observation is likely to show non-typical behaviour. This is not the best situation in which to carry out a straightforward observation. It may be, however, that observation is done deliberately at this time to look at how unknown or stressful situations affect behaviour.

- **Environmental factors such as the weather** – windy or stormy weather is known to have an effect on behaviour and make children excitable. Therefore you may get observations that are outside the norm if observing in these conditions.
- **Times of the year** – there are certain times of the year when people traditionally act out of character because they are excited, such as Christmas, and this is likely to affect observation results.

An observation needs to be a true record that is not adversely affected by anything, as this makes it easier to interpret. It also gives a fairer analysis of what is going on. Due to the nature of observations, you should not use them to prove cause and effect, as they are not controlled in the way a scientific experiment would be controlled. An observation can only provide an understanding of what is happening with a particular child at that particular time.

❚❚ PAUSE POINT   Explain clearly the advantages and disadvantages of five different research methods.

Hint   Reread this section and create a table that you can use to remember all the information.

Extend   Explain how you would apply each method to a viability study for opening a new nursery. Identify what you would need to find out and explain which method would be most effective and why.

Analysis of secondary data

Several sources can be used for secondary research, including:

- textbooks, journals and periodicals (both printed and electronic)
- the internet, particularly websites of professional bodies
- research bodies
- media sources such as newspapers and magazines
- government publications or reports, including statistics.

The topic research area will determine which type of secondary information is relevant. There is usually some secondary source material, whatever the topic. However, for more current topics, the sources are likely to be found in a professional journal or on the internet rather than in textbooks. It can take up to a year for new information to appear in textbooks.

There are also specialist research bodies, such as the Joseph Rowntree Foundation, which support a wide range of research and development projects.

Assessing the reliability of secondary sources of information is not always easy. When looking at any secondary research, think about the way in which the information has been collected. If the research methods have not been carried out thoroughly and accurately, the results will not be valid or reliable.

Secondary information can be gained from local authorities or government departments. These bodies collect a lot of data through surveys such as the national census (compiled every 10 years by the Office for National Statistics). School performance data could also be an excellent source for a research project.

Research

Find out about the most recent national census by going to the Office for National Statistics website: www.ons.gov.uk.

The following section provides information about three other organisations that may be sources of secondary data of relevance to the early years sector or early years issues.

National Child and Maternal Health Intelligence Network (CHIMAT)

CHIMAT (www.chimat.org.uk) is part of Public Health England and was set up to provide information and support to practitioners involved in the field of child and maternal health. It aims to enable the provision of health services that are cost-effective and of the highest quality, mainly by helping practitioners to improve their decision making.

CHIMAT use a lot of statistics to raise important issues. One example is Figure 4.1, which highlights the number of emergency hospital admissions due to unintentional injuries, by age group and year, from 2008 to 2013.

Discussion

Study Figure 4.1, which is from a report on the CHIMAT website that looked at reducing unintentional injuries.

1 What key finding is Figure 4.1 showing?

2 What further information might you want to see in order to draw more detailed conclusions?

3 How could you research this further?

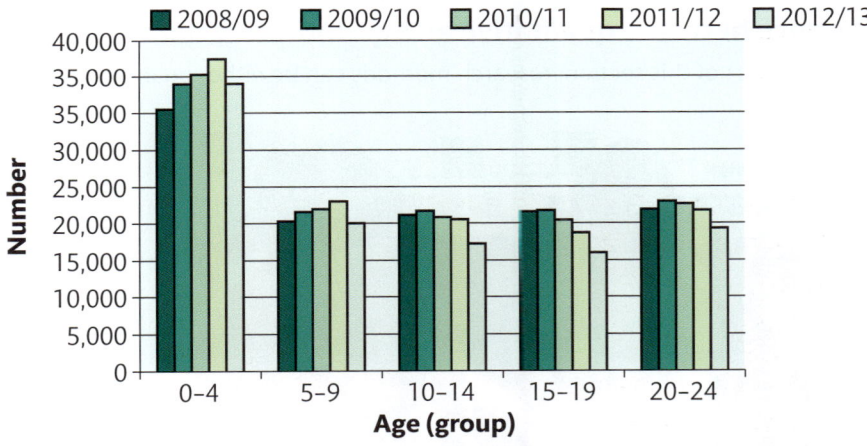

▶ **Figure 4.1:** Numbers of emergency hospital admissions for unintentional injuries by age group and year (Copyright © 2014. Re-used with the permission of the Health and Social Care Information Centre. All rights reserved)

National Society for the Prevention of Cruelty to Children (NSPCC)

The NSPCC website (www.nspcc.org.uk) has an extensive range of research reports. You can use this website to find reports of interest and practise your skills in analysing research reports.

Research

Ensuring children are safe online is extremely important in a world which increasingly uses social media. Research the NSPCC's work in this area. How do the statistics collected by the NSPCC on children's use of social networks help practitioners to ensure children remain safe?

The Children's Commissioners

The Children's Commissioners offices for England (www.childrenscommissioner.gov.uk), Scotland (www.cypcs.org.uk), Wales (www.childcomwales.org.uk) and Northern Ireland (www.niccy.org) are non-governmental organisations that work with, and on behalf of, young people, promoting and protecting their rights.

Their aim is to make life better for all children and young people, making sure their rights are respected and their views listened to – especially for more vulnerable children whose voices are least likely to be heard. Heading up each office is a named Commissioner. Depending on which country they represent, their remit is slightly different.

There are a number of publications on each Commissioner's website related to research carried out by the Children's Commissioners office, which impacts on policy and practice.

> **Research**
>
> Find the names of the current Children's Commissioners for England, Scotland, Wales and Northern Ireland.
>
> List two areas of research carried out by any of the four offices that are likely to have an impact on policy and practice in the area of early years.

The difference between qualitative and quantitative data

As we saw at the start of this section, research methods can be either quantitative or qualitative.

▶ A learner and parent are engaged in a two-way conversation. What type of research method is the learner likely to be using here – quantitative or qualitative?

Quantitative research

Quantitative research methods produce data that can be statistically analysed. They usually generate large quantities of information, and sample sizes (the number of people studied) are big. Questionnaires and surveys are generally considered quantitative research methods, as they aim to gather information from large numbers of people. To be able to handle the large amount of data, most researchers design questionnaires and surveys with questions that have a choice of specified answers.

The most effective way to make sense of the information is by presenting it in a manageable format – usually a graph, chart or diagram. This allows the reader to see patterns easily and analyse the results.

Qualitative research

Qualitative research methods, such as interviews or observations, are designed to achieve a response that has more depth. Therefore, the quality of the response is more important than the number of people who respond. These methods focus on finding out attitudes, opinions and thoughts. They allow the researcher to understand a situation in more detail.

This type of information cannot easily be analysed in a mathematical way and therefore qualitative data is not usually converted into graphs or charts. This is because a lot of the quality and meaning of responses would be lost through this process. The information is used to support arguments, and is often quoted exactly as it has been said.

Conducting effective literature searches

A **literature review** is a good place to start when you begin thinking about a research task. Carrying out a literature review means looking at material that has already been written on the topic you are researching. A literature search might include a range of sources such as textbooks, journals, newspapers, magazines and the internet.

A literature review should always come at the beginning of a piece of research, as it will give you an idea of the issues linked to your topic area, as well as an understanding of any previous research that has been carried out. It may also give you some idea of the focus of the work that has already been done and the primary research methods you should be using to take it further. Being able to compare your own findings with the information from the literature review will help to inform your conclusions and recommendations.

> **Key term**
>
> **Literature review** – an assessment of existing research around a particular issue or area of study.

> **Link**
>
> For more detailed information on ways to search for appropriate literature, see Section C1.

Identifying, analysing and evaluating source material

When you are reviewing a piece of research, as well as thinking about the primary research methods used and how effectively they have been carried out, it is important to think about the quality of the secondary source material. Secondary material needs to be relevant and primary research methods must be able to collect valid and reliable data. A good researcher will have reviewed their initial methods and made changes if necessary at the planning stage rather than spending a significant amount of time on something that has to be abandoned later. Careful identification and analysis at the planning stage will help ensure that a research project does meet the criteria it set out to cover and will allow a researcher to carry out the work needed to achieve the objectives.

This thought process can also act as a way of analysing whether a research project has the potential to achieve all of the objectives set out at the start of the piece of work.

You will need to review suitable secondary sources of research relevant to the piece of research you are being asked to evaluate. For most topics, a good place to start would be a library-based search. This should give you access to textbooks which may provide background reading. A journal search is also valuable as this will provide the most up-to-date research on the topic area. Journals often contain material before it makes its way into a textbook. You could also use an internet search but you will need to ensure you are using trustworthy sites.

To evaluate a piece of research further, once you have gathered additional secondary information, you could review the appropriateness of the primary research methods used and think about how effectively they meet the aims of the research. This is likely to include a review of the findings. You should also think about how the results are recorded and whether the report is presented in a manner which outlines the findings clearly.

B2 Planning research

Effective planning is key to the success of any piece of research. There are a number of key stages you need to go through, which are outlined below.

How to plan a piece of research

Rationale for the research

When planning a piece of research, it is important to be clear about the reason or rationale for the research. This will help you to focus closely on what the piece of research will cover.

Once you have identified the topic you want to research, you need to produce a research proposal. This should outline why you want to carry out the chosen research and what you hope to achieve. It is important to think carefully about the overall aim or question used and to make sure it is not one that leads to a 'yes' or 'no' answer. An example of a broad aim or rationale might be 'Does a parent's choice of toys impact on early gender stereotyping?'

Deciding on achievable objectives

Once you have identified the area of study, formulate your objectives (which must be achievable). The objectives should outline exactly how you intend to achieve your aims. Objectives will usually identify the methods you intend to use. Many researchers produce a detailed action plan to help them organise the research within the time-frames allocated to the work.

Selecting appropriate research methods

As you have seen, there are lots of different research methods but not every method will be relevant for every research project. You need to consider the most appropriate research methods for what you want to achieve. This will also depend on the time frame you have. It is important that any chosen method can elicit relevant, reliable results that will help the research move forward.

Selecting the target group and sample

The detailed planning of the research will involve identifying the target group to be used for each research method. The target group means the make-up of the group the research is going to focus on. Their characteristics need to be identified and might be defined by, for example, age, where they live or a particular service they use.

Once the target group has been chosen, there needs to be some form of subject selection, as it will not be possible to include everyone. This is called sampling. A sample is regarded as being representative of the target group.

There are different ways to choose the sample. These include random sampling, systematic sampling, stratified sampling and voluntary sampling.

> ▶ **Random sampling** – This occurs where each member of the population has an equal chance of being sampled. There is no particular selection; the sample is

Discussion

Talk to a partner about the characteristics that might be used to define a target group for a piece of research on eating habits. Can you come up with two other ways of defining them?

chosen at random. A lottery system would provide a random sample. For example, if trying to find out about after-school activities, a researcher would just select a number of learners from the school roll at random. All names would have an equal chance of being selected.

▶ **Systematic sampling** – This is where a sample has a pattern to it, for example, every tenth person would be a systematic sample. This could be the tenth person on a list or the tenth person who walks by.

▶ **Stratified sampling** – This method is where the people you are interested in are sampled according to a particular characteristic or **stratum**. For example, you could divide your group into different ages and ensure that your sample includes a mix from across the age range. The sample in each grouping needs to be large enough to ensure it is sufficiently representative of the population. For example, if surveying a school on the quality of school meals, a stratified sample would ensure that every year group is represented in proportion and that both males and females are represented in equal proportion.

▶ **Voluntary sampling** – This occurs where people volunteer at random to take part in the research sample. People self-select for the research and therefore often have a strong interest in the topic. This can lead to an unbalanced response.

> **Key term**
>
> **Stratum** – the level or class to which people are assigned according to their social status, education or income.

Deciding on realistic timescales

Part of planning any research activity involves appreciating the types of resources that are available, as this will influence the timescales. Many research projects have a time and resource limit. So the focus of the work has to be realistic and achievable within the available time, budget and capacity of the research team.

Many research projects fail because they are not managed effectively in terms of time. It is a common mistake to underestimate how long it takes to carry out research. Poor time management will lead to research that is badly executed. This in turn will weaken the research and may affect the end result.

A good plan sets out what needs to be done and when. It is important that there is some flexibility in the plan, however, as research does not always go to plan and changes may need to be made, either to the methods being used or the time-frame.

Deciding how research will be monitored and modified

As with any plan, it is essential that a research plan is monitored and reviewed regularly to assess progress through the project, and modified as needed.

It is important to establish right at the beginning a process for tracking progress against the aims of the research. Findings from a piece of primary or secondary research may lead you to want to explore something that you had not originally planned to at the start of the piece of work. You need to be flexible enough to change your plan as you go along, to ensure you produce the most effective piece of work.

Deciding on measures for success

Success of a research project will be based on how well the objectives are achieved. To do this, you will need to evaluate the success of your work. Evaluation is an important part of the research process. To evaluate a piece of work, you need to show an understanding of the factors that have affected the project. An effective way to evaluate is to think about each section of the research project and comment on any issues that could have affected the validity and reliability of the findings, including bias or errors.

Considering ethical issues while carrying out research

Before undertaking any primary research such as questioning, experiments or observations, you should consider the ethics of conducting the research. This includes taking into account the code of ethics that must be followed, including any issues around confidentiality. The next section of the unit covers ethics in more detail.

❚❚ PAUSE POINT   Can you make a list of characteristics that define a successful research project?

Hint   Think about all stages of a research project from identifying the project title to the evaluation at the end.

Extend   How would you use your list of characteristics to monitor the likely success of your own research project? What further actions might you take to ensure a project would have an effective outcome?

Assessment practice 4.2   `A01`

Choose one of the following scenarios.
- A nursery manager asks you to research what parents look for when choosing a nursery.
- A reception class teacher asks you to research children's play patterns at breaktime.
- A playgroup leader asks you to evaluate the success of a new piece of outdoor equipment.

1 What do you need to consider when planning your research?

2 What secondary research would you want to explore?

3 What primary research methods would you use and why?

4 Evaluate the strengths and weaknesses of your choices.

Plan
- Have I thought about the range of research methods available and decided how I can use them in relation to my chosen topic?
- Have I identified which method will provide the most effective data in the time I have available?

Do
- Have I produced any research tools I need?
- How will I ensure I carry out my research in a timely manner?

Review
- Have I reflected on my choices and how effective they were?
- Did I really understand the different research methods and how did this help or hinder me in responding to the activity?

B3 Ethical issues

Ethical principles in research reporting

Research usually involves gathering information from different people – often this information is personal, relating to an individual's decisions or thoughts. It is important that you consider the rights of the person involved in the research. This means ensuring confidentiality, so that your research subjects remain anonymous while still allowing you to represent them and their opinions accurately. This is an important consideration, as people have a right to privacy.

Ethics is all about human behaviour – it looks at whether the way something is carried out is right or wrong. It includes considering whether behaviour is morally right and the way actions affect others. Ethical issues are all the things you need to consider when conducting research with human participants to ensure their health, safety and welfare. When talking about ethics, we may also think about **attitudes**, beliefs and **values**.

Ethics is an abstract concept and understanding exactly what it is can be difficult, as it is based on attitudes, values and beliefs that are hypothetical – that is, based on ideas or thoughts. Ethics are used as guidelines when making decisions. In some situations, ethical considerations are the basis of a code of practice, which individuals in a society

Key terms

Attitudes – views or opinions about an issue or topic; these views may be positive or negative.

Ethics – the values and principles that govern the way a society operates.

Values – principles or personal rules or standards that allow people to make decisions and choose between alternatives; what a person considers to be important in life.

or group should adhere to. For example, many doctors take the Hippocratic Oath, swearing to practise medicine honestly.

Every individual has a set of ethics that define what they believe is right and wrong. These may differ from person to person. Ethics are based on the values of individuals and they will influence behaviours and attitudes as well as conscience.

The beliefs held by an individual are based on the knowledge and information they have about the world around them. They are often personal opinions based on what that individual believes to be true.

Values influence behaviour, and guide people into choosing appropriate behaviour in different circumstances. Values can also encapsulate the beliefs and accepted standards of behaviour within a social grouping.

In every aspect of research that you carry out, you will be applying ethics. Ethics also applies to the way the information that has been gathered is used. In practice this means you need to take a responsible attitude to the work being carried out and the results obtained.

Maintaining confidentiality of participants and settings

Confidentiality is an important issue. Any information that is collected through primary research methods should be confidential. Often, people involved in your research will give you personal and sensitive information about something. It is important that this information is treated with respect and only used for the stated purpose. This includes respect for people's cultural and life-choice differences. Remember that people have different opinions about what is sensitive information and what they would want repeated. Therefore, the best approach is to treat any information that is given to you in any research method as confidential. Do not repeat information to anyone in a form that can be traced back to the person who gave it. Also make sure you do not invade the privacy of those involved.

It can be very easy to forget the importance of confidentiality when chatting casually to family and friends, but you could find yourself in a difficult situation if you were overheard or if someone repeated your comments. Others will be interested in what you are doing so you should be prepared to give an overview or state your general findings but not to attribute comments to individuals.

Case study

Christa works in a family centre. She has been asked to research the impact the service is having on improving the life chances of the children who attend. To do this she needs to select participants from different social backgrounds to be able to collect data which can be compared.

Check your knowledge

1   How would Christa ensure she sets this research up ethically?

2   Write a checklist that Christa would need to follow to ensure the research is ethical.

Seeking informed consent

Anyone you ask to become involved in research has a right to know exactly what participation will involve. This means that people consenting to take part in research need to understand what the study is about, the purpose of the research and how any information they provide may be used. You might also explain how you will ensure information is kept confidential. Formal written permission may be needed before some information can be collected, especially if the research involves gaining information from children under 18 (in which case the consent of their parent or carer must be given) or researching in a particular organisation or establishment.

It is also worth remembering that participants have the right to withdraw from research at any point if they feel uncomfortable about the process. When gaining consent, you should explain to participants how they can withdraw from the research if they would like to.

The use and possible misuse of statistics and relevant codes of practice and legislation

Statistics are fascinating as they can be used both to present truths but also to assert a falsehood. Statistics can be misapplied to present information in a particular way and this can influence decisions made. Claims can be made without sufficient evidence as research findings can be manipulated.

One example of this is the controversy raised around the measles, mumps and rubella (MMR) vaccinations in the late 1990s. Andrew Wakefield, a British surgeon, produced a research paper that claimed to prove a link between the MMR vaccination and the appearance of autism in children. However, his research was only carried out on 12 children and this theory was later discredited. No other medical researchers could replicate the findings. The impact of this claim was that thousands of parents decided not to have their children vaccinated. This put them at greater risk from the illnesses the vaccine would have protected them against.

> **Research**
>
> Find out about Andrew Wakefield and the MMR vaccination research. Think about the implications for parents and children as a result of the way the research was presented to the public.
>
> What was the effect on the number of reported cases of measles in the years immediately following the Wakefield report?

Codes of practice

There are codes of practice relating to the provision of official statistics which aim to promote the correct use of statistics. The Code of Practice for Official Statistics applies to all UK bodies that produce official statistics. It sets out principles and practices that aim to ensure that statistics produced are trustworthy, high quality and of value to the public. The code also encourages bodies producing statistics to maintain their independence so reducing the possibility of bias. In addition, they promote the importance of continually improving the quality of statistics which are produced to support decision making.

Any organisation or body producing national statistics is legally required to follow this code. The full code can be found at www.statisticsauthority.gov.uk. There is a shortcut to the document on their home page.

Other bodies that carry out research, but are not producing official statistics, such as universities, often have their own codes of practice which researchers affiliated to them are expected to follow. For many bodies, the quality of their research and its validity impacts on their reputation so they have very clear rules about what is expected and how misconduct might be dealt with. When reviewing research, it is worth reflecting on the source of the data and the codes of practice the researcher would have had to follow – if any. This may influence your view about the quality of the data and its validity and reliability.

The UK Research Integrity Office also have a Code of Practice for Research. They provide a very clear checklist for researchers which enables a researcher to reflect on their research plan to ensure it meets good practice. This can be found at http://ukrio. org. This checklist could also be adapted to be used to evaluate the quality of a piece of research carried out by someone else.

However, there is no legal requirement to follow a code of practice. Therefore, when analysing someone else's research, you cannot assume it has been carried out following a code of practice. The methods and outcomes of that research, as well as their ethics, need to be reviewed to satisfy yourself that the research is valid and reliable.

Research conduct

When carrying out any research, your conduct must be completely fair and ethical. Research misconduct may occur when a piece of research is not carried out correctly. It can cover a number of issues including:

▶ fabrication or making up research findings

▶ plagiarism – where a researcher copies another person's work and passes it off as their own

▶ misreporting of research findings to present a particular picture.

You need to ensure that you always carry out your research accurately and report it with integrity.

Professional distance

The term 'professional distance' refers to the manner in which research is carried out. It is important that you maintain an appropriate relationship with your subjects and ensure it is professional at all times. These professional boundaries are important as they define the parameters in which you work and ensure that the research results are unbiased and reliable.

Protection of data – general principles

Any data collected during the course of research must remain confidential between you and the participant. You must ensure you do not reveal any responses to others – intentionally or unintentionally. This means that all information, whether paper-based or electronic, must be stored securely and safely, and cannot be linked to any individual.

When carrying out research projects that involve collecting and processing information about individuals, you need to be aware of your legal responsibilities under the Data Protection Act 1998 and the Freedom of Information Act 2000 as well as the Human Rights Act 1998.

Data Protection Act 1998

The Data Protection Act is a complex legal act that must be complied with by anyone who holds information about individuals. Any data held that can be linked to an individual comes under this act. It is essential that any personal information collected as part of your research is not shared with others or used in a way that identifies the source. Information should only be kept when there is a clear purpose for doing so.

Any data collected must only be used for the purpose stated when collecting the data. You must also ensure you avoid any invasion of privacy. Therefore, when carrying out research it is wise to depersonalise the information as much as possible so that the source of the data cannot be identified. It is also important that you destroy any source materials as soon as you have finished using them in order to maintain confidentiality.

Freedom of Information Act 2000

The Freedom of Information Act 2000 gives individuals the right to access information that is held by public bodies, often for a fee. This could be personal information or general data about a range of issues. There are some restrictions on the information that can be released.

Human Rights Act 1998 Article 8 and Section 6

The Human Rights Act 1998 is a UK law which was passed in 1998. The act mainly applies to adults but it impacts on children as well. The act identifies fundamental key rights that everyone should be able to enjoy. The Human Rights Act 1998 might influence how research is carried out.

Article 8 is one element which might have an impact when carrying out research. It focuses on the right to a private and family life. It is linked to other rights such as the freedom of expression. This article also includes the requirement of respect for private and confidential information, particularly the storing and sharing of information, which can impact on carrying out research.

Section 6 of the Human Rights Act 1998 relates to requirements on public authorities to act in accordance with the convention. Therefore any research carried out by a public authority must comply with the Human Rights Act.

Common law duty of confidentiality in English law

In England, a common law duty of confidentiality can be applied to the relationship between researcher and their research subject. It is based on an actual or assumed agreement to keep information confidential. However, it is recognised that this will not apply in certain circumstances, including:

▶ where there is a legal requirement to disclose the information, e.g. in child protection cases or in order to notify certain diseases to the public health authorities

▶ where there is a duty to the public, such as in the case of a criminal offence being committed or life-threatening circumstances

▶ where the individual agrees to the disclosure.

The common law duty of confidentiality needs to be considered alongside the requirements for confidentiality of information contained within the Data Protection Act 1998.

Legislation, policies and procedures

There are no **statute laws** covering research on humans in the UK. Therefore the law relies heavily on people giving consent to research and researchers who will carry out their research ethically. Although there are no laws specifically governing the use of ethics in research, if a researcher were to be challenged in court, there would be questions about the ethical standards that were followed.

If you carried out research on behalf of an organisation, they would probably provide **professional indemnity**, to protect you against any action relating to negligence as a result of carrying out the research. However, the organisation would expect you to follow their policies and procedures on conducting research.

When carrying out research, it is important to remember that it should only be used for the purpose for which it was initiated. If you try to apply research findings to areas outside its initial purpose, the data can be misinterpreted.

Key terms

Professional indemnity – insurance which protects professionals from being sued for mistakes.

Statute laws – written laws which are usually enacted as legislation.

 PAUSE POINT   Can you summarise how ethics impacts the research process?

Hint   Think about all aspects of the research process – planning, carrying out individual methods, including recording of data and writing up of the results.

Extend   Consider how effective planning might ensure any research is approached ethically.

Children's rights – general principles

In recent years, the importance of children's rights has been promoted. It is now recognised that the views of children should be listened to and acted on. This could influence how children are involved in research. There is a lot of debate around children's rights when it comes to being involved in research. Some people believe that children should not be part of a research activity, as they believe children cannot give informed consent. Others believe that children can be involved in research provided they are not hurt in any way as a result.

You must consider the rights of the child and all related ethical issues when using children in research. Here are four specific charters and guidelines covering children's rights that you should be familiar with.

The United Nations Convention on the Rights of the Child (UNCRC)

In 1989, governments across the world promised all children the same rights by adopting the United Nations Convention on the Rights of the Child. This convention changed the way children were viewed. They were subsequently seen as individual human beings with a distinct set of rights, and not simply objects of care and charity.

The rights apply to every child across the world regardless of where they come from or their background. They describe what a child needs to survive, grow and achieve their potential in the world. The convention has 54 articles, which cover all aspects of a child's life and set out the civil, political, economic, social and cultural rights that are entitlements for all children across the world.

All 54 articles are interlinked, with none being more important than any other. The convention also sets how adults need to work together to ensure children have these rights. You can download a summary of the convention from the Unicef website at www.unicef.org.uk.

NSPCC

The NSPCC has a useful factsheet titled *Research with children: ethics, safety and avoiding harm*. You can download it from the NSPCC website at www.nspcc.org.uk. It sets out guidelines on how to ensure that research involving children is carried out in an ethical way, including gaining consent and offering incentives. It also provides advice on how to respond to disclosures that may happen during research.

International Charter for Ethical Research Involving Children (ERIC)

ERIC is a project that aims to help you ensure that your research methods and approaches in working with children remain ethical. Their overriding principle is that the dignity of children should be maintained and their rights respected in all research.

The ERIC website, http://childethics.com, contains a lot of information and resources to guide you when working with children, as well as guidelines for improving how research is carried out.

National Children's Bureau Guidelines for Research with Children and Young People

The National Children's Bureau (NCB) is a charity that focuses on improving the lives of children and young people. Their work involves influencing government policy and giving children and young people the opportunity to be heard. The NCB believes that the most effective way to develop policies and practices that are relevant for children and young people is to involve them in the research that shapes this. They recognise that children and young people are experts about their own lives and are able to provide a valuable contribution to research related to this.

Download their Guidelines for Research with Children and Young People from www.nfer.ac.uk.

Discussion

Download the NSPCC factsheet and work with a partner to create a list of key practices that ensure an ethical approach to carrying out research with children. Discuss how you would incorporate each practice in your own research with children.

Assessment practice 4.3

Using the internet, carry out some secondary research into studies that took place at the Walter E. Fernald School in Waltham, Massachusetts during the late 1940s and early 1950s. This was a residential school for children with learning difficulties.

In one study, 17 learners, who were part of the school's science club, were asked to take part in a nutrition and metabolism study. They had radioactive iron added to their breakfast cereal.

Parents were asked for their permission to take part in the study but the available evidence suggests the full detail of the experiment – the addition of the radioactive iron – was not disclosed.

1 What ethical issues does this study highlight?

2 Could these processes be adapted in a way that would have ensured the research was carried out in an ethical manner? If yes – how? If no – why not?

Plan
- Do I understand the relevant ethical issues?
- Do I understand the study enough to be able to evaluate how the ethical issues impact on it?

Do
- Have I researched the study in more detail?
- Can I explain the ethical issues?

Review
- How effective was my research on the experiments?
- Did I fully understand the ethical issues and how did I demonstrate this?

B4 Research skills

Time management

It is important that you plan the time you have to carry out a good research project. It is easy to underestimate how long research can take, particularly primary research, where you may be relying on others to return questionnaires or you may need to carry out observations over a period of time. In addition to carrying out the research, remember that it takes time to record and analyse the results.

You can design an action plan however you like, but it is important that the plan works for you. An effective plan has a number of elements. An outline for an action plan is given in Figure 4.2.

Timeframe for the research (from start to finish)	What is my overall aim?	What do I need to do?	What materials do I need?	Have I achieved my aim?	If not, what do I need to do?
12th February–12th March	To find out how the nursery could make cooked lunch more attractive.	Plan a questionnaire to find out why parents choose a particular type of lunch for their children.	Questionnaire		

▶ **Figure 4.2:** An example of an action plan

Good time management is essential if you are going to carry out a valid research project effectively. Therefore, it is important that every research project is well planned and that you stick to that plan in order to meet the deadlines set.

Research projects often have long deadlines and it is a mistake to concentrate on work that is due in earlier to the detriment of the longer-term elements of the project.

Tips for effective time management are as follows.

▶ Start the project straight away.

▶ Develop a realistic plan, with timings, and stick to it.

▶ Work on the project at regular intervals.

▶ Monitor your progress at regular intervals; if you fall behind, allocate some additional time to the work to catch up.

▶ Talk to your tutor regularly about the research project's progress – they will help you to remain on schedule.

Organisational skills

Good organisational skills are essential if you want to produce a good piece of work within a given time-frame. A research project normally takes place over a longer period of time and consists of several pieces of work, so you need to be well organised to do this effectively.

In addition, the project will produce a lot of data and you will need to do written work. Therefore, you should have an effective way to organise your notes and research findings so that you can access them easily when you need to write up the results.

It is advisable to write up the work as you go along and not leave it until you have carried out all of your research. You may find that this written work takes longer than you think. You need to manage your time very effectively and ensure that you keep to your plan.

Non-judgemental practice

When carrying out research, you must keep an open mind and avoid making judgements about the people involved in your research, particularly if they express ideas that are different from your own. This is not always easy, as you may communicate your thoughts through your body language and facial expressions, or through the tone of your voice and the language you use. Therefore, you need to work to ensure that you appear non-judgemental in every way. Also remember to keep a professional distance from the people you are speaking to, and do not get emotionally involved in what they are discussing.

In addition, as a researcher, you must make sure you do not introduce bias by influencing participants through the way you ask questions or reply to responses given. It is likely that participants will have different views and ideas from your own so you must appear neutral and non-judgemental if you are to gain open responses and valid information from participants.

Finally, you must make sure your research is objective: try to report the facts you find out without letting your own opinions influence how you interpret the information.

Showing connections between sources of information

Researchers need to be able to show connections between sources of information and by doing so increase the validity of their conclusions. This is covered later in Section B4 on triangulation.

Methods of analysis and drawing conclusions

When you carry out your research project, you will be implementing each of the primary and secondary research methods you have chosen to use and, from this, generating your research findings. There is a variety of methods by which you can analyse data. When a large amount of data has been collected, as well as displaying this in a table or diagram, you can work out key numerical values that summarise the information. These include the statistical averages of mean, mode or median, and measures of spread, such as range. Analysis of results is covered in more detail in Section B4.

You need to make sure you carry out each research method systematically and thoroughly to get the best results you can. Good results are important so that you can draw valid conclusions. Make sure any conclusion you draw can be backed up by evidence from your research.

To draw conclusions, you should look for patterns or facts in the data you have found. You might look for similarities or differences between different results. You may draw conclusions from one piece of research that you are able to support with findings from another. Sometimes research may show that there is no connection or obvious conclusion to be drawn.

When drawing conclusions, a researcher will generally summarise what they think has been learned from the research and they will attempt to assess how strong the original **hypothesis** was. Even where the hypothesis was not proven, an effective conclusion will be able to analyse why the results obtained were not predicted. In some research situations, there may not have been an original hypothesis. In these cases, part of the conclusion will be to analyse the findings and highlight if any new information has been identified.

Conclusions may also highlight any factors that might have influenced the results achieved – causal effects, for example. When drawing conclusions, it is important to be aware of any errors in the research which may have impacted on the outcome and therefore influence the conclusion. A conclusion might also include a recommendation based on the findings of the research.

It is worth remembering that research findings may not provide clear results and can often raise more questions rather than drawing a final conclusion. When this is an outcome, it can provide opportunities and direction for further research.

Recognising potential sources of bias or error

Bias or error can happen throughout the research process. It can occur with poor planning or initial research, or through an inappropriate selection of research methods. In addition, the operation of the research methods can lead to bias or error, for example, if the sample chosen is not fit for purpose.

Given that statistics are collected for a specific reason, it is important to be aware that any data that has been collected will have been collected with a specific focus in mind. This can mean that there is an underlying slant on something which may not be obvious. This is bias. Researchers can hold particular views which may unintentionally influence the way they approach research and affect the results obtained. This can particularly be the case when the researcher is directly involved in collecting data such as in interviews.

Bias may come across in the researcher's questions, tone of voice or body language. It is important that researchers do not display their views to the participants when carrying out research as this may influence their responses. They may not answer honestly or fully if they feel the researcher might disapprove of their answers.

> **Key terms**
>
> **Hypothesis** – an unproven idea or assumption that can be tested by research.
>
> **Bias** – a tendency to allow factors, such as prejudice or discrimination for or against individuals or groups of people, to influence research and how this is carried out. This could also affect the validity of the results obtained.

For example, a researcher might feel mothers should stay at home with their children and not work. However, they might be carrying out research on the impact of working mothers on a child's development. They will need to be careful not to portray their personal views in the questions they ask or any responses the mother might give, otherwise the data gathered may not be as useful as it could be. The researcher needs to ensure they do not demonstrate bias in their approach.

Researchers can also manipulate results to reflect their own particular bias. Therefore, when reviewing any research it is important you understand the original purpose of the research and review whether the activity undertaken was structured in a way that prevents bias or error. Statistics and results need to be interpreted with care and it is often useful to use data from other sources to support any findings.

Distinguishing between fact and opinion, and identifying bias

A fact is something that is based on evidence and rational thought. It is often proven and therefore undisputed.

An opinion, on the other hand, is based on a belief or someone's personal view. Opinions can vary according to the person's knowledge, experience, culture or beliefs. Opinions are open to discussion and disagreement. Often, opinions are reinforced by emotions.

When reviewing research, it is important to keep these two differences in mind and review the results in terms of whether they are factually based or based on the researcher's own opinion. Findings based on opinions can be biased and more care may need to be taken when interpreting these.

> **Key term**
>
> **Bias** – a tendency to allow factors, such as prejudice or discrimination for or against individuals or groups of people, to influence research and how this is carried out. This could also affect the validity of the results obtained.

> **Reflect**
>
> Reflect on bias. What issues might you be biased about and how does this influence your thinking?
>
> Apply this to a research situation. How would you prevent bias in your own research?

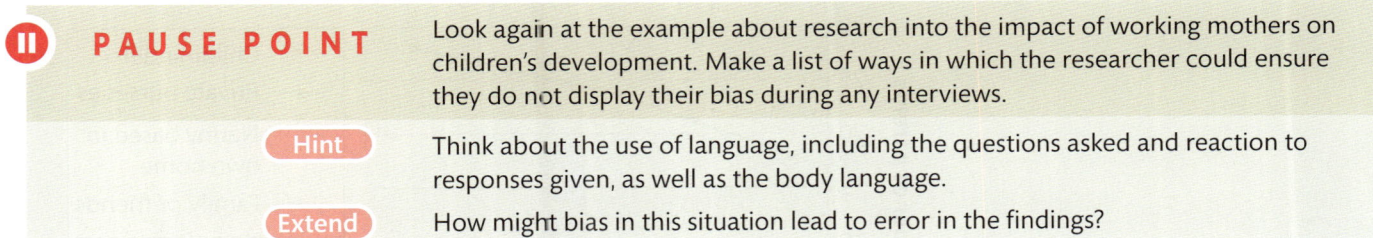

❙❙ PAUSE POINT   Look again at the example about research into the impact of working mothers on children's development. Make a list of ways in which the researcher could ensure they do not display their bias during any interviews.

Hint   Think about the use of language, including the questions asked and reaction to responses given, as well as the body language.

Extend   How might bias in this situation lead to error in the findings?

Interpreting graphs and tables produced by others

Research findings are often presented in clear and concise formats, such as tables or diagrams, which makes the information easier to read and more accessible. Understanding how graphs and charts are produced will enable you to understand the findings of any research.

Quantitative research methods generally produce a large amount of numerical data that is usually best presented using statistical diagrams.

Tables

Tables present information in a clear format, particularly where comparisons are being made. For example, if a researcher wanted to study information over a number of years and look for changes and trends, they might use a table. A table can include a lot of information in a small area. Clearly labelled tables enable the reader to understand what is being depicted.

The information in Table 4.3 shows the results of a fictional study of the number of parents using different forms of full-time childcare on a particular housing estate over a period of time. The years are shown across the top and the types of childcare down the side.

You can draw conclusions from this table about which types of care are growing and which are declining.

▶ **Table 4.3:** Forms of full-time childcare used by parents on one housing estate

Type of childcare	2011	2012	2013	2014	2015
Childminding	20	22	24	25	25
Private nurseries	18	21	24	26	28
Nanny based in own home	10	10	8	7	7
Family or friends	6	6	6	5	5

You might look at these results and decide to analyse in further depth whether there is any difference in the ages of the children who attend the different types of care, or why there is a decrease in the use of nannies compared to an increase in use of childminders and private nurseries, for example.

Statistical diagrams (or graphs)

Most research projects will present information in a pictorial format. Statistical diagrams, often generally referred to as 'graphs', are usually in the form of a line graph, bar chart, histogram, pie chart, pictogram or scatter graph.

Line graphs have horizontal and vertical axes, which are given a label. Points are then plotted on the grid. Line graphs are particularly useful in seeing trends over time. They are easy to interpret as they clearly show increases or declines but also are an effective way to compare trends. Figure 4.3 is a line graph illustrating Table 4.3.

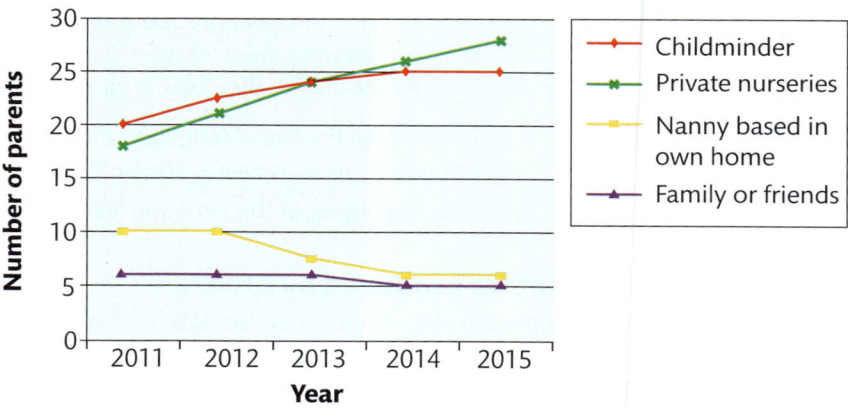

▶ **Figure 4.3:** Example of a line graph showing forms of full-time childcare used by parents on one housing estate

Discussion

Looking at the line graph in Figure 4.3, discuss with a partner what the main trends in use of childcare provision on this housing estate have been during the period 2011–2015.

As **bar charts** are easy to draw and understand, they are the most common type of statistical diagram. Bar charts show information in either vertical or horizontal bars and are particularly useful for presenting data that fits descriptive categories.

Bar charts have a number of common features.

▶ All bars are the same width.

▶ Bars may be horizontal or vertical.

▶ The bars can be drawn next to each other or with a space between each one.

▶ The height (or length) of the bar indicates the frequency (the number of items in a category).

▸ The other axis shows the descriptive categories – these describe the type of data being measured.

▸ Bar charts are often coloured to improve the presentation.

Codes may be used to label the bars, as long as a clear key or legend is included to the side of the diagram to explain what they mean. This may be useful if the labels are very long. For example, a researcher might be measuring how often a setting carries out child-initiated activities compared to adult-initiated activities, in which case they may choose to label the axis using the labels 'C-I' and 'A-I' to save space.

Figure 4.4 is a bar chart of data taken from Table 4.3 showing the types of childcare used in 2011.

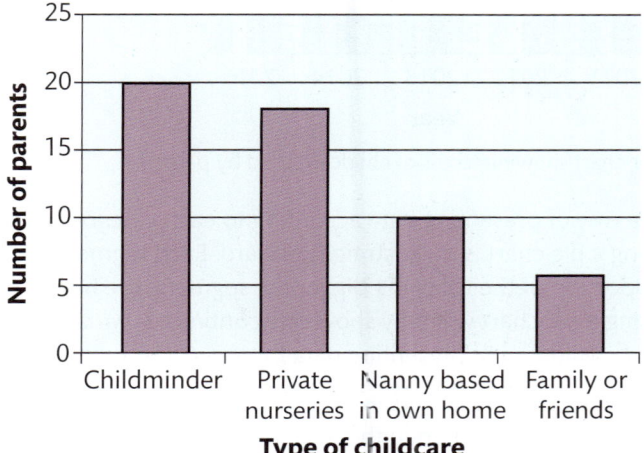

▸ **Figure 4.4:** Example of a bar chart showing types of childcare used by parents on one housing estate

Compound bar charts are particularly useful for comparing sets of data. These graphs provide a quick visual summary of the data being presented. Bar charts enable a researcher to demonstrate comparisons such as changes over time. Bar charts should enable you to see the patterns in the data which should illustrate the findings of the research. Figure 4.5 is a compound bar chart to illustrate the data in Table 4.3.

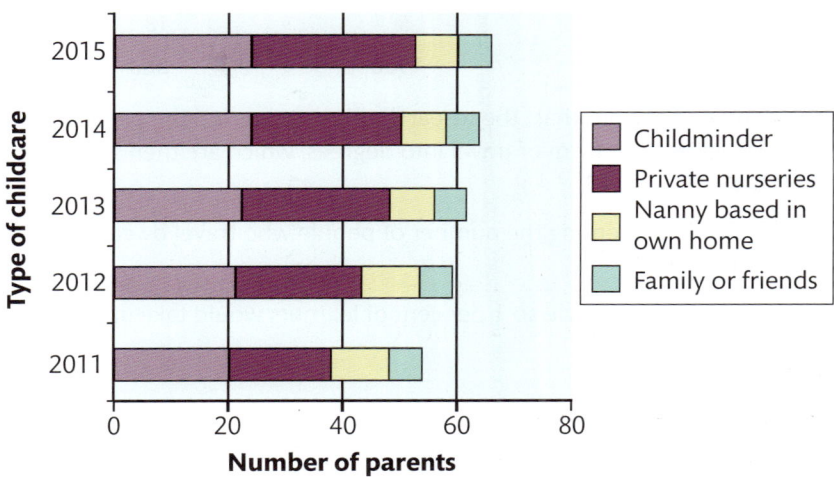

▸ **Figure 4.5:** Example of a compound bar chart showing forms of childcare used by parents

The data can also be illustrated in individual bars, as shown in Figure 4.6.

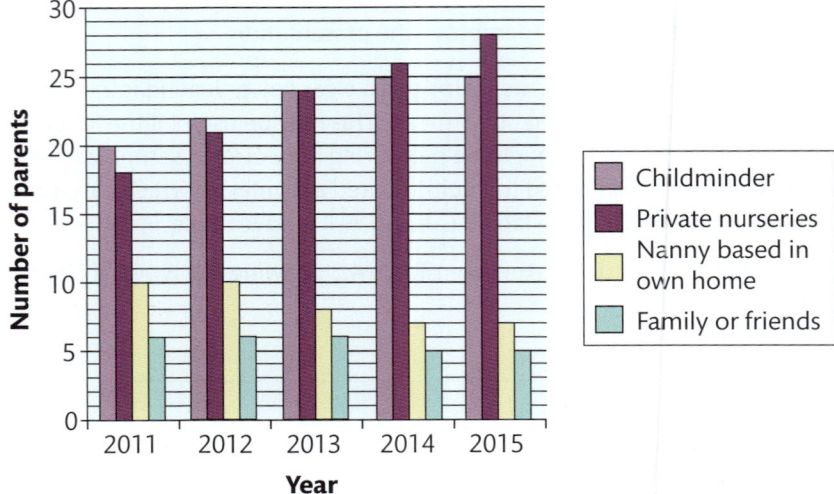

▶ **Figure 4.6:** Bar chart showing forms of childcare used by parents

Pie charts are a way of presenting data according to each category's share of the total. Interpreting a pie chart is quite straightforward. Each segment of the chart will represent a proportion of the total; the bigger the segment, the higher the proportion of the total. A single pie chart will only show one continuous variable and, therefore, they are a less versatile way of presenting data than x–y graphs or tables.

Table 4.4 shows data on how learners in three classes travel to their placements. Figure 4.7 shows the same data presented in the form of a pie chart.

▶ **Table 4.4:** How learners travel to their placements

Form of travel	Number of people	Percentage	Degrees
Bus	15	25	90
Train	3	5	18
Walk	9	15	54
Car	24	40	144
Bike	6	10	36
Moped	3	5	18
Total	**60**	**100**	**360**

In order to construct the pie chart the researcher has converted the percentages of people who travel by each form of travel into degrees, which are then shown as 'slices' of the pie chart.

The slice of the pie representing the number of people who travel by car has been worked out as follows.

There are 360 degrees in a circle so 1 per cent of learners would take up 3.6 degrees of the circle:

$$\frac{360}{100} = 3.6 \text{ degrees}$$

To work out the degrees required for learners travelling by car, you simply multiply the answer by 40, as follows.

$$40 \times 3.6 = 144 \text{ degrees}$$

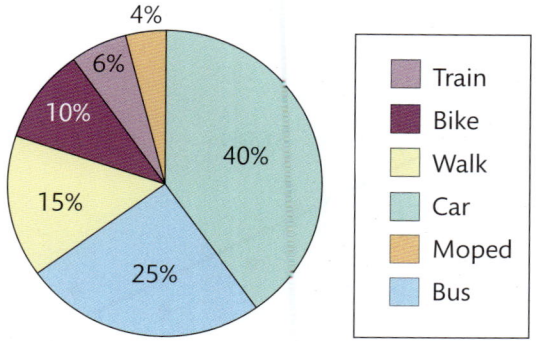

▶ **Figure 4.7:** Example of a pie chart showing how earners travel to their placements

When creating a pie chart, researchers need to make sure that they:

▶ label each sector with the percentage it represents

▶ provide a clear key or legend so the reader knows what each sector represents

▶ give the pie chart a title.

Scatter graphs are generally used where data showing two corresponding variables needs to be presented in order to see whether there is a pattern or **correlation**, such as the relationship between blood pressure and age in a group of people.

Scatter graphs may show a positive correlation, where if one variable increases, so does the other – or a negative correlation, where if one variable increases, the other decreases. Or there may be no significant correlation.

A pattern or correlation does not always indicate that changes in one variable cause the changes in the other variable, i.e. it does not always indicate cause and effect.

When the data has been plotted on a scatter graph, researchers find is useful to draw a 'line of best fit'. This is where the main clustering of the data occurs. This line can be used as the starting point for a hypothesis to link the two variables and make predictions of one value given the value of the other.

A scatter graph could be used, for example, to look for a correlation between children's reading ability and how often they are read to at home.

Figures 4.8, 4.9 and 4.10 show scatter graphs with positive, negative and no correlation, together with a line of best fit, as appropriate.

Key term

Correlation – a relationship or connection between two things.

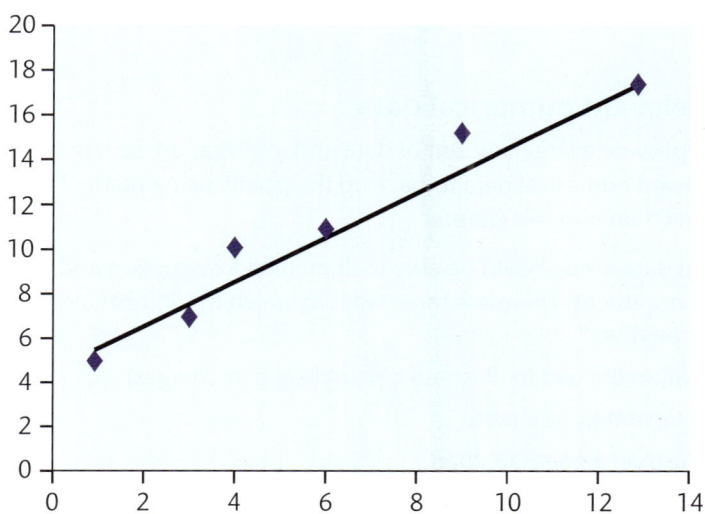

▶ **Figure 4.8:** Scatter graph with positive correlation

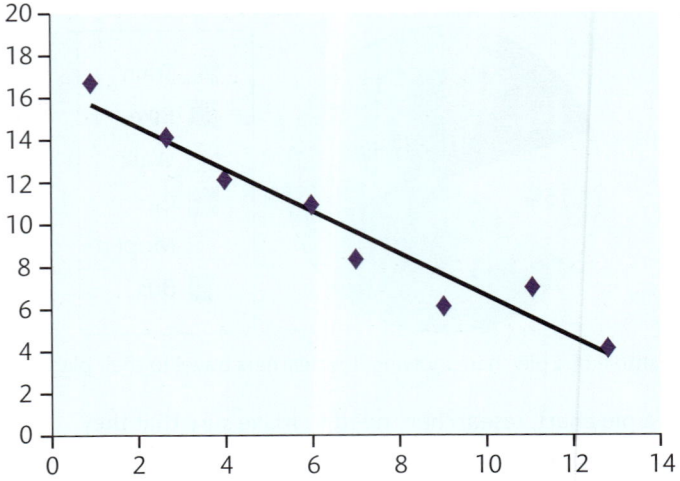

▶ **Figure 4.9:** Scatter graph with negative correlation

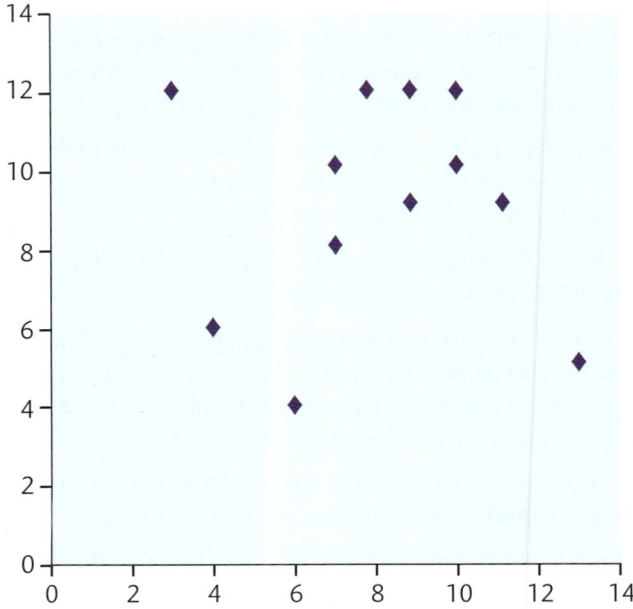

▶ **Figure 4.10:** Scatter graph with no correlation

Selecting relevant numerical data

Research can provide a large amount of data and information, so it is important to select the relevant numerical data to back up the points being made. This is covered also in Section C1 later in this chapter.

Any numerical data used should be able to illuminate a discussion and be used to support an argument. There are three ways in which this information might be presented. It could be:

▶ included within the text to illustrate a point (e.g. percentages)

▶ presented separately as a table

▶ used to construct a graph or chart.

The most appropriate method will be determined by the amount of data being dealt with and complexity of the information. The data needs to be presented in a form which is clear to the reader and enables them to interpret it easily. Poorly or inappropriately presented data will leave a reader struggling to work out what the data is telling them. Any graph or chart should be accompanied by text which explains what the graph shows. There should not be a need to explain the graph – if this is the case, it is not the best way to present the information.

Analysis of results

Analysis of the results is an important part of the research process. Research produces a lot of information, known as **data**. This **raw data** is then analysed and the findings presented so that you can draw conclusions from the results.

Raw data may be condensed or may not be presented as part of the finished project, but it must be retained for a period of time after the project is finished in case the findings are queried. Sometimes it is presented in an appendix.

Methods of analysis for data collected

As you saw earlier in this section, there are a variety of methods by which you can analyse data. As well as displaying results in a table or diagram, you can summarise information through statistical averages, percentages, triangulation and measures of spread, such as range.

Statistics

Statistics can be generated by analysing the raw data that you have collected. They allow you to consolidate, interpret and present your findings in a concise way. Presenting information in this way may allow you to make comparisons, for example, with similar information from a previous year.

For example, your research might look at how many children have a school lunch in a small primary school. If you can see a trend in the data you have collected, or the numbers of children are similar over a period of three academic years, then the school can draw conclusions about how many staff to employ to manage the demands for lunches.

Statistics need to be produced and handled with care. If your sample size is small, the statistics that can be generated from the data may not give an accurate picture of a situation overall. For example, if ten children take a test and two of them fail, it follows that eight out of ten have passed. The pass rate can be worked out as 80 per cent. However, if 100 children then sat the same test and two fail, 98 children will have passed. The pass rate will then be 98 per cent.

So, if a school reviews the results of these two tests and concentrates on the pass rates in order to inform future decisions about the design of the test, the future test might end up being different depending on how many children sat the test originally.

To get a more accurate picture, the research would need to take place over several tests, with a consistent number of candidates sitting each test. This would allow for an overall outcome from which conclusions that inform the writing of future tests can usefully be drawn and acted on.

Statistical averages

It is useful to summarise and make sense of your data by working out a representative value and also by giving a measure of the spread of the data. The representative value is called an average. There are three main types of statistical average: the mean, mode and median. To measure the spread of the data, the range is often used.

Key terms

Data – the information produced by your research methods, for example, facts, statistics, measurements or perceptions. Data has to be interpreted.

Raw data – data as it is collected, before it has been organised, analysed or interpreted in any way.

Mean

The mean is what most people refer to as 'the average'. It is the figure calculated by adding up all the values in a set and dividing the total by the number of values in the set.

For example, assume that five children got the following marks out of ten in a test: 9, 6, 4, 4, 7.

To work out the mean, add together the individual marks.

So: 9 + 6 + 4 + 4 + 7 = 30

Then, divide by the number of children:

$$\frac{30}{5} = 6$$

So the mean mark for the test is 6.

Mode

The mode is the most commonly appearing value, so the mode of the test results is 4.

The mode is a useful average when you want to know the most popular value. However, not all sets of data have a mode. Also, if there are more than two modes then the mode is not a useful average.

Median

The median is the middle value when all the values are arranged in ascending order.

The test marks in ascending order are 4, 4, 6, 7, 9. The middle value is 6, so this is the median.

Here are the marks of another group of children: 1, 6, 7, 8, 8, 10.

There are two middle numbers, 7 and 8, and the median is the mean of these, i.e.

$$\frac{7 + 8}{2} = 7.5$$

In this set, the mark of 1 is unusual.

The median is particularly useful when there are unusual or extreme values, sometimes called outliers, as the median is not unduly influenced by them.

Range

The range of a set of numbers is the difference between the highest and the lowest values, i.e. range = highest value – lowest value.

For the test marks: 4, 4, 6, 7, 9, range = 9 – 4 = 5.

For the test marks: 1, 6, 7, 8, 8, 10, range = 10 – 1 = 9.

The marks in the first set have the smaller range, so they are less variable and more consistent.

Triangulation

Triangulation is an important concept in research. It involves using at least three separate methods to collect data on a topic – for example, secondary research, an interview and an observation. The aim of this is to show that there are similarities in the findings across the three research methods, adding to the validity and reliability of the work.

Use of percentages

Percentages can be a useful way to analyse data as they allow you to show proportions of the 'overall' picture. For example, 65 per cent of children chose an ice cream and 35 per cent of children chose an ice lolly.

Key term

Triangulation – a process whereby a researcher uses at least three different sources of information in order to verify results.

Making notes and keeping records from source material

When reviewing any research, it is essential to keep well-organised notes and records of the sources you have read. This enables you to find a piece of information again quickly and easily, as well as having the correct sources to credit if referred to or quoted in a piece of written work or to list in a **bibliography**.

One way of doing this would be to have a spreadsheet where you include the details of the article or textbook together with page references and a summary of the points made/ or direct quotes. Failure to keep accessible, clear records of source materials, which are correctly referenced, could lead to plagiarism. This is where you use other people's work without acknowledgement and this could lead to work not being accepted.

Reading techniques

When reading a lot of material for a piece of work, you need to develop techniques that help you to read successfully at speed. This includes scanning and skimming texts. These techniques take time and practice to perfect. The more you practise, the quicker you will become. These techniques make you a much more flexible reader.

Skimming

Skimming is where you look only for the main idea in a piece of text. It works well with factual material and means you can read more in less time. When you skim read, your understanding is reduced because you do not read everything. You only read the information you consider important to you.

In order for skim reading to be effective, it needs to be a structured process. It is advisable to read in detail the first few paragraphs of the chapter or article you are reading to understand what it is about. This is often followed by reading the first sentence of each paragraph, which should convey the main idea of the paragraph. If the lead sentence or words in the paragraph are important to you, you can read the paragraph in full.

After this, your eyes should follow through the whole paragraph looking for words or phrases that might be of importance.

Scanning

Scanning is another useful tool to speed up your reading. With scanning you only look for a specific fact or piece of information without reading it all. To do this effectively, you need to understand the structure of the document you are reading, as well as the information you are hoping to find.

People use scanning every day, for example, when looking at the television list looking for a programme they want to watch. They know the name of the programme and will scan the listings, not reading everything until they see the title of the show they are looking for.

When scanning, you might use your finger or a ruler to help focus your attention while looking at significant amounts of information.

Conventions for presenting a bibliography and reference list

There are **conventions** to follow for writing a bibliography. Many academic journals use the Harvard system for referencing.

Here are two examples of this in practice.

Tassoni, P. (2015) *Practical EYFS Handbook*, 3rd edition, Oxford: Pearson.

Tassoni, P., *et al* (2014) *BTEC National Children's Play, Learning and Development Student Book 1*, London: Pearson.

Key terms

Bibliography – a list of all the sources you have used or referred to in your work.

Conventions – a set of agreed characteristics used in a particular situation, e.g. in writing we use full stops, capital letters, commas and sentences.

Generally, the title of the book is written in italics or bold, or underlined to make it stand out. The date is the published date of the edition you have used and this should be in written in brackets. Note the presence of commas and full stops in the reference. This punctuation should always be used.

When using a number of books, they should all be recorded in a bibliography in alphabetical order according to the author's surname.

If you refer to the books listed in the bibliography in the text of your report – for example, if you refer to the author's arguments or if you take quotes from the content – you will need to add a reference. This should be done in the main body of your report by simply writing the author's surname and the date the book was published in brackets at the end of the sentence. For example: (Tassoni 2015) or (Tassoni *et al.* 2014).

If more than one person has written a book, then the referencing is slightly different. For two or more authors, the bibliography should list all the authors. For more than two authors you can write the name of the first author followed by *et al. Et al* means 'and the others', and this form of shorthand saves you time writing all the names in the reference.

Magazine articles, journal articles and chapters in edited books are referenced in a different way as well, which is not as straightforward as books authored by one person.

> **Research**
>
> Find out the correct way to reference chapters in journal articles and magazine articles.

Producing a bibliography and reference list

When you present your research findings, you must provide a bibliography and a reference list.

Assessment practice 4.4 — AO2 AO3 AO4

1 Choose one of the research organisations listed in Section B1 (see Table 4.2) and explore their website.

2 Identify a piece of research relating to the early years sector that interests you.

3 Practise skimming and scanning the chosen article. Write a summary of the key points of the article.

4 Read the article in full.

5 What type of research methods have been used to produce data within this article?

6 How reliable are the methods used and the results they have produced?

7 What other methods would you use to explore the issue?

Plan
- Do I have all the information I need to be able to carry out this task (e.g. understanding how to skim or scan, understanding how to take notes effectively)?

Do
- Have I referenced the chosen article appropriately?
- Can I make connections between the information in the article and the research methodologies used, and can I evaluate the reliability of these methods?

Review
- Can I use my experience of this task in the final assessment task?
- Can I explain what I have learned from this task and what I would do differently next time?

C Reviewing relevant secondary research in contemporary issues affecting early years practice

C1 Selecting appropriate secondary sources

Selecting sources of reliable secondary research

There are many different sources of secondary research available, so it is important to understand what they are and which ones are reliable. Reliable sources are ones which are produced from reputable organisations. They might have a national or international reputation. Sometimes these are government-based sources but could also be from private organisations. The reliability of the sources can impact on the assessment of the validity of the research findings. An example of an unreliable source would be Wikipedia as this information can be amended by anybody and therefore is neither valid nor wholly reliable.

Sources of secondary research into the early years sector include:

▸ textbooks, professional journals and periodicals (printed and electronic)

▸ the internet, particularly websites of professional bodies related to early years

▸ research bodies and organisations (see Section B1)

▸ newspapers and magazines

▸ government publications or reports, including statistical reports.

Assessing secondary sources of information is not always easy. When looking at any secondary research, think about the way in which the information has been collected. If the research methods do not appear to have been carried out thoroughly and accurately, the results will not be valid or reliable.

Conducting electronic searches using academic search engines

Electronic searches are a good way to begin your research. An electronic search uses keywords to identify information. The number of keywords and the combination used will influence the results you get.

The internet contains a lot of information, so using keywords can help you to refine your search and reduce it to a more manageable size. You can also use the advanced search option on search engines to add more information to your search and further refine your search criteria.

Search tools and methods

You can choose from a range of general search engines, for example, Google Scholar, which has a vast database of academic titles and journal articles. The Education Endowment Foundation is also a source of relevant information – www.educationendowmentfoundation.org.uk.

One common search method is a Boolean search. A Boolean search allows you to enlarge or narrow a search by using the terms 'and', 'or' or 'not'. For example, you can search for:

▸ 'childcare AND nurseries', which will provide all records containing both

▸ 'childcare OR nurseries', which will provide all records containing both or either

▸ 'childcare NOT nurseries', which will provide all records containing childcare but not nurseries.

You can also combine the search terms for a more complex search, for example:

▶ 'childcare OR early years care AND nurseries NOT nannies'.

Considering the suitability of sources

When reviewing any secondary sources of information, you need to consider a range of issues – many of which have already been covered in this unit. Ask yourself these questions.

▶ Has the research been carried out following ethical principles? If not, how might this affect the outcome?

▶ Has participant confidentiality been maintained?

▶ Are there any conflicts of interest in the secondary sources being used? If so, what is the potential impact of that on the research? A conflict of interest might arise when a piece of research is carried out by an interested party and this may impact on the findings. For example, research on bottle feeding sponsored by a powdered milk company might be unreliable as the sponsor may have influenced the findings to suit their company's interests.

▶ Have the children and parents/carers who use early years provision been fairly represented in this research? Has the guidance on using children in research, as outlined in Section B3, been followed? If not, how will this impact on the research?

It is important you are aware of these issues to ensure you can critically evaluate any secondary sources of information you choose to review.

Selecting relevant numerical data

Researchers need to be able to select relevant numerical data to support any arguments they might be presenting. The ability to present data to support conclusions adds to the validity of the comments being made. Thought will need to go into the best way to present the information which has been gained through this process.

Examining and interpreting graphs and tables produced by others

Link

Look back at Section B4 for more details about graphs, tables and statistics.

Being able to examine and interpret graphs and tables produced by others is an important skill in analysing and evaluating research. You need to be able to look at the research and understand what the researcher is trying to highlight. You also need to be able to evaluate if the data is presented in the most appropriate way as well as analysing whether the presentation shows the information in an accurate manner.

Recognising bias in graphs, tables and statistics

As you saw in Section B4, research findings are often presented using numerical data, such as graphs or tables, and these findings can be used to produce statistics. Graphs, tables and statistics can occasionally misrepresent results and therefore the information presented may not be objective. For example, with graphs, the values on the axes can exaggerate differences, particularly if the intervals are small.

Equally, if small differences are significant, for example, if measuring chemical concentrations, small intervals on an axis may under-represent the differences.

A table might only show information which supports the argument being made, which would constitute bias as the writer would only be presenting selective information. This incomplete information is therefore presented in a way which tries to persuade the reader towards the conclusion the researcher wants. When reviewing tables of data, think about whether the table gives you the full picture with regards to the data that has been collected.

Bias in statistics can occur from both the way a sample is selected and the way in which the data is collected. The sampling method chosen can easily include bias unless the researcher is very careful in terms of the sample they have chosen. To recognise this, look at how the researcher has chosen their sample – how does the method relate to the objective of the research? For example, if a researcher is looking at parents' use of additional childcare hours on top of the government childcare vouchers, but if they only gain information from parents who do not work, the responses are likely to produce data which has a bias.

Equally, bias can be built into the way in which data is collected. For example, where a researcher is looking for a particular result, they may ask questions which reflect and lead that focus. Therefore, when reviewing questionnaires and surveys, always review the questions with reference to the focus to see if they lead a respondent towards a particular answer. For example, if a researcher was looking at road safety near a school, a question phrased 'Do you think this dangerous piece of road might be made safer with a pelican crossing?' leads the respondent to think the road is dangerous and give a certain response.

Bias can also be introduced through other issues such as the timing of when the research was carried out, the way the questions are written and the level of difficulty and also the manner in which a respondent was approached – was this by phone, post or by a researcher going door to door? Therefore, when reviewing the data, it is important to fully understand how it was collected and think about any impact this might have had. This will not mean the data is invalid but it might mean it needs to be interpreted with particular caution.

It is always important to look carefully at how data is presented and be clear about what the information is telling you. Do not take data at face value.

❚❚ PAUSE POINT

List at least five reliable sources of information when carrying out research into the early years sector.

> Hint

Remember to consider the suitability of sources.

> Extend

Carry out an internet search into safeguarding in nurseries. Review the top three results and discuss how valid or reliable the sources might be.

C2 Evaluation of research

Examining the content of secondary materials

Academic journals are an important source of research in the early years field. They usually contain the most recent thinking and research long before it can be published in a textbook. Therefore, they are an essential source of information when you are researching any topic in the field. Academic articles are usually set out in a particular way, which you need to understand. The sections are often (but not always) as follows.

▶ **Title** – The title of the project will always appear at the start of the article so that the reader is clear about what has been researched.

▶ **Contents** – A list of contents is important so the reader knows what is in the report and where to find it.

▶ **Abstract or summary** – An abstract or summary is a brief outline of what the project is about and the general approach taken to carry out the research. It is very brief, usually no longer than half a page. It is similar to the kind of overview that you might find on the back of a novel. It should tell the reader what the work is about but not all the details – those will be in the body of the report.

- **Introduction** – This briefly states the aim(s) and the research hypothesis, if this is relevant. This section includes a summary of current research findings in the field of study.

- **Body of text** – This section explains the methodology used in the study. It usually outlines and justifies the method of study chosen, stating clearly what was measured and how. It should also list any apparatus and measuring instruments used.

  There should be a brief description of the sample of participants used (indicating size, age range, location and other factors relevant to the study) and a justification of the sampling method used.

  As discussed earlier in Section B3 of this unit, ethical issues should also be covered. This section draws the reader's attention to the specific ethical issues raised by the study, for example, temporary mild deception where a participant may not be fully aware of the reason for the research, or the risk of a participant's embarrassment on performing poorly in some measure of skill.

  Finally, there is usually a description of the procedure experienced by the participant in the order in which it happened. It should include reference to the initial request for participation, a detailed description of what was done to obtain the data and reference to **debriefing**, if appropriate.

- **Results or findings** – This may include a graphical summary of results or findings (such as a table of means, or percentages), and/or appropriate chart(s), as well as an analysis of the findings in relation to the aim or hypothesis.

- **Discussion** – In this section of the report the findings will be discussed and explained in detail and evidence provided to support any conclusions drawn. The discussion section might refer the reader to the appendices, where full details of the research methods and findings should be presented.

- **Conclusion and recommendations** – The conclusion section is where the researcher draws together and sums up all the points made and produces some recommendations as a result of the findings. This usually includes a proposal for a course of action following the findings of the research.

- **Appendices** – This part of the report includes examples of materials used, raw data together with calculations, and a reference section, using the conventional form and giving references for all studies and authorities cited in the report. The appendices should include a complete list of the literature drawn on to complete the research.

Key term

Debriefing – a conversation between a researcher and participant following an experiment to inform the participant about their experience and allow them to talk about it.

Link

Look back at Section B4 on reading techniques for more details about how to skim and scan articles efficiently and effectively.

Academic reading

Reading academic texts, such as a journal, textbook or government report, is different from reading a book or newspaper for pleasure. You are trying to pick out the important points. Often you will not read an academic journal from beginning to end.

You need to find ways to read the article efficiently and effectively that enable you to survey its structure and pick out the main arguments. This is a difficult task but the more you do this, the better you will become at it. Try the reading techniques of skimming and scanning outlined in Section B4. Practising these will help you develop these skills. Also make sure that you look up and check the meaning of any technical or difficult words so that you are confident that you have fully understood the text.

Be prepared to read an article more than once, as often the contents of an academic article cannot be understood fully in one reading.

Advantages and limitations of research sources and methodologies

It is common that different research methods will have advantages and limitations. These can impact on the reliability and validity of any data collected and therefore the findings. Researchers need to be aware of this when interpreting their findings. Therefore, it is important that researchers evaluate their work.

Evaluation is an important part of the research process. To evaluate a piece of work, you need to show that you have appreciated the factors that have affected the project. As you evaluate, think about each section of the research project and comment on any issues that could have affected the validity and reliability of the findings, including bias or errors.

One way to evaluate successfully is to ask yourself a series of questions that make you reflect critically on the work you have reviewed. Try to work your way through the research process and evaluate every stage. This will ensure that you reflect thoroughly on the work you have done. Think about the following.

Secondary research

▶ Have you been able to access a suitable range of secondary research in relation to the topic?

▶ Were the sources up to date, valid and reliable? How do you know and what difference did this make to the work?

▶ How did the results for the secondary research influence your primary research?

Primary research

The following questions can be applied to most research methods as a way of evaluating the effectiveness of any primary research.

▶ Was this an effective choice of research method for the chosen topic?

▶ Was the method well planned?

▶ Was the sample used appropriate? How did this impact on the validity of the work?

▶ Did the method gain the information hoped for? If not, why not?

▶ Were the results presented appropriately?

▶ Was there any 'misuse' of the research within the project? For example, on reflection, were any of the research methods 'designed' with a particular outcome in mind? As an example, questions may have been worded specifically to elicit particular responses.

▶ Were there any errors or bias evident that might have impacted on the results?

▶ Did the researcher follow data protection and confidentiality conventions appropriately?

▶ On reflection, were there other research methods which could have been used that would have provided more effective results?

▶ If you were to continue with the research, what would you do next and why?

⏸ PAUSE POINT   Could you identify the advantages and limitations of the research methods used in a particular piece of research?

    (Hint)   Remember to reflect on both secondary and primary research methods used.

    (Extend)   Consider how any limitations identified could be effectively addressed.

Validity and reliability of results

When evaluating the results from any research, you need to assess if they are valid and reliable. These two measures are essential in assessing if research results are likely to be accurate.

Reliability can be confirmed if any significant results are more than a one-off finding and are likely to be found again if repeated. When evaluating data, you need to reflect if this is likely to be the case. You can do this by thinking about the research methods used and the sample respondents used in the research; is it likely that a similar sample could elicit similar results?

Validity is linked to whether the process that achieved the results is relevant and has been fairly carried out. Has accuracy been shown in the way in which the research was carried out? Have appropriate controls been put in place, including control groups as appropriate? Is the research method appropriate for the objective of the research?

Bias error

The possibility of bias error also needs to be evaluated. Is there any chance that the researcher could have been influenced by bias? Is there any indication of how the research process controlled potential bias error in the methods used?

Use and misuse of statistics

When assessing the validity and reliability of results, it is also important to analyse how any statistics have been used and to ensure there has not been any misuse of statistics. You might want to reflect on whether the researcher followed a code of practice as part of the research.

Ethical principles

It is also important to think about how ethics has influenced the research. Is there any possibility that the research was unethical in its implementation? How did the research ensure that ethical issues were dealt with?

Generalisability

You will also need to review if the data produced and the findings of the research are specific enough to draw firm conclusions rather than general findings. When reviewing a piece of research and its outcomes, you will need to consider if this is the case and whether there may be any causal relationships as a result of the way the work was conducted.

Link

For more information on bias error, use and misuse of statistics, ethical principles and generalisability, look back at Sections B1, B3 and B4.

Recommendations resulting from research

The results of research can lead to a range of different recommendations and can impact on work with children in many different ways. Essentially, research results enable us to have a better understanding of a child's world and help adults find ways to improve that world. They should provide an understanding of how children can be provided with the most effective care and education.

Research results can be used to:

▶ extend knowledge of different aspects of children's development and care

▶ evaluate the services provided and identify how they might be improved to meet the users' needs

▶ monitor the development of children against norms and identify ways to support their development

▶ review services provided and identify any areas where there may be gaps

▶ develop new ways of working.

A significant amount of research is commissioned by the government, and this is used to inform both policy and practice. It is through research that the quality of a child's care and education can be improved. In this way, research can have an immense influence on the life chances of children both now and in the future.

Potential areas for further development

A lot of research into early years has opportunities for further research arising from it. This might be as a direct result of the overall findings. Alternatively, it might derive from information that came out of the research methods, which might have highlighted new potential research avenues. For example, Dr Susie Formby of the National Literacy Trust carried out some research on the use of touchscreen technology in early years settings, which was published in March 2014. The conclusion was that technology is now playing a large role in the lives of children under 5 years old. It also identified that in their next survey, they would expand the questions to ask how and why early years practitioners use technology for the activities in their setting. The full report of this research can be found at www.literacytrust.org.uk.

Potential for development of working practices and provision of services

Research has always had a high potential for developing working practices and the provision of services in early years. Practitioners and policy makers recognise the importance of this stage of development and use research to inform decisions and develop practices that make the sector more effective.

There is evidence of research impacting on working practices over many years, from the development of understanding how children learn to the development of the content of the EYFS curriculum. A key example of this is the provision of free childcare for all children from 3 years old and for children from priority families from 2 years old. This is linked to research which identified the impact that structured education can have on children in terms of their early learning and subsequent achievement in school.

C3 Wider applications of research

Making recommendations for potential future areas for research

The outcomes from research can raise further questions which could become recommendations for potential future areas of research.

Suggestions for future areas of research often come out of the limitations which have been identified within the research. It is common that future research areas come from a number of different areas to address the following.

▸ To expand the original piece of work – it may be that the work was limited in terms of the sample size and therefore extending the sample would be of value to provide further validity and reliability to the results.

▸ To build on a particular finding from the research – this might be something which came out of a particular research method which was not directly related to the area of focus but is later highlighted as something which would benefit from further exploration. It could also be a finding which was not expected and therefore would be interesting to explore further.

▸ To address a particular weakness of flaw in the research – for example, a piece of research which looks at parents' views on how healthy packed lunches are might be flawed if the research only takes place with parents who provide a packed lunch.

Therefore, an area for further research might be to compare these findings with those of parents who arrange for their child to have a cooked lunch.

▶ To examine or test a theory which has arisen as a result of the research. For example, the research into the type of lunch parents provide for their children during day care might suggest that few working parents cook for their children during the working week. This could be an interesting additional piece of research.

▶ To carry out the same research in a different setting, context or with a different culture or group of people. For example, research into barriers affecting children's participation in activities at weekends, carried out with children living in a town or city, might be replicated with children living in a more rural setting. These suggestions need to be justified by their relevance to the original focus of the work. For example, if the original research was tightly focused on barriers in a town setting, there would be little value in comparing it to a village setting. Of more relevance might be to compare it to a different town setting – a different geographical area or one where there are different socio-economic groups.

▶ To address questions which remained unanswered at the end of the initial research. It is likely that the researcher identified a number of objectives at the start of the research and not all of them were achieved through the methods chosen. Therefore, future research might be the identification of additional research opportunities which might elicit answers to these incomplete objectives.

When a future area of research is proposed it should always be justified in terms of why it is a relevant area of further development.

Implications of research for early years practice and provision

Research is used in many different ways and for many different reasons. One of the main reasons is as a way of developing a better understanding of the world in which we live. As mentioned above, early years research is often commissioned by the government; it is also carried out by universities, private research companies, charities and voluntary groups. Much of the research is based on issues of political importance and interest. However, there are also a number of independent organisations who have their own funding and can carry out independent research.

Within early years, research plays an important role in moving the sector forward. Research examples include:

▶ understanding current issues
▶ developing our knowledge and understanding of current issues and practices in early years
▶ reviewing and evaluating services for children and identifying areas for development
▶ highlighting new learning theories and trialling their application
▶ reviewing the range of services available for children and identifying any gaps in provision
▶ informing and improving practices in early years
▶ informing and influencing policy
▶ monitoring developments and progress.

In addition, research is used every day by childcare practitioners to inform and support their work with the children they care for.

The range of research available is vast. It has a crucial role in developing early years practice and provision.

Assessment practice 4.5

1 Find a piece of research on an aspect of early years education.

2 Summarise the findings of this piece of research.

3 Explain how this research may influence early years practice and provision.

4 Evaluate the success of this piece of research using the questions on page 229.

5 What potential areas of future development could arise from this work and why?

Plan
- How will I find a suitable piece of research?
- How will I ensure my chosen research is valid?

Do
- Have I used techniques such as skim reading to identify the important aspects of the research?
- Have I evaluated the success of the research?

Review
- Did my choice of research allow me to cover all aspects of the task?
- Did I consider issues such as ethics, reliability and validity?

Further reading and resources

Books

Aveyard, H. (2014) *Doing a Literature Review in Health and Social Care. A Practical Guide*, 3rd edition, Berkshire: Open University Press.

Dawson, C. (2009) *Introduction to Research Methods. A Practical Guide for Anyone Undertaking a Research Project*, Oxford: How To Books Ltd.

Dunbar, G. (2005) *Evaluating Research Methods in Psychology. A Case Study Approach*, Oxford: Blackwell.

Flanagan, C. (2015) *Research Methods Companion for A Level and AS Psychology*, 2nd edition, Oxford: Oxford University Press.

Green, S. (2000) *Research Methods in Health, Social and Early Years Care*, Cheltenham: Nelson Thorne.

Roberts-Holmes, G. (2014) *Doing Your Early Years Research Project. A Step by Step Guide*, 3rd edition, London: Sage.

Websites

www.crae.org.uk – Children's Rights Alliance for England (CRAE): information about the rights of the child.

www.gov.uk/early-years-foundation-stage – **EYFS**: information about the areas of learning of the EYFS.

www.gov.uk/government/statistics – National Statistics Office: a website providing access to data collected by the National Statistics Office.

https://ico.org.uk – Information Commissioner's Office: information about the Data Protection Act, the Freedom of Information Act and the Human Rights Act.

www.naldic.org.uk – National Association for Language Development in the Curriculum: a useful forum for learning more about English as an additional language.

www.nfer.ac.uk – National Foundation for Educational Research: the NFER website contains information on educational research which aims to improve education and learning.

THINK ▶FUTURE

Janine French
Nursery
Practitioner

Janine is undertaking a course on how children learn as part of her professional development. As part of her studies, she has to research children's development.

Being able to use different research methods is vital to her role. As a key worker for five children, she has to monitor and record their progress against the early learning goals. This involves routine observations, which must be completed without influencing the outcomes. Some children are more aware of being observed than others, so she has to make sure they are fully occupied while she is observing them.

Janine often refers to secondary research to see if her observations are reflective of the norm for each child's age and stage of development. Analysing other people's findings helps her to plan activities to help the children make progress.

A new child has recently joined the nursery where Janine works. Rory has Asperger's syndrome and Janine researched the condition online before Rory started at the nursery. She made sure the information was reliable by checking the sites she had looked at were reputable and that the research methods used were valid. She then used this information to plan appropriate activities and support for Rory.

One way or another, Janine uses research methods most days in her work with children.

Focusing your skills

Early years employers will expect practitioners to demonstrate confidence in carrying out observations and other research-based skills. Whether you are hoping to go straight into work after your course, or planning to go on to higher education, you will need to be able to plan, carry out and evaluate your own and other people's research. Here are some ways to gain relevant experience.

- Choose an area of children's development that you would like to research. Visit an early years setting and observe children of different ages involved in an activity. Record carefully everything they do. (Make sure you get permission from the manager and that your records do

not include names of children.) What conclusions can you draw from your observations?

- Choose an early years topic that interests you. Carry out a literature review and summarise your findings. Ask a peer to assess your summary: do they understand what the research was about?

- Choose a stage of development (e.g. 0–3 months, 12–18 months). Research the physical development you would expect to see. Devise a checklist that you could use to assess the physical skills of children in your chosen age range.

Getting ready for assessment

Preparing for your task

Make sure you have prepared carefully for the assessment; the assessment outcomes were introduced at the start of this unit. Remember, the assessment is in two parts. For Part A, you will be given an article and you will have 18 hours over a period of 6 weeks to analyse this article and undertake your own secondary research. Part B will involve a 3-hour controlled assessment; you can take up to six pages of notes into this assessment.

Preparing for Part A

- Begin your research as soon as you are given Part A. You have up to 18 hours to complete this research (over a period of 6 weeks) and this time reflects the amount of work you will need to do.
- Read the information carefully and highlight the important areas. You may lose marks if you do not understand what you are being asked to do, or if you misinterpret the focus of the article your assessment is based on.
- Carry out your own independent research on the content of the article, using at least two secondary sources.
- Schedule your work: identify the topics you need to research and try to spend a planned amount of time on each area.
- You may take up to six pages of notes from your research into your assignment, so make the most of this. Consider typing your notes, as you will get more information onto a page compared with handwriting. If you choose to handwrite your notes, make sure your writing is legible.
- Order your notes so that you can find the information you need quickly during the controlled assessment. Number each page and divide your notes into clearly-labelled subsections.
- Note the sources you have referred to, using the Harvard referencing system so you can acknowledge them accurately in the controlled assessment if necessary.
- Alongside your research, revise the theory from the unit. You may need it during the controlled assessment. List the key areas that may be covered and make sure you have a clear timetable for your revision.
- Take regular breaks while researching or revising. Remember, most people's concentration lapses after about an hour.

Preparing for Part B

- Know the time of the controlled assessment and arrive early and prepared. Make sure you have your notes with you as well as pens, pencils and highlighter pens.
- Listen to, and read carefully, any instructions you are given. Lots of marks are lost because learners do not read questions properly.

- Most questions contain command words, so make sure you know what these words mean. Examples of command words you may find in the assessment include:
  - identify – indicate the main features or purpose of something
  - describe – give a clear, objective account of the main features or purpose of something
  - analyse – break an issue down and look at each element in depth, outlining points for and against and looking at any interrelationships.
- Before you begin writing, read the assessment at least twice. The first time, just read the question. The second time, highlight or underline the important words, or make notes on a blank page. This will help you to identify the key words and structure your answers.
- Remember, the number of marks can relate to the number of answers you are expected to give. If a question asks for two examples, do not give only one. Equally, if there are only two marks available, do not spend a long time listing every example you can think of.
- Plan your time carefully. Allow yourself enough time to answer all the questions and set yourself a rough timetable for your work. Do not spend all your time on a short 1–2 mark question and then find you have only a couple of minutes left for a 7–8 mark question later.
- Plan your answers to the longer questions. Have a clear idea of what you want to say and make sure this point comes across in everything you write.
- If you finish early, use the time to reread your answers and mark any corrections.
- Remember, you cannot lose marks for a wrong answer but you cannot gain any marks for a blank space! Try to answer every question.

Sample answers

Below is an example of the type of question you might find in the controlled assessment element, and a suggested answer.

Worked example

In this example, the set task was to read a research report issued by the National Literacy Trust about Children's Early Literacy Practices at home and in early years settings. You can access the key findings at www.literacytrust.org.uk/assets/0002/4081/EY_Key_Findings_2014.pdf. There is a link to the full report at the end of the key findings.

The report looks at children's access to books and technology as well as their reading habits. It explores the impact of these factors on their vocabulary.

You need to read the report and carry out some of your own secondary research on the topic before attempting the questions that follow.

1. What types of research methods have been used to collect data in the article?

2. How reliable are the results of the research methods?

Answers

1. The research method was a survey. The survey was conducted by an independent company, YouGov. They surveyed 1012 parents of 3–5-year-olds over a period of a month. They also surveyed 567 early years practitioners who worked with this age group over a period of 3 months. These practitioners were self-selected from a sampling process which included advertising in early years publications and social media. The survey also included a sub-sample of 183 children who took part in an assessment of their vocabulary abilities using British Picture Vocabulary Scales (BPVS).

2. The reliability would be good as the sample was random for the parents' survey and self-selecting for the practitioners. However, as this was a survey, it would be difficult to confirm the accuracy with which the participants responded. There is a possibility the parents would respond as they thought the surveyor wanted them to. There is no way to validate the information they provided.

   However, the survey is triangulated: the data provided by the parents is tested via the data provided by the early years practitioners and the results from the assessment of the children.

This response is likely to be classed as a band 2 response. It refers to the research methods in the article and shows a basic understanding of the data usage. There is limited reference to the suitability of this method of research for the research being carried out.

3. Why is research into children's literacy important in improving outcomes for children and promoting their learning and development?

4. How can this research help practitioners to apply children's vocabulary development in their own settings?

Answers

3. Research helps to highlight how social changes, such as increased access to technology, might be impacting on early learning and how this can be exploited to encourage literacy development in children. This means that if we can understand how access to books at an early age can influence literacy, and particularly vocabulary development, we can use this to help parents develop their children's skills. It is also important as it seeks to explain how development of vocabulary might be different between the genders and how technology might be used to engage boys in learning.

In addition, this research can identify best practice in early years settings and therefore develop practice.

4. This research could be used in settings to help plan activities for children, and may help practitioners to adapt the activities to meet the needs of different children. It might also inform what equipment settings choose to purchase to help learning, for example, it suggests that boys engage more using technology compared to using books. This may encourage settings to ensure they have electronic sources of text as well as traditional print books to use in literacy sessions. It also suggests that girls are more likely to be independent readers than boys, so this too might influence how settings structure this aspect of the curriculum.

These answers would also fall into band 2. They highlight the implications of the research in the sector and show how the research may be used to influence practice. More detail would be needed to move the response into the next band – for instance, how this research might provide a rationale for change within early years practice, or how parents might approach reading with their children at home.

Keeping Children Safe 5

Getting to know your unit

Assessment
You will be assessed by a series of assignments set by your tutor.

Keeping children safe from accidents and disease is an important part of your work. For parents to be able to trust you, they need to know that their babies and children are safe and that you are able to respond to emergencies that arise in your setting.

In this unit you will learn about the legislation, regulations and guidance relating to health and safety and child protection. You will also examine how early years professionals safeguard the children in their care and respond to concerns that a child is being abused.

How you will be assessed

This unit will be assessed by a series of internally assessed tasks set by your tutor. Throughout this unit, assessment activities will help you work towards your assessment. Completing these activities will not mean that you have achieved a particular grade, but you will have carried out useful research or preparation that will be relevant when it comes to your final assignment.

To achieve the tasks in your assignment, it is important to check that you have met all of the Pass grading criteria. You can do this as you work your way through the assignment. If you are hoping to gain a Merit or Distinction, also make sure that you present the information in your assignment in the style that is required by the relevant assessment criterion. For example, Merit criteria require you to analyse, assess and reflect on your own skills, and Distinction criteria require you to evaluate.

The assignment set by your tutor will consist of a number of tasks designed to meet the criteria in the table. This is likely to consist of written assignments but may also include activities such as:

▶ producing a report that examines the responsibilities of early years practitioners in relation to health and safety and safeguarding issues

▶ exploring case studies in relation to safeguarding that require analysis as well as an evaluation of actions that might be taken

▶ providing a reflective account of how you have maintained children's health and safety, prevented infections, and actions that you have taken in response to emergency situations.

Assessment criteria

This table shows what you must do in order to achieve a **Pass**, **Merit** or **Distinction** grade, and where you can find activities to help you.

Pass	Merit	Distinction
Learning aim **A** Investigate legal responsibilities and approaches to health and safety in early years settings		
A.P1 Explain responsibilities of early years professionals in keeping children healthy and safe with reference to legislation, regulations and guidance. **Assessment practice 5.1**	**A.M1** Analyse the extent to which approaches in a selected early years setting contribute to children's health and safety. **Assessment practice 5.1, 5.2**	**AB.D1** Evaluate approaches and procedures used by professionals to keep children healthy and safe in a selected early years setting. **Assessment practice 5.2, 5.3**
A.P2 Explain approaches in early years settings for promoting and maintaining children's health and safety. **Assessment practice 5.2**		
Learning aim B Explore procedures for prevention and control of infection in early years settings		
B.P3 Explain procedures used to prevent and control the spread of infection in early years settings. **Assessment practice 5.3**	**B.M2** Analyse how procedures used in a selected early years setting prevent and control the spread of infection. **Assessment practice 5.3**	
Learning aim C Examine how early years professionals safeguard children and respond to concerns that a child has been abused		
C.P4 Explain types and indicators of abuse. **Assessment practice 5.4**	**C.M3** Assess the role and responsibilities of the early years professional in safeguarding children and recognising and responding to concerns that a child is at risk of abuse. **Assessment practice 5.4**	**C.D2** Evaluate ways in which early years professionals can most effectively contribute to safeguarding and promoting the welfare of children. **Assessment practice 5.4**
C.P5 Explain responsibilities of early years professionals for safeguarding children and procedures they must follow for reporting, recording and responding to concerns that a child is at risk of abuse. **Assessment practice 5.4**		
Learning aim **D** Demonstrate how to recognise and assess hazards and risks to children and respond to emergencies in an early years setting		
D.P6 Present clear and effective risk assessments that address hazards and minimise risks to children indoors and outdoors in an early years setting. **Assessment practice 5.5**	**D.M4** Reflect on the extent to which own skills in risk assessment and responding to an accident or health emergency and emergency situation can contribute to healthy and safe outcomes for children. **Assessment practice 5.5, 5.6**	**D.D3** Evaluate own responsibilities in keeping children healthy, safe and secure relevant to legal requirements and best practice in early years settings. **Assessment practice 5.5, 5.6**
D.P7 Demonstrate skills to recognise and respond appropriately to an emergency situation in an early years setting. **Assessment practice 5.6**		

Getting started

List the ways that you can keep children safe in settings. Talk to someone with responsibility for child protection to find out what is involved in their role in safeguarding children.

A Investigate legal responsibilities and approaches to health and safety in early years settings

A1 Responsibilities to children's health and safety

Children's right to be healthy, safe and secure

Every child has a right to be healthy, safe and secure. This right is laid down in an international agreement known as the United Nations Convention on the Rights of the Child (UNCRC), which was drawn up in 1989 and came into UK law in January 1992. All countries, including the UK, that are signed up to the treaty are legally bound to implement legislation to ensure children's rights are maintained.

United Nations Convention on the Rights of the Child

The UNCRC sets out the rights and freedoms of all children in a set of 54 articles. Article 19 is about the right of children to be kept safe from harm and to be protected from all forms of abuse by those looking after them.

> **Research**
>
> Find out more about the United Nations Convention on the Rights of the Child. You can download a summary of the 54 articles from www.unicef.org.uk.

The duty of care to protect children from harm and to promote their welfare

A duty of care describes the standards of care that are expected of adults who work with children. A duty of care is a legal obligation of adults to act in a way that promotes the best interests of children, keeps them safe from harm and promotes their welfare. It also includes the obligation for an adult to do nothing that might harm a child through their actions or through their negligence.

Legislation and regulations

It is easy to think of health and safety legislation as being boring or something that is of no interest. The reality is that it underpins safe working practices in early years settings and prevents many accidents and deaths each year. Compliance is therefore essential because it has potential life-saving effects. Non-compliance, even out of ignorance, is illegal. It is considered to be an act of negligence. Prosecutions are fairly rare, but nonetheless, you have a duty of care both to yourself and the children you work with.

There are many different pieces of legislation that impact on day-to-day practice within settings. A good starting point is to look at some of the language used in health and safety and safeguarding legislation.

- **Acts** – these are written laws that Parliament has put in place.
- **Regulations** – legal requirements that have to be followed. They have their origins in **European Union Directives** and the Health and Safety Executive.
- **Statutory guidance** – the **statutory guidance** for the early years sector has special legal status and has to be taken into consideration by all providers. If an accident or incident occurs, and it is shown that statutory guidance was not followed or complied with in other ways, the person or setting would be at fault.
- **Approved Codes of Practice** – these codes of practice have similar legal status to statutory guidance.
- **Practice guidance** – this is guidance that may be followed, but it is not legally binding.

Health and safety legislation is the same in all countries across the UK but there are regulatory differences relating to early years settings. For example, there are different adult-to-child ratios across countries. It is important to be aware of the legislation that relates to the country in which you work.

Health and Safety at Work etc. Act 1974

Everyone who is in employment is covered by protection that ensures their workplace is healthy and safe. This protection is in the form of the Health and Safety at Work etc. Act 1974, which covers any workplace and places responsibilities on employers as well as employees. This piece of legislation is the reason why you may be asked to wear disposable gloves when changing nappies; by wearing them, the risk of picking up or spreading an infection is minimised.

Employers' responsibilities

Employers have to take reasonable steps to maintain the health and safety of their employees and also other people, such as learners, while they are on the premises.

Employers with more than five employees have to have a health and safety **policy** and make sure that employees are aware of it. Every employer's health and safety policy will be different, but in childcare settings it is likely that policies will have a section about the importance of eliminating cross-infection and subsequent **procedures** relating to using disposable gloves and putting waste in specific bins. In addition, the health and safety policy will probably have a section about keeping employees and children safe.

Employees' responsibilities

As an employee, you have to cooperate with your employer in relation to health and safety. Employees' responsibilities can be summed up as follows. They must:

- follow health and safety policies and procedures
- use equipment and means of protection that have been provided by the setting
- report any hazards or dangers promptly
- make sure their actions do not put others at risk.

> **Theory into practice**
>
> The Health and Safety at Work etc. Act 1974 is the reason why you are likely to have an induction period when you start work. It is also the reason why you will be instructed to keep fire exits clear, carry out **risk assessments** and report any incidents promptly.

> **Key terms**
>
> **European Union Directive** – a legislative act that countries in the European Union are required to implement in their home country.
>
> **Policy** – states the aims of the setting in relation to an aspect of early years provision.
>
> **Procedures** – detail the steps and actions that must be taken in given situations.
>
> **Risk assessment** – the process of identifying and minimising dangers and hazards.
>
> **Statutory** – required by law (statute).
>
> **Statutory guidance** – advice that settings or individuals are legally obliged to follow or pay regard to.

The Management of Health and Safety at Work Regulations 1999

These regulations require employers to carry out risk assessments on activities and equipment that might pose a serious risk to individuals' health or safety. These regulations require settings to:

▶ make a particular staff member responsible for health and safety

▶ carry out risk assessments on work activities and equipment, and take measures to minimise the risks

▶ have emergency procedures in place and ensure that employees know about them, e.g. by carrying out regular fire practices

▶ provide adequate information, supervision and training for employees

▶ carry out specific risk assessments to protect the health and safety of expectant mothers.

The Workplace (Health, Safety and Welfare) Regulations 1992

These regulations look at the physical conditions provided for employees. They include the number of rest breaks they are entitled to, the level of lighting that is required in the setting, toilet arrangements and the provision of water.

The Manual Handling Operations Regulations 1992 (as amended)

These regulations are designed to protect employees if they have to lift or handle objects or people. Employees have to carry out risk assessments for these activities. Wherever possible, employers should provide equipment that would avoid an employee doing any lifting, but if this is not possible, they should develop policies and procedures in order to make the activity safe.

▶ It is important to follow health and safety guidance when picking up babies and toddlers

In early years settings, this may result in staff going on training courses, or being given clear instructions about what they should, and should not, do in terms of lifting children or equipment.

 **PAUSE POINT** Why are the Manual Handling Operations Regulations important in early years settings?

Hint Think about times when staff may need to lift children or equipment in the course of their work.

Extend Find out how most early years settings comply with these regulations.

The Reporting of Injuries, Diseases and Dangerous Occurrences Regulations 2013

These regulations, known as RIDDOR, state that employers are responsible for reporting any injuries, diseases or other incidents that have seriously affected their employees to the **Health and Safety Executive**. As the full implications of an accident or incident may not be known at the time, employers will provide a health and safety accident book, which has to be filled in if there is an accident or incident.

> **Key term**
>
> **Health and Safety Executive** – an independent national body that regulates health, safety and illness in the workplace.

Health and Safety (First Aid) Regulations 1981 (as amended)

These regulations require that employers provide a first-aid box and have sufficient staff trained to deal with first-aid incidents and to contact the emergency services.

Note: early years settings also have to comply with separate legal requirements that require them to employ first aiders who have been trained in paediatric first aid. Settings also have specific health and safety policies that you must follow.

The Regulatory Reform (Fire Safety) Order 2005

This piece of legislation states that whoever is in charge of the setting must carry out a risk assessment relating to fire, making sure that there are clear ways of escaping the building, including ways for people who may be vulnerable, such as children or people with mobility needs. The workplace also has to be equipped with fire-fighting equipment and smoke alarms, and a person has to be appointed to be in charge of fire safety. In many settings, this will be the person in charge of health and safety.

▶ Look out for the 'running man' symbol. It is required by law to indicate how to get out of a building in the event of a fire

The Control of Substances Hazardous to Health Regulations 2002

These regulations are known as COSHH. They require employers to make sure that risk assessments and procedures minimise the dangers of hazardous chemicals. COSHH regulations apply to cleaning products as well as industrial chemicals. As part of the regulations, hazardous products have to be managed in ways that will keep children safe. This is why many settings have locked cupboards or rules that prevent children from going into the kitchen.

Food hygiene regulations

England, Scotland, Wales and Northern Ireland have food hygiene regulations that came into force in 2006 as a result of several European directives. As each home country has its own regulatory powers, you will need to find out about the food hygiene and handling regulations for your home country. The regulations are similar across all of the home countries as they incorporate European directives. Therefore, in this section, we will look at the regulations solely for England.

The Food Safety and Hygiene (England) Regulations 2013

Here are some of the key points in the Food Safety and Hygiene (England) Regulations that affect practice in early years settings.

▸ Early years settings and schools may need to register with, or gain approval from, the local authority if they are providing food to children.

▸ Early years settings are required to keep premises where food is prepared clean and hygienic (see Figure 5.1).

▸ Equipment should be kept in good working order, clean and disinfected.

▸ A food management system has to be in operation and records should be kept to show that food is stored, handled and disposed of hygienically and safely.

▸ Settings are required to train and supervise staff who are involved in the preparation and handling of food.

▸ Food has to be kept and stored at a safe temperature, which will depend on whether it is being frozen, chilled or kept warm.

▸ Precautions have to be taken to prevent pests and insects coming into areas where food is prepared and stored.

▸ **Figure 5.1:** Would you want your meal to be prepared here?

Keeping records

Early years settings are required by law to keep up-to-date records to show that food safety management is taking place. As well as good record-keeping, staff members should make sure that they report anything that might cause a spread of infection, such as an accident in the toilet, if a child is vomiting or if a child is not feeling well. In addition, staff must report if they have had diarrhoea or vomiting. If they are responsible for food preparation or serving of snacks, they should not return to work until they have been free of the symptoms for 48 hours.

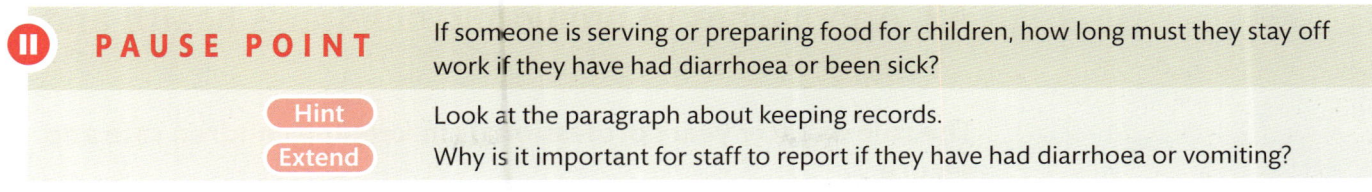

❚❚ PAUSE POINT   If someone is serving or preparing food for children, how long must they stay off
work if they have had diarrhoea or been sick?

Hint   Look at the paragraph about keeping records.

Extend   Why is it important for staff to report if they have had diarrhoea or vomiting?

The requirements of the statutory early years curriculum relevant to health and safety

As with food hygiene regulations, each home country has its own requirements
in relation to safeguarding procedures, recruitment of staff and health and safety.
The safeguarding and welfare requirements of the early years foundation stage (EYFS)
in England are legally binding. There are several legal requirements for early years
settings that include:

▶ adult-to-child ratios

▶ recruitment and vetting procedures to ensure suitability of adults working with
children

▶ arrangements for collecting children

▶ health and safety, including suitable premises, risk assessments and hygiene

▶ maintaining safety on outings.

The responsibilities of early years settings to have policies relevant to health and safety

Early years settings have policies to cover a range of topics, including child protection,
safe recruitment, information sharing and data protection. It is usual for these policies
to be written down so that everyone working in the setting, and parents, know how
the setting operates to keep children safe.

In addition to policies, settings also have to develop procedures that staff, volunteers
and, where relevant, parents need to follow. As you saw earlier in this section,
procedures are the practical ways in which policies are put into place. A good example
of a how a policy is implemented is the procedures that are put into place to ensure
safe recruitment of staff and volunteers. Early years settings need to have procedures
in place to ensure that each member of staff and volunteers are safe and sufficiently
qualified to work with children.

Assessment practice 5.1   A.P1   A.M1

A local businesswoman is thinking about setting up a
day care nursery. She needs your help to find out about
legislation relating to children's health and safety.

She has asked you to:

- identify legislation, regulations and guidance that is
relevant to early years settings

- explain the key points of each type of legislation

- consider a particular setting and analyse the effects
of legislation, regulations and guidelines on the
children's health and safety.

Plan
- What information is the most relevant for this task?
- Where can I go to gain additional information?

Do
- Have I considered the effects of legislation in a setting
I am familiar with?
- Am I managing my time effectively?

Review
- Have I evaluated my work and am I confident that it
fulfils the set task?

A2 Approaches to promoting children's health and safety

The role of early years professionals in keeping children safe and secure

As early years professionals, you have a responsibility to keep children safe. There are several skills and practices that are important when doing this.

Supervision

Supervision is one of the key ways in which you can ensure that children are kept safe. Make sure that the level of supervision is correct for the age and stage of children. In general terms, babies and toddlers need very close supervision, but as children become older the level of supervision required may change depending on what they are doing.

Close supervision and engagement

Close supervision requires adults to be alongside children. Babies and toddlers will need this level of supervision most of the time, but children aged 5–8 years will only need it during certain activities, such as going on an outing or when cooking.

▶ Is this level of supervision appropriate for the age of the children and the type of play they are engaged in?

Supervision within sight

There are times when it is safe for children to play within sight of adults, but not necessarily in close proximity to them. Being away from adults is good for increasing children's independence. This level of supervision is useful once children are 3 years old and are engaging in low-risk activities.

Awareness

Children aged 4–8 years will not need close supervision all of the time, but they will need an adult to know where they are and what they are doing. There are many ways of doing this. Adults can watch children at a discreet distance or go over and chat to them from time to time about what they are doing.

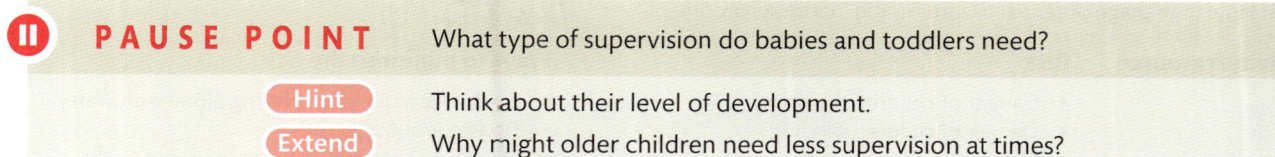

PAUSE POINT   What type of supervision do babies and toddlers need?

Hint   Think about their level of development.

Extend   Why might older children need less supervision at times?

Keeping up-to-date registers

One of the requirements of the EYFS and other early years frameworks, and a responsibility of all schools, is to keep accurate and up-to-date registers. Registers have to be completed at the start of each session, and if children leave before the end of a session this should be indicated. Registers are needed to ensure safe evacuation of children in the event of a fire or other emergency.

Role modelling safe behaviour

Children can learn about staying safe by watching the way that adults behave and also by hearing their reasoning about why certain things keep us safe. For example, an adult may tell a 4-year-old child that they are going to check that the door is closed so toddlers cannot get out. This, combined with the action of closing the door, is likely to help the 4-year-old child remember to close the door.

The power of role modelling also means that you need to think hard about what children see you do. Smoking is a good example. Smoking is banned in early years settings, but if you go outside to smoke, children must not see you.

The importance of observation

It is important to observe individual children as this will help you to understand their stage of development and also how they play with objects – relying on milestones alone is not a good idea.

As well as using observation in relation to safety, you should always be observant in case children are showing signs of becoming poorly or tired. When children are in the early stages of being poorly or tired, their behaviour can change and they may become less aware of risks or less spatially aware. For example, a child who can usually steer a wheeled toy well may knock into another child or may be less careful.

Recognising and reporting hazards in indoor and outdoor environments

In all early years settings, adults spend a lot of time trying to prevent accidents from occurring. In this section we will look at the types of **hazards** that can exist in an early years setting and how to recognise and report them when they occur.

A hazard is anything that could cause harm, for instance, a pond in an outdoor play area. A **risk** is the probability that someone could be harmed as a result of the hazard, for example, there is a risk of drowning.

> **Key terms**
>
> **Hazard** – something in the environment that could cause harm.
>
> **Risk** – the probability that someone could be harmed by a hazard.

Hazards in the indoor environment

There are some areas, resources or activities that have the potential to be hazardous for children in early years settings. Table 5.1 shows some key hazards in the indoor environment, the risk(s) they pose and ways the risk(s) can be minimised.

Table 5.1: How to manage potential hazards in the indoor environment

Area/activity/resource	Risk	Ways to minimise the risk
Water	• Danger of children drowning • Danger of children slipping	• Do not leave children playing alone with water • Tip water out after use • Make sure that spills are wiped up promptly
Sand	• Danger of sand going into children's eyes • Danger of children slipping	• Do not use sand with babies and toddlers • Make sure that children know they must not throw sand • Be ready to intervene if children are throwing sand • Make sure that spills are wiped up promptly
Playdough	• Danger of children eating the playdough – salt is harmful to babies and young children • Danger of infection	• Do not give to babies and children who are still mouthing • Make sure that dough does not smell like food as children may be encouraged to eat it • Change dough frequently • Make sure that children wash their hands
Mark making: pens, pencils, paintbrushes	• Danger of children poking themselves in the eye with the resources	• Do not give pencils to babies and toddlers • Prompt intervention if older children are using the resources inappropriately
Scissors, hole punchers and staplers	• Danger of children getting puncture wounds and cuts	• Make sure resources are out of reach of babies or toddlers • Show children how to use the equipment correctly • Provide child-safe scissors
Dressing-up clothes – belts and similar items	• Danger of strangulation if children engage in play using belts, e.g. pretending to take a 'dog' for a walk – one child may put a belt around another child's neck to act as the dog lead • Danger of belts hitting children's eyes or face	• Explain to children that belts and similar items can cause children injury • Be aware of how children are playing with items
Bathrooms and toilets	• Danger of children drowning • Danger of cross-infection	• Directly supervise babies and toddlers • Supervise and intervene if children are using either area as a play area • Make sure that children wash and dry their hands properly
Physical care routines/ bathing and nappy changing	• Danger of children drowning in the bath • Danger of children being scalded by hot water • Danger of children falling off a changing mat	• Do not leave any young children unattended during bathing • Adults only should supervise children during bathing – do not give older children this responsibility • Run cold water first, then add hot water into the bath • Check temperature of the water before putting babies into baths. The water should be lukewarm at around 36–37°C • Be organised when nappy changing so you do not have to leave the child alone • Consider changing older babies and toddlers on a mat that is placed on the floor
Entrances and doorways	• Danger of children escaping onto the road • Danger of children going home with strangers or parents who do not have custody of them	• Set out clear procedures for the collection of children • Keep entrances and doorways locked or secure • Make sure that staff and parents understand the importance of security
Windows	• Danger of children falling out	• Make sure that windows above ground floors can only be opened slightly • Make sure windows that have tables/cots/other climbable objects under them are kept locked

▶ **Table 5.1:** How to manage potential hazards in the indoor environment – *continued*

Area/activity/resource	Risk	Ways to minimise the risk
Cooking activities	• Danger posed by the use of knives, hot stoves and ovens	• Keep babies and toddlers away from the kitchen • Show children how to use knives properly • Explain to children about hazards present in the kitchen • Make sure cupboards that contain dangerous items are locked • Do not leave children in the kitchen unattended • Use saucepan guards
Toys and objects scattered on the ground	• Danger of children falling over the resources	• Keep 'walkways' clear • Pick up objects that are likely to be a hazard • Explain to children the importance of not leaving things on the floor • Encourage children to tidy resources away
Adult behaviours: hot drinks and handbags	• Danger of scalding children if hot drinks spill onto them • Danger of children taking medicines and/or lighters out of adults' handbags	• Keep hot drinks out of reach and out of sight of children • Put lids on hot drinks • Put handbags out of reach or locked away in a cupboard

Specific hazards in home settings

In home settings there are some specific hazards that you need to be aware of.

Pets

Pets need to be kept away from food preparation areas. When you first meet parents, you will need to ask whether the presence of a pet is likely to cause any allergic reactions in their children. In addition, cats and dogs should not be left alone with babies and young children.

Kitchens

Many homes will have a kitchen-diner arrangement, which means that children are eating in the kitchen or going in and out of it to use a table. Great care needs to be taken to make sure that objects such as knives and kettles are kept out of reach. Children should never be left in the kitchen without supervision.

Mixed-age groups

In many ways it is wonderful for settings to allow babies to play alongside toddlers and older children, but it does create some challenges. First of all, remember that toddlers are likely to want to hold, cuddle or even hit a baby. This means that babies should never be left alone with toddlers or even young children. The other challenge is around the provision of equipment and resources. What is safe for a 4-year-old child may not be suitable for a baby. This means that planning is very important; settings should think about having set areas where certain toys belong.

Hazards in the outdoor environment

Today, it is recognised that babies and children need to spend time playing outdoors. Being outdoors is very beneficial for their health and well-being, but it also raises safety issues. You will now look at how to ensure children are safe outdoors.

Checking the outdoor area for hazards

Before babies and children are taken to an outdoor environment, it is usual for the area to be checked. This is because incidents could have occurred overnight, boundaries may have been broken or damaged, and litter or dangerous objects could have been dropped. In addition, animals such as foxes and cats may have been in the area and **defecated**.

Here are some key points to check in outdoor areas.

▶ Is the area secure? Check fences and gates.

▶ Are there any signs of debris, broken glass or litter? Sweep up if necessary.

▶ Is the equipment in a good state? Remove old or broken equipment if necessary.

▶ If there is a sandpit area, is it clean? Rake and replace the sand if necessary.

▶ Is equipment such as slides and climbing frames dry? Dry the equipment if necessary.

Common outdoor hazards

Babies and children should spend some time each day playing outdoors. This means that you need to be aware of common outdoor hazards. Table 5.2 shows potential hazards and how the risk caused by the hazard can be minimised and managed.

Key term

Defecate – excrete faeces (solid waste) from the body.

▶ **Table 5.2:** How to manage potential hazards in the outdoor environment

Area/piece of equipment	Hazard	Ways to minimise the risk
Ice on paths	• Child falling	• Have salt ready for cold weather
Slides/climbing frames	• Child falling off the equipment • Child being pushed off	• Make sure rungs/steps are dry and clean • Supervise and check that children are using the equipment safely • Make sure clear rules are in place for turn taking on the equipment
Swings	• Child falling • Child banging his/her head	• Locate swings in specific areas away from where children may be walking • Supervise children and make sure clear rules are in place for turn taking
Wheeled toys such as tricycles	• Child falling • Collisions with other children	• Provide cycle helmets • Create specific areas where wheeled toys can be used
Fencing/gates	• Children escaping if gates are left open or if there are gaps in fencing • Strangers entering if gates are left open or if there are gaps in fencing	• Check fences thoroughly • Make sure that gates are securely fastened. Do not rely on parents to remember to close them
Water activities	• Danger of child drowning • Danger of child slipping	• Do not leave children playing alone with water • Tip water out after use • Make sure that spills are wiped up promptly
Sand	• Danger of sand going into children's eyes • Danger of children slipping • Possibility of contamination from animal faeces	• Do not use sand with babies and toddlers • Make sure that children know they must not throw sand • Be ready to intervene if children are throwing sand • Make sure that spills are wiped up promptly • Make sure that sand is covered when not in use • Before children play, check sand for possible contamination such as animal faeces or urine
Plants	• Poisoning • Children being poked, or poking themselves in the eye with sticks	• Check that you have no poisonous plants in reach of children • Make sure there are rules about how children can use sticks – they are not for fighting

Outings

Good planning and organisation are required if you are thinking about taking children on an outing. It is important when planning an outing, but also during the outing, that dangers and hazards are carefully identified and managed. You should always try to visit the venue ahead of an outing so that you can carry out a risk assessment and familiarise yourself with where you are going – especially if it is an all-day trip.

Table 5.3 shows some of the common dangers and hazards and how they might be minimised.

▶ **Table 5.3:** How to deal with potential hazards on outings

Danger/hazard	Steps to minimise/deal with potential hazards
Traffic	<ul><li>Babies and toddlers should be wearing reins</li><li>The ratio of adults to children must be sufficient</li><li>What is going to happen on the outing and the 'rules' children must follow should be explained</li><li>Adults and children should consider wearing fluorescent jackets so that motorists can see them</li><li>Use all crossing points</li><li>Visit the route and assess risks before the outing</li></ul>
Abduction by strangers (very rare)	<ul><li>The ratio of adults to children must be sufficient</li><li>Children should be closely supervised at all times</li><li>Adults should take responsibility for particular children</li></ul>
Children wandering off	<ul><li>The ratio of adults to children must be sufficient</li><li>Children should be closely supervised at all times</li><li>Adults should take responsibility for particular children</li></ul>
Bites and stings	<ul><li>Take a first-aid kit</li><li>Keep children away from litter bins</li><li>Teach children not to touch dogs or cats that are not their own pets</li></ul>
Dehydration	<ul><li>Take plenty of drinking water</li><li>Monitor children's intake of water in hot weather</li></ul>
Sunburn/sunstroke	<ul><li>Follow sun protection guidelines</li></ul>
Children with ongoing medical conditions	<ul><li>Take children's medicines with you on the outing</li><li>Take a mobile phone</li><li>Take emergency numbers and appropriate records for the children with medical conditions</li><li>Observe children for signs that medication is needed, e.g. inhalers, insulin</li></ul>
Motion sickness (on cars, buses, trains)	<ul><li>Find out from parents beforehand whether their children suffer from motion sickness</li><li>Allow sufficient time to stop during the journey</li><li>Take a bucket, disposable gloves, an apron, disposable wipes and plastic bags to put soiled clothes in</li><li>Take a spare change of clothes</li></ul>
Toileting accidents	<ul><li>Give children plenty of opportunities and reminders to go to the toilet</li><li>Take a bucket, disposable gloves, an apron, disposable wipes and plastic bags to put items in</li><li>Take a spare change of clothes</li></ul>

▶ **Table 5.3:** How to deal with potential hazards on outings – *continued*

Danger/hazard	Steps to minimise/deal with potential hazards
Accidents	• Risk assess the outing beforehand • Closely supervise children • Ratio of adults to children must be sufficient • Make sure that adults take responsibility for individual children • Take a first-aid kit • Take emergency contact numbers • Take a mobile phone
Rainy, cold weather	• Check the weather forecast and postpone if possible • Ask parents to bring in warm, waterproof clothes • Take plenty of spare clothes with you • Use all possible shelters • Change timings of the outing so you can spend more time indoors
Food poisoning/allergies	• Make sure that children wash their hands before eating • In hot weather, bring ice packs to keep food cool • Give parents information about how to avoid food poisoning in packed lunches • Make sure that adults know which children have food allergies • Supervise children at mealtimes

Reporting hazards

Section 7 of the Health and Safety at Work etc. Act 1974 sets out the responsibility of everyone working in an early years setting to keep themselves, and everyone else in the setting, safe. This applies to the person's actions or to their failure to act. This means that you have a legal duty to report hazards immediately whether they are found indoors or outdoors. Any hazard that poses immediate risk should be removed immediately or, if this is not possible, you should keep children away from the area. It is important that you report any hazards promptly to your supervisor, manager or the health and safety officer. Most settings have a procedure for this, so you will need to find out what this is in your setting. Following the report on a hazard, your concerns should be recorded in a health and safety book. The relevant risk assessment will also need to be updated.

Equipment and resources that can be used to minimise hazards

Some pieces of equipment can prevent accidents. They are only useful if they are used consistently and in accordance with the manufacturer's instructions. They are never an alternative to supervision or good health and safety practices. Table 5.4 lists some examples of useful safety equipment.

▶ **Table 5.4:** Useful safety equipment

Equipment	Features
Safety gates	Restrict children's access to areas such as stairs and kitchens
Cupboard locks	Restrict children's access to cupboards where cleaning equipment or medicines are kept
Safety corners	Cover sharp edges on furniture, preventing eye and head injuries
Cycle helmets	Provide protection against head injuries when children are on scooters or bicycles
Smoke detector	Signals that there is smoke in the environment and so can save lives
Fire blanket	For use in kitchens to throw over items that are on fire
Fire extinguishers	A number of different types; used to put out small fires
Harnesses	Prevent babies and toddlers from falling out of highchairs and pushchairs – make sure that children can be released quickly if needed
Reins	Prevent toddlers from wandering off or into traffic
Window and door locks	Prevent toddlers and young children from falling out of windows or 'escaping'
Car seats	Required by law in cars to transport children to the age of 12 (or 1.35 m in height). They can prevent serious injuries in the event of an accident. Car seats have to be properly installed and be of the right design for the age/weight/height of the child

The importance of appropriate resources and equipment

The equipment and resources you choose for children must be appropriate for their age and stage of development. Children under 18 months will, for example, play with objects by mouthing them. Therefore, small objects that are fine for older children to play with will be dangerous for babies and toddlers.

The appropriateness and safety of resources and equipment must be regularly checked through a rolling programme of inspections. A tricycle that was safe a year ago may have moving parts that have become loose. Anything that is found to be unsafe should be put out of reach of children immediately.

The importance of maintaining accurate and coherent records

Maintaining accurate and coherent records and reports is a duty of anyone working with children. With respect to children's health, safety and welfare, this includes records of medication, accidents and incidents.

How and by whom records should be completed will depend on the policies of the setting in which you work. The policies will be based on the statutory requirements, which, in turn, will be inspected by Ofsted, the regulatory body, if you are working in England. Ofsted states that any serious incidents or accidents should be reported to them within 14 days of the incident.

Recognising and assessing risk to children's health, safety and welfare

Early years practitioners need to recognise and assess any risk posed to children's health, safety and welfare. By knowing what dangers there are in the setting – indoors and outdoors – early years professionals can take appropriate steps to eliminate or minimise them. As you saw in Section A1, the process of identifying hazards and minimising or eliminating them is called risk assessment. Good risk assessment involves carefully evaluating the level of risk and deciding on the necessary precautions to take. This process is vital when working with babies and children. It can prevent accidents from occurring.

Remember, recognising and assessing risk is a legal requirement. You have a duty of care towards children, which includes keeping them safe. If an accident occurs and insufficient risk assessment has taken place, you may be prosecuted.

The importance of passing on concerns about the practice of colleagues

When it comes to health and safety, you should be aware of inappropriate actions of other adults and understand what your responsibilities are in relation to this. If, for example, a colleague is not properly supervising children when outdoors, or not managing risks carefully, this would need to be reported to a senior member of staff.

In the unlikely event that no action was taken by the management team and children were still at risk, the next step would be to contact an outside regulatory organisation. In England, this would be Ofsted, while in Wales it would be the Care and Social Services Inspectorate. Reporting the failings of an early years setting is sometimes known as **whistleblowing**.

> **Link**
>
> In Unit 3 we looked at toys, resources and equipment that were suitable for babies and children at different ages and stages of development. Look back at Section A to remind yourself of the important points.

> **Link**
>
> Section D1 of this unit looks in detail at the risk assessment process, including how to identify hazards, deciding who may be harmed and how, evaluating risks and deciding on precautions.

> **Key term**
>
> **Whistleblowing** – raising concerns about the actions of an individual, group or organisation.

The importance of child-centred provision

While keeping children safe is a priority in early years settings, environments still have to be child-centred and support children's overall development. Until a few years ago, there was a focus on total risk elimination in early years and play settings. This has now been revisited because it has been shown that children did not benefit from this approach – they did not learn the skills needed to keep themselves safe. For example, children who have not walked on an uneven surface will not know that they need to moderate their speed when doing so.

Today, it is accepted that children need physical challenges in their environments and opportunities to explore and experience risk management. It is recognised that where settings totally eliminate risk and, therefore, challenge for children, there is a greater likelihood of accidents taking place because children become bored and use toys and resources inappropriately. A balance has to be struck between maintaining a stimulating and child-centred environment, but also one that is essentially safe.

Recognising the individual needs of children

When keeping children safe it is important to focus on their individual needs, to ensure that provision is inclusive and that they are treated equally. While you can make general observations about how children play and what they are likely to do, knowing more about individual children is important. It may be that a child is more impulsive than other children within a nursery or finds it hard to see potential dangers.

For children who have additional needs in terms of keeping them safe, it is important not to become too restrictive. Otherwise their opportunities to learn and explore will be limited and you will inadvertently be providing a barrier to inclusion and equality. Instead they may need additional supervision and reminders, or more adult involvement. For some children with disabilities, it may be helpful to seek advice from other professionals such as occupational therapists – they should be able to make suggestions about how to include a child in an activity safely.

Discussion

There is an argument that children today are over protected and this is one reason why they are not allowed to play outdoors. Do you think this is true? Discuss this issue in small groups and share your feedback with the rest of the group.

Assessment practice 5.2 A.P2 A.M1 AB.D1

An early years setting has asked you to provide information for new volunteers about the role of the early years practitioner in keeping children safe.

Your information needs to:

- explain approaches that early years practitioners can use to promote and maintain children's health and safety
- analyse the extent to which the identified approaches are likely to maintain and promote children's health and safety
- consider the strengths and weaknesses of the approaches to keeping children healthy and safe.

Plan

- Where can I find relevant information and how can I check this is still current?
- How long do I need to collate and analyse the information required for the task?

Do

- Am I presenting the information accurately and concisely?
- Am I managing my time effectively?

Review

- Can I justify why I have decided to approach this task in the way that I have?
- Have I evaluated my work and am I confident that it fulfils the set task?

B Explore procedures for prevention and control of infection in early years settings

B1 Statutory requirements and procedures for infection prevention and control

As part of keeping children safe, it is important to prevent them from becoming unwell. There are many steps you can take to reduce or eliminate the source and transmission of infection in early years settings, starting with your own personal hygiene. Personal hygiene is important as you touch food, resources and, of course, the children. Figure 5.2 shows how you can make sure your personal hygiene is as good as it can be.

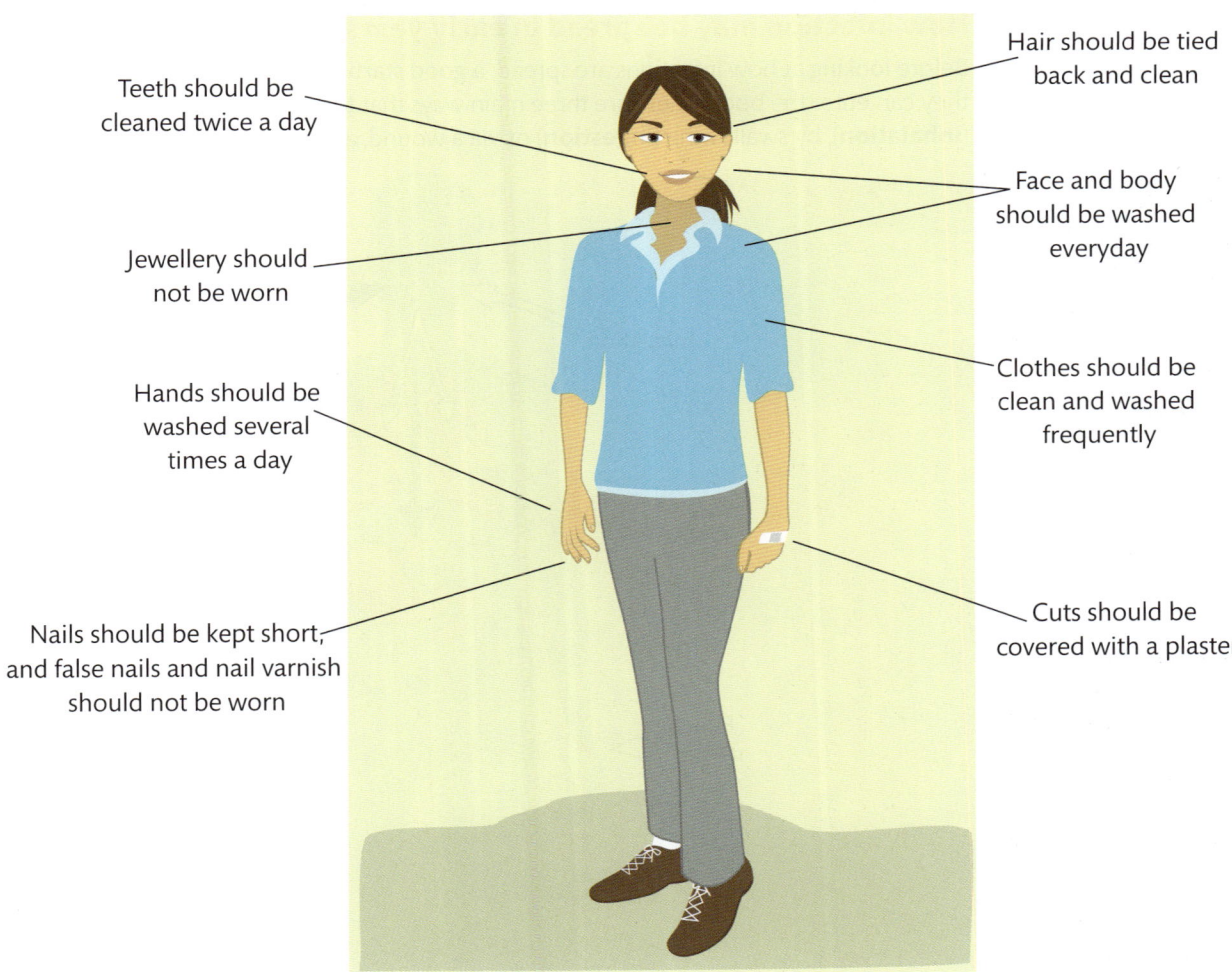

Teeth should be cleaned twice a day

Jewellery should not be worn

Hands should be washed several times a day

Nails should be kept short, and false nails and nail varnish should not be worn

Hair should be tied back and clean

Face and body should be washed everyday

Clothes should be clean and washed frequently

Cuts should be covered with a plaster

▶ **Figure 5.2:** It is important that your own personal hygiene is good so that you do not spread infection

Current legislation, regulations and guidance

In England, the safeguarding and welfare requirements of the EYFS state that early years settings have a duty to maintain hygiene procedures in order to keep children safe and healthy and to prevent infection. While no specific procedures are given for early years settings to follow, it is a legal requirement to prevent infection.

Link

See Section A1 in this unit for the key regulations and requirements relating to food safety and hygiene.

Theory into practice

Find out how your work placement prevents and controls the spread of infection. You may find it helpful to look at their policy and procedures.

1 Who manages the day-to-day cleaning in the setting?

2 What is the procedure to be followed if a child is sick?

Key terms

Ingestion – swallowing.

Inhalation – breathing in.

In England, early years settings are required to follow the guidelines set out by Public Health England. In Wales, the guidelines are issued by Public Health Wales. In Northern Ireland, guidelines are issued by the Food Standards Agency. When there are outbreaks of serious infections or food poisoning, early years settings have to report these to the relevant local agency, e.g. in England, food poisoning outbreaks have to be reported to the local environmental health team.

The importance of policy and procedures for infection prevention and control

To prevent the spread of infections such as chickenpox or gastroenteritis, early years settings need to have policies in place to prevent children from returning to a setting too early after being infected. The exclusion policy does vary from setting to setting, but many early years settings follow the guidance from the regulatory or advisory body in their home country, e.g. Public Health England.

How infection may be spread in early years settings

Before looking at how infections are spread, a good starting point is to understand how they can enter the body. There are three main ways that this can happen: by breathing in (**inhalation**), by swallowing (**ingestion**) or via a wound, as shown in Figure 5.3.

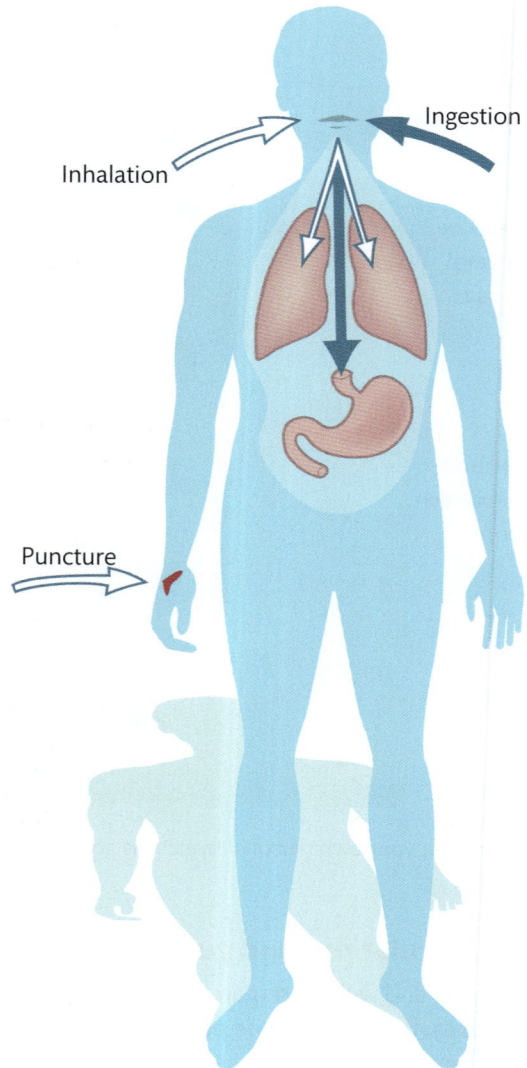

▶ **Figure 5.3:** The three main ways in which infection can enter the human body

There are some specific ways that infections can spread, as you will now see.

Airborne

Some **microorganisms** that cause disease are spread by tiny droplets in the air when someone who is infected coughs or sneezes. The droplets are then breathed in or swallowed by another person, causing that person to become infected. Airborne droplets are extremely fine and can travel considerable distances. Colds, **norovirus** and measles travel this way.

Key terms

Microorganisms – living organisms, including viruses and bacteria, that are too small to be seen with the naked eye.

Norovirus – a common stomach bug that causes severe diarrhoea and vomiting.

Some microorganisms, for example, influenza, form in heavier droplets and so closer contact with the infected person is needed to pick up the disease.

You can pick up microorganisms including influenza by touching an object that has been touched by an infected person. The influenza virus lasts for up to 48 hours on hard surfaces. It is, therefore, important to regularly clean objects such as door handles and light switches.

Direct contact (skin-to-skin and head-to-head)

Some diseases and parasites can be passed between people by skin-to-skin contact, for example, scabies. Others can be transmitted by head-to-head contact, for example, head lice.

Faecal/oral transmission

Infections, especially food poisoning, can spread when someone has passed faeces, wiped themselves and then not washed their hands thoroughly. The faecal microorganism is then on their hands and can be ingested or spread to others by touching other people or objects.

Blood/body fluid transmission

Serious diseases such as HIV and hepatitis can be transmitted through the transfer of blood and bodily fluids from one person to another, although this is rare in early years settings.

Common childhood infections and how they are spread

A range of common infections occur in early years settings. It is worth understanding how they are spread and also how they can be minimised. Table 5.5 shows some common infections and how you can prevent them from being spread.

▶ **Table 5.5:** Common infections, how they are spread and steps that can be taken to minimise them

Infection	How it is spread	How it can be minimised
Chickenpox	Airborne particles and close contact	• Ventilation of rooms • Hand washing • Prompt recognition that a child has the infection • Quarantine of the child and exclusion for 5 days
Influenza	Airborne particles and close contact	• Ventilation of rooms • Hand-washing procedures for adults and children • Prompt recognition that a child has the infection • Quarantine of the child and exclusion until child is fully recovered
Diarrhoea and vomiting caused by food poisoning	Bacteria spread in food and also by touch	• Hand-washing procedures for children and adults • Good food hygiene at all points during food preparation and cooking process, including storage of food • Prompt recognition that a child has food poisoning • Quarantine of the child and cleaning of everything that they have been in contact with • Use of paper towels rather than general towels • Cleaning of toilets and bathroom areas
Diarrhoea and vomiting caused by norovirus	Virus spread through touch and close contact	• Hand-washing procedures for children and adults • Sterilisation and cleaning of toys and resources • Cleaning of toilets and bathroom areas • Use of paper towels rather than general towels • Quarantine of the child • Exclusion of the child for 48 hours after the last episode of vomiting or sickness
Common cold	Virus spread through airborne particles and close contact	• Good ventilation • Hand-washing procedures for children and adults • Use of disposable tissues

Ⅱ PAUSE POINT   Can you identify two ways in which bacteria and viruses might get inside our bodies?

Hint   Think about the terms 'inhalation' and 'ingestion'.

Extend   List at least two more ways in which disease can be transmitted.

Infection prevention and control procedures

Infection control is about managing the spread of infection and preventing bacteria, parasites, viruses and fungi from infecting others. Although a common cold is usually harmless, other diseases such as norovirus, E. coli and influenza can be fatal for babies and young children. This is because their immune systems are still developing. In addition, you may care for children who have ongoing health problems and whose immune systems are not very strong as a result.

> **Key term**
>
> **Infection control** – the process of minimising the spread of infection.

Hand-washing routines for adults and children

If there is one message that is universal about infection control, it is the importance of hand washing. As practitioners, you need to be role models for hand washing. From very early on, children need to be taught to wash their hands and this activity has to be supervised until adults are sure that children are doing it properly every time. In order for you to teach children to wash their hands properly, it is important that you know how, and when, to wash your own hands. The step-by-step guide in Figure 5.4 shows the correct routine for washing hands thoroughly. It is advised that liquid soap and disposable paper towels are used in early years settings.

Adults and children should wash their hands thoroughly:

▶ after going to the toilet
▶ before eating or drinking
▶ after touching any animals
▶ after going outdoors
▶ after playing with sensory materials
▶ when hands look grubby.

Additionally, adults should wash their hands:

▶ before preparing food
▶ after touching raw meat or fish
▶ before and after a nappy change
▶ after changing children's clothes
▶ after dealing with waste.

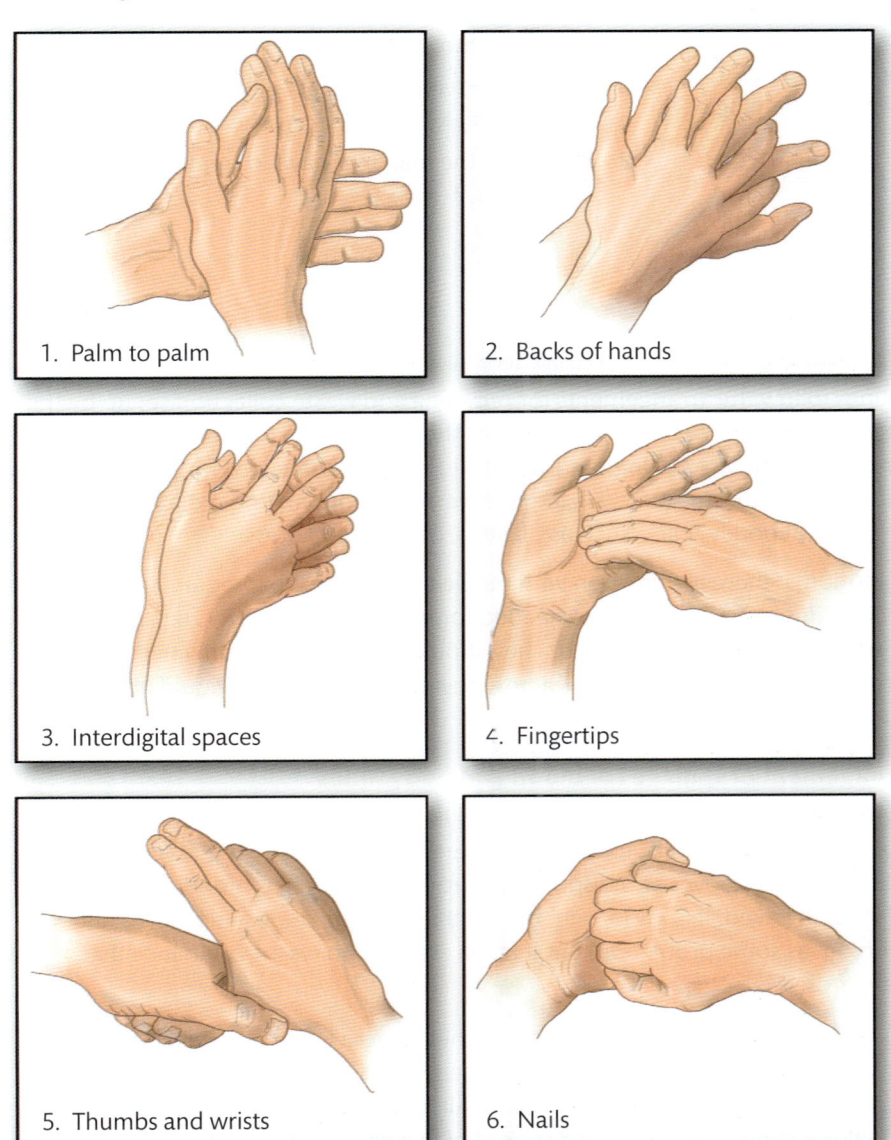

1. Palm to palm

2. Backs of hands

3. Interdigital spaces

4. Fingertips

5. Thumbs and wrists

6. Nails

▶ This child is learning about hand washing from the adult supervising him

▶ **Figure 5.4:** A step-by-step guide to hand washing

Personal protective clothing/equipment (PPE)

To prevent the spread of infection, early years settings provide protective clothing such as disposable gloves and plastic aprons. Protective clothing is important as it prevents bacteria and viruses from entering your body, but also prevents the spread of infection via your hands or your clothing.

You should use disposable gloves and aprons for nappy changing, dealing with toileting accidents, cleaning and dealing with waste. It is important that you dispose of the gloves each time you have finished an activity with them. For example, gloves should be changed each time you change a child's nappy.

Case study

Breaking the rules

Kylie has been told to wear a disposable apron and gloves when she is assisting children with toileting in the nursery where she works. Most of the time she does this, but sometimes she can't really see the point. After all, in her own home she doesn't when she's helping her nieces and nephews.

One day, her manager sees that she is not wearing protective clothing and reprimands her. The manager records it as a disciplinary incident.

Check your knowledge

1 Explain why the risk of infection is different in a nursery setting compared to a family home.

2 Using the Health and Safety at Work etc. Act 1974, analyse why Kylie is breaking the law.

3 Why does the manager have to treat this incident so seriously?

Safe handling and disposal of waste

Settings follow the arrangements for recycling and waste collection set up by their local authority, but they should also have their own waste disposal procedures. It is usual for group-care settings and schools to have separate bins for paper waste, food waste and hazardous waste. Hazardous waste includes anything that has been in contact with bodily fluids, such as plasters, nappies and dressings.

In addition, if there are children with medical conditions that require injections, a specially designed 'sharps' bin is needed for needles and syringes. Bins for hazardous waste are normally colour coded. They should be kept away from children and instructions from the waste contractor must be followed. You should not flush waste down the toilet.

Management of spillages of blood and body fluids

It is likely that you will be handling body fluids on a regular basis if you work with babies or young children. To avoid the spread of infection, you should always wear disposable gloves and disposable aprons when there is blood, vomit, urine or faeces involved. It is important to note that wearing disposable gloves and aprons gives some protection, but it is still essential to wash your hands thoroughly afterwards.

You should also change or wash your clothes if there is any possibility that there has been contamination. Anything you use when dealing with body fluids, such as cloths, should be thrown away after use. All items that have been used to deal with body fluids should be correctly disposed of in a colour-coded hazardous waste bin. These bins are usually yellow and nappies, wipes and plasters should be put inside. Nappies are usually wrapped before being disposed of in the bin.

In your work with children, you are likely to have to wipe children's noses. Disposable tissues are needed for this task and again, to avoid spreading infection, you should wash your hands afterwards.

❚❚ PAUSE POINT What items of personal protection clothing should be worn when changing a nappy or cleaning up toileting accidents?

> Hint Think about how you can protect your clothes and hands from becoming contaminated.

> Extend Make a list of all the items in your setting that could be considered as hazardous waste.

Decontamination and cleaning of environment, equipment and toys

Environments that children are in should be cleaned regularly, as well as areas where the children do not usually enter, such as the kitchen. This applies to resources, such as equipment and toys, too. In some settings, cleaners come in after the children have left, but the staff team must still take responsibility for the cleanliness of the environment during the day. If you work as a nanny or childminder, you need to take responsibility for keeping the environment clean and hygienic. Table 5.6 shows cleaning procedures for early years settings.

> **Key term**
>
> **Detergent** – a cleaning product that is water soluble. Unlike soap, it doesn't form a scum.

▶ **Table 5.6:** Cleaning procedures in early years settings

Area or equipment	How often should it be cleaned?	Cleaning method
Basins and taps	• Daily and whenever needed	• Hot water and **detergent**
Bins	• Daily	• Hot water and detergent
Carpets	• Daily	• Vacuum daily • Steam clean every 6 months in group-care settings
Floors	• Daily	• Hot water and detergent • Only use disinfectant if there has been a toileting accident, or if blood and vomit are present
Tables and chairs	• Daily	• Wipe with disposable cloths
Nappy changing mats	• After use	• Wipe with disposable antibacterial cloths
Bedding	• Every few days or immediately if soiled	• Soiled washing should be handled wearing disposable gloves and apron. Solid waste should be flushed down the toilet. Linen should then be put into a plastic sack and tied until ready for washing at 60°C • Each child should be allocated their own bedding
Soft toys	• Weekly	• Hot water and detergent, and then rinse
Plastic toys	• Weekly or preferably after use where they have been mouthed by babies	• Hot water and detergent, and then rinse
Water trays	• Water should be changed after use	• Tray should be dried if not in use
Water toys	• Wash and dry after use	• Hot water and detergent, and then rinse
Sand tray indoors	• Sand should be sieved regularly • The tray should be washed and dried when the sand is changed	• Sand needs changing every month • Wash tray with hot water and detergent
Sand outdoors	• Rake the sand on a daily basis	• Keep covered when not in use • Check for animal faeces • Change when discoloured
Playdough	• Children should wash hands before and after use • Playdough should be replaced after every session (ideally)	• If an outbreak of gastroenteritis occurs, use of playdough, water and sand play should be stopped

▶ These children are enjoying handling dough – but are their hands and the dough clean?

Theory into practice

What regular cleaning practices take place in your work placement? Who is responsible for carrying them out?

Cleaning equipment

Separate cleaning equipment is needed for toilets, bathrooms, kitchens and play areas. The cleaning equipment can be colour coded for identification or can be stored separately. This is to avoid cross-contamination.

Disposable wipes are recommended, otherwise cloths should be changed daily. Mops should be washed through with hot water and detergent, and left to dry.

Food and kitchen hygiene

Under the food hygiene regulations, it is a requirement for anyone handling, preparing or serving food for the public to have been trained in food hygiene. This includes nurseries and other early years settings. Food poisoning in young children can be serious, and even fatal.

Table 5.7 shows some of the key features of good food hygiene but you can find more information on the Food Standards Agency website at www.food.gov.uk.

▶ **Table 5.7:** Good practices for maintaining food hygiene

Feature of food hygiene	What to do
Safe storage of food	• Cooked and raw food should be kept separately at all times, ideally in separate fridges • Fridges and freezers should be kept at recommended temperatures • Use by dates should be observed and unused food should be thrown away promptly
Maintaining a hygienic environment	• Regular disinfectant of surfaces and floor • No pets in the kitchen • Washing of all utensils involved in food preparation • Separate chopping boards and utensils for the preparation of meat, fish and poultry
Maintaining personal hygiene	• Hand washing before touching or serving any food • Hand washing after touching raw meat, fish or poultry • Tying back and covering of hair, removal of rings and nail varnish • Use of aprons • Covering of any cuts with blue plasters
Cooking	• Cooking meat, poultry, fish and eggs thoroughly • Re-heating of food only in accordance with recommended temperatures and guidelines
Allergies	• Identifying children who have dietary allergies • Ensuring that foods that may act as allergens are not used within the kitchen or are used and prepared in controlled conditions • Serving food correctly to avoid children being given food that may cause a serious allergic reaction

Link

Revisit Section A1 in this unit to see the key points in the Food Safety and Hygiene (England) Regulations that affect practice in early years settings.

Research

Visit the Food Standards Agency's website. See if you can answer the following questions.

1 At what temperature should fridges be kept?

2 Where in a fridge should vegetables be kept?

3 How long should someone avoid preparing and serving food after a stomach upset?

4 How long can hot food be kept warm and at what temperature?

The immunisation programme for children and its role in infection control

Many serious childhood infections can now be prevented through children receiving a **vaccine**. This is known as vaccination. When children are vaccinated against a disease, the body creates the necessary antibodies so that if they are exposed to the disease, they are **immune** to it. When most children are vaccinated against a disease, the bacteria or virus responsible for it have fewer opportunities to infect and, therefore, reproduce. Vaccination is considered to be a key way in which diseases can be controlled and potentially wiped out.

Table 5.8 details the immunisation programme that is offered to children in England at the time of writing and is detailed on the NHS website. However, it is worth noting that some children who have pre-existing medical conditions, such as cancer or epilepsy, may not be able to be vaccinated.

Key terms

Immunisation – the process by which someone is protected against an infectious disease.

Vaccine – a very weak dose of an infectious organism that is injected into someone in order to prevent a disease.

▶ **Table 5.8:** The NHS vaccination schedule for babies and young children (Source: Public Health England, Summer 2016)

Age	Vaccine
2 months	• 5-in-1 (DTaP/IPV/Hib) vaccine against diphtheria, tetanus, whooping cough (pertussis), polio and Hib, which can cause pneumonia • Pneumococcal (PCV) vaccine (a bacteria that can cause pneumonia and meningitis) • Meningitis B • Rotavirus vaccine (an infection that causes diarrhoea and sickness)
3 months	• 5-in-1 (DTaP/IPV/Hib) vaccine (second dose) • Rotavirus vaccine (second dose)
4 months	• 5-in-1 (DTaP/IPV/Hib) vaccine (third dose) • Meningitis B • Pneumococcal (PCV) vaccine (second dose)
12–13 months	• Hib/Men C booster, given as a single jab containing meningitis C (second dose) and Hib (fourth dose) • Measles, mumps and rubella (MMR) vaccine, given as a single jab • Pneumococcal (PCV) vaccine (third dose) • Meningitis B
2 to 6 years old (including children in school years 1 and 2)	• Annual flu vaccine
3 years and 4 months, or soon after	• Measles, mumps and rubella (MMR) vaccine (second dose) • 4-in-1 (DTaP/IPV) pre-school booster, given as a single jab containing vaccines against diphtheria, tetanus, whooping cough (pertussis) and polio

Maintaining accurate records and reporting

It is good practice for early years settings to keep accurate records and reports of all matters relating to infection control and cleaning schedules. Records and reports should include risk assessments linked to food hygiene and to cleanliness in relation to the maintenance of environments and resources.

Some types of infection require children to be kept away from the setting for a period of time. This depends upon the infection and the advice for each is very specific. For instance, children with diarrhoea and vomiting should be kept away for 48 hours after the last episode. For mumps they must be excluded for 5 days after the onset of swelling. More serious infections such as measles and meningitis C, once they have been diagnosed, must be reported to a named person at the local authority by the child's doctor. Detailed information on exclusions and infections that must be reported can be found on the Public Health England website: www.gov.uk/government/organisations/public-health-england.

Discussion

In some countries, children cannot attend school unless they have been vaccinated. Do you think that the UK should adopt this approach? Discuss this with a partner and then share your feedback with the rest of the group.

There is a duty for early years settings in England to report any outbreak of food poisoning to Ofsted and also, where appropriate, to the local health protection team. There may also be local regulations that early years managers need to know about that require settings to report infectious diseases to Ofsted or the local Public Health England.

Accidents must also be reported and recorded – see Section D2 of this unit for more information.

Assessment practice 5.3   B.P3   B.M2   AB.D1

A childminder has asked you for information about how infections can be prevented and her role in preventing the spread of infections. She also needs to know how legislation and regulations will influence the procedures she uses to control the spread of infection in her setting.

Produce an information sheet that:

- explains the procedures used to prevent and control the spread of infections in early years settings
- analyses how these procedures prevent and control the spread of infections
- considers the strengths and weaknesses of the procedures used.

The sheet should include practical ways of preventing the spread of infections. You should discuss nappy changes, cleaning routines and the disposal of waste.

Give examples of procedures in early years settings, showing how they follow guidance from the relevant infection control regulations.

Plan

- Where can I go to gain additional information and to check that information is still current?
- What resources do I need to complete the task and how can I get access to them?

Do

- Am I presenting the information accurately and concisely?
- Am I recording any problems I am experiencing and looking for ways to resolve queries?

Review

- Can I identify how this learning experience relates to work I might do in the future in the early years sector?
- Can I explain what skills I used to complete the task and which new ones I developed?

C Examine how early years professionals safeguard children and respond to concerns that a child has been abused

C1 Types and indicators of abuse

Types of abuse

There are four types of abuse recognised in law: physical abuse, neglect, emotional and sexual abuse. Other forms of abuse fall within these four types, such as domestic abuse and female genital mutilation. Many children who are abused experience more than one type of abuse.

Physical abuse and injury

Physical abuse happens when a child is intentionally physically hurt or injured. For instance, hitting a child with hands or implements, kicking, burning, scalding, suffocating, throwing objects at a child or shaking them are all classed as physical abuse. Physical abuse also describes acts that induce illness in a child, including poisoning.

Neglect

The legal definition of neglect is the persistent failure to meet a child's basic physical and/or psychological needs. This happens when a child is not provided with adequate food, shelter, clothing or medical care. Neglect also includes an adult not meeting a child's developmental, educational or emotional needs or protecting them from harm.

Emotional abuse

Emotional or psychological abuse happens when a child suffers persistent ill-treatment that affects their emotional development. It may involve making the child feel frightened, unloved, worthless or in danger. Emotional abuse may happen on its own, but it often takes place with other types of abuse.

Sexual abuse

Sexual abuse happens when a child is forced or persuaded into sexual activities or situations by others. It may involve physical and/or non-physical contact. Physical contact may be penetration (rape) or touching the child's body for sexual gratification. Physical contact also includes masturbation or touching a child inappropriately, even if it is outside their clothing. Non-physical sexual abuse involves forcing or enticing a child to look at sexual materials and sexual activity, or watching a child undress. For sexual abuse to happen adults do not have to be in close proximity to a child; there is a growing problem of sexual abuse happening via the internet.

Domestic abuse

Domestic abuse happens between adults or older children in the family and is not directly aimed at children. It can encompass different types of abuse because it may involve violent behaviour, sexual attacks and coercive and controlling behaviour. Children can be deeply affected even if they do not witness the abuse directly but only see the results, such as a parent who is upset or injured. Research shows that children in families where domestic abuse takes place are more likely to be subjected to abuse themselves.

Female genital mutilation (FGM)

FGM is a specific type of child abuse towards girls, most commonly aged between 5 and 8 years old. It is a dangerous medical procedure involving the removal of the external female genitalia (sometimes referred to as female circumcision). It is carried out for cultural and religious reasons in order to control sexuality of women and can have a lifelong impact on their physical and emotional well-being.

Why it is important to be vigilant for signs of child abuse

National Society for the Prevention of Cruelty to Children (NSPCC) statistics show that in 2014 more than 56,000 children in the UK were known to be at risk of abuse. Research suggests that this is by no means an accurate picture of what is happening and for every child identified to be at risk there are another eight children who are still suffering abuse. This means that, for many children, adults are not recognising the signs. Although the number of deaths from child abuse is falling, there is an increase in sexual abuse. The most common form of abuse is neglect. Statistics show that one child per week is dying from malnutrition.

Vigilance plays a crucial role in protecting children from harm and neglect, and in promoting their welfare. Being vigilant requires you to get to know the child and their parents so that you become aware of changes in their circumstances that might put additional pressure on the family. Vigilance means that even small clues, signs, hints or minor injuries that are unusual should be picked up. Being vigilant can result in support for the child and/or family being put into place at an early stage, which will help reduce the risk of further harm.

Key term

Vigilance – keeping a careful watch on children and being alert to signs that show they may be at risk of harm or abuse.

It is a statutory requirement of the EYFS that each child has a key person assigned to them. In a small group, discuss the role and responsibilities of the key person and identify why this role is important for child protection.

Indicators of abuse

When a child is experiencing abuse, there are often tell-tale signs. Each child is unique, so they will show signs of abuse in different ways. It is important to remember that it is not the behaviour in itself that causes concern but how it has changed. A child who is usually quiet may become more active, or an active child may become withdrawn.

Changes in personality or behaviour

You may notice that a child:

▶ starts to wet or soil themselves after they have become dry
▶ starts to show unwanted behaviour such as rocking their body, or twisting or pulling out their hair
▶ comforts themselves more often by sucking their thumb or carrying a piece of blanket or toy
▶ is reluctant to play with others and make friends
▶ becomes aggressive or passive and withdrawn.

Changes in behaviour may not indicate a particular type of abuse, but could indicate that a child has been disturbed by something that has happened to them.

▶ It is important that you look out for any signs of injury or changes in a child's behaviour

Physical marks and injuries

Young children frequently have bumps or falls and as a result they will have bruises or grazes, often on their knees or forehead. These marks can usually be explained. Physical signs where there is no explanation, where the reasons given are contradictory or happen frequently are a cause for concern. Be particularly alert to unusual injuries that would not occur accidentally, such as grasp marks. Figure 5.5 shows the type of injuries that may indicate abuse.

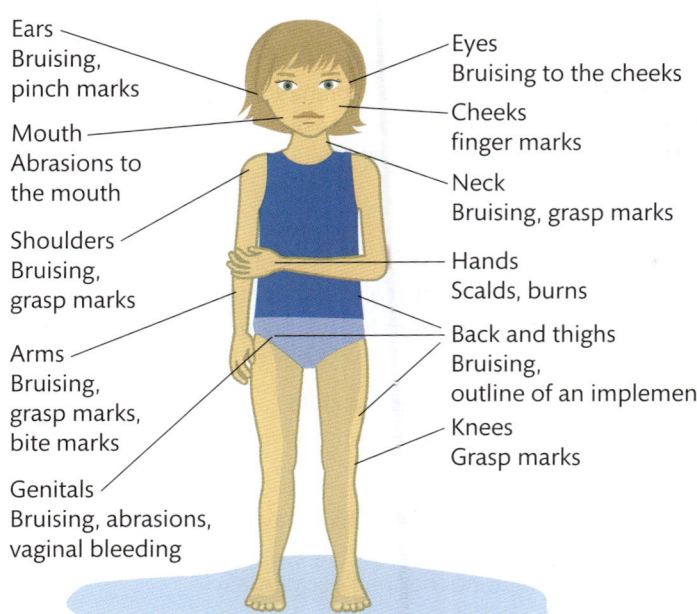

Ears
Bruising,
pinch marks

Mouth
Abrasions to
the mouth

Shoulders
Bruising,
grasp marks

Arms
Bruising,
grasp marks,
bite marks

Genitals
Bruising, abrasions,
vaginal bleeding

Eyes
Bruising to the cheeks

Cheeks
finger marks

Neck
Bruising, grasp marks

Hands
Scalds, burns

Back and thighs
Bruising,
outline of an implement

Knees
Grasp marks

▶ **Figure 5.5:** Injuries that may indicate abuse

The signs identified in Figure 5.5 do not always mean that abuse is happening, as there may be other explanations. For example, what appears to be bruising may be a birthmark. Even so, signs of injury must never be ignored. If you are in any doubt, they must be reported or a child could be put at risk.

Signs of neglect

Neglect can show in a child's appearance and behaviour. Signs may include a child who:

▶ is underweight or overweight for their age

▶ has illnesses that have been left untreated

▶ is unusually tired

▶ has poor personal hygiene

▶ shows they are hungry by eating unusually large amounts, eating quickly or taking food from others

▶ wears dirty clothing, or unsuitable clothing for the weather.

Inappropriate behaviour or language for age and stage of development

It is important that you are able to recognise when behaviour is inappropriate for a child's age and stage of development. In the early years it is natural for very young children to show interest in their own body parts. They will use personal or childlike terms to describe them. From the age of 3 years old they will play games such as mummies and daddies or hospitals. When they reach 5 years old they will become interested in the bodies of their friends. Children naturally touch or rub their own genitals from time to time.

It becomes a cause for concern if behaviour becomes compulsive or if it is not appropriate for a child's age or stage of development – for example, if they use explicit sexual terms or indicate by what they say, or the way they act, that they may have seen sexual acts.

Being unusually dependent on a key person

When children are unhappy or frightened they will seek reassurance from the person they trust most. In early years settings this is likely to be their key person. Children build strong relationships with their key person but will gradually become less dependent on them as they develop.

If children fail to develop independence or revert back to dependence, it can indicate that they are feeling insecure and need reassurance. These concerns should always be investigated. There could be a feasible explanation, such as illness or the death of a family member, but where there is no clear explanation concerns should always be passed on.

> **Safety tip**
>
> When children seek comfort, you must always maintain a professional relationship. Settings should have clear guidelines to follow that explain appropriate physical contact for the age/stage of a child.
>
> Ensure that you are never left alone with a child.

Ⅱ PAUSE POINT   Note down five physical indicators that a child may be suffering from abuse.

Hint   Think about injuries that might not happen accidentally.

Extend   Why is domestic abuse between adults classed as abuse of children?

> **Key terms**
>
> **Disclosure** – when someone tells you, or makes it known in another way, that something (for instance, abuse) has happened.
>
> **Disposition** – a person's temperament or nature.
>
> **Regress** – to move backwards to a previous stage.

Disclosure of abuse by a child, parent or other adult

Disclosure by a child

Some children may **disclose** that they have been, or are being, abused. More often, a child may make comments that hint that all is not well. For instance, they may mention that they have watched an 'adult' film or that they don't like being collected from nursery by a particular person. A child may start to say something and then clam up. For example, they may say, 'I've got a secret…' They may just give a hint, for example, 'I don't like Peter coming into my room.' You must be receptive to these types of comments.

Disclosure by a parent or other adult

Parents or other adults may approach you to tell you that they are concerned a child may be being abused. You must let them know that you will need to share any information with your manager or the person in the setting who has designated responsibility for child protection.

Always seek advice when:

▶ a child's development has slowed or even **regressed**

▶ a child lacks interest, for example, they are not taking part in play

▶ a child becomes clingy

▶ a child appears unusually tired

▶ a parent raises concerns about their child's behaviour, development and/or welfare

▶ a child is showing inappropriate behaviour towards adults, such as overfamiliarity.

How abuse may impact on children's health and development

The effects of abuse will be different depending on the type of abuse and the child's **disposition**. Each type of abuse can seriously affect children's health and holistic development: emotional, social, physical and cognitive. Children who have been abused may be underweight or take longer to crawl, walk or talk compared to children of the same age. The early years are critical, so anything that prevents a child from learning may have lasting consequences for their attainment.

Physical abuse can cause temporary or permanent injury. Broken bones, scalds or burns affect not only a child's health and physical development but also their self-esteem. Non-accidental head injuries (often caused by shaking) may cause neurological impairment or even death.

Children who have been abused often feel that it is their fault and this feeling causes them to think badly of themselves. Children can develop a poor self-image, have low self-esteem and lack confidence. They may find it more difficult to cope with the normal transitions that happen in their lives, such as transferring to primary school.

In the longer term, research suggests that abuse or neglect has serious effects on emotional and social development. Adults who were abused as young children often experience difficulties in building relationships, including intimate relationships. They also suffer from a higher incidence of mental health problems. Abuse can result in self-harm or even suicide.

People who may abuse children

Anyone who has contact with children can abuse them. There are often preconceptions held about who is likely to abuse children. Common beliefs include that it is men who sexually abuse children or that step-parents are more likely to abuse children than birth parents. These beliefs are unfounded. The abuse we read about in the papers is often carried out by strangers, but this is actually very rare. In most cases, abuse is carried out by people known to the child: a parent, family member, family friend or someone who works with the child. Adolescents may also abuse children who are younger than themselves.

Although abuse happens across all sections of society and across all cultures, there are factors within a home that increase the risk of abuse. These factors include:

▶ domestic violence
▶ drug or alcohol abuse
▶ mental health problems
▶ lack of knowledge about child development/children's needs
▶ poverty/unemployment.

C2 Safeguarding children

Legislation, policies and procedures relevant to child protection in early years

As you have already seen, everyone working with children has a duty of care to protect them from harm and to promote their welfare. This responsibility includes you, as a learner, even if you are not employed by the setting.

> **Link**
>
> Look back at Section A1 in this unit to remind yourself how, in 1989, the UNCRC treaty set out the rights and freedoms of all children in 54 articles.

Legislation

Table 5.9 sets out the current key legislation that establishes children's rights to be safe and the responsibilities of children's settings and services. These are civil laws that work to safeguard and promote the **welfare** of children and which underpin working guidelines. There are also criminal laws, which deal with people who have abused children.

> **Key term**
>
> **Welfare** – holistic needs, including health and well-being.

Act	Purpose
Children Act 1989	This act identifies the responsibilities of parents and established the duty of early years professionals to identify and meet the individual needs of children. It introduced the concept of welfare of the child being paramount when decisions are made about them. It includes two important sections that focus specifically on safeguarding children. Local authorities must provide services for safeguarding and promoting children's welfare. • **Section 17** states that local authorities must put services into place that 'safeguard and promote the welfare of children within the area who are **in need**'. • **Section 47** states that the Local Authority has a duty to investigate when there is 'a reasonable cause to suspect that a child ... is suffering, or is likely to suffer, significant harm'.
Education Act 2002	This act sets out the responsibilities of local education authorities, governing bodies, head teachers and all those people working in schools to ensure that children are safe and free from harm.
Children Act 2004	This act came into being in response to reviews of high-profile cases of child abuse where it was shown that children had been failed by services. It introduced the requirements for: • services to work more closely together • a shared process for the assessment of children's needs • a shared database of information that is relevant to the safety and welfare of children • a Local Safeguarding Children Board to be set up in every area (LSCB) • support to be put in place earlier for families experiencing problems.

> **Key term**
>
> **In need** – refers to children who are unlikely to maintain, or be given the opportunity to maintain, a reasonable standard of health or development, or children whose health could be impaired without the support of local authority services. It includes children who are disabled.

Statutory frameworks

Statutory frameworks give guidance on how laws should be implemented in early years environments. In England there are two key documents that you should become familiar with: *Statutory Framework for the Early Years Foundation Stage* (2014) and *Working together to safeguard children* (2015). If you are working in Wales, refer to *All Wales Child Protection Procedures 2008* or *Safeguarding Children – Working Together Under the Children Act 2004* (2007), and if you work in Northern Ireland, look at *Co-operating to Safeguard Children* (Northern Ireland Order) 2003.

Statutory Framework for the Early Years Foundation Stage

The framework for the EYFS gives guidance for working with children from birth to 5 years. Section 3 of the document sets out the safeguarding and welfare requirements for early years settings and services, including the duty to:

▶ provide an environment where children can grow and learn

▶ keep children safe and secure

▶ promote good health

▶ take steps when there are concerns about a child's safety and welfare.

Working together to safeguard children 2015

This guidance sets out the duty of care for all organisations, including those that are voluntary, that provide services for children up to the age of 18 years. This includes, for instance, education services, social workers, health services, leisure services and the police. The document focuses on the importance of shared responsibility and how agencies should cooperate to safeguard children and promote their welfare.

It has two key principles:

▶ safeguarding is the responsibility of all those working with children

▶ a child-centred approach is essential for services to be effective in keeping children safe and promoting their welfare.

Policies and procedures

Policies and procedures in early years settings are written to help adults protect children and promote their welfare, but they must comply with current legislation and statutory requirements. With particular regard to child protection, there are additional requirements that children's settings must have in place, which are:

▶ a policy and procedure for safe working practices that meet the requirements of the Local Safeguarding Children Board

▶ a policy and procedure for whistleblowing, when professionals have concerns about the practice of colleagues

▶ a lead professional with designated responsibility for child protection

▶ processes for safe staff recruitment and ongoing monitoring, to include enhanced disclosure through the Disclosure and Barring Service (DBS)

▶ a programme of child protection training for all staff.

e-safety

Recently, as a result of increased use of the internet and electronic communication systems, children are being put at more risk of harm.

Childcare settings are now required to have a policy and procedures on e-safety, including monitoring procedures and having filters in place to ensure that children do not access unsuitable materials and information online.

Research

Visit www.gov.uk and search for *Working together to safeguard children*.

This document will help you to understand your shared responsibility for keeping children safe from abuse. In particular, refer to page 12 to identify children and families who would benefit from early help, page 16 on sharing information and Chapter 2 for the roles and responsibilities of early years settings and other professionals.

Link

Section A1 of Unit 11 looks at the DBS in more detail.

Look back at Section A2 of this unit to remind yourself what whistleblowing means.

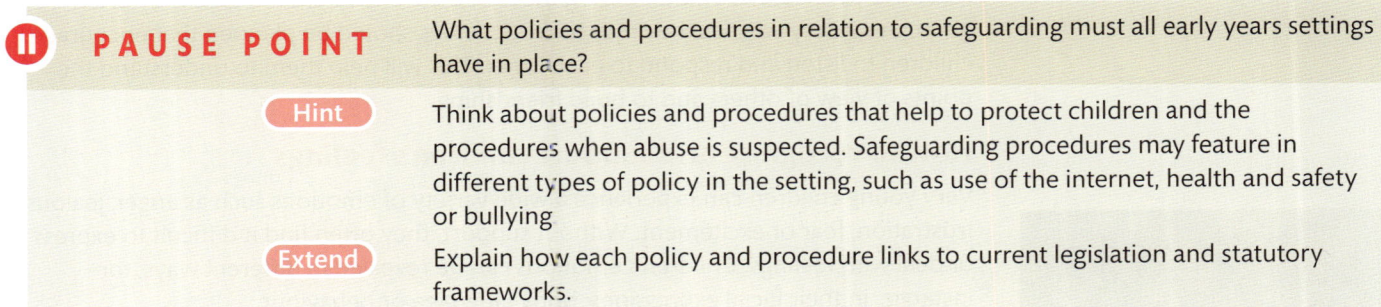

⏸ PAUSE POINT   What policies and procedures in relation to safeguarding must all early years settings have in place?

Hint   Think about policies and procedures that help to protect children and the procedures when abuse is suspected. Safeguarding procedures may feature in different types of policy in the setting, such as use of the internet, health and safety or bullying

Extend   Explain how each policy and procedure links to current legislation and statutory frameworks.

The role of observation in recognising changes in children's behaviour

As you have seen already, observation is an important part of the early years professional's role. It is typically used to understand children's stage of development, how they learn and their interests. Observation helps professionals get to know individual children and how they behave in different situations and environments. It can be a useful tool in understanding that children are unhappy or possibly being subjected to abuse, through seeing subtle changes in behaviour or physical signs.

Why children may be more vulnerable to abuse

You must be extra vigilant if you work with babies or children who have a disability. NSPCC statistics relating to children under 1 year show that they are eight times more likely to be killed than children in all the other age groups, accounting for almost half of serious case reviews. Children who are disabled are three times more likely to be abused than non-disabled children. The abuse may also be more difficult to recognise, as they may show signs that can be confused with symptoms of a physical or learning disability.

Babies and children who have a disability are at higher risk because they:

▶ are dependent on others for all of their care

▶ are not able to communicate that they have been abused

▶ require intimate care.

Statistics relating to children under 1 year old show that they are eight times more likely to be abused than older children – accounting for almost half of the **serious case reviews**.

The importance of children having their voice heard

Article 12 of the UNCRC states that all children who are able to express themselves should have the right to do so freely. Early years professionals must always take the child's views into consideration. Involving children in decisions about themselves shows them that you value what they say, their opinions and ideas. These may be everyday decisions such as the activity they want to take part in or life-changing decisions about their future. Of course, not all children can express themselves easily. They may be very young or have communication difficulties. If so, they can be helped to communicate by using signing, objects of reference or pictures. In some situations, when a child's family is not able to speak, or it is not appropriate for them to speak for the child, an **advocate** may represent their views.

When planning routines, time should be set aside for individual children to be with their key person and have their undivided attention. This can happen naturally during mealtimes or when helping children with their personal care. It is important to be receptive to children's chatter during these one-to-one interactions as they often give clues to any worries they may have. Activities should be planned that encourage children to listen and respond to each other. This will help them to understand the points of view of others and to build friendships.

How to recognise and support children's feelings

Very young children can experience a wide variety of emotions such as anger, jealousy, frustration, fear or excitement. Without support, they often find it difficult to express or deal with feelings. Children's emotions can be revealed in different ways, for instance, in their facial expressions, body language or behaviour.

Babies can be soothed to reassure and calm them. As their vocabulary expands, children can be helped by giving them the words to use to describe the way they feel. For example, you could say, 'I know you felt sad when Dad left but he will be back soon to take you home for dinner', or 'I know you are angry because Adam is playing with the car but it will be your turn next.' This will give children the message that it is fine to have these feelings and that you can empathise with them.

At times, children can be overcome by their emotions and this can result in negative behaviour. If they lose control they can become quite frightened. Young children may stamp their feet, scream, cry or have temper tantrums. When angry or jealous, children may display physical aggression towards other children or adults.

It is important that the adult recognises the cause of the child's feelings and supports them to express their feelings in an appropriate way. Physical play can be a safe way for children to release their emotions, for instance, kicking a ball, climbing, or playing with soft and flexible (malleable) materials.

▶ Why is it important to reassure a child who is feeling distressed?

Link

Unit 1 and Unit 7 have more information about children's social and emotional development.

The importance of supporting social and emotional development

Children's emotional and social development involves them having an awareness of themselves and how they relate to others. Children need to be nurtured in their early years as their personality and temperament develop. The environment has a direct influence on the way that children feel about themselves; they will thrive when they are made to feel safe and secure. When children are confident, independent and have good self-esteem they are more able to cope with the everyday difficulties they may come across. Children who are independent and self-confident are more likely to tell an adult when they are unhappy or frightened. It is important that their social and emotional development is promoted through every aspect of their care.

Here are some examples of how you can support children's social and emotional development.

▶ Provide challenging activities that give children a sense of achievement and help to develop their self-esteem and confidence.

▶ Give children choices to develop their confidence about making their own decisions.

▶ Encourage physical activities, for instance, running, climbing and sit-and-ride toys, to boost children's energy and feelings of well-being.

▶ Use stories, circle time and emotion cards to support children in expressing their feelings.

▶ Teach and encourage personal care skills to develop children's independence.

▶ Provide opportunities and experiences that help children to build friendships.

▶ Use art, music and movement activities to help children release their anxieties and explore their feelings.

Ⅱ PAUSE POINT   Explain how a safe and secure environment supports children's emotional development.

> **Hint**   Identify times/situations in your own setting where children have the opportunity to talk and express their feelings.

> **Extend**   Plan an activity for one child or a small group of children that will support their emotional development.

How to be an approachable adult

Think about someone you know with qualities that make them approachable. It is likely to be someone who always has time for you, has shown you respect and is genuinely interested in what you do. They demonstrate active listening because they are keen to hear your views and then take what you say into consideration. They may not always agree with you but they will be consistent and fair.

In an early years setting these qualities are essential. The key person provides for all the child's needs when the parent is not there. Although it is important for them to build a strong relationship with the child, the adult needs to remember that this relationship is different from the relationship between a child and their parent.

Although the relationship should always remain professional, it is essential that the adult knows the child's background and interests so they can demonstrate a genuine interest in the child; The key person should know and talk about things that interest the child; for example, they could suggest making a train out of junk boxes because they know the child loves travelling by train.

How to empower children

It is not always possible to prevent abuse, but adults can reduce the risk of abuse happening by providing an environment that helps children to protect themselves. Children will feel more confident disclosing their fears in an environment that encourages supportive relationships and recognises and celebrates individuality.

Games and activities are a good way to help children protect themselves. They can also be used to support children who have been abused. Activities can provide indirect support by developing children's confidence and self-esteem, or by helping them to release negative feelings. They can be used to empower children to protect themselves, say 'No' and make safe choices in difficult situations.

How to support children to protect themselves through games and activities

The following types of activity empower children to protect themselves.

▶ Body-awareness activities such as puzzles, identification games, songs and rhymes about bodies, and learning about the 'underwear rule'.

▶ Activities that teach children to be assertive. For example, teaching children to say no to inappropriate or harmful behaviour by using puppets, stories, drama or body-awareness songs such as 'My body belongs to me'.

▶ Activities that teach children not to keep secrets by helping them to understand the difference between surprises (e.g. about presents and parties) and secrets (e.g. being told not to tell about being hurt or touched inappropriately).

▶ Activities that teach children what to do if they are lost, such as circle time, the use of drama or use of puppets.

▶ Activities that explore feelings, such as producing anti-bullying or 'group rules' posters. Older children should be given the opportunity to discuss what they understand by the term 'bullying'.

> **Research**
>
> Find out about how to use the underwear rule with young children – the NSPCC website will provide more information.

C3 Responding to concerns about abuse

How to respond to a child who discloses abuse

It is always upsetting if you find out that a child has been harmed or neglected but it is important not to show your own emotions. Facial expressions and body language can give mixed messages. If an adult appears shocked, the child is likely to feel that they are in the wrong, or even that they 'deserved' the abuse. It is the child's feelings that are important and these feelings should be recognised and acknowledged.

Think about how you would respond verbally if a child tells you they are being abused. Your first response is really important and it can affect how well a child copes. Your response should give the message that the child has done the right thing in telling you. For instance, you could say, 'I'm glad that you have told me', or 'You have done the right thing to let me know that you are worried.' You can also show that you understand their feelings. For example, you could comment that what has happened must have made the child feel scared or unhappy.

Responses should be open to avoid leading the child into giving a particular answer. For example, rather than ask, 'Did your dad hit you?' you may ask, 'How did you get those bruises?' You may feel angry with the abuser but you should not make comments or pass judgements on the person who has been named. Instead, focus on reassuring the child that the action was wrong and that you will tell someone who can help them.

Always:

▶ take disclosure seriously

▶ remain calm and listen carefully

▶ avoid using leading questions

▶ reassure the child that they are not to blame

▶ tell children that you will have to tell someone who can help them

▶ write down what you have observed or what has been said as soon as possible

▶ pass information to the person who is responsible for child protection.

Never:

▶ promise to keep information a secret

▶ interrogate or ask further questions, as this could affect investigations

▶ make promises to children or adults who tell you about abuse

▶ discuss what has happened with other colleagues or the child's family.

How to respond when others have concerns about the welfare of a child

If you are approached by a parent, colleague or others who have concerns about a child, the information should always be taken seriously. They may be worried about talking to you and need reassurance that they have done the right thing. You must explain that it is your duty to pass on concerns even if they ask you not to, or say that they will report it themselves.

How to respond if there are accusations or concerns about colleagues

If you have concerns that a colleague or professional is abusing a child, or that their practice is impacting on a child's welfare, your actions should be the same as if the abuser were a parent, family member or stranger. You must act immediately to protect children by informing the lead professional in your setting who has responsibility for safeguarding, or the manager. If you are unable to approach either person because they are involved in abuse or poor practice, you will need to contact social services.

This type of reporting is known as whistleblowing (see Section A2 for a definition of whistleblowing). These are difficult situations, but your first priority must always be the child. It is important that you do not discuss what has happened with others who do not need to know. However, you may need to seek support for yourself from the person within your setting who has safeguarding responsibilities or a professional from an outside agency.

▶ If you have any concerns, you must get advice from your manager or the person responsible for child protection

The importance of responding appropriately to concerns

Every early years setting must have a safeguarding policy that explains the setting's commitment to keeping children safe and promoting their welfare. It should also describe how it intends to do this. Procedures give clear guidance to staff on how to respond to concerns in different child protection situations. For instance, the policy may state that the setting has a commitment to reporting concerns about children, and procedures should show how the concerns are recorded and reported. Failure to comply with a setting's policy for safeguarding will delay support and may put children at increased risk of harm or abuse.

Why it is important to believe a child

Children will rarely lie about child abuse. It takes a child a lot of courage to tell someone what has happened to them. More often, they will only hint at what is happening because they are afraid of the abuser or may think that they won't be believed. Imagine how a child may feel if an adult just dismisses something they have said as being a lie or exaggeration.

Some adults may feel a reluctance to believe a child because they:

▶ have assumptions about abuse that make them less likely to believe some children – for example, they may believe that professionals would not abuse their children

▶ know and like the adult

▶ find it difficult to believe that an adult could act towards a child in a particular way

▶ assume that the behaviour is acceptable in some cultures

▶ are concerned that they are interpreting what has been said incorrectly and that they are making a fuss.

If you do not believe children it will make them less willing to repeat their fears to you or other adults. This can result in abuse going undetected for some time and put children at further risk.

Remember, it is not your role to decide if a child has been abused. You must avoid judgements and jumping to conclusions – only share the concerns you have. However, you must always respond when you notice typical physical signs of abuse or changes in a child's behaviour.

Why professionals must follow the reporting procedure of the setting

It is your duty to pass on concerns using the correct procedures and it is vital that you know about and follow reporting procedures in your own service or setting. Reports should be passed to the named professional in the setting with responsibility for safeguarding as soon as possible.

You must ensure that reports are written clearly, carefully and factually. They should include:

▶ the child's name and date of birth
▶ the time and date when signs were noticed or abuse was disclosed
▶ others who were present
▶ what happened, including anything that was said
▶ your own signature and the date.

This is because the report may need to be used in future reviews, child protection conferences or even court cases. You should always be objective in your comments and avoid making any value judgements. For example, 'Chloe's clothes smelled strongly of urine' is preferable to 'Chloe is always dirty and neglected'. It is important that you report the words that the child has used and do not change them into 'adult speak'.

How information should be recorded and shared

Procedures give guidance on when and how information must be recorded, stored and shared, and who has access to it. Settings must establish a process for recording welfare concerns about individual children. This is called a welfare or safeguarding file and it must be kept separate from confidential but 'non-sensitive' information such as a child's contact details.

Each separate piece of information, such as a change in a child's behaviour or an injury, helps to build up a picture of the child's developmental welfare – a bit like a jigsaw puzzle. This provides the person in the setting who has safeguarding responsibilities with an overview of concerns that have been raised. Information may include:

▶ concerns about health and welfare
▶ assessments and records of discussions about a child's health and welfare, including face-to-face conversations, telephone calls or meetings
▶ formal plans such as an individual education plan (IEP) or child protection plan
▶ copies of letters sent or received about a child's welfare.

The information must be kept confidential and only accessed and shared with people who need to know: the lead professional in the setting with safeguarding responsibilities and, where there is cause for concern, children's social services.

It is important that any information entered into the safeguarding file is written accurately and clearly. If information is not clear or does not show accurate dates, for instance, it will be more difficult to make decisions or timely referrals. A key piece of information that is missed out or cannot be deciphered could have serious consequences for a child's safety and welfare. Inaccurate information could even affect the outcome of a court case where there has been abuse.

Responding to concerns

Samirah is an early years professional working in a private nursery with children from 6 months to 5 years. Earlier today, Claire, one of the work placement students at the nursery, came to her and said that she was worried. She had seen Naomi, a colleague, taking some of the children into a screened-off area to change them rather than changing them in the designated changing area. Claire asked Samirah not to say anything as she didn't want to lose her work placement and not be able to finish her course.

Check your knowledge

1 What should Samirah say to Claire?

2 What action should Samirah take next?

3 Which policy could Samirah refer to?

4 What could be the result of Samirah's actions?

5 Why is it important that Samirah acts immediately?

6 What could be the long-term impact for children at the nursery if Samirah does not act?

Child protection procedures

The process of investigation

If the person in the setting who is responsible for safeguarding believes that a child may be at risk, they must immediately report their concerns to the children's social care department in their local authority. They may speak to a social worker on the telephone but concerns must be put in writing within 48 hours. The social worker will then decide if an early help assessment is required within one working day.

Assessment

An early help assessment involves an assessment of the child's developmental needs in agreement with parents. An assessment may be carried out where there are concerns about a child's well-being and/or a family's ability to meet their child's health or developmental needs. A professional, who could be a family support worker or key person, will be identified to lead the assessment. Relevant people, from different agencies and the child's parents, will contribute information about the child. The purpose is to put targeted support into place to reduce the risk of harm or abuse.

Where it is considered that a child is 'in need', statutory intervention will be required and the case referred to children's social care. A Child in Need meeting will be held, which will be chaired by a social worker. This may involve other services but, most importantly, it will involve the child and their parents. This instance may arise, for example, where a parent has been unable to take sufficient care of a child because they are unemployed or have mental health problems. In these cases, under Section 17 of the Children Act 1989, a care plan will be put into place identifying services that can work with the family to ease the problems, reduce the risk of abuse and promote the child's welfare.

When there is sufficient concern that a child has been harmed or is likely to be harmed, a strategy discussion will take place to decide whether enquiries must be initiated under Section 47 of the Children Act 1989. The strategy discussion will be followed by a more in-depth core assessment of the child's needs. If it is considered that the child remains at risk of harm, a Child Protection Conference will be held.

Link

See Table 5.9 in Section C2 for more information about Section 17 and Section 47 of the Children Act 1989.

Child Protection Conference

A Child Protection Conference is led by a manager from children's social care or the NSPCC. It is attended by professionals from a range of relevant services such as health, social care and early years providers. The purpose of the Conference is to review the child's needs and the level of risk of harm or abuse to the child, and discuss the action that should be taken. A child who is thought to be at continued risk will become the subject of a Child Protection Plan. If a child is thought to be at immediate risk, the local authority can apply for an Emergency Protection Order (EPO) to remove the child from the family or to remove the perpetrator of abuse.

Child Protection Plan

Once it has been agreed by the conference that the child should be the subject of a Child Protection Plan, there will be a meeting of key professionals led by a named professional, usually a social worker. The purpose of the plan is to keep the child safe from harm. The plan should address the child's immediate needs, taking their long-term needs into consideration. It may also include information on the support to be given to family members to help them safeguard the child.

The plan must:

▶ be based on the information learned about the child and their family during the core assessment

▶ identify the interventions that are necessary to give the best outcome for the child

▶ identify the services, professionals and the child's parents or carers, and their role in supporting the plan

▶ be regularly reviewed.

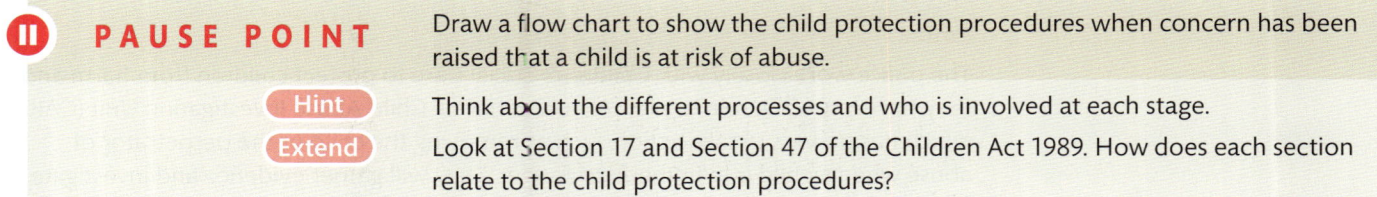

Ⅱ PAUSE POINT   Draw a flow chart to show the child protection procedures when concern has been raised that a child is at risk of abuse.

> Hint   Think about the different processes and who is involved at each stage.

> Extend   Look at Section 17 and Section 47 of the Children Act 1989. How does each section relate to the child protection procedures?

How agencies work together to safeguard children

Individual agencies may have information about a child and their family which in itself is not concerning but when shared builds a picture of the child's overall needs. In many cases, children's needs can only be met through different agencies, so it is critical that they plan and work together. Research shows that children are safeguarded most effectively when they are listened to, and their interests and needs are firmly at the centre of collaborative assessment and planning. The document *Working together to safeguard children* (2015) gives guidance on how this collaboration should be achieved.

Following the death of Victoria Climbié in 2000, a report from Lord Laming (2003) concluded that services had failed to share concerns about her welfare. As a result, the Children Act 2004 sets out the statutory duty for services to work more closely together. Even so, concerns remain. Reports following serious case reviews, such as the death of Daniel Pelka in 2012, continue to highlight that there are weaknesses in information sharing.

Local authorities have responsibility for the welfare and protection of children in their area. They are required to coordinate children's services in partnership with a wide range of services. Services may include public services such as the police, private organisations such as specialist health professionals and voluntary organisations such as advocacy services. The roles and responsibilities of key agencies are now described.

Local agencies involved in safeguarding

Although the roles of individual services are clear, child protection cannot be provided by agencies in isolation. It is important to stress that everyone working in early years environments, including volunteers, have a personal and joint responsibility to safeguard children, see Figure 5.6.

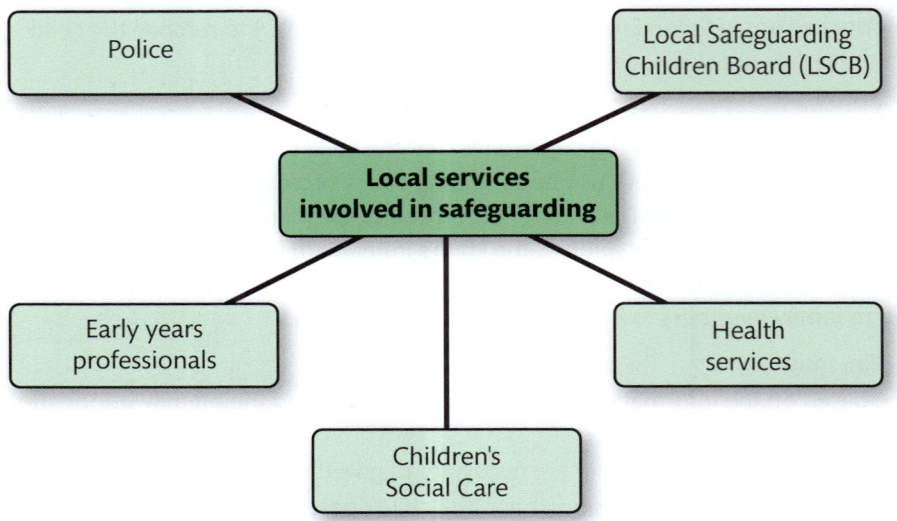

▶ **Figure 5.6:** Local services involved in safeguarding

Police

The police work closely with Children's Social Care to protect children from harm and they have a specific role to play. All forces have a Child Abuse Investigation Unit (CAIU), which has powers to take action such as removing the child or the perpetrator of abuse when a child is in immediate danger. They will gather evidence and investigate when it is thought a crime has been committed.

Children's Social Care

Children's Social Care (CSC) has a key role in safeguarding and promoting the welfare of children who are in need. To do this it must work in partnership with parents and other agencies. Social workers lead on assessments at each stage of child protection procedures, recording information and taking decisions (with their manager) on further action. They are also responsible for conducting interviews with children and parents.

Health services

Health professionals, in particular GPs and doctors in emergency departments, may examine children who have injuries they suspect to be non-accidental. They have a duty to alert CSC when abuse is suspected. Health professionals will carry out medical examinations and, if necessary, give evidence in court.

Local Safeguarding Children Boards (LSCBs)

The Children Act 2004 requires there to be a LSCB in every local area. Each board is made up of experts from the range of children's services. The LSCB has a statutory duty to oversee the work of key agencies in the context of child protection. They develop policies and procedures for the recruitment of people who work with children and monitor and evaluate training.

An important aspect of their work is to conduct a serious case review when a child dies as a result of abuse or neglect, and for serious cases of sexual abuse and/or when a child has sustained a life-threatening injury. You can access reports of serious case reviews on your local authority LSCB website.

The role of the National Society for the Prevention of Cruelty to Children (NSPCC)

The NSPCC is a charitable organisation. Its role as its name suggests, is to work to protect children from abuse. The NSPCC is the only charitable organisation that has the statutory power, alongside the police and children's social services, to take action when children are at risk of abuse. The NSPCC also:

- provides services to support families and children
- provides a helpline for people to call who are worried about a child
- provides a helpline for children in distress or danger
- raises awareness of abuse through its website, advertising campaigns and training materials
- works to influence the law and social policy to better protect children
- shares expertise with other professionals.

Assessment practice 5.4

C.P4   C.P5   C.M3   C.D2

Case study

Brad is 4 years old and has been in the reception class for 2 months. He is often late for school and is sometimes brought in by his older sister.

Leyla, Brad's teacher, is concerned that Brad appears underweight. Leyla arranged for a meeting with the school nurse but Brad's mum didn't turn up.

In the last few days, Brad has appeared particularly tired. One of the other children complained that Brad had taken her snack from her bag. Today, Leyla has been told by a parent that Brad's parents often shout at him for making a mess and leave him out in the garden when it is cold.

1 Write a report that:
- identifies the types of abuse that may be happening
- examines the behavioural and physical indicators that suggest types of abuse
- gives detailed advice on the procedures for responding, recording and reporting that Leyla should follow.

2 Assess Leyla's overall responsibility to safeguard and promote Brad's welfare in the setting, including how she should work with other professionals at each stage of the child protection procedure.

Plan
- What are the success criteria for the task?
- Do I need clarification about my knowledge and understanding of abuse and the role of professionals?

Do
- Am I reading effectively so that I can identify the key information to complete this task?
- Am I able to make links between the situations in case studies to procedures, roles and responsibilities?

Review
- Can I draw information together to reach a reasoned conclusion?
- Can I recognise whether I have met the criteria for this task?

D Demonstrate how to recognise and assess hazards and risks to children and respond to emergencies in an early years setting

Link

Refer back to Section A2 of this unit, particularly Tables 5.1, 5.2 and 5.3, to remind yourself of the potential hazards of resources and activities in indoor and outdoor environments.

D1 Risk assessment in early years

Hazards in early years settings

There are many different hazards in early years settings that you need to be aware of.

Some types of commonly used toys and equipment can also be hazards, as shown in Table 5.10.

▶ **Table 5.10:** Dangers you should check for in equipment and resources

Items/materials	Danger
Toys and resources made from plastic	• Plastic can become brittle with age and snap
Toys and resources with moving parts, e.g. wheeled toys	• Moving parts can become weakened over time • Screws can become loose
Toys with batteries	• Batteries can leak. When toys are not in use, batteries should be removed and stored in a locked place
Resources or equipment that require electricity	• These resources should be checked every year • Any wear and tear or malfunctioning, e.g. flickering lights, will mean that the resource or piece of equipment should be removed

Common types of injuries to children of different ages

Thousands of children are admitted to hospital every year as a result of injuries sustained in accidents. Table 5.11 shows some common accidents with examples of how they may have occurred.

▶ **Table 5.11:** Common childhood accidents

Accident/injury	Possible cause of the accident/injury
Poisoning	• A child finds some medicine lying around
Bite or sting	• A child is bitten by a dog in the park • A child is stung by a bee, wasp or other insect while playing outside
Chemical burn	• A child touches some bleach that has been put in a bucket and left unattended
Cut	• A child finds a penknife that has been dropped and left on the floor
Crushing	• A child is in a car park and is not seen by a driver
Electrocution	• A child pushes their finger into a lamp fitting
Fall	• A child falls from an open window
Introduction of a foreign body	• A child swallows a nail
Suffocation	• A child puts a plastic bag over their head, pretending it is a mask
Drowning	• A child is playing in a paddling pool and slips face forward
Burn	• A child finds some matches and lights one
Scald	• A child tries to move a mug of tea as it is on their book

How injuries might be avoided

As you can see, young children are injured in many ways. While it is a part of normal childhood for children to have some bumps and bruises, it is essential that you are aware of how to prevent serious injuries. This applies to care of children in group settings as well as in home-based environments.

Supervising and being alert

A key way to keep children safe is to know what they are doing and what and who they are playing with. This means being alert at all times. Most early years settings have a key person system. If you are a key person, you need to take responsibility for your children and keep an eye on what they are doing.

> **Theory into practice**
>
> Does the key person in your work setting take responsibility for where individual children are?

New equipment, resources and activities

When you introduce new equipment, resources or activities, it is important that you are particularly vigilant. Although you may think a resource is safe, a child may do something with it that is unexpected.

Ages and stages of children

The ages and stages of children and understanding their capabilities should have an impact on your risk assessments, the level of supervision you provide and your choice of resources and equipment. In home-based care settings, in particular, mixed ages of children can cause difficulties.

Table 5.12 outlines key characteristics and behaviours of babies and children at different ages/stages that may be hazardous, and the implications these characteristics have for your practice.

▸ **Table 5.12:** Key characteristics of babies and children and the implications they have for your practice in terms of risk assessment

Age/stage of children	Key characteristics/behaviours	Implications for your practice
Non-mobile babies	• They will wriggle and roll so may fall off raised surfaces • They will take any object to mouth	• Do not leave babies on raised surfaces • Babies should be supervised closely unless they are asleep
Mobile babies	• Mobile babies can move very quickly • They will explore and touch everything in their range • They will mouth any object found on the floor or at their height • They will pull themselves up onto furniture and other items that may not be stable • They will attempt to climb stairs • They have no sense of danger	• Keep floors vacuumed and free of objects that could be choking hazards • Remove tablecloths and furniture or equipment that is unstable • Use stair gates • Babies should be supervised closely unless they are asleep
Toddlers	• They may still be mouthing up until 18 months • They are restless and exceedingly active • They will copy the actions of older children and adults • They are determined • They love climbing • They love throwing • They can move fast • They may climb out of their cot or bed to play and explore • They have no understanding of danger • They are impulsive	• Make sure there are plenty of activities that will engage them, especially climbing and throwing • Keep medicines out of reach • Create child-friendly areas • Provide close adult supervision at all times • Do not leave toddlers unsupervised unless they are asleep

Age/stage of children	Key characteristics/behaviours	Implications for your practice
3–4-year-olds	<ul><li>They will play with others but may squabble or become very excited</li><li>They may engage in superhero play and try to hit each other or jump from heights</li><li>They may copy what they have seen adults do, e.g. attempt to use lighters or feed a baby</li><li>They have limited understanding of danger and may forget instructions</li></ul>	<ul><li>Be ready to step in if play becomes very boisterous or children are getting cross with each other</li><li>Be aware of your actions in terms of giving children ideas</li><li>Be ready to keep repeating rules and expectations</li><li>Increase adult awareness and close supervision for some activities</li><li>Children need close supervision when they are very excited or tired</li></ul>
4–8-year-olds	<ul><li>They will play cooperatively, but may show off to peers or become excited by ideas</li><li>They may engage in superhero play</li><li>They may engage in risky behaviours if they are bored or the environment is not stimulating enough</li><li>They have more awareness of safety, but still need reminding of rules</li><li>They enjoy having some responsibility and independence</li><li>They are starting to understand the concept of 'rules'</li></ul>	<ul><li>You should recognise that children's behaviours can change according to who they are with</li><li>Make sure that the play environment continues to be stimulating and physically challenging outdoors</li><li>Talk to children about rules and the reasons behind them</li><li>Close adult supervision will be required for some activities. Adults need to be aware of what children are doing at all times</li></ul>

Ⅱ PAUSE POINT Why might the risk of choking or swallowing an object be higher among mobile babies and children under 18 months?

Hint Look at Table 5.12 and see the age-related characteristics in relation to how they explore.

Extend What are the key differences in terms of the role of the adult between keeping toddlers safe and keeping older children safe?

The role of risk assessment in identifying hazards

As you saw in Section A of this unit, risk assessment is the process of identifying and minimising hazards in the environment. It is a key way in which you can help to keep children safe.

Risk assessment is a process that can be done informally as well as formally. Formal risk assessments are needed when the risks are thought to be significant. The risk assessment should be written down but you will need to follow the specific risk assessment procedure for your setting. This will be based on the requirements of the country in which you work.

The process of risk assessment is quite straightforward.

1 Look at an area, activity or resource and identify what hazards or risks may be associated with it. Think about what the consequences of an accident may be. It can be worth thinking about common types of accident while doing this. (Some settings use a rating scale to identify the level of risk.)

2 Decide to whom the risk might apply and how they could be harmed. Remember, something that is safe for older children may be dangerous for younger ones.

3 Evaluate the risk and decide how it will be managed (what precautions will be put in place), e.g. supervising children more closely or putting equipment away after use.

4   Record this information accurately and coherently on a sheet.

5   Sign and date the sheet.

6   Make sure the precautions are implemented.

The same process applies to assessing both indoor and outdoor provision, but assessments for outdoor provision may need to take account of the weather. This is because each type of weather may create new hazards. A slide in dry weather is a different proposition to a slide that is wet because it has been raining. A surface that is safe in dry weather may become hazardous in icy conditions.

Reviewing and updating assessments

As well as carrying out risk assessments for individual 'one-off' activities, settings also need to do regular risk assessments on areas within their setting. These risk assessments need to be reviewed and updated when necessary. Most settings review them annually but they will need to review them more often if there are changes made to the areas. Changes may include intakes of younger children or a larger number of children. It is important that risk assessments are also reviewed in the light of any accidents.

> **Theory into practice**
>
> Find out who is responsible for risk assessments in your workplace. Do you have specific forms that are filled in? Where are these kept?

Assessment practice 5.5   D.P6   D.M4   D.D3

You have been asked to present information to a group of childcare learners about how to carry out a risk assessment and minimise risks in an early years setting, both indoors and outdoors.

Your information should include:

- a range of risk assessments covering different ages and stages of children, both indoors and outdoors
- an analysis of how these risk assessments would help keep children safe
- an evaluation of the effectiveness of your approach to risk assessment.

Plan

- What information is most relevant for this task?
- Where can I find additional information?

Do

- Am I presenting the information accurately and concisely?
- Am I managing my time effectively?

Review

- Can I justify why I have decided to approach this task in the way that I have?
- Have I evaluated my work and am I confident that it fulfils the task?

D2 Recognising accidents and emergencies

Although the following information covers how to respond to accidents and emergencies, it cannot take the place of a valid, recognised first-aid qualification. Until you have been on a first-aid course, you should be very careful about any actions you take in an emergency, because the wrong action could cause more harm to the casualty. If in doubt, summon help first.

How to respond to non-emergency common injuries

Most often you will need to deal with common injuries such as grazes, bruises or splinters. Grazes should be washed in clean water only to remove dirt and gravel. Antiseptics should not be used. Some children are allergic to plasters, so injuries should be left uncovered. If the graze or cut is bleeding it should be washed and covered with a sterile dressing until it stops and then you should seek advice from a first aider. Bruises can be helped with the use of cold compress. The area around splinters should be washed and left so that they work their way out. You must always follow procedures of the settings and if in any doubt advice should always be sought from a first aider. Remember to wash your own hands and put on protective gloves before dealing with minor injuries.

How to recognise an emergency situation

It is important that when an emergency situation arises, everyone working with children quickly reacts to it in a calm but careful manner. There are some situations when it will always be essential to call for assistance from a colleague or to call the emergency services directly. It is worth remembering that an emergency situation may not necessarily involve a child; it may be a situation involving another adult, e.g. an adult may have cut themselves.

Emergency help should be called for if:

- there is a fire or explosion
- a child is trapped
- there has been a traffic incident
- there is a bomb threat
- someone is using violence or threatening violence
- serious damage is being caused or could be caused to property
- a criminal has been disturbed or apprehended
- there is danger to life
- there is a serious injury
- someone has chest pains
- someone is having difficulty breathing
- someone has a severe allergic reaction
- someone is bleeding heavily
- someone is fitting or has a concussion
- someone is drowning
- someone has been poisoned.

How to call for assistance from colleagues and emergency services

Depending on the emergency, you may need to seek assistance from a colleague or from the emergency services. It is essential at all times to remain calm and also to speak clearly and concisely so that either your colleagues or the emergency services can quickly find out what course of action needs to take place.

Calling for emergency help

To call for the emergency services in the UK, you are required to ring 999 or 112. Calls to these numbers should only be made in the event of an emergency that requires the presence of an ambulance, the police or fire services. For gas leaks, you should contact the emergency number for the gas services, which is 0800 111 999.

Making a call

If you have to call the emergency services, it is important that you do so promptly but also calmly. Under stress, it is very easy to forget information and so remaining as calm as you can is essential. The emergency services are used to taking calls and will ask you a series of questions in a set order, as follows.

1 The service that you require – this allows the call to be handled by the correct service.
2 The address and, if possible, the postcode or a nearby landmark – this allows the emergency vehicles to be dispatched.
3 The number you are calling from – this allows them to call back if the connection is broken. It also helps them to eliminate hoax calls.

4 What has happened – this allows the dispatcher to send the correct emergency service. If an incident involves a child you should let the operator know this. Do not waste time by trying to talk about what has happened before the operator has taken down the address as this can slow down the dispatch of the emergency vehicle.

Ambulance

If a child is unwell or there is an accident, you should give their age, sex and any medical history. Provide information about the symptoms and what has happened to cause the accident. You should also say what has been done so far and what is happening to the child at the time. Ideally, you should try to make the call close to the child so that you can pass on any instructions to them or follow instructions with them.

Police

If someone is being violent or is threatening violence, you should try to call the police from a safe place. You should make it clear why you need immediate help, for example, by explaining the level of the threat and the type of actions that are taking place.

If you see criminal activity, you should not confront the perpetrator.

Fire and rescue service

In the event of a fire or explosion, only call 999 or 112 once you are out of danger yourself. You should give the location of the fire and say if the building has been evacuated or anyone is trapped. You should not go back into the building.

In the event that a child is trapped, consider calling an ambulance as well. You should give clear details of how the child is trapped and what parts of their body are trapped.

Accidents and emergencies

Accidents can happen and it is important to know what you should do when they occur. The main aim of first aid is to keep someone alive so that they can receive medical treatment.

As well as understanding the principles of first aid, it is essential that you attend paediatric first-aid training. Ideally, only first aiders should give children first aid, including mouth-to-mouth resuscitation. The exception to this is when there is no first aider available and a child's life is in danger. In this section, you will look at the basic principles of first aid that are recommended at the time of writing, but do remember that advice can change.

There are signs that indicate a child will need immediate medical attention following an accident or an incident. Note that some of these signs are the same as those that indicate a child may have a serious illness, for instance:

- no pulse
- not breathing or having difficulty in breathing
- unconsciousness
- lips and fingertips turning blue
- heavy bleeding
- a limb that sticks out at an awkward angle
- a head injury or concussion
- a burn or scald
- swelling of the face and/or neck (may indicate an allergic reaction/poisoning)
- cold and clammy skin
- a fever
- a convulsion or fit.

PAUSE POINT Make a list of five signs that indicate emergency help may be required.

Hint

Think about signs that the child is not breathing or the heart is not beating.

Extend

Explain why it is essential for immediate action to be taken rather than to wait and see if the child will recover.

DR ABC

The acronym 'DR ABC' has been adopted to help people remember the priorities when there is an accident.

D is for Danger

You should always assess the danger to you and to others before taking any action.

R is for Response

See if you can get a response from the child. Try speaking loudly or gently shake the child's shoulders. If there is a response, but the injuries seem significant, call an ambulance immediately by ringing 999 or 112. Stay with the child, treating the injuries if you know what to do. Keep talking to the child and monitoring their responses.

A is for Airway

If there is no response from the child, shout for help and make sure that someone calls 999 or 112. Then, open the child's airway. This will help them to breathe.

If no one is around, open the child's airway and then follow the guidelines for breathing and circulation/compressions before calling the emergency services.

To open a child's airway, tilt the child's head back by placing one hand on the child's forehead and two fingers underneath the child's chin. Figure 5.7 shows this action in practice. If you are trying to open a baby's airway, only tilt the baby's head back slightly as babies have narrow airways.

Note: you should not tilt a child's head back if you have any suspicions that the child's neck is injured, for example, if the child has fallen from a height or has been in a road traffic accident.

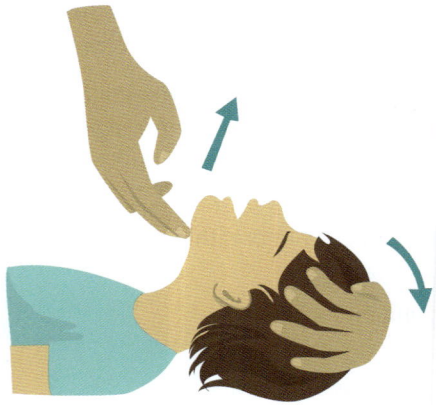

▶ **Figure 5.7:** If a child is not conscious, you should open their airway

B is for Breathing

Quickly check that the child is breathing. Put your head close to their face and see if you can feel the child's breath on your cheek. While listening and looking for breathing, call out for help.

C is for Circulation/Compressions

If you cannot feel any breath, you will need to give the child five rescue breaths. You should then check for signs of life, for example, swallowing, movement, breathing and speech. If there are no signs of life, you should carry out 30 chest compressions. If you are alone, carry out chest compressions and rescue breaths at a ratio of 30 : 2 for one minute and then dial 999 or 112.

Afterwards, if the child is not responding by showing any sign of life, give them two breaths and then 30 chest compressions. Keep doing this until the ambulance arrives.

Note: you are more likely to do harm by not giving chest compressions to a child that needs them than giving chest compressions to a child that does not need them.

Giving rescue breaths (children over 1 year)

▶ Make sure the child's airway is open.

▶ Pinch the child's nose.

▶ Put your mouth around the child's mouth to create a seal.

▶ Breathe steadily into the child's mouth. Each breath should be delivered slowly (over 1–1.5 seconds). Make sure the child's chest rises and falls with each breath.

Giving chest compressions (children over 1 year)

▶ Press down on the lower half of the child's sternum with the heel of one or two of your hands depending on the size of the child. It is important to avoid pressing down on the child's abdomen.

▶ Press the chest down to one-third of its depth.

▶ Do this at a rate of 100 to 120 times a minute.

Giving rescue breaths (babies under 1 year)

▶ Make sure the baby's airway is open.

▶ Place your mouth around the baby's mouth and nose to create a seal.

▶ Blow gently into the baby's mouth. Each breath should be delivered slowly (over 1–1.5 seconds). Make sure the baby's chest rises and falls with each breath.

Giving chest compressions (babies under 1 year)

▶ Use two fingers to press down sharply on the lower half of the baby's sternum. It is important to avoid pressing down on the baby's abdomen.

▶ Press down at least one-third of the depth of the chest.

▶ Do this at a rate of 100 to 120 times a minute.

❚❚ PAUSE POINT   What is the acronym to remember if there is an accident?

> Hint   Think about doctors and the alphabet.
>
> Extend   Explain why it is important to look out for any ongoing danger before attempting basic first aid.

Responding to serious injuries

Table 5.13 shows how to respond to accidents and serious injuries. Remember, you should only respond if you have been trained in first aid unless there is no one else around and the situation is life threatening.

▶ **Table 5.13:** How to respond to different serious injuries

Type of injury	How to respond
Burns and scalds	• Put the affected area under the cold tap for 10 minutes • If skin is broken, wrap the affected area in cling film and call 999 or 112
Severe bleeding	• Check if anything is embedded in the wound – if there is, do not attempt to remove it • If nothing is in the wound, press firmly down using a clean cloth if one is available • Lift up the wounded area so that it is higher than the child's heart • If something is in the wound, press on each side of the wound to apply pressure to minimise bleeding • Call 999 or 112
Suspected fractures – legs and arms	• Suspected broken leg or back injury: do not move the child. Call 999 or 112. Keep the child warm with a blanket • Suspected broken arm: sit the child up. Put a pad between the child's arm and the chest. Support the arm with a sling or scarf. Go straight to hospital
Choking baby (under 1 year)	• Lie the baby face down along your arm with your hand supporting the baby's head. Using the heel of your hand, give five firm back blows between the baby's shoulder blades • Stop after each blow to check if the obstruction is cleared from the baby's mouth • If the obstruction is not clear after five back blows, lie the baby along your forearm on their back, keeping their head low and supporting their back and head • Using two fingers, give up to five chest thrusts. To do this, push inwards and upwards (towards the baby's head) against the baby's breastbone. The area you should push is one finger's breadth below the baby's nipple line • Check if the blockage has cleared after each thrust • If the blockage is still not clear after three cycles of back blows and chest thrusts, dial 999 or 112 and continue the cycle of back blows and chest thrusts
Choking child (over 1 year)	• Stand behind the child and make sure the child is bending over forwards. Using the heel of your hand, give five firm blows between the child's shoulder blades. After each blow, check to see if the blockage has cleared • If the blockage has not cleared after five blows, give up to five abdominal thrusts. Stand behind the child, place your arms around their waist and bend the child over forwards. Make a fist and place it directly above the child's belly button. Then, place your other hand on top and thrust both hands backwards into the child's stomach with a hard, upward movement • Stop after each thrust to check if the blockage has cleared • Note: do not use abdominal thrusts on pregnant women or people who are obese • If the blockage is still not clear after three cycles of back blows and abdominal thrusts, you will need to call for help • If you are with other people, ask one person to dial 999 or 112 • If no one is around, dial 999 or 112 yourself • Then, continue with the cycles of back blows and abdominal thrusts until help arrives
Severe allergic reactions (anaphylaxis)	• Symptoms: e.g. a rash, swelling of the lips and/or tongue, noisy breathing or difficulty breathing • If the child has an EpiPen®, administer it if you have been trained and have permission to use it. Check that it is in date • Call 999 or 112 • Move the child away from the source of the allergic reaction, e.g. milk, nuts • Keep the child upright
Electrocution	• Check that the child is not still in contact with the source of the electrocution – if so, push the child's body away from the source with a wooden pole or another object that is not made of metal • Check for a pulse and breathing and follow DR ABC, as necessary • Call 999 or 112
Dehydration	• Symptoms: dark urine, headache, dizziness, listlessness, dry nappies, fast breathing • Provide oral rehydration solution or diluted squash • Seek medical attention if the child does not improve or if a baby is affected
Poisoning – swallowing harmful substances	• Symptoms: vomiting, stomach pains • Do not attempt to treat yourself • Take the child straight to hospital. If possible, take the suspected poison with you
Foreign objects in the nose, ears and eyes	• Take the child to hospital to remove the foreign object • If a duplicate item is available, take this along as well

▶ **Table 5.13:** How to respond to different serious injuries – *continued*

Type of injury	How to respond
Stings and bites	• Bee sting – scrape out the sting using a fingernail; avoid puncturing the venom sac. Do not use a pair of tweezers or fingers • If the child shows signs of an allergic reaction (see above), seek emergency help • Minor bites and stings – wash affected area with soap and water. Place a cold compress over the affected area • If the area becomes red or itchy, seek medical attention
Fever	If a child has a temperature: • remove layers of clothing • keep the room cool and well ventilated • take the child's temperature and record it; repeat every hour or more regularly if symptoms change • offer a paracetamol or ibuprofen-based medicine, if permission has been gained from parents • offer the child sips of cooled boiled water For a baby, seek immediate medical attention: • for a raised temperature above 38°C if the baby is under 3 months • for a raised temperature above 39°C if the baby is over 3 months • if the baby has a fever (above 38°C) with cold hands and feet • if the baby displays unusual crying or screaming • for convulsions For a child, seek medical attention: • for a temperature above 40°C • for a fever with cold hands and feet • if the child complains of a headache • if the child complains that their eyes hurt
Sickness – vomiting	• Reassure the child. Clean area using disposable gloves and aprons Seek medical attention if: • you think the child has swallowed a harmful substance • there is blood in the vomit • the child is becoming dehydrated • the child has a raised temperature • the child has had a blow to the head • the child has any symptoms requiring urgent attention (see 'Accidents and emergencies' heading in Section D2)

The effects of extremes of cold and heat

Children's bodies are less able to cope with extremes of temperature than adults.

Hypothermia

Hypothermia occurs when children's body temperature drops. Always seek medical attention if this happens. Signs of moderate hypothermia in children include:

▶ constant shivering

▶ tiredness, low energy and eventual confusion

▶ cold or pale skin

▶ fast breathing (hyperventilation).

Signs of hypothermia in babies include loss of energy and listlessness, being cold to the touch and refusal to feed. Babies may otherwise look well.

While you are waiting for medical attention, move the child somewhere warm, remove any wet clothing and wrap them in warm blankets or towels.

Extremes of heat

When the weather becomes very hot, children can become dehydrated (see Table 5.13), they are at risk of sunburn (if steps are not taken to protect their skin) and they may also develop heat exhaustion.

Signs of heat exhaustion can include:

▶ tiredness and weakness

▶ feeling faint or dizzy

- a decrease in blood pressure
- a headache
- muscle cramps
- feeling and being sick
- heavy sweating
- intense thirst
- a fast pulse
- urinating less often and having much darker urine than usual.

If children are showing these signs, seek medical attention. In the meantime, place the child in a cool place and out of the sun. Cool their skin with a wet sponge or flannel. Encourage them to drink fluids.

The common triggers and how to respond to anaphylaxis

Some children and adults can have extreme allergic reactions that are potentially fatal. The extreme reaction may include swelling of lips and mouth, and difficulty in breathing. This type of reaction is known as anaphylaxis.

Parents normally notify an early years setting that a child is in danger of this type of extreme reaction. Significant precautions are taken to avoid children coming into contact with whatever is liable to create such a reaction.

Examples of substances that can cause anaphylaxis in some individuals include:

- nuts, e.g. peanuts
- cow's milk
- shellfish
- eggs
- insect stings such as bee stings
- some types of fruit including strawberries, bananas, kiwis.

Table 5.13 shows how to respond to anaphylaxis.

PAUSE POINT   Give three examples of substances that can cause anaphylaxis in some children.

Hint   Think of allergy labels you see on food products.

Extend   Explain the steps to take if a child is showing signs of anaphylaxis.

The content of a first-aid kit in an early years setting

There are no mandatory requirements as to what should be in a first-aid kit in an early years setting. A first-aid box is usually green with a white cross and should be kept accessible to adults, but out of reach of children. The quantity of individual items in a first-aid box will depend on the number of children in the setting. Many early years settings also make sure that they have a digital thermometer in a first-aid box so they can accurately assess a child's temperature.

The typical contents of a first-aid box in an early years setting are:

- one first-aid guidance card and contents list
- resuscitation face shields
- individually wrapped adhesive dressings (plasters) of assorted sizes
- sterile eye pads
- triangular bandages – individually wrapped

- small, medium and large sterile dressings
- low-adherent dressing with perforated plastic surface (i.e. Melolin)
- roll of hypo-allergenic tape (i.e. Micropore)
- sterile gauze swabs (for cleaning wounds) and sterile wet wipes
- finger bandage and applicator
- round-ended scissors
- disposable non-latex gloves.

Useful additions could include: two small plastic bags (for disposal of soiled wipes and dressings); notepad and pencil; safety pins; and a foil blanket.

After an accident or emergency, remember to check the first-aid kit and replace any items that were used. It is also important to check regularly that items in the first-aid kit are still 'in date'.

Policies and procedures for dealing with emergency situations

Every setting needs to have policies and procedures in place that explain to staff, parents and anyone who visits the setting what they should do in a range of emergency situations. This means that if there is an emergency, it can be dealt with quickly and correctly without anyone panicking. Policies and procedures need to be reviewed and updated if circumstances change or following an emergency or incident.

Fortunately, serious accidents, emergencies and illnesses are relatively rare, but it is still important to know what you should do if you are ever faced with any of these situations. At the start of this section, you looked at how to call for emergency help. You will now look at what to do if you need to evacuate a building or respond to a situation where a child goes missing or how to deal with access to the setting by an unauthorised person.

Whatever the emergency or situation, it is important that you stay calm at all times and reassure the children in your care.

Access by unauthorised persons

There may be times when you see someone you do not recognise in the building or outdoor areas. If you are not concerned about their behaviour, ask them if you can help them. This should allow you to find out their reason for being there. You should then accompany them to the place or person they have said they are there to visit. If at any time you are concerned by their behaviour or doubt their reasons for being there, seek help from others.

Emergency evacuation

Every setting needs to have a policy in place that states in what circumstances the building should be evacuated, for example, as the result of a fire, gas leak or bomb threat. As well as a policy for evacuation, settings also need to have procedures in place for staff to follow if an evacuation is required. The procedures will explain in detail what adults need to do and where they need to go. You will look at the practicalities of evacuating a setting later in this section.

There are several reasons why you may need to evacuate a building. Procedures to follow in different situations are suggested below.

- A bomb threat – evacuate to the fire assembly point unless otherwise directed.
- Flooding – move to a higher floor in the setting or to high ground.
- A gas leak – do not turn any electrical appliances on or off, or let anyone in the area smoke or use lighters or matches. You should also keep doors and windows open.

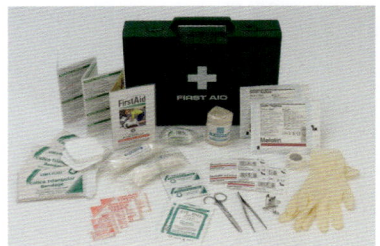

▶ Remember to check regularly that items in your first-aid kit are 'in date' and to replace anything that you use

- A person who is being violent or threatening (this might include an intruder or someone who does not have authorised access to the setting) – if safe to do so, you should evacuate the building and take the children to a safe place – this may not be the designated fire assembly point. If this is not possible, you should try to find a room or place in which you can lock yourselves away.
- An explosion – evacuate the building. This may mean moving to somewhere other than the designated fire assembly point.
- A fire – evacuate to the fire assembly point.

General principles for evacuating children safely

Your setting should have a comprehensive evacuation and fire plan and you should familiarise yourself with it. You should also check that you know where the nearest doors are and the escape route for the part of the building in which you are working. It is important to follow procedures within the setting as this can avoid confusion; it also means that every adult knows what they need to do and which children they need to take responsibility for.

If you are working with babies, you may have an evacuation crib. Make sure that this is always available and that you know how to use it.

Table 5.14 shows a list of 'Dos' and 'Don'ts' when evacuating children.

▶ **Table 5.14:** General principles for safely evacuating children

Do	Don't
Raise the alarm immediately	Panic or scream
Leave by the nearest exit	Waste time by picking up personal possessions or getting coats
Give clear instructions to the children	Ignore the alarm because you think it is a practice
Take a register with you	Forget to take the register
Respond to an alarm immediately even if you think it might be a practice	Run
Remember to check all areas of the setting, e.g. the toilets if you are with older children	Let the children out of your sight
Close doors behind you if there is no one following you (in the event of a fire)	Go back into the building until the all-clear is given
Go straight to the assembly point if it is safe to do so	Block fire exits under any circumstances
Keep the children with you	Lock fire exits under any circumstances
Let the appointed fire officer know if anyone is missing	

Ⅱ PAUSE POINT   Identify three things that you should do when evacuating children.

   Imagine that you were in a building and had to keep you and the children safe..

   Why is it important to repeatedly practise evacuation procedures in early years settings?

Actions to take if a child is missing

Parents expect us to keep their children safe and we should take every precaution to prevent children from going missing. The reasons why children might go missing include:

- a gap in a fence
- a child being picked up by another adult
- a child getting out through open doors or windows
- a child wandering off and away from others during an outing.

It is also important to recognise that some children can be thought to be missing when they are actually still on the premises or a parent has collected them early. This might happen because:

▶ a member of staff has asked the child to come and do something without letting other staff members know
▶ the child has gone to the toilet
▶ the child has gone home without staff realising or the register being amended
▶ the child has gone to play outdoors without staff being aware
▶ staff have forgotten that another adult is with the child.

Settings should have a policy that deals with what to do in the event of a child going missing as part of their child protection or safeguarding policies, and it is important that you follow this. This policy is likely to be informed by local or national policies.

If you suspect that a child is missing, it is essential that you stay calm. Panicking means you are less likely to be logical and methodical. The list below gives the usual procedures that settings follow both indoors and outdoors, but you will need to check if procedures differ in your setting.

What you should do indoors

▶ Act quickly. Check whether the child is really missing – call their name, look properly for them in the room. If you are with a colleague, ask them to help you.
▶ Alert your supervisor or senior team.
▶ Carry out a thorough search of the building and outdoor area, including cupboards and sheds.
▶ While this search is happening, another adult should take a register of the remaining children and they should be kept safe.
▶ If the child is not located, call the police on 999/112.
▶ Parents must also be contacted by a senior member of staff.

What you should do outdoors

▶ Act quickly. Check whether the child is really missing – call their name and check if other adults have seen the child.
▶ Search the immediate area and call the child's name regularly.
▶ At the same time, another adult should keep all of the other children together and take a register or head count.
▶ If the child is not found, call the police on 999/112 and wait for advice. Be ready to give a description of the child including their name, age and what they were wearing.
▶ Call the setting and speak to a senior member of staff. They, in turn, should contact the child's parents.
▶ If the setting is close by, other adults from the setting could search beyond the immediate area.

Case study

Missing child

Tom works at a large day nursery. The nursery has free flow in and out of doors. There are 34 children in the setting. Tom is responsible for an activity and decides to look for Carla, who he thinks will enjoy this activity. Tom looks around the room, but cannot see her.

Check your knowledge

1 What should Tom's next actions be?
2 Why is it important that Tom acts quickly?
3 What should happen if, after an initial search, Carla is not found?

Reporting the incident

If a child has gone missing, even if only for a short amount of time, the incident has to be recorded and also reported. The setting will do this according to the requirements of the inspectorate in the home country; for example, a missing child incident in England should be reported to Ofsted.

A review of policies and procedures will also need to take place in the setting. In some cases, there may be disciplinary actions if a staff member is thought to have been negligent.

The importance of staying calm and reassuring children

When an emergency or an evacuation takes place it can be particularly frightening for children. It is important that adults stay calm for both the child or children involved and children who are onlookers. If adults shout or rush around, children will become even more frightened, which could make the situation worse and may even put others at greater danger. Keeping the voice steady and at a low level while giving clear instructions will help children to feel reassured.

Even if children who are not involved are removed from the area they will continue to be concerned. Children have vivid imaginations and may think that the incident will happen again or that the child or children involved are more seriously hurt than they really are. Adults should be honest with children about what has happened, explaining in words appropriate to their age and stage of development. Children may need reassurance for some time afterwards and will need the opportunity to talk about their fears.

How to record, report and share information

It is important that all accidents and incidents are recorded and reported to parents. Serious incidents or accidents should also be reported to organisations such as the Health and Safety Executive or to the inspectorate of your home country.

As part of its health and safety policy, each setting will have procedures dealing with how to report accidents and incidents, and you will need to follow them. Information that needs to be filled in promptly after an accident or incident includes:

▶ the date
▶ the time and location of the accident or incident
▶ the name of the child/adult involved
▶ the name of the adult in attendance
▶ a description of the incident/accident and cause
▶ the injuries, if any, to the child
▶ the first-aid treatment, if any, that was given and by whom
▶ a signature.

Minor accidents

However minor an accident, parents need to know what has happened to their child. Most settings will let parents know at the end of the session if a child has had a bump, bruise or a fall. They will give parents a piece of paper that contains details of the accident so that, if necessary, they can take it to the hospital. This is usually given to the parent by the child's key person or the manager of the setting.

Assessment practice 5.6

D.P7 D.M4 D.D3

Reflect on a situation where you have shown your skills in responding to an emergency situation. You may use an example from a real emergency or a simulated response such as where you have taken part in an evacuation procedure or dealt with an accident during a first-aid course.

1 Produce an account of how you responded to the accident or health emergency, giving details for each stage.

2 Reflect on the extent to which your own skills and decisions helped to minimise the risk to the child's or children's health and safety and maintained the safety of observers.

3 Evaluate your own responsibilities to respond appropriately when there is an emergency situation, with reference to health and safety legislation and regulations.

Plan

- Which of my experiences in early years settings will be the most relevant for this task?
- Where might I go to get feedback on my skills?

Do

- Am I presenting the information accurately and concisely?
- Am I managing my time effectively?

Review

- Can I justify why I have decided to approach this task in the way that I have?
- Have I evaluated my skills accurately and am I confident that it fulfils the set task?

Further reading and resources

Books

DK Publishing (2014) *First Aid Manual*, 10th edition, London: Dorling Kindersley.

Parker, L. (2012) *The Early Years Health and Safety Handbook*, 2nd edition, Oxon: Routledge.

Websites

www.barnardos.org.uk – Barnardo's: information about the charity's work to support vulnerable children and their families.

www.sunsmart.org.uk – Cancer Research UK SunSmart: advice about how to keep safe in the sun.

www.education.gov.uk – Department for Education: look for the resources titled *Working together to safeguard children* (2015), *What to do if you're worried a child is being abused* (2015), *Safeguarding Disabled Children* (2009).

www.hse.gov.uk – Health and Safety Executive: guidelines and advice about health and safety including latest legislation.

www.nspcc.org.uk – NSPCC: information and advice about how to keep children safe and identify signs of abuse.

THINK ▶FUTURE

Jay Hussein

Day care manager

Jay has been working in day care for nearly ten years. As a manager, he has to take health, safety and safeguarding very seriously. Parents naturally expect him and the team to keep their children safe. If any incidents hit the headlines, they become particularly nervous about how safe their children are in the day care setting.

The key to health and safety as well as child protection is to ensure that all staff are up to date, well-trained and that they understand the policies and procedures for every area. Every time a new member of staff is recruited, Jay spends a lot of time going through the information and the reasons for every procedure. He also updates the policies and the procedures regularly as best practice does change. In addition, he has to make sure that the setting is complying with the latest regulations. This may sound boring, but he takes satisfaction that the policies and procedures may save a child's life!

Focusing your skills

Risk assessing a play activity

It is important to be able to risk assess a play and learning activity. Here are some simple tips to help you do this.

- Look at the age and stage of the child's development.
- Think about the implications for how they might use any of the equipment or resources, such as babies putting things in their mouths.
- Think about the implications for their behaviour, for example, 2-year-olds are impulsive and babies do not follow instructions.
- Think about each part of the play and learning activity and consider where the hazards might be, such as getting dressed or tidying up.
- Finally, for each hazard that you identify, work out how to minimise the danger. In some cases this might mean adapting the play and learning activity.

Skills to develop in relation to safeguarding

Practise the following things related to safeguarding while you are in your setting.

- Become more aware of your listening skills when you are with children. Also consider your own body language. Ask a colleague to observe your interactions and give you feedback.
- Think of ways you can promote children's confidence and self-esteem. How do you give praise and let children know they are doing well?
- Develop your own confidence in talking to professionals from outside agencies. You could ask them questions that will help your understanding of aspects of your course.

Children's Physical Development, Care and Health Needs

6

Getting to know your unit

If children are fit and healthy, their learning and development is supported and they are more likely to be happy.

In this unit, you will learn about the physical development and physical care needs of children and look at how to support their healthy development. You will consider how to plan routines and activities that meet children's individual needs, help them to be independent and encourage them to make healthy choices. You will also learn how to recognise and respond when children are unwell and look at ways of supporting children who have long-term medical conditions.

How you will be assessed

This unit will be assessed by a series of internally assessed tasks set by your tutor. Throughout this unit, assessment activities will help you work towards your assessment. Completing these activities will not mean that you have achieved a particular grade, but you will have carried out useful research or preparation that will be relevant when it comes to your final assignment.

To achieve the tasks in your assignment, it is important to check that you have met all of the Pass grading criteria. You can do this as you work your way through the assignment.

If you are hoping to gain a Merit or Distinction, also make sure that you present the information in your assignment in the style that is required by the relevant assessment criterion. For example, Merit criteria require you to analyse and discuss, and Distinction criteria require you to assess and evaluate.

The assignment set by your tutor will consist of a number of tasks designed to meet the criteria in the table. This is likely to consist of written assignments but may also include activities such as:

▶ responding to a case study, which will allow you to show your understanding of how children at different ages will have different physical development needs as well as care needs, and how these needs might be met

▶ planning a reflective account linked to your work placement that shows how you have supported a child's physical development

▶ producing a report that considers the role of early years practitioners in meeting the needs of children who are unwell or who have a long-term health condition.

Assessment criteria

This table shows what you must do in order to achieve a **Pass**, **Merit** or **Distinction** grade, and where you can find activities to help you.

Pass	Merit	Distinction
Learning aim **A** Understand the physical development and care needs of children and approaches to their healthy development		
A.P1 Explain the importance of care routines for meeting children's physical care needs to support a healthy lifestyle. **Assessment practice 6.1**	**A.M1** Assess the extent to which care routines and play activities support and promote physical development and encourage a healthy lifestyle for children. **Assessment practice 6.1, 6.2**	**A.D1** Evaluate the value of care routines and play activities for supporting and promoting children's physical development and encouraging a healthy lifestyle. **Assessment practice 6.1, 6.2**
A.P2 Explain how different types of indoor and outdoor play activities are used in early years settings to support and promote the physical development of children at different ages and stages. **Assessment practice 6.2**		
Learning aim **B** Plan and support routines and activities to meet children's physical development and care needs		
B.P3 Plan care routines and physical play activities to meet the needs of a selected child. **Assessment practice 6.3**	**B.M2** Analyse the planned care routines and play activities in relation to their contribution to children's physical development, care needs and promotion of independence and a healthy lifestyle. **Assessment practice 6.3, 6.4**	**B.D1** Demonstrate effective self-management and professional conduct consistently in planning and supporting care routines and activities that meet the physical development and care needs of a child. **Assessment practice 6.4**
B.P4 Support care routines and physical play activities to promote development, independence and a healthy lifestyle. **Assessment practice 6.4**		
Learning aim **C** Investigate how to recognise and respond to children who are unwell and support children with ongoing health conditions		
C.P5 Explain how to recognise the signs of ill health in children and the procedures that should be followed in early years settings. **Assessment practice 6.5**	**C.M3** Justify procedures for recognising and supporting children who are unwell. **Assessment practice 6.6**	**C.D2** Evaluate, giving justifications, the role of the professional in early years settings in the effective use of procedures for recognising and supporting children who are unwell and in supporting children with ongoing health conditions. **Assessment practice 6.6, 6.7**
C.P6 Explain how professionals in early years settings support children with ongoing health conditions for positive outcomes for their health and holistic development. **Assessment practice 6.7**	**C.M4** Analyse the role of the professional in early years settings to support children with ongoing health conditions for positive outcomes for their health and holistic development. **Assessment practice 6.7**	

Getting started

Make a list of care routines that you think are important to children's health and development. For each one, see if you can provide a reason why it is important. When you have finished this unit, see if there are any that you missed.

 **A** **Understand the physical development and care needs of children and approaches to their healthy development**

A1 The physical needs of children

Basic needs of children

It is easy to forget that babies and children cannot learn, relax and play if their basic physical needs are not met. Figure 6.1 shows the physical needs of babies and children.

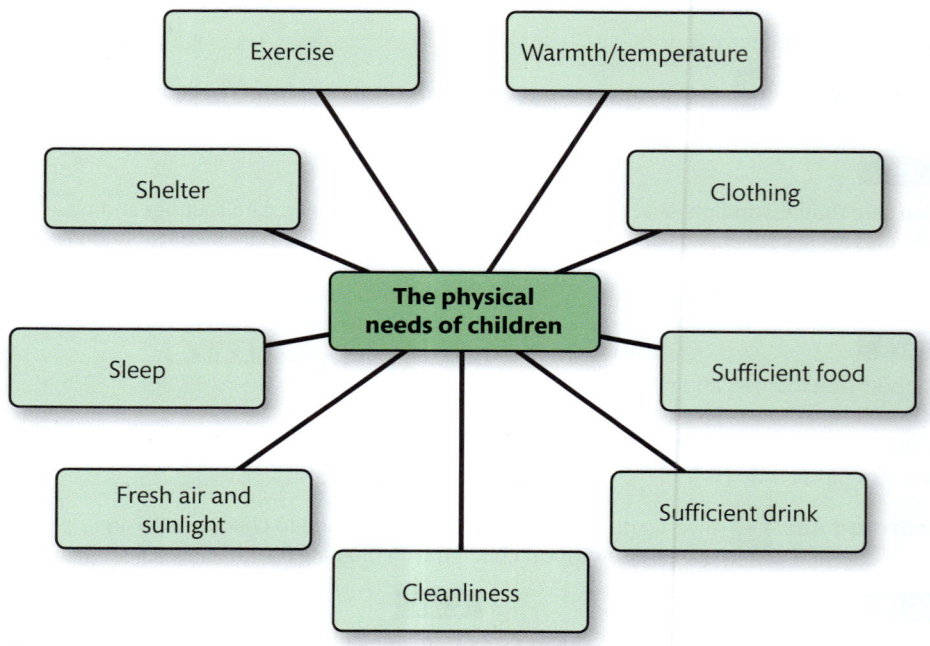

▶ **Figure 6.1:** The physical needs of babies and children

In addition to these basic physical needs, you also have to think about temperature and ventilation when providing an environment for children. Ideally, the temperature indoors should be 18–21°C, with babies' sleeping spaces at 16–18°C. Ventilation is important indoors to prevent airborne illnesses and to make sure that the air is sufficiently oxygenated.

When any of children's physical needs are not met, their development, health and well-being are likely to be affected. If, for example, children are too hot or too cold, they may find it hard to concentrate. If they do not have enough sunlight, they may develop **rickets**, which is a bone disease. Children should also live in good housing because when they are exposed to damp or live in unsafe homes, they are more likely to develop a **respiratory disease** such as **asthma** or have accidents.

Maslow's hierarchy of needs

Abraham Maslow (1908–1970) was a psychologist who was interested in understanding people's behaviour and motivation. He studied people who were high achievers and came to the conclusion that it was only possible to reach high levels of personal and career fulfilment if other needs were met first. Maslow showed this through a hierarchical model similar to the one shown in Figure 6.2. The idea is that the basic physiological needs on the bottom layer have to be met before the next layer of needs can be met. When Maslow's work was published in 1943 it was influential in many areas, and notably for large employers. Maslow's model is useful in reminding us that children cannot learn or benefit from settings unless their physical and emotional needs have been met.

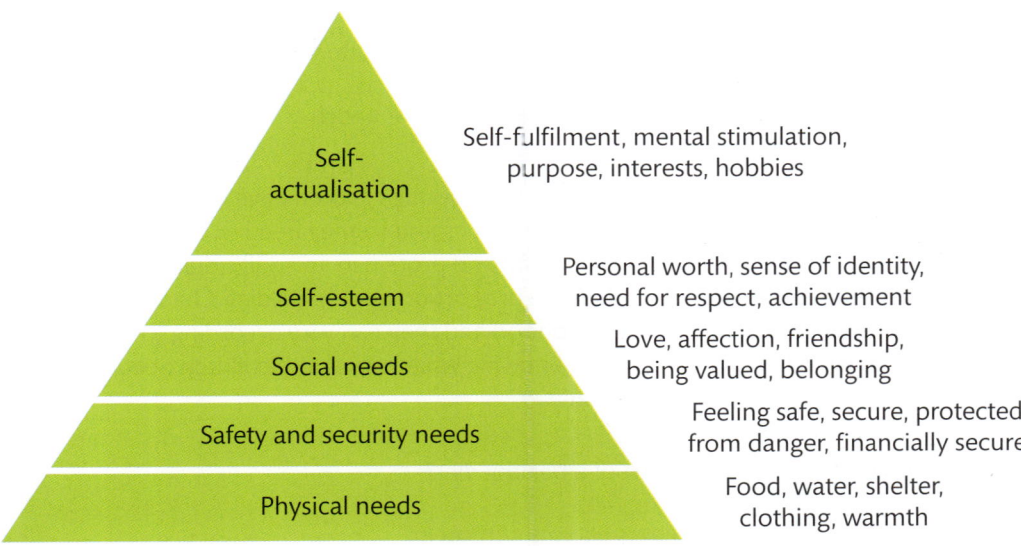

▶ **Figure 6.2:** Maslow's hierarchy of needs

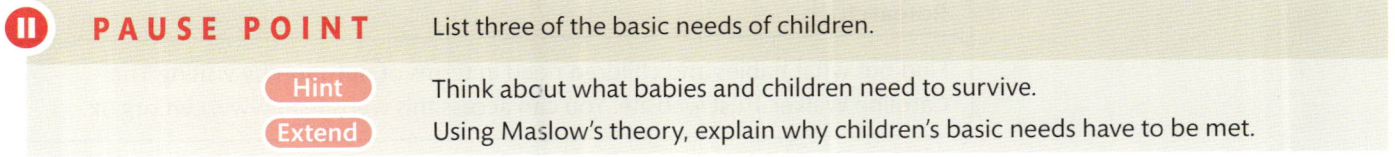

Ⅱ PAUSE POINT   List three of the basic needs of children.

（Hint）   Think about what babies and children need to survive.

（Extend）   Using Maslow's theory, explain why children's basic needs have to be met.

The importance of meeting children's physical needs at different ages and stages

Children's physical needs can impact significantly on their development. It is important that you not only identify the physical needs of children, but also understand their importance and how they change as a child grows and develops.

A nutritious diet

The development of babies and children is affected by what, and how much, they eat. Food and drink intake supports the physical and brain growth of babies and young children, and also provides them with sufficient energy to move. It therefore helps to develop their physical skills. Food and drink are also important for good health, and children who are **malnourished** or **undernourished** are more likely to have periods of ill health.

On the other hand, babies and children who have too much food and drink and insufficient exercise, even if the food is otherwise healthy, are likely to develop health problems later in life that are associated with being overweight, such as heart disease.

> **Key terms**
>
> **Malnourished** – having a lack of proper nutrients.
> **Undernourished** – having insufficient food/nutrients.

What is a healthy diet?

It might seem easy to suggest that children should have a healthy diet, but recognising what, and how much, children should eat is actually quite complex. This is because children's needs change according to their age and level of activity. A good starting point is to understand that food and drink provide us with nutrients. A healthy diet is, therefore, one in which children have the right balance of nutrients for their age/stage in order to support exercise, growth and development.

Nutrients are often grouped into:

▶ protein – good for growth and repair of cells
▶ carbohydrates – good for energy
▶ fats – good for energy and to absorb some vitamins
▶ minerals – necessary for a range of different functions, such as calcium for bone development
▶ vitamins – necessary for a range of different functions, such as vitamin C for healthy skin.

Changing needs

It is important to understand that babies and young children have different nutritional needs from adults. Adults have larger stomachs and so they need to eat less often than babies and children. The proportion of fat and protein in an adult's diet in comparison to other nutrients is also lower than the proportion in a child's diet. Children's nutritional needs change during childhood and they can vary according to the child's activity level. When planning meals, knowing what babies and children need at different ages is, therefore, essential.

PAUSE POINT   Why is protein needed as part of a healthy diet?

Hint   Think about why bodybuilders eat lots of protein.

Extend   What other four groups of nutrients are needed for a healthy diet?

Research

Find out what babies and children need in terms of nutrition by visiting The Caroline Walker Trust website. You can access this website at www.cwt.org.uk.

Rest and sleep

Sleep and rest are vital to children's health and well-being. Sleep is needed for healthy brain function and growth, and to enable the body's cells to repair themselves. It is also needed to regulate the hormones that are responsible for growth and even appetite. Sleep and rest are needed for other reasons, as you will now see.

▶ **Concentration** – brain function is helped or hindered by sleep. When children are tired they find it harder to concentrate.

▶ **Memory/learning** – during sleep, the brain reviews the day's events and this seems to be important in terms of putting down memories. Children who are not sleeping sufficiently are likely to find it harder to learn because they will not remember as much.

▶ **The immune system** – sleep plays a part in supporting the immune system. During sleep the body repairs cells and fights infection. Children who are not sleeping sufficiently are more likely to have colds and other infections.

▶ **Controlling emotions and impulses** – young children tend to be impulsive and **emotionally labile**. A lack of sleep exaggerates this and so children who are not sleeping sufficiently are more likely to show impulsive behaviour. Linked to this is sleep's ability to provide children with a sense of well-being.

▶ **Obesity** – The Family Lifestyle, Activity, Movement and Eating (FLAME) study looked into the relationship between how long a child sleeps and their weight. The results, published in 2011, suggest that children who are not getting sufficient sleep run the risk of becoming overweight, and even obese. Scientists are still working on the correlation between sleep and weight gain, but it is thought to be related to the hormones that are responsible for appetite and metabolism. Also related is the fact that being tired increases lethargy and so decreases interest in physical activity.

How much sleep?

Although children vary in how much sleep they need, there are some useful guidelines. Table 6.1 shows the guidelines for children aged 3 months to 5 years.

▶ **Table 6.1:** How much sleep children need at different ages (Source: *Information for parents: Sleep*, p.5 © Crown copyright 2010)

Age	Naps	Night-time	Total
3 months	5 hours	15 hours	20 hours
4–12 months	3 hours	11 hours	14 hours
1–3 years	2 hours 15 minutes	11 hours	13 hours 15 minutes
3–4 years	1 hour 30 minutes	10 hours 30 minutes	12 hours
5 years	None	10–12 hours	10–12 hours

Signs that a child is tired

Babies and children will show you when they are tired. Look out for the following signs:

▶ irritable behaviour, having tantrums or becoming whiny and uncooperative

▶ crying for no clear reason

▶ a lack of concentration

▶ dark rings around the eyes.

Helping children to sleep

You can only fall asleep when your body relaxes and feels safe. This means that children who are tired may find it hard to sleep in an environment that is noisy or unfamiliar. You can help babies and children to sleep by providing them with familiar objects such as their own sheet or cuddly toy, and by making sure that the environment feels calm.

Research

Find out more about the latest research into the links between childhood obesity and sleep by looking at the FLAME study on the British Medical Journal website: see www.bmj.com.

Children's Physical Development, Care and Health Needs

▶ These children all have their own beds and blankets and an adult will stay with them so they feel safe

● **PAUSE POINT**   List three signs that a child might be tired.

Hint   Think about how you feel and act when you are tired.

Extend   Explain the impact on children's development if they are not having enough sleep.

Exercise

Babies and children need exercise, among other things, to improve their lifelong health. This does not mean formal movements or PE lessons, but opportunities to move around or, in the case of non-mobile babies, to be able to kick and move their arms. Figure 6.3 shows the benefits of exercise to children's overall development.

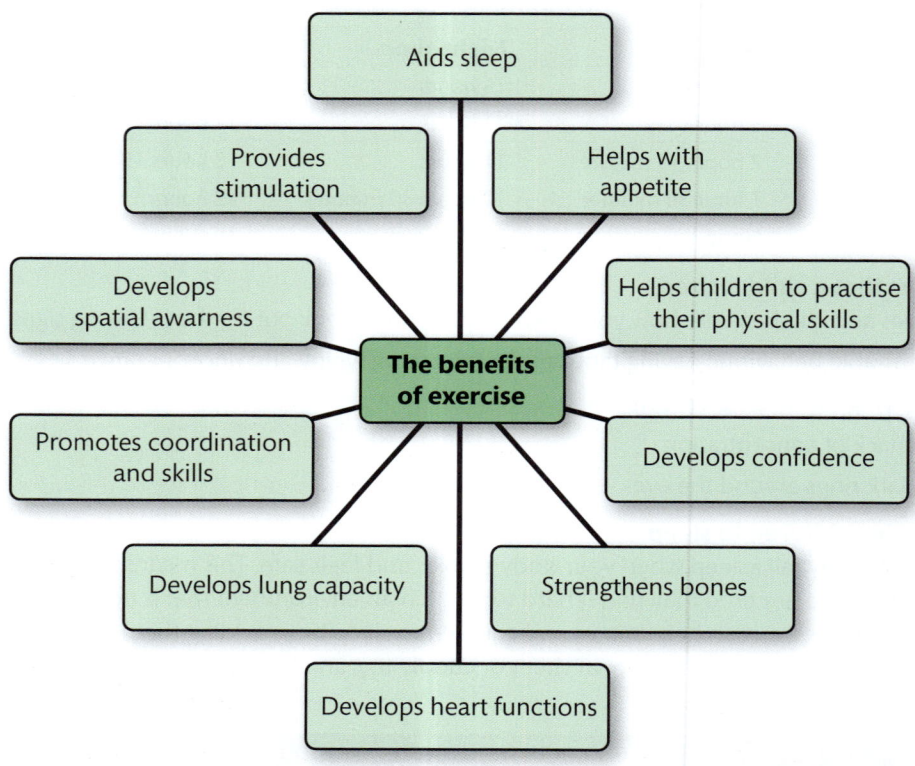

▶ **Figure 6.3:** The benefits of exercise

How much exercise?

Over the past few years, there have been concerns that young children are not having sufficient opportunities for vigorous exercise. At the time of writing, the UK government recommends that children under 5 years old, who are walking, are physically active for at least 3 hours per day; children aged 5–18 years should spend an hour over the course of the day engaged in physical activity. This might be walking, running, using wheeled toys or generally engaging in some form of play. When planning for children's physical activity, it is worth knowing that young children need a stop-start approach. Their lung and heart capacity means that they will find it hard to maintain vigorous activity for long periods. This is why toddlers are in and out of their pushchairs, for example – one moment they will be sitting down and the next they will be up walking or running about.

Skin care

Skin is an organ that has many purposes, one of which is to protect the body from infection. This means that keeping skin clean and healthy is essential. Children have different types of skin and many children have skin conditions, so it is essential for early years professionals to find out from parents how they should look after children's skin. For example, a child with severe eczema may not be able to use soap on their hands or face, and children with dry skin may need to use moisturisers or oils.

Hand washing

Developing good hand-washing routines with children is important to prevent infections and stop germs spreading. It also gets them into a habit for when they are older. Remember the following guidance.

▶ Keep nails short.

▶ Wash hands after going to the toilet, after playing outside and after touching animals.

▶ Wash hands before eating or drinking.

▶ Use a nail brush if there is dirt under the nails.

▶ Dry hands thoroughly – each child should have his or her own towel or paper towel.

Ⅱ PAUSE POINT   What are the key points about keeping hands clean?

Hint   Think about when and how to wash and dry hands.

Extend   Explain the role of hand washing as part of infection control.

Washing the face and body

Bath or shower time is usually a source of great pleasure for children and is often part of a bedtime routine at home. If you are employed in a child's home, it may become your responsibility, although many parents enjoy this part of the day with their children.

The bottom and genital areas of children need to be washed each day, although older children should be encouraged to wash these parts themselves. Each child should have their own towel and flannel to prevent the spread of any infection. After the bath or shower, the skin needs to be thoroughly dried to prevent soreness. Younger children have folds of skin under their arms and neck that need to be patted dry.

Although many children have a bath or shower before going to bed, they will still need to have their hands and face washed in the morning. Younger children will need to have their faces and hands washed after meals.

Bathing babies

As well as being a key aspect of the routine for caring for babies, bath time is often great fun for them. Most babies love being in the bath and benefit from playing in the water. They learn from the sensory experience of touching the water and also develop muscles while kicking and splashing around.

Making sure that bath time is safe

Although bath times can be fun, they can also be dangerous – some babies drown or are scalded by hot water. The following safety advice must always be followed when bathing babies and young children.

▶ Never leave babies or young children alone when they are near or in water.

▶ Always check the temperature of water. It should be around 37–38°C: warm, but never hot.

▶ Make sure that any toys for the bath are suitable for the age of the baby.

Preparing for bath time

Good preparation and organisation is essential when bathing a baby. Everything should be laid out before starting to undress the baby. The room needs to be warm (20°C) as babies chill quickly. Adults also need to check they are not wearing anything that might scratch babies' skin – for example, a watch or jewellery. An apron is often useful, as babies tend to splash. Figure 6.4 outlines how to bathe a baby.

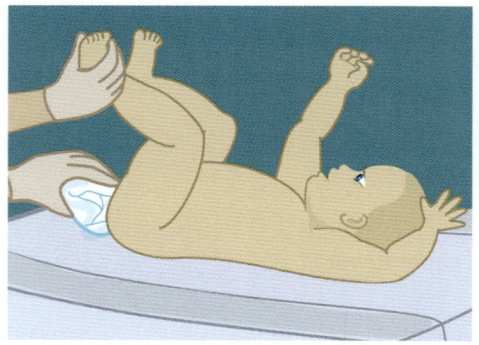

1 Put the baby on a flat surface. Undress them and take off the nappy. Clean the nappy area.

2 Wrap the baby gently but securely in a towel so that the arms are tucked in.

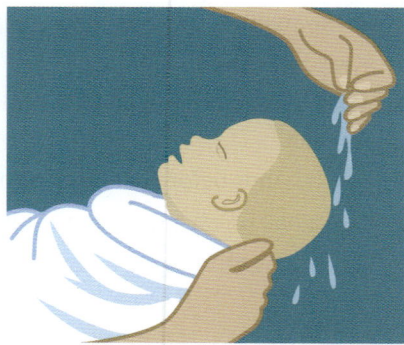

3 Hold the baby over the bath and wash the head and hair.

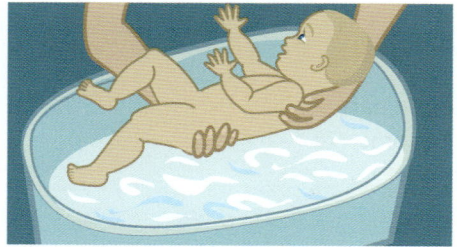

4 Take off the towel. Holding the baby securely under the head and round the arm, lift them into the water.

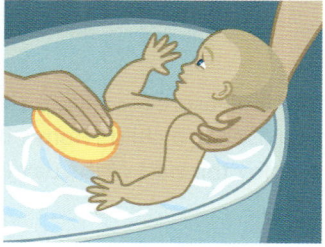

5 Use your spare hand to wash the baby.

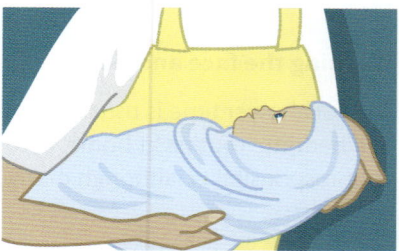

6 Lift the baby out of the bath, supporting the baby under the bottom. Quickly wrap them in a warm towel.

▶ **Figure 6.4:** A step-by-step guide to bathing babies

Changing nappies

Changing nappies will be part of the role of most early years professionals. It is extremely important for babies and children because skin infections and nappy rash may occur if it is not done properly. Ideally, nappy changes should be done mostly by the child's key person. Figure 6.5 shows how to change a nappy.

Nappy rash

Nappy rash is common in babies. It comes up in the genital area as a bright red rash, which often starts as a spotty rash. If left untreated it may turn into sores. It is painful and so early years professionals must do everything they can to prevent babies and toddlers from developing it. This means changing soiled nappies promptly, having frequent nappy changes and keeping an eye out for any changes to the skin. You should also let parents know as sometimes a change in diet or skin product can be a trigger. Many parents and practitioners also find that babies who are teething are more prone to nappy rash.

One of the best treatments for nappy rash is to leave the nappy off so that the skin can dry and heal. With parents' permission, barrier cream can be used, but the most important thing is that the skin is kept as clean and dry as possible.

1 Wash and dry your hands. Get everything that you need to hand and put on disposable gloves. Remember to tell the child what you are going to do, and keep communicating with them throughout.

2 Lift the child onto a changing mat and remove the dirty nappy. Place it out of reach of the child.

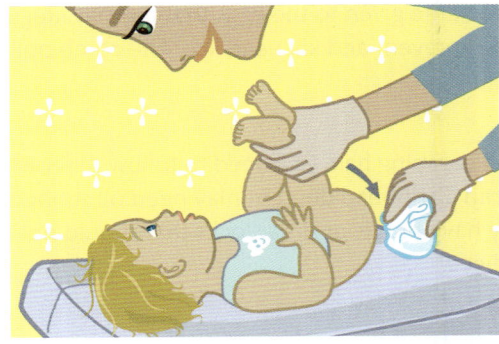

3 Clean the area carefully, making sure that you wipe from front to back. Use a clean wipe or piece of cotton wool for each wipe.

4 Dry the area and apply barrier cream, if requested by parents. Put on a new nappy and fasten. Take the child down from the mat.

5 Safely dispose of the dirty nappy and disinfect the changing area. Dispose of your gloves.

6 Wash your hands thoroughly.

▶ **Figure 6.5:** A step-by-step guide to changing nappies

Sun care

As part of skin care, adults working with children should keep them safe from the sun. While it is important for children to spend time outdoors, and also to benefit from the vitamin D that being in the sun offers, UVA and UVB rays can damage skin. You will look at how to support sun protection for skin in Section B2.

Link

Sections B1 and B2 provide more information on how to plan care routines for toileting and nappy changing, and how to support progression out of nappies..

Toileting routines

Most children are out of nappies at around 3 years. In early years settings it is good practice for children to go to the toilet when they need to. It is also good practice to encourage children to be as independent with their toileting as possible. Good toileting routines are important to avoid children from becoming constipated or developing urinary infections.

Care for hair

Children's hair needs to be kept clean as babies and young children can get quite a lot of food and other things in their hair. While looking after children's hair is usually the responsibility of parents, there are some early years professionals, such as childminders and nannies, who will, as part of their work, regularly look after children's hair. When caring for children's hair, it is important that parents' wishes and advice is respected.

Head lice

In recent years, there has been an increase in outbreaks of head lice in preschool settings and in schools. Head lice are parasites that live close to the scalp. They are also sometimes known as nits, which is the name given to the eggs that they lay. Regular combing with a fine-toothed comb can prevent and kill head lice. The comb pulls the lice out and damages the eggs.

Brushing and combing hair

If you are responsible for washing and combing hair, you need to follow parents' wishes. For example, children of African Caribbean descent may need oil rubbed into their hair and some children may have braids or dreadlocks that should not be brushed. Remember the following advice.

▶ Hair should be combed or brushed twice a day.
▶ Make sure that you check for head lice or nits.
▶ If hair is tangled, start with a wide-toothed comb and then use a brush.

To make brushing hair more enjoyable for children:
▶ give toddlers a doll of their own with hair to brush
▶ encourage older children to brush their own hair
▶ let children look in the mirror while you are brushing.

Care of teeth

Dental hygiene is important in young children. Teeth help children to eat and they are also important for clear speech. Teeth impact the way we look; children who have poor teeth or no teeth are likely to become self-conscious as teenagers or adults.

Most parents will be responsible for the day-to-day cleaning of their children's teeth but there are some early years professionals, such as nannies and childminders, who may be responsible for cleaning teeth. Teeth cleaning should begin once a baby has their first tooth. Teeth should be brushed twice a day, once at bedtime and once at another time in the day, often after breakfast. While children can be interested in joining in, it is important that adults do the 'two minute' clean until children are 7 or 8 years old.

Here is some general advice for cleaning young children's teeth.
▶ Clean teeth a little while after food has been eaten so as not to brush food into the gums.
▶ Use a small-headed toothbrush with fluoride toothpaste.
▶ For children under 3 years, put a smear of toothpaste on the brush. For children aged 3–6 years, use a pea-sized quantity.
▶ Brush teeth gently and in circular movements.

Preventing dental decay

More children now than ever are showing early signs of dental decay. To prevent dental decay, children need periods of time when there is no food or drink (except water) on their teeth. This is because food and drink increases the amount of acid in the mouth, which is the starting point for dental decay. The amount of acid is gradually neutralised after eating, but this process cannot happen if teeth are continually exposed to food/drink (except water). Remember, foods and drinks containing natural sugars (such as fruit and fruit juices), as well as foods and drinks containing refined sugars cause higher levels of acid to be created. Dentists therefore recommend that foods and drinks with natural and refined sugars should be consumed mainly at mealtimes.

Follow these guidelines to help prevent tooth decay in young children.

▶ Provide only water in between meals.

▶ Milk and diluted fruit juice should be drunk at meal times rather than continuously sipped.

▶ Snacks should be free of sugars, including sugars from fruit.

▶ Foods containing sugar should be offered only at meal times.

❚❚ PAUSE POINT   What are the key points for preventing dental decay in young children?

Hint   Think about what young children should eat and drink at mealtimes and snack times.
Why should children be offered water rather than juice between meals?

Extend

The interrelationship between health and growth and physical development

Being healthy helps children to feel good about themselves, which supports their confidence and sense of competency. This means that health and well-being are often linked when we consider their impact on children's development. Interestingly, children who have continued poor health are more prone to depression, and so steps to promote children's health will have an effect on their well-being.

Good health is important for babies' and children's all-round development. When babies and children are poorly, they are less likely to want to play with others, interact and explore their environment. This lack of stimulation will, in turn, delay their cognitive and social development as they will not be gaining new experiences or interacting well with others. Babies and children who feel unwell are also less likely to cope with the trials and tribulations of the day and so are more prone to have tantrums, cry or become frustrated.

For children of school age, taking time off school due to illness may mean that they fall behind with learning to read as well as other aspects of the curriculum.

It is important to support children with medical conditions, because their long-term development can be affected for the reasons just described.

Link

For more detailed information about how to support children with ongoing health conditions, see Section C3 of this unit.

Reducing the risk of sudden infant death syndrome (SIDS)

If you are responsible for putting babies down to sleep, you should follow the latest guidelines to prevent sudden infant death syndrome (also known as cot death or SIDS). At the time of writing, these guidelines include preventing the baby from overheating by making sure the room is cool and not using cot duvets or bumpers. You should also place babies on their backs with their feet touching the end of the cot. This is known as 'feet to foot'. It is important to know that smoking plays a part in cot deaths. You should not handle a baby for 20 minutes after you have last smoked because the baby will breathe in your exhaled air, which will be low in oxygen.

> **Research**
>
> Find out about the latest guidelines for putting babies safely to sleep from The Lullaby Trust website: see www.lullabytrust.org.uk.

Assessment practice 6.1   A.P1   A.M1   A.D1

Nina is working as a nanny for a family with a baby of 8 months and a 2-year-old. She wants to find out more about children's physical care needs.

- Explain the importance of physical care needs for children.
- Assess the impact on children's development when their physical care needs are met.
- Evaluate ways in which Nina might be able to meet the physical care needs of the two children she is working with.

Plan

- What information will be the most relevant for this task?
- Where can I find additional information?
- How long will I need to collate and analyse the information required for the task?

Do

- Am I presenting the information accurately and concisely?
- Am I managing my time effectively?

Review

- Can I justify why I have decided to approach this task in the way that I have?
- Have I evaluated my work and am I confident that it fulfils the set task?

A2 Approaches to supporting physical development and care needs

The importance of observation and assessment

Observation and assessment play an extremely important role in supporting development. By looking carefully at babies' and children's physical development, you can assess what their developmental needs are. You can also think about whether children are showing any signs of developmental delay that may need further investigation. For observation to be of any use, you do need to know what typical development looks like for most children. This means that it is worth revising your knowledge of normative development.

Link

See Unit 1 for more information about typical or normative development. Also see Unit 9 for more detail about the processes of observation and assessment.

You also need to talk to parents, as children often show some aspects of their physical development outside the setting.

By observing children, you can also think about other areas of their development – such as their confidence levels and whether they are keen to try out new experiences. In addition, you can begin to identify children's interests and plan activities that take these into account.

Case study

The importance of observing and assessing children

Purmina is 18 months old. She loves playing with her sit-and-ride toy. Her key person has spotted that she is coordinating her feet movements to push the toy along with both feet. She is also moving quickly and knows when to stop and turn the toy. Her key person talks to Purmina's mother who tells her that, at home, Purmina tries to get on her brother's tricycle. They agree that it is time for Purmina to try out a simple tricycle that requires pushing rather than pedalling, but which she can steer.

Check your knowledge

1 Why is it important for Purmina's key person to observe and assess her development?

2 Why is it helpful for the key person to talk to Purmina's parents?

3 How will this observation and assessment help Purmina's development?

Environments that support children's physical development

There is no single template as to how to provide an environment to support children's development. The key elements when planning environments for children's physical development include the following.

▶ **Space** – to practise many large (gross) and locomotive skills, such as running and throwing, children need sufficient space. This is one reason why taking children outdoors is considered to be important.

▶ **Time and encouragement** – many of the skills that children need to master take time to develop. You only have to watch a baby trying to crawl to realise the amount of effort and motivation that is involved. This is one reason why adults need to support and encourage children.

▶ **Resources** – to support children's physical development, a good range of resources are needed. These are best chosen according to the skill that is being developed, but also according to the stage of development of each child. If resources are put out that children do not have the skills to access, there is a danger that they will become frustrated or that they may harm themselves. The various resources that can help children learn to use a bicycle are shown on the following page.

Step by step: Learning to ride a bicycle

7 Steps

1 Brick trolley

2 Sit-on toy

3 Sit-on toy with steering

4 Tricycle without pedals

5 Tricycle with pedals

6 Bicycle with stabilisers

7 Bicycle

Routines for physical care

Years ago, group-care settings had very tight routines around children's physical care. These mainly met the organisation's needs rather than individual children's; for instance, children were told when to go to the toilet and had to eat everything on the plate at mealtimes.

Today, things have changed. Physical routines are more child-centred and individual. Early years professionals also work in partnership with parents and respect their wishes. However, early years settings still need to make sure that children's physical needs are met during a session or during the day. This means that it is usual for children to spend some time outdoors but they can have naps or water whenever they need them.

Play and activities to promote physical development

Play is an important tool to support children's physical development because children are likely to practise movements as they are enjoying play. Many resources and activities that support development of the muscles used in fine and large (sometimes referred to as gross) motor movements can be set up in indoor and outdoor environments. Tables 6.2, 6.3 and 6.4 show activities and resources that can be used indoors and outdoors.

Babies

In cold or damp weather, babies need to be dressed warmly but they should still spend time outdoors so they can benefit from fresh air and the opportunity to be in a sensory environment.

▶ **Table 6.2:** Activities for babies that support fine and large motor movements

Fine motor movements (including fine motor and hand–eye coordination)	Large motor movements (including balance)
Treasure basket play	Paddling pool
Sensory play	Baby gym
Shakers	Swings
Rattles	Roll-a-ball games
Looking at books	Knock-down bricks and beakers
Activity mat	Tree stumps to allow babies to cruise

Toddlers aged 1–2 years

Toddlers are very active and so need opportunities to move around.

▶ **Table 6.3:** Activities for toddlers aged 1–2 years that support fine and large motor movements

Fine motor movements (including fine motor and hand–eye coordination)	Large motor movements (including balance)
Heuristic play	Climbing frames
Mark making	Some wheeled toys – sit-and-rides
Paint	Soft play cushions
Playing in water and sand	Throwing (beanbags and soft balls indoors)
Sensory play, e.g. gloop	Swings

> **Theory into practice**
>
> Look at the indoor and the outdoor environment in your work placement. Consider how each of the environments support children's physical development.

> **Link**
>
> You looked at some of the key elements of physical care in Section A1 and you will look in more detail at how to plan routine care in Sections B1 and B2.

▶ This child is being helped onto a climbing frame. How is the activity helping his physical development?

Children aged 2–8 years

As children develop, their need for space increases when playing with wheeled toys or during other vigorous activities. Some settings, such as schools, have large indoor spaces that are helpful in this respect.

▶ **Table 6.4:** Activities for children aged 2–8 years that support fine and large motor movements

Fine motor movements (including fine motor and hand–eye coordination)	Large motor movements (including balance)
Construction, e.g. block play	Parachute games
Mark making, chalking and drawing	Moving to music
Painting	Throwing and catching (beanbags in limited spaces)
Role play (this may include elements of large motor movements)	Soft play
Sand and water play	Circle games, e.g. 'The farmer's in the dell', 'The hokey cokey', musical statues

Theory into practice

Observe what activities are available to promote the development of children's fine and large motor movements in your setting. Create a table like the one below and fill it in to show whether these opportunities are indoors or outdoors.

Fine motor movements		Gross motor movements	
Indoor	Outdoor	Indoor	Outdoor

ⅠⅠ PAUSE POINT Give two examples of activities that might support a 3-year-old's hand–eye coordination.

Hint Think about activities for 3-year-olds in your setting – which ones relate to hand–eye coordination?

Extend Explain why play is important in supporting children's physical development.

Ways to use the indoor and outdoor environment to support physical development

When planning the layout of a setting and specific activities, you should consider the range of physical skills that children can gain through play, both indoors and outside. There are many ways of doing this, but it can be helpful to make a list of skills and then think about activities and resources that will support these skills.

It is also important to observe and assess children to ensure that any activities or resources are developmentally appropriate for groups of children as well as individual children. Table 6.5 suggests ways of using indoor and outdoor environments to support children's physical development. It is usual to find that larger movements and vigorous exercise take place outdoors where there is more space.

▶ **Table 6.5:** Examples of how to use the indoor and outdoor environment to support physical development

Skill	Indoors	Outdoors
Balance	<ul><li>Opportunities to sit on the floor or on cushions</li><li>Opportunities to stand to do activities, e.g. sand and water tray</li><li>In baby rooms, handrails or stable furniture to help babies stand and walk</li></ul>	<ul><li>Swings</li><li>Slides</li><li>Obstacle courses</li></ul>
Coordination of large movements	<ul><li>Small wheeled toys such as pushchairs or brick trolleys</li></ul>	<ul><li>Opportunities to throw</li><li>Wheeled toys including trikes and scooters</li></ul>
Fine motor skills	<ul><li>Sand and water play</li><li>Construction play</li><li>Small-world play</li><li>Cooking activities</li><li>Opportunities to develop self-care skills at mealtimes</li><li>Role play</li></ul>	<ul><li>Opportunities to care for garden, e.g. planting seeds, and pets</li><li>Play with natural materials, e.g. sand and water</li><li>Role play</li></ul>

How to ensure inclusive provision

Inclusive provision is about making sure that children of all ages benefit from physical activities. This includes children who may have physical needs, mobility needs or learning difficulties. It may also include children who are not confident and need reassurance and encouragement from adults.

In order to ensure inclusive provision, the adults in a setting should have a positive and can-do attitude. The next important thing is to identify the needs of each child. There are many ways to do this, including observing the child and talking to parents and other professionals who may be involved with them. Once individual needs have been identified, you must consider how to adapt, change or add in new resources to meet them.

Many voluntary organisations can provide advice or even equipment to support children with additional needs.

Gender and culture

In addition to supporting children who may have additional needs, you must ensure that provision is inclusive for children regardless of their gender and culture. This is important, because if children are not taking part in the full range of physical activities and play there is a danger that their development will be restricted. To check that all children are able to access provision, observe children over a period of time as they play. You may spot that some equipment is only used by certain children.

Settings report that some girls choose not to play with wheeled toys or take part in ball games as they get older. If this is the case, consider whether the equipment could

Reflect

How does your work setting support inclusive practice?

form part of a wider activity – for example, setting up a role play shop outdoors and using the tricycles to do 'deliveries'. The involvement of adults can also influence children's play preferences. For example, if an adult starts off a skipping game and invites children to come and join in, wider participation is more likely.

How to provide children with appropriate physical challenges

One of your roles when supporting children's physical development is to provide sufficient opportunities to help children develop further. Table 6.6 shows some of the activities that can provide children with physical challenges and help them learn and develop physical skills.

▸ **Table 6.6:** Activities that can provide children with appropriate physical challenges

Fine motor movements 0–2 years		Fine motor movements 2–8 years	
Skill	**Activity**	**Skill**	**Activity**
Hand coordination: grasping; moving objects from one hand to the other	• Rattles • Self-feeding • Play with sensory materials such as gloop (from 6 months) • Activity mat	Pincer grip	• Tweezers, pipettes • Sewing, pegboards
		Strengthening hand preference	• Routine activities that require an active hand and a stabilising hand, e.g. dustpan and brush, drying a beaker
Hand–eye coordination	• Pointing to pictures in books • Turning pages in books • Self-feeding • Baby gym • Pop-up toys • Playing with water	Hand–eye coordination	• Turning pages in books • Self-care skills such as dressing, eating • Sewing • Construction toys, e.g. LEGO® • Drawing and painting • Playing with malleable materials, sand and water • Junk modelling
Large motor movements 0–2 years		Large motor movements 2–8 years	
Skill	**Activity**	**Skill**	**Activity**
Strengthening of limbs and muscles	• Baby gym • Activity mat • Bath time • Playing with water • Playing in ball pool • Throwing soft balls	Locomotive skills and balance	• Climbing frames • Running • Obstacle courses • Movement to music
Locomotive movements and balance	• Baby swing • Brick trolley • Sit-and-ride toys • Climbing frame	Balance	• Tricycles, bicycles, pushchairs and other wheeled toys requiring steering • Ball games involving catching and throwing • Games such as 'The hokey cokey'

Risk assessment to balance physical challenge and safety

In Unit 5, we looked at the process of risk assessment. When providing physical challenges for children to support their physical development, the risk assessment process remains important.

Link

You may find it helpful at this point to look back at Sections A2 and D1 of Unit 5 to remind yourself of the principles of carrying out a risk assessment.

Settings have to balance risk against their legal duty to take reasonable steps to prevent accidents. The test of what is reasonable or not is linked to what a 'reasonable person' thinks is acceptable. This, in turn, is likely to link to the age of the child and how significant the risk is. For example, giving a marble to a baby would present an unreasonable level of risk, but it would be reasonable to let a 6-year-old child play with marbles. For children to develop physically, they need sufficient challenge in their activities. If there is insufficient challenge, there is a danger that children will become bored or frustrated. Figure 6.6 shows the benefits of providing risk and challenge in settings.

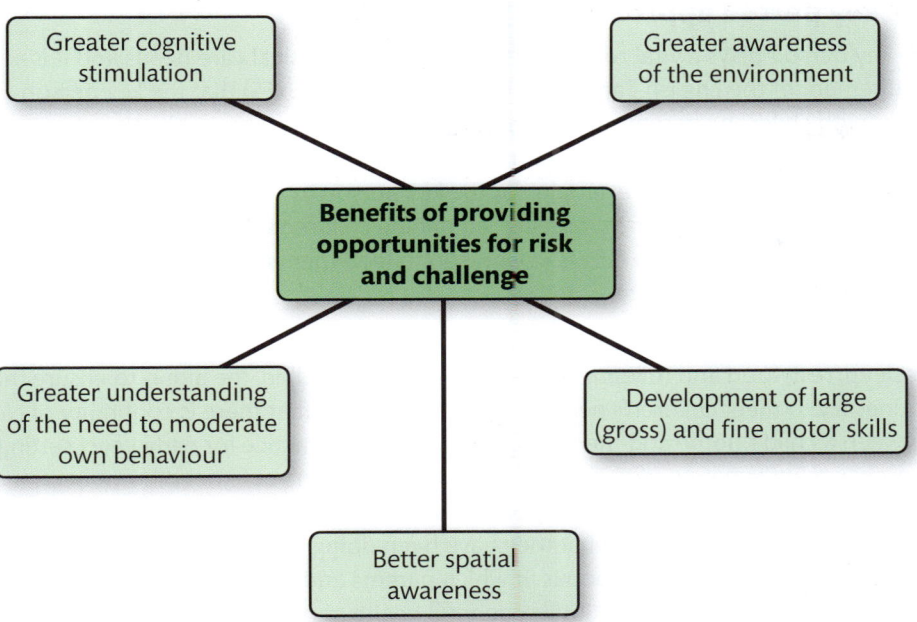

▶ **Figure 6.6:** The benefits for children of providing opportunities for risk and challenge in settings

Deciding on the level of risk

When deciding how much risk and challenge is acceptable, you have to consider several factors.

▶ **The age/stage of the child** – Babies and toddlers have little awareness of safety and are very impulsive. We also know that until 18 months or so, babies and toddlers put things in their mouths. However, the majority of older children are often more aware of their surroundings and have more self-restraint.

▶ **Risk assessment** – It is important to identify the risks in order to make a decision about what is appropriate. As part of the risk assessment, you should consider what the physical impact/injury for the child would be if an activity went wrong. A slight bump or bruise is likely to be acceptable for an older child but the possibility of concussion or a serious wound is not.

▶ **Group size and composition** – When young and older children are together and sharing the same space, it is important to think about what resources can be used and what activities can take place. A toddler can easily stumble into the path of an oncoming bicycle or football, for instance.

Health and safety procedures for physical care routines

Every setting has its own health and safety procedures in relation to physical care routines. These have to be followed to ensure your personal safety and that of the children. Lifting a child incorrectly can, for example, cause back injury and not using personal protective equipment might spread infection.

> **Link**
>
> In Section B1, you will look at how to ensure health and safety when providing physical care, including infection control.

The key person approach

The key person plays a vital role in meeting children's physical care needs and it is a requirement of the English Early Years Foundation Stage (EYFS) that the key person works with children's parents and carers. Other early years frameworks also stress the importance of strong key person or key worker approaches in relation to physical care. It is good practice, for example, for the key person to be involved in toileting and nappy changing as this is important in maintaining children's dignity. In the same way, it is also good practice for a baby's key person to feed them as this helps to strengthen attachment bonds.

The key person should also talk to parents about how they meet their children's needs for sleep, rest, food and toileting at home. Wherever possible, the aim is to ensure that settings try to meet children's needs in the same way, so that there is continuity of care between a child's home and the setting. It is also good practice for early years settings to exchange information with parents about how children's care needs have been met in the session. This is particularly important with babies and toddlers who are not able to talk to their parents about what they have been doing. Most early years settings use daily diaries or home–setting books in which parents and early years professionals can record information about food intake, general health and toileting.

PAUSE POINT   What is the role of the key person in supporting children's physical care?

Hint   Think about how the key person works with children and their parents.

Extend   Explain the link between maintaining children's dignity and the role of the key person in carrying out physical care activities.

Physical care routines as learning and development opportunities

Physical care routines such as dressing, combing hair and toileting all take some time. This means that they are perfect opportunities for adults to support children's learning in a variety of ways. One of the most important is the opportunity to develop children's language. By chatting and listening carefully to children during a nappy change or at mealtimes, there is the opportunity for children to have ten or more minutes of sustained conversation. This is one of the reasons why it is important for a child's key person to be responsible for most or all of the physical care routines.

If adults are able to draw children's attention to what is happening, and why, there is also the possibility of children learning through these routines.

Link

In Section B2, you will look at practical examples of how care routines can support children's learning.

Theory into practice

How does your work placement use care routines as learning and development opportunities?

How to support children and parents/carers to make healthy lifestyle choices

Increasingly, early years settings have a role in supporting children and their families to make healthy lifestyle choices. This is done in a variety of ways, including having a healthy food policy at the setting. As a result of this policy, foods served in the early years setting will be healthy and children will be encouraged to try new fruits and vegetables. Many early years settings provide nutritional information for children and their families by putting out leaflets and using wall displays.

Early years settings also help parents find out about the need for their children to have sufficient sleep and exercise. In some early years settings, parents are offered information sessions and signposting to professionals who may be able to help them further.

Case study

Sleep support for parents

Adam is nearly 4 years old and rarely sleeps more than nine hours at night. He is clearly tired and as a result his behaviour is difficult to manage. Bedtimes are a battleground because Adam wants to stay up with his teenage brother, with whom he shares a room. His mother is desperate to tackle his sleep habit and has tried without success to cope alone. She is embarrassed about seeking help as she feels that everyone will think she is a bad parent. When the early years setting offers an information session for all parents about sleep, she decides to attend and is relieved to find that she is not the only parent who struggles at home.

Check your knowledge

1   How much sleep should Adam be having at his age?

2   Explain the importance of early years settings offering information to parents about sleep and other issues.

3   Evaluate the impact on Adam and his family if his mother is able to access more information and support.

How to work in partnership with parents/carers to provide for children's individual needs

Parents are likely to have preferences about what should happen when their child sleeps, which nappies and skin products to use and also what their child should wear. Parents will also know about any allergies that their children may have or particular needs that may affect their child's health and comfort, such as ongoing health conditions or special dietary needs. In particular, food allergies that might put a child at risk have to be noted carefully and many early years settings have procedures in place to ensure that children are not given foods that might contain allergens.

Many aspects of babies' and children's routines need to be continued when children are in early years settings, particularly their sleeping and feeding routines, so it is important that you consult with parents about these things.

Also remember that parents' wishes may be linked to cultural and religious practices. An example of this would be people of the Muslim faith who would prefer any washing to be done under running water. This means that their children will need to be showered rather than bathed. In the same way, cultural or religious practices might influence the dietary requirements of a particular child.

Assessment practice 6.2

Nina (the nanny from assessment practice 6.1) also wants to know about meeting the baby's and 2-year-old child's physical development needs. She is particularly interested in physical activities both indoors and outdoors, as well as finding out more about how to support their care needs.

- Identify a range of activities that will support the baby's and 2-year-old child's physical development needs.
- Analyse the impact of the activities on their overall development.
- Evaluate how care routines and physical activities can promote children's physical development.

Plan

- What information will be the most relevant for this task?
- Where can I find additional information and check that information is still current?

Do

- Am I presenting the information accurately and concisely?
- Am I managing my time effectively?

Review

- Can I justify why I have decided to approach this task in the way that I have?
- Have I evaluated my work and am I confident that it fulfils the set task?

B Plan and support routines and activities to meet children's physical development and care needs

B1 Planning for physical care routines and activities

Planning for a child's physical care or creating a programme of activities to support a child's development are part of the responsibilities of any early years practitioner. However, it is important that this is not done in isolation. This means that you need to work closely with other colleagues and also the parents or carers of the children you look after. This is particularly important with babies and toddlers who will not be able to tell you, for example, what they have eaten and whether they have been to the toilet.

How to exchange and record information about children's physical care needs

Adults need to work together to exchange and record information about children's physical care needs. In most early years settings, systems of daily recording and exchanging information are used so that everyone who is caring for the children knows about:

▶ naps and sleep
▶ toileting
▶ food and drink intake.

With older children, daily records are not normally kept, but any changes to children's regular care needs are recorded and information is exchanged. This means that parents of a child who has not wanted anything to eat at lunchtime would be told about this, as it may be that the child is starting to be poorly. By sharing and exchanging information, children's physical care needs can also be balanced. For instance, a child who has missed their usual nap time may need to go to bed earlier while a child who has not eaten any breakfast at home will be given an earlier snack by the early years setting.

To record physical care needs on a daily basis for younger children, most settings have a simple home–setting book or send out slips of paper. Parents are also encouraged to let the setting know about their child at home. This can happen using a home–setting book or parents may prefer to let the child's key person know.

What to remember when recording information

Each setting will use a different format to record babies' and toddlers' physical care needs. However, you should always ensure the following when recording information.

▸ Make sure that you are recording information about the correct child.

▸ Write the time as well as the event that took place.

▸ Write concise and precise information, e.g. 'Millie slept between 2.00–2.40 p.m. this afternoon' or 'At 10.45 a.m. David took 180 ml of his feed'.

How to plan care routines

There are many factors to bear in mind when creating a plan for physical care routines for children.

First, find out about a child's individual needs from their parents or carers, or existing key person. Based on the information you gain, work out a daily routine for meal and snack times, sleep and rest, and opportunities to visit the toilet or nappy changes.

Here are some general guidelines.

▸ Think about the child's age and stage of development.

▸ Look at the latest guidelines in relation to sleep, naps and physical activity.

▸ Think about how long each care routine is likely to last.

▸ Think about each child's need for exercise and time spent outdoors.

▸ Record the proposed daily routine and talk to parents and colleagues about whether it is suitable.

Figure 6.7 shows an example of a daily physical care routine for a child aged 18 months with older siblings, being cared for by a nanny.

7:30 a.m.	Arrival of nanny – breakfast if required
7:45 a.m.	Clean teeth, wash face and hands
8:00 a.m.	Check nappy before going out on school run with older children
8:30 a.m.	Use pushchair/walk to school to drop off older children
9:00 a.m.	Walk through park and play on swings and roundabouts
10:00 a.m.	Home – check nappy and have snack
10:30 a.m.	Nap time
12:15 a.m.	Wash hands and face before lunch
12:30 a.m.	Lunch time and check nappy
1:00 p.m.	Play – in garden if weather is good
2:45 p.m.	Check nappy
3:00 p.m.	Use pushchair/walk to school to collect older children
3:45 p.m.	Home – snack for child and older siblings
4:00 p.m.	Check nappy
5:30 p.m.	Meal time
6:00 p.m.	Shower, clean teeth, change nappy and change into nightwear

▸ **Figure 6.7:** An example of a plan for a physical care routine

Once you have created a physical care routine and you are starting to follow it, think about how effective it is. A good routine that will provide a child with a healthy lifestyle should not feel rushed or pressured. It is also worth remembering that as children grow and develop, their physical care needs change and so new routines will need to be created.

How to plan for challenging, safe activities to support physical development

Planning for children's physical development should start with a good knowledge of their current level of development. This is why observation and assessment (as we saw in Section A2) is very important. In addition, many early years frameworks, including the EYFS in England, also have curriculum outcomes for physical development. This means that early years settings plan activities that are linked to the curriculum that they are following.

When planning activities for children, it is also important to think about their current interests and what they are keen to do. This helps children to be motivated. As many physical skills are acquired through practice, it is essential that children enjoy what they are doing.

It is also important when planning to think about individual children's level of development. If an activity is not sufficiently challenging, children become bored and may start to show unsafe behaviours. It is also important that while an activity is challenging, it is still within grasp of a child. If it is too difficult, children may give up.

You also need to think about specific skills that children may need to work on. This means planning enjoyable activities that might support this skill. Look back at Table 6.6 in Section A2 to see how skills can be linked to different activities.

Link

Section A2 looks at how to provide children with appropriate physical challenges and the importance of risk assessment to balance physical challenge and safety.

Case study

Balancing challenge with safety

Little Gems nursery is planning the environment for the next week. It is June and the weather forecast looks promising. The staff are thinking about planning a series of activities based on water. They are considering creating a waterfall and also perhaps having a paddling pool for the toddlers on one or two days. Indoors, they are thinking about putting water in buckets rather than in water trays so that children can explore water in a different way.

Everyone in the setting is excited about this theme, but they need to carry out a risk assessment as the activities are not part of the usual environment. They also need to consider how each risk will be managed.

The team quickly identify the risk of drowning and also the potential of falls caused by water creating slippery surfaces. In addition, with the weather forecast suggesting hot weather, the team need to consider how to prevent sunburn.

Check your knowledge

1 Why is it important during the planning process for risk assessment to be considered?

2 Explain ways in which the setting might decide to manage the key risks that they have identified.

3 Why is it important when planning the environment to consider a range of factors such as the weather?

 **PAUSE POINT**   What factors are involved in planning challenging, safe activities to support physical development?

Hint   Think about children's skills and enjoyment.

Extend   Why is it important that children enjoy the physical activities on offer?

Discussion

Today there are concerns that children are not doing sufficient physical activity, especially outdoors. Some people think that parents are over protective. Others blame the increased use of television, computer games and tablets.

What do you think is to blame? How would you go about increasing physical activity among children?

Discuss these questions in a group and share your feedback.

Formats for recording care routines and activity plans

There is no particular format for recording care routines or activity plans. So settings tend to develop them in very individual ways. It is, however, usual for early years settings that care for babies to have individual routines for each baby. This is because each baby is likely to have different sleep and feeding patterns. Recording individual routines allows for continuity of care.

In group-care settings, the overall routine is likely to be recorded in a timetable format, especially where different groups of children are sharing spaces such as outdoor space or hall time. Figure 6.8 shows an example of a care routine for a nursery school attached to a school.

Sunnyfields Nursery
Daily care routine

9:00 a.m.	Register with key person on arrival Choice of play activities indoors and outdoors until 10:45 a.m.
9:30–10:45 a.m.	Snack bar open for self-service. Staff member reminds children to wash hands before eating.
11:00–11:30 a.m.	Mondays, Wednesdays and Fridays: hall time for dance/using simple apparatus Tuesdays and Thursdays: children remain in provision playing indoors and outdoors
11:40 a.m.	Story and rhymes in key person groups
11:50 a.m.	Preparation for going home Children are supported to dress themselves independently and collect their belongings
12:00 p.m.	End of session

Toileting arrangements
- Children who are in nappies are changed when required
- Children are free to go to the toilet at any point during the session but are reminded if necessary

▶ **Figure 6.8:** An example of a care routine for a nursery school attached to a school

How to ensure health and safety in provision of physical care

The process of making sure that the physical care needs of children are met involves some tasks that carry a potential risk. It is important that early years professionals are aware of these risks so that they can ensure their own health and safety and also the health and safety of the child. For example, lifting a baby or toddler up onto a raised surface in order to change a nappy can potentially put a strain on the early years professional's back unless it is done properly. There is also a risk to the child of falling from the raised surface. During each physical care task, you should carefully evaluate the risks to both you and the child, and then take the necessary steps to minimise them.

Infection control

As well as the potential for physical risks during physical care routines, it is essential to avoid the possible risk of infection, especially from tasks related to nappy changing or toileting. It is for this reason that disposable gloves and aprons are provided in early years settings. Good hand-washing procedures should also be in place. These procedures protect both the child and the adult.

> **Link**
>
> You may want to remind yourself of the infection prevention and control procedures you looked at in Section B1 of Unit 5.

Assessment practice 6.3 | B.P3 | B.M2

Nina, the nanny working with a baby and a 2-year-old, is concerned about how, in practice, a care routine can be planned.

- Identify the care routines that are needed for a baby and a 2-year-old.
- Think about the likely duration of each routine. Then plan an overall routine.
- Evaluate the effectiveness of this routine and its likely impact on the children's health and well-being.

Plan
- What information will be most relevant for this task?
- Where can I find additional information?

Do
- Am I presenting the information accurately and concisely?
- How can I evaluate the effectiveness of the routine?

Review
- Can I justify why I have decided to approach this task in the way that I have?
- Have I evaluated my work and am I confident that the routine would be effective?

B2 Support physical development and care needs

How to empower children and support their independence

Good care routines are respectful of babies and children. They help them to understand the process, and where possible to be involved in it. In practical terms, this means always talking to babies and children when you are with them and finding ways to involve them in a routine. For example, babies can hold items during a nappy change or start the process of wiping their own faces during a cleaning routine. Finding ways of involving children means that they can start the process of learning to care for themselves. It also makes the experience more pleasant for them and can reduce their anxiety.

The following tips are useful when carrying out care routines.

▶ Let babies and children know what is going to happen.
▶ Always talk to babies and children during physical care routines, using a warm and sensitive voice.
▶ Explain the importance of what you are doing as soon as children can understand.
▶ Find ways of involving the child and, if possible, give them choices.
▶ Look for ways in which the child can do some parts of the process.
▶ Try to find ways to ensure some privacy during toileting.
▶ Look for ways of making physical care routines fun.

How to support routines for sleep and rest

Falling asleep is easier for babies and children when there is some sort of routine. Sleep routines allow babies and children to feel safe and, therefore, to relax. The ability to relax is key to falling asleep. To help babies and children fall asleep, it is important that adults spend time with them beforehand so that they feel emotionally secure. It is also helpful if adults choose things to do with children that are calming. There is little point in expecting children to fall asleep immediately after they have been running around.

▶ This parent is making the routine of putting shoes and socks on fun

Bedtime routines

The following bedtime routine for the home is recommended by many health visitors to help babies and children get into the habit of sleeping:

1 Mealtime
2 Give the child time to play and relax with you
3 Bath or shower the child
4 Change the child into nightwear
5 Child cleans teeth
6 Take the child into the bedroom, which is darkened slightly
7 Put the child into bed/cot
8 Share a story with the child
9 Reassure the child
10 Leave the bedroom.

Theory into practice

Sleep routines

Talk to three parents about how they settle their child for sleep and find out the following information.

• Does their child have a set bedtime?
• How do they manage the bedtime routine?
• Do they have, or have they ever had, any difficulties in getting their child to sleep?

Creating an environment for naps

Bedtime routines are also important in group-care settings, where it is important to create both a routine and an environment that help children to take naps.

It is good practice to have a separate area for children to sleep in. This area should feel calm, tidy and homely. Children should also have their own bed, which is always in the same place. Ideally, the room should be darkened. As with the home routine for bedtime, children benefit from a strong routine in group care.

As some children struggle after waking up, it is a good idea to have a routine to help them. A story and a hug while a child is waking up can work well. Also consider offering children a drink of water, as some children will be dehydrated.

Comfort objects

Some children will be used to having a comfort object such as a dummy, special blanket or toy with them in order to sleep. You should find out from the child's parents what the child needs and how any comfort objects are usually used.

How to support mealtimes

Mealtimes should be social occasions and times when children can enjoy eating. It is good practice to sit with children while they are eating so you can model how to use utensils and interact with others. Children should also have opportunities to show independence. This means that most settings will encourage children to pour their own drinks and to serve themselves food.

Encouraging healthy food choices

Dieticians recommend that all food served to children in early years settings is nutritious and healthy, so children are making choices between healthy foods rather than between healthy and unhealthy foods. It is also recommended that children are introduced to a range of different vegetables and flavours. Adults can help this process by role modelling eating a wide range of vegetables and also being open to trying new combinations and flavours.

How to support toileting routines and progression out of nappies

The role of the adult is important in helping children with toileting and moving out of nappies. Firstly, adults have to remain calm and very child-centred. Children are likely to have more accidents or refuse to go to the toilet when they are unsure of adults' reactions. It is also important that the toileting environment is a pleasant one and maintaining toileting areas is the responsibility of adults. Not only should areas be clean and hygienic, they should also be attractive.

As part of supporting toileting, adults need to recognise any signs that children are becoming constipated. Constipation can be caused by lack of hydration, insufficient fruit or vegetables and other forms of fibre in the diet, or due to a child feeling nervous and resisting going to the toilet. In some cases, constipation may be linked to a medical condition. If the early signs of constipation are not recognised, it can become increasingly difficult and painful for a child to pass a stool. This in turn can make things worse and some children can develop long-term problems with constipation.

The signs of constipation include:

▶ soiling of clothes
▶ small, hard stools ('rabbit droppings') or very large stools
▶ foul-smelling wind
▶ loss of appetite.

If you have concerns that a child is becoming constipated, it is important that parents are alerted so that they can seek medical advice. Often, constipation can be reversed if children take in more fluid and have more opportunities to eat fruit, vegetables and other fibrous foods.

Progression out of nappies

There is no set time when children should be ready to move out of nappies. Anywhere between 18 months and 3 years is fairly typical. It is important that parents understand this age range and do not feel pressurised to start toilet training their children until they are physically and emotionally ready. A successful process requires the child to recognise they need the toilet and to get there in time. If children need constant reminders, or are having accidents, the full process has not been achieved.

Signs of readiness

When children are ready to move out of nappies, the process can be very quick. Most children are clean and dry within four or five days and no longer have accidents or require constant reminders. Children's physical maturity, their individual motivation and their language development will all have an effect on their readiness to move out of nappies. The starting point though is always to check that children have bladder maturity and can retain urine for a period of time. Unless this is in place, children will be physically unable to manage the process of moving out of nappies.

Look out for the following things to help you decide whether or not a child is ready and work closely with parents to make sure the time is right.

▶ Children's physical maturity:
  - Is the child's nappy dry for a long period, e.g. two hours?
  - Does the child release urine in significant quantities?
  - Can the child walk upstairs on alternate feet?
  - Can the child manage simple undressing?

▶ Children's motivation:
  - Is the child keen to move out of nappies?
  - Is the child interested in potties/toilets?

▶ Children's language:
  - Does the child have sufficient language to signal that they need to use the toilet?

Ⅱ   PAUSE POINT   List four signs that children might be ready to move out of nappies.

Hint   Think about signs of physical maturity, motivation and language.

Extend   Why is bladder maturity needed before a child can move out of nappies?

Starting off the process

When you think the child is ready to progress out of nappies, it is worth removing the nappy and having a potty or two strategically placed in the room. Let the child know where they are but do not keep reminding them. A low-key approach, which is calm, relaxed and matter-of-fact, works well. Too much emphasis on the child being a 'big boy' or 'big girl' can make it harder to put the child back into nappies if required. Too much pressure can also mean that the child becomes anxious and this anxiety can, in turn, prevent the child from relaxing sufficiently to pass urine.

If the child has an accident, simply clear it up without comment. When the child manages to get to the potty and perform, praise them but do not overreact. When the child goes to sleep or, if staying near a potty in this way is not possible, put a nappy back on the child. Within a day or so, it will soon become clear whether the child is ready. If a child is not ready, it is better to return to nappies for a few more weeks and then try again.

How to use everyday care routines as learning and development opportunities

In Section A2, you looked at the importance of using care routines as learning and development opportunities. There are many ways of doing this, as Table 6.7 shows.

▶ **Table 6.7:** How everyday activities with babies and children can provide learning opportunities and developmental benefits

Activity	Learning opportunities	Developmental benefits
Nappy changing	• Interaction between child and adult • Opportunities for baby or child to contribute, e.g. holding clean nappy	• Supports language development • Helps baby or child to build an attachment towards their key person • Helps baby or child to feel part of the process
Feeding a baby a bottle	• Close physical contact • Eye contact • Interaction	• Helps baby to build an attachment • Gives baby pleasure • Helps promote baby's receptive language
Mealtimes	• Interaction between child and adults • Talk about food, e.g. colour, size, shape • Encouragement for serving themselves and self-feeding	• Supports language development • Gives child a healthy attitude towards food • Helps child develop concepts of number, size and colour • Promotes social development • Helps child's fine motor skills
Getting dressed	• Interaction between child and adult • Talk about features of clothes, e.g. colour, shape, number of buttons • Encouragement for child to dress themselves	• Supports language development • Helps child to build an attachment • Helps child learn concepts of colour and number • Develops fine motor skills • Helps child to develop self-care skills and confidence
Going for a walk	• Interaction between child and adult • Encouragement for children to get dressed and go out • Talk about what children see during the walk	• Supports language development • Helps child to learn about their surroundings • Develops large motor skills • Supports development of healthy bones and muscles • Promotes a healthy lifestyle

 PAUSE POINT Give an example of how a care routine could be used as a learning opportunity.

 Hint Think about communication and how the child could get involved.

Extend Explain how the concepts of colour and number could be incorporated into a care routine.

How to ensure infection control

You looked at infection control in Unit 5, Section B1. Consider this section now with reference to care routines.

A good example of infection control is the use of personal protective equipment, for example, disposable aprons and gloves during toileting and nappy changing. Separate bins should also be used to dispose of materials that have been in contact with bodily fluids. Good infection control is also important during mealtimes.

Theory into practice

Make a list of the ways that your work placement avoids the spread of infection during care routines.

How to support sun protection for skin

Children and adults need some sunlight because it is a major source of vitamin D. However, babies' and children's skin burns easily in the sunlight and UVA rays from the sun can cause cancers. Most settings will have a policy relating to sun protection that should be based on the latest guidelines. Early years settings will ask parents to provide items used for sun protection, such as sun hats and sun-cream. They will also ask parents for written permission to apply sun-cream.

At the time of writing, the following is recommended for the summer months.

▸ **Shade** – make sure you put babies and children in the shade whenever possible.

▸ **Sunglasses** – provide sunglasses that will protect eyes against UVA rays.

▸ **Sun-cream** – use a high-factor sun-cream, and use it generously. Use non-allergenic creams and be ready to apply according to the manufacturer's instructions.

▸ **Clothing** – whenever possible, keep children covered up in loose, long-sleeved cotton clothes.

▸ **Hats** – use sun hats to protect babies' and children's heads from the sun.

> **Research**
>
> Find out about protecting children's skin from the sun by visiting the Cancer Research UK website: www.cancerresearchuk.org.

PAUSE POINT   List three ways in which children's skin can be protected from the sun.

 Hint   Think about how you would protect your own skin from the sun.

Extend   Explain why children's skin particularly needs protecting from the sun.

Assessment practice 6.4   B.P4 B.M2 B.D1

Make a list of the care routines and physical play activities that you have been involved in at your work placement.

Write a reflective account of your role in each routine and activity. Your reflective account should:

- explain your role in each of the care routines and physical play activities
- analyse how you supported the health and physical development of the children and how you promoted their independence and understanding of a healthy lifestyle
- evaluate your overall performance in relation to the provision of care routines and physical play activities and how they meet the needs of the child.

Plan

- Have I made a note of the care routines and activities I have been involved in?
- How can I gather feedback on my performance?

Do

- Have I considered all the activities I am involved in?
- Have I gathered feedback from other people about my performance?

Review

- Have I written an account in a reflective way that covers both my strengths and weaknesses as a practitioner?
- Have I provided examples to support the analysis of my performance?

 ## C Investigate how to recognise and respond to children who are unwell and support children with ongoing health conditions

C1 Signs of illness

There will be times when you need to deal with a baby or child who is unwell. Recognising that the child is poorly and knowing what to do is very important, especially in the rare event of a life-threatening disease. This section looks at how to recognise and respond to babies and children who are unwell. However, it cannot take the place of a valid, recognised first-aid qualification. Until you have been on a first-aid course, you should be very careful about any actions you take in an emergency, because the wrong action could cause more harm to the casualty. If in doubt, summon help first.

Recognising signs of illness

It is important to recognise the signs that babies and children are either becoming ill or are poorly. Babies and very young children rely on us to notice that they are becoming, or are, unwell as they cannot tell us.

Figure 6.9 shows some of the key signs that might alert you to a baby or child being unwell or incubating an illness. Some of these signs, as you will see, are indicators that emergency attention is required.

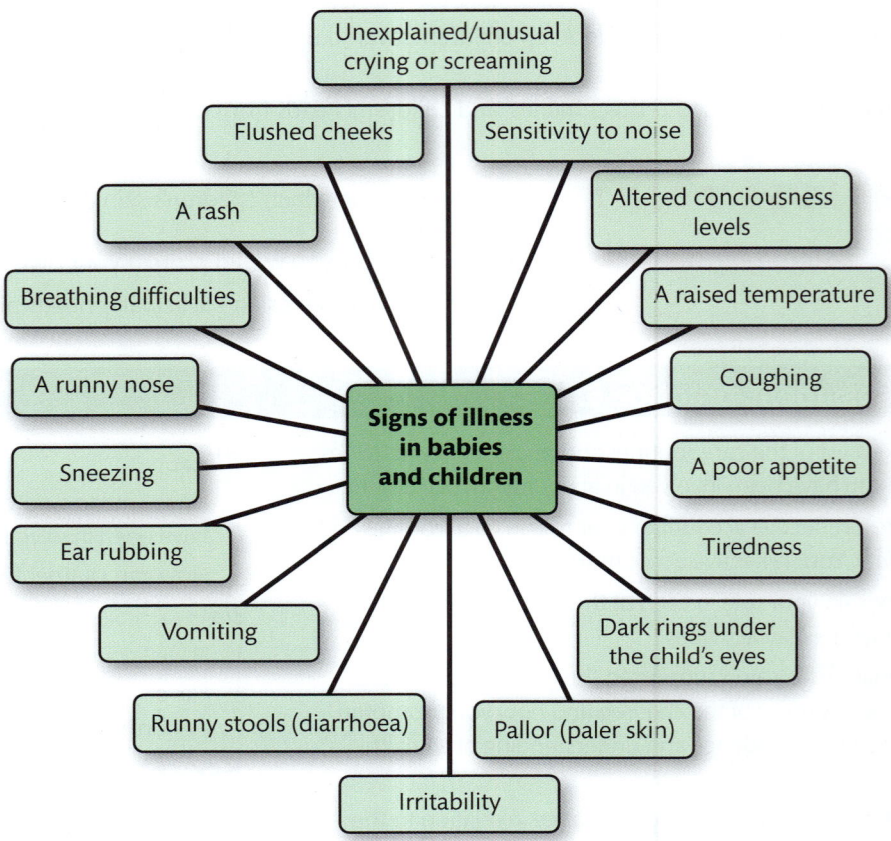

▶ **Figure 6.9:** Signs of illness in babies and children

Behavioural signs of illness

Behavioural signs of illness are often early indicators that a child is becoming poorly. In order to identify changes to children's behaviour that might be linked to illness, it is important to know the child well. This means that it is often the child's parents or the child's key person who are best placed to spot the signs.

Behavioural indicators may include a child being irritable or tearful. Take note if children who are usually quite outgoing, bubbly or sociable are withdrawn or uninterested in playing with others. Changes in a child's sleep or feeding patterns may also show that the child is becoming unwell. Many children who are unwell want to nap or find it hard to wake up from a sleep. They may also lose interest in food or only want to eat foods that are easy to swallow. The latter is usually a sign of a sore throat, which often precedes many childhood illnesses.

Even if a child is not showing other signs of being poorly, it is important to share changes in their usual behaviour with parents so that they can keep a closer eye on the child when they return home.

⏸ **PAUSE POINT**   List three signs that may indicate that a baby or child is not well.

Hint   Think about obvious symptoms but also changes in behaviour.

Extend   Why is it important to quickly identify a baby or child who may be ill?

Symptoms that require urgent medical attention

Some symptoms are important to notice and then act on immediately. Most childhood illnesses are mild but there are some, notably meningitis, which have sudden onset and can be fatal if not treated quickly. All of the following symptoms indicate that a baby or child should be seen immediately by a doctor. Some of these symptoms are associated with meningitis and sept caemia. Remember, if you notice that a baby or child's skin looks blotchy or a rash is appearing, press a glass to it. If the rash does not fade under pressure, you should immediately summon emergency help.

Babies

Babies' immune systems are not fully developed and so infections can quickly overcome them. It is important to call for help quickly if there are signs that a baby is becoming very poorly. All of the following symptoms indicate that a baby should be seen immediately by a doctor:

▶ raised temperature – above 38°C if the baby is under 3 months or above 39°C if the baby is over 3 months
▶ a fever (above 38°C) with cold hands and feet
▶ unusual crying or screaming
▶ convulsions
▶ floppiness and unresponsiveness
▶ pale, blotchy skin or blueness of skin
▶ an intense response to light
▶ drowsiness – trance-like state
▶ refusal of food
▶ vomiting or vomit that contains blood
▶ fast breathing or difficulty in breathing.

Children

Children can often fall quite ill within a few hours, so it is important to recognise not only when a child is off colour, but also when their illness is becoming severe. All of the following symptoms indicate that a child should be seen immediately by a doctor:

▶ temperature above 40°C
▶ fever with cold hands and feet
▶ child complains of headache
▶ child complains that their eyes hurt
▶ unresponsiveness or drowsiness
▶ child screams and dislikes light
▶ pale blotchy skin or blueness of skin
▶ child complains of stiff neck
▶ violent and prolonged vomiting or vomit containing blood
▶ fast breathing or difficulty in breathing.

PAUSE POINT List four signs that indicate that a baby needs immediate medical attention.

Hint Think about changes in temperature and skin, and level of consciousness.

Extend Why might a baby's health deteriorate more quickly than an adult's?

Assessment practice 6.5 C.P5

Nina, the nanny working with an 8-month-old baby and a 2-year-old, is a little worried that she might not be able to spot the signs of illness. She has asked you to prepare some information for her.

- Identify the key signs of illness.
- Analyse the importance of identifying illness promptly in children.
- Evaluate how early years practitioners can have an impact on children's health through the prompt identification of illness.

Plan
- Where can I find information about signs of illness in children?
- How confident do I feel in my ability to complete the task?

Do
- Am I presenting information in a way that will be accessible?
- Am I managing my time effectively?

Review
- Can I identify how what I have learned during this task relates to my future work with children?
- Can I clearly state whether my work meets all the criteria for the task?

C2 Responding to children who are unwell

The importance of having policies and procedures for supporting children who are unwell

Every early years setting has a policy and procedures for adults to follow when children are unwell. The policy and procedures focus on:

▸ preventing infection from spreading to other children

▸ care and attention for the child who is unwell

▸ informing parents about their child's illness

▸ exclusion periods for children who have been unwell

▸ reporting the illness to other organisations and authorities where appropriate (see the section below on statutory reporting of infectious diseases).

The policy outlines the approach to supporting children who are unwell. The procedures give adults working with children a step-by-step guide about what to do. It is good practice also for parents to be aware of the policy and procedures that are in place so that they know what will happen if their child becomes poorly.

If you work in a setting, it is important that you follow the procedures to ensure that a child who is unwell is properly cared for, but also to prevent the spread of infection.

Theory into practice

Look at your work placement's policy on children who are unwell.

- In what situations will parents be asked to collect their children immediately?
- What steps does the setting take if a child is showing early signs of being poorly, but is not very unwell?

Procedures for seeking medical help

As part of the policy for supporting children who are unwell, early years settings also have procedures in place in the event that medical help is required. In most settings, when children need medical attention, the child's key person will either call the parent to ask that they collect the child to take them to the doctor, or in the case that a child's condition is serious, an ambulance will be called by whoever is best placed to do this. This is usually a senior member of staff or the child's key person.

Procedures do vary from setting to setting, so it is important to always find out in your setting what would happen if a child needed medical help.

Procedures for reporting and recording illness

An essential aspect of your role is to know about and follow your setting's policy for reporting and recording illness in children.

Reporting signs of illness promptly is important, so that procedures to stop the spread of infection can be implemented. It is usual, for example, for the child to be moved to an area away from other children. You may need to contact the child's parents and, in serious cases, seek medical help.

It is important to record illness. It is usual to write down the date and time of the illness, the child's name, the symptoms, and the actions that were taken (which may include giving medication). Where a baby or child has a temperature, you should record the temperature, how it was taken and the time it was taken, and keep doing this until the child leaves your responsibility. You should also do this with episodes of diarrhoea and vomiting.

The information that has been recorded should be passed to the parent so that they know what steps have already been taken and also so that they can see how the illness is affecting their child. Where medical attention has been sought, this information should be passed to the medical professional treating the child.

 PAUSE POINT   What information should be recorded if a child is ill?

 Hint   Think about the details that a parent or medical professional might ask for.

Extend   Why should this information be passed onto to the child's parents or the medical professional treating the child?

How to call for urgent medical help

In Unit 5, you looked at how to call for urgent help in an emergency. Always try to stay calm so that you can give clear information. In some cases, urgent help may mean calling for a colleague, but an ambulance should always be called if the child is showing any of the signs listed in Section C1. It is always better to err on the side of caution – in the case of some illnesses, such as meningitis, a delay may be life-threatening.

> **Link**
>
> Section D2 of Unit 5 has more detail about how to call for urgent medical help.

How and when parents are informed about illness

Parents need to know if their child is unwell. This is one reason why it is important to maintain up-to-date contact details for parents. Parents should also, as part of the admissions process, have given written consent for emergency medical treatment.

It is usual for settings to contact parents immediately when it is recognised that the child is unwell. Where a child has a slight complaint, such as not eating as much as usual, this may be noted, and the parents informed when they arrive to collect the child. When parents arrive, let them know if there are restrictions on when their child can return to the setting.

When contacting a parent, remember the following.

- Check that you are talking to the child's parent.
- Clearly explain the symptoms.
- Clearly explain what measures have been taken.
- Let the parent know whether their child needs immediate collection or, in the case of an emergency, where their child is.

If a child has been hospitalised, a member of staff should have accompanied the child and should meet the parents at the hospital.

Case study

Letting parents know about their child's illness

Jamie is 4 years old. He is at nursery when his key person notices that he has a fever and also a rash. She thinks that he may have chickenpox. She sits with him in a separate room from the other children and calls his father. During the phone conversation, she is reassuring but makes it clear that Jamie does need collecting from nursery.

Check your knowledge

1 Why is it important that the key person is reassuring but gives a clear message to Jamie's dad?
2 Explain why Jamie needs to be taken home.
3 Why did the key person separate Jamie from the other children?

How to support children who are unwell

Being poorly is distressing for babies and children. Many babies and children want the reassurance of being with their parents. While waiting for parents to arrive, it is important to give the child reassurance. Babies and children should not be left alone, not only because they could take a turn for the worse, but also because they need this reassurance from you. Remember to:

- make the baby or child as comfortable as possible
- explain to them what is happening to their body and what is going to happen next
- offer a comforter, if a child has one
- stay calm and positive
- follow the baby or child's mood, e.g. recognise if they do not want to communicate
- observe the child closely and be ready to get emergency help if the child's condition deteriorates or you see any of the symptoms described earlier.

Steps to take if a baby or child has a temperature

If a child has a temperature, you should:

- remove layers of clothing
- keep the room cool and well ventilated
- take the child's temperature and record it; repeat every hour or earlier if symptoms change
- offer a paracetamol- or ibuprofen-based medicine, if permission has been gained from parents
- offer the child sips of cooled boiled water
- get emergency help if the temperature rises to the temperatures given in Section C1.

Research

Find out how to take a child's temperature using the following instruments:

- a fever strip
- a digital thermometer in the mouth/under the armpit
- a digital thermometer in the ear
- a traditional thermometer in the mouth/under the armpit.

Find out the advantages and disadvantages of using different methods to take a child's temperature.

Precautions to prevent the spread of infection

It is essential to take precautions to prevent the spread of infection when children are unwell.

▶ **Isolate the baby or child** – The first step to take if illness is suspected is to keep the baby or child separate from other children. Otherwise, the infection may be passed from one child to another, either through contact or through the air. Some large settings, such as schools, will have a designated room for unwell children.

▶ **Ventilate** – It is a good idea to keep the setting well ventilated by opening a window to disperse/dilute airborne infections.

▶ **Wear disposable gloves and aprons** – If a child has diarrhoea or has vomited, gloves and aprons should be worn to clean the toilet or area affected; you should then dispose of the gloves and aprons immediately. If the child's clothing needs changing or the child needs washing, use a new set of gloves and aprons.

▶ **Use disinfectant to clean areas affected** – Toilets and any areas affected by faeces or vomit must be cleaned immediately with disinfectant. Items used to clean the areas should be disposed of or disinfected. Items that the child handled before becoming ill should also be disinfected. In addition, where vomiting and/or diarrhoea has occurred, the whole setting should be thoroughly cleaned, with particular attention paid to door handles, toys and food utensils.

In cases where babies and children show other symptoms such as tiredness or headaches, the area where they have been isolated should be cleaned thoroughly after they have left.

▶ **Wash hands** – It is essential that adults who have been with the child wash their hands frequently, especially after coming into contact with the child. Other children who have been playing, or in contact, with the child should also have their hands washed.

> ❚❚ **PAUSE POINT**   What are the key ways in which the spread of infection can be prevented when a child is ill?
>
> **Hint**   Think of these key words: isolate, ventilate, clean!
>
> **Extend**   Why, in group-care settings, is it particularly important that steps to minimise the spread of infection are taken immediately?

Exclusion periods

To prevent the spread of infections such as chickenpox or gastroenteritis, early years settings have policies in place to prevent children from returning to the setting too early after being infected. The exclusion policy does vary from setting to setting, but many early years settings follow the guidance from Public Health England.

Table 6.8 shows the different exclusion periods for different diseases.

▶ **Table 6.8:** How long to exclude children with infectious diseases (Source: *Guidance on infection control in schools and other childcare settings*, 2014 © Crown copyright 2014. Reproduced under the terms of the Open Government Licence v2.0)

Disease	Exclusion period
Chickenpox	Until all vesicles (fluid-filled spots) have crusted over
Diarrhoea and/or vomiting	For 48 hours after the last episode of diarrhoea or vomiting
Flu (influenza)	Until recovered
Impetigo	Until lesions are crusted and healed or 48 hours after commencing antibiotic treatment
Measles	For four days from the onset of rash
Mumps	For five days from the onset of swelling
Whooping cough	For five days from starting antibiotic treatment, or 21 days from onset of illness if no antibiotic treatment

Statutory reporting of infectious diseases

There are some illnesses that have to be reported to the authorities by law. These are known as **notifiable diseases**. Reporting is usually done by the child's family doctor at the point of diagnosis. They will report to the local public health office in the area. In England, all notifiable diseases have to be reported to Ofsted and, if two or more children have food poisoning, this also has to be reported. The list of notifiable diseases is frequently changing and so it is important that you remain up to date.

Policy and procedures for giving medicines

Every setting should have policies in place for the administration of medicines. In England, these policies must be based on the statutory EYFS framework. Policies for settings in England:

▶ require parents to provide written consent for each medicine that is to be administered

▶ state that all medicine that is being administered must be recorded and reported.

Early years settings, therefore, have procedures in place to keep records of medication that has been given to children. In the case of medications that are occasionally given to children because of a known medical condition such as asthma, or because of a severe allergic reaction, settings have procedures in place to make sure parents know that these medications have been given to their children.

Most settings also refuse to give children medicines that are not in their original package, for example, cough syrup in a clear bottle.

Remember to check the following when giving medicine.

▶ Check that there is written parental consent in place for the medicine that you are administering.

▶ If possible, find out what the medicine is for.

▶ Make sure that the medicine is labelled with the child's name and that you are giving it to the right child.

▶ Make sure that the medicine is in date and has been stored correctly.

▶ Follow the dosage instructions and the correct method of administration.

▶ Record the date, time and dosage, and sign your name.

▶ Check that the baby/child does not have any adverse reactions.

▶ Store the medicine as per the manufacturer's instructions and out of reach of other children.

⏸ PAUSE POINT   List four of the key points to remember when giving medicines to children.

Hint   Think about the checking and recording procedures that are important.

Extend   Explain why it is important that records are kept when children are given medicine.

Assessment practice 6.6   C.M3   C.D2

An early years centre wants new members of staff to understand how to support children who are unwell and the procedures that they should follow. They have asked you to provide the relevant information.

- Explain the importance of following policies and procedures, including infection control and provision of medicines.
- Analyse the impact on children when early years professionals are effective in supporting children who are unwell.
- Evaluate the role of the early years professional in supporting children who are unwell.

Plan

- Do I understand what I am learning and why it is important?
- Do I have any existing knowledge that will help me with this task?

Do

- Am I recording any problems I am experiencing in completing the task and looking for ways to clarify queries?
- Have I considered my own experiences when evaluating the role of early years professionals?

Review

- Can I explain which parts of this task I found hardest?
- Do I realise where I have learning or knowledge gaps and do I know how to resolve them?

C3 Support for children with ongoing health conditions

Many babies and children have ongoing health conditions. These conditions can be anything from eczema and asthma through to sickle cell anaemia. This section looks at some of the most common health conditions and the principles behind working with children who have health issues.

How to work in partnership with parents and carers

Meeting children's individual physical care needs should be done in close consultation with parents and carers.

Children may have ongoing health conditions, such as eczema or dietary needs, which need careful management and/or additional support. It is important to work with parents to find out all of the information you require about children's needs when they first come into a setting. In turn, you will need to regularly share information with parents about their children. Children's needs may change over time but by discussing them on a regular basis with parents or carers, and by recording the information carefully, practitioners can ensure these needs are met.

It is essential to listen to parents carefully, take notes and make sure that you understand the condition, how it is managed and what you need to do. You may need to ask parents the following questions.

- What is the name of the medical condition?
- What are the symptoms/effects?
- How long has the child had the medical condition?
- Are there any triggers that we need to be aware of?
- How will we know when the child is getting worse, or needs medication or emergency help?
- What should we do in case of emergency?
- How can we reassure your child?
- How and when should the medication be used?
- Where should the medication be stored?

PAUSE POINT   Give three reasons why it is important to work in partnership with parents when their children have ongoing health needs.

Hint   Think about examples of useful information that might need to be exchanged.

Extend   Why is it important not to assume that two children with the same health condition will have identical needs?

How to keep accurate and coherent records of medication requirements

It is a requirement of the EYFS and other early years frameworks that records are kept every time medication is given to children by adults. The type of medicine, the dosage and the time and date have to be recorded, as well as the name of the person who gave the medicine to the child. It is important to keep accurate records and to record details promptly for several reasons.

- It enables adults to check that medication has been given to the child and that this has been done at the correct time.
- If there is a medical emergency, there is a record showing what medicines have already been administered.
- It prevents any confusion about exactly what has been given to the child and when.

How to minimise the impact of illness on learning and development

Some children with ongoing health conditions can miss out on learning as their health condition may mean that they are tired, or they miss sessions due to medical appointments or because they are poorly. You can minimise the impact on learning and development in several ways.

- Share with parents the activities that have been planned for the child so that parents can do these at home, if appropriate.
- Send toys and resources home so that children have access to some of the play opportunities that they may otherwise miss out on.
- When children are in sessions, increase the amount of adult interaction during play.
- Plan to repeat specific activities for the child that will help them to acquire any skills, knowledge or concepts that they may otherwise have missed.

Maintaining friendships

As children develop friendships, usually from the age of 3 years, it is important to maintain these friendships when children are not able to join in. You can do this by talking about the child to their friends and using photographs and film clips as reminders. You could also encourage the children to write or send items to each other. With parental permission, it might be possible to maintain contact using Skype or by telephone. When children return to the setting, it may also be helpful to plan an activity where pairs of children can work together with an adult, e.g. cooking.

How to ensure inclusive provision

Years ago, settings often refused to take children with serious ongoing medical conditions or would insist that parents come on-site to give medication to their children themselves. This meant that some children could not access education and services.

Today, under anti-discrimination legislation, this is no longer the case. However, simply admitting a child with an ongoing medical condition does not necessarily mean that the setting is being inclusive. Settings must be aware of individual children's physical and emotional needs. Good practice means that children who have ongoing medical conditions should not be made to feel different in a setting and that, wherever possible, thought is given to making sure the child feels fully part of the setting, for example, by adapting routines.

The case study shows how two settings have managed children with diabetes.

Case study

Inclusive provision

Gregory and Rajeet are both 4 years old. They attend different preschool settings but both have type 1 diabetes. This means that they need injections of insulin before they eat and need to eat regular snacks.

The staff team at Farmhouse Nursery spent a long time with Gregory's parents discussing Gregory's needs. They wanted to make sure that Gregory did not feel isolated or miss out in any way. The preschool suggested that they would introduce a rolling snack time, but prompt Gregory to eat his snack at a certain time. That way his condition would be managed but he would not have to eat alone. The staff asked Gregory's parents how they felt about this.

The manager at Minnows preschool was horrified when Rajeet's mother said that he had diabetes. She asked

his mother to send in a factsheet explaining what the condition was and what it meant for the setting. The manager decided that it would be unfair on the other children to disrupt the routine of the setting. She told Rajeet's mother that she should send in a box of snacks for Rajeet and that he could sit out in the cloakroom to eat them.

Check your knowledge

1 Which setting is working in an inclusive way, and why?

2 What effects might the settings' approaches have on each of the children?

3 What effects might the settings' approaches have on each child's parents?

How to meet the needs of children with ongoing health conditions

There are some health conditions that are quite common. It is helpful for all early years practitioners to be aware of them and also how to support children who may have them. As with all areas of physical care, it is important to talk to parents to find out about how the health condition affects their child.

Asthma

Asthma is a respiratory condition that affects one in eleven children in the UK. During an asthma attack, the airways are narrowed and mucus can form, which further prevents air from reaching the lungs. Asthma can be fatal and so it is important to know what you should do if a child has an asthma attack. You should also know what can trigger an individual child to have an asthma attack, and how their asthma affects them. As you saw earlier, working with parents is important to gain this knowledge.

How asthma as a condition is managed

When a child is diagnosed with asthma, a decision will be made about whether the condition should be managed by giving the child a **preventer inhaler**. Many people refer to this type of inhaler simply as a preventer.

Preventer inhalers are used daily and are unlikely to be taken into settings unless a child is going on an overnight stay. Preventers reduce, but do not eliminate, the possibility of a child having an asthma attack. They are of no use during an asthma attack.

Reliever inhalers are used during an asthma attack. They work by enlarging the airways, so helping to facilitate breathing. Reliever inhalers are usually blue. Parents and others may call them Ventolin inhalers. Reliever inhalers can save a child's life during an attack.

If you are caring for a child with asthma, make sure that you have a reliever inhaler for them that is in date and remember the following information.

▶ Reliever inhalers must always be kept near or with the child.

▶ Reliever inhalers must not be locked away.

▶ Take the child's reliever inhaler with you if you go outdoors, on a trip or leave the building.

Nebulisers

Nebulisers are used in hospitals and in emergencies. They are machines that create a mist containing the same drugs as a reliever inhaler. The child wears a mask to breathe the mist in. The fine mist helps the drugs work more effectively.

Spacers

Spacers are often given to children to help them take their inhalers more easily. They are effectively plastic tubes. At one end there is a mouthpiece and at the other end there is a hole to slot the inhaler into. The inhaler is depressed and then the child breathes in. Figure 6.10 shows you what a reliever inhaler looks like when it has a spacer attached to it.

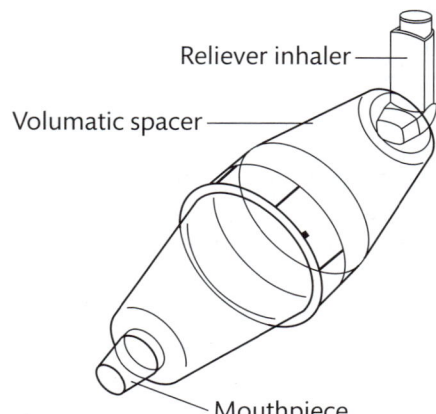

▶ **Figure 6.10:** This reliever inhaler is attached to a spacer, which makes it easier for the child to breathe in the drug

Recognising the signs of an asthma attack

It is important that you find out from a child's parents what the signs are that their child is likely to have, or is having, an asthma attack. This is because although there are some common signs such as wheezing, not all children will present with these. The following list shows the common signs associated with an asthma attack. Some, but not all, of these signs are likely to be present:

▶ wheezing
▶ difficulty in catching breath
▶ chest pains
▶ persistent coughing
▶ difficulty in talking
▶ rapid breathing
▶ anxiety and panic.

What to do if a child is showing signs of an asthma attack

If a child is showing signs of an asthma attack, you should do the following.

1 Reassure the child and stay calm.

2 Get the child to sit down and discourage onlookers.

3 Get the child's reliever inhaler; this should always be kept with or near the child.

4 Give the inhaler a quick shake. Attach the inhaler to the spacer if provided.

5 Encourage the child to take one or two puffs while breathing in.

6 If the child does not start to feel better, the inhaler should be taken again at a rate of two puffs over two minutes – one puff at a time. The child should take up to a maximum of ten puffs.

7 If the child is not feeling better, call an ambulance.

8 After ten minutes of waiting for the ambulance, and if the child is still unwell, use the inhaler again as in Step 6.

Asthma can be fatal, so it is important to summon emergency help if:

▶ a child is not responding to their reliever inhaler
▶ a child's lips or fingernails are turning blue.

Common triggers and how to reduce them

Table 6.9 shows some common triggers of asthma and ways of preventing or minimising them. This is not an exhaustive list and you will need to find out from parents what triggers their individual child.

▶ **Table 6.9:** Common triggers of asthma and ways of preventing/minimising them

Trigger	Steps to reduce/minimise
Dust and associated dust mite droppings	• Keep the setting clean • Wash cuddly toys • Wash bedding at 60°C
Strong perfumes	• Do not wear strong perfumes • Do not use cleaning products, soaps or sensory materials that contain heavy perfumes
Pollen	• Keep children indoors if the pollen count is high or be ready with an inhaler
Mould and fungi	• Make sure that any problems with damp in buildings are dealt with • Do not have rotting fruit and vegetables lying around • Keep rooms well ventilated

▶ **Table 6.9:** Common triggers of asthma and ways of preventing/minimising them – *continued*

Trigger	Steps to reduce/minimise
Exercise	• Although children do need to take exercise, some children will need a puff of their inhaler beforehand • Children may need time to rest • Be aware of children's breathing
Colds	• Be aware that a child is more likely to have an attack
Change of weather	• Sudden changes of weather can create problems • Wrap children up – if children are going from warm to very cold, see if they wish to pull a scarf up over their mouth to start with
Stress and emotion	• Some children have asthma attacks when they are very upset • Make sure that time is spent settling children in • Make sure that you prepare children for any changes that may cause distress

Theory into practice

In your work setting, where are the 'reliever' inhalers kept for children who have asthma?

Research

Find out more about asthma by visiting the Asthma UK website: www.asthma.org.uk.

Eczema

Eczema is very common in childhood. According to the NHS, one in five children has eczema, with most children having it in early childhood. Eczema causes the skin to become itchy, dry, red and cracked. There are many types of eczema but the most common form is atopic eczema.

Areas of the body often affected by eczema include:

▶ wrists and crook of arms

▶ back of knees

▶ neck

▶ around eyes and ears.

Knowing the child's irritants and how to avoid them

Although it is unclear what causes eczema, we do know that it tends to follow a pattern of flaring up and then calming down – although children's skin may well be dry in the periods when the eczema is not present. Flare-ups can be caused by triggers, although what will trigger an episode for an individual child will vary. Some common triggers are:

▶ soaps/detergents

▶ rough clothing

▶ food allergies (especially in babies)

▶ overheating

▶ a skin infection

▶ dust mites (and their droppings)

▶ pet fur

▶ pollen.

Remember that if you are working with a child who has eczema, you should find out from the child's parents if there are any identified triggers.

 **PAUSE POINT**   List five common triggers for eczema.

Hint   Think of things that may irritate or react with the skin.

Extend   Why is it important that settings minimise the triggers that might affect individual children's eczema?

Supporting a flare up

Below are typical treatments for eczema.

▶ **Emollients** are often suggested or prescribed for babies and children with eczema. These are applied as a cream to the affected areas even when there are no flare-ups.

▶ Topical corticosteroids in cream form are often prescribed during a flare-up and need to be applied sparingly. If you are asked to apply a **topical corticosteroid**, follow the manufacturer's instructions and make sure you wash your hands thoroughly.

▶ Antibiotics may also be prescribed if the skin becomes infected.

Reducing the risk of infection

Eczema causes the skin to be very itchy and babies and children find it hard not to scratch. If the skin is broken as a result of the scratching, there is a danger of infection. To prevent this from happening:

▶ try to make babies wear mitts or special sleepsuits

▶ keep babies' and children's nails short

▶ keep the skin clean and dry after washing

▶ make sure babies' and children's hands are washed.

Effects of eczema on the child and family

Eczema prevents babies and children from sleeping well because it is so itchy and can become very sore. This is likely to impact on their behaviour and development. It can also affect children's feelings about themselves as they recognise that their skin is different from other children's.

Eczema can also have an impact on the family. It is very distressing for parents to see their children suffering and many parents will find that they have to reassure and comfort their children in the night. This means that the whole family can become sleep deprived. In addition, parents need to take extra care when washing their children, and give extra time for applying emollients.

Recognising the impact of eczema is important as it could mean that children may want to have a daytime nap or need reassurance when their skin is particularly itchy.

Diabetes

Diabetes is a potentially fatal condition that is caused by the body not producing sufficient insulin. Insulin is produced by the pancreas. It is needed by the body to control the amount of glucose in the blood. Glucose is important as it gives cells energy. Too much or too little insulin can create problems for the body.

Diabetes is a lifelong condition. There are two types of diabetes: type 1 and type 2. Typically, children under 8 years old who suffer from diabetes have type 1.

Type 1 diabetes occurs when the body is unable to produce any insulin. This means that the body cannot process glucose and so it is a very serious condition. Signs that a young child has type 1 diabetes include lack of weight gain, thirst and extreme tiredness. Type 1 diabetes is not caused by a child's lifestyle or food choices.

Once a diagnosis has been made, parents will be shown how to check their child's blood glucose level and how to inject insulin. To start with, the child will also need to follow food guidelines or a diet.

Controlling diabetes

Diabetes must be controlled carefully. There is a balancing act between how much insulin the child needs and how much food (which in turn creates glucose) the child eats. If a child is diabetic, you need to follow parents' instructions carefully.

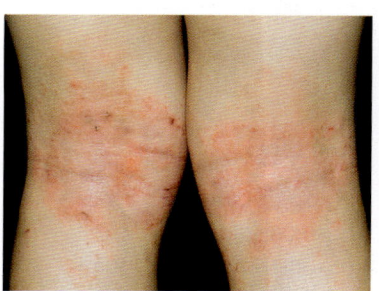

▶ This child suffers from eczema on the backs of her legs. Are there any other parts of the body where you think eczema is more likely to be present?

You may also need training as to how to inject the child with insulin and check their glucose level. Most consultants will encourage the child to do this for themselves as soon as they are old enough, so that they are more involved in the management of their condition. In addition to insulin injections, food intake has to be regulated. The modern approach is to avoid giving children a strict diet, but to make sure they eat within guidelines, which may limit the intake of certain foods, such as sugar.

How much food a child needs to eat and how much insulin they need will vary day-to-day according to their activity level.

Reporting and recording

In order to control diabetes, information must be shared accurately between the setting and parents. It is important to know how the child is, what has been eaten and what dosages of insulin have been given. As diabetes is potentially life-threatening, it is likely that parents will have a system of recording insulin dosages and glucose levels that you will need to contribute to.

Balancing children's diet and exercise

Find out from parents what the child needs in terms of their diet. It is usual for children to need frequent snacks and smaller meals so that food intake is spread across the day. This keeps the glucose level stable. You must also find out which foods are restricted. It is important to speak to parents about what to do if the child is likely to be engaging in more physical activity than normal. This is because children who will be using more energy will need more food in order to prevent hypoglycaemia.

The signs of hypoglycaemia in a child

Where there is an imbalance between glucose levels and insulin, a child may develop **hypoglycaemia** (often known as a 'hypo'.) Hypos are very serious and have to be responded to immediately.

Hypoglycaemia can have a sudden onset, so it is important to be observant and to keep something sugary, such as a sweet, on hand. If hypoglycaemia is not treated quickly, children can lose consciousness. Older children will be able to recognise the signs of hypoglycaemia themselves.

Signs include:

- shakiness
- sweating
- hunger
- difficulty seeing
- lack of concentration
- headache
- change in temperament, e.g. being moody
- loss of colour
- drowsiness.

Note: if a child loses consciousness, emergency help must be called.

How to respond to the signs of hypoglycaemia

The priority is to give the child something high in sugar. This might be a sweet or sugary drink, or sugar in a glass of water. Do not give any diet drinks or products as these do not contain sugar. Chocolate is not ideal but if nothing else is available, use it.

Once the child becomes more responsive, wait for 10–15 minutes and then check their blood glucose levels. If the blood glucose levels are still low, give the child a further drink or sweets. Check the blood glucose levels again after a further 20–30 minutes.

You may also need to give the child a snack such as a piece of fruit or cereal bar, but this will depend on the advice of parents.

Parents should always be told that their child has been hypoglycaemic as they may need to follow this up with the child's doctor or specialist, especially if there have been several events.

Assessment practice 6.7

C.P6 C.M4 C.D2

A children's centre is keen to make sure that all staff understand how to support children who have ongoing health conditions. They have asked you to provide information on this topic.

- Explain the importance of working closely with parents when children have health needs.
- Analyse how providing an inclusive approach to meeting children's health needs can support their overall development.
- Evaluate the role of the early years professional in supporting children with ongoing health conditions.

Plan
- What information will be the most relevant for this task?
- How long do I need to collate and analyse the information required for the task?

Do
- Have I presented the information in a way that will be accessible to staff at the centre?
- Am I managing my time effectively?

Review
- Can I justify why I have decided to approach this task in the way that I have?
- Have I evaluated my work and am I confident that it fulfils the set task?

Further reading and resources

Books

Crawley, H. (2006) *Eating Well for Under-5s in Child Care. Practical and Nutritional Guidelines*, 2nd edition, St Austell: The Caroline Walker Trust.

Crawley, H. (2014) *Eating Well for 1–4 Year Olds. Practical Guide*, 3rd edition, St Austell: The Caroline Walker Trust.

Duffy, A., Chambers, F., Croughan, S. and Stephens, J. (2006) *Working with Babies and Children Under Three*, Harlow: Heinemann.

Fitzhenry, T. and Murphy, K. (2015) *Time to Move*, London: Featherstone Education.

Virgilio, S. J. (2006) *Active Start for Healthy Kids. Activities, Exercises, and Nutritional Tips*, Illinois: Human Kinetics.

Websites

www.asthma.org.uk – Asthma UK: information and advice about asthma and its prevention and treatment.

www.cancerresearchuk.org – Cancer Research UK: information about sun protection for children.

www.diabetes.org.uk – Diabetes UK: information and advice about supporting children with diabetes.

www.eczema.org – National Eczema Society: information and advice about helping children with eczema to manage the condition.

www.cwt.org.uk – The Caroline Walker Trust: advice and guidance about children's nutritional requirements.

www.lullabytrust.org.uk – The Lullaby Trust: information and advice about increasing babies' safety during sleep.

THINK ▶FUTURE

Annie Sharp

Childminder

Annie has been a childminder for nearly five years. She started her career in a day care setting but after she had her own baby she decided that she needed a slight career change. She loves being able to provide a homely setting for children. They do a range of activities to promote physical activity and nearly every day they go to the local park. There is a great playground for the children that is suitable for all ages; it even has a baby swing! Annie takes a range of children of different ages so she has quite a lot of care routines – everything from hair combing through to bathing babies.

As Annie spends a lot of time with children, she is good at spotting the first signs of children becoming poorly. She is able to work closely with parents when children are unwell. Sometimes, if a child is off colour but not seriously ill, parents can still drop the child off, providing, of course, Annie is not taking any other children that day. This flexibility is one of the reasons why some parents use childminders.

Focusing your skills

Helping children to enjoy eating fruit and vegetables

Fruit and vegetables are essential as part of a healthy diet. Here are some tips when introducing children to a new fruit or vegetable for the first time.

- Provide plenty of choice – children are more likely to try out new things when there is a selection.
- Encourage children to touch and handle the fruit or vegetable before it is prepared.
- Involve children as much as possible in the preparation of the food.
- Cut the fruit or vegetables into very small pieces.
- Role model eating the food and talk to them about how it tastes.
- Invite children to self-serve.
- Do not put pressure on children if they are not interested.

Changing cot bedding

It is important that cot bedding is kept clean and fresh. To help you with this, remember the following things the next time you change cot bedding.

- Wear disposable gloves if sheets or blankets are soiled.
- Remove cot bedding carefully. Fold sheets and blankets inwards.
- Wipe down the mattress according to the setting's procedure. Allow the mattress to air.
- Wash hands before touching clean sheets and blankets.
- Put a base sheet over the mattress, making sure that there are no creases.
- Fold the top sheet and blanket down the cot so that they will only cover the baby's chest. Firmly tuck the sheet and blanket in at the base and in on one side. This should prevent the baby from being able to slip down underneath the covers and cuts the risk of cot death from overheating.

Children's Personal, Social and Emotional Development

7

Getting to know your unit

Babies and children need love, attention and careful support to thrive. This helps them to make relationships, express their feelings and emotions appropriately, and gives them the confidence to try out new skills. When children have the support that they need, they go on to make friends, cope with strong and sometimes conflicting thoughts and emotions, and are able to show qualities such as perseverance and resilience.

Understanding how to support children in this area will be key to your day-to-day work. In this unit, you will look at different roles and responsibilities, including the key person approach, and influences on children's behaviour. You will then explore how you can support children through transitions and significant life events. You will also look at different ways of supporting and promoting positive behaviour.

How you will be assessed

This unit will be assessed internally by a series of tasks set by your tutor. They will include practical tasks that will need to be carried out on placement, and that link to your Practical Evidence Portfolio. Throughout this unit, assessment practice activities will help you work towards your assessment. Completing these activities will not mean that you have achieved a particular grade, but you will have carried out useful research or preparation that will be relevant when it comes to your final assignment.

To achieve the tasks in your assignment, it is important to check that you have met all of the Pass grading criteria. You can do this as you work your way through the assignment.

If you are hoping to gain a Merit or Distinction, also make sure that you present the information in your assignment in the style that is required by the relevant assessment criterion. For example, Merit criteria require you to analyse and discuss, and Distinction criteria require you to assess and evaluate.

The assignment set by your tutor will consist of a number of tasks designed to meet the criteria in the table. You may be asked to produce:

▶ a report describing the work of early years professionals in supporting children's personal, emotional and social development

▶ a portfolio of evidence showing how you have applied the knowledge and skills from this unit in your own early years setting.

Assessment criteria

This table shows what you must do in order to achieve a **Pass**, **Merit** or **Distinction** grade, and where you can find activities to help you.

Pass	Merit	Distinction
Learning aim A Investigate approaches in supporting children's personal, emotional and social development and influences on behaviour		
A.P1 Explain how to develop relationships with children in early years settings that support their personal, emotional and social development. Assessment practice 7.1	**A.M1** Assess the success of approaches used in early years settings in developing effective relationships that support children's personal, emotional and social development. Assessment practice 7.1	**A.D1** Evaluate the key person approach in terms of how it may overcome negative influences on children's personal, emotional and social development. Assessment practice 7.2
A.P2 Explain the benefits of the key person approach in meeting children's personal, emotional and social development needs. Assessment practice 7.2		
A.P3 Explain factors that may impact on children's personal, emotional and social development. Assessment practice 7.3	**A.M2** Assess the influence of theories of attachment on the key person approach in early years settings. Assessment practice 7.2	
Learning aim B Explore how to prepare and support children through transition and significant life events		
B.P4 Explain how children may be affected by transition and significant life events. Assessment practice 7.4	**B.M3** Assess the contribution of early years professionals in preparing and supporting children through transition and significant life events. Assessment practice 7.4	**B.D2** Evaluate factors that contribute to the development of children's resilience to transition and significant life events. Assessment practice 7.4
B.P5 Explain how to prepare and support children in early years settings for transition and significant life events. Assessment practice 7.4		
Learning aim C Support and promote children's positive behaviour		
C.P6 Promote and support children's positive behaviour appropriate to children at different ages and stages of development in an early years setting. Assessment practice 7.5	**C.M4** Justify approaches used in own practice in supporting and promoting children's positive behaviour. Assessment practice 7.5	**C.D3** Demonstrate personal responsibility and effective self-management and professional conduct consistently in supporting children's positive behaviour appropriate to their age and stage of development. Assessment practice 7.5

Getting started

Make a list of **transitions** that are likely to happen in the first five years of children's lives, for example, starting school. At the end of this unit, see how many more transitions you can add to your list.

A Investigate approaches in supporting children's personal, emotional and social development and influences on behaviour

A1 Roles and responsibilities

Curriculum requirements

It is a requirement across early years curricula for children to be supported in their personal, social and emotional development (PSED). In the Early Years Foundation Stage (EYFS) statutory framework in England, PSED is one of the three prime areas of learning, as it is considered essential in order for children to learn and develop well.

In addition to being responsible for supporting children's emotional well-being, there is a statutory requirement (under the safeguarding and welfare requirements of the EYFS statutory framework) for early years settings to allocate a **key person** to each child. In other early years frameworks within the UK, there are similar requirements, although they do not have the same legal status. In Wales, for example, the term 'key worker' is used instead of key person.

Research

Find out about the curriculum requirement for promoting children's personal, social and emotional development in the country where you intend to work. See if you can answer the following questions.

1 Is there a curriculum area that covers PSED?
2 Is there a requirement for children to be allocated a key person or key worker?

Policies and procedures

There is a range of policies and procedures relating to PSED that many early years settings have in place. Firstly, as part of their admissions policy, many settings have a settling-in policy and accompanying procedures. These set out how children will develop a relationship with their key person and settle into the setting. Some early years settings also have policies relating to when parents can leave their children when they first join.

In addition, early years settings are likely to have policies and procedures about promoting children's positive behaviour. For settings in England, this is a requirement of the EYFS. Behaviour policies usually identify the importance of taking a positive approach to children's behaviour and set out strategies for doing this. The procedures that are linked to behaviour policies detail what steps adults will take in the event that children show unwanted behaviour. Consistency is important in promoting children's behaviour, so it is important that all adults know about the procedures in their setting.

> **Theory into practice**
>
> Find out about the behaviour policy in your work placement setting.

Personal, social and emotional development theories

There are a range of theories that consider children's personal, social and emotional development. Over the years these theories have informed practice in early years settings.

Theories of personality and self-esteem

In Unit 1, you looked at the development of self-concept and self-esteem. You saw how children learn about themselves mainly through the way that others respond to them. This is often referred to as the 'looking glass' effect. It has major implications for the way that adults respond to and work with children. If children frequently see and hear that adults are not positive about them, they are likely to come to the conclusion that they are not likeable people. On the other hand, children who gain genuine warmth, respect and high regard from adults are more likely to develop a positive self-concept. In Susan Harter's model of self-esteem, the development of a strong self-concept is essential as it means that when the child becomes older, they are more likely to develop strong self-esteem.

▶ **Praise** – children need to be praised for their achievements, but not all praise should be conditional on success. Children need to feel liked and valued for 'just being'.

▶ **Warmth** – children can tell when adults really like them and feel warm towards them. Adults who are warm towards children listen to them, are interested in what they are doing, but also offer appropriate physical contact and are often playful.

▶ **Acceptance** – it is impossible for children to show positive behaviours every minute of every day. Accepting that children will sometimes forget to say 'thank you' or may not feel like being cooperative is therefore important. Children who are repeatedly made to feel guilty are less likely to become confident.

▶ **Avoiding comparisons** – as part of children feeling that they are cared for and accepted unconditionally, it is important not to keep making comparisons between children. 'I've just asked James to do the same thing and he didn't make a fuss' is the kind of comment that can be quite damaging if used repeatedly.

▶ **Encouraging self-efficacy** – it is useful if children, even as babies and toddlers, feel that they are involved but also able to do things for themselves. This might be simple tasks such as feeding and helping with dressing themselves but also choosing what to play with. This is sometimes known as **self-efficacy** and helps children to feel that they are capable and competent. This in turn supports a strong self-concept.

> **Key term**
>
> **Self-efficacy** – the understanding that you are able to do things for yourself.

> **Link**
>
> Look back at Section D1 of Unit 1 to find out more about the development of self-concept and self-esteem.

In your work setting, look out for different ways in which children are given opportunities to do things for themselves to promote their self-efficacy.

Attachment – a special relationship or bond between a child and someone who is emotionally involved with them.

Theories of attachment

The key focus of all theories of **attachment** is that babies and children need to have strong bonds with the adults who play a prominent role in their lives. This starts with their parents, but also includes family members and adults who look after them when they are separated from their parents. It is thought that the need for children to develop strong attachments in their early years is instinctive. When children have strong attachments within their family, but also with the adults who care for them in early years settings, they are likely to learn more easily, develop strong social skills and show less unwanted behaviour.

Over the years, several significant pieces of work have looked at attachment processes and their importance in early childhood. You looked at these in Unit 1 and it is worth revisiting them. A summary of the key points of attachment theories and research is shown in Table 7.1.

▶ **Table 7.1:** Summary of the main attachment theories

John Bowlby	• A strong primary attachment is key to children's later emotional and social development and well-being • Children show separation anxiety when their main attachment figure is not available for them
Mary Ainsworth	• The quality of main attachments can vary • Children who have secure attachments are better placed to deal with stressful events
James and Joyce Robertson	• When children are separated from their main attachments, they can cope if they have already developed another attachment; this is the basis of the key person system

See Section A2 of this unit for more information about the importance of strong attachments.

Use the internet to find out more about theory of mind. You may find it useful to print out any relevant articles so you can refer to them later.

Theory of mind

It is thought that children's ability to understand what others might be thinking is a key skill in their social development. This ability is sometimes referred to as theory of mind (ToM) and it is thought that children who may have an autism spectrum disorder have difficulties in this specific area. Several researchers have been looking at this, including Uta Frith and Simon Baron-Cohen.

Theory of mind allows a child to work out what others might be feeling and why, even if the other's thoughts are different to theirs. There is a well-known test that can be used to see if a child has developed ToM, known as the Sally Anne test. It would seem that most children have acquired this by 4 or 5 years old.

Understanding that it takes a while for children to develop ToM is useful for practitioners. It means that you cannot always expect very young children to interpret the reasons why others are doing things or to understand the impact of their own actions on others.

While it is thought that ToM is linked to children's cognitive development and so cannot be 'fast tracked', you can help children by explaining what others might be thinking and feeling, e.g. 'Sarah hasn't got anyone to play with. Do you think that she might be feeling sad?'

Theory into practice

In the Sally Anne test, a child is shown two dolls, Sally and Anne, and a story is told and acted with the two dolls. The child sees Sally put some marbles in her basket and then go out to play. The child then sees Anne take Sally's marbles from the basket and put them in a box. Then Sally is brought back in. The child is asked where Sally will go to find her marbles. Children who are starting to acquire theory of mind will point to the basket as they understand that Sally does not know that the marbles have been moved to the box.

- Try out the Sally Anne test with children of different ages and see which children are starting to develop theory of mind.

The role of observation and assessment

One of the ways in which adults can support children's personal, social and emotional development is by being aware of their needs and next steps. There are many times when this becomes particularly important.

Transitions and significant events

It is essential to observe children during transitions and significant events. Being in a new place and potentially being separated from a parent or carer is stressful for children. Observing a child will mean that any nervousness or uncertainty shown by the child can be picked up and the adult can immediately offer reassurance. As part of observing children during transition, you need to be able to recognise that children have genuinely developed strong relationships with their key person, with older children and their peers.

Assessing progress

You have seen that children's social and emotional development usually changes over time. Although toddlers find it hard to play together, children will usually have developed some friendships by the age of 4 years. It is important to recognise the progress that children have made so that they can be given opportunities to further develop their skills, or thought can be given as to why they have not made the expected progress, if this is the case.

▶ Children usually develop some friendships by the age of 4 years

Monitoring changes in behaviour

Children's behaviour needs to be observed for several reasons. First, you need to think about whether children are showing behaviours typical of their age/stage of development. This should help you to ensure that activities and expectations are appropriate.

How children are feeling and coping with stress often plays out in their behaviour. It is therefore helpful to monitor changes in behaviour, as this might be a sign that a child is finding it difficult to cope with a change within the family such as the birth of a sibling, the separation of parents or change of setting. Finally, another reason for monitoring behaviour is to consider whether a child is showing any behaviours that may indicate that they have been, or are being, harmed.

Professional boundaries with children

While it is important that you build strong relationships with children and their parents, there are certain professional boundaries that you need to keep. Children and their parents rely on you and this requires you to remain professional though friendly.

Appropriate physical contact

It is important that physical contact remains appropriate and in line with a child's age and stage of development. You must also ensure that you are working within your setting's policy and in line with parents' wishes.

Safe working practices

Although it is important to offer children physical contact, you need to be aware of doing so in a way that is appropriate and empowers them. Appropriate contact is very much dependent on the age of the child and the setting that you are in. You will need to find out and follow your setting's policy, but it is likely that the policy will state that physical contact should only occur when you are in sight of other adults. Of course, this will not be the case if you are working in home-based care.

Offering contact

Babies and young children need physical contact in order to support their emotional development, particularly if they spend long periods of time away from their parents. Holding a child's hand or allowing a child to cuddle up to you while you share a story can send out reassuring signals to a child. Physical contact has been shown to reduce anxiety, and hence cortisol levels, so it is important when children are upset.

It is good practice to offer physical contact and to observe a child's immediate reaction – if you offer a hand, the child may indicate that they are not interested by shaking their head or moving away slightly. Insisting on physical contact is highly inappropriate unless a child's life is in danger.

Recognising children's wishes

Babies and toddlers often indicate that they need a cuddle by reaching out to you. It is important that you follow their wishes as this helps them to learn that they are in control of what happens to their bodies. It is also important to let a child's hand go or put a toddler back on the floor at the first indication that they have had enough. Table 7.2 shows some examples of appropriate physical contact with children of different ages.

> **Research**
>
> Table 7.2 shows examples of appropriate physical contact. However, guidance is likely to vary between settings. Find your setting's policy for appropriate physical contact and make sure you understand what you can and cannot do.

▶ **Table 7.2:** Examples of appropriate physical contact

Age of children	Type of contact
Babies	• Should be picked up and cuddled • May be kissed (subject to parental wishes) but never on the lips • May sit on adult's lap
Toddlers	• May be picked up and cuddled at toddler's request • May sit on adult's lap
Preschool children	• Hand holding, snuggling in next to an adult – in some settings, sitting on an adult's lap is allowed • May be cuddled if the child requests it
School-age children	• Hand holding • May be hugged, but only if the child is seriously upset

Use of language

The language that you use when you talk to children and their parents is important. While you can be warm in the tones that you use, it may not always be appropriate to use some terms of endearment. Equally, it is important that even when you are irritated by children's actions, you control your language and model appropriate responses.

▶ Is the level of physical contact between the practitioners and children acceptable?

Details of your personal life

Children and parents like to hear some details about your life but it is important to be careful about how much you say. This is a sensitive area, but overall nothing you say should cause any concern to either a child or a parent; your focus is to work with them and so parents should not feel they need to care for you or have concerns about your suitability.

Case study

Too much information

Jaydee is 4 years old. Her mother noticed that she was unusually quiet when she picked her up. That night at bedtime, Jaydee asked what happened if someone was 'off their head'. Her mother asked her who had said this. Jaydee replied that one of the staff had told a group of children to be quiet because she had a headache and another member of staff had called over that she shouldn't have 'got off her head' the night before.

Check your knowledge

1 Why was this language and conversation inappropriate in the setting?

2 Why was Jaydee's mother upset on hearing that this had been said?

3 How might this comment affect the trust between Jaydee's mother and the staff in the setting?

The importance of trusting relationships with children and families

When children are away from their parents and carers, they have to trust you. This means that one of the roles of early years practitioners is to build trust with parents. One of the ways that you can build trust with parents is by showing that you genuinely care and like their children. It is also important for parents to see that their children are happy and enjoy being with you. This means that you need to create strong and trusting relationships with children.

It is essential that you create the right conditions for children to develop strong relationships with you. This is vital if you are a key person to a child, as your role is to create a strong attachment. There are many skills that contribute to this, some of which you looked at in Unit 2, as part of how to communicate with children.

Link

See Unit 8 for more information about how to work with parents and others in early years.

Eye contact

Babies and children are primed to notice your eyes, and strong eye contact is linked closely to building relationships. Often with children that you do not know well, it is a good idea to 'gaze' and then look away. This is because sustained eye contact with someone you do not know well can feel uncomfortable.

Sensitive communication, listening and showing empathy

Sensitive communication requires a number of skills, including being able to listen carefully, showing interest in what a child is saying or, in the case of babies, being interested in what they are pointing at. Sensitive communication is also about your tone of voice and whether you sound warm, interested and kind. Children also need you to be **empathetic**, which is about the way that you show your understanding of how they are feeling. It is good practice, for example, if a child is looking sad after waving goodbye to a parent, to acknowledge this rather than 'chivvying' the child along. It may be that you ask the child if a cuddle is needed as well as reassuring the child that the parent will come back later.

Key term

Empathetic – showing empathy (the ability to feel or understand the emotions of others).

Playfulness

Babies and children often have a strong sense of humour. This means that it is helpful if adults have a playful style when this is appropriate. This may mean smiling or pretending to do something that makes a child laugh. Playfulness does need to be appropriate, as children may copy your actions.

▶ A playful style will help you to engage with the children in your care

How to communicate effectively with parents and/or carers

It is essential to work in partnership with parents and carers. In Unit 8, you will look in more detail at the skills that are needed in order to communicate with parents and carers. These include positive body language, sensitive communication and also the need for confidentiality.

When it comes to communicating with parents or carers about children's emotional and social development, it is worth recognising that this area is a sensitive topic. Most parents and carers are anxious to ensure that their child has friends and is settled within the setting. It is, therefore, important that you listen to parents' and carers' concerns and also use the knowledge gained from observations to talk through with them how their child is doing. It may be that their child needs additional support or that their responses are typical for their age.

> **Link**
>
> See Unit 8 for more information about communicating with parents and carers.

Ways to support children's emotional well-being and resilience

There are several ways in which adults can work with children to help them feel secure and also develop independence. Having a sense of independence will in turn help to make children more **resilient**.

Providing choices

Providing choices for children can help them to develop self-efficacy. This is because they learn to make decisions for themselves. How much choice children should be given, and over what, needs to be tailored to the child's stage of development. It is not fair for children to be given a choice only for the adult to intervene because their choice was inappropriate – choices have to be genuine ones! Child-initiated play is

> **Key term**
>
> **Resilient** – able to recover quickly from different or difficult situations.

one of the key ways in which most early years settings give opportunities for children to make choices. In addition, there are other simple ways of giving children choices, for example:

▶ cooking activities – choosing what to put into a salad or how to bake a cake

▶ books – choosing which books to share with an adult

▶ mealtimes – choosing where to sit and even the colour of plates or beakers.

Developing independence and praising effort

From the earliest age, as well as providing opportunities for choice, children need opportunities to develop independence. This may be through child-initiated play, rather than just adult-directed activities, but also through day-to-day activities such as dressing, serving their own food, pouring drinks and choosing when to go to the toilet. It often takes more time for a child to feed and dress themselves, but it is extremely important for children's emotional development and, as you saw earlier, it supports children's sense of self-efficacy. In order to support children's independence, it can be helpful to make sure that children have sufficient time, but also that their efforts are noticed, praised and acknowledged. This may be in the form of praise, but also through making a commentary of what the child can now do for themselves.

Routines and realistic boundaries that develop a child's sense of security

Most babies and young children thrive on a little bit of predictability. Having some routines is important for children as it helps to develop a sense of security. Not every moment of the day needs to be regulated as this can be stifling and unstimulating, but there are some key points where establishing a routine can be helpful. Figure 7.1 shows these routines. Mealtimes and snack times should be opportunities when babies and children can develop some skills for independence, such as feeding themselves.

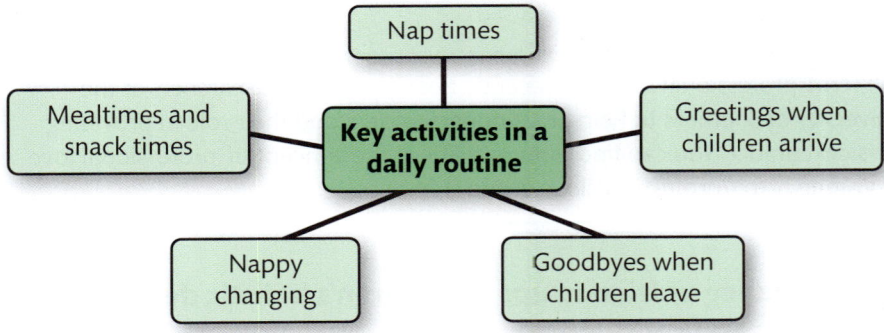

▶ **Figure 7.1:** Routines during the day

Realistic boundaries

Children seem to need boundaries in order to become secure. They need to know what is and is not acceptable behaviour within the setting. Boundaries should relate closely to the children's age and stage of development, so while you might expect a 4-year-old child with typical development to wait to take their turn when playing a game, you may need to remind a younger child or accept that a toddler will struggle to wait.

Boundaries should be set with a clear rationale, such as health and safety, fairness and being considerate towards others. The rationale should be explained calmly to children. With older children, it is good practice for them to be involved in some boundary setting as this is good for their own development. They may, for example, be able to provide rules for where a ball game should be played or how they will ensure that everyone can join in an activity.

The importance of age-appropriate physical contact to support emotional development

As discussed earlier in this section, touch is an important way for babies and young children to gain reassurance and feel secure. This is why young children will often want a hug or to sit on an adult's lap when they are feeling sad, frightened or when they are missing their parents. For babies, touch is extremely important and when they are away from their primary carers, it is vital that they are held, rocked and cuddled. Not providing physical contact to children who clearly need or desire it is harmful, as physical contact is an essential part of attachment and is needed for healthy development.

Having said this, it is essential that physical contact is appropriate, and adults working with children have to understand that there are boundaries to ensure that children are kept safe from abuse. A good rule of thumb is to understand that physical contact should never be imposed on a child. This means that while an adult might offer their hand to a child who is worried, the adult should wait for the child to take their hand rather than automatically take it. In the same way, a baby who has been happily held, but then indicates by wriggling that they have had enough, should be placed back on the floor immediately. The level of physical contact on offer depends on the age of the child, their emotional needs and also the context. Generally speaking, the younger the child, the more physical contact is needed. It is important always to find out about your setting's policy on physical contact, which will be part of their safeguarding policy. Few group-care and school settings, for example, allow staff to kiss children, although nannies and childminders may do this because the context is different.

The importance of friendships to children's holistic development, self-concept and confidence

Friendships are very important to children as they develop. This starts early on with babies being very excited by looking at other babies. Toddlers will often enjoy copying and playing alongside other toddlers. **Reciprocal** and **cooperative friendships** begin when children are around 3 years old.

Friendships help children in a variety of ways. First, they are the bedrock of many play activities, which in themselves can support children's overall, or holistic, development. Children's self-concept is developed through friendships as they note how their peers respond to them. Children who have positive responses from peers are likely to become more confident in dealing with others. Children who have a shaky start, on the other hand, might have less confidence about approaching and playing with other children. By the age of 5 years, most children should have at least one strong friendship. If not, it is worth looking at ways of supporting the child.

Observing friendships

From around 3 years, it is helpful to note whether children are starting to make friends or whether any child is being regularly excluded from play. This is important because a child who is regularly excluded may be missing out on gaining confidence and the developmental benefits that having friends brings.

How to support children to develop social skills

Children need a variety of social skills in order to develop relationships and friendships. There are some features that other children look for in choosing a playmate. Figure 7.2 shows these features.

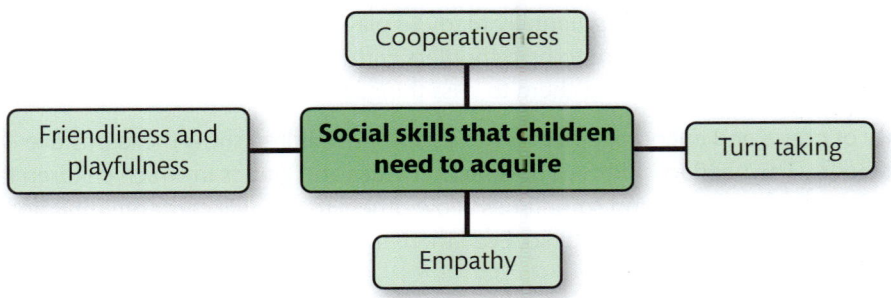

▶ **Figure 7.2:** Social skills that children need to acquire

It is probably not possible to 'teach' empathy, but it is possible to create conditions for children that will support its development and encourage them to make friendships. Children who have strong attachments will find it easier to be empathetic. They have been 'cared for' and 'understood' and this in turn helps them to show these qualities towards others. This is why children having a strong attachment to their key person is so important in early years settings.

Encouraging friendships

From around 3 years of age, having friends to play with becomes very important for children. There are many reasons why some children find it easier to make friends than others. These include children's level of confidence and how easily they are able to show friendliness. Friendliness is important as it is a signal to other children that a child wishes to play and be with them. Friendliness is characterised by relaxed body language, open gestures and often a lot of smiling.

Children who are very anxious about being with other children often give off closed and fearful body language and this in turn sends out negative messages to other children. This can develop into a vicious cycle in which the child becomes less confident about joining in with other children.

You can support children to show friendliness by helping them to feel confident. You may do this by organising activities in which they have particular responsibilities and also planning activities that are naturally 'fun' so that children are likely to smile and giggle. Helping children to smile and giggle often helps them to connect with each other.

Acting as a role model

Another characteristic that popular children have developed is the ability to show kindness and thoughtfulness. This is a characteristic that children can learn by role modelling adults.

If they see adults being kind and thoughtful towards others, they are more likely to adopt these behaviours. If, on the other hand, they see adults who seem unsympathetic or, even worse, laugh at or mock others, this behaviour is likely to be copied.

As well as seeing role models, as children become older they can benefit from adults who point out how others might be feeling. They may read a book and ask a child about how the character in the book might be feeling and see if the child can relate this feeling to a time in their own lives.

Being cooperative

As children's friendships develop through mutual play and activities, it is important that you help them to learn the skills of being cooperative. Children who try to dominate games or want only their ideas to be used by the group are likely to be unpopular playmates, as are children who always want to be first or sulk if they lose. These are not easy skills to acquire and they do take time, which is one reason why toddlers are often not developmentally ready to play cooperatively with others. Having said this, it is important to help toddlers with this process and you may begin by looking for opportunities for them to pass things to each other or take turns.

Plenty of praise and encouragement is needed when children show these positive behaviours. The need for adults to do small activities and games in which children take turns, learn to be patient and sometimes allow others to win will carry on until most children are around 5 years old or so. Even then, the odd reminder is still needed from time to time.

The style that adults use when reminding children about being cooperative is important too. If adults become cross or make the child feel guilty, they may associate being cooperative and thus thoughtful with feeling uncomfortable.

❚❚ PAUSE POINT   Identify two characteristics that will help a child to make friends.

Hint   Think about the qualities of your close friends.

Extend   Evaluate the role of the adult in supporting children's friendships.

Supporting children's group learning and socialisation

For many children, friendships develop fairly easily if they have acquired social skills and the confidence needed to interact with others. If you observe that a child does not appear to have friends, consider why this might be. It may be that the child has lower levels of language and so is not able to join in or is too boisterous or just shy. If any of these are the case, the first step is to work on the underlying reasons. In addition we can do some of the following.

Playing alongside

It can be helpful to play alongside a child while they are with others so that you can model play behaviours such as listening to others, joining in and taking turns.

Giving hints

With children from around 5 years old, it may also be appropriate to give them hints about how to join in children's play. They may, for example, try to dominate a game or just ask children to change what they are doing. A quiet reminder about being a 'follower' rather than always trying to 'lead' a game might be in order.

In addition, you may also have to collaborate with children's parents. Many parents of children once they get to 4 or 5 years old become concerned if their children are not making friends. It might be useful to share strategies and also to find out how the child reacts at home. Some children, for example, may have made good friends with older children outside the setting and it may be that they prefer playing with older children where games might be more demanding or exciting.

▶ How is this adult supporting the children to make friends?

Some children who are used to getting their own way at home and who are not given opportunities to be thoughtful and flexible can find it harder to make friends in a setting. If this is the case, it may be a good idea to discuss it with the parents and suggest that they work on this at home as well.

How prejudice and discrimination may impact on a child

All forms of prejudice and discrimination have a negative effect on children's lives. Indeed, prejudice can lead to discrimination. When discrimination occurs, it means that children are being denied the care and education to which they are entitled.

Discrimination, for any reason, can seriously affect children's social and emotional development. Even very young children can pick up on the attitudes and actions of adults or, in some cases, of other children. This can make children feel as if they do not belong, which can have a long-term effect on their ability to build friendships. Children who are excluded or feel that an activity is 'not for them' will easily lose confidence in their own ability. It will affect how they view themselves, which can lead to low self-esteem and possibly lower levels of achievement in their learning and development. It is, therefore, important to challenge discriminatory behaviour and promote respect for others.

The importance of challenging discriminatory behaviour and promoting respect for others

As you have seen, the impact of discrimination on children's development can be significant, particularly in relation to their self-identity and self-esteem. It is therefore good practice for early years settings to take an inclusive approach to working with children. This means thinking about meeting individual children's needs, but also challenging discriminatory behaviour. Examples of discriminatory behaviour may include comments that children make to each other, as well as when children tell another child that they cannot join in. While many young children will not understand the impact of what they say and do, early years practitioners should gently intervene.

It is also good practice for early years settings to have equality policies and these will include the procedures that should be followed in the event that an adult working in the setting shows discriminatory behaviour. Challenging another adult's behaviour can be a sensitive area, so it is important that you refer to the equality policy and procedures for the setting where you work.

Preventing bullying

Happily, bullying is rare in the early years, although children may be dominated by other children or unhappy because they do not have a friend to play with. With children of school age, bullying can occur and so it is important to be aware of it and take steps to prevent it.

All schools have policies designed to prevent bullying and also pick up on bullying. The policies have procedures that identify steps to take if you notice that a child might be being bullied or if you are told about a bullying incident.

As well as following procedures, it is important for adults to model cooperative behaviours and to praise these when they see them in children. It is also important to be aware of children who are unhappy in their home lives, perhaps because of changes to the family structure. Supporting these children is important, as such children are at risk of being bullied or alternatively using bullying as an outlet for their own emotions.

Signs that a child might be bullied include the following:

- appearing quiet or withdrawn
- tearfulness or angry outbursts
- difficulty in sleeping, or bedwetting when previously dry.

Assessment practice 7.1 A.P1　A.M1

A nursery is creating an information pack for new staff members to help them understand the broad issues around promoting children's personal, social and emotional development. They feel that a good starting point would be for practitioners to be aware of the general roles and responsibilities within the setting.

They have asked you to provide:

- a description of the curriculum requirement for children's personal, social and emotional development and the role of policies and procedures in early years settings
- an analysis of the ways in which adults can support the development of children's social skills
- an assessment of how the approaches used to develop effective relationships in early years settings can support children's personal, social and emotional development.

Plan

- What information might a new member of staff need about roles and responsibilities?
- Where can I find up-to-date and relevant information?

Do

- Have I chosen information that is relevant?
- Am I using my skills of analysis of evaluation?

Review

- Can I justify why I have decided to approach this task in the way that I have?
- Have I evaluated my work and am I confident that it fulfils the set task?

A2 The key person approach

Statutory requirements for the key person approach

As you saw at the start of the unit, in England, a statutory requirement of the early years curriculum framework is for early years settings to provide a key person for every child. Although it is not a statutory requirement in other home countries, early years settings in Wales and Scotland do in practice have a key person or key worker (Wales) approach. This is to comply with the minimum standards set out for registration and inspection. In Northern Ireland, it is also considered good practice for early years settings to have a key person system and there is an expectation that early years settings should adopt this approach.

How the key person approach is applied in different types of setting

> **Link**
>
> Unit 11 has more information about the role of the key person.

The way in which the key person or key worker approach is applied in different settings can vary according to the type of setting that a child is in and also the length of time that they are there. The essentials of being a key person, however, remain the same regardless of home country or setting. The role of the key person/key worker is always about providing consistent emotional support for children and also being there to support and share information with children's families.

Day care

Most day care settings take children from 6 months, or sometimes earlier, through until they start school. It is usual for day care to operate for at least 10 hours per day and for 50 weeks a year. As staff are likely to be working a 37- to 40-hour week with holidays and time off for lunch breaks, it is rare for one person alone to act as key person to a particular child. A way of working known as a 'buddy' system is therefore often used.

A buddy system means that the key person role is shared between two staff members. The idea is that when one key person is not available, the other member of staff can step in. This allows for continuity of care and means that children do not suffer separation anxiety because their key person is not there.

Sessional care

Many children in preschools and maintained nurseries attend sessions of around 3 hours each day. In many preschools and nurseries, the child is likely to be allocated a single key person, but another member of staff may frequently step in to support the child in their absence.

Home-based care

Most, but not all, childminders and nannies work alone and so act as the sole key person for children. Childminders may have children for sessions or children may come for 40 or 50 hours a week. Where children are looked after by more than one childminder, it is more common for the child to develop special bonds with both adults and so both people may become key for the child.

Crèches

There are many different models of crèches, ranging from those that only see children for very short periods to those that see children for regular sessions. It is good practice for children who attend regularly, but for short sessions, to have a sole key person, but also to become familiar with other staff. When children attend 'one-off' sessions, they may be allocated a key person who will reassure and comfort them, but in such a short time, it is unlikely that an attachment can be made.

Reception classes

In many reception classes, the teacher is the key person for all of the children as they have the responsibility to work with and share information with parents. In some schools, teaching assistants or nursery nurses may act as key persons in terms of building close relationships but then pass on information about the child to the teacher so that they, in turn, can report to parents.

Theory into practice

There has been much debate as to whether a teacher with 25 or so children can make genuine attachments to children given the pressures of time. Find out how schools in your area operate a key person system.

The role of the key person in establishing and developing attachments

As you have seen, to help babies and children cope with the effects of separation from their parents, it is good practice for every child to be allocated a key person.

A key person takes particular responsibility for a child's emotional needs by encouraging the child to make an attachment with them. This special relationship helps the child to gain comfort and reassurance in their parents' absence. As well as working intensely with the baby or child, it is also the role of the key person to develop a relationship with the child's family. In this way, the child's physical and emotional needs can be closely met. From 2012, in England, the key person also has a role in supporting parents to engage in learning activities at home that will complement those in the early years settings.

The importance of strong attachments

The earliest attachments between parents and children seem to be the most significant, as they are often intense and enduring. As you have seen, attachments with other adults who spend frequent and long periods with babies and children (such as in day care) are also important to children's overall well-being.

The development of further attachments

There is something very interesting about the nature of child–adult attachments. It would seem that they give babies and children confidence that allows them to go out, explore and try new things, and also cope better in stressful situations. They are more likely to relax and this in turn helps them to sleep. It also helps them develop further attachments and relationships. Children with secure attachments seem to find it easier to trust and accept the care and attention of other adults as well as other children. They also seem better placed to give care and attention, and show empathy.

> **Link**
>
> Go to Unit 1, Section D1 to find out more about how attachments are formed.

Effects on physiological and psychological stress levels

All babies and children need to feel loved, reassured and nurtured – it is important to their overall development. This usually comes from their parents or primary carers, but children need this to continue when they are separated from them. Practitioners can 'step in' to support children when their parents are not with them.

Research completed over a number of years, including that of Bowlby, Ainsworth and the Robertsons (see Table 7.1), shows that children become distressed if they are separated from their parents and no substitute attachment is available. When you are stressed, a hormone called cortisol is released. Though all of us secrete cortisol, high levels of cortisol that are sustained over a period appear to be associated with a suppressed immune system and therefore poorer health. Research has shown that children who are separated from their parents without a substitute attachment are more likely to have raised levels of cortisol. The effects of this are thought to put children at increased risk of illness and may also affect their ability to learn.

In addition to these **physiological effects** of stress, there are **psychological effects** too. These include confidence and the ability to control emotions. It would appear that children who are separated from their parents and have no substitute attachment may find it hard to cope with separations in the future, as the distress is in some way remembered.

Contribution to development in other areas

In Unit 1, you looked at attachment theory and how babies and children need to develop strong bonds with their parents or primary carers. When children are separated from their parents, even for a few hours, they need to have strong attachments with those looking after them. As you have seen, strong attachments help babies and children to feel secure, loved and understood. Table 7.3 gives practical examples of how strong attachments can influence development in other areas.

> **Key terms**
>
> **Physiological effects**
> – effects that change or influence normal bodily functions.
>
> **Psychological effects**
> – effects that change the pattern of behaviour or thinking.

▶ **Table 7.3:** How strong attachments can contribute to development in other areas

Social and emotional development	
Making relationships	Children who have strong attachments find it easier to make relationships with others. They learn to trust other people and also to understand others' needs and feelings. Children who have poor attachments may find it harder to make meaningful relationships. As children learn a lot by playing with other children, this can be problematic
Confidence	Children need a degree of confidence so that they can try out new things. Children are more likely to have confidence if they feel loved and nurtured
Showing consideration for others: behaviour	Where children have strong attachments, they find it easier to show appropriate behaviours for the situation they are in. This comes over time, but children will find it easier if they have been shown consideration and warmth at an early age
Controlling emotions	Everyone at all ages can feel angry, irritated, sad or react impulsively. Being understood can help children to manage these feelings as they develop
Physical growth and development	
Sleep	Children are more likely to relax and find it easier to sleep
Feeding (babies)	Children are more likely to feed well and so thrive
Large and fine motor skills	Children are more likely to develop new skills and to explore their environment. Their confidence will allow them to try to do things for themselves
Cognitive development	
Concentration and perseverance	When babies or children are insecure or worried, they cannot focus their attention on what they are doing. They may be easily distracted or give up quickly. This reduces how much learning they can gain from what they are doing, e.g. if a child gives up after two minutes of looking at a jigsaw puzzle, they will have missed out on learning about shapes and problem-solving
Confidence	Trying out new games, play or tasks will help a child learn new skills or think differently. If children are insecure, they are less likely to try out new things and so miss out on learning
Language development	
Developing receptive and expressive speech	Children who are strongly attached will often spend time listening and talking to the people to whom they are attached. They may spend time with them chatting and listening to stories and so acquire more language
Practising speech with other children	Children practise language by playing with other children, especially from 3 years onwards. As attachment affects children's ability to make and maintain friends, some children may miss out if they cannot form good relationships with others

 **PAUSE POINT**   Explain how children's attachment can influence their communication and language development.

 Hint   Think about your relationship with the people you spend time talking to.

Extend   Give examples of how strong attachments can positively influence children's overall development.

How attachment theorists have influenced current practice

The importance of secure attachments and the need for children to have a substitute attachment when their parents are temporarily unavailable has shaped early years practice in many ways. Today, much of the good practice you see in early years settings relating to settling in children and preparing them for significant events in their lives has come about through an understanding of the work of attachment theorists such as John Bowlby, Mary Ainsworth and James and Joyce Robertson.

Recognising separation anxiety

Before attachment was fully understood, distressed children who were crying because their parents were no longer there were often seen as showing unwanted behaviour. Today, we know that distress is indicative of a child having a strong attachment and needing reassurance. We also know from John Bowlby (1907–1990) that separation anxiety is harmful for children and so steps should be taken to avoid children being distressed, for example, by preparing them for transitions. This is why settings should have settling-in policies that help children to feel comfortable with at least one member of staff before separation takes place.

▶ It is important to prepare children for transitions so they do not become upset when their primary carer leaves

Supporting parents

The work of Mary Ainsworth (1913–1999), which you looked at in Unit 1, shows that children's attachments to their parents may not always be secure. The need to support parents with babies and young children is now a focus for early years. Attempts are made to recognise those mothers and families who, for a variety of reasons, may find it hard to form an attachment. This recognition is done by a variety of services including midwives during pregnancy and shortly after birth, health visitors and also family doctors. Groups such as baby massage, often held in children's centres, can help to support parents and carers in developing good attachments with their children. Early years professionals are also encouraged to offer support and identify when parents may need to access further help.

Substitute attachment

James Robertson (1911–1988) and his wife, Joyce Robertson (1919–2013), were concerned that the effects of separation on young children were not recognised. James Robertson began filming children's behaviour when they were separated from their mothers, who were going into hospital. James Robertson made eight films showing children of different ages and receiving a range of care. In some of the films, the children are staying with the Robertsons, and Joyce Robertson takes time to soothe, comfort and meet children's emotional as well as physical needs. In other films, children are staying with responsive foster carers. Outcomes for children who could form substitute attachments were considerably better than for those who had no adult supporting them. The idea behind offering children a substitute attachment is the basis of the key person system that is now used in early years settings.

Link

Go to Unit 8, Section A1 to find more information about the reasons why some parents may be emotionally unavailable to their children and as a result may find it hard to form an attachment to their child.

Research

Find out more about the Robertsons' work by reading about the films that were made at the time. You can access the Robertson Films website by going to www.robertsonfilms.info.

How the key person system supports effective relationships with parents

The key person role is not just about working with children. When key person systems work well, they are the starting point for effective relationships with the setting. Parents and carers become used to, and enjoy meeting, the person who is directly looking after their child. From this starting point, parents can develop a wider relationship with the setting. The benefits of effective relationships with parents include:

▶ strong involvement and interest in the care and education of the child

▶ confidence and trust in what the setting is doing

▶ effective information sharing.

In addition, effective relationships can benefit families who need additional support. Using the relationship with the key person, parents can be signposted to other services and advice, including those run in children's centres such as dads' clubs, job clubs and 'stay and play' sessions.

Communication with parents

Good communication with parents and carers helps you to work in partnership with them and, as part of this, to provide continuity of care and approach. Key persons should therefore be good at talking and building a relationship with parents so that information can be shared easily.

As you saw in Unit 6, you may need to talk to parents about subjects such as diet or skin products, or their approach to helping their child fall asleep. You may also need to work with parents to provide consistent approaches to managing unwanted behaviour. This requires good communication skills and active listening, as well as empathy and warmth. Where relationships between key persons and parents are strong, children seem to find the transition between home and setting easier.

In England, key persons are also expected to take a role in supporting parents with learning activities at home, such as teaching children to read, cook and play games. Many will share resources and ideas with parents and tell them what their child has enjoyed within the setting. This helps parents and carers to develop a trusting relationship with the setting.

Indicators of good attachment between child and key person

When children have a strong attachment with their key person, they are likely to show several attachment behaviours.

▶ **Eye contact** – babies and children make eye contact with people they are attached to. Toddlers will, for example, glance up from a play activity to check that 'their' adult is still there.

▶ **Proximity** – babies and toddlers often want to stay close to their key person and if they play out of sight, they will quickly come back into 'range'.

▶ **Seeking behaviours** – when there are strong attachments, children seek out their key person. They may want to show them something that they have done or ask or demonstrate that they want their key person to play with them.

▶ **Reassurance** – a good test of attachment is whether a child looks for reassurance from their key person if they are feeling upset. Children may also only be ready to separate from their parents if they know that they can be cuddled by their key person.

- **Physical contact** – as you saw earlier, babies and young children need physical contact. It helps them feel reassured and is good for their emotional well-being. Having said this, babies and children will only accept physical contact from people that they are comfortable with and with whom they have a bond.

- **Noticing and objecting to absence** – where a child has a key person, they should notice whether or not that person is present. Older children may be disappointed if the key person disappears, but younger children may cry or even show signs of separation anxiety unless there is a 'buddy system' in place. Key persons with strong bonds are likely to find that their key children will wait by the door if they go out of the room.

- **Observing attachment behaviours** – if you are a key person to a child it is important that you check that your key child has attached to you. If this has not happened, you should reflect on your body language, style of interaction and also how you are showing interest in the child, for example, by getting down to their level. You should also think about how you are working with parents to gain information from them about how best to form a relationship with the child.

Link

Go to Unit 1, Section D1 to find more information about separation anxiety.

Theory into practice

In your work placement, ask if you could observe a toddler or a 3-year-old child to see if they are showing signs of attachment to their key person.

▶ Can you see how comfortable this child looks with his key person?

The benefits for children's development of the key person approach

There are numerous benefits for children's development when the key person approach is used effectively in settings. Firstly, it helps children to settle in and feel secure, and prevents them from becoming anxious. This is a prerequisite if children are to learn and enjoy their time in an early years setting. In addition, where there is an effective key person approach, children find it easier to socialise and develop relationships with other children because their own emotional needs are being met.

Interestingly, an effective key person approach also supports the process of children's learning. This is because children who are relaxed and happy find it easier to learn and they may also be more motivated to try new things because they enjoy being with their key person.

Some of the most significant benefits of the key person approach on children's development are linked to children's language development. Babies' and children's early language development is closely linked to the relationships they build with adults. A strong key person relationship helps babies and children with this area of development in the following ways.

- **Amount of exposure** – when babies and children have strong attachments to their key person, they spend time interacting with them. This exposure and strong attachment helps them gain language, and makes the learning fun.

- **Tuning in** – it is essential that babies and toddlers spend time with their key person. This is because they are 'tuning in' to the tones and meanings of words. As we all speak using different tones and may also use different expressions, a baby who is being handled and spoken to by several different people may not be as quick to 'tune in' to the meanings of words.

▶ **Acknowledging and responding** – it can be difficult to understand what babies and toddlers are trying to say. This is because of speech immaturities. If you spend time with the same children, it becomes easier for you to understand them. A strong relationship with the children's parents also means that you may know what children's home words are for things and also what they have been doing. If children repeatedly find that their vocalisations are not being responded to, they are likely to talk less.

Assessment practice 7.2 | A.P2 | A.M2 | A.D1 |

A nursery is keen to ensure that its key person approach is effective and that all members of staff understand their role and its importance. You have been asked to look at this topic and put together an information pack, which:

- explains the benefits of the key person approach to meet children's development needs
- analyses and assesses the links between the key person role and theories of attachment
- evaluates how the key person approach can overcome negative influences on children's personal, emotional and social development.

Plan

- Do I have all the information I need about the key person approach?
- Do I understand the impact of the key person approach on young children's development?

Do

- Have I chosen information that is relevant?
- Am I using my skills of analysis and evaluation?

Review

- Can I justify why I have decided to approach this task in the way that I have?
- Have I evaluated my work and am I confident that it fulfils the set task?

A3 Influences on children's behaviour

As babies and children develop, so too does their behaviour. During this process, adults have an important role in helping children to show positive behaviour that is appropriate for their stage of development and that reflects the context they are in. In this section you will explore how you might work with children to support their positive behaviour, and consider what factors you should take into account and strategies that might be used.

Cultural and social perspectives

Working out what is appropriate behaviour for children is very interesting and quite complex. Our behaviours change according to whom we are with, where we are and how we are feeling. This means that you would probably behave differently with your friends at a party than you would if you were studying in a library.

In addition, people have different cultural and social expectations of what is appropriate behaviour, many of which they have 'inherited' from their own upbringing. It is important to be aware of different perspectives in relation to behaviour because you will need to work with parents, colleagues and other professionals, and children benefit from consistency. Three areas in particular are interesting when it comes to expectations of children's behaviour.

Differing views of childhood

People have very different views and beliefs about how children should behave. Some are based on spiritual beliefs such as reincarnation and others on social traditions. Here are some questions that may make you think about your own values and beliefs.

▶ Should there be strict boundaries set by adults or should children be free to explore and set their own boundaries?

▶ How much respect should children pay to adults? Should children be free to ignore them?

▶ Are children competent and independent learners or do adults have to teach children everything?

Social norms and values

Every society has its own values and these become linked to social codes of behaviour. These are based on tradition as well as other things such as religion. As the UK is very diverse, you will find that there is a range of social norms and values. Look at the following statements and see what you think about them.

▶ Children should be made to sit at the table at mealtimes.

▶ Saying please and thank you is important.

▶ Taking your shoes off when you enter a home is essential.

Gender expectations

The way that cultures, individuals and society expect boys and girls to behave can be different. This can be reflected through the type of play and resources that are provided, but also through the clothing that is given. Look at the following statements and see if you recognise them.

▶ Boys are more active than girls.

▶ Girls are better at sitting down than boys.

▶ Boys like being outdoors.

▶ Girls try to please adults.

The influence of cultural and social perspectives on adult responses

As well as recognising different cultural and social perspectives, it is important to understand that these are likely to shape adults' responses towards children's behaviour. An early years professional may insist that a child sits at the table until the end of the meal because this was the norm in their childhood. Gender expectations are also interesting: it is sometimes thought that adults subconsciously curb girls' exuberant behaviours while not doing this with boys, saying 'boys will be boys'.

It is important for you to be aware of your own thoughts about children's behaviour and, where necessary, make sure that they do not lead to discrimination. It is also helpful to think about whether another adult's reaction to a child's behaviour is based on their own cultural and social perspective.

Avoiding conflict

The different opinions that people have about 'socially acceptable' behaviour can lead to conflict among adults unless they are explored and some clear expectations are established. This is why early years settings have behaviour policies that are shared with new staff, but these policies should also be shared with parents.

Links between behaviour, language and cognitive development

You have seen that what you expect of children is linked to social and cultural perspectives, but it is important to understand that children's behaviour is also closely linked to their cognitive and language development. This means that even with encouragement and a positive environment, there are some things that children do that are simply 'normal' for their stage of development.

Effect of language on behaviour

Most children aged between 2–3 years take an incredible language journey. At the start of this journey, they are likely to be highly impulsive and find it difficult to share attention or possessions with others. If their language develops well, you should see quite a change in their behaviour after their third birthday. This is linked to language development, which in turn seems to help their cognitive development. From around 3 years, most children seem to be able to wait a little and do some simple sharing. Parents will find that they are more cooperative with simple tasks and that they have fewer tantrums.

Language delay

Where children have language delay and so are not able to express themselves, the usual milestones for positive behaviour are unlikely to be met. This is because language helps children to manage their behaviour and be less impulsive. So a 4-year-old child whose language level is similar to that of a 2-year-old child is likely to show many of the behaviours that characterise a child who is 2 years of age.

Theory into practice

With permission, talk to staff in your setting about children whose behaviour is atypical. Is there a link to their use of language?

Expectations in relation to a child's age or stage of development

Although all children are unique, it is worth knowing the usual patterns of behaviour for the age group of the children you are working with. This should help you to establish fair expectations. Table 7.4 shows examples of what you might expect at different ages, goals for behaviour and also the role of the adult. Note that this is a guide only and that an individual child's behaviour might be affected by levels of language and other factors.

Link

Unit 1 has more information about how a child's behaviours may be affected by language and a range of other factors.

▶ **Table 7.4:** Expectations at different ages, goals for behaviour and the role of the adult

Age	Stage of development	Goals for behaviour	Role of adult
1–2 years	• Actively explores environment • Imitates adults in simple tasks • Repeats actions that gain attention • Alternates between clinginess and independence • No understanding that toys or other objects may belong to others	• To play alongside other children (parallel play) • To carry out simple instructions such as 'Can you find your coat?'	• **Good supervision** is necessary as children of this age do not understand the dangers around them • **Distraction** works well in stopping unwanted behaviour, as children often forget what they were doing, e.g. if a child wants another child's toy, offer a different one instead • **Praise** will help children to understand how to get an adult's attention in positive ways and to develop good self-esteem • **Being a good role model** is important as children learn behaviour by imitating those around them

▶ **Table 7.4:** Expectations at different ages, goals for behaviour and the role of the adult– *continued*

Age	Stage of development	Goals for behaviour	Role of adult
2–3 years	• Easily frustrated and may have tantrums • Dislikes adult attention being given to other children • No understanding of the need to wait • Finds sharing difficult • Rapid physical and emotional learning • Tries to be independent	• To wait for needs to be met, e.g. at mealtimes • To share toys or food with one other child with adult help • To play alongside other children • To sit and share a story for five minutes • To say 'please' and 'thank you' if reminded • To follow simple instructions with help, such as 'Wash your hands'	• **Good supervision and anticipation** are vital when working with this age range. Children try to be independent but lack some of the physical and cognitive skills they need. This makes them frustrated and angry. Adults need to anticipate possible sources of frustration, and support children either by offering help or by distracting them, e.g. a child who is trying to put their coat on may need an adult to make a game of it so the child does not become frustrated • **Praise and encouragement** will help children to learn what behaviour adults expect from them. Some unwanted behaviour that is not dangerous should be ignored so that children do not learn to use it as a way of getting adult attention • **Consistency** is needed as children will try to work out what the limits are on their behaviour • **Being a good role model** helps children as they model their behaviour on others around them. This is especially important as children act out their experiences through play
3–4 years	• Follows simple rules by imitating other children, e.g. collects aprons before painting • Able to communicate wishes • Enjoys activities such as painting • Enjoys being with other children • Can play cooperatively • Enjoys helping adults	• To follow rules in games when helped by an adult, e.g. playing lotto • To say 'please' and 'thank you' often without reminder • To take turns and share equipment • To follow adults' instructions most of the time, e.g. 'Let Simon have a turn' • To help tidy away	• **Praise and encouragement** build children's confidence and make them more likely to show desirable behaviour • **Explanation** of rules should be given, as children are more likely to remember and understand them • **Good supervision** is still needed: although children are able to do many things for themselves, they remain unaware of the dangers around them. Most of the time children will be able to play well together, but squabbles will break out • **Being a good role model** will help children learn the social skills they need to resolve arguments and express their feelings
4–5 years	• Plays with other children without help from adults • Is able to communicate feelings and wishes • Understands the need for rules	• To ask permission to use other children's toys • To comfort playmates in distress • To say 'please' and 'thank you' without a reminder • To tidy up after activities	• **Providing stimulating activities and tasks** that allow children to develop confidence is important. Children are keen to help adults and enjoy being busy. Tasks such as setting the table allow children to feel independent • **Praise and encouragement** help children feel good about themselves, which is important as they are often starting school. Children need to feel that they can be 'good' • **Explanation** helps children to remember and understand the need for rules or decisions • **Being a good role model** helps children to learn social skills – they will copy what they see
5–8 years	• Has strong friendships • Can argue back • Copies behaviour of other children, e.g. may swear or spit • Understands the need for rules and plays games that have rules • Understands the difference between right and wrong • Has many self-help skills, e.g. getting dressed, wiping up spills	• To follow instructions from adults • To apologise to others • To listen to others **From 6 years** • To work independently and quietly in educational settings • To be helpful and thoughtful	• **Praise and encouragement** avoids children looking for other ways of gaining attention. Praise is needed as children become more aware of others and compare themselves critically • **Explanation** helps children to understand the reasons for rules and decisions. They also need to consider the effect of their actions on others. As children become older, they are likely to argue back and clear boundaries need to be enforced • **Being a good role model** is important, as children try to understand more about adults. Speech and actions are modelled increasingly on adults whom children admire • **Providing activities and responsibilities** helps children 'mature' and learn more about their capabilities. Small responsibilities help independence and confidence, e.g. ask them to pour drinks for other children

⏸ **PAUSE POINT**   Give an example of a typical behaviour of a child aged 2 years.

Hint   Remember that 2-year-olds find it hard to regulate their emotions.

Extend   Compare the typical patterns of behaviour between children who are 2 and 3 years old.

Short-term factors that may affect behaviour

Children's behaviour is not constant. Like adults, they become tired, hungry and have days when they do not feel like interacting or sharing. This means that while adults may have some ideas about what is usual in terms of expectations of behaviour, they have to be aware of short-term factors that will influence a child's behaviour at any given time.

Tiredness

All children and adults need sleep. Children who are feeling tired or have not slept sufficiently are likely to show the behaviours outlined in Figure 7.3.

Appear withdrawn · Be uncooperative · Act impulsively

Be unwilling to share

Tired children may:

Have difficulty in concentrating

Be forgetful

Have tantrums, eg outbursts of anger, laughter or crying

Be argumentative · Be tearful

▶ **Figure 7.3:** Tiredness can affect children's behaviour in many ways

Hunger

When you are hungry, your blood glucose levels drop. This affects the brain's capacity to function. As impulsivity and emotions are governed by our neural activity, this can mean that children will show behaviours that are otherwise unusual for them. When children eat diets that are high in sugar, their blood glucose level is likely to fall suddenly – this can account for quite dramatic mood swings.

Boredom

The brain likes to be stimulated. When children are bored and lacking stimulation, they are likely to do things that will literally give their brains a boost – they may run around, do things that make sounds and do things that feel exciting for them. It is therefore essential that you are thoughtful about what type of activities and resources are available for children and whether they are sufficiently fascinating, exciting and stimulating.

The likelihood of children showing unwanted behaviours is therefore high during periods when they are waiting around for things such as meals, snacks or lining up. This is why it is good practice for early years settings to plan carefully for these routine events and to see them as learning opportunities. Some settings, for example, sing rhymes when children are waiting for lunch or encourage children to be involved in laying the table or serving.

Reflect

Look at the characteristics that children may show when they are tired. How many do you recognise when you are feeling tired?

PAUSE POINT   Explain why boredom might be a factor when children show unwanted behaviour.

Hint   Think back to your own childhood.

Extend   Give an example of how waiting for a meal to be served might be turned into a learning opportunity for a young child.

Illness

When children are feeling poorly, they are more likely to show behaviours that are uncharacteristic. Often it is only after the child's symptoms begin to show that you recognise that the child was probably not well, so it is important to be observant and take note of uncharacteristic behaviours.

Bullying

As you saw earlier in the unit, bullying is rare in early years, but can occur with school-age children. It is important to be thoughtful about whether a child might be experiencing friendship difficulties or being bullied. Look out for children who become withdrawn, are angry or seem to be intent on hurting others, especially younger children. If you suspect that a child is bullying or is being bullied, you should raise this as an issue with the child's key person, who will need to talk to the child's parents.

Abuse

You know that some children are victims of abuse. Ongoing abuse and the consequences of abuse can change children's behaviour. In Unit 5, you looked at the signs that might indicate that a child is being abused and you saw that as well as physical indicators there are often things that can be noticed in a child's behaviour. If you spot a change in a child's behaviour towards other children, or in their general demeanour, it is important to follow this up. It may be that other circumstances, such as a family problem, are causing the difficulty, but it is essential not to rule out the possibility that there might be abuse. You should report any concerns to the lead person named in your setting's child protection policy.

Long-term factors that may affect behaviour

There are some long-term factors that might affect children's behaviour. Understanding these can help you to support children more effectively.

▸ **Chronic illness** – children with **chronic illnesses** may struggle at times to show positive behaviour. There are many reasons for this, including tiredness and the effects of drugs, but also the condition itself. Eczema, which is common in children, can prevent a child from sleeping properly. During a flare-up, the itching itself can be unbearable and may result in a child becoming frustrated and angry.

▸ **Anxiety** – there are multiple reasons why children may be affected by anxiety, including home circumstances, transitions or trauma. Children who are anxious may show a variety of behaviours including attention seeking, withdrawal and impulsiveness.

▸ **Not settled** – you have looked at the importance of key persons and, as you will see later in this unit, it is very important to support children with transition. When a child is not fully settled in, they find it harder to show positive behaviour. It may be that the child will not share, or show anger, but they may also exhibit attention-seeking behaviour.

▸ **Poor attachments** – children who have poor attachments to their primary carers are more likely to show unwanted behaviours, for a variety of reasons. You have

---

Link

Look back at Unit 5, Section C1 to find more information about the signs of abuse.

Key term

Chronic illness – a long-term medical condition.

---

seen already that a strong attachment to a primary carer is required for healthy emotional development. One of the many benefits of strong primary attachments is that they provide a template for how to behave towards others. This means that children with poor attachments may not know how to relate to other children. In some cases, children with poor attachments may show attention-seeking behaviours, as well as frustrated or aggressive behaviours towards others.

Transition and significant life events

Many children are looked after by several adults over the course of a week. While some children can manage a number of transitions, it is not always ideal and can sometimes create disturbances in children's behaviour. It is worth remembering that every transition brings a new environment or a different relationship as well as different expectations from adults. As you will see in Section C, children thrive on consistency and so changes can be problematic.

Some children navigate transition well, but other children struggle to 'belong' or to remember the routine and expectations of each setting. In addition, if there are any difficulties within the child's own family, this will make it particularly hard for the child to show positive behaviour. Figure 7.4 outlines how children's behaviour can be affected if they find transition difficult.

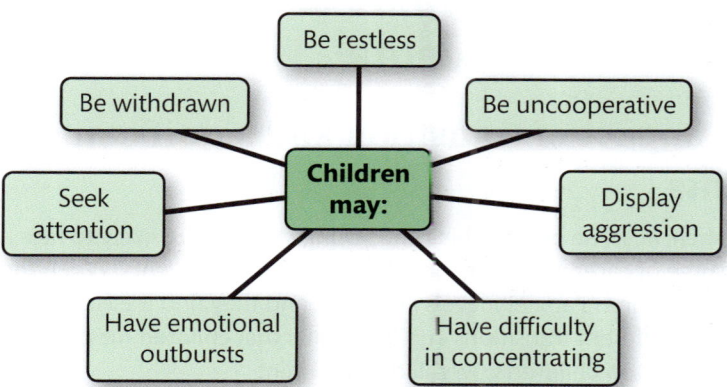

▶ **Figure 7.4:** How difficulties with transition may affect a child's behaviour in a child's life, especially in relation to adults who may be looking after them

Link

Section B has more information about transition and significant life events that children may experience.

Supporting children

If you feel that a child is struggling because of the transitions they are making or because of a significant event that has affected them, you should try the following.

▶ Talk to parents about any changes in the child's life and how things are working.

▶ Gain suggestions from parents about how to support the child.

▶ Find out more about the routines and expectations of other settings.

▶ Spend more time with the child so that a strong attachment can be built.

▶ Try to create a special routine for when the child arrives, e.g. hang up their coat, share a story and then lay the table together.

A children's centre is reviewing its behaviour policy and procedures. It wants to ensure that everyone understands the influences on children's behaviour. You have been asked to provide information and analysis that they can use for a training session.

The information needs to:

- describe the factors that may impact children's behaviour
- analyse the difference between short- and long-term factors on children's behaviour
- evaluate the impact on children's personal, social and emotional development when adults understand influences that affect children's behaviour.

Plan

- Do I have all the information I need about influences on children's behaviour?
- Do I understand how the factors affecting behaviour impact on children's development?

Do

- Have I chosen information that is relevant?
- Am I managing my time effectively?

Review

- Can I justify why I have decided to approach this task in the way that I have?
- Have I evaluated my work and am I confident that it fulfils the set task?

Explore how to prepare and support children through transition and significant life events

B1 The impact of transition and significant life events

As we have seen, at some point babies and young children are likely to face a transition such as a change of carer or setting, or more significant life events. When these are managed well, children's anxiety levels are lower and they find it easier to adapt. This section looks at different transitions and life events that children may experience and the effects of these on children's overall development.

Transitions and significant events that children may experience

Almost all children will experience transitions between different settings and between an early years setting and a school. Some children will experience other significant events in their lives outside a setting, such as moving house, the birth of a sibling, a family breakdown or even the death of a family member.

Events that are common to children

Recognising the many transitions that children make, including those on a day-to-day basis, can help you to plan for them and also find ways of lowering children's anxiety.

Day-to-day transitions

Moving from home to setting is a transition for children. In addition, there will be many children who may be moving from home to setting and then to another setting later in the day. An example of this would be a child who goes to a childminder, who then takes the child on to nursery or school.

As well as 'formal care and education', it is also important to recognise that many families use friends and relatives. This is known as **informal care**. This may mean that as well as seeing a childminder and a teacher, the child might be picked up by a friend of the family for the rest of the afternoon.

> **Key term**
>
> **Informal care** – childcare provided by friends or family who are not registered childcare practitioners.

How many transitions?

Andrea is 4 years old. Her parents work full time, but they have managed to organise childcare for her every day. Before school on Mondays, Tuesdays and Wednesdays, she goes to a childminder who has children in the same school. She also goes to an after-school club on those days. On Thursdays, before and after school, she goes to her grandmother's house and her grandmother takes her to a swimming class. On Friday, she is sometimes taken to school by her father if he is free; otherwise, she goes to a neighbour's flat and the neighbour takes her to school with their own children. On Friday afternoon her aunt picks her up.

Check your knowledge

1   How many different transitions is Andrea experiencing in the week?

2   How many adults will she be with over the course of a week?

3   Why is informal care a major part of many children's lives?

Day-to-day transitions within settings

As adults, it is easy to forget that even relatively small transitions within the same setting can be stressful for children. In school, children make transitions between classrooms, playtime, assembly and hall time. In some nurseries and preschools, children may go to particular areas for certain periods of the day or to certain staff members for some activities. These are all transitions.

▶ These children are ready to go outside. This is a transition from the classroom

Changes in environment

Some children find any changes that take place in a familiar environment difficult. This may include moving around furniture or activities. It is worth noting which children find even these relatively moderate changes upsetting as it may be that they still need to develop a bond with their key person or that additional reassurance is needed. For some children who have specific social or communication difficulties, small changes in the environment can make them feel anxious. It is worth using resources such as visual timetables or photographs, or creating personal books that will help them adjust to any changes.

When it comes to babies and younger children who need naps, it is never a good idea to change the sleep environment. This is because while changing the environment can be stimulating for children and good for learning, stimulation and sleep do not go together!

Moving from one setting or practitioner to another

As children grow, they are also likely to experience a change in their key person. They may move from a preschool into a school or from a childminder into a preschool. It is worth remembering that transition does not have to be a physical change of environment – for example, children who are looked after at home will face a transition if their au pair or nanny leaves. In day care it is usual for children to change rooms as they become older. This again is a significant transition.

Changes in friendship groups

As children grow, they are likely to develop strong friendships with peers. When children change settings, early years professionals or groups, remember that they may be changing friendship groups as well. As children develop attachments to other children, this can be stressful for them.

Birth of a sibling

Many children face a change to their family structure. One of the most common changes is the birth of a sibling. For children, a change to their usual family structure can be very stressful.

Events that are particular to some children

Looked-after children

Looked-after children are likely to experience multiple transitions. First, they will be in the care of the local authority and have left the family home. They are also likely to be in **foster care** placements and these may not last long, depending on the child's and the foster family's situation. Some children may then go on to be adopted.

> **Key terms**
>
> **Foster care** – temporary care in foster families for looked-after children who are not with their parents.
>
> **Looked-after children** – children whose care is the responsibility of the local authority.

Changes to family structures

Some children may face a change to their family structure because of divorce or relationship breakdown. A parent's new partner and their children may also change the dynamic of a family.

- **Moving from one family to another** – as well as managing day-to-day transitions, some children move from one family to another. This may happen because parents have shared custody and children stay with one parent for some of the time and then move to another.
- **Loss of significant people** – children may suffer the bereavement of significant people in their family.

For children, change to their usual family structure is likely to be very stressful.

> **Research**
>
> Find out about Winston's Wish, an organisation that supports children who are facing, or have suffered, a bereavement of someone close to them. You can access the organisation's website at www.winstonswish.org.uk.

Effects of transitions and significant events on children's holistic development

Each type of transition may affect children, although the effects may be relatively short-lived if there is otherwise consistency in attachments with the important adults in their lives. This means that moving home may be problematic, but if children are still in the same setting, in the same friendship group and with the same family and practitioner attachments, it would be unusual for children to remain stressed. On the other hand, a child whose parents have separated and is now moving between two family units is likely to need longer-term support.

Table 7.5 shows some of the possible effects of transitions on children. Note that some of those listed apply only to transitions that are causing the child enormous levels of stress, such as a bereavement.

▶ **Table 7.5:** Possible effects of transitions on children

Type of transition	Possible effects
Physical	• Disturbed sleep and sleeping patterns, including waking in the night, refusal to go to bed • Disturbed eating habits, including over-eating or becoming anxious about food • Toileting accidents when they had been clean and dry in the day, bedwetting (enuresis) • Attempt to go back into nappies – by young children who were just toilet trained • Frequent illnesses such as cold, flu • Regression or refusal in self-care tasks such as feeding and dressing • Repetitive movements, e.g. head banging, sucking and rocking
Communication and language	• Stammering • **Selective mutism** • Withdrawal • Lack of interest in communicating with others, including peers
Cognitive	• Difficulty in concentrating • Forgetfulness • Difficulty in following instructions • Lower interest in activities
Emotional	• Increase in temper tantrums for children under 4 years • Temper tantrums in older children • Increase in impulsivity • Crying and tearfulness • Outbursts of anger often directed at those with whom the child has a strong attachment • Clinginess sometimes combined with angry gestures, such as hitting
Social	• Attention seeking through unwanted behaviours • Antisocial behaviours that are unusual for the child and not age-appropriate, e.g. biting, spitting • Withdrawal or lack of interest in joining other children for play • Solitary play activities

Key term

Selective mutism – where a child does not talk although they have the ability to do so.

B2 Support transition and significant life events

Strategies to prepare children for transitions and significant events

There are many strategies that you can use with children to prepare them for planned and unplanned transitions or significant events. How you support children will depend on your discussions with parents, the type of transition and also the children's age and stage of development.

Discussions

Table 7.5 shows the many effects that transition can have on children. Transitions can create stress for children, so your role is to look for ways of minimising stress and also supporting children through them. The starting point for this is to work closely with parents so that you know what is happening in children's lives and how they are reacting.

Children do remember stressful separations and so when talking to parents about current transitions, it is important to find out if children have already experienced other transitions and how these worked out. Below are some points that may be useful when discussing events and transitions with parents.

▸ What is currently happening, and how is the child feeling or reacting?
▸ What does the child know about what is due to happen?
▸ How does the parent feel about the transition?
▸ Has the child had past experiences of transitions – what were they and how did the child react?
▸ How does the child normally react to stress?
▸ What helps the child to cope with stress?

Discussing what is going to happen can help children to prepare. How much information you give them may depend on the type of transition, as some things may be quite overwhelming and children may need time to digest information and ask questions. A useful strategy can be to ask general questions to find out children's current knowledge and understanding of the transition.

The timing of any discussion is important too. Telling young children too far in advance can make them anxious, but leaving things until just before they happen can be equally problematic. That is why it is helpful to work with parents so that timescales and messages are agreed.

Books

There is a range of books that can help children understand more about a transition that is about to take place. Books can sometimes be used to help children make connections and as a way of allowing them to raise questions. A book about the arrival of a baby brother might prompt a child to say that their mother has a big tummy and she is going to have a baby too! Books can also be used after a transition to help children explore their emotions and feelings. This can be particularly helpful for transitions such as bereavement, divorce and separation.

Photographs/online resources

As well as books, photographs can be helpful. A child who is anxious about going on holiday may be interested to see photographs of an airport, while a child who is going to a new nursery might be interested in seeing a photograph of their new key person.

In addition to using photographs, it is also possible to use online resources to support children. This might mean using a 'streetmap' function to show a child the outside their new school or visiting a website to show the child a film clip of the inside of a hospital.

Storytelling

Simple stories can also be used to help children prepare for changes in their lives. Stories may be about a character of a similar age and situation so that a child understands the connections.

The importance of building effective relationships with children and their families

Wherever possible, you should be looking for ways for children and their parents/carers to get to know you before they start in the setting. This is why, in most early years settings, time is spent with children before they join you. Ideally, the key person should focus on playing and building a relationship with the child.

Activities to build relationships with children

There is no single way of building a relationship with a child, but it is important that during the settling-in process, the key person finds a way of 'befriending' the child. This requires responsiveness and acute observational skills. If you rush a child, for example, by touching them before they are ready, they are likely to become fearful. Here are some activities and strategies you could try to help build relationships.

▶ This father is using a story to help prepare his child for school

Visits to the setting

Children and parents need to visit before they start at the setting to look around, explore and meet children and staff. It is also helpful for children to know where things are on a visit, especially toilets and changing rooms as well as toys and resources. It is helpful if visits are done when the setting is working smoothly so that parents and children can see a calm setting. It is good practice for the key person to spend time with the child and the parents on these visits. This allows the child to start building a relationship with the key person.

Many children need more than one visit to the setting. It can be helpful to give parents instructions on what they should do at each visit, with the aim that, little by little, the child becomes used to spending time with the key person while the parent is close by but not heavily involved.

Home visits

Many early years settings carry out home visits. Ideally, they should be made by the child's key person. The idea is to see the child in their own home, where they and their parents may feel more relaxed. When children are relaxed, they are more likely to talk or play with someone that they do not know and thus a relationship can be built more easily. Home visits often allow parents to ask questions or share information that they might not have wanted to raise when surrounded by other adults. During the home visit, the key person should interact and play with the child. It can be helpful to take a photograph of the visit so that the child has a memory of this when they start at the setting.

Puppets

Puppets can help young children form a relationship with their key person. This is because they are intriguing for young children and so temporarily deflect the child's focus away from their parent onto the key person. Children will often touch a puppet, make friends with the puppet and then with you.

Blowing bubbles

Children of all ages seem to enjoy bubbles. Blowing bubbles so that a child can catch them can be very engaging and can encourage a child to approach you and ask you to blow some more.

Cooking

Older children often find it easier to make relationships when they are involved in an activity with other children. Cooking is a great activity as children are busy and there is likely to be plenty of talk.

PAUSE POINT   Explain how a home visit may support a child's transition.

Hint   Think about the importance of a child feeling relaxed.

Extend   Think of a practical activity that might help children to build a relationship with an adult.

How to work with colleagues and other professionals to offer support during transitions and significant events

For some types of transition, you will need to work with colleagues or other professionals in order to help the child and the family.

Visits to other settings

Sometimes you may need to help children make the transition to another setting or to another staff member. You may provide support by taking the child to visit the new setting or staff member they will be working with. This will require parental consent. It is important when doing this to allow the future key person to spend time with the child. You may stay next to the child so that they feel safe, but keep a 'low profile' so that the future key person can get to know the child. This can be a good time to share information and answer questions about the child.

Welcoming a child's future key person

It is common for reception teachers and other people such as childminders to visit early years settings to see their 'future' children. It is important that you are welcoming to visitors and that you help them get to know children. Often this is a good time to share information informally with them. As with other aspects of sharing information, it is important to gain parental consent before doing this.

Sharing information

You may need to seek information from another service or professional. All information sharing that is specific to the child and the family requires parental consent, unless there is a child protection issue. If no consent is given, general information about the structure of the service and advice about supporting transitions can be given but no specific information about the child or the family can be shared.

The type of information that you may need, or others will need from you, will very much depend on the type of transition the child is experiencing. It can be worth preparing questions or information in advance of having a conversation with a colleague or other professional so that you can focus your discussion on the key points. The following are some general points that might be raised when sharing information:

▶ structure and role of the service or setting

▶ specific policies or **ethos** within the setting

▶ how long the child has been coming

▶ what the child enjoys doing

▶ how the child reacts to stress

▶ how you can comfort or reassure the child.

> **Key term**
>
> **Ethos** – the philosophy or approach used by a setting, which will affect the setting's practice.

Remaining in contact

Where children and their families are using several settings or services, it is important to have ways of staying in contact. This requires parental consent, but it is worth seeking, as when a child is moving from one setting to another it is important for the various key persons to keep in contact. This is sometimes done using a notebook that travels with the child in which activities, incidents and thoughts are jotted down. It is good practice to do this with the child.

How to support the settling-in process

Settling in at a new setting needs to be viewed as a process. You have seen that babies and young children are likely to have separation anxiety if they have not made a substitute attachment before their parents leave them at the setting. This means that the focus of settling in should be on facilitating this attachment. As children do not make immediate attachments, a series of visits either to the setting or to the child's home will need to be made so that the child becomes used to seeing their key person and interacting with them.

Once this process is under way, it can be useful to check whether the child is starting to feel comfortable with their key person. Parents can be asked to withdraw their attention little by little. They may start by picking up a magazine while the key person and child are playing. Then they may wander across to the other side of the room. If the child is happy to keep on playing, the parent might be able to tell the child that they are popping out for a couple of minutes. When the child is able to cope with this and be reassured by the key person, it is likely then that longer periods of separation can begin to take place. It is good practice to go at the child's pace wherever possible, but key to this is that the child and the key person need to develop a relationship.

Case study

Collecting information

Asia is due to start at a new childminder's on Thursday. She was previously at a nursery, but she was unhappy. The childminder has asked if she could gain some information about Asia from the nursery, but the parents have not given consent. They have not yet told the nursery that Asia will be leaving. The childminder believes that it would be helpful to find out more about the nursery's routines and ethos and so she prepares some questions and makes a phone call to the nursery. She tells the manager that she is a childminder and she may at some time in the future be minding one of the children. She does not reveal the name of the child or any information that might allow the nursery to identify her. She asks the manager if she can ask a few quick questions. She asks about the opening times of the nursery, how they help children to fall asleep and other questions relating to the routine and care of children.

Check your knowledge

1 Why was the childminder unable to ask questions about Asia?

2 Why was it still important that she found out about the day-to-day running of the nursery?

3 How might she use the information to help Asia make the transition?

Indicators that a child has settled in

The starting point for settling in is whether the child can separate from the parent without immediate distress. It is important though to recognise that this in itself is only one facet of settling in. Figure 7.5 shows other things that we should be looking out for, for example, whether the child is happy to join in with activities in the setting. Note that if you do not observe these, it may be that the child needs longer with their key person or, in rare cases, that the child needs a different key person.

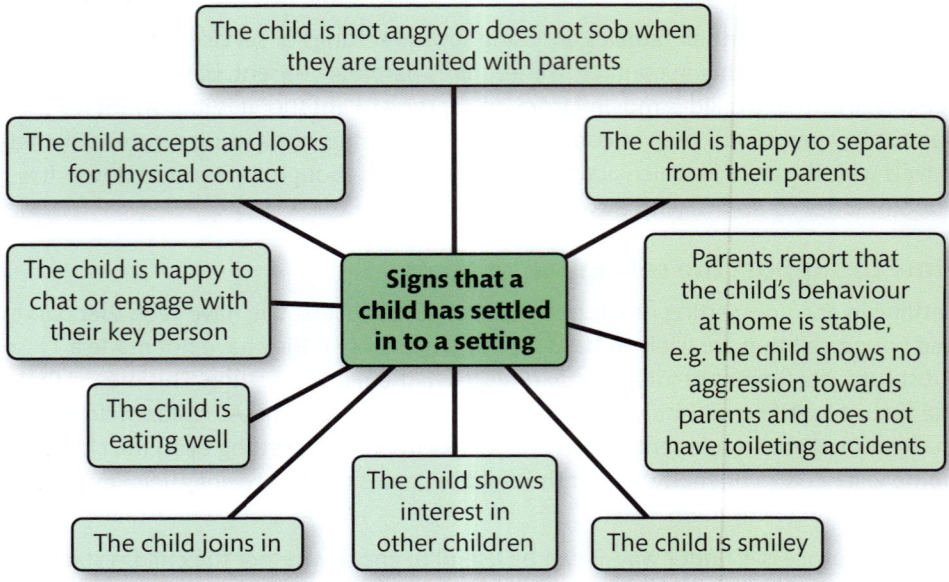

▶ **Figure 7.5:** Signs that a child has settled in

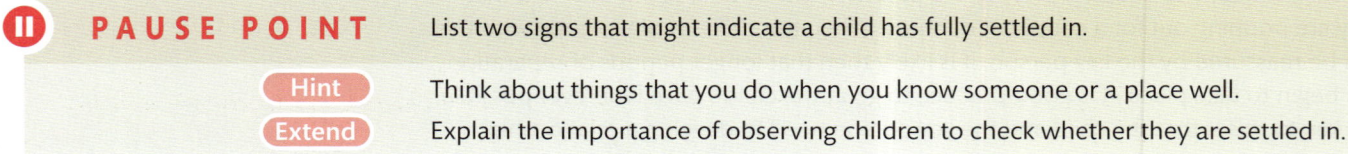

⏸ **PAUSE POINT**   List two signs that might indicate a child has fully settled in.

Hint   Think about things that you do when you know someone or a place well.

Extend   Explain the importance of observing children to check whether they are settled in.

The importance of recognising signs of concern or distress

Table 7.5 in Section B1 showed how stress caused by transitions might affect a child. It is important to keep an eye out for these and also to find out from a child's parents about the child's behaviour at home. Finding out how a child is doing at home is important, as this way you can build a picture of their overall reaction to the current transition. Though it is usual for children to take a while to adapt to new situations, if a child appears to be showing serious signs of distress, it is important that careful thought is given as to how to help the child.

It may be that in extreme cases, such as food refusal or selective mutism, referrals are made to other services. These can be arranged through a family doctor or sometimes a children's centre, but would need parental consent. In the case of looked-after children, the child's social worker should be informed in addition to the person with the direct care of the child. Recognising that children's distress is not temporary and that the symptoms are significant is essential to prevent the child experiencing further distress and potentially worsening symptoms.

Factors that support resilience

The ability for children to adapt and cope with stressful events is linked to their levels of resilience. There are many factors that can influence children's resilience. There is some thought that there is a genetic component, but environmental factors also seem to be significant. Firstly, children's stress responses are linked to how adults have reassured and supported them in the past. This means that children who have had consistent and warm relationships with adults are more likely to be able to deal with stress, especially where adults have remained calm under pressure. In addition, children seem to cope better with stress when they understand what is about to happen or what is happening. This is why it is good practice to talk to children as well as to reassure them.

Children benefit from regular routines and consistency as this helps them to anticipate what is due to happen and therefore what is expected of them. An inclusive environment, where children's needs are anticipated and where every child feels valued, also seems to promote resilience.

Assessment practice 7.4

B.P4 B.P5 B.M3 B.D2

A network of childminders is interested in the impact of transitions and significant life events on children's development. They are also interested in ways of supporting children through transitions.

- Describe the range of transitions and significant life events that children may experience.
- Analyse the impact on children's development of transitions and significant life events.
- Explain how to prepare and support children in early years settings for transition and significant life events, and assess the contribution that early years practitioners can make to this process.
- Evaluate the factors that can contribute to a child's resilience to transition and significant life events.

Plan

- Do I have all the information I need about transitions and significant life events?
- Do I understand the ways in which practitioners can support transitions and significant life events?

Do

- Have I chosen information that is up-to-date?
- Am I using my skills of analysis and evaluation?

Review

- Can I justify why I have decided to approach this task in the way that I have?
- Have I evaluated my work and am I confident that it fulfils the set task?

C Support and promote children's positive behaviour

One aspect of children's social development is learning to show positive behaviour. This includes sharing, being cooperative and taking turns. The extent to which children can show positive behaviour will depend on their age and stage of development, including their levels of language. Other factors such as tiredness, anxiety and lack of adult attention can also affect children's ability to show positive behaviour. This means that sometimes in order to promote positive behaviour, adults working with children have to think about the reasons behind a child's unwanted behaviours. In this section you look at how you might support and promote positive behaviour, including the strategies that are commonly used in early years settings.

C1 Support and promote positive behaviour

Policies and procedures of the setting for managing and promoting positive behaviour

Every setting should have a policy that describes how positive behaviour is to be promoted, as well as procedures for reporting and dealing with unwanted behaviour. It is good practice for such policies to focus on developing children's positive behaviours rather than just on unwanted behaviours.

It is important that you follow the policies and procedures in your setting. These may include guidance as to how adults in the setting should behave, including remaining calm, role modelling thoughtful behaviour and also ensuring that the environment and activities are suitable for each child's stage of development. The behaviour policy should also look at what should happen if specific incidents occur, such as biting, offensive name-calling or swearing.

The way in which incidents are reported and recorded varies from setting to setting. While small incidents of unwanted behaviour are not usually logged, anything significant, including injuries to other children, is usually recorded. It is good practice to note down the names of children that were involved, anything significant that happened before the incident took place, and how the incident was resolved or handled. The name of the adult who dealt with the incident should also be logged, as well as the time and the date. In large settings, where there are a number of adults working with children, the key person should always be told about any significant incidents. This allows them to plan activities and/or adapt routines in order to prevent further incidents. Informing the key person is also important so that parents can be advised of what happened at the end of the session.

> **Research**
>
> Find out how your setting handles incidents of unwanted behaviour and whether there are expectations of staff as to their conduct.

How social learning theory informs practice

Albert Bandura's work on social cognitive theory, also known as social learning theory, has many implications for helping children to show positive behaviour. First, his work shows the importance of children learning from adults, simply by observing them. This is why many settings' policies have clear guidelines for staff conduct, such as showing respect and manners, and not shouting or being aggressive towards children.

> **Link**
>
> Unit 1, Section D1, has more information about social learning theory.

In addition, social learning theory explains why toddlers and young children will not automatically be able to behave in the same way as adults. This is a source of frustration for parents and practitioners as they might expect that if children have observed them being patient or taking turns in a game, they will be able to do the same. Social cognitive theory suggests that several elements have to be in place at the time of the **modelling**, including an appropriate level of development of the child. Having said this, it is reassuring that when children repeatedly see others showing attitudes such as kindness, friendliness and thoughtfulness, they seem to eventually model these behaviours as they grow and develop.

> **Key term**
>
> **Modelling** – demonstrating an action, gesture or behaviour so that a child can observe and later imitate.

Using social learning theory in your work with children

If you model behaviours that are within the developmental grasp of children, they are more likely to be able to show them. This means that simple things such as tidying away toys can be modelled and then children are encouraged to join in. They may not be developmentally ready to do it for a long period of time, but they should be able to join you until their attention wanes. In the same way, if adults model picking up coats or other items from the floor, some older children will also do this.

Children can also learn behaviours from other children. For example, if you identify a child who is showing positive behaviour, it is worth pointing it out to other children. This is likely to encourage them to show similar behaviour, assuming that this is within their developmental grasp.

It is also clear from Bandura's later work that for children to follow modelling behaviour, it is helpful if they are developmentally ready and have the opportunity to repeat what they have seen soon afterwards.

Strategies to promote positive behaviour at different ages and stages of development

We have seen that being positive when working with children can support their behaviour. Different strategies work well to promote positive behaviours that are appropriate to children's age and level of development.

In this section, we will start by looking at several strategies that settings use, some of which work best with particular age groups. We will then explore how a theory of managing behaviour known as operant conditioning can be used with children.

Distraction

Distraction is often used to help toddlers and even older children focus on something else. You may, for example, get a puppet out of the bag to distract a toddler who is determined to climb on a table. Distraction works by engaging the child in another activity that is equally or more appealing. As children get older, distraction does not always work, but it is worth considering. If you find that you are relying on distraction as a technique, it may be that the environment, activities or resources available are not sufficiently engaging for children.

Negotiation

Once children are starting to talk, it can be helpful to negotiate with them. Ideally, you should explain the situation and allow children to offer up their own suggestions. This style of working gives children responsibility and makes them feel more involved. The good news is that when children start to set their own rules, they are more likely to follow them, as the case study on negotiating shows.

Case study

Negotiating with children

Three 7-year-old children are playing football, but the ball keeps hitting some glass doors. The adult talks to the children. The children are keen to continue playing, although the adult does not offer an alternative suggestion. The adult asks them to think about how they can play in such a way that it does not interfere with other children's games or hit the glass doors. The children have a think and then offer to play with a softer ball. The adult considers this and they agree to try it out.

A few minutes later, the adult asks them if they are still enjoying the game and congratulates them on coming up with the solution.

Check your knowledge

1 Explain how the adult gave the children responsibility for setting their own boundaries.

2 What were the overall benefits of this approach?

3 Why was it useful for the adult to acknowledge their behaviour?

Praise

Toddlers and children can be helped to show positive behaviour if they are given sufficient encouragement and acknowledgement. This often comes in the form of praise. Ideally praise should be offered during or shortly after the behaviour as it seems to have more effect. It is also helpful if children can make the link between the praise or positive attention and their behaviour, as this helps them to understand what they need to do again. For example, an adult might say 'Well done! You waited for Arthur to have his turn first.' As children develop, it is important to help them learn to acknowledge their own positive behaviour. This might be done through saying to a child, 'Were you proud of yourself?', or 'Did you notice how pleased Daniel was when you let him take his turn?' This is important, as children have to learn to take responsibility and also internally acknowledge their own positive behaviours.

❚❚ PAUSE POINT

Why is it important that adults help children to understand the link between praise and their actions?

Hint   Think about why it is useful on placement to be told when you have done something well.

Extend   Explain why, over time, older children need to learn to reflect on their own behaviour.

Operant conditioning techniques

Operant conditioning techniques include positive reinforcement (for example, rewards), intermittent reinforcement, unexpected reinforcement and not reacting to children. The use of star charts is an example of secondary reinforcement.

Positive reinforcement

Positive reinforcement should, in theory, encourage children to repeat behaviours. Most settings use the following methods of positive reinforcement:

- praise
- rewards – stickers, certificates, being allowed to choose equipment
- attention – smiles, eye contact, clapping.

Intermittent reinforcement

A powerful model of reinforcement is known as intermittent reinforcement. You looked at this in Unit 1 and saw that it can create longer-lasting behaviours in children. This model of reinforcement is useful when praising children, as it means that they do not expect praise every time they show positive behaviours, and so avoids the scenario whereby children stop doing something because they are no longer praised.

Intermittent reinforcement can also be a cause of unwanted behaviours in children. This is worth exploring if you have found that a persistent behaviour is being shown. It might be that the child has had some intermittent reinforcement, which means that their behaviours are now longer lasting. If intermittent reinforcement is suspected, it is important to maintain absolute consistency and to talk to the child about their actions.

In some cases, it can be easier to try a strategy that is sometimes referred to as 'changing the script'. This means literally changing the situation so that it is impossible for the child to repeat the behaviour. The case study on intermittent reinforcement provides a good example of how 'changing the script' can be used as an approach.

Unexpected reinforcement

Adults do not provide all of the reinforcements. Children can have positive reinforcement from sensations that they have discovered. This explains why children love bouncing on sofas, throwing sand and splashing in puddles. Reinforcements from sensations are very powerful for children and they are likely to find it hard not to repeat the actions even when told to stop. This means that at times it might be appropriate to distract children with alternatives and if necessary to remove items that are causing dangerous or inappropriate behaviour.

Link

Go to Unit 1, Section D1, to find more information about operant conditioning methods.

Case study

Intermittent reinforcement

A day nursery is having difficulty with a 3-year-old child who keeps climbing on the table at lunchtime. The other children laugh when he does this. On some days staff are quick to stop him, but on other days they do not react quickly or decide not to pay any attention.

After a couple of weeks, staff realise this is becoming an issue. What started as a 'one-off' behaviour has become a daily occurrence and the child tries to climb even when staff are ready to stop him.

The manager suggests that the staff should use a different approach. She suggests that instead of having lunch at the table, a picnic mat should be put on the floor. The children are all very excited by this and the 3-year-old child is given the job of putting out the plates. Lunch goes very smoothly!

Check your knowledge

1   How was this child's behaviour being reinforced, and by whom?

2   Why was this an example of intermittent reinforcement?

3   How was 'changing the script' used as an approach and why did it work?

Theory into practice

- What do children in your work placement enjoy doing that needs to be stopped by adults?
- Can you work out what makes it so pleasurable for the children?
- Can you think of other ways in which the children could gain the same stimulation but in a safer context?

Not reacting to children

Operant conditioning suggests that in situations where there is no negative or positive reinforcement, behaviours may disappear. This is the basis of the advice that there may be times when you should not react to children's behaviours but turn away instead. This is effective if children are trying to seek your attention by using inappropriate behaviours such as hitting your arm or threatening to tip a bucket of plastic bricks onto the floor.

While this is a very effective method of working with young children, it also takes a little practice on the part of parents and practitioners, as quite often our 'natural' reaction is to respond to the child. This unfortunately gives children eye contact and a reaction, which can ironically act as a positive reinforcement.

Star charts

Star charts are very popular as a way of changing children's behaviour. They can work well, but only if they are used when children are developmentally ready and also if they are designed well.

Star charts are secondary reinforcers. Children get a small reinforcement by being praised at the time, but the real purpose is that the stars or stickers on the chart build up and at some point are converted into a reward. This is often not meaningful for children until they are 4 or 5 years old. (This is why young children will often prefer a single sticker rather than a pound coin that could buy them a roll of stickers, even when you explain it to them.)

When star charts are used with children who do understand them, they can support a change in children's specific behaviours in a long-term way.

Link

Go to Unit 1, Section D1, to find more information about secondary reinforcers.

Advantages and disadvantages of operant conditioning techniques

You have seen some of the advantages and disadvantages of different operant conditioning techniques.

Generally, operant conditioning methods of helping children to show positive behaviour can be effective, although it is important that you understand them and only apply them when you are sure that children are developmentally able to show the behaviours.

Positive reinforcers work well if they are used at the time of the positive behaviour that you want to encourage further. Leaving praise or attention until much later is not a problem, but it will not be as effective.

However, it is also important that children develop an internal model of being thoughtful, kind and aware of others. The danger of continual praise or rewards is that some children show positive behaviour in order to 'get something' rather than for its own sake. It is therefore helpful to encourage children to reflect on the importance of their actions.

> **Reflect**
>
> Using food as treats for children can cause poor eating attitudes in adulthood. It is thought that where children are regularly rewarded with food treats, they are more likely to eat sugary and other unhealthy foods later – either as comfort foods or because they have developed the attitude of 'being good or working hard = food'.

The importance of a positive attitude, consistency and collaboration

There are many things you can do that can help children show positive behaviours.

Positive attitude

A good starting point is your own attitude towards children and also your work. Adults who have a positive attitude are more likely to appeal to children and this makes it easier to form a strong attachment. This in turn can help children to show positive behaviours and seek attention in appropriate ways.

A positive attitude also helps to keep a good pace within the setting. This is important because it stops small incidents from blowing out of proportion and then creating new problems. It also pays to have a good sense of humour and not to take things personally.

Few toddlers and young children plan to show unwanted behaviours. They are normally the result of age-related impulsiveness, frustration or attention seeking.

Consistency

Toddlers and young children need consistency, in many ways. First of all, children need adults to be consistent in the way that they act and in their tone of voice. They also need adults to be calm. All these things make children feel more secure. This is particularly important to remember if you are working with children who have multiple transitions over a week or are facing a significant upheaval within their family structure. The bottom line is that children need to feel that they can depend on adults.

In addition, for children to show positive behaviour, our expectations of them need to be consistent. This is particularly important for children under 4 years of age. 'Exceptions' or 'special occasions' are not helpful for 2- and even 3-year-old children as they struggle with this as a concept. It is easier for a toddler if they know that they always have to put an apron on before painting or that they are never allowed to climb on the furniture.

Case study

Keeping a positive attitude

Fran is having problems in her personal life. She has come into the nursery tired and annoyed with her boyfriend. She has not slept well and is not looking forward to the day ahead. When one of the children arrives and wants a hug, she says in an irritated voice that she is not a teddy bear. The child looks crestfallen. Later, when she spots one of the children throwing the knives and forks on the dinner table to the floor, she decides that she can't be bothered to say anything. A little later on during lunch, she spots that one of the children has spilt water onto the table. She shouts that the child is doing it on purpose.

Check your knowledge

1 How might Fran's attitude affect the children's emotional well-being?

2 In what ways is Fran being inconsistent?

3 How might her inconsistency affect the children?

4 Why is it important for practitioners to remain professional regardless of their personal circumstances?

Collaboration with parents and others

As well as consistency within your own practice, it is helpful wherever possible to collaborate with others so that there can be overall consistency for children. You may ask parents to share their views with you and also explain the ethos of how you manage behaviour in the setting. It is not always possible for all aspects to be consistent, but the aim is to achieve as much consistency as possible.

As well as sharing information about approaches to things such as mealtimes, dressing and sharing, you also need to work with parents to find out what might be happening that may be impacting on a child's behaviour. Working together on any aspects of a child's behaviour that is proving difficult can mean that a consistent approach is taken to things such as biting or mealtimes. Where children are in a range of settings, discussions with others will also be essential, assuming you have parental consent. It may be that practices are different in the various settings and you may need to take these on board when you are working with the child.

Finally, some families will also get additional support from outreach workers, family liaison teams or health visitors. Knowing what has been agreed as an approach at home will be very helpful and again, with parental consent, it is a good idea to contact others who are working with the child and family.

How to help children develop positive attitudes

Children learn the majority of their social skills through observing adults and being guided by them. This means that early years professionals play an important role in helping children to develop positive attitudes. You should help children learn how to respect and value others, and to understand that children are all different.

You can do this in a variety of ways, including role modelling thoughtfulness and respect, and praising children when they are kind and helpful towards others. You can share books with children that explore how to respect others and be thoughtful.

Children also need to develop an awareness of the similarities and differences between people. Your aim should be to teach them that while everyone is unique, we all have the right to be treated with respect and dignity. A good starting point is to help children explore the differences and similarities between themselves in ways that are age-appropriate. This might mean looking at food and toys, and helping children to see that while they may have different preferences, there will be similarities between them too. Books are a good way of helping children understand that other families may lead different lives to theirs.

How to use observation and assessment to support positive behaviour

Observation and assessment are useful tools to support children's positive behaviour. For some children, you might work out that there are patterns in their behaviour. It might be that a child tends to show unwanted behaviour at the same time each day or in the company of certain children. Wherever possible parents need to work with you on this as they may be able to shed some light on what is happening. You may notice, for example, that on Tuesdays a child's behaviour is different, but then find out from a parent that on Monday nights the child's grandparents come round and on this night they go to bed late.

There are many ways that you might use observations and assessment to build up a picture or pattern of a child's behaviour.

Event samples

This is a recording method whereby you keep a note of certain behaviours each time they occur. The time, date and other information needed to find out what is happening is recorded. This way, it is possible to see the frequency of incidents and also if there is a pattern to them. As part of recording an event sample, it is also useful to record which adult responded to the unwanted behaviour and how they dealt with this. This can help adults to think about being consistent in their responses.

Event samples can also reveal whether any strategies that are being used are helping to reduce the number of incidents.

Diaries

It can be helpful for the setting and parents to keep diaries, day by day or session by session. These can be used as longitudinal records to see if you can notice any patterns, and also when and where they occur. Diaries are usually kept over a few days or even months. Diaries can also be used as a way for the setting and parents to keep in touch with each other and make comments about what is happening.

How to work with parents and carers to support children's positive behaviour

One of the ways in which you can help children to show positive behaviour is for all adults to be fairly consistent in their approach. This means that wherever possible, you need to work with parents and carers to support children's positive behaviour. This is particularly important when children are showing specific behaviours such as attention seeking. The starting point is to share information with parents so that together you can build a picture of how the child is behaving, both in the early years setting and at home. Together you may work out specific triggers for behaviours or underlying reasons why a child is finding it hard to show positive behaviour, for example, tiredness or sibling rivalry.

As a result of information sharing, it is useful for agreed strategies to be drawn up and then put into action, with regular updates taking place. In some instances, you may find that while a child is fine in an early years setting, parents report difficulties at home. In such cases, settings may suggest some strategies to try at home or may give parents information about where they can get additional help. This might include advice from health visitors or local parenting classes.

How to work with colleagues and other professionals to support positive behaviour

You have seen that a consistent approach within early years settings is important to support children's positive behaviour. This is why it is always vital to follow the behaviour policy and procedures within your setting. As part of supporting children's

Link

You look in more detail at how to use event samples in Unit 9.

▶ Observation and assessment are useful ways to help you build a picture of a child's behaviour

positive behaviour, adults in early years setting also have to keep their colleagues informed about children's behaviour on a day-to-day basis. This information sharing means that adults will know how the child is feeling and responding, and this in turn will help them to respond more sensitively to the child.

For some children who have specific needs that affect their behaviour, other professionals may need to be involved. A child, for example, who has witnessed domestic abuse may have difficulties controlling their anger and so strategies to help this child may have been drawn up by a counsellor or psychologist. When other professionals are involved, it is important to follow their advice and also to share information about how any programmes of support are working.

Assessment practice 7.5   C.P6 C.M4 C.D3

A nursery chain wants to ensure that all adults working in its nurseries understand how best to promote and support children's positive behaviour. They have asked you to explain how you promote children's positive behaviour.

- Describe a range of strategies that you have used to promote and support children's positive behaviour, with reference to children's ages and stages of development.

- Justify, giving examples, the approaches you have used to support and promote children's positive behaviour.

- Evaluate your own effectiveness in promoting and supporting children's behaviour in ways that are appropriate to their ages and stages of development, to include consistent positive role modelling and professional conduct.

Plan
- Am I confident that I understand strategies that promote and support positive behaviour?
- Do I understand the role of the adult in promoting and supporting positive behaviour?

Do
- Have I analysed a range of different approaches to promoting and supporting positive behaviour?
- Am I managing my time effectively?

Review
- Can I justify why I have decided to approach this task in the way that I have?
- Have I evaluated my work and am I confident that it fulfils the set task?

Further reading and resources

Books

Dowling, M. (2014) *Young Children's Personal, Social and Emotional Development*, 4th edition, London: Sage.

Elfer, P., Goldschmied, E. and Selleck, D. (2012) *Key Persons in the Early Years. Building Relationships for Quality Provision in Early Years Settings and Primary Schools*, 2nd edition, Oxon: Routledge.

Garhart Mooney, C. (2009) *Theories of Attachment: An Introduction to Bowlby, Ainsworth, Gerber, Brazelton, Kennell and Klaus*, Minnesota: Redleaf Press.

Lindon, J. (2012) *Understanding Children's Behaviour 0–11 years*, London: Hodder Education.

Websites

www.nurseryworld.co.uk – Nursery World: the website of *Nursery World* magazine. Search for the headline 'Love, love, love' to find the article referenced in this chapter.

www.robertsonfilms.info – Robertson Films: these films are referenced in Section A2 of this chapter.

www.winstonswish.org.uk – Winston's Wish: an organisation that supports children who are facing, or have suffered, a bereavement.

THINK ▶FUTURE

Sussana Agresta

Nursery manager

Building up strong bonds and relationships with families is a real focus for the nursery where Sussana works. The children often come to the nursery as babies and stay until they start school. The staff can spend more time with some of the children than their parents do, as some children are at the nursery for 50 hours a week, 48 weeks of the year. Sussana knows that it is the team's responsibility to make sure that all of the children develop strong bonds with their key person.

By the end of their time at the nursery, many children and their parents view the staff as family members. The focus on relationships is important as they act as a template for children's later friendships. Strong relationships are important in promoting positive behaviour. The nursery staff know children so well that they can quickly identify when they are tired or unwell, and work out how best to support them during transitions and any significant life events.

Focusing your skills

Promoting positive behaviour

Being able to help children show positive behaviour is an important role for adults working with children. Remember though, all children find it easier to show positive behaviour when they are not tired or hungry.

Tips for helping children aged 1–3 years manage their own behaviour

- Give children simple 'at the time' instructions.
- Distract children from situations that are difficult for them.
- Praise children when they show kindness or thoughtfulness.
- Remove temptations, for example, toys children may squabble over or any items of food that may cause them to 'nag'.
- Create an environment and a routine that keep children of this age group busy.

Tips for helping children aged 3–5 years manage their own behaviour

- Praise children when they are showing positive behaviour but always tell them what it is they have done well.
- Remind children about the expectations for behaviour, for example, 'Don't forget to tidy up when you have finished playing'.
- Discuss with children the expectations for their behaviour before they start an activity.
- Encourage children to find their own solutions to possible difficulties that might affect positive behaviour, for example, how they are going to share resources or take turns.

Working with Parents and Others in Early Years

8

Getting to know your unit

Babies and children are surrounded by people who play an important part in their lives. These people may be the child's parents or carers, grandparents or other family members. In addition, many families have other professionals who support them and their children. For example, children may go to more than one setting, such as a childminder and a preschool, or may be supported by health professionals, social workers or outreach workers.

As early years professionals, it is important that you understand all of the different roles that are played by adults in children's lives and also that you work with parents, colleagues and other professionals in a cooperative way.

How you will be assessed

This unit will be assessed by a series of internally assessed tasks set by your tutor. They will include practical tasks that will need to be carried out on placement, and that link to your Practical Evidence Portfolio. Throughout this unit, assessment practice activities will help you work towards your assessment. Completing these activities will not mean that you have achieved a particular grade, but you will have carried out useful research or preparation that will be relevant when it comes to your final assignment.

To achieve the tasks in your assignment, it is important to check that you have met all of the Pass grading criteria. You can do this as you work your way through the assignment. If you are hoping to gain a Merit or Distinction, also make sure that you present the information in your assignment in the style that is required by the relevant assessment criterion. For example, Merit criteria require you to analyse and discuss, and Distinction criteria require you to assess and evaluate.

The assignment set by your tutor will consist of a number of tasks designed to meet the criteria in the table. This is likely to consist of a written assignment but may also include activities such as:

▶ producing a guidance document for new learners about to start a work placement in a setting

▶ writing case studies or giving examples from a placement to demonstrate your understanding

▶ using observations you have carried out during your placement

▶ creating materials that could be used to train new staff.

Assessment criteria

This table shows what you must do in order to achieve a **Pass**, **Merit** or **Distinction** grade, and where you can find activities to help you.

Pass	Merit	Distinction
Learning aim A Explore partnership work with parents in early years settings		
A.P1 Explain the impact of parental rights, views and experiences on partnership work in early years settings. **Assessment practice 8.1**	**A.M1** Assess the influence of parental rights, views and experiences on approaches to developing effective partnerships in early years settings. **Assessment practice 8.1**	**A.D1** Evaluate approaches to effective partnership work with parents in an early years setting and benefits for children and their families. **Assessment practice 8.1, 8.2**
A.P2 Explain approaches for developing effective partnerships with parents in early years settings. **Assessment practice 8.2**	**A.M2** Analyse the importance of partnership work with parents to meet the play, learning and development needs of children in early years settings. **Assessment practice 8.2**	
Learning aim B Explore partnership work with colleagues and other professionals in early years settings		
B.P3 Explain approaches to working in partnership with colleagues and other professionals in early years settings. **Assessment practice 8.3**	**B.M3** Assess the extent to which partnership work with colleagues and other professionals can benefit children and families **Assessment practice 8.3**	**B.D2** Evaluate partnership work with colleagues and other professionals and the extent to which it contributes to meeting the needs of children and their families. **Assessment practice 8.3**
B.P4 Explain the benefits for children and families of working in partnership with colleagues and other professionals in early years settings. **Assessment practice 8.3**		
Learning aim C Demonstrate effective partnership work with parents and others in early years settings to meet the needs of children		
C.P5 Demonstrate effective partnership work with parents in own workplace setting. **Assessment practice 8.4**	**C.M4** Assess own partnership work with colleagues or other professionals and parents in meeting the needs of children in own workplace setting. **Assessment practice 8.4**	**C.D3** Demonstrate effective self-management and professional conduct consistently in partnership work with colleagues or other professionals and parents. **Assessment practice 8.4**
C.P6 Demonstrate effective partnership work with colleagues or other professionals in own workplace setting. **Assessment practice 8.4**		

Getting started

How many professionals who work with children can you name? Do you know what they do and how they work to support families? At the end of this unit, come back to this task and see if you answer the question differently.

A Explore partnership work with parents in early years settings

A1 The impact of parental rights, views and experiences on partnership work

The term 'parent' should be viewed as a very broad one. Although some children do live with both natural parents, many live with a carer who is not their parent. This could include step-parents or others who have parental responsibility for them or who are looking after them. It might also include foster carers, grandparents or staff in residential homes. This section looks at the important role that parents and carers play in children's lives.

Legislation relevant to parental rights and responsibilities

The importance of parents or other carers in children's lives was established and set out in the Children Act 1989 (revised in 2004). It was stated that, wherever possible, children should remain with their parents. Under the act, parents and others who have parental responsibility have the right to make decisions for and about their children in the following areas:

▶ the name of the child

▶ the child's religion

▶ the child's education

▶ the child's medical treatment

▶ where and with whom the child should live

▶ money and property belonging to the child.

Although not stated in the Children Act 2004, there is also an expectation that parents and carers will protect their children and keep them healthy and safe. Parents also have to ensure that children receive education from 5 years of age until the end of **statutory** schooling. If parents do not manage to do this, they may face prosecution and/or lose their powers of parental responsibility under separate legislation.

Key term

Statutory – required by law (statute).

Research

Find out school leaving ages in the UK by going to the UK government website: www.gov.uk.

Then find out more about the expectations that are associated with parental responsibility by visiting the 'Parental rights and responsibilities' page on the Gov.UK website.

Link

Go to Unit 5, Section C2, Table 5.9, where you will find out more information about the Children Act 1989 and 2004.

Children's welfare is paramount

Although you have seen that parents and carers have the right to make particular decisions when it comes to their children, if their actions are not in the interests of the child, such as refusing medical treatment on their behalf, these rights can be suspended. This is because the guiding principle of the Children Act 2004 is that the **welfare** of the child is paramount. When the child's welfare is compromised, parents' or carers' wishes can be overruled.

Key term

Welfare – holistic needs, including health and well-being.

Parental responsibility

The term 'parental responsibility' has legal status and it may apply to people who are not a child's birth parents. Parental responsibility is given automatically to:

▶ the child's birth mother

▶ the child's father, if he is married to the child's mother

▶ the child's father, if he is named on the birth certificate.

Otherwise legal steps will need to be taken for parental responsibility to be accorded to the father. The father can acquire parental responsibility if:

▶ a Parental Responsibility Agreement is made with the mother

▶ he obtains a Parental Responsibility Order from the court

▶ he obtains a Residence Order from the court

▶ he becomes the child's guardian.

Step-parents can also acquire parental responsibility if:

▶ a Parental Responsibility Agreement is made with the agreement of those who have parental responsibility

▶ a Parental Responsibility Order is given by the court when the step-parent is married to the child's mother.

In addition, the local authority can gain parental responsibility if the child is taken into care or there are concerns about the child's welfare.

Other people, such as family members and foster carers, can also gain parental responsibility. Again, this happens through the court and is often given in cases when the child is considered at risk or where the child's parents have died.

Ⅱ PAUSE POINT   Who is automatically given parental responsibility?

Hint   Think about the person who gives birth.

Extend   Explain how having parental responsibility can influence the decisions that are made about a child's life.

Adoption

Where a child has been adopted, all parental responsibility is transferred to the child's adoptive parents. It is important when working with children to know who has parental responsibility and whether there are any Residence Orders or Care Orders in place.

Research

Find out about Victoria Gillick's challenge to her local health authority in a case known as *Gillick v West Norfolk and Wisbech Area Health Authority* (1985). The case centred on the parental right to prevent a local health authority from giving contraception to underage young people.

Parent–child relationships

Professionals, practitioners and teachers come and go, but most parents or carers are a constant presence in their children's lives. It is the parents/carers who know their child well and who support them through happy and sad times. This is why the phrase 'enduring relationship' is used when describing the bond between parents and their children. Parents act as role models and, therefore, children will often develop similar attitudes and values to their parents. Figure 8.1 shows the ways that parents help and support their children.

The bond between parents or carers and children is usually strong, but it is also complex. Many parents will say that they have both strong positive and negative emotions when it comes to their own children. Parents need to be reassured that strong feelings of love, but also anger, are normal.

The recognition that parents play such a pivotal part in children's lives should be shown in every part of your work with parents. It is good practice to listen to their ideas and feelings, and involve them in the provision of their child's education.

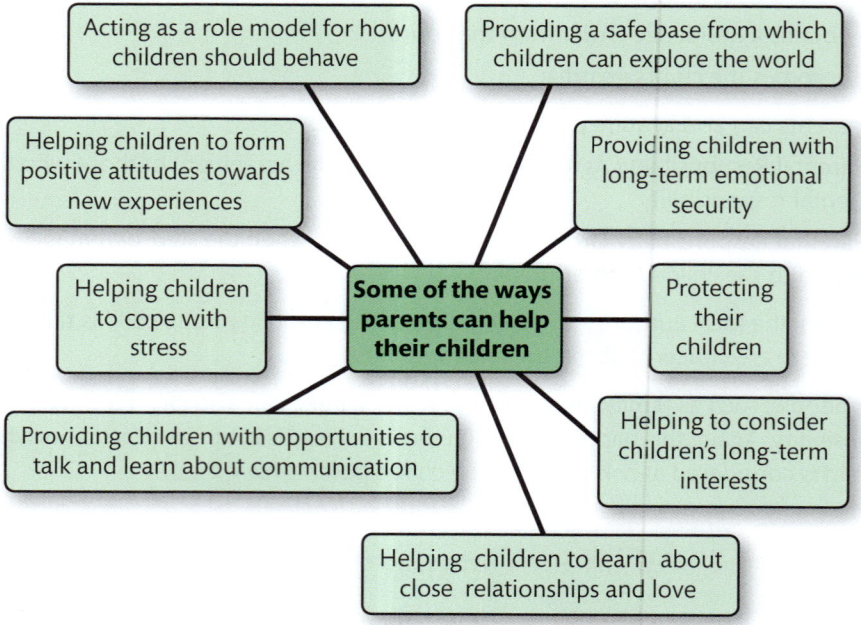

▶ **Figure 8.1:** Some of the ways in which parents help their children

The impact of the home learning experience on the outcome for children

Children learn a variety of attitudes and practical skills from their parents. Parents, therefore, play a huge part in supporting children's emotional development and later in their academic achievements. This has been recognised by educators for a long time, but more recently it has been demonstrated by a piece of research known as the EPPE Project.

The EPPE Project

EPPE stands for the Effective Provision of Pre-School Education (although over time this name has changed to Effective Pre-School, Primary and Secondary Education – EPPSE). Between 1997 and 2003 the project tracked a group of 3,000 children who were 3 years old at the start of the project. The children and their families were selected from a range of socio-economic groups. Many of the children attended some type of preschool education but some stayed at home.

The researchers carried out in-depth studies of the children's histories and then evaluated the home environment and also the preschool environment in cases where children were attending a preschool.

There were many findings from the EPPE project as it reported year on year. A major and quite famous finding was that 'what parents do is more important than who they are'. It found that 'while parents' social class and levels of education were related to child outcomes, the quality of the early years home learning environment (HLE) was more important'.

The Home Learning Environment

The EPPE project evaluated what the researchers called the 'Home Learning Environment'. They found that where parents did some or all of the following activities, the benefits for children were strong:

▶ sharing stories
▶ singing songs and nursery rhymes
▶ painting and drawing
▶ taking children on visits, e.g. to the library or park
▶ letting children play with friends at home
▶ teaching children numbers and the alphabet
▶ playing with numbers and letters.

Effects of the EPPE Project

The EPPE Project has helped professionals realise the importance of parents' involvement in early education. This in turn has meant that more settings are starting to see parents as 'partners' in children's learning. It is now good practice for practitioners and settings to look for ways of encouraging and supporting parents by explaining the type of activities that can help their child.

The study of the same 3,000 children continued until 2008 under the new name of Effective Pre-School, Primary and Secondary Education (EPPSE).

Research

Find out more about the EPPE Project by looking at a summary of the research findings on the Institute of Education website: www.ucl.ac.uk/ioe.

The impact of parents' own experiences

Children's outcomes are believed to be partially linked to parents' own experiences. Where parents have had high levels of education and where their experiences have been positive, they are more likely to pass these attitudes onto their own children. Interestingly, the EPPE Project found that as well as children's home learning environments making an impact on early development, so too did the mother's level of education. In addition, a parent's own upbringing can make a difference to their children's development. A parent who was always read to as a child is more likely to do so with their own children. In the same way, a parent whose own parents encouraged them to try out new things, do their homework and who had high expectations may well pass on these attitudes to their offspring.

How parental views about childhood affect their parenting style

Parents are not all the same. Often, they have very different opinions about what is right for their child and also how children, in general, should be brought up. These views may be based on their culture, lifestyle or own experience of being parented. You will look more at different parenting styles later in this section.

Recognising that parents will have very different views is important because it is easy to fall into the trap of making assumptions. Children coming from different families will have had a range of experiences.

It is worth exploring some typical areas where there are differences in parenting style and looking at the opposing views. Note that many parents will sit somewhere in the middle on some, or all, of these issues. When looking at these areas, it is important to remember that parents like to either be in control or give an amount of control to their children.

▸ **Education** – parents are likely to have different attitudes towards the importance of education. For some parents, formal learning and education in schools is of paramount importance, yet others, for a variety of reasons, may feel differently. For example, some parents feel that schools do not stress the importance of being an individual and others may feel that learning to read, write or study is a waste of time as practical skills are more important.

> **Research**
>
> A growing number of children are being educated by their parents at home. Find out more by visiting the website for a charitable organisation called Education Otherwise™, which supports home education: www.educationotherwise.net.

▸ **Screen time** – some parents may restrict television viewing and tablet or laptop use, or not allow it at all. Other parents may install a screen in their child's bedroom and be happy for them to use it.

▸ **Mealtimes** – some parents want their children to sit down at the table at set mealtimes. Others are happy for their child to eat in front of the television or when they are hungry. Some parents have strong feelings about what their child should eat (for example, a vegetarian diet), whereas others follow their children's own food preferences and may even provide alternative meals.

▸ **Bedtimes and routines** – some parents have set bedtimes for their children. Other families may not prioritise bedtime, allowing children to set their own. In some families, routines are not always established and there may not be fixed times for doing everyday activities such as washing and dressing.

▸ **Gender roles** – some parents choose toys according to the gender of their child. They may be uncomfortable with play that breaks gender stereotypes, for example, boys playing with pushchairs and girls playing with construction toys.

Some parents actively try to make their children play with toys that are not traditionally associated with their gender. Some parents also choose clothes that reinforce traditional gender stereotypes, for example, camouflage clothes for boys and pink fairy dresses for girls. However, some parents actively dislike clothes that reinforce gender stereotypes.

▸ **Attitude to risk** – some parents have a relaxed attitude to health and safety. They may let their children play out of sight or not use safety equipment as long as the child is happy. Meanwhile, other parents are conscious of health and safety, and may not let their child play out of sight or take risks.

▸ Some parents have a bedtime routine with their children, which may include reading a story

❚❚ PAUSE POINT   List three areas where parents may have varying views on how to bring up their children.

Hint   As a child, what were you allowed to do or prevented from doing that may have been different from your friends?

Extend   Consider why it is important for early years settings to be aware of parents' views.

Parenting styles

All of us have had an experience of childhood and being parented. This means that parents will be affected by what has happened to them as children. This experience may have been positive, mixed or even difficult; whatever the experience, it will affect their conscious and subconscious behaviours.

Some parents deliberately try to use different strategies or take a very different approach from that of their parents. Others find that they parent in a very similar fashion to their own parents.

Three broad styles of parenting are traditionally described: authoritarian, permissive and authoritative. If parents do not follow the authoritative style, they often alternate between authoritarian and permissive. This is particularly common where a parent's own parent was authoritarian.

▶ **Authoritarian** – this style of parenting is one where parents may be distant and attempt to limit and control their children. They may not provide explanations for rules and may punish children if they do not conform.

▶ **Permissive** – this style of parenting is one where children are given freedom and there are few boundaries on their behaviours or actions.

▶ **Authoritative** – this style of parenting is one where the parent feels comfortable with their role and is ready to set boundaries, but also negotiate with the child. The parent allows the child some freedom and choice, but only in areas that will not impact on the child's health and well-being.

Although parents are often inconsistent in their own style of parenting, it is thought that overall, children benefit when parents are authoritative. It seems to help children to feel emotionally secure, but also independent and confident.

Mixed styles in families

Of course, when there are two parents and sometimes step-parents involved in parenting, there can be conflicts and differences in approach. This can be a source of conflict for some parents and, in turn, can lead to children not gaining the stability they need.

Parenting classes

Many early years settings and organisations in the community offer parenting classes. These classes are run to help parents feel more confident about their parenting skills. Parents who are confident and equipped with some knowledge about child development often find it easier to cope with the stresses of parenting. The effects on children's development are also positive when parents feel comfortable and confident about their own ability. Parenting classes are sometimes seen as something only for 'failing parents', but many settings now offer these information sessions on activities to support the home learning environment in addition to topics such as sleep, feeding and behaviour. These subjects are often the top issues for parents.

Research

Visit mumsnet, a well-known website that is regularly visited by parents: www.mumsnet.com. Why do you think this website is so popular?

Neglectful

While the three traditional parenting styles are usually used to describe most of the ways that parents respond to their children, there are some parents who are considered not to have their children's interests at heart. In the case of neglectful parents, they may not be able to provide their children with emotional or physical security. Children may not be fed, washed or provided with appropriate clothing. Where children's safety is at risk, neglectful parenting becomes a child protection issue.

Link

See Unit 5, where child abuse and neglect are covered in more detail.

Disengaged

Disengaged parents may not know about or be interested in furthering their children's development. They may not spend enough time interacting with their children, encouraging their skills or engaging in any of the home learning activities that you looked at earlier in this section. There are many reasons why parents may be disengaged, including depression, social isolation and hostility towards educational establishments.

Factors that may make parents emotionally unavailable

Most parents or carers form strong attachments with their children and are able to cope with the stress of being a parent. However, there are some things that may interfere with establishing this security and strong attachment. It is worth remembering that being a parent or carer is not just about providing for children's physical and care needs. It is also about being **emotionally available**.

There are many factors that prevent parents from being emotionally available and responding appropriately to their children. For some parents, not being able to respond to their children will be a short-term difficulty, but for other parents, this may be a longer-term issue. You will now look at these factors.

Depression

Depression changes a parent's state of mind as there is a chemical imbalance in the brain. When a parent is depressed, it is hard for them to create the conditions for strong attachment. They may not 'feel' the full range of emotions and so give the warmth, love and energy that babies and young children require. The effects of this on babies and children can be significant, particularly in terms of speech and language and also emotional development.

There are many causes of depression, including relationship breakdown and postnatal depression. Depression is often something that people find difficult to talk about or get help for. As depression is very common, some settings provide information about mental health services so that parents can seek appropriate help. Figure 8.2 shows the common signs of depression.

Mental health issues are still seen as **taboo** and some parents are scared that social services will remove their children. This is highly unlikely, but it remains a perception among parents.

Key terms

Emotionally available – able to respond, support and deal with the emotions of others.

Taboo – a custom that prevents discussion of a particular practice or association with a person, place or thing.

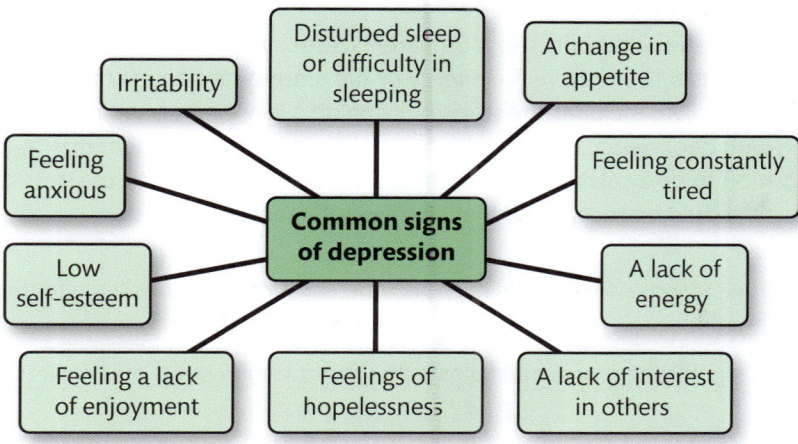

▶ **Figure 8.2:** Common signs of depression

Postnatal depression

Postnatal depression can occur in women in the weeks following birth. Many women know that they are not feeling 'right' but do not seek help. They may go through the motions of caring for their baby, but struggle to bond. This will cause difficulties with attachment for both the child and the mother.

Once recognised, postnatal depression responds well to treatment, but if left unchecked it can have long-term effects on the child and parent.

Substance misuse and addiction

Alcohol and drugs affect the chemical reactions in the brain. This means that parents who are substance misusers and/or addicts may not be able to parent their children effectively. In the case of addiction, the parent's focus may not be on the child, but on securing the substance or alcohol. Substance misuse and addiction is often the reason why children will be removed from a parent.

Relationship breakdown

Where there is a relationship breakdown between parents, especially one that is bitter and contested, it is likely to create stress, tension and, in some cases, depression. Parents may also be so involved in their own emotions that they may overlook or not be able to respond to their children.

In addition, there can be effects on the relationship between the absent parent and the child. If children do not have regular contact with a parent, there is a danger that the period of absence will result in the child 'detaching' from the parent.

Research

Find out what help is available to support families where there is relationship breakdown by visiting the website for the National Association of Child Contact Centres. You can access this website at www.naccc.org.uk.

Illness

A serious illness, such as cancer, can mean that parents, however much they wish to, may not be physically well enough to give their children sufficient time and energy. Where there is serious illness in the family, this may also mean that the physically fit parent may be preoccupied in caring for the parent who is unwell. They will probably also be coping with their own emotions.

Other factors, including low income

Any event or situation that puts stress on parents, especially over a long period, may mean that parents may not have the energy or the emotional stamina to be available for their children. This includes the stress of living on a low income, which in turn is associated with depression. Parents who have had a close bereavement may again not be in a position to be available for their children. Although the effects of stress can be short term, it should be recognised that stress is a trigger for depression.

How approaches in the setting may differ from those of parents

In Section A2, you will look at some of the barriers that can affect **cooperative** working and effective partnerships with parents. In addition to these, it is important to recognise that there may be times when the approach of an early years setting is different from the approach taken by parents. As you have seen, parents have a variety of different views and approaches to things such as screen time, mealtimes and risk. In some cases, parents may look at the approach that an early years setting takes to working with their child and feel less confident in their own parenting ability. This could impact on the relationship between the early years professional and the parent, which in turn could affect a child's progress in terms of their learning and development.

For example, parents who struggle to get a child to eat at the table may question their parenting skills when they find out that their child happily eats at the table in the nursery. Similarly, a preschool may report that a child in the setting never has tantrums, but when at home with a parent, the child often has tantrums. It is important, therefore, to be aware that parents' and carers' confidence can be affected by your actions. Make sure you look for ways in which parents can be supported, if they so wish. They could be invited to spend time in the setting so that some of the strategies that early years professionals in the setting use can be shown and explained.

Current research on the value of parental involvement

Through the EPPE Project's research, you have seen that parental involvement plays an important role in children's learning. To date, the EPPE Project is the key piece of research that is cited in the UK in relation to parental involvement. The project not only recognised the role of parents, but also concluded that early years settings had a role in sharing information with parents and supporting learning at home.

In England, the EPPE Project influenced the early years curriculum. There is now a statutory requirement for early years settings to provide information about activities that support home learning. This means that early years settings will make suggestions for play opportunities and activities that parents might like to do at home. For children who are due to join the reception class, this might include simple board games where children roll the dice so that they can practise the skills of recognising numbers and moving a counter accordingly. In order to help children recognise sounds in words, parents might be encouraged to play games such as 'I Spy' or games that encourage children to listen such as musical statues.

In addition to the EPPE Project, governments have, over the years, published research reports looking at parental involvement and its effectiveness in supporting children's education programmes. While no single research stands out in the way that the EPPE Project does, the conclusions of various research reports seem to suggest that parental involvement is key to supporting children's development.

> **Research**
>
> You may be interested in the research report entitled 'Review of best practice in parental engagement', which documents research findings about parental involvement. Download the report by visiting www.gov.uk and typing the title of the report into the search field.

Assessment practice 8.1   A.P1   A.M1   A.D1

A children's centre is organising an inset training day for new members of the team about working in partnership with parents. You have been asked to provide an overview about the role of parents in children's lives and the importance of collaborative working.

Your overview should:
- explain how parental rights, views and experiences affect how early years settings work in partnership with parents
- assess, using examples, how parental rights, views and experiences influence the quality of partnership with parents
- evaluate the benefits of effective partnership work with parents on children and their families

Plan
- Have I understood how parental rights affect current practice in early years?
- How long do I need to collate and analyse the information required for the task?

Do
- Have I researched theories and current practice in relation to partnership working with parents?
- Am I managing my time effectively?

Review
- Have I used appropriate examples to support my reasoning?
- Have I evaluated my work and am I confident that it fulfils the set task?

A2 Approaches to effective partnerships with parents

As you have seen, parents can make a significant contribution to their children's development. This means it is good practice for early years professionals to work in partnership with parents. This requires a range of skills as well as a good understanding of some of the issues involved. In this section, you look at approaches to working effectively with parents.

Responsibility of early years professionals to work in partnership with parents

Some of your work with parents will be shaped by the statutory early years framework that is being used in the setting, along with relevant policies and legal requirements. A good example of this is the legal requirement in England for early years settings to carry out a progress check on 2 year olds and a duty to inform parents about the result of the assessment. In the same way, the SEND (Special Educational Needs and Disability) code of practice in England is clear that children cannot be referred to professionals without parental consent.

When it comes to information sharing, our work with parents also needs to comply with the Data Protection Act 1998 (the act is covered in more detail later in this section and in Section A1 of Unit 11). Such requirements provide clear directives as to our professional responsibilities when working with children and their parents. It is therefore important when you work in an early years setting to read policies carefully and to ensure that you understand their implications when it comes to working with parents.

While you have professional responsibilities towards parents, you also have a duty of care towards children. Occasionally, there can be a conflict between the two. In such cases, the welfare of children outweighs the rights of parents.

> **Theory into practice**
>
> In your work placement, what are your professional responsibilities towards parents in relation to:
> - reporting accidents
> - concerns about children's progress
> - data protection?

Recognising the limitations of your responsibilities

While there are requirements to work in partnership with parents, you also have to be aware of your limitations. This is particularly important where there are developmental concerns about a child or where parents are struggling with caring for their children. Where a child or parent would benefit from specialist input or advice, it is important that you refer parents to these services. Otherwise there is a danger that you may give inaccurate information to parents by mistake. This could prevent families from gaining the correct support they need and potentially cause harm to a child. This could lead to a breakdown in trust between the family and the setting or a service to which they have been referred.

Friendly, not friends

You should be friendly with parents but you cannot become their friends. This is because it clouds your relationship with them and may mean that the needs of children stop being your main focus. This is particularly important to remember if a parent tells you that they are not coping.

> **Case study**
>
> ### Friendly or friends?
>
> Alun is working as an assistant in a nursery. He has good relationships with the children's parents. He gets on particularly well with one parent who is having personal relationship problems. After listening to the parent's problems, Alun gives her advice about what she should say to her partner. The following week, the parent complains to the nursery manager, saying that because of Alun's advice, her partner has now left.
>
> **Check your knowledge**
>
> 1 How has Alun crossed the line between being friendly and friends?
> 2 Why was it inappropriate for Alun to give the parent relationship advice?
> 3 Find out the name of an organisation that specialises in relationship counselling.

The benefits of good communication

Communicating well with parents and carers is central to developing a genuine partnership with them. Every practitioner needs to have strong communication skills, not just the individuals who regularly work with specific children. This is because parents may ask a question to a member of staff who is not the child's key person.

It is important that communication is seen as an ongoing process as it is needed for relationships to be maintained.

The benefits of effective communication are significant and include the following.

▸ Parents will find it easier to trust the staff and so separation may be easier.

▸ Parents are more likely to exchange and share significant information with you that may help you to meet children's needs.

▸ Good communication helps parents and staff to discuss children's development and allows parents to play a part in the tracking of their child's development.

▸ Staff and parents can find it easier to ask questions or make comments without being misunderstood.

▸ Parents are able to become engaged with the care, learning and development of their children. This can have a positive effect on children's achievement.

▸ Good communication reduces the likelihood of misunderstandings and allows for quick clarification if they do arise.

▸ The setting is more likely to receive honest feedback that can inform its work and policies.

▸ Parents are more likely to access information that has been signposted.

▸ Everyone benefits from having a more harmonious environment.

Ⅱ PAUSE POINT Identify five benefits of effective communication with parents.

Hint Think about different types of information that need to be shared between the setting and parents.

Extend Discuss how effective communication with parents impacts on the development and well-being of a child.

The features of good communication

Many people associate communicating with parents with verbal methods such as talking and writing. Interestingly, communication with parents is not always about words. Non-verbal communication such as smiling, gestures and nods is also important. Quite often the starting point for relationships is the non-verbal communication that takes place. Through your body language, facial expressions and gestures, parents will come to a conclusion about whether or not they can trust you and whether or not they are valued.

There are some universal features that are important for good communication and **interpersonal skills**. Table 8.1 shows the key features of good communication and why they are important.

▸ **Table 8.1:** The key features of good communication skills

Feature	Why is it important?
Warmth/**empathy**	It encourages parents to talk to you and develop a relationship with you
Sincerity/honesty	It encourages parents to trust you
Interest	It is essential if parents are to share information with you
Active listening	It is essential if parents are to feel that their ideas, emotions and comments are being taken on board. It is also important as it helps you to understand parents' needs and feelings

Key terms

Empathy – the ability to feel or understand the emotions of others.

Interpersonal skills – the skills required for building relationships.

▶ This practitioner is showing warmth and interest. How can these things help you to build and maintain a professional relationship with parents?

Communicating appropriately and with empathy

Table 8.2 shows some of the many ways that you can communicate with parents. The 'comments' column shows things that you need to be aware of when using the different types of communication.

▶ **Table 8.2:** Ways to communicate with parents

Communication methods	Comments
Face-to-face interactions	• Useful for sharing and giving information as you can see the other person's reaction • May not be best for conveying complex information that someone else will need time to consider or see written down, e.g. in order to make decisions
Phone	• Can be difficult to interpret the other person's reactions and assess whether they have understood the meaning • Choice of words and tone is very important • Allow for quick responses • In some situations, notes should be taken at the time of a call so a record can be made. In this case, remember to record the date and time of the call
Sign language	• British Sign Language is a recognised language and allows someone to communicate fully if they are not able to hear
Letters and memos	• Useful as they allow the reader to take time and absorb the information • Likely to be kept after for future reference • Style and tone must be considered carefully to avoid misunderstandings • Important to check for spelling mistakes
Emails	• Useful if a more relaxed style is needed • Not everyone will have access to a computer or will store/print out emails: you cannot be sure the other person will keep a record of the email
Text messages	• Useful for an instant update for parents • Tone and language must remain professional • Only a dedicated work mobile should be used to send text messages
Audio-visual recordings	• Can be used to help parents 'see' or 'hear' their children and so provide a way of sharing information with them

Face-to-face communication and body language

The majority of communication with most parents happens face to face. Most parents will come and look around a setting before joining, for example, and many, but not all, will drop off and collect their children. Parents are also likely to come in if they have any issues. Understanding active ways in which you can communicate effectively is therefore important, as is your body language and attitude. You will now look at specific ways that help you to communicate effectively.

▶ **Proximity** – this is about the distance between you and the person you are communicating with. If you are too far away from another adult it is hard to demonstrate interest and warmth, but if you are too close it may be uncomfortable. Note that there are cultural differences as well as personal differences that affect how much space should be left between you and another person. You need to be observant and notice when you are too close or too far away from someone. For example, the person you are talking to may try to move back a little bit from you or they might move a bit closer.

▶ **Orientation** – this relates to your body's position. Standing or sitting slightly at an angle when communicating with adults is helpful as it means that both of you can break off eye contact if you want to and it allows the communicating style to be less direct.

▶ **Posture** – this is also important, whether you are standing or sitting. Leaning forwards slightly in a chair shows, for example, that you are interested, while leaning backwards may make the other person think that you are bored.

▶ **Smiling** – it is important to smile when you are communicating with parents as this is usually seen as a sign of warmth and interest.

▶ **Facial expression** – this is a strong element in communication. People can show a lot of feelings through their faces and a good communicator will not only notice other people's facial expressions, but will be aware of their own. Facial expressions can show warmth, empathy, interest and signs of listening.

▶ **Eye contact** – eyes are powerful tools when interacting with someone and they can show interest, sincerity and warmth. Eye contact is powerful, so it is important not to stare or be too intense as this can feel threatening. The level of eye contact that is appropriate can vary from culture to culture and it is important to be sensitive to this.

▶ **Tone of voice** – this is stronger than the words that are actually said, both in face-to-face interactions and in communication over the phone. Tone can say a lot about what someone is really thinking. Good communicators use warm tones and do this by thinking warm thoughts. Smiling as you talk on the telephone will also give you a warmer tone.

▶ **Active listening** – the term 'active listening' is often used to describe the way in which good communicators do not just listen, but they think about what they are hearing. They also closely observe body language, gestures and other signals that are sent out by the child or adult. Active listening requires that you give your full attention to the other person and focus not just on what they are saying, but *how* they say it. Active listening is essential when encouraging young children's speech and also when dealing with potentially difficult situations with other adults.

Reflect

How good a listener are you? Try spending some time listening to a friend without interrupting or changing the topic of conversation.

▶ Parents often drop their child off at the setting. What is the practitioner on the right doing to communicate effectively with this mother and her child?

Barriers to effective communication

Although the principles of communication are straightforward, there are many potential barriers to communication. It is important that you are able to recognise these barriers and find ways of overcoming them. Figure 8.3 shows some of the key barriers.

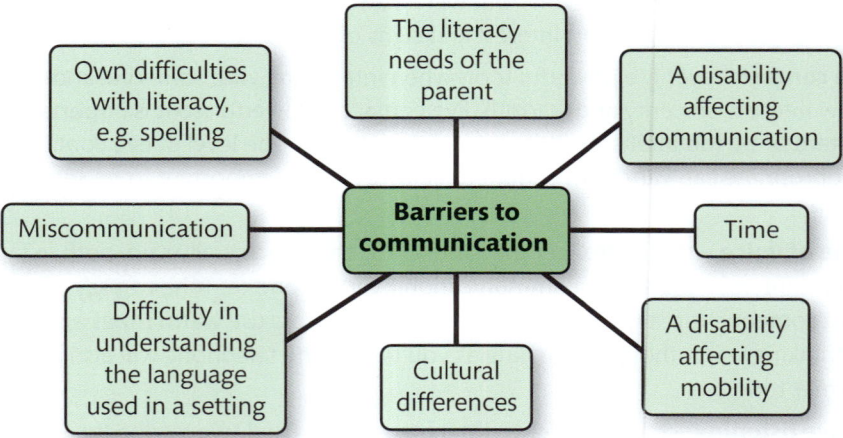

▶ **Figure 8.3:** Barriers to communication

Strategies to overcome barriers to effective communication

It is important that when you identify possible barriers to communication, you look for ways to overcome them. This needs everyone in the setting to have a can-do approach. In particular, it is important to avoid making assumptions about a parent's level of understanding. You must always be respectful and you should be prepared to be flexible in your approach. It is also important to consider the individual needs of parents and/or carers and you should take time to reflect on your interactions with them to consider whether the ways in which you communicate could be improved.

Table 8.3 shows the common barriers to communication listed in Figure 8.3 and the ways in which they may be overcome.

▶ **Table 8.3:** Strategies for overcoming communication barriers

Barrier	Strategies for overcoming the barrier
Limited time with the parents and/or carers or they do not drop off and pick up their children	• Use home–setting books • Email parents and/or carers • Phone parents and/or carers • Hold information sessions at flexible times, e.g. evenings or weekends • Update the setting's website with news, if relevant
The parent(s) and/or carer(s) has/have a disability affecting communication	• Invite a signer to support the parent and/or carer • Find out how to meet the parent's/carer's needs, e.g. better lighting, larger print or speaking more clearly • Check that the setting complies with the Disability Discrimination Act 2005
The parent(s) and/or carer(s) has/have a disability affecting mobility	• Choose a place that suits the needs of the parent and/or carer • Find out how to meet the parent's/carer's needs, e.g. adjust the height of chairs, help with doors, provide ramps • Check that the setting complies with the Disability Discrimination Act 2005
The parent(s) and/or carer(s) may have difficulty in understanding the language used in a setting	• Provide an interpreter or invite the parent and/or carer to bring a friend to act as interpreter • Translate key documents • Use information and communication technology, such as translator pens or welcome cards • Look for local support to help you, e.g. local authority teams with ethnic and minority support
The literacy needs of the parent(s) and/or carer(s)	• Do not assume that all parents and/or carers are comfortable reading and writing • Offer to fill in forms without embarrassing parents/carers • Look for ways of presenting information orally
Own difficulties with literacy, e.g. spelling	• Ask a sympathetic colleague to check documents such as letters • Use a dictionary/spellcheck • Consider getting further help with your literacy
Cultural differences in communication style, e.g. choice of language, proximity, eye contact	• Respect that people communicate in different ways and use different styles • Be sensitive, and if and when appropriate, adapt your own style of communication to reflect that used by the parent and/or carer
Miscommunication	• Clarify meaning as soon as possible • Apologise for any misunderstanding, if appropriate • Reflect on how miscommunication can be avoided in future, e.g. by avoiding educational jargon or thinking about the tone of your writing

Ⅱ **PAUSE POINT**   Identify five barriers to communicating with parents.

> Hint

Think about why a parent and/or carer may not be able to understand what has been written or what is being said.

> Extend

Using examples, discuss the importance of finding practical solutions to communication barriers.

Strategies for building effective relationships with parents

Good relationships with parents and carers do not just 'happen'. They require thought, skill and reflection. In this section, you will look at practical ways in which you can work effectively with parents. Note that parents can be anyone with parental responsibility or who has a special role in the child's life. This may include grandparents or foster carers.

When parents or carers have strong relationships with their child's key person and other practitioners within the setting, they are likely to feel more confident about leaving their child with you. This will help when settling the child in and supporting separation. They are also more likely to share information with you, which can be used to ensure that the child's individual needs are met. This allows for continuity of care between the home and childcare setting. Parents who have strong relationships with staff are also more likely to feel comfortable about asking questions. Finally, many early years curricula, such as the Early Years Foundation Stage (EYFS) in England, now expect early years professionals to provide information to parents so that they can support their child's development at home. This is difficult to achieve unless parents and practitioners have a good working relationship.

Partnerships with parents vary from setting to setting according to the type of setting and ages of the children. However, the following approaches are often used.

Shared working

Shared working is the concept of parents and settings working closely together. This approach is considered to be best practice in early years. Many settings will do the following things to achieve shared working.

▶ **Key person approach** – a key person has responsibility for the emotional well-being of a child and will have a close relationship with them. They should also develop a strong relationship with parents. When using the key person approach, the key person should greet the parent and the child, and pass on any important information to the parent. In the past, the key person in some settings took on a record-keeping role, but it is now understood that in order to prevent babies and young children from being harmed by separation, they need a strong substitute relationship.

▶ **Open-door policy** – many settings operate an open-door policy. This means that parents can come into the setting at any time to be with their child or discuss anything they wish with staff members.

▶ **Progress reports** – most settings have times when they meet with parents to talk about their child's progress. This might be during the day or in the evening.

▶ **Stay and play** – some settings offer stay-and-play sessions where parents with younger children can get to know the setting or where parents who have a little time can stay and play with their children before leaving them.

Developing a trusting partnership

It is important that quite quickly, practitioners and parents build up a trusting partnership. One of the main ways in which this takes place is through accurate information sharing. It is good practice for parents to be given updates on their children's progress, but for a trusting relationship to take place, parents need to be given accurate information.

▶ Stay-and-play sessions are great opportunities for parents to see what their children are doing. They also help staff and parents to get to know each other

---

Case study

The importance of accurate information sharing

Freddie is 2 years old and has been in the preschool for 3 months. His key person has always reassured his mother that his language development is typical for his age. His mother continues to have some concerns though because she has seen that other children of a similar age are using more words and are more interested in communicating. During a routine progress check with the health visitor, it turns out that Freddie's language is not typical for his age and the health visitor

suggests that he may need additional support. The next day Freddie's mother asks the key person why this has not been picked up before. The key person says she did realise that Freddie's language was delayed, but that she did not want to upset his mother.

Check your knowledge

1 How might Freddie's mother be feeling?
2 Why might Freddie's mother no longer trust what the key person says?
3 Why is it important for parents to be given accurate information?

How to exchange and share information safely

In order to work effectively with children, a lot of information is shared between parents and early years settings. This includes important information such as known medical conditions, allergies and phone numbers to be used in the event of an emergency. There are also times when parents share information that is particularly personal or sensitive, such as when parents split up or where there are ongoing difficulties with older siblings. Every early years setting has policies and procedures in place in order to maintain the confidentiality of personal information that is shared. In addition, early years settings have to comply with the Data Protection Act 1998. The act covers computer records as well as handwritten records. You will look at the purpose and key principles of the Data Protection Act later in this section.

As well as ensuring that sensitive information is kept confidential, it is also important to ensure that information you give to parents is accurate and will not cause any health and safety issues. A nursery might, for example, share with parents that their child enjoys water play and suggest that they could do this at home. It is important for them to let parents know that this should always be a supervised activity to prevent any risk of drowning.

Case study

Sharing information safely

Anna is a student working in the baby room of a nursery. After feeding a baby who has a long-term medical condition, she is told to log the amount of feed that the baby has taken and to note how much medication was given. She forgets to give the medication but later writes down that it has been given.

The next day, she hears that the baby was taken to hospital in the night.

Check your knowledge

1 How might Anna's actions have compromised this child's safety?

2 Why is it important for information to be shared accurately with parents?

3 Explain the importance of parents being able to trust early years settings.

How to provide information to support children's development at home

Parents play an important role in their children's lives. The EYFS framework and other early years frameworks recognise this by requiring early years settings to encourage parents to support their child's development and learning at home. Early years settings do this by telling parents about the types of play and activities that their child has enjoyed and by giving them ideas of how they can build on these at home. Some early years settings also have displays and share leaflets that have suggestions about books and games that will be helpful for children's development.

Support must be provided sensitively so that parents do not feel that they are being judged or criticised. This is one reason why strong relationships and good communication with parents is important. When providing information to support children's development at home, it is important to think about the following.

▸ **Knowledge base** – parents may have different levels of knowledge about child development and the importance of play. For a parent who is well informed, being told what they already know may come across as patronising. It is therefore worth talking to parents to find out how much they already know and what they are already doing to support their child's development.

- **Spare time** – some parents lead very busy lives and they may not have much spare time. Again, through discussion with parents, you can make suggestions that fit with their lives and are realistic.

- **Interests** – suggestions for activities and games are likely to work better if they are based on what children and their parents already enjoy doing, This means that it is good practice to find out from parents about their child at home and what they do together.

- **Sharing feedback** – wherever possible, it is helpful if parents are able to share information about how any suggested activities have worked. This means that they can be tweaked or built on in the early years setting. You can also learn about the types of activity parents and their child have most enjoyed, and, using this information, make more relevant suggestions. Sharing how things have gone can also be motivating for parents.

Ways to encourage parents to engage in their child's play, learning and development

There are a number of practical ways that early years settings can work with parents to support home learning. Many early years settings try a range of strategies.

- **Information sessions** – many settings hold sessions where parents can learn about aspects such as managing sleep, choosing schools or the early years curriculum.

- **Lending toys, resources and books** – some settings lend parents toys, games and books to use at home. This helps parents who may not know what to buy to support their child or who may not have the money to do so.

- **Leaflets, DVDs and other articles** – many settings put out a range of information that parents can take home or borrow.

- **Discussions** – it is a requirement for settings using the EYFS framework in England, and also good practice in other countries, for the key person to discuss with parents ways of supporting their child's progress at home. They might share activities that the child has enjoyed and benefited from in the setting.

> **Theory into practice**
>
> Find out what initiatives your work placement setting has introduced to support working with parents.

Parental involvement

In addition to sharing information and resources with parents, it is also good practice for early years settings to involve parents in the life and work of the setting. The following activities are common ways to do this.

- **Volunteer opportunities** – many settings encourage parents to act as volunteers. For some parents, being a volunteer helps them to develop a new career. Volunteer opportunities may include cooking with children, helping out in the office or fundraising.

- **Parent committees** – some settings are managed and run by parents and others will have a parent committee that supports the work of the setting by giving feedback and/or raising funds. Parent committees help early years settings to stay in touch with parents and ensure that the setting is genuinely meeting children's needs.

- **Social events** – social events can be linked to fundraising or they can simply encourage families and staff to get to know each other. It is important to vary the type of events and hold them at a range of times so that more families can join in.

▶ **'Bring a grandparent or friend' day** – parents are important in children's lives and so too are many grandparents. An event that encourages grandparents into the setting can help practitioners to meet and talk to children's extended family and friends.

Factors that impact on the participation of families in settings and how to overcome them

There are many reasons why not all parents will wish to work in partnership with you. Although this may be disappointing, it is important to remember that it is totally within parents' rights not to engage.

Understanding the reasons why parents are not always able to participate can sometimes help to overcome the barriers. Usually this occurs, as you have seen, through good communication skills and stronger relationships between parents and staff, especially the key person–parent relationship.

Case study

Coping with learning difficulties

Alessie is a single parent with learning difficulties. Social services have been supporting her since the birth of her son, Jamie, 2 years ago. Over the past few months, Alessie has found it hard to care for Jamie who is an active and impulsive 2-year-old child. Concerns have been raised about his welfare.

At a recent case conference, it was decided that Alessie could continue to have care of Jamie as long as he continued to attend nursery regularly. Alessie is worried about taking Jamie to the nursery. She has told her social worker that everyone is bound to think she

is a bad mother. She is also worried that she will not understand or cope with forms that have to be filled in. Her own experiences of education were not good as she was bullied at school. The social worker goes with Alessie and Jamie to the nursery for the first time.

Check your knowledge

1 What are the key factors that might affect Alessie's participation in the setting?

2 Explain what the setting will need to do in order to help Alessie participate.

3 Why will it be important for Jamie's key person to establish a trusting relationship with Alessie?

Time

Today, many parents work, which means that they may not be able to drop off and collect their children from settings. They may not have time to read books or diaries that are sent between home and the setting or to volunteer to help. It is important not to assume that parents are just not interested.

If time is the issue, you may have to work around parents' needs and times. This may mean more flexible meeting times or more communication using phone and email.

Theory into practice

Many day care nurseries have working parents who may not have much time. Find out the strategies that nurseries use to communicate and work in partnership with parents. For example, you could ask a key person how they maintain contact with parents and whether they do things such as using a home setting book.

Confidence

Some parents may not feel confident in early years settings. This might be because they do not feel welcome or because they have had a previous poor experience. Some dads in particular can feel that they do not belong in what is sometimes a female-dominated environment.

It is useful to make sure that parents who come for the first time are warmly greeted and time is taken to put them at ease. It is also important for all-female settings to look for ways to make dads feel welcome. Some settings have 'dads' days' or run social events and information sessions aimed at dads.

Literacy

It is always important to remember that not all parents can read and write easily. Some parents may worry that they may be asked to do something they are not comfortable with, for example, fill in a form or read a book to their child.

Reflect

Think about how you communicate information in your placement setting – is all of the information written down? Could you use photos or video clips as well? Think also about involving outreach workers who may be able to signpost basic skills classes.

Expectations

You cannot assume that parents always have the same expectations as you. Some parents may not understand that the setting does want to involve them. They may think that only 'favourite' parents are able to participate. They may also be new to the area or have joined the setting during the year and may not know anyone. Some parents do not think that they 'belong', as settings are run by professionals. They may also not know what is expected of them and so unless settings make an effort to regularly talk to parents about how they can become involved, the participation of some parents in the setting may be low.

Settings should be a welcoming environment. Think about the signs in your placement setting. Are there many 'do not' notices around? Good key person relationships can help parents feel more welcome and key persons can personally invite a parent to join in with activities.

Reflect

How friendly and welcoming is your placement? What makes it welcoming? Are there any ways that you feel the environment could be improved?

Legislation, policies and procedures relevant to confidentiality and data protection

If you are working well with parents, they are likely to share information that is quite personal. This may be written information, such as admission forms, but also comments on a day-to-day basis.

Unless there is a child protection issue, such information has to be treated as highly confidential. If you gossip about what parents have said or talk about it to others in the setting who do not need to know, you are likely to endanger your relationship with the parents. You are also likely to make the parents mistrustful of other professionals in the future. Most settings will have a policy on confidentiality and you should always follow it. Breaching confidentiality is usually a disciplinary matter.

You saw earlier in this section that information needs to be shared and that this needs to be done safely. Parents and children have rights under the Data Protection Act 1998 and it is therefore important that you understand the scope of the act.

The Data Protection Act 1998

The keeping of records, storing of data and passing on of information is strictly regulated by the Data Protection Act 1998. The act covers both paper-based and electronic records. It is designed to prevent confidential and personal information from being passed on without a person's consent.

The act originally applied only to information that was stored on computers, but it has been updated to include any personal information that is stored, either on paper or on screen. Under the act, organisations that collect and store information must register with the Information Commissioner's Office. Anyone processing information must also comply with the eight enforceable principles of practice shown in Figure 8.4. In terms of working with children and their families, this means that most information that is collected and held in an early years setting will be confidential. It also means that you need to have systems in place to make sure that information is up to date and that access is secure.

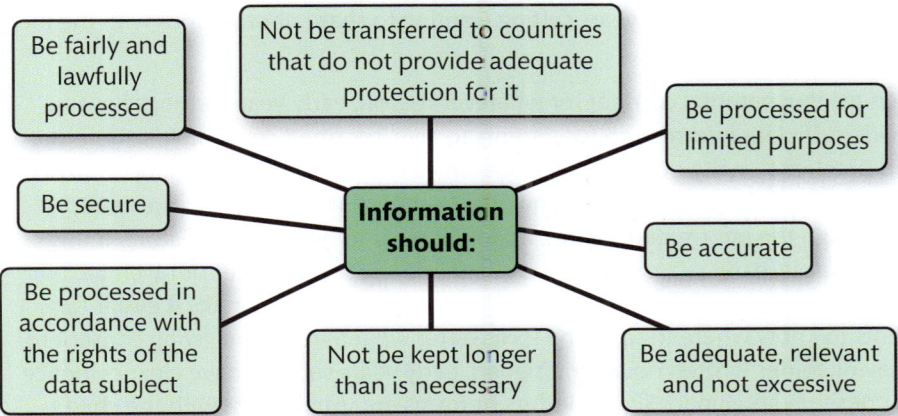

Be fairly and lawfully processed

Not be transferred to countries that do not provide adequate protection for it

Be processed for limited purposes

Be secure

Information should:

Be accurate

Be processed in accordance with the rights of the data subject

Not be kept longer than is necessary

Be adequate, relevant and not excessive

▶ **Figure 8.4:** The eight enforceable principles of data protection

---

Research

For more information about the Data Protection Act 1998, visit the website for the Information Commissioner's Office: https://ico.org.uk.

Case study

Maintaining confidentiality

Erdem's mother wants to invite a child to Erdem's birthday party. She cannot find the phone number of the child although Erdem and the child have played at each other's houses before. Erdem's mother asks Janice, the nursery assistant, whether she could just pop into the office and get the phone number for her. Janice can see that this is a genuine request as Erdem's mother does know the other parent's address.

Check your knowledge

1 What should the nursery assistant do?

2 Explain why it is important that confidentiality is upheld.

3 Consider what Janice should say to Erdem's mother.

Ways to obtain parental consent for referrals and sharing of information

There are many times when early years settings need to gain parental consent. These include going on outings, carrying out observations and assessments, and giving medication.

Parental consent is also needed if you wish to seek the advice of other professionals about an individual child's development or if you wish the child to be referred to another service such as the speech and language team or educational psychology. In most situations, once parents understand why you wish to share information, or to gain a referral about their children, they will willingly provide their consent. However, it is always worth remembering that parents can choose not to agree. Some parents refuse consent because they do not accept that their child has a need to see another professional, while others may wish to organise the referral themselves.

There are other occasions when parental consent may be required. This might include students on placement wanting to use information about a specific child in their research, or the early years setting wanting to share photographs with the local newspaper.

When gaining parental consent for whatever reason, early years settings have to provide sufficient information for parents to give informed consent. It is therefore good practice to write down the reasons why a course of action is being proposed, the benefits to the child and also any other benefits. It is also good practice to talk through the information before asking parents to provide a signature. If this is not possible, early years settings send out information by letter or by email, but still require a parental signature. A form is usually provided to make it easier for parents to know where to sign. The form states what parents are giving consent to. By having things written down and signed, early years settings have clear evidence that consent was gained. Signed letters or forms are usually kept with the child's records, or, in the case of an outing, in a folder in which all documents relating to the outing are kept.

> **Link**
>
> See Unit 5 for more information about child protection and safeguarding.

While it is a requirement to respect parents' wishes and for settings to gain consent before sharing information or referring a child to another service, there is an exception when there is a child protection issue. In the case where a child's immediate well-being or physical safety is at stake, an early years setting can contact other professionals. This is quite rare and if it takes place, early years settings will follow their child protection and safeguarding procedures.

II PAUSE POINT

Give an example of a situation where an early years setting may seek the written consent of a parent to share information about a child.

Hint Think about other professionals and the information they may need to know.

Extend Consider the impact on the relationship between an early years setting and a parent where information is shared inappropriately without parental consent.

How to respect the emotional attachment that influences parents' choices and behaviours

When looking at how to work with parents it is important to understand the deep emotional attachment that most of them have with their children. Many of their actions, choices, behaviours and concerns are influenced by this attachment. This section looks at attachment from a parent's perspective.

Link

Go to Unit 1, Section D2, and Unit 7, Section A2, to find more information about the importance of attachment.

Separation

Parents are instinctively wary of being separated from their children. This is particularly true when children are under 4 or 5 years old. The actions outlined below show some of the behaviours rooted in attachment that parents may exhibit.

▶ **Goodbye rituals** – some parents need to know that they are doing the best for their child right up until the point that they leave them at a setting. They may take the child's coat off and hang it up for them before being ready to hand the child over. Other parents may need their child to give them a certain number of kisses or goodbyes. Goodbye rituals are important to parents and should be respected.

▶ **Rushing off** – some parents cope with separation by rushing off quickly. This is not a sign that they do not care, but is usually because they want the separation to be over quickly. Show parents that you understand this is important before you suggest that their child needs a slightly longer goodbye.

▶ **Staying behind** – some parents cope with separation by staying for as long as they can or even not leaving the premises. Although this might not be helpful for the child, it is an attachment behaviour and you will need to be empathetic if you feel that this behaviour needs moderating. Some settings support parents who are finding separation difficult by organising coffee mornings or encouraging parents to take voluntary roles in the setting.

How to support separation and provide continuation of care

For parents to feel confident that their child will be happy and settled, it is important that you work closely with them when they leave their children. It is also essential that parents are confident that the care they provide at home will be continued within the setting.

Settling-in process

It is good practice for early years settings to encourage a settling-in process. The aim of this process is for the child to develop a strong attachment with their key person, which will allow the parent to leave knowing that their child will not become distressed. In Unit 7 we looked at the importance of the key person relationship in regard to children's emotional development.

The length of the settling-in process will depend on many factors including the child's age and previous experience of being cared for by someone else. By taking time to settle the child in, early years settings will also find that they can get to know parents too.

Supporting separation

As you saw above, parents have different ways of coping when they leave their children. During the settling-in process, early years settings should help parents to find a way of saying goodbye to their children that works for both parent and child. This might mean that parents will choose to find their child's key person and spend a little time playing together before leaving; or some parents may choose to leave quickly once their child is with the key person.

Continuation of care

There are three common areas that parents often have concerns about when they leave their child with other adults: food, warmth and safety, and friendship. It is helpful to understand the significance of these and also to find ways to respect parents' wishes.

- **Provision of food** – parents need to feed their children. This is instinctive and universal. Parents, therefore, will want to know if their child has eaten enough and may be concerned if their child has not eaten at all. Some parents who provide packed lunches may put in too much food – just in case!

- **Providing warmth and safety** – another concern of parents is whether their children are warm and safe. This is why some parents resist their children playing outdoors when it is cold or damp, or notice if their child's coat is not properly done up. It is also why some parents overdress their children. Understanding these concerns and also sharing information with parents about the benefits of outdoor play is important.

- **Friendships and loneliness** – parents need to know that their child will not be alone or have no friends. As children become older, the issue of friends becomes important to parents. They may ask their child who they played with. Making sure that you greet children when they first come in and take care of them before they settle in will reassure parents. It can also be worth taking photographs of them playing with other children or noting this activity down in a home book.

▶ Can you tell that these children are enjoying playing together?

Challenging discriminatory behaviour and promoting respect for children and families

All early years professionals have a duty, not only to protect children from **discrimination**, but also to actively promote respect for others. Discrimination can be institutional (where the policies or procedures within an institution discriminate against certain groups of people) or individual. Discrimination can be practised by adults working in a setting, by people from outside organisations, or by others such as parents and carers. Discrimination can have a negative effect on children's lives because it can mean that they are denied the care and education to which they are entitled. By challenging discriminatory behaviour and promoting respect, you are dealing with the immediate effects that discriminatory behaviour can have on children. This will, in turn, improve their long-term outcomes.

Key term

Discrimination – not giving equality of opportunity to groups or individuals because they belong to a particular group.

Discrimination should always be challenged. If you ignore it, it could be assumed that you condone discriminatory language or behaviour. Consider how a child or their family might feel if they experience discrimination that is ignored. They may feel that you share the same views or believe that the discriminatory treatment is normal practice.

It can be difficult to challenge discrimination, particularly if it is institutional within an early years setting. In this case, you will need to raise it with a senior manager or Ofsted, the official body for inspecting and regulating settings. To be able to challenge discrimination you will need to have a good understanding of legislation and the policy, procedures and practice in your own setting. If you feel confident that you know what good practice is, you will be able to deal more effectively with concerns about discrimination.

There are many ways in which you can actively show respect for parents. These are linked to communication skills, which you have already considered in this unit. They include acknowledging parents by smiling, nodding or making eye contact when they arrive, carefully listening to their point of view and being courteous, e.g. holding doors open for them, or offering to help if they are struggling with a buggy. In addition, it is important to learn more about parents' culture, language and way of life in order to show that you value and respect them. By being interested, you can show others that you value every child and family in the setting.

How to signpost services for parents

There are times when parents might benefit from additional information. They may wish to find out about parenting courses, leisure activities in the area or about additional services for children. They may also want to gain further information in relation to health care of their children, or to make a referral to another service. It is therefore good practice for early years settings to help parents know how to access information and services. This is sometimes referred to as **signposting**. There are many ways that you can do this.

> **Key term**
>
> **Signposting** – giving guidance about how to access additional services or information.

Leaflets

Most settings look out for leaflets that they can put out for parents to pick up about services, organisations and groups in their local areas. Good links with other professionals and organisations should make it easy to keep the leaflets and information up to date.

Websites

Many organisations have web addresses. These web addresses can be displayed clearly for parents somewhere in the setting, or you can write the addresses down for individual parents. It is important parents understand that you are not responsible for the content of the information on websites or the advice given.

Drop-in sessions

In some settings, drop-in sessions are organised so that other professionals and services can meet parents in the setting. This is particularly true of children's centres, which may have job advisers and provide access to health professionals.

Being sensitive

While sometimes parents may approach you to ask for additional information or how best to contact a service, at other times, it might be the early years setting who approaches parents. When it is thought that parents might benefit from additional information or the involvement of another service, it is essential that conversations with parents are handled sensitively. Parents must not feel that they are being judged or that the suggestion of additional information is because the setting feels that they are inadequate in some way. Some early years settings will just draw a parent's attention to a poster or leaflet at an appropriate moment, or it will be the role of the key person who already knows the parent to carry out the signposting.

Assessment practice 8.2 | A.P2 | A.M2 | A.D1

As part of the second session of the inset training day at the children's centre, new team members are asked to consider practical approaches to working in partnership with parents and the benefits these bring. Prepare a report for the session that:

- explains, with examples, practical ways in which effective partnerships with parents can be built in early years settings
- analyses how working in partnership with parents can support the play, learning and development needs of children
- evaluates, with examples, how approaches to effective partnership work with parents can benefit children and their families.

Plan
- What are the key approaches used in early years settings to work in partnership with parents?
- Where can I find examples of different approaches?

Do
- Am I using examples to support my work and reasoning?
- Am I managing my time effectively?

Review
- Have I used analysis and evaluation when considering approaches and benefits of parental partnership?
- Have I evaluated my work and am I confident that it fulfils the set task?

B Explore partnership work with colleagues and other professionals in early years settings

B1 Approaches to effective partnerships with colleagues and other professionals

Many children and their families have contact with, and are supported by, other professionals. For example, children may go to more than one early years setting or their families may be supported by services provided by a children's centre. For some families, social workers have a leading role in coordinating services if they need support caring for a child with disabilities, or if they have been identified as needing additional support. This section looks at the responsibilities that other professionals have and the role they play in children's lives.

Roles and responsibilities

Health professionals

There are a range of health professionals that children and families may be in contact with. It is helpful to understand their roles and responsibilities and how they support individual children and their families. Some health professionals, such as midwives and health visitors, will have routine involvement with children and families as part of their role in promoting children's health. Other health professionals, such as dieticians and speech and language therapists, will become involved only if the child or family has a specific need.

Midwives

Midwives play an important part in the lives of families. They provide antenatal care, help to deliver the baby and also visit the baby in the 10 days following birth. In some areas, mothers will have the same midwife for antenatal, delivery and postnatal care. In other areas, mothers will see community midwives for most of the antenatal and postnatal care, but will see hospital midwives for some antenatal checks and delivery. Midwives provide support and advice for new mothers, but they also have a role in child protection. They may recognise signs of postnatal depression as well as other strains on the family, and will pass this information to other health professionals and social services if appropriate.

Health visitors

Health visitors have an important role in all families' lives. Health visitors visit families in the weeks following a child's birth. They provide advice and information to parents about topics such as weaning, behaviour and sleep. Health visitors also have a role in monitoring children's development. They may carry out developmental checks as well as weigh and measure children. These activities are often carried out in health clinics, children's centres and also in children's homes.

Health visitors also have a role in child protection. They may spot signs that parents or carers are not coping with their role or that children are failing to thrive. Depending on the assessment of families' needs, health visitors may regularly visit families where there are concerns. The health visitor role is now often supplemented by a community nursery nurse who will visit families to do routine checks.

▶ Health visitors play a key role in families' lives. What do you know about their role?

Speech and language therapists

In Units 1 and 3, you explored the usual patterns for the development of children's speech and communication. Speech and language therapists work with children and their families where a child's speech is delayed or they need support in order to communicate. Speech and language teams have an important role in providing information to other professionals. They may run courses or visit settings to advise on how to increase opportunities for adult–child interaction. Referrals to speech and language therapists can be made by a variety of professionals, and in some cases by the parents themselves. Early years professionals can also make a direct referral with parents' consent or parents can be advised to talk to their family doctor (GP) or health visitor.

Dieticians

Dieticians work with children and their families where information and support is needed about children's diet. This may be because a child is not gaining sufficient weight or is overweight. Dieticians will also be involved in supporting families whose children have diabetes, coeliac disease or food phobias. Given that increasing numbers of children have weight problems, dieticians may also provide information about healthy eating to the community and to early years settings.

Referral to a dietician is usually provided by a GP, paediatrician or other health professional.

Paediatricians

Paediatricians are qualified doctors who specialise in the health of babies, children and young people. Many paediatricians are based in hospitals. Babies and children who are unwell, or have problems including sleep, bowel control or other medical conditions, are likely to be referred to a paediatrician by the child's GP or health visitor. Paediatricians may also be involved in child protection issues as they may examine the child following an unexplained injury or suspected abuse.

▶ Why might this baby require the attention of a paediatrician?

Portage

Where children have identified disabilities or learning needs, parents may be offered 'portage'. Portage is where children are visited in their homes by a portage worker who will work with them and their parents. Portage workers are often volunteers. Together with parents, they will set small goals and work towards them. Portage workers usually work with children under 5 years old. Close involvement and collaboration with parents is important to the scheme's success because parents will need to carry on exercises with their children after the visits. Referrals to portage are usually made by social workers and health professionals.

Physiotherapists

Physiotherapists work with children who need support with their physical development and movement. Their aim is to maximise children's movements. Physiotherapists work closely with parents and may also work with early years staff. They may provide exercises, equipment and advice as well as suggest modifications that might be needed in order for children to access the provision. Children may be referred to physiotherapists by paediatricians, family doctors and other health professionals.

Sensory impairment team

Children with sensory impairment such as hearing or sight problems are usually supported by members of the sensory impairment team. They work with parents and early years settings to help children maximise their senses or to access provision. The sensory impairment team may visit a setting to suggest modifications, tips and equipment that will help children learn.

PAUSE POINT Make a list of three health professionals who might be working with a child.

Hint Think about difficulties that children may have with their development or their health.

Extend Consider why it is important for early years settings to be aware of health professionals that are involved with the family.

Social care professionals

Some families need additional support and so a range of professionals will be working with them. In some cases, families will have referred themselves to these services and professionals. In other cases, there may be a statutory obligation for a local authority to support families where children are identified as being **in need**.

The definition of 'in need' in terms of local authority statutory obligations is a child who:

▶ needs local authority services to achieve or maintain a reasonable standard of health or development

▶ needs local authority services to prevent significant or further harm to health or development

▶ is disabled.

It is worth noting that children with disabilities are categorised as 'in need' by the Children Act 1989, and local authorities have an obligation to allocate a social worker to assess the child's and the family's needs regardless of the financial or social situation of the family.

Social workers

Social workers can work for organisations such as the NSPCC as well as for local authorities. As social work is a large area, most social workers will work in different specialisms or in different teams. There may, for example, be social workers who specialise in fostering and adoption, and others who work with vulnerable families.

Key term

In need – refers to children who are unlikely to maintain, or be given the opportunity to maintain, a reasonable standard of health or development, or children whose health could be impaired without the support of local authority services. It also includes children who are disabled.

Social workers are likely to spend time assessing the needs of the child and the family, organising services and meeting with other professionals who are involved with the family.

Family support workers

Family support workers work with families and provide practical support and advice. They are usually employed by local authorities and will work closely with social workers. Family support workers often work with families as a result of referrals from social workers or from other agencies involved with the family.

Police liaison officers

Police liaison officers often work closely with social workers and other professionals when abuse is suspected and needs investigating. In addition, some police liaison officers work to support families where crimes have been committed or there are incidents such as road traffic accidents that impact on the family.

Outreach workers

Outreach workers often work closely to support families who may otherwise not access advice and services. Some outreach workers are based in children's centres and may help parents with parenting, life skills and also child development. Outreach workers often meet parents in other early years settings or in the local community and build up a relationship with them. Some outreach work is done as a result of referrals from social workers, early years professionals and health visitor teams.

Home-Start volunteers

Home-Start is an organisation that supports families with young children. Volunteers, often experienced parents, will visit families once a week. They provide practical as well as emotional support. Families can self-refer or parents can be offered a referral from health visiting teams, early years settings and social workers.

> **Research**
>
> Find out more about Home-Start by visiting www.home-start.org.uk.

Early years educators

Within early years settings where there are teams, it is likely that there will be a range of professional roles linked to early education. Early years educators are likely to be on the management team at the setting and may be the decision makers in terms of the educational direction of the setting. The nursery manager is likely to be in this category. The term 'early educators' is sometimes used as an umbrella term to encompass the range of ways in which adults may work with children and their families to support early education. It is useful to understand the different roles and responsibilities of each role.

Special Educational Needs Coordinator (SENCO)

The term SENCO stands for Special Educational Needs Coordinator. A SENCO is someone who oversees the support of children within a setting who have additional needs. There is a legal requirement for all early years and school settings to have someone in this role. Their key responsibilities are to liaise with parents and other professionals, to ensure that the special needs policy of the setting is adhered to and to help colleagues meet and support the needs of children.

Key person

The role of the key person is to provide additional support and develop a special relationship with individual children and their families. There is a legal requirement within the EYFS for every child to have a key person. The EYFS also states that in addition to helping the child feel secure, the key person must encourage parents to support their children's learning at home. The key person will also coordinate the planning and observations for each of their key children.

Early years teachers

Some settings have an early years teacher on their staff team. Early years teachers provide additional knowledge and expertise about the education and development of children. In some settings the early years teacher will take the lead in planning activities and will be supported in this role by other staff.

Early years professionals

Early years professionals are staff who have additional knowledge and training in early years. They are likely to be on the management team of the setting and may be the decision maker in terms of the educational direction of the setting.

Teachers

Where early years teams are based in schools, or are part of a school's early years provision, there will be some liaison with the primary teachers in Key Stage 1. The role of teachers is to lead and be responsible for class teaching.

Strategies for working in partnership

Most adults working with children need to work together with other people. This begins with the parents or carers, but is also likely to include work colleagues and professionals from a range of disciplines. You will now look at the importance and principles of cooperative working and partnership working.

Cooperative working

Cooperative working is primarily about good communication between different professionals, colleagues and also parents and carers. It means that service providers and individuals work side by side in order to provide services, meet families' needs and also keep children safe in child protection cases. When working cooperatively, each professional will keep in contact with the other, but will maintain their own focus and responsibility for the work.

Partnership working

Partnership working is in theory slightly different. It suggests a greater degree of coordination and that organisations or professionals are working more directly together. This is pretty automatic in an early years setting when the team has the same aims and objectives. Occasionally, professionals from different services will engage in partnership working. An example of this is the way that some speech and language teams produce materials for parents jointly with early years teams. This partnership working means that both services come together to work on a joint project and that they have equal and combined responsibility.

> **Key terms**
>
> **Cooperative working** – working with a family, but taking responsibility for different tasks.
>
> **Partnership working** – combining expertise to work jointly with a family.

Multidisciplinary teams

The term **multidisciplinary teams** is used to describe times when professionals from a range of services come together to deliver services to children and families. Sometimes teams are based in the same building and will plan services and interventions for children together, or they may have close contact with each other. Children and families who have a high level of needs will often be involved with multidisciplinary teams. For example, a child who has a life-limiting health condition and also specific learning needs may be supported by a range of professionals who need to dovetail their interventions and plan together to best support the child.

> **Key term**
>
> **Multidisciplinary teams** – teams involving professionals from a range of services who work in close association with each other, and plan services and interventions together.

Victoria Climbié and Peter Connelly

Sadly, in the past, cooperative working and subsequent communication was often not in place. This was a contributory factor in many high-profile deaths of children. One high-profile case was that of Peter Connelly, and before this the case of 8-year-old Victoria Climbié, who was tortured and then killed by a great aunt. After the Climbié killing, an inquiry was held, led by Lord Laming. The enquiry found that doctors and social workers were not sharing information. The Laming inquiry made a number of recommendations, many of which have been acted on and turned into legislation in England, for example, in the Children Act 2004. In the other home countries, similar approaches have been taken.

Since the Laming inquiry, there has been a renewed focus on ensuring that services for children and young people are more coordinated to improve children's life chances and outcomes. This is one reason why children's centres often provide a wide range of services, including speech and language therapy, employment advice and health care.

The new focus on multidisciplinary teams has also meant that there are more multidisciplinary approaches towards child protection. A good example of this is the Local Safeguarding Children Boards that have been set up in England. These boards work with local early years settings and schools, and consist of police, social services and health professionals. One of the positive benefits of multidisciplinary work has been more opportunities for early years professionals to meet and learn more about other professions and, in some cases, gain knowledge and further skills.

> **Link**
>
> Go to Unit 5, Section C3, to find more information about the role of Local Safeguarding Children Boards, the Laming inquiry and the Children Act 2004.

> **Research**
>
> Find out about the Peter Connelly case by carrying out an internet search.
>
> 1   Why was the public shocked by this case?
> 2   Why is this case a good example of a breakdown in cooperative working?

The benefits of cooperative working

If professionals work effectively with colleagues in their own setting and with professionals from other agencies, children's life chances and outcomes will be improved. Child abuse can also be prevented when different agencies work together and share information. Abuse, if not prevented or quickly recognised, can damage children for life and so working together can make a real difference. There are also other important benefits for children and families.

One of the most important outcomes is the potential for children and families to have efficient support that is organised and tailored around their needs. Information sharing also means that parents do not have to repeat pieces of information about their children every time a new professional works with them. Additionally, collaborative working creates a climate of trust between parents and professionals because parents can feel that everyone is working in the best interests of their children. Close working also prevents misunderstandings, miscommunications and again this contributes to the climate of trust.

Figure 8.5 shows many more of the benefits of working cooperatively. Key benefits for parents are that services are coordinated and they feel listened to.

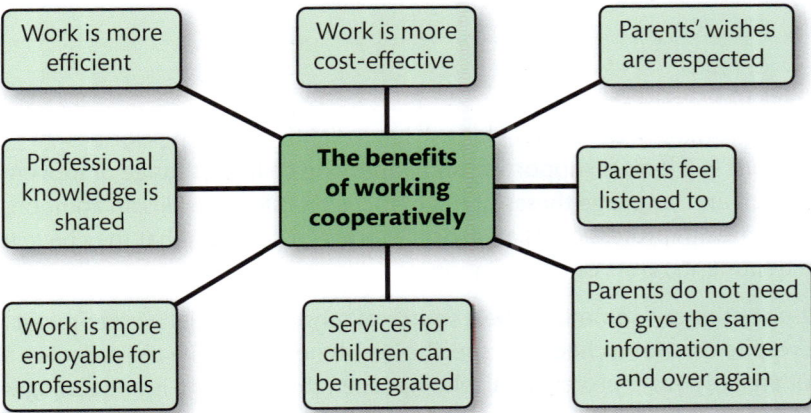

▶ **Figure 8.5:** The benefits of working cooperatively

Although children and their parents benefit from cooperative working, so too does everyone involved. For example, professionals can learn skills and information from each other and, in some situations, knowing what others are doing with the child and family complements professionals' own work, so improving outcomes for the child.

Teamwork

If teams in a setting work cooperatively, it usually makes work more enjoyable and reduces stress in the workplace. This, in turn, is likely to rub off on children and their families because a happy workplace is more likely to be positive and welcoming. Where staff are unhappy or do not understand their roles and responsibilities, misunderstandings can occur, which means that the needs of children are less likely to be met.

Barriers to effective working with colleagues and other professionals

Although it is easy to say that cooperative working should take place, the reality is that it requires significant effort and organisation. When people are not sharing the same physical environment, and do not have the same roles, experiences and knowledge, cooperative working becomes more challenging. Even colleagues in some large settings find that they do not always know what is happening.

Understanding the potential barriers to cooperative working is, therefore, a good first step. Once you are aware of the potential difficulties, you can start to look for ways to overcome them.

Time

Most people working with children are busy. Professionals in different disciplines may not work the same hours or be able to attend meetings.

Cooperative working

Maisy is 3 years old. She was born with significant health problems and also a learning difficulty. Her social worker has organised support for her and the family, which means that she has portage, **respite care** and also a place at a local nursery. Maisy's key person is in frequent contact with her parents, social worker, physiotherapist and also other health professionals.

Maisy's parents are relieved that she and they are getting this support.

Check your knowledge

1 Why is it important that Maisy's needs are met promptly?

2 What are the benefits to Maisy's family when professionals are working cooperatively?

Differences in priorities

Professionals working in different fields will have slightly different priorities. A physiotherapist will look at supporting and improving children's range of movements while a speech and language therapist might focus on listening skills. In addition, caseloads for health professionals and social workers may mean that they have to prioritise treatments, visits or consultations.

Different priorities can sometimes be a source of tension. A social worker might organise respite care for a child with specific health needs, to give the parents a short break, but an early years professional who has seen that the child is not coping well with different transitions and changes might feel that stability is more important for the child. If this concern is raised using the communication channels available through partnership working, it might be possible to find an alternative solution. For instance, a care worker could come in to stay with the child through the night, to allow the parents a night off while ensuring the child's environment is stable and the parents are available in an emergency.

Differences in approaches and ethos

As well as having different priorities, different professionals have their own procedures, policies and ways of working. Information systems and administrative processes are also likely to be different. Simple things such as making contact may require going through an administrator first, or decisions might need to be approved by managers. A 'quick turnaround' for one professional might mean an hour; however, for another it might mean a week. This can lead to frustration and miscommunication if professionals do not know how the other services are set up.

Overcoming barriers to effective working

Some strategies can help professionals to overcome difficulties in cooperative working. These strategies include:

- finding out about the roles and responsibilities of other professionals and colleagues
- finding out if anyone is acting as the **named person** for a child's family

Key terms

Respite care – short-term care with the assistance of professional carers.

Named person – a person who is the main point of contact.

▶ taking time to build up a working relationship with others – be friendly and show respect for their work and ideas

▶ not making assumptions about the way others might work or the timescales they use

▶ not making assumptions that others have the same information as you.

When and how information should be shared with colleagues and other professionals

Cooperative working requires good communication and the sharing of information. On the other hand, families have a right to expect that information they share about their family is treated in confidence. This means there are issues around how, with whom and when information should be shared. A good starting point when thinking about information sharing is to look at your own setting's policies and procedures in relation to the sharing of information. The following principles are usually embedded in policies and procedures.

▶ The welfare of the child is paramount and so in cases where a child's life or welfare is at risk, or likely to be so, parental consent is not required to share information.

Example: A 4-year-old child comes into the setting with burn marks on the back of her legs and knees. The child's social worker is immediately contacted.

▶ Parental consent is required before making referrals to other services. If you refer children or talk about them to others without parental consent, you are likely to be in breach of the Data Protection Act 1998. Remember that you can only share information with other services when you have reasonable concerns that the child's welfare is in jeopardy.

Example: Jason's key person is concerned that he has difficulty in making a 'g' sound. She asks Jason's mother if she can make a direct referral to the speech and language team. Jason's mother says that she thinks he will grow out of it. The key person respects this decision, but instead finds out more about speech immaturities in general from the speech and language team.

▶ Only relevant information should be shared with others. This means that when there are complex family needs, only information that will impact on another professional's ability to do the work should be shared.

Example: Hannah's key person knows that Hannah's brother has been convicted of theft. She does not share this information when talking to the physiotherapist about Hannah's fine motor movements.

▶ Information is only passed to those who have a direct need or involvement with the child and the family. This is sometimes called the 'need to know' approach. Although it might be important for information to be shared, it should only be passed on to those who have a direct need or reason to have it. In settings, this might mean that only the key person and the manager may hold certain information that will not be shared with the rest of the team.

Example: It is suspected that Harry may have been physically abused by one or both of his parents. The investigation is in its early stages. Social workers have only told the manager of the setting and Harry's key person.

▶ Information is accurate and up to date. If necessary, check whether this is the case with parents or other individuals before passing it on. If you are not sure of the accuracy, you should indicate this.

Example: Greta is 5 years old. She is finding it hard to settle in at school. With the parent's consent, the school phones Greta's preschool. Greta's key person at the preschool says that Greta used to get very anxious about going to the toilet, but the key person stresses that this might have changed since.

▶ Information is kept secure. You should think about how information is shared and how it is likely to be kept secure. Everyone 'handling' personal information has this duty under the Data Protection Act 1998.

Example: A social worker has asked to see a child's developmental records. She gives the setting assurances that the records will not be passed on to any other service, but if she thinks the information will be useful to another service, she will refer the other service directly back to the early years setting.

PAUSE POINT

Identify four principles that inform policies and procedures about information sharing.

Hint

Think of the key points about sharing information and the importance of keeping a child safe.

Extend

Why is it important to understand an early years setting's policy in relation to information sharing?

How to ensure data protection in cooperative work

Link

Look back at Section A2 of this unit to find more information about policies, procedures and statutory guidance for data protection.

You saw in Section A2 that the Data Protection Act 1998 sets out clear requirements regarding personal information. It is, therefore, important that you ask parents before you share information with other professionals, except where the child's welfare is seriously at risk. It is also important to pass on only information that is needed and to do so securely so that other people with no interest in the child or the family do not see it. Most settings will have policies and procedures in place and you should always follow them.

Purpose of multidisciplinary meetings

There are times when it is important for professionals from a range of services to meet together to develop a strategy or plan for the child and their family. Meetings may be called because of child protection issues, because children need a wide range of support due to complex disabilities or medical conditions, or because a family is in need of additional support. These meetings are sometimes called 'case conferences'.

Key term

Multi-agency – involving staff from different agencies working together.

There will also be times when a review of what has already been put in place is required. As **multi-agency** meetings can be difficult to organise, they are usually kept to a minimum and some information sharing and decision making may sometimes be done without face-to-face meetings.

Before the meeting

It is usual for the service convening the meeting to organise the arrangements – time, date and place. They should also state the purpose of the meeting and give clear indications of any background reports that need compiling or any pre-reading that is needed. Meetings should be held with the consent of parents unless the child's welfare is at risk. The convening service should nominate the chair and draw up the agenda.

It is also good practice for parents to attend meetings so that they can provide information, but also because decisions should not be made without them. This includes meetings in respect of child protection. Some parents may not be able to attend, but they should be given the opportunity to nominate someone to attend for them.

At the meeting

If you are attending a multidisciplinary meeting, make sure you arrive punctually, have read any background documents or have prepared information to share.

At the start of the meeting it is good practice for the chair to outline what is going to happen during the meeting. This is particularly important when parents are attending.

Apologies for those who are absent should also be read out. It is also usual for everyone to introduce themselves and their roles. Minutes or notes from the meeting should be kept. This allows anyone who was not present to know what conclusions were reached in the meeting.

The usual pattern of many meetings is first to consider the current situation and what has happened since the previous meeting (if there has been one) before deciding on a plan of action. The plan of action should be clear and everyone should know what actions they are individually responsible for. Before the meeting ends, times and dates for a follow-up meeting (if needed) should be set.

▶ These people are representatives from a range of children's services. What are the benefits of them working together?

After the meeting

The service that convened the meeting should circulate the minutes of the meeting promptly. If a formatted action plan has been written, this should also be sent out. Everyone involved should then try to complete the actions or tasks that have been agreed. Any difficulties should be promptly shared with others if this is likely to affect their input.

> **Theory into practice**
>
> Find out about the types of meeting that your placement settings are involved in. Involvement could include coverage of:
> * special educational needs
> * child protection
> * supporting children with disabilities.

Assessment practice 8.3   B.P3   B.P4   B.M3   B.D2

The children's centre is made up of a large team. It is also used as a base for multidisciplinary work and so the manager is keen as part of the inset day to explore the issues around working with colleagues and other professionals. You have been asked to:

* explain, with examples, how early years settings approach working in partnership with colleagues and other professionals
* explain the potential benefits to children and their families of partnership working with colleagues and other professionals
* assess, using practical examples, how partnership work with colleagues and other professionals might benefit children and their families
* evaluate the extent to which partnership working with colleagues and other professionals contributes to meeting the needs of children and their families.

Plan
* Do I know the key ways in which early years settings are likely to work in partnership with colleagues and other professionals?
* Do I understand the key issues and barriers to partnership working?

Do
* Am I using examples to support my work and reasoning?
* Am I managing my time effectively?

Review
* Have I used analysis and evaluation when considering approaches and benefits to children and their families of partnership working between colleagues and other professionals?

C Demonstrate effective partnership work with parents and others in early years settings to meet the needs of children

C1 Demonstrate effective partnerships with parents

In Sections A and B of this unit, you looked at the knowledge and skills needed to work effectively with parents and other professionals. In order to complete the assessment for this unit, you need to demonstrate that you can put this knowledge into practice. This section gives you suggestions as to how you might do this.

Develop and maintain effective relationships with parents

In order to demonstrate that you can develop and maintain effective relationships with parents, you will need to talk to your manager or the person responsible for your early years placement. They can guide you to work in ways that are compatible with the procedures and policies of the setting. It may be that you begin by watching how other staff work with parents before venturing solo!

Use appropriate verbal and non-verbal communication

You could begin by looking at the non-verbal as well as verbal communication strategies that are used in the setting to work with parents. Think about how staff convey to parents that they are actively listening to them. It is always worth remembering that even small gestures, smiles and a greeting to a parent are important when developing a strong communicative relationship.

Recognise and use strategies to overcome barriers to effective communication

Think about the parents that you are working with in your setting. What are the key barriers to communication that exist? These may be different from one placement to another. For example, in one setting some parents may not bring their children to the sessions, but use a childminder or another family member. Think about how the setting, and therefore you, could overcome these barriers to help ensure there is effective communication. This might mean using a form of technology or some of the other suggestions that you looked at in Section A2.

Share information complying with policies, procedures and statutory guidelines

As information sharing is an important area, you need to show that you can follow the policies and procedures of your setting at all times. You should also make sure that you have revised the Data Protection Act 1998 to understand how it applies to the information in your setting.

Before sharing any information with parents, it is a good idea to check with colleagues which information is confidential and to learn from them about how they exchange information. If you work in England, a two-way exchange of information is actually a statutory requirement of the EYFS. A two-way exchange of information means that not only should you talk to parents, but you need to demonstrate that you listen and take on board what they say about their child. When you manage to achieve a two-way exchange of information with parents, you will find that their input can help with understanding their child's behaviours, as well as making planning interesting. There are two areas in particular where a two-way exchange of information is essential.

▶ **Children's needs and interests** – while you might tell parents about what you have observed their child doing and enjoying in the early years setting, a two-way exchange of information means that parents will comment on your thoughts and also talk to you about what their child enjoys doing when they are with them.

▶ **Observations and assessments of development** – it is a statutory requirement of the EYFS in England that parents are kept informed of their child's progress. This means that observations and, in particular, assessments of development are shared with parents. While you might talk about what you have observed and the progress that the child has made, parents may have observed other aspects of development.

Value parents' contribution to their child's development

You have seen that parents are the experts when it comes to their own children's development. Parents show this in a variety of ways, by, for example, knowing when their children are becoming ill or when their child seems a little out of sorts. Parents also know about their children's interests and friendships, as well as their strengths and weaknesses.

One of the key ways in which you can demonstrate that you value parents' knowledge is by taking an interest in what they tell you about their children through conversations. This includes comments made in passing as well as by directly asking them interested questions.

Recognise and respect emotional attachment that influences choice and behaviours

In Section A2, you looked at the way that parents' attachment to their children influences how they separate from them and also how they respond to their children.

It is worth spending some time observing different parents so that you can see how this plays out. By understanding how parents respond to their children, it is easier to recognise when parents' responses are guided by their attachment. You can show respect for parents by giving them time to say goodbye or by being non-judgmental as they 'indulge' their children when, for example, helping them to put their coat on.

Demonstrate awareness of your own limitations when giving advice

As a learner, you have clear limitations as to your knowledge and also your responsibilities within the setting. Think about what these limitations are and how you might make sure that you can demonstrate your awareness of them. For example, in answer to a parent's question, you might say that you will need to refer to another colleague. Or you may ask a colleague within a placement a question to clarify your understanding before going to talk to a parent.

Encourage parents to take an active role in children's play, learning and development

As you have seen, it is good practice for early years settings to provide suggestions and advice to parents so that they can support their children's development at home. You have looked at different ways in which settings might do this, including lending books, suggesting activities and talking to parents about what they already do with their children. You will need to find out how your setting works with parents and also how they tailor advice and suggestions according to the needs of the parents and their interests.

C2 Demonstrate effective partnerships with colleagues and others

While you are on placement you will need to show that you are able to work effectively with other professionals.

Demonstrate understanding about the roles and responsibilities of colleagues and other professionals

A good starting point when meeting another professional or colleague is to talk to them about their role within the setting or more generally. Section B1 outlined the roles of different professionals, but you may find it interesting to hear about how they work in practice. It can be useful to keep a note of the name and also the role of the professionals that you have met so that you are clear about how their work links to the early years setting's work.

Communicate effectively to share accurate information about children's needs and development

It is important that you are able to communicate effectively with others about children's development and other needs. This might include contributing to planning through suggestions (verbal communication), but also through writing. It may also mean talking to others about what you have noticed about individual children.

To communicate effectively, you will need to be accurate in what you say or write, and also ensure you choose the best communication method for the situation. Sometimes that may mean making a comment to a colleague, but at other times you may need to use a written form of communication.

Show awareness of when and how information should be shared

As well as sharing information to benefit children, you also know that sharing information is important to ensure the smooth running of an early years setting. When you start at an early years setting, you need to find out about the current forms and procedures for sharing information about things such as accidents, planning activities and stock control, as well as forms that need to be filled in for gaining parental consent. You should also learn from watching others about when and how to do this so that information is passed on promptly.

Maintain confidentiality when recording and sharing information

You have looked at the importance of confidentiality with parents, but it is also an important issue when working with other professionals and colleagues. A good starting point is to read your setting's confidentiality policy, but also to check with others before you record anything or share information.

If you are working in a privately run early years setting, there may also be commercial sensitivities. For example, you may not be able to tell other people about the costings of children's places or how the day-to-day business is run.

Assessment practice 8.4

A potential employer wants to know more about how effective you are in relation to working in partnership with parents, colleagues and other professionals. You have been asked as part of the interview to prepare the following information.

- Using examples, explain how you have demonstrated effective partnership work with parents, as well as colleagues or other professionals, in a work placement setting.
- Using examples, assess your strengths and weaknesses in relation to partnership work to meet the needs of children.
- Using examples, evaluate ways in which you have consistently demonstrated self-management and professional conduct in partnership work with colleagues and other professionals and parents.

Plan
- What examples of working in partnership with parents, colleagues or other professionals can I use?
- What strategies can I use to assess and evaluate my partnership working?

Do
- Am I using examples to support my work and reasoning?
- Am I managing my time effectively?

Review
- Have I used analysis and evaluation when considering my effectiveness in partnership work?
- Have I evaluated my work and am I confident that it fulfils the set task?

Further reading and resources

Books

Crowley, M. and Wheeler, H. 'Working with Parents in the Early Years' in Pugh, G. and Duffy, B. (2013) *Contemporary Issues in the Early Years*, 6th edition, London: Sage Publications.

Gasper, M. (2010) *Multi-agency Working in the Early Years: Challenges and Opportunities*, London: Sage Publications.

Lindon, J. (2012) *Parents as Partners: Positive Relationships in the Early Years*, 2nd edition, London: Practical Pre-School Books.

Sylva, K., Melhuish, E., Sammons, P., Siraj-Blatchford, I. and Taggart, B. (2004) *The Effective Provision of Pre-School Education (EPPE) Project: Final Report*, London: Institute of Education.

Whalley, M. (2007) *Involving Parents in their Children's Learning*, 2nd edition, London: Sage Publications.

Websites

www.educationotherwise.net – Education Otherwise™: support and resources for home education.

www.gov.uk – UK Government: information about school leaving ages and research into the effects of parental engagement.

www.home-start.org.uk – Home-Start: support and advice for families with difficulties.

https://ico.org.uk – Information Commissioner's Office: information about the Data Protection Act.

www.ucl.ac.uk/ioe – Institute of Education: information about the EPPE Project.

www.mumsnet.com – Mumsnet: information, advice and forums for parents.

www.naccc.org.uk – National Association of Child Contact Centres: information about the help available to support families through relationship breakdown.

www.pre-school.org.uk/providers – Pre-school Learning Alliance: information and advice for childcare practitioners in a range of settings.

THINK ▶FUTURE

Alena Petrou

Manager of a children's centre

Alena has been working in a children's centre for five years. It is a very exciting place and she has enjoyed working with colleagues from a range of professions. The children's centre offers a range of services to children and their families. There are first-aid courses, baby massage, parenting classes, and information and advice sessions with a range of professionals including GPs, health visitors and speech and language therapists. The team includes outreach workers and Alena and her colleagues liaise closely with other childcare providers in the town.

To make sure that everyone knows what is available and what is happening within the centre, there are regular catch-up sessions. This brings everyone together as a team. Although the professionals are not always working alongside each other, it is important to understand each other's roles and responsibilities. There are strict policies and procedures about confidentiality and every new member of staff has to read and understand these as part of their induction. A careless word would mean the end of the trust that parents have in Alena and her colleagues.

Focusing your skills

Tips for working effectively in partnership with parents

- Always greet the child and parent warmly. However busy you are, try to smile or wave to them.

- Give information to parents promptly and make sure you are always honest with them. For example, tell the parents if their child has missed them during the day or if their child has not eaten.

- Reassure parents. Let them stay at the setting for longer if they need to or take photographs of their child throughout the day.

- Show interest in the child. Ask parents questions about what the child enjoys doing at home and what the child likes to eat, and find out tips on how to settle the child.

- Show interest in the parent. Ask about their weekend or previous evening when the parent drops their child off at the setting, or ask how their day has been when they pick up their child.

Tips for working in partnership with colleagues and other professionals

- Try to understand the role of the colleague or professional in the setting or when working with a child.

- Recognise that you may have different priorities, but find ways of respecting what they do.

- Be friendly, show respect and be ready to learn from colleagues and other professionals.

- Promptly follow up on discussions and any areas on which you have agreed to work.

Observation, Assessment and Planning 9

Getting to know your unit

As a professional working with children you will need to observe, assess and plan for their development, interests and strengths. Observing children is quite a skill but, once mastered, it is fascinating and rewarding. By making observations you can begin to understand a child and start to think and plan for their needs and interests. This requires knowledge of both child development and play. It also requires an understanding of the curriculum framework that is being used in your setting.

In this unit you will look at the importance of this process and how to observe and plan learning activities for children, based on the conclusions of your observations.

How you will be assessed

This unit will be internally assessed by a series of tasks set by your tutor. They will include practical tasks that will need to be carried out on placement, and that link to your Practical Evidence Portfolio. Throughout this unit, assessment practice activities will help you work towards your assessment. Completing these activities will not mean that you have achieved a particular grade, but you will have carried out useful research or preparation that will be relevant when it comes to your final assignment.

To achieve the tasks in your assignment, it is important to check that you have met all of the Pass grading criteria. You can do this as you work your way through the assignment.

If you are hoping to gain a Merit or Distinction, also make sure that you present the information in your assignment in the style that is required by the relevant assessment criterion. For example, Merit criteria require you to analyse and discuss, and Distinction criteria require you to assess and evaluate.

The assignment set by your tutor will consist of a number of tasks designed to meet the criteria in the table. This is likely to consist of a written assignment but you may also need to produce evidence such as:

▶ a report about the importance of observation, assessment and planning

▶ observation records of young children

▶ activity plans for identified children based on observations

▶ a report evaluating the ways in which your activity plans support children's play, learning and development

▶ a presentation to your peers and tutor, explaining your planning and delivery.

Assessment criteria

This table shows what you must do in order to achieve a **Pass**, **Merit** or **Distinction** grade, and where you can find activities to help you.

Pass	**Merit**	**Distinction**
Learning aim **A** Understand the importance of observation, assessment and planning in work with children		
A.P1 Explain the importance of observing and assessing children in early years settings to plan how to support their individual play, learning and development needs. **Assessment practice 9.1**	**A.M1** Assess the significance of methods of observation in early years settings for reliable assessment of the child's play, learning and developmental needs. **Assessment practice 9.1**	**A.D1** Evaluate the influence and importance of observation, assessment and effective planning for play, learning and development in early years settings. **Assessment practice 9.1, 9.2**
A.P2 Explain influences on planning for play, learning and development in an early years setting. **Assessment practice 9.2**	**A.M2** Analyse influences on planning for play, learning and development in an early years setting. **Assessment practice 9.2**	
Learning aim **B** Carry out and record observations of children to make accurate assessments		
B.P3 Present detailed plans to observe the play, learning and development of a child in an early years setting using appropriate methods. **Assessment practice 9.3**	**B.M3** Justify the observational methods used to record the play, learning and development of a child in an early years setting. **Assessment practice 9.3**	**B.D2** Evaluate own practice in the planning, creation and implementation of activities in terms of how they supported the observed child's play, learning and development. **Assessment practice 9.4**
B.P4 Present full and effective records to show accurate observations of a child's play, learning and development. **Assessment practice 9.4**		
B.P5 Explain an observed child's stage of play, learning and development, making use of relevant theories. **Assessment practice 9.4**		
Learning aim **C** Create, implement and review activity plans for children		
C.P6 Present and implement activity plans appropriate for the observed child to support their play, learning and development. **Assessment practice 9.5**	**C.M4** Analyse the extent to which the plans and implemented activities supported the child's play, learning and development. **Assessment practice 9.5**	**C.D3** Evaluate how the plans and implemented activities supported the child's play, learning and development with justified observations. **Assessment practice 9.5**
C.P7 Review the effectiveness of the planning methods, plans and implemented activities in supporting the child's play, learning and development. **Assessment practice 9.5**		

Getting started

Do you know how many different types of observation methods there are and why they might be used? List the methods that you know about already. By the end of this unit, see if you can add to your list.

 **A**

Understand the importance of observation, assessment and planning in work with children

A1 The importance of observation and assessment

Observing and assessing children is key to effective professional working. In this section, you will look at the many reasons why early years professionals and others observe and assess children.

There are many reasons for observing and carrying out assessments on children, shown in Figure 9.1.

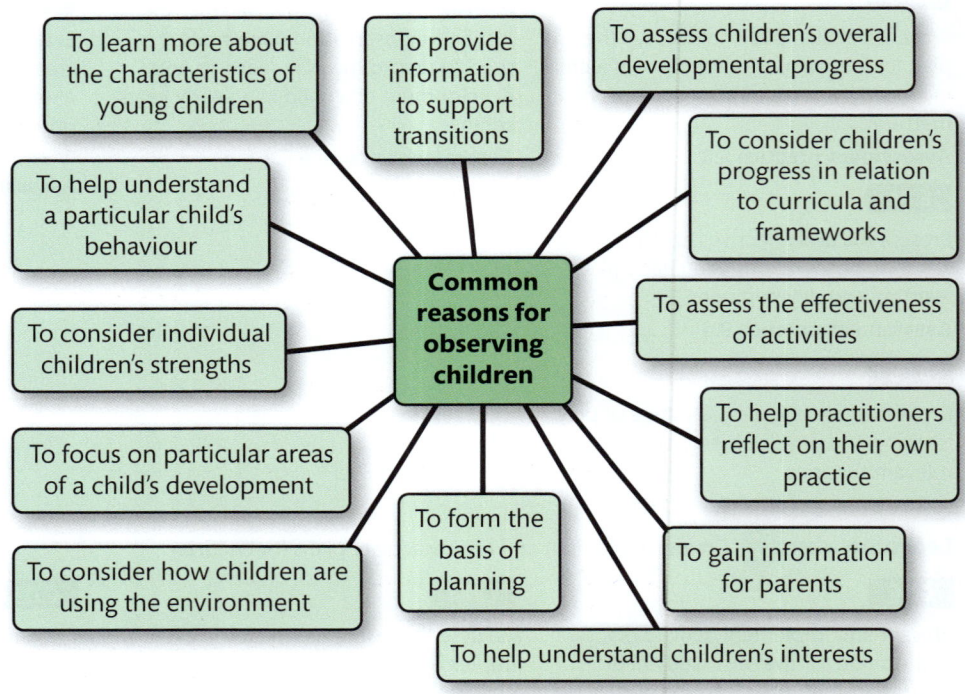

▶ **Figure 9.1:** The common reasons for observing children

Assessments are particularly important as a tool to:

▶ share information with parents about their child

▶ provide information for other professionals

▶ learn more about children's needs and interests

- track children's progress in relation to **developmental milestones** and curriculum outcomes
- plan for next steps and shape learning opportunities for children
- identify when a child's development is atypical or when a child needs additional support
- help you reflect on your own practice.

Key term

Developmental milestones – typical skills that most children have acquired at given ages.

Current assessment requirements

As you can see in Figure 9.1, observations and assessments are used to help plan activities, resources and play opportunities for groups and individual children. Observations and assessments are also needed to ensure that children are making progress within the curriculum framework of their home country. For example, a 3-year-old child living in England is likely to attend a setting that is using the Early Years Foundation Stage (EYFS), while a child of the same age living in Wales is likely to be in a setting using the Foundation Phase.

For children in England, the EYFS Profile is an assessment that is carried out by teachers towards the end of the reception year. The EYFS Profile requires teachers to make judgements about children's progress in relation to the early learning goals. These are targets that have been set by the UK government (applicable to England only) and it is hoped that most children will be able to meet them by the end of this stage.

Since 2013, teachers have been recording whether children are working towards, have met or have exceeded the early learning goals. The judgements that teachers make must be based on observations that have taken place throughout the year.

Sharing information with parents and other professionals

Working closely with parents and other professionals is essential in early years practice.

- **Parents** – working closely with parents is essential in early years practice. Parents have a right to know how their child is progressing and what they have spent time doing. As you will see later in this section, wherever possible, parents should contribute to the observation and planning process, as they will also have knowledge and ideas about their child.

Link

Unit 8 has more information about how important it is to work closely with parents and other early years professionals.

- **Other professionals** – observations and assessments may also be shared with other practitioners and professionals to support any transition. Transitions may include children moving to a new setting, or day-to-day transitions such as children moving between a nursery in the morning and a childminder in the afternoon. Remember though, that observations and assessments can only be shared after parental consent has been gained. You may provide information about how best to help the child settle or ideas for resources and activities that the child enjoys. You may also pass on records about the child's progress in relation to a curriculum framework, where appropriate.

Understanding children's needs and interests

Observing children helps you learn more about them and so should, in theory, help you to work more effectively. For example, you might spot a left-handed 4-year-old child, so you will need to remember to put out left-handed scissors for them to use; or, when observing another child, you might notice a movement they make that shows when they need the toilet. These are examples of small day-to-day needs, but observing a child might also reveal that they require more significant support, such as speech and language therapy. Identifying a need for this kind of support should happen as early as possible in the child's life, as this has been shown to result in more positive outcomes.

It is useful not to fall into the trap of only observing children when there is a problem or concern. Observations should also tell you about children's strengths and interests, and this information can be used to help plan play and other activities for them.

Tracking children's progress in relation to developmental milestones

Observation and assessments of children are also used to follow children's development in relation to developmental milestones (also referred to as normative development). These developmental milestones, which are often used by health professionals as well as by early years practitioners, have been widely researched and so are considered to be very reliable. Using developmental milestones is particularly important in the early years where early identification that a child is not showing usual patterns of development may indicate that a child needs additional support.

Tracking children's progress in relation to curriculum outcomes

As well as using observations to assess children in relation to developmental milestones, early years settings following frameworks such as the EYFS are also required to monitor children's progress in relation to outcomes outlined in the framework. A good example of this is the requirement mentioned above for reception teachers in England to carry out an assessment as to whether children have met the early years goals in the different areas of learning and development within the EYFS. The EYFS and other early years frameworks can therefore be reliable sources of developmental milestones, as they indicate expected stages of development at different ages.

Planning for next steps

Another reason for observing children is to plan for their next steps. This might mean building on their current interests or recognising that they need additional reinforcement activities so they can become secure in a skill, such as using scissors. In addition, by identifying children's next steps you can also think about how to shape learning opportunities for them. It might be that you have recognised a child needs practice in counting and so you may draw their attention to the number of cars they like playing with. In this way you can shape the learning opportunity to meet the child's needs.

Identifying atypical development or additional support needs

You know it is important to track children's development against normative developmental milestones. In addition, you should also be using observations and assessments to consider whether a child has any additional support needs that may indicate atypical development.

It may be that the child is lacking confidence and so needs to have planned opportunities that will make him or her feel successful. Alternatively, you may recognise that a child's language development seems to be atypical for their age, which may result in the child needing a referral.

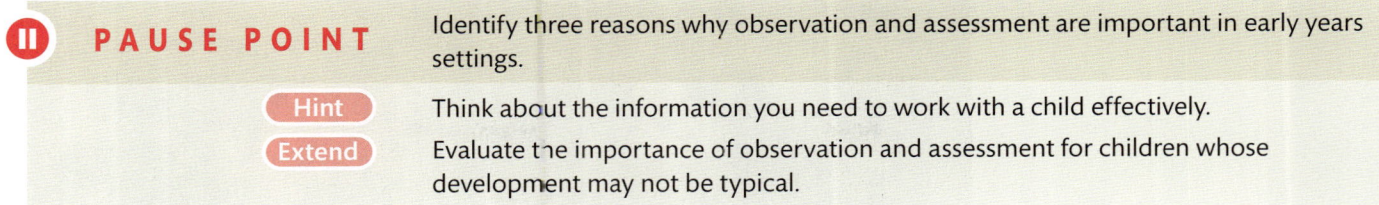

PAUSE POINT   Identify three reasons why observation and assessment are important in early years settings.

Hint   Think about the information you need to work with a child effectively.

Extend   Evaluate the importance of observation and assessment for children whose development may not be typical.

The role of formative and summative assessment

It is good practice for settings to observe children during play and adult-directed activities, and to use the information gained to support the planning process. Two types of assessment are generally used in settings: **formative assessment** and **summative assessment**.

> **Key terms**
>
> **Formative assessment** – assessment that takes place during the learning process on an ongoing basis, or 'assessment for learning'.
>
> **Summative assessment** – assessment of what a child knows and can do at the end of a period of learning, or 'assessment of learning'.

Formative assessment

Formative assessment is where a child's progress is tracked on an ongoing basis. Most settings will do some observations and immediately use the information to consider what the child's next steps might be in particular areas of the curriculum or their development. Formative assessment supports short-term planning.

Summative assessment

Most settings will periodically review a child's progress in all areas of the curriculum. This often takes the form of an overall report. Summative assessment allows for an overview of the child's progress, interests and development. Summative assessments are helpful in long-term planning.

They are also likely to be shared with other settings when the child is due to move, but this can only take place with parental consent. In England, settings following the EYFS are required to produce two summative assessments: one when the child is 2–3 years old and another when the child has finished their reception year.

Discussing children's progress with parents and carers

It is recognised that parents and carers are partners with you in the care and education of their children, so you should involve them in every area of your work. Parents are key to helping you fully understand a child's interests, needs and overall development. They should, if they wish, be involved in the ongoing observation and assessment of their children and you should ensure that you regularly discuss their children's progress with them. It is good practice to find out about what children do when they are at home and what parents have noticed about their children's interests and development. This is important because children often behave differently at home than they do in the setting. At home, children may be more relaxed and also have different opportunities. For instance, they are likely to interact with siblings or other family members. They are also likely to do a range of different activities such as helping in the garden, going shopping or going to the park. Some children may also speak a language at home that is different from that used in the setting.

▶ Parents should be kept informed about their child's progress

The involvement of parents may take different forms according to the age of the child, the type of setting and the parents' wishes. All settings should provide written summaries of the child's progress as well as parents' meetings, but it is good practice to do far more than this. There are many ways in which settings work alongside parents in the observation and assessment process. Table 9.1 shows some of these.

▶ **Table 9.1:** How settings can work alongside parents

Ways settings work alongside parents	How they are helpful
Sharing photographs, film clips and sound recordings	As children do different things at home, some settings invite parents to share photographs, film clips and sound recordings with them
Observations in the home	Some parents may be interested in observing their child and looking out for particular milestones when their child is at home
Sharing observations with parents	It is good practice for settings to show and talk about observations on or near the day they have been carried out
Observations in the setting	Some settings invite parents to observe their child in the setting. They may give parents some points to look out for
Summative assessment	Some settings create summative assessments using parental input. Others create specific sections in which parents can make comments about their child

Discussing children's progress with key person, colleagues and other professionals

You have seen that it is essential to share with parents/carers information about their children's progress. As well as sharing information with parents, you may also at times discuss a child's progress or a significant observation with others who are involved in the care of the child. This is particularly important in group-care settings when several adults may be involved with an individual child. An early years practitioner will tell the child's key person if they have spotted the child doing something for the first time or if they notice that the child is playing with a new group of friends. Passing on information in this way can help the key person understand more about the child.

As well as discussing information with colleagues, there may also be times when early years practitioners will talk to other professionals about a child's progress. This can only take place with parental consent, as you have seen in Unit 8.

Issues to consider when observing and assessing children

There are three main issues to consider when observing children:

▶ confidentiality

▶ participant bias

▶ gaining permission from parents and/or supervisors.

It is important to understand these before you begin observing and assessing children.

Gaining permission

The starting point of any observation is to gain permission. As observation is integral to working effectively with children, settings usually have an agreement with parents that observations and assessments can take place. Digital observation methods such as photography and film are increasingly being used, and parents may sometimes opt out of allowing these methods or may impose strict conditions on how they can be used.

If you are on placement, you should ask your supervisor for permission to carry out an observation. In order that permission can be given, it is helpful for parents or supervisors to know:

▶ the purpose of the observation

▶ the method of observation

▶ how the information gained will be used

▶ who will have access to the observation.

Confidentiality

Information recorded during observations must be treated as confidential. It is also worth noting that it comes under the scope of the Data Protection Act 1998.

Research

Find out more about the Data Protection Act 1998 and what it means for you and your setting. You can find out more on the website of the Information Commissioner's Office: https://ico.org.uk.

It is usual for settings to have policies in place that say who can look at children's records and assessments. This may include the key person, the manager and of course the parents. Most settings operate a **need-to-know policy**.

If you submit observations as part of an assignment, it is important to change the names of children and settings. This avoids a child being identified by others who have no direct reason to know about the child. The need for confidentiality is one reason why digital methods, such as photography or film clips, are not likely to be appropriate for observations submitted as part of an assignment.

Participant bias

When you carry out an observation, it can be very hard to remain objective. This is called **participant bias**. There are many possible reasons for participant bias.

▶ **Relationship with a child** – when an observer has a relationship with a child, they are likely to have subconsciously made judgements about the child based on what they already know. This means they may miss things that do not 'fit' this existing picture. Participant bias is also seen in assessments of children, as someone who knows a child may mark that child favourably or, sometimes, be more critical in their assessment.

Key terms

Need-to-know policy – a way of making sure that personal information is only provided to those people who genuinely 'need to know'.

Participant bias – where an observer is subconsciously recording information in a subjective way.

- **Values and beliefs** – observers may have certain beliefs about groups of children, which make it hard to observe them objectively or make accurate assessments. An example of this is gender. If an observer subconsciously believes that girls are more cooperative than boys, the interpretation of a girl answering back to an adult may be different than it would be for a boy.

- **Information from other adults** – you have seen that parents and others are important sources of information in the assessment process. However, observers who have already been given information about a child can find it hard to observe that child objectively. They may pay more attention to information that concurs with what they have been told than to information that contradicts this.

- **Developmental knowledge** – having a good knowledge of development is important, as without it observers may not pick up on behaviours that are atypical or of interest. On the other hand, if an observer has a particular interest in certain areas of behaviour, they may focus on these to the exclusion of others.

- **Method of recording** – some methods of recording are 'open', and allow the observer to decide what is of interest and which behaviours to note down. This makes it easier for participant bias to be shown. Other methods of recording where children are asked if they can do certain things can also skew results as children can feel nervous, which can affect what they are able to do.

> **Link**
>
> See Section B1 for more information about different ways of recording information.

Avoiding participant bias

It is difficult to avoid participant bias, but being aware that it may occur is the first step. In addition, it can be useful to choose a variety of recording methods for a clearer overall picture. It is also important to listen carefully to alternative points of view about a child and to consider these when next observing the child.

 PAUSE POINT　Identify three issues to consider when carrying out observations and assessments.

Hint　Think about what might influence the observer or the results of observations.

Extend　Choose one of the issues you have identified and consider how you could overcome this in your own observations and assessments.

Assessment practice 9.1　　　　A.P1　A.M1　A.D1

An early years setting wants to improve its observation, assessment and planning system. It has decided to give all staff appropriate training and an information pack. You have been asked to put together information that will act as an introduction to this area of responsibility. You should:

- explain the importance of observation, assessment and planning in early years
- consider how different methods of observation enable practitioners to provide reliable assessments of a child's play, learning and development needs
- evaluate, with examples, the extent to which observation, assessment and planning can impact on an individual child's development.

Plan
- Do I understand why observation, assessment and planning are important?
- Where can I find additional information to put into the training pack?

Do
- Am I selecting information that is relevant for an early years setting?

Review
- Have I shown that I understand the impact and importance of observation, assessment and planning on children's development?
- Have I used the skills of analysis and evaluation in my work?

A2 Planning for children's development

How observations and assessments are used to inform planning

One of the key reasons why early years settings observe and assess young children is to be able to plan effectively to meet their needs. By observing children's interests, early years settings can plan resources and activities that are likely to be of interest to individual children and also groups of children. A child may be interested in playing with toy dinosaurs and so a maths game involving dinosaurs might be created to support this area of development.

Through careful assessment of individual children, early years settings can help to ensure that the activities and resources that they have put out are safe, but also developmentally appropriate. A child, for example, who is still mouthing beyond the usual age and stage, might be given resources that will not represent a choking hazard, while a child who is showing exceptional fine motor skills might be given opportunities to use more intricate construction toys.

In addition, observations and assessments can be used to plan a programme of activities and interventions that target specific skills that a child needs to gain, as the case study shows.

Case study

Planning for individual needs

Jason is 3 years old. Through assessments, his key person has recognised that Jason has not yet acquired a strong hand preference. Typically, most children have developed this by 2½ years. His key person has also observed that over the past couple of weeks Jason is very interested in cooking. She has therefore planned a series of cooking activities that require both hands to be used at the same time, but with each hand having a different role, e.g. grating cheese, peeling bananas and pouring milk into a cup. She has also incorporated washing up and drying dishes into her planning, as these activities can also strengthen hand preference.

Check your knowledge

1 Explain why it is important for Jason's hand skills to be assessed.

2 Discuss the role that observation and assessment have played in the planning of these activities.

3 Why will it be important for Jason's key person to continue to observe and assess his hand preference?

The use of planning

Reflecting children's developmental stage, play and learning needs

Children can learn a lot from simply playing and being with adults, but it can also be helpful to plan specific activities and play opportunities that impart a variety of different skills and knowledge. To ensure this happens, professionals working with children need to carry out their planning based on children's developmental stages, their play and learning needs, as well as their interests. Where a curriculum is being followed, planning will also ensure that any activities meet the requirements of the curriculum.

As well as ensuring that children's needs are met, planning has other advantages. In group settings, it helps staff to be organised and prevents situations in which the children's needs may be overlooked. Planning can also give everyone, including children, a focus and create a more stimulating environment that aids children's overall development.

Meeting children's additional needs

Planning is essential to ensure children's individual needs are met. Children who may need to be planned for in this way include those who have additional needs such as development delay and those who may need additional reassurance. In some cases, you may also need to plan specifically for children who have English as an additional language and/or are new to learning English.

Planning for children who have additional needs is normally done in the medium and short term. This is partly because children's needs and interests can change quite quickly. For some children who have a learning difficulty or global delay, more specialised plans will be needed. These are known as individual education plans (IEPs).

Individual education plans

Individual education plans (IEPs) are usually compiled with the input of a Special Educational Needs Coordinator (SENCO) and the child's parents or carers. The plan will show some particular developmental areas that will be the focus of activities, usually over a period of 4–6 weeks. Children's IEPs will help support the setting's short-term plans, so it is important that suggested activities from the IEP are also included in group planning.

Children's interests and circumstances

Children play more and learn more when they are relaxed. If the play activity they are offered reflects something they are interested in, they are likely to pay closer attention and the learning will be more effective. Learning is also more likely to happen when children can see that their culture and family circumstances are reflected in the play environment and the activities they are taking part in. Therefore, settings need to review plans and planning methods to ensure that they reflect individual children's cultures and family circumstances.

Balancing adult-directed and child-initiated play

Observations and assessments of children are used by early years settings to help them create a balance between adult-directed and child-initiated play on both an individual and group basis. A child, for example, who has a communication and language difficulty, may be encouraged by an adult to engage with activities that involve other children and which may be led by an adult. The balance of adult-directed and child-initiated play may also be considered when a child's progress is analysed according to gender or other characteristics. It may be that some children are not developing sufficiently in specific areas and need an introduction to other types of play and activities. An adult-led activity may act as a good starting point. A good example of this would be a nursery that decides to arrange a visit to a local garden centre to introduce a new theme into the children's role play.

Factors that influence planning

There are many factors that influence what you plan in the long and the short term with the children you work with. In some ways, planning is a little bit like a jigsaw puzzle, as there are many pieces to consider. Getting all the pieces in the right order means that children's developmental needs can be met alongside their interests, while ensuring that they make good progress. Figure 9.2 shows the information required in the planning process.

Current framework or curriculum requirements

In settings that follow a curriculum framework, planning will be heavily influenced by it. In England, for example, settings using the EYFS will need to plan activities that cover all of the seven areas of learning, with the aim of helping children reach the early learning goals. In schools, children may be working towards literacy and numeracy goals, depending on the curriculum that is being followed.

Link

You can find out more about the EYFS in Unit 11.

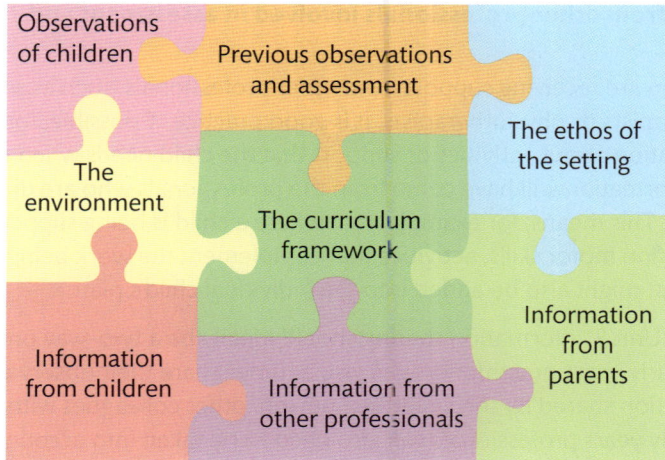

The environment

Observations of children

Previous observations and assessment

The ethos of the setting

The curriculum framework

Information from children

Information from other professionals

Information from parents

▶ **Figure 9.2:** Information that supports the planning process

Most inspectorates that look at how settings implement a curriculum framework will look at the planning in the setting. They are likely to check not only that all parts of the curriculum are being delivered but that plans are appropriately tailored to meet individual children's needs. To show that this is happening, your setting may have a tracking system in place to help staff plan activities in a balanced way, including between adult-directed and child-initiated activities. You may also find that plans for individual children are drawn up that show how, over a period of time, the setting will support their progress.

Research

1 Find out about the requirements for planning that relate to the curriculum being followed in your setting.

2 Find out more about the EYFS or the early years framework that is used in your home country, for example, the Foundation Phase in Wales.

Observations of children

There is little point in planning any activities or play opportunities unless you are sure that they are suitable for children and they will enjoy them. By carrying out observations you can work out what developmental needs children have and what their next steps might be. You can also observe their interests and think about what they enjoy doing.

Previous observations and assessment of children

As well as carrying out observations on children, you can also use your evaluations of activities they have previously been involved in to help you with your planning. For instance, a small group of children who enjoyed playing a particular card game may enjoy playing a similar game.

Discussions with parents and/or carers

Parents and/or carers can often help you in your planning. They may have long-term goals for their child and, wherever possible, you should try to support them. In addition, parents/carers may give you information about what they see their child doing at home and have ideas about how to build on these interests and strengths.

Information from children

You should also involve children in planning as much as you can. You may listen to children's ideas about the equipment, resources and activities they would like to use or do. You can also learn about children's interests and preferences from observations.

Information from other professionals involved in assessment and observations

Where children are receiving support from other professionals, such as speech and language therapists or physiotherapists, it is good practice, if possible, for settings to use information about activities or support that the child needs when preparing plans. This information will have come from the professionals who are directly working with the child. This means, for example, that where a child is being supported to develop their fine motor skills, activities that complement the work being done by a physiotherapist might also be added into the individual child's plan.

As you saw in Unit 8, information sharing should ideally be a two-way process and it is likely that early years practitioners will also at times share their observations of the child. Information shared by the child's key person, other colleagues within the setting and other early years professionals will also need to be taken into account when planning for children's learning needs.

The ethos of the setting

Some settings have their own very distinct ethos and this is reflected in the curriculum. A Forest School setting might plan to take children out into the woods to support their acquisition of outdoor skills. Similarly, a Montessori setting would follow the methods outlined by Maria Montessori, and their planning would be tailored accordingly.

> **Link**
>
> Look back at Unit 3, Section B2, for more information about the different curriculum approaches to play.

The environment

One of the key factors which affects planning is the environment. The term 'environment' is being used loosely here to include space, resources and also the number of adults available. In some settings, space is tight and so careful planning has to take place to maximise learning opportunities. A good example of this is in some childminding settings, where it is simply not possible to put out every resource. Instead, the practitioner has to consider carefully what children need and also what they are likely to enjoy doing.

Where space is limited, it is usual for activities and resources to be rotated so that children can still have access to a wide range of opportunities. Similarly, some early years settings use a shared space such as a hall or outdoor area. This is quite typical in school settings. Again, there has to be careful planning to ensure that opportunities to use shared spaces are maximised.

Another common factor that affects planning for most early years settings is timing. Where children have 3-hour sessions or do not attend a setting every day, careful consideration is needed when planning to ensure that the early years framework is being fully covered. It is also important to make sure that children who attend part time do not feel that they have missed out on activities such as cooking or outings.

> **Theory into practice**
>
> Think about your work placement setting. What environmental factors have to be taken into account during the planning process?

Methods used to plan for children's development

There is a number of ways in which settings carry out planning, but the one thing they have in common is that they are all based on the planning cycle. As such, it is worth looking at this cycle first.

The planning cycle

The planning cycle is sometimes referred to as the Planning, Observation and Evaluation cycle: first you plan an activity or play opportunity, then you observe children's responses to it. The responses will allow you to evaluate the activity, which provides information to help you to plan more effectively in the future.

Early years settings are free to decide how they plan for their children. There is a requirement in the EYFS that settings should plan for individual children based on their needs and interests. As a result, most early years settings create individual plans for children who need additional support as well as plans for the whole group. Many settings will plan a week at a time and adapt these plans over the week. These plans may show adult-led activities for individual and small groups of children, as well as plans for the environment to support child-initiated play. For example, making sure there is always a range of resources that will provide a sufficient challenge.

Long-term planning – groups

Most settings will have some type of long-term planning. Some settings' long-term planning is done every 3 or 4 months, although others may plan for a year at a time. Long-term planning helps settings to schedule in specific activities or topics, outings and festivals. Where a curriculum is being followed, such as those in schools, long-term planning will also be linked to any curriculum expectations for the year group. Long-term planning for most settings centres around the whole group rather than individual children, as it is only very general in nature.

Short-term planning

Most settings will also have some form of short-term planning. This is usually to show what groups and individual children will be doing over a relatively short period of time – for example, a week or a day. Short-term planning is likely to show links to curricula frameworks and also to children's developmental needs and interests. Short-term planning often consists of more than one type of plan.

▶ **Weekly plans** – many settings have weekly plans. These show the activities, play and outings planned for that week. They may also include specific activities for individual children as well as for groups of children.

▶ **Daily plans** – some settings also produce daily plans. These show the activities, play opportunities and routine for the day in more detail. They may also be used to indicate which adults will be working with which groups of children, and where.

▶ **Activity plans** – these show single activities or groups of activities and are drawn up to support individual children's developmental needs, or to help groups of children make progress within a curriculum area.

Continuous provision sheets

Most settings offering early years provision will provide a play-based curriculum. The term 'continuous provision' is used to describe the way that resources and activities for play are provided continually both indoors and out. This allows children to choose what to play with and is one way in which settings can provide both adult-directed and child-initiated play simultaneously. As most settings have plenty of toys and resources that cannot all be made available all the time, many will plan what to put out on either a daily or a weekly basis. Resources and activities are likely to be chosen to give children access to several types of play. Settings may also link their provision to the curriculum framework in the planning. Where resources or activities are put out with specific children in mind, this might be indicated on the sheet. An example of a continuous provision sheet is shown in Figure 9.3.

Activity	Monday	Tuesday	Wednesday	Thursday	Friday
Small-world play	Cars + sawdust	Cars (ML+ST)	Dinosaurs Turf ←———→		
Role play 1	In the living room ——————————————————————————→				
Role play 2	←——— At the hairdressers'		Develop through week ——————→		
Board games and jigsaws	2 x 4 pieces (ST)				
Sensory materials	Gloop ←———→		Soap flakes?		
Mark-making area	At the printers' ←	Develop through week ——————————→			
Water	Clockwork toys				
Dough	Cake cases + buttons (LT)				
Sand	Buttons				
Construction	Wooden blocks				
Exploration and investigation	Digi microscope (collect things on walk)				
Creative area	Collage + Junk modelling (ST) ———————————			Visit to scraps ——→	
ICT	Beebots (BT)	Digi microscope ———————————————→			Beebots
Other	Sewing kits ←———→		Marble run		

▶ **Figure 9.3:** A continuous provision sheet. The sheet is added to and changed based on children's observed interests. These interests can be marked with children's initials

Learning journeys

Many settings have combined observation, assessment and planning for individual children by using **'learning journeys'**. The idea behind these is to build up a portfolio of children's progress and interests that can be shared, not only with parents/carers, but also with the children themselves. Most settings that use learning journeys find they are a great way of bringing together observations and planning. Figure 9.4 shows how a snapshot observation accompanied by a photograph is used to record an area of learning. These can form the basis of an assessment, along with some ideas about activities that can be planned as a result of the observation.

Observation	Ayse found her shoes when I said that it was time to go outdoors. It took her a moment, but she was able to work out which shoe went on the correct foot. She managed to fasten the buckles without any support. She was very pleased with herself.
What does the observation mean?	Ayse can now put on most of her clothes and shoes herself.
What next?	• Give Ayse time so that she can get dressed herself. • Show her how to use a zip and find dressing-up clothes that have zips. • Look out for role-play clothes that will help her to practise using buttons, zips and buckles.
Links to the EYFS	PSE Self-care (30–50 months) PD Using equipment and materials (30–50 months)
Notes for the next observation	CLL Look out for examples of mark making and also record speech.

▶ **Figure 9.4:** An example of a learning journey

Observations are carried out fortnightly by each child's key person to review the different areas of development. Every 6 weeks, a summative record is produced to show the child's progress in each of the areas of learning and development based on these observation sheets. At planning meetings, key persons talk about what activities, needs or interests their key children have. These are then incorporated into the weekly plans.

> **Key term**
>
> **Learning journey/learning story** – a way of assessing and planning for children's development using a narrative approach that can easily be constructed and shared with parents and children.

How to review plans and planning methods

As with other areas of work with children, it is important for settings to review the effectiveness of their planning systems. This is because when planning systems are working well, children's individual needs are met and activities are sufficiently challenging. This in turn means children are likely to be making good progress. Settings need to consider whether their planning reflects the needs, strengths and interests of the children and also the requirements of the curriculum framework they are using. Children's individual needs should also be reflected within group planning. This can be demanding, as there is often a tension between creating a manageable system, where staff are not spending too long on paperwork, while ensuring planning is sufficiently detailed and robust. This is one reason why settings will continually review and try to improve their planning systems.

Here are some questions to help you review plans and planning systems.

▸ Are each child's interests and strengths reflected in the planning?

▸ Do plans reflect the education requirements of the curriculum being used?

▸ Are plans used and referred to by adults working with children?

▸ Do plans take account of children's family circumstances?

▸ How do plans show what will be happening in the setting on a day-to-day basis?

▸ How are plans shared with and contributed to by parents?

Assessment practice 9.2 — A.P2 A.M2 A.D1

As part of the second training session for staff on observation, assessment and planning, the manager has asked you to focus on factors and influences on planning for play, learning and development. Your information should:

- explain the factors that affect planning for play, learning and development
- analyse the influences on planning for play, learning and development in an early years setting.

Finally, at the end of this session, the manager has asked you to present an evaluation of the observation, assessment and planning process, with examples from an early years setting.

Plan
- Do I understand how observation and assessment processes feed into planning?
- Do I have sufficient information about the factors that influence planning in early years settings?

Do
- Have I presented my information clearly and accurately?
- Will my information be useful and accessible to early years staff?

Review
- Have I provided relevant information and used examples to support my work?
- Have I shown the skills of analysis and evaluation?

B Carry out and record observations of children to make accurate assessments

B1 Observation recording methods

There are many different methods of observing and assessing children. In this section, you will look at several different methods, the reasons why they might be used and their benefits and drawbacks.

Methods of observation recording

Each observation technique has its own advantages and limitations, so it is useful to learn to use several. While there are different techniques, remember that observing children is always about collecting information. Therefore, knowing what you need to learn about the child is important when choosing a technique. There are two broad methods of data collection: closed data methods and open data methods.

▸ **Closed data methods** – closed data methods focus our attention very narrowly. A good example of a closed data method is a checklist, which usually consists of groups of statements. The observer reads the statements and then considers whether or not this is what they are seeing while they observe the child. Closed data methods are considered to be less subjective than open data methods. Their major drawback is that they can focus your attention so narrowly that data might be missed; for example, whether children smile as they skip. Closed data methods tend to be good for assessing children's skills and achievements.

▶ **Open data methods** – open data methods allow you significantly more freedom, as the observation format is not as narrow. The observer is able to focus on whatever takes their attention. This increases the likelihood of subjectivity, but does mean you might gain more information about children. Snapshot observations are examples of open data recording. In this type of observation, the observer jots down what is perceived as interesting when watching a child.

Figure 9.5 shows some commonly used methods of observation.

▶ **Figure 9.5:** Popular methods of observation

Checklists/tick charts

Checklists, or tick charts, are a popular closed method of observing children because they are easy to use and understand. Checklists are used in many settings by a range of professionals, and they comprise a list of prepared statements. In some settings these statements relate to the curriculum framework, or they may be compiled to include developmental milestones.

When to use this method

Checklists or tick charts can be used when you need to look at a child's skills or knowledge. This is a good method to use if you want to see how much progress a child has made, as the same tick chart can be used a few weeks later. For example, in the classroom a checklist may be used to see how many letter sounds a child knows. Checklists are often used to compare a particular child's development or knowledge with children of a similar age.

How to use this method

You need to carefully read through the listed tasks or skills before beginning the observation. When you observe the child, note whether or not a child is able to do each with a tick or remark. This is an observation technique that can either be done unobtrusively (by simply watching the child and hoping they will show the skills to be recorded) or by asking the child a specific question or to demonstrate certain skills such as writing their name.

Figure 9.6 shows an example of a checklist.

Theory into practice

Find out what types of observation methods are used in your work placement. Divide these into open data and closed data methods.

Child
Child's age .... Observer ....
Date of observation .... Time ....

Activity	Yes	No	Comments
Puts together three-piece puzzle			
Snips with scissors			
Paints in circular movements			
Holds crayons with fingers, not fist			
Can thread four large beads			
Turns pages in a book one by one			
Can put on and take off coat			

▶ **Figure 9.6:** An example of a checklist

Ⅱ PAUSE POINT Identify three disadvantages of the checklist method.

> Hint Think about why checklist methods may not always be accurate.
> Extend Consider why many early years settings use checklist methods.

Time samples

Time samples are interesting and versatile. They provide information about a child's activity at regular intervals (e.g. what a child is doing during a session at ten-minute intervals). Time samples can be structured and written in code form, or they may be freer, with observers simply using a running commentary style as the sample is taken. Figure 9.7 shows an example of a time sample recording sheet.

When to use this method

This is a useful method to use to look at a child's activity overall or as part of a session. It is less intensive than target child observations or the written narrative methods and leaves the observer free to look at other children between samples. It is a good method for observing children's all-round development in a range of contexts. For example, you may observe social interaction while the child is playing indoors with the sand, followed by outdoor play using a range of equipment. Time samples can also be used to observe children's interests and concentration span.

How to use this method

The starting point for this method is to decide how structured the time sample needs to be. A structured recording will mean you need to draw a sheet in advance and familiarise yourself with codes. You will also need to decide how often you will sample the child's activity – this may depend on the length of time you intend to observe them for. For example, you may use five-minute intervals for observations that last for less than an hour, or 15-minute intervals for all-day observations. It is unlikely that sample times greater than 15 minutes will be very informative.

Name of child Bryony Matthews			Date of birth	20-08-12
Date of observation	14-9-2016	Start time	10.00 am	End time	11.00 am

Purpose of observation Plays + interaction with other child?		
10.00	Book corner. Alone taking books out of shelves and making piles	③
10.05	Book corner, with adult. Tidying books. Rolling on floor	②
10.10	Book corner. Adult reading story. 2 x other children with BM. BM moves away slightly	⑤
10.15	Book corner. Adult + BM talking. Pointing out pictures. Pushes other child away	⑤
10.20	Sand tray. Standing watching 3 x children at play. Eye contact	②
10.25	Water tray. 2 x other children (ST + TM) Hitting water with hands. Smiling at ST	③
10.30	ST passes BM a funnel. ST smiles, uses funnel, laughs (water tray)	④
10.35	Book corner. Alone. Rolling on floor lifting rug around her	②
10.40	Book corner. Alone. Tapping books on shelves one by one	②
10.45	Snack table. Waiting for turn. Watching 2 x others pour drinks	③

▶ **Figure 9.7:** A time sample recording sheet. This observer is using a code number to record the intensity of the child's engagement as well as recording what the child is doing every five minutes

Once you have determined the range of the time sample, the next step is simply to record what you see when it is time to observe. While it can be interesting to observe the child in the meantime, it is important only to record at the sample times.

Advantages of time samples

▶ They provide information about children's activity over a relatively long period.
▶ They can be used to provide information about children's overall development.
▶ They can give an indication of children's interests and levels of concentration.

Disadvantages of time samples

▶ They do not record information about what a child is doing outside the sample time.

Written narrative/running record

This method is probably one of the most straightforward. It requires the observer to put what is being seen into writing. There is a surprising amount of skill required though, as it can be hard to find descriptive language and write it down quickly enough to keep up. The speed at which the observer must write means that only a small amount of information can be recorded and its selection is likely to be very subjective. The language used to record it is also subjective. Observers will not have time to consider vocabulary carefully and may put down the first word that comes to them that they feel fits the situation. For instance, they may use 'snatches', which is more emotive than 'takes quickly'. Most observers using this method find it helpful to pause from time to time to finish off sentences. Afterwards, notes will need to be rewritten so they are legible.

When to use this method

This is a versatile method, often used as a starting point for future observations. You can choose to record any area of development, or look at a child more holistically and note down things of interest as they occur.

How to use this method

You will need a reliable pen and notepad. Begin by noting the start time of the observation as well as the context. Then, as you watch the child, write down what you are seeing. This method is sometimes referred to as a 'running commentary'. Most observers find they need to stop after a few minutes, as they are unable to write quickly enough to record everything a child is doing or saying. It is good practice to note the time of each stop and start so that anyone reading it later does not assume that the commentary is continuous. It is also usual for the writing to be in the present continuous tense, for example, 'he is going towards the door' rather than 'he went towards the door'.

Advantages of written narrative

▶ This is quite an open method of recording, so it can provide quite a lot of information.
▶ No preparation is required.
▶ This method provides a 'portrait' of a child and so is popular with parents.

Disadvantages of written narrative

▶ This way of recording can be quite subjective, as it is impossible to record everything a child does and says while observing them.
▶ It can be hard to write quickly and to choose words well, so this technique requires practice.

Snapshot observations

This method is a variation on written narrative, and has been used widely by early years settings. The idea is the child is observed very briefly, perhaps a minute or so, because the adult has seen something of interest the child is doing or has decided in advance the child needs to be seen in a particular area of play or showing a particular skill. This short observation is often written on a sticky note. Snapshot observations are also used as the starting point of the 'learning journey' method of assessment and planning.

Advantages of snapshot observations

▶ They do not take long to write.
▶ Parents like to see what their child has been doing and these snapshots provide accessible information.
▶ They allow for spontaneous observation and recording.

Disadvantages of snapshot observations

▶ They are very short and may not provide sufficient, detailed information.
▶ They may be subjective, as this is an open method of observation.

Target child observations

Target child observations note the actions and responses of a particular child over a continuous period of time. Target child observations require the observer to be very focused and to work intensively. The observer uses codes to ensure they can record what the child is doing minute by minute.

Link

Go to Section A2 in this unit to find more information about the 'learning journey' method of assessment and planning.

When to use this method

This method is often used to learn about individual children and, while it can be used to provide a holistic observation, it is often used to focus on children's social and language interaction.

How to use this method

This is an observation method that does need to be planned ahead. It requires the observer to focus on only one child and means the observer is not able to work with other children at the same time.

1   Start by deciding which child is to be observed.

2   Prepare or photocopy a record sheet (see Figure 9.8 for an example).

3   Read through and check that you can remember the codes to use.

4   Write the start time on the sheet and use a stopwatch or clock to keep time.

5   For each minute, record what the child is doing. Use codes to ensure that you can keep up.

Individual child-tracking observation

Name of child   *Hamza*   Observer   *Steph*   Date   *22/10/16*

Age of child   *3* yrs   *2* months   No. of adults present   *2*   No. of children present   *6*

Free play/structured play/directed activity

Time	Description of activity	Language	Grouping	Level of involvement
10.00 am	TC scooping sand using left hand repeated movements	TC →	P	4
10.02	TC burying r. hand, scooping with other	→ TC ←	I	4
10.03	TC nods head. Other child copies TC, TC smiles	C → TC	P	3

Key

Grouping	Language		Level of involvement
WG = Whole group	TC → A	Balanced interaction between adult and child	1 = No activity
SG = Small group			2 = Frequently distracted
P = Pair	TC → C	Balanced interaction between target child and another child	3 = Fairly continuous activity
I = Individual			4 = Absorbed in activity
	A → C	Adult interacts with more than one child	
	C → TC	Another child interacts with target child	
	→ TC ←	Target child talks to himself/herself	
	TC →	No interaction	

▶ **Figure 9.8:** An example of a target child observation record sheet

Advantages of target child observation

▶ It provides detailed information about a child's activity over a continuous period.

▶ Codes are used to enable the observer to write more efficiently. These can be made up by the observer to suit the observation.

Disadvantages of target child observation

▶ The observer needs to be familiar with the coding system and practise using it.

▶ It can be difficult for others to understand the notes if non-standard codes are used.

Digital recordings

As technology has become increasingly cheap and easy to use, many settings are now using digital methods to record children. There are many advantages to using these methods. However, as with all methods of recording, it is vital to gain parental/carer consent and ensure all recordings are kept secure.

Good organisation is also required for these methods, as it can be easy to forget when recordings were made. Settings using this method often create a digital folder for each child so that recordings are not lost and can be kept in date order.

Using a camera

Using a camera either to photograph or film children and young people is becoming increasingly popular as an observation technique. Either photography or filming can help you notice details that you might otherwise miss.

When to use this method

This method can be used to film groups of children as well as individual children. If you wish to film children with sound, it is important to choose situations in which there is not too much ambient noise. It is also important to be aware of any children who may wander into view whose parents have not given permission for them to be recorded in this way.

How to use this method

This is a straightforward method, as you only need to decide what to film and then get started. However, it is worth practising first to ensure you can use the equipment easily. Remember to check that the camera has sufficient battery power. It is important to write down the time and date of the observation or to set the camera up so it does this automatically. It is also important to get children used to being filmed first; otherwise they may be more interested in what you are doing than in carrying on with their play or activity.

Advantages of using a camera

▶ It is easy to review what children are doing and notice details.

▶ This method is popular with parents, as they can see what their children have been doing.

▶ Older children can use this as a medium to show you what is important in their lives.

Disadvantages of using a camera

▶ Confidentiality can be an issue. Children can only be filmed with parental/carer consent. This includes children who are not the focus of the observation but who may stray into the shot.

▶ Recordings have to be kept secure.

▶ Background noise may prevent you from hearing what children are saying.

▶ Photographs only give limited information. It is not possible to know what the child did or said in the moments leading up to the photograph or film, or immediately afterwards.

▶ Using a camera is a popular observation technique

Sound recordings

It is now easy to record children's speech onto a variety of devices including mobile phones, MP3 players and other gadgets.

When to use this method

Sound recordings work well for recording children's speech. It is particularly useful to make several recordings of the same child over time as a way of checking that their speech is progressing.

How to use this method

Choose a quiet place and note the name of the child and the date, either on a piece of paper or into the recording device. Talk to the child naturally to encourage them to respond as usual. If a child's speech is unclear, either because of their age or stage of development, make sure that you recast what has been said. This is good practice – it is essential that anyone else listening to the recording afterwards can understand what the child was trying to say. For instance, 'We go guirrel?' may be recast as, 'Yes, we are going to see the squirrels later'.

Play back the recording to check it is sufficiently clear, then transfer it into the child's digital folder.

Advantages of sound recordings

▶ Recordings can be done while you are with the child, which makes this a time-efficient way of recording.

▶ Parents and carers can hear their child's speech develop if several recordings are made over time.

▶ Parents and carers can make recordings of their child's speech at home. This can be useful if the child speaks a language different from that used in the setting.

▶ Where there are suspected speech and language difficulties, recordings can be played to other professionals as part of the referral process.

Disadvantages of sound recordings

▶ It can be difficult to hear what children are saying in noisy environments.

▶ It is not possible to see the child's body language or facial expression, or to see the context in which speech is taking place.

▶ If recordings do not specify the time, date and name of the child, it may not be clear later when they were made or who was speaking.

PAUSE POINT   Identify three reasons why sound recordings might be used in early years settings.

Hint   Think about the importance of assessing language.

Extend   How could sound recordings be used to monitor children's progress in language?

Sociograms

Sociograms are used with children from around 4 years old to look at patterns of friendships within groups. By asking children about their friendship preferences, a chart is created that shows which children are frequently named, whether friendships are reciprocated and whether certain children find it difficult to name friends or are not named themselves.

> **Key term**
>
> **Sociogram** – a recording method whereby children indicate their friendship preferences.

When to use this method

Talk to children one at a time when no other children are with them. Ask them to name their friends and, if necessary, use a prompt question such as, 'Who do you like playing with?' Remember to give children enough time to respond, and record the names that are given by each child. Then create the sociogram chart.

How to use this method

It can be interesting to use sociograms as a starting point for further observations. Consider following up with those children who are not named by other children or who had difficulty in naming any friends. It is also important to follow this up with information from parents and colleagues who may have seen children play with each other or who may have heard children talk about other children.

Advantages of using sociograms

▶ They can provide an indication that some children need more support in making friends.

Disadvantages of using sociograms

▶ This can be a very unreliable method to use with 4-year-old children, who will often base their answers on whoever they have just played with.

▶ It can be more reliable with older children, but there is a danger that older children will mention names simply to please the questioner.

> **Theory into practice**
>
> Ask your placement supervisor how friendships are monitored in your setting. Why might sociograms be problematic with very young children?

Event sample observations

Event samples are sometimes referred to as 'frequency counts'. The aim of these observations is to find out how often a specific type of behaviour or response takes place and also the context in which it occurs. They are often used when a child is showing unwanted behaviour, but may also be used more broadly. They can help a practitioner to work out the reasons for certain responses, and also provide evidence to show whether responses or incidents are increasing or decreasing. Event samples are **non-contemporaneous**, as recording takes place after the event or incident has occurred.

When to use this method

Event samples focus narrowly on the particular response of a child. For example, you might decide to investigate how often a child has a tantrum and the context in which this occurs, or you might look at how often a child interacts with other children.

How to use this method

A sheet that directs the user to the type of information to be collected has to be drawn up. There are no standard formats, as the recording columns need to reflect the observer's information requirements. Commonly collected information includes the date and time as well as the context. Figure 9.9 shows an event sample focusing on the number of times a child interacts with other children in a setting. In this situation, it will be important to see whom the child talks to and for how long. It will also be useful to find out whether the child initiates the contact or if the other children do.

Event	Time	Activity of child	Social group	Language used	Comments
1	11.07	Playing in the water tray	Sam, Katie, Mustafa, Ben	'Look, look! Water fell.'	Sam leaned over and said this to Mustafa and Ben
2	11.16	Playing with two beakers in the water tray, trying to transfer water between the two	Sam, Mustafa, Ben	'Water splash, splash, splash.'	Sam was showing Mustafa, while splashing Ben

▶ **Figure 9.9:** Part of an event sample showing how often Sam interacts with other children

Once the record sheet is drawn up, it is only filled in when the specific behaviour or response is noted. In settings where several adults might work with a child, the person who was working with the child at the time could fill in the record sheet.

Advantages of event samples

▶ They can help us understand the frequency and patterns of a child's behaviour or responses.

▶ They can be a way of monitoring the success of strategies by providing a baseline.

▶ They produce detailed information on the behaviour being observed, can indicate events that may trigger the behaviour and confirm if there is the need for concern.

Disadvantages of event samples

▶ Others may need to fill in the record sheet if the observer is absent.

▶ They require the observer to concentrate on one child for a long period of time.

▶ The child being observed might know they are being observed and this could affect the outcome.

Participant and non-participant observation

A participant observation is one where the observer is involved with the child at the time. They may, for example, join in the child's play or ask the child a question. Some observation techniques, such as checklists, are likely to use participant observations because sometimes it is quicker or simpler to ask the child to do something, for example, 'Can you count these ladybirds?' The key drawback to a participant observation is that what the child does or says may alter because of the adult's involvement or presence. A child may become nervous or may try extra hard to achieve something to please the adult. This can alter the results. To avoid this, it can be helpful if participant observations are done by someone who is familiar to the child.

Other observations, such as target child observations, are likely to be non-participant. The observer tries to be discreet and observe what the child is doing without becoming involved. The main drawback of this approach is that, unless the observer is behind a screen, children might still feel that they are being watched and may moderate their behaviour. It can also be a slow way of ascertaining what the child can do. For example, if a child's counting is being assessed, you have to wait until they engage in an activity in which counting plays a part.

Information from other sources

Strictly speaking, the term 'observation' relates only to what you have actually seen and recorded at a particular time. In practice, the term is used more widely and covers information gained in retrospect or from indirect sources; for example, it might include something a parent or carer tells you. As previously mentioned, information that is not actually seen and recorded at the time is described as non-contemporaneous.

Advantages of non-contemporaneous information

Information from others can help you build a holistic picture of a child in a range of situations and over a period of time. This is important, as you cannot be with the child in every situation or for every hour of the day. Other people can also provide additional viewpoints and so potentially counter participant bias.

Disadvantages of non-contemporaneous information

The biggest disadvantage of non-contemporaneous information is, because no direct recording is available, you cannot be sure it is accurate or reliable. For example, a child may tell you what has happened but may not include details that you would have wanted to focus on. You may not be given a full picture of what has happened, or an event might be exaggerated. In addition, parents and others may have different expectations of children and this can colour their reporting. For instance, parents may say their child has shown very difficult behaviour when, actually, the behaviour is quite typical for the child's age range.

Information from parents, carers and others

Parents or carers and colleagues see children in different situations and so may have different views of a particular child's development. Information from parents or carers can be gained from questionnaires, structured face-to-face interviews or informal chats. Some practitioners also encourage parents to observe their children at home using a recording method such as filming.

Advantages of using information from parents and others

Parents or carers and other professionals will see children in different situations and so may provide information that would otherwise be difficult to collect. In the case of other professionals, you may not have the expertise to collect the information yourselves, while they do.

Disadvantages of using information from parents and others

Parents and carers may show participant bias, as they want to present their child in the best light or try to second-guess what the setting wants. It may be hard to verify the accuracy of observations or to understand the context in which they have taken place.

Selecting appropriate observational methods

It is important to choose the right method of observation, so begin by thinking about what type of information you are trying to collect. For example, if you are focusing on a child's speech and language, you might decide to carry out a sound recording as well as a time sample. This will give information about how the child talks in relation to their age and stage of development, as well as whom the child communicates with and how often over the course of a session.

Here are some questions to consider.

▶ **What is the purpose of the observation?** – As you have seen, there are many reasons why you may carry out observations. It is important to think about the specific purpose of the observation and how the information gained from the observation will be used. If, for example, an early years setting wants to observe whether or not boys and girls all access a range of play opportunities, then a method of recording that looks at group activity over a period of time might be chosen.

▶ **What information do I need to collect?** – This is important because some areas of development or types of behaviours lend themselves to certain types of observational methods.

▶ **How much time do I have to spend recording?** – Some recording methods take more time than others. Some can be done alongside working with children, whereas others work better when the observer is not directly involved. How much time is available is therefore important, especially in busy settings.

▶ **How reliable must the recording method be?** – While we should always aim for accurate observations, sometimes the reliability is particularly important. This might be the case where your observations will be used to determine whether or not a child is referred to other professionals, or where your information will support the work of other professionals.

▶ **Do I need a combination of recording methods?** – A combination of recording methods can help to give a better all-round picture of a child. If you do not know very much about a child, a combination of methods might be a good idea.

▶ **Do I want open or closed methods of recording?** – You have seen that open and closed methods each have their advantages and disadvantages. The purpose of the observation will probably determine which method you use.

▶ **How skilled am I at using the recording method?** – Everyone has favourite recording methods and ones that they find easier than others. If an observation is very important, you may decide to use a method that you are comfortable with. On the other hand, in other circumstances, you may decide to practise a recording method in order to become more skilled.

❚❚ PAUSE POINT   Identify four factors to consider when carrying out observations.

> Hint   Think about factors that will affect the results of your observations as well as the practical issues involved.

> Extend   Evaluate the importance of carefully planning your observations.

B2 Carry out and record observations of children

How to carry out observations

In order to achieve a Pass grade in this unit, you will need to demonstrate that you are able to use a range of observation methods with children. These will be used to carry out assessments that will feed into activity plans. It is therefore important that you practise each of the different methods that you looked at in the previous section.

You have seen that there are many factors involved in the planning of observations. You will need to present a detailed plan of how you intend to carry out observations, along with a justification of your choices. It is therefore important to spend some time thinking about which children you may observe, as well as the methods that might generate plenty of information. In addition, you should also consider the following factors.

Awareness of observer influence

In terms of observer influence, you will need to consider all aspects that might influence the outcome of the recording. This includes how you intend to record information in ways that will reduce the possibility of children changing their responses because they know that they are being observed. You will also need to consider how you will minimise potential subjectivity, especially if you have already been told about the child or have worked with the child beforehand.

Timing

In your detailed plan that shows how you intend to carry out observations, you will also need to consider whether or not the recordings will be made at certain times, or whether you will carry out a recording spontaneously because you have noticed something significant that the child is doing. As recordings are likely to take place in the work placement setting, you will also need to ask your placement supervisor's advice and permission as to when and where recordings can be carried out.

Environmental variables

In your planning, you should also think about environmental variables that might influence children's responses. These may include unusual activities in the setting, as some children may become more excited, or a change of weather. Children also interact differently according to who they are with, so you may need to consider, for example, whether a child's best friend is absent.

How to present records of observation

As observations will be used to support planning and assessment, it is important that they are presented in ways that are easy to understand and refer back to. The following should be considered when presenting records of any observations that you carry out.

▸ **Legibility** – it is important that records of observations are neat and legible, so that other people can understand them. Observations may be read by parents and/ or carers, key persons and other professionals such as inspectors. As part of your course, you may also have to present observations as part of an assignment. These must be neat and legible.

▸ **Accuracy and detail** – it is important that information is recorded accurately and, wherever possible, in detail. This can take practice, but it is essential, as otherwise there is a danger that inaccurate conclusions will be drawn about a child's interests, needs or development.

▸ **Non-judgemental tone** – it may be hard, but you should aim only to record what you see or hear – without elaboration and without using words that imply a judgement. You should not state what did not happen, such as 'he did not say thank you', as this was not observed.

▶ **Non-subjective** – you will already have worked with many of the children that you observe. It is likely that subconsciously you have reached some conclusions about individual children. It is important, however, during the recording process to imagine that you are meeting this child for the first time and to consciously put aside any pre-existing thoughts. This will allow you to record in a non-subjective way.

▶ **Date of observation** – it is important to write down the date the observation was carried out. This helps observations to be put in order and allows you to see the progress that children are making. It also helps the observation to be seen as valid.

▶ **Age of child** – it is usual to note the child's age at the beginning of the observation. This is usually recorded in years and months (for example, 4 years 3 months). This helps anyone reading the observation to see how what has been observed relates to the typical development.

▶ **Contextual information** – it is usual to note down information that helps the reader understand the full picture of what was happening at the time. You should note down the context in which the activity took place and what the type of activity is. For example, what the child was doing or what was happening when the observation began: 'four children were around the sand tray and an adult had just added some more sand'.

▶ **Number of children/adults present** – record the number of children and adults around the child at the time of the observation. This is important because children's behaviour changes according to the group size and who they are with.

▶ **Purpose of the observation** – it can be helpful to write down the reason for carrying out the observation, as this helps anyone reading it to see what the focus of the observation was meant to be. For example, 'the observation was carried out to determine whether child X talked more when alone with an adult or in a small group'.

❚❚ PAUSE POINT   Identify five features of accurately presented observations.

> Hint   Focus on what would make an observation invalid.
>
> Extend   Consider why contextual information may have an impact when drawing conclusions from observations.

Reflect

Observation and assessment of children are a key part of many qualifications. Think about the following when you are planning your observations and assessment.

1   Clear aims and relevant method – the more focused you are as an observer, the more accurate and detailed your observation record will be.

2   Open methods of recording – open methods allow you to collect a wide pool of information about a child. Closed methods, such as checklists, provide less insight into a child's responses but are still valuable in providing information about groups of children in a setting.

3   Detail – more detailed information provides more evidence to support your conclusions.

Assessment practice 9.3

Ask your placement supervisor if you can practise your observation technique. With the support of your supervisor, choose a child to observe and decide on four different methods to use to observe their development.

- Draw up a detailed plan of observations that you intend to carry out.
- For each recording method, justify your choice.
- Evaluate your plan, considering how well the combination of recording methods will help to assess the child's development.

Plan
- When can I talk to my placement supervisor?
- Do I understand the issues involved in observing children?

Do
- Have I drawn up a detailed plan for my observation of the chosen child?
- Have I discussed my plan with my placement supervisor?

Review
- Have I justified my choice of recording methods?
- Have I evaluated my plan for observing the child?

B3 Make accurate assessments of children

Observing children is just one part of the process of assessing children and making plans for their play and development. Once you have observed children, you need to interpret what you have recorded. This is an important step, as the conclusions that you draw should influence the short-term planning for the child. Your conclusions will also be used to help parents and others understand the child's developmental progress. Importantly, they might also help to identify when a child may need additional support. This section looks at ways in which you might draw these conclusions.

Identifying a child's stage of development from observations

One of the key reasons for observing children is to check that they are making developmental progress. Looking at developmental milestones (or norms) may help you realise that a child's development is completely typical for their age group. On the other hand, looking at the developmental milestones may help you realise that the child needs additional support.

Developmental milestones are looked at particularly carefully in children's earliest years. This is because the early identification of needs often makes a significant difference to later outcomes. One of the reasons why early identification is so important is that different areas of development are interlinked. For example, a child with atypical speech and language development may find it hard to control their behaviour and so may not be invited to play with other children.

Checking developmental milestones is especially important when you look at young children's behaviour. A child with a peer group whose behaviour is in advance of expected development may appear to be 'difficult and uncooperative' when, in reality, their behaviour is within the expected range for their age.

Looking at developmental milestones can also help you to be aware of what the child needs to go on and do. This might help in planning equipment and activities, and also checking that you are providing sufficient challenges.

How to identify a child's stage of development from observations

When looking at developmental milestones, a good starting point is to check the developmental milestones given for the child's age in reference books, and see how they relate to the skills and knowledge the child showed in the observation. For instance, if the child was busy pouring sand from one container to another, how do these fine motor skills relate to the expected developmental norms or milestones?

Link

Go back to Section A1 to remind yourself what developmental milestones are.

Once you have established how the child's fine motor skills relate to the developmental norms, you can then write a conclusion that shows the correlation. This has the advantage of showing the reader how the conclusion was reached. One way of doing this is to start by stating what you have observed and then quoting directly or indirectly what is stated in a reference book or on a trusted website. An example is shown in Figure 9.10, where a learner has made an indirect reference to the author Carolyn Meggitt's work in support of her observation.

> Janie, aged 3 years, repeatedly poured sand from one container to another. She often did this without spilling any. According to Carolyn Meggitt, this is typical of this age group.

▶ **Figure 9.10:** An example of an indirect reference

Making links to milestones

Once you have made a note of the specific skills and knowledge that a child has shown through their actions, behaviour and language, the next step is to make your own links to developmental norms. You will need to find a reliable source of milestones that are age-related. This book, for example, has some charts that you may find useful.

You will then need to look at what skills and knowledge are expected for the age of the child and draw some conclusions. This might require you to use a 'best-fit' judgement at times. For example, a milestone for fine motor skills might say 'uses seven bricks to make a tower', but the child you observed was stacking beakers instead of using bricks. It is also worth looking at the milestones that relate to older as well as younger children than the child you were observing, to see if they provide a better match.

Drawing conclusions and recognising the need for additional support

Part of the assessment process is to draw some conclusions. Where a child is not showing the development that is expected for the age, it may be that the conclusion will be to give the child more opportunities to practise the skill, or a range of resources that will encourage the child to play in different ways. You may also conclude that you need to be involved more with the child or to work with the child in different ways. In some cases, your conclusion may be that the child needs additional support or a referral to another professional. If this is the case, it is likely that other observations will be carried out to ensure that an accurate assessment has been made.

As well as looking out for children who may need additional support, the assessment process may also draw conclusions about the child's interests and preferences. Using these conclusions, it is possible to plan for the provision of toys, activities and resources that will support their known interests and preferences in new ways.

Recognising children's needs, interests and preferences

Open recording styles of observation, such as filming, written record or target child observations, are particularly useful when looking at children's developmental needs, interests and preferences. When looking at an observation, think about the following.

▶ **With what or whom did the child spend the most time?** – This may indicate a friendship preference or a play interest.

- **What level of engagement did the child show?** – High levels of concentration and perseverance, especially during child-initiated play, are often indicators of interests and play preferences.
- **Facial expression** – Children may smile, laugh or look intensely interested in things. This may indicate an interest or play preference.

As with development, you should try to show the link between the interests and preferences you have observed and your conclusions. In some cases you may realise that although you have seen the child smile or laugh, you have not recorded it. This is not good practice because, in theory, you are drawing conclusions about something for which you have no evidence. This is one reason why it is important when starting out to keep practising observation. The more you do it, the more skilled you will become. Read the observation in Figure 9.11 by Akbar, an early years professional, to see a good example of an observation record.

> During the observation I saw Michael spend most of the hour playing with a toy shark, which he used in both the sand and the water trays. He also asked if he could take it to the snack table with him.
>
> *Akbar, an early years professional*

▶ **Figure 9.11:** An example of an observation note

PAUSE POINT

Identify how developmental milestones are used as part of assessing children's development.

Hint
Think about why you observe children. What is the main reason?

Extend
Discuss the importance of using reliable sources of information when making links to developmental milestones.

Linking observations to the curriculum framework

One of the key reasons why observations are undertaken is to consider whether children are showing expected progress in either developmental areas or curriculum areas. These are often interlinked. In order to be able to identify a child's stage of development, it is important to read carefully what has been recorded. Think about what skills or knowledge a child is showing through their actions. A child, for example, who says 'My Nan tooked me to the shoe shop yesterday,' is demonstrating an understanding of time as well as the ability to construct simple sentences. The error in the use of 'tooked' is also significant. Picking out what is significant in observations does require practice. In some cases, you may not have recorded information in sufficient detail or the type of observation method does not lend itself to identifying a stage of development or a specific curriculum area.

As you saw in Section A1 of this unit, there are two types of assessment carried out in early years settings: formative assessments and summative assessments. Assessments are conclusions that are drawn about the child and are based on observations.

Formative assessment

A formative assessment is an ongoing record of the child's development. To record a formative assessment, you need to consider what you feel each observation shows after you have carried it out. This can be quite concise. You should then link it to an area of learning in the EYFS (or the curriculum in your own home country) and then consider what the child's next steps might be.

Summative assessment

A summative assessment is literally a 'summing up' of the child's progress, development and interests. Most early years settings will do a summative assessment every 3–4 months. In a summative assessment, each area of the child's development is considered and looked at in line with expected developmental norms. The rate of the child's progress will also be looked at.

Most early years settings have a format for recording summative assessments. Summative assessments are important and so it is important to be accurate and precise when writing them. The format can vary from setting to setting so it is always worth asking a supervisor to show you how the setting in which you work records these assessments.

Using the curriculum framework to consider next steps

As well as providing developmental information, observations also have to be used to help plan activities and experiences to support the child further. This is often in relation to the curriculum framework being used in the setting. Many settings design observation sheets that include a section titled 'Next steps'. This is where ideas for what could be planned next to support a child's progress or interests may be written.

A good starting point is to look at the information from the observation and then pick out which parts relate to the curriculum framework being used. You may, for example, have observed a child playing a board game. From this observation, there could be several links to the curriculum framework. You might consider their social skills, as the game required them to take turns, and also whether the child understood the concept behind the game.

Once you have identified possible areas to consider, you will then need to look in detail at the curriculum framework and consider what to provide next for the child. It may be that the child would benefit from playing the game again, as they enjoyed it, but would also benefit from further practice in recognising numbers.

Suggestions for next steps

After nearly every observation, you should think about what the observation has told you about the child and what else could be planned to support the child further. You should consider the child's interests when doing this, as well as suggestions contained in the curriculum framework. It can also be helpful to look at the developmental milestones, which may suggest what the child is likely to be working towards. Information and ideas from parents are also important, based on what they know about their children.

Suggestions for activities, resources and play opportunities do not have to be very detailed, but should be sufficient to be followed up in the planning process. It is also good practice to make links to the observation so it is clear what the next steps have been based on. Read the example in Figure 9.12 written by Steven, an early years professional.

> Lorna showed that she enjoyed dropping things and having the attention of an adult. This game could be repeated, but extended by providing other objects for Lorna to drop. The adult could also name the object each time they returned it to Lorna, as this might help her to learn a new word.
>
> *Steven, an early years professional*

▶ **Figure 9.12:** An example of how to use information to support a child's future learning

Relating theories of play, learning and development to observations

Through observations, you can also think about how a child's play and interests link to theories of play, learning and development. By looking at the information gained from the observations and thinking about the theories, you are more likely to understand the reasons behind the behaviours that children have shown.

This can help you to be more strategic in guiding behaviour. It can also help you see what the child needs from you in terms of planning and further experiences. You have already looked at some key theories of development and play in Units 1 and 3, and you are likely to be able to see these in action when you watch babies and children.

The importance of relating theories to what you observe children doing is one reason why you are asked to record this as part of the observations you submit during training.

How to relate theories to observations

As with relating developmental milestones to records of observations, the key is first of all to read through the observation carefully. You should then look in reference books for theories of play or child development and consider whether you can see any links. Record these links by explaining what you saw, which theory of play or development it may link to and why you have made this association. Read the example in Figure 9.13 written by Sarah, an early years professional.

Link

Look back at Units 1 and 3 to find more information about theories that link to development and play schemas.

Theory into practice

Find out whether your setting observes children at play and relates these observations to play schemas.

> Hasan repeatedly dropped his spoon on the ground and each time giggled when an adult picked it up for him. I think that the attention he gained from the adult acted as a positive reinforcement and so prompted him to repeat this behaviour.
>
> *Sarah, an early years professional*

▶ **Figure 9.13:** An example observation note

More than one theory at work

In most observations, you should see that there is more than one theory at work. Children may use objects to symbolise other objects, such as using a cupful of sand to stand for a cup of tea. They may also look for adult support, attention or praise. In addition, the way that they play may give them particular cognitive benefits.

Analysing observations

Meghan is 18 months old. She has been given a washing-up bowl full of coloured dried rice. She has been dropping toy animals into the rice and covering them over. She has then taken great pleasure in uncovering them and showing them to her key person. She has spent 15 minutes repeating this play.

After looking again at Units 1 and 3, see if you can relate theory to practice by answering the following questions.

Check your knowledge

1 Why does Meghan repeat these actions?

2 What play schema does this relate to?

3 Why does she keep showing the animals to her key person?

4 What skills is she learning and practising through this hiding and finding?

Assessment practice 9.4   B.P4   B.P5   B.D2

Using your plan from Assessment practice 9.3, carry out your chosen observations. Present full and effective records to show accurate observations of the child's play, learning and development.

Using these observations, write a detailed assessment of your findings. Your assessment should directly link to the observations. You should:

- explain the observed child's stage of play, learning and development, with references to developmental milestones
- consider how the observed child's development links to the early years curriculum in your country
- discuss how the observations of the child link to theories of child development
- evaluate your own practice in planning, creating and implementing activities in terms of how they support the observed child's play, learning and development.

Plan
- Have my recording methods generated sufficient information to make assessments?
- Have I identified developmental milestones that I can use to carry out an assessment?

Do
- Have I read through my observations and highlighted possible links to theories and curriculum outcomes?
- Have I linked my observations to my assessment of the child?

Review
- Have I made an accurate assessment of the child's development, based solely on what I have observed?
- Have I drawn links to theories and developmental milestones?

C Create, implement and review activity plans for children

C1 Create activity plans

Activity plans are used in many settings to help promote the acquisition of specific skills and knowledge. Learning how to create, implement and review an activity plan provides you with a valuable thought process that is useful on an almost daily basis. In this section, you will look at how you might create, implement and review plans.

Purpose of, and rationale for, the activity

A good activity plan is really a way of organising your thoughts about providing for children. Figure 9.14 lists the things to think about when creating an activity plan, including the reason behind the activity (its purpose) and why you have chosen that particular activity (the rationale).

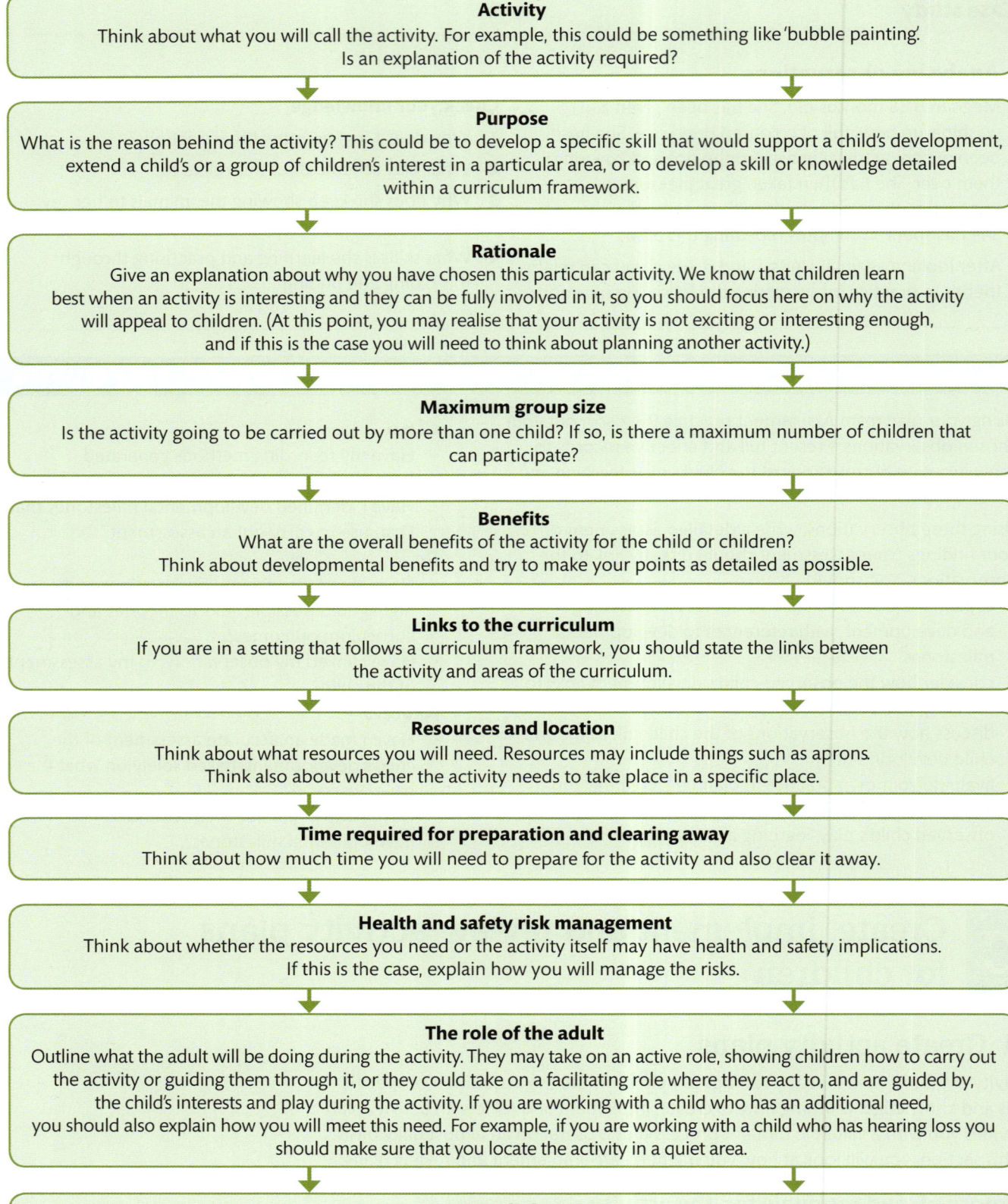

Activity
Think about what you will call the activity. For example, this could be something like 'bubble painting'.
Is an explanation of the activity required?

Purpose
What is the reason behind the activity? This could be to develop a specific skill that would support a child's development,
extend a child's or a group of children's interest in a particular area, or to develop a skill or knowledge detailed
within a curriculum framework.

Rationale
Give an explanation about why you have chosen this particular activity. We know that children learn
best when an activity is interesting and they can be fully involved in it, so you should focus here on why the activity
will appeal to children. (At this point, you may realise that your activity is not exciting or interesting enough,
and if this is the case you will need to think about planning another activity.)

Maximum group size
Is the activity going to be carried out by more than one child? If so, is there a maximum number of children that
can participate?

Benefits
What are the overall benefits of the activity for the child or children?
Think about developmental benefits and try to make your points as detailed as possible.

Links to the curriculum
If you are in a setting that follows a curriculum framework, you should state the links between
the activity and areas of the curriculum.

Resources and location
Think about what resources you will need. Resources may include things such as aprons.
Think also about whether the activity needs to take place in a specific place.

Time required for preparation and clearing away
Think about how much time you will need to prepare for the activity and also clear it away.

Health and safety risk management
Think about whether the resources you need or the activity itself may have health and safety implications.
If this is the case, explain how you will manage the risks.

The role of the adult
Outline what the adult will be doing during the activity. They may take on an active role, showing children how to carry out
the activity or guiding them through it, or they could take on a facilitating role where they react to, and are guided by,
the child's interests and play during the activity. If you are working with a child who has an additional need,
you should also explain how you will meet this need. For example, if you are working with a child who has hearing loss you
should make sure that you locate the activity in a quiet area.

Vocabulary
In some settings, you may be asked to write a list of vocabulary that you will need to attempt to use
with the child/children during the activity, so bear this in mind when planning your activity.

▶ **Figure 9.14:** Things to think about when creating an activity plan

Formats for recording planned activities

There is no single format for creating an activity plan. In some settings, paperwork for activity plans is kept to a minimum, while in others more emphasis is placed on this. Whatever format is used in your setting, the process of planning an effective activity remains the same. It is likely that your tutor will give you a sample format to help you get used to the process of creating plans. As you have already seen, you will have a number of things to think about, such as resources, the role of the adult, links to the curriculum and the reason behind the activity. Figure 9.15 is an outline of a sample activity plan that you can use or adapt. If you decide to create your own format, make sure you allow sufficient space for detailed planning.

Activity	
Aim and rationale	
Links to curriculum	
Resources	
Location	
Health and safety	
Individual needs	
The role of the adult	
Additional comments	

▸ **Figure 9.15:** A sample activity plan

While there are no set formats for activity plans, plans that are effective have a number of features. These include the following.

Links to curriculum framework

Plans that work well are always linked to the curriculum framework. This means that you will need to read carefully and have a good understanding of the curriculum framework that is being used in the country in which you work.

It is important that links to the curriculum are accurate. For example, any activity supporting handwriting in the EYFS used in England comes under 'physical development' rather than 'literacy'.

Theory into practice

Look at an activity plan in your setting. How is the plan linked to the early years curriculum?

Role/involvement of the early years educator/professional

In the plans that you construct during the course, you will need to consider the role of the adult. You may, for example, set up an activity and then act as a facilitator. Or, in the case of an activity such as cooking, you may lead the activity.

Link

Revisit Unit 3 to consider the role of the adult in play and activities.

Types of resources

For an activity to be successful, it is always important for any essential resources to be available and in sufficient quantity. In your plan, think about what resources are needed and also check that they will be available at the time needed.

Discussions with key person, colleagues, parents and carers

It is good practice when planning activities to get input from others; in a busy early years setting, plans have to take account of others' views and ideas. It is important to discuss your ideas with the child's key person as well as your placement supervisor, as they will already know about the child's interests and may be able to anticipate the child's likely responses to the activity. It is also important to talk to colleagues to ensure the activity plan does not clash with what they have planned, and to allow them to consider whether any of their key children would benefit from the activity, or to alert you to any reasons why some children may not be able to participate (for example, children with allergies to particular resources).

It is good practice to talk through plans with parents or carers. They may be able to advise on their children's interests and previous experiences as well as on more practical matters such as known allergies to substances, for example, shaving foam, hay or foods for cooking.

Health and safety risk management

The safety of children is paramount and so in the planning process you should also think about how you will keep children safe. This involves identifying potential hazards, which includes hygiene risks. Unit 5 looks in more detail at how to prevent accidents and also at the process of risk assessment.

Link

Look back at Unit 5 to remind yourself of the role of the adult in minimising risks and hazards.

The importance of planning

Anna is a student on placement in an early years setting. She needs to carry out some activities with a child as part of her coursework. She has not been very organised and has not asked her placement supervisor for permission, advice or guidance.

She sees the child who she wishes to work with and encourages him to come and make a card with her. Anna helps herself to some collage materials from the store cupboard but, during the activity, the child tips these materials onto the floor and starts to put the

sequins in his mouth. The placement supervisor sees this and quickly removes the child from the activity.

Later that day, a member of staff complains that some of the collage resources that she wanted to use with a group of children are missing.

Check your knowledge

1 Identify the key errors in Anna's approach to planning.

2 Explain why it is important to discuss planning with colleagues.

3 Evaluate the impact on children's learning and development when plans are not effective.

C2 Implement activity plans

If you have written a good activity plan or gone through a strong thought process, most of the work of setting up and organising the activity should be straightforward. You should already know what you need in terms of resources, where you might go and, importantly, what benefits the activity is likely to offer the child. All that remains is to implement the plan, which is a skill in itself and depends on a few basic principles.

The role of the adult

While planning activities based on observations and assessments is important, the role that adults play during the activities is equally important. There are several ways in which adults can extend children's learning and also ensure that planned activities are effective. You will now consider some of the ways in which adults can support children.

How to encourage children's participation

Good activities should involve children fully. Their participation is important as they are more likely to gain from an activity when they join in and participate. To help children participate, think of ways of involving them early on in the activity. This might include getting them to help set up an activity and encouraging them to make suggestions. It also means the design of the activity should allow for choice, suggestions and plenty of participation by the children themselves. Interestingly, in activities such as writing, painting or playing a board game, children are more likely to participate if adults sit and join in rather than just supervising.

How to support and extend children's learning and thinking

You have seen that children need plenty of opportunities for interaction and, as part of this, children also need opportunities for their thinking to be extended. This means that the style of the adult's interaction should help children to make connections between what they are doing and past experiences, as well as allowing children to reason and predict. This style of working is known as 'sustained shared thinking' and requires great sensitivity and the use of well-timed questions.

For example, when you are blowing bubbles you may ask a child to speculate on what size the next bubble may be. You may also experiment with the child to see whether blowing quickly or slowly makes a difference to the size of bubbles. In this way, blowing bubbles becomes an opportunity for the child and the adult to explore an activity together to make meaningful conclusions.

Theory into practice

Find out about the way that your setting plans activities for children. Ask if you can complete or contribute in some way to the planning process so that you can familiarise yourself with how plans are recorded.

Providing opportunities for children to talk

Children benefit from talking as they are learning. Simply listening to an adult is not likely to help their learning process. If you have planned an adult-directed activity, you will need to make sure that children have plenty of opportunities to talk spontaneously and freely, such as chatting while they are cooking with you.

Making activities enjoyable

You know that children are most likely to learn, concentrate and persevere when an activity is fun. This means that you should constantly monitor their reactions and reflect on whether they are engaged in the activity. This might also mean you have to adapt the activity or even, in some cases, abandon it.

Adapting activities if children are not engaged

Most experienced early years professionals will tell you that children are very creative and will often find inspiration and have ideas that you had not thought of. It is good practice to be flexible, and not to worry if children learn or discover something other than what you planned, or are not as engaged in the activity as you may have thought they would be.

In addition to children changing the activity, unexpected events such as the arrival of snow, a rainbow or a hamster on the loose may mean that carrying on with the planned activity may no longer be appropriate. Being ready to adapt and change your plans is therefore important.

PAUSE POINT
Identify three ways in which you can support children when implementing your activity plans.

Hint
Think about how you can get the best out of children and extend their understanding.

Extend
How important is it to be spontaneous when carrying out an activity?

C3 Review activity plans

Evaluating the effectiveness of activities

Reviewing plans and activities is important, as it enables you to evaluate how effective they have been in meetings the needs of children and in supporting their play, learning and development. It helps to improve your planning, and also enables you to think about children's possible next steps.

Measures for success

As you have seen, plans for activities and resources should have a clear purpose. It is therefore important to think about how you can measure whether or not they have achieved this purpose. This is particularly important when planning activities that are linked to curriculum outcomes or when supporting children who have additional needs. A measure for success might be that a child can undo a large button after playing a game where toys have been hidden in cloth bags that need to be unbuttoned. As part of your evaluation of a plan, you should think carefully about what has been achieved and whether or not the purpose of the activity has been fulfilled. In some cases, you may find that there have been unplanned opportunities for learning, as children often pick up or notice other things about an activity.

As part of your overall evaluation, you should think about the following points.

How engaged were the children during the activity?

This is quite a good starting point. Children who were very engaged and who participated well are likely to have benefited. If this was the case, it may be that you could build on this activity again for a particular child or group of children. On the other hand, you may have found that a child or some children lost interest. This might mean that a different approach is needed with those children in future.

As you know that language is connected with learning, you might also like to reflect on how much speech individual children used and to whom they spoke, or, in the case of babies, vocalised.

How did the activity link to the curriculum framework?

If you made links to the curriculum framework, think about whether these links were correct. It may be that more was covered than you expected. Most settings keep track of the parts of the curriculum that have been covered.

Which aspects of the activity and the plan were successful, and why?

It is important to understand why activities with children work well and how effective the activity was in supporting a child's play, learning or development. This gives you useful insights for future planning. Factors that affect the success of an activity include the type of resources used, the level of challenge or novelty, the way in which the adult was involved and to what extent the activity built on children's interests.

▶ Why is this adult-directed activity working well?

What aspects of the activity could be improved?

While some activities go to plan, others do not. There is a huge number of reasons for this. It might be that the timing or the location was not good. It could be that the number of children was too great or that your style was too controlling. Some activities may not have been sufficiently appealing or challenging for children, or there may not have been enough variety or interest in the resources.

You also know that young children are affected by who they are with. It may be that your relationship with the child or children is not sufficiently developed for them to feel totally at ease. This is particularly important to reflect on when you are working with children under 3 years old.

Consideration of other's views

It is good practice to consider the views of parents/carers as well as the child's key person and colleagues. This can be done by discussing with them the child's responses to the activity and what was noticed during the activity. This allows parents or carers, key persons and colleagues an opportunity to share their ideas for future planned play and activities. Working together in this way makes it more likely to develop future plans that will meet children's interests and needs. This way of working also encourages parent/carer partnership.

What did the children think of the activity?

It is important to take children's views about activities into account when evaluating activities. With older children, you can talk to them directly about what they most/least enjoyed about the activity and which aspects they found the most/least interesting. With younger children such as babies and toddlers, you will need to gain their views by observing their reactions during an activity and reflecting on them afterwards. A good tip is to take some photographs during an activity, as this will help you to see how enthusiastic the children were when you reflect on the activity.

PAUSE POINT   Identify three indicators that an activity might be effective.

Hint   Think about the children's responses, links to the curriculum and also where you might get further feedback.

Extend   Explain the importance of evaluating activities.

Planning the next steps

Planning is a continual process, as through observation and evaluation you need to consider the next steps for children. It is usual for next steps to be considered alongside parents, the child's key person and any other colleagues who are involved with the child. Parents may make suggestions based on their knowledge of the child at home. When it comes to the child's key person or colleagues, they will be aware of the child's previous experiences, interests and also how they respond to different activities. In addition, the child's key person and colleagues may have more experience of working with children or be aware of the complete range of resources that are available within the setting. By taking into consideration the views of others, your next steps are more likely to be accurate.

Next steps for the children

As part of the planning, observation and evaluation cycle, you should always be thinking about the next steps for children following on from activities. It could be that a child really enjoyed the activity and it would be worth repeating it, or perhaps a child struggled with a concept or skill and so adapting the activity or thinking of a new approach might be important. If you spotted that children were keen to use the resources differently, you might think about how to organise this. It is also important to find out from children directly whether they enjoyed an activity and playing with certain resources.

Next steps for you

You should spend time thinking about what you have learned from the activity. Perhaps you have learned about the importance of preparation or about children's interests at certain ages. It may be that you have learned what to do if an activity is not enjoyable for children. It can be helpful to spend time talking to an experienced practitioner about what happened during the activity, as their thoughts might help you gain more insights.

Writing up a review of an activity

It is easy to make statements such as 'all the children enjoyed this activity', but it is good practice to provide a reason for your statement and to make it as detailed as possible. See Figure 9.16 for an example.

> Zoe and Thomas were engrossed in the activity and were disappointed when it was lunchtime. I think that this indicates that this activity worked well for them. Damian, on the other hand, lost interest within five minutes or so and I feel that this activity may not have been sufficiently challenging for him.
>
> *Grace, an early years professional*

▶ **Figure 9.16:** An example of an observation note

Assessment practice 9.5   C.P6   C.P7   C.M4   C.D3

Using the observations and assessment that you have carried out, create and carry out activity plans to support the child's play, learning and development.

- Present the activity plans and your rationale for deciding on these play and learning activities.
- Review and analyse the effectiveness of the play and learning activities.
- Evaluate how the plans and implemented activities supported the child's play, learning and development, with justified observations.

Plan
- Where can I find information about the types of activity and play that will support this child?
- When can I carry out these activities at a time that will suit my placement?

Do
- Have I spoken to my placement supervisor and carried out my activities?
- Have I gathered feedback from a variety of sources to assess the effectiveness of the activity plans?

Review
- Have I analysed the effectiveness of my activities?
- Have I shown that I can evaluate my ability to observe, assess and plan for a child's play, learning and development?

Further reading and resources

Barber, J. and Paul-Smith, S. (2010) *Early Years Observation and Planning in Practice*, London: Practical Pre-School Books.

Brodie, K. (2013) *Observation, Assessment and Planning in The Early Years – Bringing it all Together*, Maidenhead: Open University Press.

Dubiel, J. (2016) *Effective Assessment in the Early Years Foundation Stage*, 2nd edition, London: Sage Publications.

Hobart, C., Frankel, J. and Walker, M. (2009) *A Practical Guide to Child Observation and Assessment*, 4th edition, Cheltenham: Nelson Thornes.

Tassoni, P. (2012) *Penny Tassoni's Practical EYFS Handbook*, 2nd edition, Oxford: Heinemann.

THINK ▶ FUTURE

Cathy Marks

Preschool staff manager

The preschool where Cathy works has a very good observation and planning process. As a manager who used to work in the National Health Service, Cathy is very keen for staff to be aware of children who are not making the usual developmental progress. She always advises her staff to look at the developmental milestones before they begin to observe a child, especially if they are new to working with the age group or they have not been with them for a while.

The team tries hard to make sure that information gained from observations is not just put in a child's folder and then forgotten. Each week, when staff are doing their short-term planning, children's key persons will contribute ideas for activities, toys and resources based on what they know their key children need. The team also shows this on the planning sheet by adding the child's initials in the appropriate place.

Focusing your skills

Observations: common questions and answers

Here are some frequently asked questions about observations. These handy tips will help you carry out more effective observations.

What can I do to stop a child from coming up to me when I am observing other children?

- This is a common problem. Try telling children that you are busy but will talk to them or play with them later. If this does not work, try using closed body language and avoid making eye contact with them.

I have tried to use target child observation but I keep forgetting the codes.

- You can devise your own codes if you find this easier. If you do this, you will need to rewrite the observation later, substituting conventional codes, or include a clear key explaining what your codes mean.

I observed that a child who is now 4 years old does not have hand preference. I am not sure what activities I should plan. Help!

- Hand preference can be strengthened with activities that require both hands, but where one hand stabilises an object and the other is active, for example, unscrewing a bottle or peeling a banana.

When should you share observations with parents/carers?

- It is good practice to share observations with parents/carers as soon as you have carried them out. Some parents/carers may be interested in reading or seeing your observations, while others will prefer you to explain to them what you have seen.

My setting does not write up observations with theories and links to milestones. Why does my tutor ask me to do this?

- Learner observations and conclusions are often more detailed than those used in settings, because they are designed to train you in the process of observing and thinking about children. The idea is that later on, you will be able to use these skills without having to write down everything you know.

Reflective Practice 10

Getting to know your unit

Learning to think about, and question the effectiveness of, your work with children is now considered an important part of being a professional. Reviewing your strengths and weaknesses and checking that your knowledge is up to date helps to ensure that you give children the best start possible.

This unit is about knowing how to recognise your strengths and weaknesses and how to take steps to improve your practice, especially in relation to promoting children's learning and development. In this unit you also consider different theories and approaches for reflective practice.

How you will be assessed

This unit will be assessed by a series of internally assessed tasks set by your tutor. Throughout this unit, assessment activities will help you work towards your assessment. Completing these activities will not mean that you have achieved a particular grade, but you will have carried out useful research or preparation that will be relevant when it comes to your final assignment.

To achieve the tasks in your assignment, it is important to check that you have met all of the Pass grading criteria. You can do this as you work your way through the assignment.

If you are hoping to gain a Merit or Distinction, you should also make sure that you present the information in your assignment in the style that is required by the relevant assessment criterion. For example, Merit criteria require you to analyse and discuss, and Distinction criteria require you to assess and evaluate.

The assignment set by your tutor will consist of a number of tasks designed to meet the criteria in the table. This is likely to consist of a written assignment but may also include activities such as:

▶ producing a report on the importance of reflective practice, including the approaches and theories that can be used by early years practitioners

▶ preparing a reflective account in your Practical Evidence Portfolio linked to your work placement, which shows that you can use reflective practice to improve your work with children.

Assessment criteria

This table shows what you must do in order to achieve a **Pass**, **Merit** or **Distinction** grade, and where you can find activities to help you.

Pass	Merit	Distinction
Learning aim **A** Understand the purpose of reflective practice in relation to improving early years provision and practice		
A.P1 Explain the purpose of reflective practice in early years. **Assessment practice 10.1**	**A.M1** Assess how reflective practice contributes to professional development in early years. **Assessment practice 10.1**	**AB.D1** Evaluate how theories and approaches to reflective practice support an improvement in professionals' knowledge, skills and practical competence in early years settings. **Assessment practice 10.2**
Learning aim **B** Investigate theories and approaches for reflective practice		
B.P2 Explain theories for reflective practice. **Assessment practice 10.2**	**B.M2** Assess how theories and approaches are used in supporting early years practice in own workplace setting. **Assessment practice 10.2**	
B.P3 Explain approaches for reflective practice for personal development. **Assessment practice 10.2**		
Learning aim **C** Develop reflective practice skills in an early years setting		
C.P4 Discuss own skills, attitudes and experience relevant to work in early years settings. **Assessment practice 10.3**	**C.M3** Analyse influences on the development of own knowledge, skills and practical competence. **Assessment practice 10.3**	**C.D2** Evaluate the extent to which own reflective practice has impacted on the experience of children and families in own early years setting. **Assessment practice 10.3**
C.P5 Demonstrate reflective practice in relation to own work in an early years setting. **Assessment practice 10.3**	**C.M4** Demonstrate effective reflective practice in relation to own work in early years settings. **Assessment practice 10.3**	**C.D3** Evaluate the effectiveness of reflective practice in supporting continuous quality improvement in early years settings. **Assessment practice 10.3**

Getting started

What do you think your strengths and weaknesses are when working with children? How good are you at encouraging children's learning and development? When you have finished this unit, see whether you feel your answers to these questions are still an accurate reflection of your practice.

 A **Understand the purpose of reflective practice in relation to improving early years provision and practice**

A1 How early years professionals use reflective practice

All adults working with babies and children are encouraged to think about the way that they work. This is known as **reflective practice** and it is considered an essential way of improving practice and of improving provision for children. In this section you will look at how early years professionals use reflective practice and how it can help you to become a more effective practitioner.

The term 'reflective practice' is used to describe the process by which practitioners become aware of their limitations and gaps in their knowledge, as well as their strengths and good qualities. Reflective practice should be used in all areas of your professional work with children and their families. This is shown in Figure 10.1.

Our role with children
By thinking about the effectiveness of the way that we work with children, including the way that we support children's learning and development, we can tailor our approach to suit their interests and needs.

Planning to meet children's needs
By considering the effectiveness of our observations and plans we may be able to develop new and improved systems of planning and recording. These systems may be faster or more effective.

Working with parents and other professionals
By thinking through how we work with parents and other professionals, we may be able to develop stronger partnerships with them.

Understanding children's behaviour
By reflecting on the way that we respond to children's behaviour we can develop new strategies.

Aspects of our work that benefit from reflection

Meeting the needs of individual children
By reflecting on the way that individual children learn in the setting and our role in their development, we should be able to meet their needs more effectively.

Improving provision
Reflective practice can allow early years settings to reflect on the quality of their provision for children. This is important to ensure that the quality of care and learning for children is high. Self-evaluation of practice is also needed in preparation for inspections.

Working with colleagues
Reflecting on the way that we interact with colleagues can help us to create better relationships and more effective teams. This can also help us to enjoy our work more.

▶ **Figure 10.1:** How early years professionals use reflective practice

What is meant by reflective practice?

The idea of reflective practice is relatively new to early years. It is a way of working that can improve practice considerably. For years it has been known that the quality of our work has a huge impact on children and their families, but finding ways to develop and maintain this quality was not easy. Inspections, reports by line managers and ongoing staff training have all been tried. However, today it is felt that the best person to help you work effectively with children is yourself.

A continuous cycle

The process of reflective practice can be seen as a cycle, as it is continuous and never ending. Figure 10.2 shows this continuous cycle. Interestingly, you may find that experienced practitioners say they are still learning. This is because every child is different, every family is different and there are often changes to resources, the curriculum and approaches to early education. Reflective practice covers every aspect of your work, including your relationships with parents, colleagues and other professionals, as well as the importance of promoting children's overall learning and development.

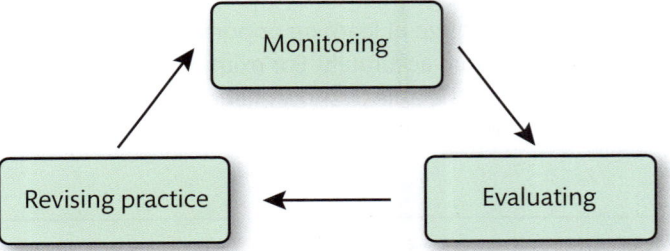

▶ **Figure 10.2:** The continuous cycle of reflective practice

Monitoring

This is about being aware of what you are doing when you are with children. You may look at children's reactions or consider how children are using equipment or enjoying an activity. Monitoring is also about being aware of children's outcomes and progress, then relating this to your practice and those used in the setting. As well as self-monitoring, you can also gain feedback from a range of sources such as parents, colleagues and children.

Evaluation

As you monitor and gain information from a wide range of sources, you need to evaluate its significance and then consider whether any aspect of your practice requires changing.

Revising own practices

As a result of ongoing evaluation, experienced practitioners will often try out new ideas, change their practices or change the routine or equipment of the setting. In some cases, you will need to change your own behaviours or style of working with children. You may also need to change your attitudes, approaches and beliefs about how best to work with children.

Improving your own skills and subject knowledge

There are many reasons why reflective practice is important in the workplace. If you are a reflective practitioner, not only will you improve outcomes for the children you work with, but you will also develop your own skills and career.

Link

Go to Section B2 in this unit to find more information about gaining feedback from parents, colleagues and children.

When you first begin working with children, you will face a steep learning curve. You will need to adjust to working in a new environment as well as learning how to use the skills and knowledge that you acquired in your training. Being able to be a reflective practitioner and using the process that you will look at later in this unit will help you become more confident and, of course, competent.

Reflection will also help you to keep developing, as you will start to think about what new skills and areas of knowledge you would like to develop further. You may become interested in working with children who have additional needs or you may want to learn more about working with babies, for example.

Just as reflective practice is continuous, so your learning should be continuous too. As well as continuing to develop your own skills, knowledge and practical competence to help you work with children, it is also important to think about any gaps in your education and try to fill them. For example, you may have disliked science at school and, therefore, may not have gained much knowledge in this subject, or you may not have had the opportunity to learn a foreign language or to work with IT.

Having knowledge across many subject areas is thought to be important. Not only does it make you more confident but it also helps your practice with children, as you are more likely to find a wider range of learning opportunities in the environment and be able to use language more accurately. For example, if a practitioner has some knowledge of science, they may be able to show children that a brick wall retains heat at the end of the day and give an accurate explanation of why this is.

Research

Research the opportunities available to improve your subject knowledge in a particular area. Use online sources and books as well as courses offered in your local area as a starting point.

Reflect

Look at the following subject areas.
- English
- Mathematics
- Music
- History
- Science
- Modern foreign languages
- Information Technology (IT)
- Cookery

1   On a scale of 1 to 5, with 1 being poor, how confident are you that you have good knowledge of the subject?
2   Consider which areas you would prioritise for improvement.

Extending children's learning

Reflection can be used to support your personal and professional development. However, the most important reason for using reflection is to improve the quality, type and range of early learning experiences for children. These should be made as effective as possible to aid children's development.

You know that children who have sensitive and reflective adults with them are more likely to have their learning extended. These adults are likely to be more skilful at forming relationships. They are also likely to be good at recognising the best way of responding to individual children's interests and needs, and thus extending their learning. Reflective practitioners also think about trying out new ideas and approaches that might extend children's learning. For example, a practitioner who spots that a pair of children have been watching a spider's web might reflect on what other activities could be planned to support the children's interest. The practitioner might, for instance, find a book about spiders or see if the children want to make their own web out of string.

Supporting continuous quality improvement

While the basic needs of children have not changed for centuries, society and the perception of childhood are constantly changing. In addition, new developments from research into children's learning have influenced the curricula and expectations of work with children. There are also changes to legislation in areas such as health and safety, employment and the rights of children. It is therefore important that settings and individual practitioners keep abreast of developments and are ready to reflect on, change and improve their practice. This needs to be a continuous process, which is planned and organised.

<table>
<tr><td>⏸</td><td>**PAUSE POINT**</td><td>Identify four reasons why settings use reflective practice.</td></tr>
<tr><td></td><td>Hint</td><td>Think about how the quality of an early years setting might be affected if it never reflected on its practice.</td></tr>
<tr><td></td><td>Extend</td><td>Consider why reflective practice might be important in helping early years settings cope with societal and political changes.</td></tr>
</table>

Factors that shape behaviours, beliefs, values, attitudes and approaches

Reflective practice may lead to you changing your behaviours and attitudes. It is easy to say this but often harder to do it in practice. This is because quite often your own existing behaviours, attitudes, beliefs and values led you in the first place to use the approaches you take with children and families. Simple things, such as whether or not you encourage children to finish everything on their plate at mealtimes, are likely to be a result of your set of beliefs, attitudes and values; in this case those towards food, which in turn may be linked to approaches that your parents and other carers took with you.

Behaviours, attitudes and beliefs are powerful. This means that they can have the ability to prevent you from being able to effectively reflect on your practice and change and develop as a result. For example, if you strongly believe that children should be 'taught', it might mean that you are resistant to practices that encourage children to be independent and to learn for themselves through child-initiated play. This would mean that practice in the setting may be too formal.

As well as your own behaviours, beliefs and attitudes, you should not forget the people you work with have their own set; and so for change to take place, you may have to find a way of collectively changing your approach.

A good starting point when engaging in reflective practice is to understand the impact that your behaviours, beliefs, values and attitudes have on your current approach and ways of working.

Reflect

Look at the following situations. Consider what your initial reaction is likely to be. Then, think about how your approach is linked to your beliefs, values and attitudes.
- A child is bouncing on a sofa.
- A child is walking around drinking from a beaker.
- A parent is on the phone while her son is trying to tell her something.
- A child does not want to join the story time and instead is throwing beanbags at the sitting children.
- Two children are squabbling over a tricycle even though there is a spare one.

How reflective practice can bring about change in behaviours, beliefs, values, attitudes and approaches

You have seen that behaviours, attitudes and beliefs can affect the way that you work with children and their families. The process of reflective practice is important as it can change not only the way in which you work but also your behaviours, attitudes and beliefs. This is because many of your attitudes and behaviours have evolved without any conscious thought. By consciously considering what you do and think, and the reasons behind your thoughts and actions, you can actively change the way you do things and, as a result, your own beliefs and attitudes.

Case study

Jason has worked in day care for a number of years. He has always encouraged children to eat all the food on their plate and has believed that children should not be offered pudding if they haven't finished their main course. This was the way he was brought up.

Recently, he has been on a training day about young children and nutrition. The dietician showed how rates of childhood obesity have increased and provided information about creating long-term healthy attitudes towards food in childhood. At first Jason was resistant to the new information, but then, through a process of reflection, began to realise that some of his practices

might not be supporting children's attitude to food. Within a few weeks, mealtimes were transformed. Children were encouraged to self-serve and to try out new foods. Pudding was no longer given a high profile or used to reward children.

1 Why were Jason's original attitudes and beliefs a barrier to best practice?

2 Explain how children have benefitted from Jason's reflective practice.

3 Identify a time when your beliefs and attitudes have been changed through the process of reflection.

The importance of continuous reflection

Reflection is something that you should be doing all the time in order to continue building on progress and developing any ideas that have come about from your original reflections. Reflection is also important to check that changes in your practice are working as you had hoped.

This is particularly important because sometimes you may make changes that work well with a particular group of children or a specific child, but you may need to revise these changes at a later stage. Although children's interest levels may increase when you first introduce a new activity or resource, they are likely to decrease once children have become accustomed to them. Through the process of observation, reflection and monitoring, you can create a more dynamic environment that is keenly matched to children's interests and levels of development.

▶ This team is reflecting on the quality of the toys in the setting

The role of others in supporting reflective practice and continual personal and professional development

Reflective practice and continual personal and professional development should be done with the support and feedback of others. This might include colleagues or line managers but also professionals from other agencies, such as speech and language therapists or family outreach workers. Gaining feedback, suggestions and information can help you to reflect on and improve your practice by focusing your attention on particular areas. In addition, if you attend a training course or enrol on a new qualification you will also meet other practitioners working in early years settings who have different approaches to yours. By exchanging ideas with these colleagues and learning about other approaches, you can further develop your practice. Sometimes, conversations with others can also support your personal development. You may, for example, find out how others in a similar role deal with stress, managing their time and finding ways to relax.

Shared understanding

In settings where reflection is built into the routine of the day, a more dynamic and interesting work environment is created. Practitioners can collaborate and discuss different options, approaches and ideas for working with children. This professional discussion can support a team's development, but also the individual development of team members. The impact on practices within the setting is usually very positive and a culture of open discussion and readiness to try out new ideas will emerge.

Engaging in continuing professional development

Just as reflection is a continuing process, our professional development needs to be ongoing. The term continuing professional development, or CPD, is used to describe the way that practitioners need to remain up to date with current practice and also develop their skills and knowledge. This is important as the early years sector is constantly changing. There are often new initiatives brought in by governments, including changes to early years curricula. A good example of a recent initiative in England is the funding of nursery provision for 2-year-olds, which has resulted in many settings needing to change their way of working. There are also sometimes changes in the way that settings are inspected. By attending training, reviewing documents and learning more about current expectations and best practice, early years practitioners can adjust to the changes more easily.

In addition to government changes to policy, curricula and inspections, the pattern of family life also changes. This means that the early years sector has to change in response. A good example of this is the introduction of overnight care in a few settings.

Theory into practice

Ask an experienced member of staff from your work placement what changes have occurred in the setting over the past five years.

- How has the inspection process changed?
- What changes to the curriculum have taken place?

What type of CPD have they undertaken to keep their knowledge and practice up to date?

Assessment practice 10.1   A.P1 A.M1

An early years setting that has recently had a poor inspection result wants to improve their practice. To do this, the manager wants to create a culture among staff of reflective practice.

You have been asked to support a training session for staff. Using examples, your information should:

- explain the purpose of reflective practice in early years
- assess how reflective practice contributes to professional development in early years.

Plan
- Do I fully understand the purpose of reflective practice?
- Do I understand the benefits of reflective practice?

Do
- Am I using examples to show the impact of reflective practice on professional development?
- Am I presenting information in an effective way?

Review
- Have I clearly explained the purpose of reflective practice?
- Have I shown analytical skills in my work?

Investigate theories and approaches for reflective practice

B1 Theories for reflective practice

In earlier units, you have learned that there are many theoretical and philosophical approaches to children's learning and development. It is important to think about how these relate to your own approaches with children and which ones are most relevant. There may then be opportunities for you to attend training courses to explore the most relevant theories in more detail to support your reflective practice.

A good example might be a practitioner who works in a preschool deciding to explore in more detail the Montessori approach to children's learning and development. By reading into the approach in more detail, attending a training course and visiting a Montessori group, the practitioner is able to reflect on whether any elements of the approach would be useful in developing the preschool's practice.

There are a number of different theories specifically relating to reflection and reflective practice. These models can be used to help you think about your practice. There is no 'right' model, but by exploring different models, you will learn more about different ways of reflecting.

The Schön model

Donald Schön suggested that reflective practitioners can work in two ways to develop and improve their practice: reflection in action and reflection on action.

Reflection in action

This is about how you might think about and adapt your practice at the time. This is often called 'thinking on your feet' and is likely to occur when something unexpected happens that challenges your usual way of working. A good example of this is when an activity you have done several times with children fails to gain the usual positive response from a new child. You may have to quickly consider why this might be and then test out new ways of working. You would, therefore, be learning from this.

Reflection on action

The other method that Schön described is reflecting on what you have done afterwards. You may explore what you did and why, and decide whether it was the best way of working.

The two types of reflection are not necessarily independent of each other because if you have altered your way of working at the time (reflection in action), you may afterwards take time to consider whether there were any other strategies or approaches you could have taken (reflection on action).

The Gibbs reflective cycle model

The Gibbs reflective cycle is a way of structuring your thoughts and reflections. It is very useful to use after a particular situation, such as following an activity you felt had not worked out well. By using the cycle, you should be able to reach some conclusions to help you think how you could work differently in the future. Figure 10.3 shows this cycle.

After a situation, incident or activity (this could be either positive or negative) you need to think about what happened, your feelings about it and evaluate what was good about it or what was not good about it. You then need to go on to analyse why it occurred in the way it did. Finally, you need to draw some conclusions from the situation, incident or

Link

Go to Units 1, 2, 3 and 7 to revisit theories and philosophies of children's learning and development.

activity. You can include this in an action plan. Although it is possible to use Gibbs' cycle by yourself, it is often best to have a partner to do it with. Having someone else sitting with you to clarify your thoughts and ideas can make the process easier.

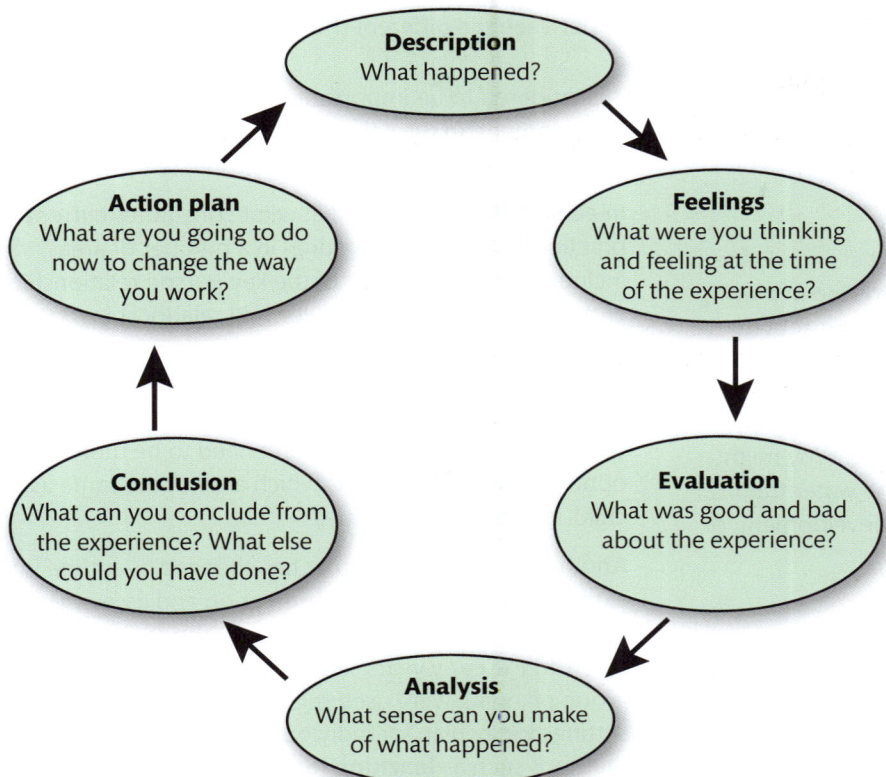

▶ **Figure 10.3:** Gibbs' reflective cycle model

Kolb's learning cycle

Kolb's learning cycle is a useful model for reflection. It is based on the idea that you learn from experiences and then adapt your thoughts and actions accordingly. Learning from and reflecting on your experiences is sometimes called 'experiential learning'. Although in theory you can start at any point of the cycle, most reflection begins with the experience as this provides a trigger for thinking. Figure 10.4 shows this cycle.

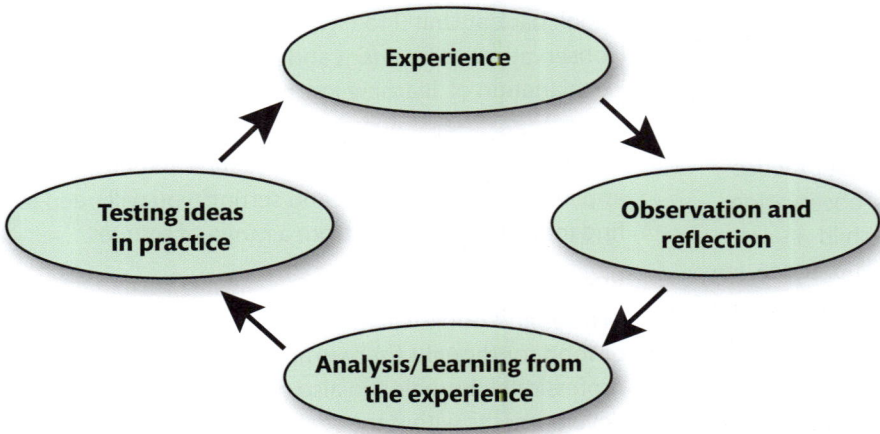

▶ **Figure 10.4:** Kolb's learning cycle

PAUSE POINT   Explain the key points of two different theories of reflective practice.

> **Hint**   You have looked at Schön's, Gibbs' and Kolb's models.
> **Extend**   What are the key differences between the different theories of reflective practice?

We will now look at how you use the learning cycle. In this instance we will use the example of setting up an activity for children to play in a water tray.

Experience

The learning cycle always starts with an initial experience. In this example, the children were not interested in playing in the water tray despite you having planned an activity there.

Observe and reflect

The next stage is to reflect on the experience. Why might the children not have been interested in the water tray? Did you underestimate their age/stage of development, or were they tired?

Analysis/Learning from the experience

Use your observations and reflections to help shape your future plans and ideas. What else could you do? Could you have chosen different materials, or a different time? This analysis will help you form new ideas to help you develop in the future.

Testing ideas in practice

Once you have developed your new ideas, you should try to put them into action. The next step would be to start the process all over again using the information gained from the first cycle of reflection. This ensures the process of learning and reflection is continuous.

B2 Approaches to reflective practice

Seeking information about current best practice

When reflecting on your practice you need to be aware of current best practice in relation to promoting children's learning and development. Key aspects of best practice include playfulness and play opportunities, observation, assessment and planning, as well as adult– child relationships. By being aware of current best practice, you can analyse what you and your setting are doing in each of these aspects, then compare your practice to it.

Best practice does change over time, so it is important to keep up to date. Best practice can change for a number of reasons, including government policy and changes in what

is considered to be important for children's learning and development. In turn, these changes affect how the early years framework is delivered and inspected.

In earlier units, you looked at what constitutes current practice (at the time of writing) in a number of areas, including the importance of the key person relationship and the need for quality adult–child relationships. Interestingly, these have not always been a focus for inspection, but they are now. In the same way, there is an ongoing debate about what type of play opportunities children need and whether there need to be more play opportunities led by adults which are not the same as child-initiated play activities.

Another area of practice that has changed over time is the extent to which planning, observation and assessment are carried out in settings and the methods used to do these. In the early years sector, long-term planning and group planning were used regularly, however, many settings today plan for individual children using short-term methods such as **learning journeys**.

> **Key term**
>
> **Learning journey/learning story** – a way of assessing and planning for children's development using a narrative approach that can easily be constructed and shared with parents and children.

> **Link**
>
> Look back at Unit 9 to find more information about observation, assessment and planning, and an explanation of 'learning journeys'.

In order to find out about best practice and how it can be applied to your own work and setting, you will need to find information, ideally from a range of sources.

Reading articles and books

Articles and books can provide you with new information or food for thought for new activities. Magazines and professional journals can also make you aware of new developments within the sector, so it is a good idea to find the time to look through them.

Research

Find out the titles of three magazines or journals that are published for the early years sector. Which ones does your setting subscribe to? Are any available in your local library or online?

Television, radio and the internet

Television, radio and the internet can be good sources of information about issues in early years, or subjects or topics that link to early years. For example, you might find a radio programme that is discussing the topic of disability or a documentary on television about particular social or developmental difficulties that some families face. The internet can also be a very useful source of information, especially as there is a wide range of websites set up and run by practitioners with an interest in early childhood development. Some websites and forums can also offer an international perspective as its members come from all over the world. If you decide to use the internet, it is important you consider carefully whether the information you are reading and seeing is accurate.

Meeting other professionals

Many early years teams organise 'cluster groups', which enable practitioners from a particular area to meet up. Meeting other professionals in this way can help you to explore different ideas and reflect on your practice. Sometimes other professionals will tell you about how they have brought in a new system or piece of equipment to their setting, and their experiences can help you to explore your own ideas.

Research

Find out if there are any professional networks in your area. Contact your early years team, education department or a national organisation such as the Professional Association for Childcare and Early Years (PACEY): **www.pacey.org.uk**.

You could also get in touch with Early Education, a charitable organisation that supports families and the professional development of people working in early childhood education: see **www.early-education. org.uk**.

Attending training

Training courses can provide you with new ideas and thoughts about practice. Many settings will organise their own internal training sessions, either by closing for a day or as part of ongoing staff meetings. In addition, most early years advisory teams provide training courses, as do many national organisations such as Early Education. It is important to attend training in areas of your work that you feel strong in as well as those where you know your knowledge needs to be updated. This is because it is easy to become so comfortable with one way of working that you overlook other possibilities.

It is useful to write up your notes and thoughts following a training event. You can then look back at your notes and share them with colleagues.

Shadowing others

Sometimes you can reflect on the way in which you work, by noticing how other people handle situations, plan activities and relate to children. The term 'shadowing' is used to describe observing what others are doing in order to learn. Looking at how others work should not be about comparison or it can become too negative. It is about reflecting on others' and your own strengths. This can be done in your own setting with experienced colleagues or those who have particular specialisms or interests. It can be helpful, after watching others, to take the time to sit with them and talk about what you have seen. This will help you to understand the reasons behind their actions and also to learn any tips from them.

▶ What are the benefits of shadowing a more experienced colleague?

Visiting other settings

It is also useful to watch others who are working in a similar setting in order to gain a different perspective and learn about their approaches. When visiting other settings, it is important to be respectful and polite even if you are unsure of their way of working. Interestingly, most people who visit other settings find that they come away with new thoughts or ideas.

Improving practice by visiting other settings

Joachim works at a day care nursery but is spending the morning in a local preschool. He is particularly keen to find out more about how the preschool encourages children's communication and language development. He has been invited to the preschool as a result of making contact with the supervisor during a local network meeting. During the morning, he picks up many ideas and is interested in the different approaches that are being taken to support children who have English as an additional language. He also likes the way that the key persons spend set times with their key children. The staff are very friendly and quite open. Next week the supervisor of the preschool is due to visit his nursery.

1 Why is it important for Joachim to have an open mind during the visit?
2 How will Joachim benefit from seeing another early years setting in action?
3 How will the children in Joachim's nursery benefit from his visit to another setting?

Sources of information on your own practice

There are a number of different ways in which you can gain awareness of your own practice and how you are doing.

Feedback from colleagues

Listening to others can provide you with vital information that will help you to reflect on your practice. Feedback works best if you trust the people giving it and if they feel that they can give you an honest point of view. Listening to feedback carefully and avoiding being defensive is a skill in itself. It is easy to defend the reasons why you do things, but the key is to remember that the focus is on moving on and improving performance.

Feedback from children

You can gain feedback from children of all ages by simply noting down their reactions to what you do and by noticing what seems to engage them. Toddlers and older children can also tell you about activities that they enjoy and you can use photos to help them remember things that they have done with you.

Feedback from parents and carers

You can ask for feedback from parents or carers. Parents/carers may notice how their child's speech has developed

and which activities or ways of working seem to have been effective.

Seeking a critique of your skills, knowledge and competence

In order to analyse your skills, knowledge and competence, it is important that you gather information about your performance. This will mean that you need to ask others to critique your work. There are many ways of doing this, as you will see.

Observations

Being observed by others such as colleagues, tutors or inspectors may seem scary, but it can provide a valuable source of information. You may also find that your line manager carries out observations as part of the quality assurance process within your setting. Gathering information from others who have seen you in action is helpful because they may notice habits that you have acquired, such as saying 'okay' at the end of a sentence or not giving children sufficient time to respond. If you are being observed by colleagues, you may wish to talk to them about what you would like them to focus on. This might include your posture, tone or eye contact.

Mentoring

Mentoring is a useful way of gaining information about your practice. A **mentor** is usually someone who is more experienced than you who can guide your practice, provide information and give you feedback on your work. Mentoring systems are usually set up by employers and it is common to have a mentor when you first join a workplace or if you are new to the sector. It is usual for mentors not to be directly managing their **mentee**. This makes it easier for the mentee to go to them with questions, concerns or to seek advice.

Key terms

Mentee – the person who is being mentored.
Mentor – someone who guides and supports a less experienced person and gives feedback on their work.

Critical friend

The term 'critical friend' is used to describe someone that you trust and like who may provide feedback that will help you to improve your performance. The critical friend approach is useful because, even though some of the feedback might be critical, it is likely to be constructive and well meant. This means it is often easier to take on board. A critical friend might observe your practice directly or may look at other aspects of your work, including observations of children or planning activities.

Peer reviews

Many early years settings encourage or facilitate peer reviews. This is when practitioners who work directly with you are asked to share information that can be used to critique your skills. Peer reviews can work well, as the people you work with on a day-to-day basis will have seen you at work and will also understand the challenges that you face. Peer reviews can be helpful as part of a range of sources of information about your performance.

Assessment of children's outcomes

By tracking children's progress, you can consider whether your practices are effective. If there are several children that you have responsibility for who are not making the expected progress, you may need to consider whether you need to improve opportunities for promoting their individual learning and development.

Appraisals

All early years settings carry out appraisals on their staff. An appraisal is a review of both your work with children and as part of a team. An appraisal should help you to identify your strengths, weaknesses and areas for your future development. The appraisal process is usually led by the manager or deputy manager of the setting and involves feedback from your colleagues, observation of your work as well as feedback you provide about your own work. At the end of an appraisal process, a plan is drawn up that may identify targets and ways in which you can work towards them.

Ⅱ PAUSE POINT	Identify four ways in which you may gather information that will help you to critique your skills.
Hint	Think about your work placement and ways in which you might find out how well you are doing.
Extend	Evaluate the importance of gaining information from a range of sources.

How to gather and record information to help you engage in continuing professional development

Most people benefit from having input, encouragement and feedback. There are many ways of gaining support for your own continuing professional development, as Figure 10.5 shows.

▶ **Figure 10.5:** Where to get the support you need to help with your professional development

Training

Training courses are valuable sources of support and information. You may go on a short course organised by your local early years team, college or national organisation. You may also decide to take a course of further study resulting in a qualification. This may be helpful in progressing your career or in allowing you to move into another area.

Websites

Websites and social media can give you support, but you must be aware of confidentiality issues and also your setting's policy in relation to social media. This means that you may not be able to share everything you are doing on a website. On the other hand, you may find suggestions for practice and information about what others have tried.

Tutors

While you are studying, your tutor will be a good source of support. They may observe you as you work and give you feedback. They may also help you to draw up an action plan and suggest ways of developing your practice a step at a time.

Supervisors

Your line manager or supervisor in the setting may be a good source of support. They may be very experienced and able to give you suggestions for how to put your ideas into practice. They may also be able to arrange further training for you or put you in contact with other practitioners.

Recording information or feedback

It is always worth recording the information that you have gained about your practice. Not only should you do this to be able to show a potential employer or an inspector that you are keeping up to date with your practice, but you may want to revisit some information to support your personal development. While you may be provided with handouts from some formal training courses, at other times you may take your own notes. It is always a good idea to write down a date and also the name of the training course and the trainer.

If you visit a website to seek information, make a note of what you have looked up, or bookmark it on your computer, so you can revisit the website later (as it is easy to forget). Similarly, if you have found a leaflet or magazine article that is of interest, keep a note of it so that you can easily find it again. Some employers require that you maintain a CPD log and as part of the performance appraisal process may ask you to show evidence that you have been keeping up to date.

Recognising influences that might affect your own practice

As part of your reflection process, you need to be able to recognise factors that might be affecting your practice. If you don't recognise them, they can sometimes lead you to be defensive about your practice or overcritical.

Experiences

Your own experiences will affect your practice. Firstly, what you have seen on placement or in your working life will be a major influence. This is one reason why it is a good idea to visit a range of settings so that you can see different approaches. In addition, past experiences of being criticised or being given feedback may also determine your immediate reactions.

Values

Your own values and beliefs about childhood and how children should behave will affect your practice. Interestingly, this often shows in the way that you manage children's behaviour. If you are aware of your own underlying values, you may find it easier to be open-minded.

Own education

Some people's own education may influence the way they work with children. A good example of this is play-based education. This is now the approach taken in all of the home countries' curricula. If your own education was more formal, it may be that your tendency is to intervene or try to structure play unnecessarily. Understanding how you were educated and comparing it to the current ways of working would be a good starting point.

▶ These children are being taught formally. If you experienced this type of education, how might it affect your own practice?

Case study

Evaluating practice

Kay has been working with toddlers for a year. She recently attended a course about working with 2-year-olds. She realised that she had not been spending sufficient time talking to the children and that she had not been monitoring their language. At the start of the training day, she was sure that she would not learn anything new and was cross that she had to get up earlier than usual to attend.

After the training day, she returned to work upset and demotivated. Her manager noticed the change in her attitude and Kay told her that she was feeling useless and was considering resigning. Her manager explained that working with children was a learning process. Together they discussed what elements of the course could be implemented immediately and they agreed to talk about Kay's progress after a week or so.

1 How might reflection help Kay improve her practice?
2 Why might Kay's new knowledge improve the quality of outcomes for the children?
3 Why is it important for Kay to be supported by her manager?

Assessment practice 10.2

| B.P2 | B.P3 | B.M2 | AB.D1 |

The early years setting that wants to introduce staff to reflective practice has asked that as part of the training day, staff learn about theories and approaches to reflective practice. Using examples from your work placement, put together training information that:

- explains theories for reflective practice
- explains how to use approaches to reflective practice for personal development
- assesses how theories and approaches are used in supporting early years practice
- evaluates how theories and approaches to reflective practice support an improvement in professionals' knowledge, skills and practical competence in early years settings.

Plan
- Do I understand a range of different theories and approaches to reflective practice?
- Can I give examples of reflective practice from my own workplace setting?

Do
- Have I thought about how to present information effectively?
- Have I chosen examples that will illustrate the points I am hoping to make?

Review
- Using examples from my work placement, have I shown the benefits of reflective practice?
- Have I used the skills of analysis and reflection?

C Develop reflective practice skills in an early years setting

C1 Reflective practice skills

There are many skills you need in order to evaluate your own practice. The key reflective practice skills are shown in Figure 10.6.

Objectivity, open-mindedness and being self-critical without negativity

Two of the most important reflective practice skills are the ability to be objective and open-minded. If you close your mind to any information that you have gained, you will not be able to make progress. However, you also need to avoid being too self-critical and negative as this can sap your confidence. The key when evaluating your own practice is always to bear in mind that the aim of reflection is to move forward.

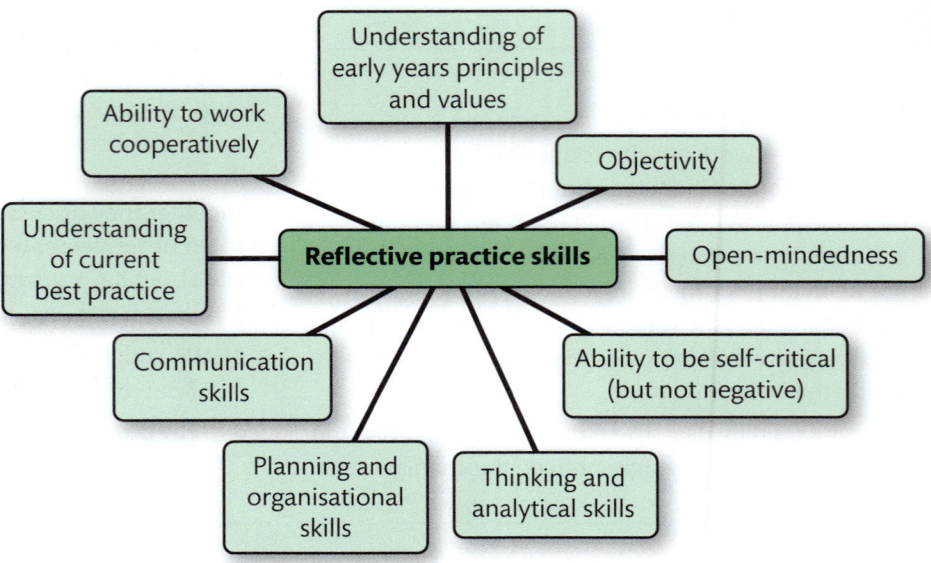

▶ **Figure 10.6:** The key skills you need to develop to become an effective reflective practitioner

Thinking and analytical skills

Another important aspect of being a reflective practitioner is to be able to think about and analyse information. You have seen that you may gather information about your work in a variety of ways, including peer reviews, observations of your work and also through comments that others make. Being able to analyse these and think about how to change or adapt your work is essential. It may be that through thinking and analysis you realise you need additional support or advice about how best to work with a child. Or it may be that you realise you need to gain further knowledge about a specific area such as stammering in order to support a particular child.

Planning and organisational skills

Reflective practitioners are able to plan and organise themselves. They are able to think ahead and work out what knowledge, skills or information they need and create a plan of action. Planning and organisation may be as simple as recognising that a child seems to be anxious if there are lots of other children arriving at the same time and, after reflecting and talking to the child's parents, arranging a slightly quieter drop-off time.

Planning and organisation skills are important if you decide that you need further training. You will need to find out what courses are available and organise your time so that you can go on a training course.

Communication skills

You have seen the importance of communication skills, both verbal and non-verbal, in other areas of working with children and their families. These remain important when it comes to reflective practice for a variety of reasons. Firstly, when you work directly with children and their families, you need to consider what they are saying and showing in their body language in order to correctly reflect on your practice with them.

Communication skills are also important when you receive feedback about your performance from others. If your own body language or tone of voice is defensive, you may not be given honest feedback from a peer or critical friend. On the other hand, if your communication skills are strong and include active listening, you may notice a slight hesitation, which could indicate that your supervisor is thinking about saying something critical. Although it can be difficult to hear, it may actually benefit your work with children in the long run.

Principles and values for working in early years

A reflective practitioner needs to be aware of the key principles and values in the early years sector. For example, in Unit 5 you learned that we have a duty of care towards children. You have also seen the importance of equality and inclusion in your work with children.

Reflective practice means thinking about these principles and values, as well as your own beliefs and values.

You then need to consider whether, in reality, they can be seen in the way that you work with children and the approach that your early years setting takes.

Current best practice in early years

You have seen already in this unit that it is essential to stay up to date with current best practice. You have also seen that the early years sector is a changing one and so a reflective practitioner needs to remain up to date and aware of changes in approach and government policy. A reflective practitioner also has to consider how to apply current best practice to their own setting.

Working cooperatively with colleagues, children and families, and other professionals

Early years practitioners do not work in isolation. It is easy to focus only on your work with children, but the adults around you are just as important. Reflective practitioners think about how well they are developing relationships with parents and to what extent they are able to share information and therefore meet children's needs. Similarly, reflective practitioners think about how the quality of their work contributes to that of the overall team.

C2 Demonstrate reflective practice skills

You have considered the importance of reflection and personal and professional development in your work with children, and also the skills and tools needed to do these things. In this section, you will look at how you might put these theories into action. In order to achieve this unit, you will need to create a portfolio of evidence that shows you can reflect on your own practice, knowledge and skills. Your tutor will have shown you the Practical Evidence Portfolio that accompanies this course and it is important you begin using it as soon as you start your work placement. It will help you to demonstrate how you have begun to build and develop the skills you need to work with children and continually improve your practice.

 PAUSE POINT   Identify six skills that are important in reflective practice.

    Think about your work placement and the skills that you need to work effectively.

Extend   Analyse your own level of skill for each of the areas that you have identified.

Selecting and using appropriate theories and tools of reflection

One of the ways you can show evidence of reflection is by writing reflective accounts and evaluations of your work. Later in this section you will look at how to write reflective accounts. However, the starting point is to decide which theories and tools of reflection will work best in different situations. You should therefore revise the three theories that you looked at in Section B1 and consider how you might use them.

In addition, there are other tools that you can use for reflection, which we will look at now. They are SWOT analysis, action plans and SMART targets.

SWOT analysis

A SWOT analysis is a planning method and stands for:

S = Strengths
W = Weaknesses
O = Opportunities
T = Threats.

Most SWOT analyses are used by settings and groups. However, it is possible to use the process to help you gain an overall picture of your current position.

Strengths

Consider what your overall strengths are. If you are not sure, sometimes it is easier if you ask a friend or classmate to say what they think your particular strengths are. There may be some you haven't thought of.

Weaknesses

Consider what your current weaknesses are. This can include knowledge and skills as well as working relationships that are not as strong as they should be. They might also include organisational skills such as timekeeping, or gaps in your education such as spelling or writing.

Opportunities

Assuming you address your weaknesses, think about the opportunities available to you for the future. This might include career opportunities such as a promotion or moving to a different setting.

Threats

Assuming that you did not address your weaknesses, what are the possible threats to your career or work with children? For example, if you do not improve your timekeeping, you will be asked to leave or if you do not pass your qualification, you may not be able to work with children.

Using a SWOT analysis

Once you have completed your SWOT analysis, you must start to think about what areas you should focus on to improve your work with children. It can be worth drawing up an action plan using your SWOT analysis and deciding on some priorities.

PAUSE POINT   What does the acronym 'SWOT' stand for?

Hint   The 'O' is for opportunities!

Extend   Use a SWOT analysis to identify your current knowledge of this unit.

Action plans

When you have decided on an area of practice that you need to develop, the next step is to create an action plan. This is important because the process of drawing up a plan can help you to focus your ideas and thoughts. It also provides a framework within which you can monitor and review your progress. Many people draw up an action plan alongside a manager, tutor or someone they trust within the setting.

Creating an action plan

There are five simple steps to take when drawing up an action plan.

1 Decide in detail about what you wish to change or develop. Base this on your evaluation. These will become your goals.
2 Break down each of your goals into smaller tasks and think about what you need to do to complete each task – if you have many goals and therefore many tasks, you may create an action plan for each goal.
3 For each task, set yourself a target for when you hope to complete it.
4 Write down a date or dates when the plan will be reviewed to check on progress.
5 Provide a timescale by which all of the tasks will be completed and the goals achieved.

SMART targets

The acronym 'SMART' is often used when creating plans. The aim of SMART goals or targets is to help people focus clearly on what they want to achieve and avoid situations where goals are unrealistic. SMART stands for:

S = Specific
M = Measurable
A = Achievable
R = Realistic
T = Time bound.

Specific

Try to make sure in your planning that you have thought clearly about what you need to learn, experience or develop. Phrases such as 'become better at talking to children' are too vague, but 'making eye contact and getting down to a child's level' would be better.

Measurable

Consider how you will know whether you have achieved this part of your plan. For example, you may want an individual child to approach and interact with you more frequently. You could measure how often this happens now and then set a target, such as at least five times during the day. Or you may want to support a child who uses Makaton, but not know many signs yourself. Your target in this case might be to learn 50 signs.

Achievable

When thinking about your plan, make sure that it is possible to complete each target.

Realistic

There is always a danger of being over enthusiastic and optimistic at the start of any project. Think about how you normally cope and check that your plan will meet your needs and suit the way in which you learn and work.

Time bound

Thinking about how long each part of the plan will take is essential. Many people need a set start and end time to help them work effectively. Working out a realistic timescale will help you remain motivated.

> **Research**
>
> As well as the tools for reflection that you have already considered, others have been created by specific organisations. An example of this is the self-evaluation form that Ofsted have to help early years settings, including childminders, think about their practice. You can access the form at www.gov.uk by searching for 'Early years self-evaluation form'. Note that you need to create a personal Government Gateway account before you can access the form.
>
> Look at the self-evaluation form – what could you learn from completing it? How could you use this in your setting? It is worth finding out whether your early years setting has any tools that they have developed from other sources or have been given.

Keeping a reflective diary

To complete this unit, you will need to show you can reflect on your own learning in many different aspects of your work with children. A reflective diary can be used as a tool to help you develop the skills of reflection. As most people's practice improves over time, it is worth keeping a reflective diary so you can see how far you have progressed over time in the following areas:

▶ your understanding of your own roles and responsibilities
▶ health and safety in early years
▶ promoting children's learning and development in different areas
▶ working with colleagues.

There are no set formats for a reflective diary, but it is usual to make an entry each time you have attended your placement. It is worth recording briefly what you have done, how you feel it went and what you have learned. Over time, you should be able to look back on your diary and realise that you have made progress in many areas. This in turn should allow you to write a reflective account about your learning in the workplace.

In addition to keeping a reflective diary, you could also look for tools that deal with specific areas of practice. These tools might be available from your local authority or through other organisations that support early years practice. Tools may include, for example, the Eat Better, Start Better programme, which is run by the Children's Food Trust and looks at how settings can promote healthy eating.

Your own role, responsibilities and limitations

In order to reflect on your practice, you need to be aware of your role and responsibilities, and also the limitations of your responsibilities. As a learner, your role and responsibilities might be quite limited at the moment, but you should be aware of them in order to be able to reflect upon your work. You should also identify any limitations of your role at present which will change once you have qualified.

One of the areas where you are likely to have some responsibility is in the planning and carrying out of activities and tasks with children. This is an important area to reflect on because for activities and tasks to effectively support children's learning and development, they need to be carefully tailored to meet their individual needs. By reflecting on activities and tasks, you can find ways to be more effective in supporting and promoting the development of individual children.

You looked at observation and planning in Unit 9 and it may be worth revisiting this unit when reflecting on activities and tasks with children. While carrying out activities and tasks, you might like to try to use Schön's 'reflection in action' model to ensure they meet the needs of individual children and so promote and extend their learning and development. Here are some points you might like to bear in mind while planning and carrying out activities.

▶ What is the purpose of this activity?
▶ How will it link to children's known interests?
▶ What resources will be needed?
▶ How will children be able to participate during the activity?
▶ How responsive are individual children?
▶ What do I need to do to improve children's participation or learning?
▶ How might I use my reflections to adapt future activities and tasks to meet the needs and development of individual children?
▶ How could I adapt my plans to extend children's learning or development?

Following an activity, you should consider how well it went and what you could learn from it. Focus on all elements of the activity, including how carefully you planned, prepared and thought about the children's needs, stages of development and ages. You should also think about how your planning and activity linked to the current EYFS requirement that 'Practitioners must consider the individual needs, interests, and stage of development of each child in their care, and must use this information to plan a challenging and enjoyable experience for each child...' (Source: Statutory Framework for the EYFS, page 8, paragraph 1.6). If you are not using the EYFS, you will need to link to the learning requirements of the curriculum used in your home country.

You should also reflect on how you felt during the activity and what the positive aspects were, as well as any areas for improvement. As part of your reflection, you should identify ways to improve your practice for the future.

Reflect on the effectiveness of theories for your own reflective practice

As part of your reflective practice, you should be able to make links to theories and philosophies of learning and development. There are many ways you might do this.

Try out a new technique or approach based on a theory or philosophy

If you have adopted a theory or philosophy for the first time, you should reflect on its effectiveness. This might be in order to experiment with new ways of working with children. For example, you might use a star chart to work with a 7-year-old child to create a system of positive reinforcement.

Visit another setting

You may reflect on what you have seen when you work in a placement whose approach to extending children's learning and development is based on a particular philosophy or theory. A good example of this is if you were to visit or have a placement in a Steiner Waldorf setting and see first-hand how they work with children and the impact their approach has on children's outcomes. As part of your reflection, you would consider what elements you might try to retain, even if you are working elsewhere.

Understand how a theory or philosophy is influencing your practice

There may be times when you reflect on how a theory or philosophy is directly influencing your practice and consider how effective it is. It may be you use a lot of modelling to help children learn new concepts. You could consider for which children this proves effective and whether or not you need to adapt your way of working or use other approaches.

▶ It is useful to reflect on the effectiveness of new practices, such as using a star chart for the first time

Reflect on own practice in working cooperatively with others

If you have strong working relationships, colleagues and other professionals are more likely to give you feedback, advice and also allow you to shadow them. They may also suggest sources of information that will help you develop further. As part of the reflection process, you need to reflect on how well you work cooperatively with others and what contribution they make to your professional development. There are many ways in which you may find out about your practice in relation to others, and we will look at two of these here.

Self-evaluation

You could observe other people's responses to you and note whether you seem to fulfil their expectations of you. The danger with this approach is you may be too subjective and not pick up on subtle cues.

Feedback

The best way to gain information in terms of your effectiveness in working with others is by asking them to evaluate your practice, either as part of a face-to-face interview or asking them to fill in a questionnaire.

Reflect on own practice in promoting diversity, equality and inclusion

Promoting diversity, equality and inclusion is an important part of the early years practitioner's role. It is, therefore, an area for reflecting on your own practice. You might like to consider the following points when reflecting on this aspect of your practice.

▶ How knowledgeable are you about the different issues that surround diversity, equality and inclusion?

▶ What sources of information could you access to help you learn more?

▶ In your practice how is your awareness of diversity, equality and inclusion reflected?

- How do you ensure that all children are valued as you interact with them?
- How do you ensure that families feel welcome and valued?
- How do you ensure in the planning and implementing of activities that they reflect children's interests, cultural differences and family circumstances?

Developing a Practical Evidence Portfolio (PEP)

A reflective account is a critical description and evaluation of an activity, event or situation. For this unit, you will need to write several reflective accounts showing that you can analyse, evaluate and reflect on your practice in promoting children's learning and development. The skills and experiences you need to reflect on are those within the Practical Evidence Portfolio. You also need to show you are developing your skills of reflection and professional development.

How to write a reflective account

This involves three elements.

Description

First, provide a description of what happened. This sets the scene and gives the reader and yourself a chance to understand the circumstances. It also provides evidence that you have completed the core competency, especially if you have asked your supervisor to sign your reflective account when you have finished.

Analysis

Your next step is to interpret what happened. It is useful to look at the models of reflection to help you. An analysis might include your feelings, what went well, how it linked to theory and why things did/did not go to plan. You should focus on how competently you carried out the core aspects of practice.

Evaluation

You should conclude with what you have learned from this experience and how you intend to change or develop your practice. This shows that you are able to develop your own skills of reflection. You should explain what practical steps you might take to improve or develop your practice, or what you might try to do to further your learning. You should also consider how, by reflecting on your practice, you will be able to better promote children's learning and development.

Adapt practice in response to taking part in reflection

You should show that you have started to adapt your practice as a result of what you have learned through the process of reflection. You might make suggestions of what you intend to do differently or you may be able to write about how you have already changed your practice and how effective that has been.

Use feedback received from children, colleagues and others to improve own practice

In your reflective accounts you should show you have been gaining a range of feedback from your colleagues and tutors but also from the children and families you are working with, and that you are actively using it to improve your practice. You should also identify how you intend to, or how you are currently, improving your own practice. This might be, for example, by undertaking additional training, doing some of your own research or gaining some extra work experience.

Assessment practice 10.3

C.P4   C.P5   C.M3   C.M4   C.D2   C.D3

As part of their training day on reflective practice, the early years setting has asked you to provide some examples of where you have used reflective practice in your own work to improve your professional practice. They would like this information to help reinforce their staff's understanding of how reflective practice supports continuous quality improvement. Your information should be based on your own reflective practice and should:

- discuss your skills, attitudes and experience relevant to your work in early years settings
- analyse influences on the development of your own knowledge, skills and practical competence
- demonstrate effective reflective practice in relation to your own work in early years settings
- evaluate the extent to which your reflective practice has impacted on the experience of children and families in your early years setting
- evaluate the effectiveness of reflective practice in supporting continuous quality improvement in early years settings.

Plan

- Which areas of my practice might I reflect on in order to show the process of reflective practice?
- How long will it take me to produce reflective accounts?
- Where can I gain support in order to develop my skills of reflective practice?

Do

- Am I choosing examples of my own reflective practice which illustrate the process well?
- Am I presenting my information in a relevant and concise way?

Review

- Have I used the skills of evaluation in my work and used relevant examples to support my work?
- Have I shown how reflective practice plays an important role in supporting continuous quality improvement?

Further reading and resources

Books

Brock, A. (2014) *The Early Years Reflective Practice Handbook*, Abingdon: Routledge.

Reed, M. and Canning, N. (eds.) (2010) *Reflective Practice in the Early Years*, London: SAGE Publications Ltd.

Macleod-Brudenell, I. and Kay, J. (eds.) (2008) *Advanced Early Years for Foundation Degrees & Levels 4/5*, 2nd edition, Essex: Heinemann.

Lindon, J. and Trodd, L. (2016) *Reflective Practice and Early Years Professionalism: Linking Theory and Practice*, 3rd edition, London: Hodder Education.

Websites

www.early-education.org.uk – The British Association for Early Childhood Education: a range of resources designed to support early years practitioners.

www.gov.uk – UK Government: information about the Early Years Foundation Stage framework.

www.pacey.org.uk – Professional Association for Childcare and Early Years (PACEY): news, information and support for early years professionals, to promote best practice.

THINK ▶FUTURE

Xiaoyuan Li
Nursery manager

The nursery is very keen to remain an outstanding setting. As a manager, Xiaoyuan believes that the nursery's success is partly down to the professional development the staff undertakes. Each staff member is regularly given opportunities to reflect on their practice and to draw up an action plan. Sometimes, the whole setting focuses on particular areas. This year the nursery is looking at care routines. Next year, it will be looking at outdoor play.

To help with improving practice, each staff member is paired with a colleague. They look at each other's work, give suggestions and help each other in drawing up an action plan. The nursery is also part of a cluster group and through this network staff see what other settings are doing. This works very well and recently the nursery has been twinned with a nursery in Finland – the staff are aiming to learn more about how they work with children.

Focusing your skills

Supporting peers using peer-to-peer observation

One of the ways in which early years settings maintain and improve the quality of practice is through peer review. It may seem daunting to be asked to review a colleague's work, but if you can do so sensitively, you may support their professional development. In addition, reflecting on a colleague's work can help you to think about your own practice.

Preparation matters

Find out in advance what area of practice is going to be looked at. This will allow you to carry out your own research so you know what is considered to be best practice in this area.

It is also helpful to speak to your colleague about whether there is something they would like to focus on.

Observing a colleague working with a child

Ask your colleague if they would prefer you to be discreet in your observation or whether they would like you to join in. If they would prefer you to participate, be careful not to take over the activity or to change the children's responses. You must remain able to observe and analyse your colleague's work.

Before feeding back to your colleague

Reflect on what you have seen and decide what the key points of your feedback will be. Think about the key aspects of their work that are positive and what makes them so. Choose two or three points where you think there may be room for improvement.

Feeding back to your colleague

Choose a time when you can both take time to discuss the observation. Start by asking how your colleague felt and what they thought. Talk through your observation, highlighting the aspects of their work that were positive. Give feedback about areas where you thought there might be room for improvement. Be precise and give clear reasons for your thoughts. Ask your colleague for their reaction, allowing them time to reflect and think. Expect that they may query what you have said or explain the reasons behind their actions.

The Early Years Foundation Stage 11

Getting to know your unit

Assessment
You will be assessed by a series of assignments and a paper set by your tutor.

The Early Years Foundation Stage (EYFS) is the statutory framework for practitioners in England, which covers the curriculum, development and welfare requirements for children up to the age of 5 years. If you are working with this age group, you will need to have a firm understanding of its principles, structure and requirements, and the rationale behind each of the seven areas of learning.

You should also know how to plan for play and activities that are both adult-directed and child-initiated, and that support children's progress towards the early learning goals at the end of the EYFS. In this way, you will be able to ensure that you meet the needs of all the children in your setting and enable them to reach their full potential.

How you will be assessed

This unit will be assessed internally by a series of tasks set by your tutor. The assignments set by your tutor may take the following forms:

▸ creating a training programme that evaluates the legal status, structure and purpose of the Early Years Foundation Stage and the requirements relevant to children's learning and development, assessment, safeguarding and welfare

▸ a reflective account of the skills used in supporting children's progress towards the early learning goals and in safeguarding and promoting their welfare.

The assessment activities within this unit are designed to help you improve your understanding of the theory you will need to complete your assignments. Completing these activities will not mean that you have achieved a particular grade, but you will have carried out useful research or preparation that will be relevant when it comes to your final assessment.

To pass this unit you must ensure that you have covered all the Pass grading criteria. You can see these listed in the table below. If you are seeking a Merit or Distinction grade then you must make sure you have presented the information in your assignment in the style required, for example, Merit criteria ask you to analyse and assess, while Distinction criteria ask you to evaluate.

Assessment criteria

This table shows what you must do in order to achieve a **Pass**, **Merit** or **Distinction** grade, and where you can find activities to help you.

Pass	Merit	Distinction
Learning aim **A** Understand the legal status, principles, themes and aims of the Early Years Foundation Stage		
A.P1 Explain the legal status of the EYFS and process of inspection. **Assessment practice 11.1**	**A.M1** Analyse how the structure, principles, themes and aims of the EYFS shape practice in early years settings. **Assessment practice 11.1**	**A.D1** Evaluate importance of a Statutory Framework for the EYFS for children's life chances. **Assessment practice 11.1**
A.P2 Explain the structure, principles, themes and aims of the EYFS. **Assessment practice 11.1**		
Learning aim **B** Examine the learning and development and assessment requirements of the Early Years Foundation Stage		
B.P3 Explain how learning and development and assessment requirements of the EYFS influence the development of educational programmes. **Assessment practice 11.2**	**B.M2** Assess the extent to which the learning and development and assessment requirements of the EYFS prepare children for school at the age of five years. **Assessment practice 11.2**	**BC.D2** Evaluate the impact of the EYFS requirements for learning and development, assessment and safeguarding and welfare on practice in early years settings. **Assessment practice 11.4**
B.P4 Explain how educational programmes in an early years setting provide opportunities across areas of learning in the EYFS. **Assessment practice 11.2**		
Learning aim **C** Examine the safeguarding and welfare requirements of the Early Years Foundation Stage		
C.P5 Explain the safeguarding and welfare requirements of the EYFS. **Assessment practice 11.3**	**C.M3** Assess the importance of meeting safeguarding and welfare requirements for children's learning and development. **Assessment practice 11.3**	
Learning aim **D** Apply skills to support children's progress towards early learning goals and to meet safeguarding and welfare requirements of the Early Years Foundation Stage		
D.P6 Plan, lead and record play and educational activities towards early learning goals. **Assessment practice 11.5**	**D.M4** Demonstrate confidence and independence to plan, lead and record play and educational activities towards early learning goals across areas of learning. **Assessment practice 11.5**	**D.D3** Demonstrate effective self-management and professional conduct consistently in adhering to the educational and safeguarding and welfare requirements of the EYFS. **Assessment practice 11.6**
D.P7 Demonstrate adherence to safeguarding and welfare requirements in the EYFS. **Assessment practice 11.6**	**D.M5** Demonstrate consistent adherence to safeguarding and welfare responsibilities in the EYFS. **Assessment practice 11.6**	

Getting started

Take a few minutes to write a brief account of what you already know about the Early Years Foundation Stage (EYFS) – why it was introduced, its structure, the curriculum itself and how and when children are assessed.

Share this with a partner and compare your understanding.

A Understand the legal status, principles, themes and aims of the Early Years Foundation Stage

A1 The legal status of the Early Years Foundation Stage (EYFS)

The scope and legal status of the EYFS

Taking its basis from the Childcare Act 2006, the EYFS is a statutory framework that was introduced in 2008 and reviewed in 2014, with the aim of improving outcomes for children in the early years and setting the standard for all early years providers.

The EYFS is made up of a curriculum that includes learning and development requirements, as well as specific safeguarding and welfare requirements. The EYFS applies to a range of settings and providers in England. This includes all those caring for children from birth to the end of the academic year in which they have their fifth birthday. This means it is very important for early years providers to understand their legal status. The EYFS documentation defines all these settings as Ofsted-registered providers on the Early Years Register. This includes childminders, nurseries and preschools, all schools in England that are attended by young children and all providers registered with an early years childminder agency.

Legislation behind the safeguarding and welfare requirement regulations in the EYFS

The legal status of the EYFS is based on a number of different pieces of legislation, all of which have gradually improved the safeguarding and welfare requirements for children. The requirements mean children have more rights and there is a greater emphasis on agencies working together for their benefit. The relevant legislation is outlined in the following 'Research' box.

> **Research**
>
> Before you start work on this unit, make sure you read, and are familiar with, the 2014 EYFS documentation. Find out more about the requirements of the EYFS by downloading the EYFS statutory framework, which can be found on the Foundation Years website under Resources: see www.foundationyears.org.uk/.
>
> You should have a hard copy of this document to refer to, as it will help you in your work.

Children Act 1989 and 2004

One of the key aims of the Children Act 1989 was to clarify the laws affecting children and to give a greater focus to children's welfare. It aimed to achieve a better balance and closer partnerships between authorities and parents/carers, and gave more individual rights to the child, separate from their parents/carers.

The Children Act 2004, introduced after the death of Victoria Climbié, built on the Children Act 1989 and was closely linked to the publication of 'Every Child Matters', which set out to integrate services for children. Under this legislation, local authorities such as the police, health service and youth justice system must work together and cooperate with one another, sharing information to promote the well-being of children and young people so that their welfare is protected.

Data Protection Act 1998

The Data Protection Act 1998 covers the way early years settings handle information about children. Under this act, information gathered by the school or setting in the context of safeguarding and child protection must **only** be used for that purpose. If any individuals concerned, or their parents or carers, wish to know information that is held about them, they have a right to access it.

There are only a few exceptions to this, which are:

▶ information that may cause serious harm or risk of abuse to the child or another individual

▶ information given to a court or in adoption or parental order records

▶ copies of examination scripts or marks prior to their release

▶ unstructured personal information, or information that is held manually and not in school or setting records.

Childcare Act 2006

The Childcare Act 2006 was the first piece of legislation that focused on early childcare and early childhood services by requiring local authorities and their partners to work together. It aimed to reduce child poverty by supporting parents to get into work and to reduce inequalities and improve outcomes for all children up to the age of 5. It also introduced the EYFS, which came into effect in England in 2008. This act gives the requirements of the EYFS a legal force.

Safeguarding Vulnerable Groups Act 2006

The Safeguarding Vulnerable Groups Act 2006 provides the legislative framework for a vetting and barring scheme for people who work with children and vulnerable adults. Early years settings have a duty to make a referral to the Disclosure and Barring Service when a member of staff is dismissed because they have harmed a child or put a child at risk of harm.

The purpose of the scheme is to minimise the risk of harm posed to children and vulnerable adults by those who might seek to harm them through their work (paid or unpaid).

> **Link**
>
> Remind yourself of the content in *Unit 5 Keeping Children Safe*. You will look at safeguarding and welfare requirements in more detail in Section C1 of this unit.

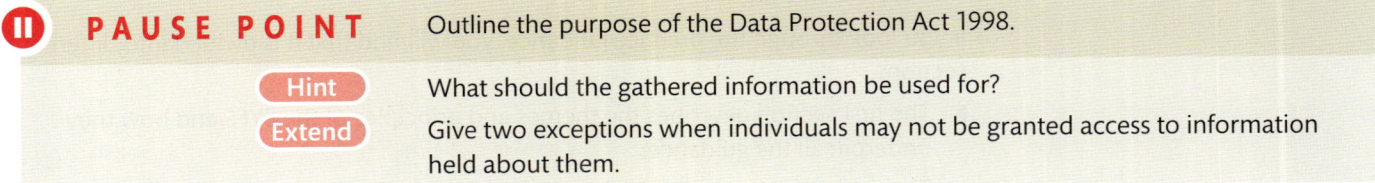

❚❚ PAUSE POINT   Outline the purpose of the Data Protection Act 1998.

      Hint   What should the gathered information be used for?

      Extend   Give two exceptions when individuals may not be granted access to information held about them.

Equality Act 2010

The Equality Act replaced nine acts of parliament over several decades. It applies to schools and early years settings, and in particular the way in which they treat children and prospective pupils, so that all children have the same opportunities.

Settings that are governed by the EYFS

As you saw at the start of this section, the EYFS is for all early years providers caring for children from birth to the end of the academic year in which they have their fifth birthday. This includes all maintained and non-maintained schools, all independent schools and all providers on the Early Years Register such as childminders, nurseries and preschools. They must all be Ofsted registered.

Definitions of terminology

The terminology used in the EYFS documentation can be confusing. It is important that you are able to understand the terminology and know where to find information about it in the documentation so that you understand its purpose.

The statutory guidance

The statutory framework is the most important part of the documentation as it sets out the legal requirements of the EYFS and its overall structure.

It is divided into three sections:

▶ the learning and development requirements – these set out the different areas of learning as well as the early learning goals within each aspect

▶ the arrangements for assessment

▶ the legal requirements relating to safeguarding and welfare.

The specific legal requirements relating to safeguarding and welfare

The specific legal requirements relating to safeguarding and welfare are part of the statutory guidance document and outline what your setting is **legally required to do** under the EYFS to ensure the safety and well-being of children. The requirements are specific to children.

You need to make sure that these requirements are being met at all times and in different areas. For example, the specific legal requirements for outings are that a risk assessment must be carried out prior to taking children on a trip and that they must be kept safe. As well as the safeguarding and welfare requirements, settings will also have other more general legal requirements, for example, disability discrimination.

Good practice guidance

The practice guidance found in 'Development Matters in the Early Years Foundation Stage (EYFS)' is published by the British Association for Early Childhood Education and supported by the Department for Education to help settings implement the EYFS. It is non-statutory – that is, you do not have to follow it. However, it is useful and gives different ideas and suggestions to support practitioners in delivering the EYFS. You can download it from the Resources section of the Foundation Years website: www.foundationyears.org.uk.

If you look through the practice guidance, you will find that it is divided into different sections.

▶ The first section describes the themes and principles of the EYFS and how they underpin all the guidance.

▶ The second section provides information on how to use the guidance to support children's learning and development, and how observation, planning and assessment are linked together.

▶ The third section describes the characteristics of effective learning and how they run through the different areas of learning and development.

Research

Use the statutory guidance to find out the specific legal requirements for equal opportunities and behaviour management.

▶ The final section outlines the characteristics of effective learning alongside the key themes and gives useful guidance on what adults can do to support children in each area. It then goes on to do the same for the areas of learning and development.

The overall structure of the EYFS

As you have seen above, the EYFS statutory guidance is structured so it can be broken down into three sections.

The learning and welfare requirements are based on four overarching principles that should influence all areas of practice in early years settings. You need to bear all of these in mind when working with children so that you can ensure you adhere to them. These overarching principles are that:

▶ every child is unique
▶ children learn to be strong and independent through positive relationships
▶ children should be provided with a positive and enabling environment
▶ children learn and develop in different ways and at different rates.

Source: Adapted from the Statutory Framework for the Early Years Foundation Stage (2014) p6 © Crown copyright 2014

The learning and development requirements

The learning and development requirements cover:

▶ the seven areas of learning and development
▶ the early learning goals, which are a summary of the knowledge, skills and understanding that all young children should have gained by the end of the academic year in which they turn five.

The seven areas of learning and development

The educational programmes and curriculum of the EYFS are set out within a framework of seven areas of learning and development. The requirements describe how settings should promote the learning and development of children in their care, so that they are 'school ready' and able to move into reception and Year 1. Figure 11.1 shows the seven areas of learning.

Each of the seven areas are subdivided, for example, literacy is divided into reading and writing, and mathematics into numbers and shape, space and measures.

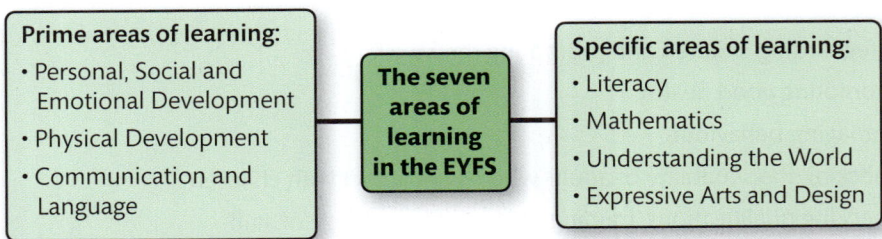

Prime areas of learning:
• Personal, Social and Emotional Development
• Physical Development
• Communication and Language

The seven areas of learning in the EYFS

Specific areas of learning:
• Literacy
• Mathematics
• Understanding the World
• Expressive Arts and Design

▶ **Figure 11.1:** The seven areas of learning in the EYFS

The early learning goals

The early learning goals are designed to show where each child should be in each area of learning at the end of the EYFS. For example, under reading, the early learning goal reads: 'Children read and understand simple sentences. They use phonic knowledge to decode regular words and read them aloud accurately. They also read some common irregular words. They demonstrate understanding when talking with others about what they have read.' There are 17 early learning goals in total.

Source: Statutory Framework for the Early Years Foundation Stage (2014) p11 © Crown copyright 2014

▶ What area(s) of learning could these children be working on?

Link

To find out more about early learning goals, see Section B1.

Key terms

Formative assessment – assessment that takes place during the learning process on an ongoing basis, or 'assessment for learning'.

Summative assessment – assessment of what a child knows and can do at the end of a period of learning, or 'assessment of learning'.

The assessment requirements

Assessment requirements may be ongoing – **formative assessment** – or structured – **summative assessment**. This means that assessment will take place throughout the EYFS, but that children will also be assessed at two specific points: between 2 and 3 years, and again at the end of the final term of the year in which the child reaches five. This is known as the Early Years Foundation Stage Profile (EYFSP). Children aged between 2 and 3 years will only be assessed in the three prime areas (personal, social and emotional development, physical development and communication and language). The requirements for assessment will be covered in more detail later in this section.

The safeguarding and welfare requirements

Early years providers need to take steps to ensure that all children in their care are kept safe and well. They should create settings that are welcoming, safe and stimulating so that children are able to enjoy their learning.

The areas covered under the safeguarding and welfare requirements of the EYFS include:

▶ safeguarding children and promoting their welfare
▶ promoting good health
▶ managing behaviour
▶ checking the suitability of adults who have contact with children
▶ checking qualifications, training, skills and knowledge of staff
▶ staff : child ratios
▶ key people
▶ before/after-school care and holiday provision
▶ childminder agencies
▶ ensuring that the premises and facilities are safe and secure, and meet health and safety requirements
▶ special educational needs
▶ promoting equal opportunities
▶ maintaining records, policies and procedures.

PAUSE POINT　Explain the difference between formative and summative assessment.

> Hint　You might use them at different stages in the EYFS.

> Extend　How do different settings carry out formative assessment?

The purpose and process of inspection

Providers who are registered on the Early Years or Childcare Register, whether early years or childcare providers or childminders, need to follow the statutory framework of the EYFS. This means that they must meet the legal requirements of the Childcare Act 2006 in order to remain registered, as well as the learning and development requirements.

Early years and childcare settings are regularly inspected (every 3 to 4 years) as part of the Ofsted framework, to look at how well they meet the requirements of the Early Years or Childcare Register and the standards of the EYFS. The amount of notice given for a visit will depend on the early years setting. Group providers normally receive no notice, whereas childminders and early years classes within primary schools are likely to receive a few days' notice.

As part of the inspection process, inspectors will ask to see the setting's **self-evaluation form**. Managers should complete this form with staff on a regular basis to ensure they are looking at the quality of provision and how well they are meeting the needs of children and improving outcomes for them.

The self-evaluation form also gives guidance on the types of question inspectors will ask providers when looking at the quality of provision in the setting. Ofsted recommend that settings complete the form thoroughly as it will give them some idea about the aspects they think are working well, and those that they are working towards improving.

Inspectors also carry out observations at the setting, look at paperwork, interview staff, parents/carers and children, and assess how well the children's learning and development are progressing. They then provide feedback on:

▶ how well the early years provision meets the needs of the range of children who attend

▶ the contribution of the early years provision to children's well-being

▶ the leadership and management of the early years provision.

Each of these areas is given a grade. At the time of writing, these grades are:

▶ grade 1 (outstanding)

▶ grade 2 (good)

▶ grade 3 (requires improvement)

▶ grade 4 (inadequate).

All inspections are published on the Ofsted website so that the process is transparent and parents, carers or others are able to view the results.

As part of the inspection process, practitioners need to provide information to Ofsted, including the type of setting, the number of children and the number of hours for which childcare is provided. Inspectors check that settings are meeting a number of requirements, including those shown in Figure 11.2.

> **Key term**
>
> **Self-evaluation form** – a form that settings fill out on a regular basis showing how they intend to review and improve their provision.

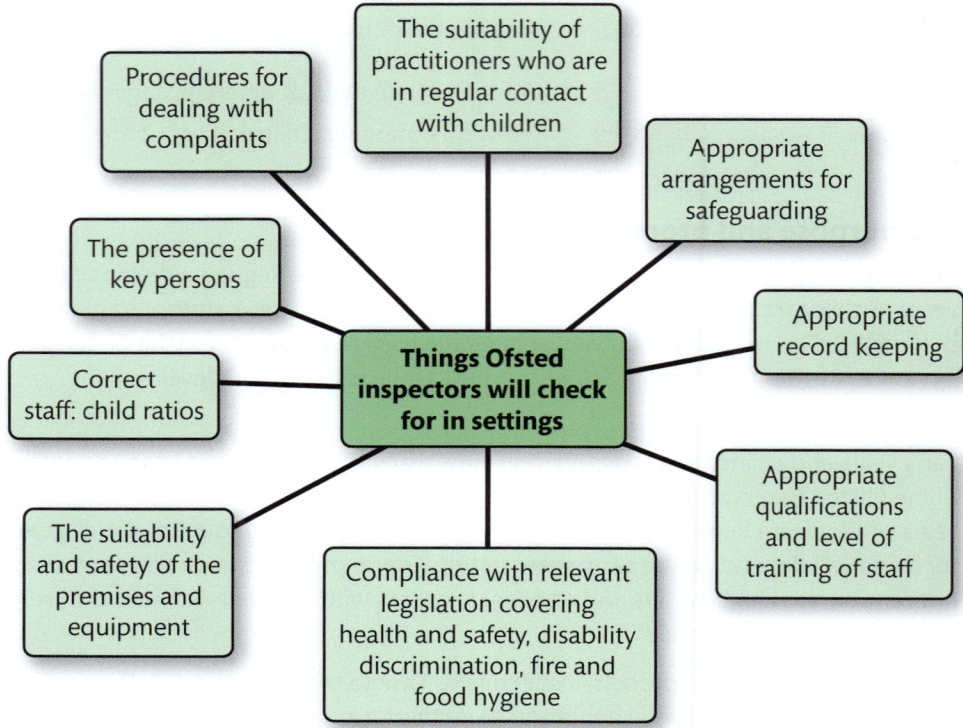

▶ **Figure 11.2:** The things Ofsted check for in a setting

As they are legal requirements, the Ofsted inspection will assess all aspects of the setting under the headings in Figure 11.2, checking paperwork and looking at all statutory requirements. Settings can apply to have exemption from some aspects of the requirements, for example, if an individual child's family has a religious or philosophical view that is in conflict with the learning and development requirements, or if the setting is unable to fully meet the learning and development requirements due to temporary restrictions in their facilities. However, no setting may be exempted from the welfare requirements for any reason, as these requirements deal with child safety.

You can download a copy of the Early Years Inspection Handbook at www.gov.uk.

Assessment practice 11.1   A.P1 A.P2 A.M1 A.D1

Create a reference document for new early years practitioners that:

- summarises the legal status, structure, principles, themes and aims of the EYFS and describes how its delivery is inspected
- explains the requirements for the assessment of children's progress
- analyses how the structure, principles, themes and aims of the EYFS shape practice in early years settings, and evaluates the potential impact of the EYFS on outcomes for children.

Plan

- What features should I include in my reference document?
- How much detail do I need?

Do

- Do I understand my thought processes for devising the reference document and can I explain why I have decided to approach it in a particular way?
- Can I set milestones and evaluate my progress and success at these intervals?

Review

- Can I go through the reference document with new practitioners and check their understanding of the EYFS?
- Can I identify when this may be useful in the workplace?

A2 Principles, themes and aims of the EYFS

The overarching principles and themes of the EYFS

The principles of the EYFS are designed to guide the work of all early years practitioners and influence and shape practice in early years settings. They are divided into four guiding themes, each of which has a principle behind it. They are shown in Table 11.1.

▶ **Table 11.1:** The themes and principles of the EYFS

Theme	Principle behind the theme
The unique child	Every child is a unique child, who is constantly learning and can be resilient, capable, confident and self-assured
Positive relationships	Children learn to be strong and independent through positive relationships
Enabling environments	Children learn and develop well in enabling environments, in which their experiences respond to their individual needs and where there is a strong partnership between practitioners and parents and/or carers
Learning and development	Children develop and learn in different ways and at different rates. The framework covers the education and care of all children in early years provision, including children with special educational needs and disabilities

Source: Adapted from the Statutory Framework for the Early Years Foundation Stage (2014) p6 © Crown copyright 2014

The unique child

You should be able to show that you are meeting the individual needs of children in different ways – through your role as a child's key person, getting to know families and parents/carers, and demonstrating an understanding of the needs of the child. The curriculum framework requires you to show inclusive practice and encourage the development of children's communication and language skills so that they are able to develop their understanding and self-expression. Planning should show that the setting reflects the interests and views of individual children, for example, by taking their views into consideration.

Positive relationships

You should support children in developing positive relationships with their parents and carers as well as others. The curriculum framework requires you to do this through planning for children's personal, social and emotional development, as well as through meeting their needs on a daily basis when managing feelings and behaviour and considering the needs of others.

Enabling environments

You should ensure that relationships with those outside the setting – for example, other professionals and visitors from the community – are strong and positive, and that you act as a good role model for children. The curriculum framework requires you to ensure that the learning environment – both indoor and outdoor – is rich and varied and will support each child's development through a range of learning opportunities. You also need to show that you plan for, assess and observe children to demonstrate that you are meeting their needs.

▶ Do you think this child and practitioner have a positive relationship?

Learning and development

You need to be able to plan for all areas of the Foundation Stage curriculum while being mindful of the fact that they are interrelated and should reflect children's interests. Children develop and learn in different ways and at different rates.

You should also take into account the importance of play, which is the key way in which children learn. The curriculum framework requires you to provide children with active learning opportunities, which allow them to make their own connections and discover things for themselves.

How principles are reflected within the early education curriculum requirements

It is important to think about each principle of the EYFS in relation to the children you are working with at all times. This will help you make sure that you keep the principles at the forefront of your practice. The principles should also be reflected within the early education curriculum as you carry out your work with children.

Remember:

▶ every child is a unique child – you need to show how individual children's progress is monitored and assessed, and how you do this alongside colleagues, parents, carers and other professionals

▶ children learn to be strong and independent through positive relationships – you should always demonstrate good relationships with children and other adults in the setting

▶ children learn and develop well in enabling environments – the learning environment should be a stimulating and positive reflection of children's work and support their learning; all children should be represented

▶ children develop and learn in different ways and at different rates – you should make sure the curriculum is differentiated to take into account the needs of children.

The importance of applying the principles to practice

The EYFS principles are guiding themes that should shape your practice in all early years settings. You need to show how you are applying the principles to your practice and you should have a clear idea about how they run through all of your setting's work with children. It would be a good idea to look regularly at the principles to make sure you can show how they are being applied to your practice.

You should also ensure that your setting complies with the legal requirements of the EYFS to create a stimulating, inclusive and enjoyable environment. These are set out in the statutory guidance and include:

▶ child protection
▶ suitable people
▶ staff qualifications
▶ staff : child ratios
▶ health
▶ equal opportunities
▶ accident or injury.

Theory into practice

Look carefully at your setting's policies and make sure you are familiar with the legal requirements of the EYFS.

How settings apply principles to practice

Your setting needs to show how the EYFS principles are applied in its daily practice by:

▶ planning for children

▶ providing children with a key person

▶ working with parents.

Planning for children

There should be a clear structure to planning in your setting, which shows how the early years curriculum is organised as well as how it is meeting children's individual needs.

⏸ PAUSE POINT   Look at some examples of short-term planning. How do they meet children's individual needs and map to the early years curriculum?

Hint   Plans should be annotated and used as working documents.

Extend   Make sure you are aware of where planning documentation is kept so that you can refer to it when needed.

Providing children with a key person

Each child in your setting should have an adult who is their main contact. This key person should know the child well and have good relationships with them and their parents/carers so that both the child and their parent/carer knows who to go to if there are any issues. The key person should also encourage parents and carers to support their child's development at home. They should ensure that children's learning and care is tailored to their individual needs.

Link

Look at Section C1 to find out more about the key person role.

Working with parents

The EYFS statutory framework places an emphasis on the importance of information sharing between parents/carers and the setting. Parents should be encouraged to share information about their child's development at home, and early years settings should provide information about:

▶ how the EYFS is being delivered

▶ staffing

▶ their child's key person

▶ all policies and procedures that are followed.

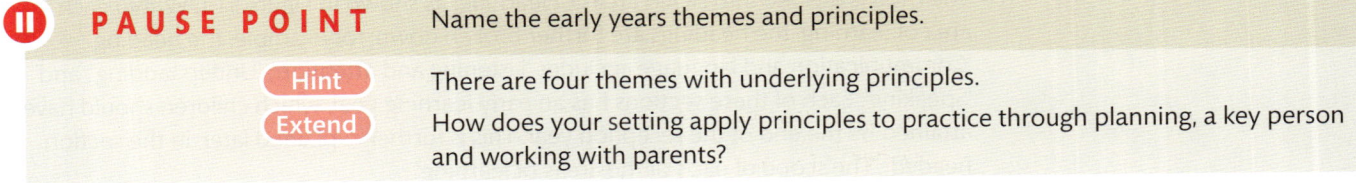

⏸ PAUSE POINT   Name the early years themes and principles.

Hint   There are four themes with underlying principles.

Extend   How does your setting apply principles to practice through planning, a key person and working with parents?

The aims of the EYFS

The EYFS sets the standards that settings must meet in order to support children to meet their full potential. The introduction to the statutory guidance sets out what the EYFS seeks to provide and its main aims.

The key aims include the following.

▶ **Promote school readiness** – the EYFS aims to 'promote teaching and learning to ensure children's "school readiness"' and give them a 'broad range of knowledge and skills that provide the right foundation for good future progress through school and life'.

▶ **Reduce inequality** – the EYFS aims to provide 'equality of opportunity and anti-discriminatory practice, ensuring that every child is included and supported'.

▶ **Promote health, safety and safeguarding** – the EYFS 'sets the standards that all early years providers must meet to ensure that children... are kept healthy and safe'. The steps that providers must take to keep children safe and promote their welfare are within Section 3 of the guidance, 'The safeguarding and welfare requirements'.

Source: Adapted from the Statutory Framework for the Early Years Foundation Stage (2014) p5 © Crown copyright 2014

 PAUSE POINT   Think about how your setting meets the three aims of the EYFS.

Hint   Look at your setting's policies for equal opportunities, health and safety, and safeguarding or child protection. Consider the knowledge and skills that will support children in becoming 'school ready'.

Extend   Find out about other settings and how they ensure school readiness.

 B

Examine the learning and development and assessment requirements of the Early Years Foundation Stage

B1 Learning and development requirements

The requirement for planned, purposeful play

The EYFS has been developed to incorporate the different areas of children's development within seven areas of learning. These areas of development must be delivered through planned, **purposeful play**. When planning activities under the EYFS, settings need to make sure play is a key part of the delivery. Play is essential for children's development because it:

▶ builds children's confidence

▶ encourages children to think about problems

▶ helps children relate to others.

The areas of learning

The EYFS is divided into seven areas of learning, as shown in Figure 11.1. Within each area of learning, the headings are further broken down; for example, the heading 'Communication and language' includes 'Listening and attention', 'Understanding', and 'Speaking'. Each of these sections has an early learning goal, which children should have attained by the end of the reception year. This is further explained later, in the section headed 'The scope of each of the areas of learning'.

> **Key term**
>
> **Purposeful play** – play which allows children to investigate and experience things, and 'have a go'.

The rationale behind each of the areas of learning in terms of supporting children's overall development

Table 11.2 shows the relationship between the seven areas of learning and the areas of child development. As can be seen from Table 11.2, the prime areas of learning relate directly to the main areas of child development. These areas are considered to be those that are particularly important in building children's capacity to learn.

The specific areas of learning, which develop the breadth of children's skills in the areas of literacy, mathematics, understanding the world, and expressive arts and design, should be developed as children become more competent in the three prime areas. If you are working with the youngest children, you should be focusing on the three prime areas, as they are the basis for subsequent, successful learning.

▶ **Table 11.2:** The relationship between the seven areas of learning and the areas of child development

Area of learning and development	Area of child development
Prime areas of learning and development: • personal, social and emotional development • physical development • communication and language	The **prime** areas of learning relate directly to the main areas of child development, which are: • social and emotional development • physical and sensory development • cognitive and language development
Specific areas of learning and development: • literacy • mathematics • understanding of the world • expressive arts and design	The **specific** areas of learning should be developed as children become more competent in the prime areas of learning

By the time they reach the end of the EYFS, children should be spending the same amount of time on each area of learning so that they continue to develop their confidence in the three prime areas while also developing in the specific areas.

If children give cause for concern in any of the prime areas at any time during the Foundation Stage, they should be given increased support so that they are less likely to be unprepared for the start of school. In this situation, parents and/or carers would need to be informed and staff should consider whether other agencies should be involved so that the child and their family can have further support, within or outside the setting.

The scope of each of the areas of learning

Each area of learning and development in the EYFS is expanded into two or three different strands to show the scope or breadth of what children should develop during their time in the Foundation Stage. For example, literacy is split into reading and writing, mathematics into numbers, and shape, space and measures.

Personal, social and emotional development, one of the prime areas, is split into three strands, as follows:

▶ self-confidence and self-awareness

▶ managing feelings and behaviour

▶ making relationships.

Source: Statutory Framework for the Early Years Foundation Stage (2014) p11 © Crown copyright 2014

Children should be supported in each strand as they progress towards the early learning goal associated with it. For all areas of learning and development, and their separate strands, see the statutory framework for the EYFS, Section A1.

Link

Revisit Unit 1, where you will find more information about how children under 5 years develop.

Link

See the 'Early learning goals' section to find out more about these goals.

The relationship between the prime areas of learning and the specific areas of learning and how they are interrelated

Look again at Table 11.2. As you look at each of the different areas of learning and development, it should be clear that they are interrelated. This means children who are learning through play will develop in more than one area. For example, a child who is playing with playdough with a group of children will be developing their physical (fine motor) skills; their communication and language skills; their personal, social and emotional skills; and their expressive arts skills through their imagination. They will also be developing relationships with others, exploring and learning in an active way through play. As the different areas of learning are so interrelated, planning for different areas of the EYFS is usually topic based.

Topic-based planning has long been used as a way to introduce activities to young children. It enables you to use ideas that are familiar to children in order to create a focus and link things together. Although it is not usually possible to cover every aspect of learning within a topic, it is a useful starting point. When you are planning, make sure you cover separately any learning areas that cannot be included as part of the topic.

Early learning goals

Early learning goals are the statements associated with the strands within each area of learning in the prime and specific areas. These are what providers are helping children to work towards by the end of the academic year in which they turn five. They summarise 'the knowledge, skills and understanding that all young children should have gained by the end of the Reception year.'

Source: Statutory Framework for the Early Years Foundation Stage (2014) p7 © Crown copyright 2014

Here are the early learning goals for personal, social and emotional development.

▶ **Self-confidence and self-awareness** – children are confident to try new activities, and say why they like some activities more than others. They are confident to speak in a familiar group, will talk about their ideas, and will choose the resources they need for their chosen activities. They say when they do or don't need help.

▶ **Managing feelings and behaviour** – children can talk about how they and others show feelings, talk about their own and others' behaviour, and its consequences, and know that some behaviour is unacceptable. They work as part of a group or class, and understand and follow the rules. They adjust their behaviour to different situations, and take changes of routine in their stride.

▶ **Making relationships** – children play cooperatively, taking turns with others. They take account of one another's ideas about how to organise their activity. They show sensitivity to others' needs and feelings, and form positive relationships with adults and other children.

Source: Statutory Framework for the Early Years Foundation Stage (2014) p11 © Crown copyright 2014

▶ It is important to give children opportunities to play cooperatively and form positive relationships with one another

The strands and early learning goals for each of the prime and specific areas of learning and development are listed in the statutory framework document.

The characteristics of learning

The three characteristics of effective teaching and learning are as follows.

1 **Playing and exploring** – the way in which children investigate and experience things, and 'have a go'.

2 **Active learning** – the process by which children concentrate and keep on trying if they encounter difficulties, and enjoy their achievements.

3 **Creating and thinking critically** – when children have and develop their own ideas, make links between ideas and develop strategies for doing things.

These characteristics should form the basis of child-initiated activities. Early years practitioners should look at the different ways in which children learn and should reflect on these when planning and assessing children. When carrying out observations of children, it is sometimes helpful to note down the **way** in which they learn as well as **what** they are learning.

Although interconnected, children's overall development is usually considered in relation to the following prime areas.

▶ Personal, social and emotional development – how the child relates to others and is developing emotionally, including feelings and behaviour.

▶ Physical and sensory development – how the child is developing physically, to include both fine and gross motor skills, and development of the five senses.

▶ Communication and language – how the child is developing intellectually/cognitively, or how they are learning, to include their language development.

Ⅱ PAUSE POINT   Name three ways in which children learn.

     Hint   Think about the characteristics of effective learning.

     Extend   Find out how your setting assesses and records the way in which children learn.

The importance of balancing adult-led and child-initiated activities

As an early years worker, you should be aware of the importance of balancing child-initiated and adult-led activities. Much of the EYFS is based on the need for play to be part of children's learning and for adults to encourage children to develop their independence.

However, children also need to be guided and supported by adults as they are challenged by new concepts and ideas. As children work towards the end of the Foundation Stage, the balance of activities should gradually move more towards those that are led by adults, so that children are ready for more formal learning in Year 1.

B2 Assessment requirements

> **Link**
>
> Before you read this section, you may like to remind yourself of the content in Unit 9.

How assessment is used to plan for individual children's progress within the EYFS

Section 2 of the EYFS statutory guidance is devoted to assessment. It is important for parents and carers, healthcare practitioners and educationalists that you regularly check children's learning and development, particularly during their earliest years. This is because it is a time of rapid growth for children, physically, emotionally and in terms of general cognitive development. If there are any issues, they should be picked up as early as possible so that they can be addressed. Parents and carers should work hand in hand with the setting to monitor children's development. Healthcare professionals may also liaise with providers, particularly if there is an issue that adults in the setting are able to support.

In groups, download the Ofsted document, 'Early years and childcare registration handbook' – you will be able to find this using a simple internet search. Choose one of the headings to focus on.

1 Are all of the requirements under your chosen heading being carried out in your setting?

2 How could all staff in your setting be clear about what they need to do to meet Ofsted requirements?

3 Present your findings to the class.

⏸ PAUSE POINT Make a list of the ways that you work with parents and carers to ensure that children are assessed and monitored effectively throughout the EYFS.

Hint Think about contact with parents/carers before children start at the setting. In what ways does this contact continue to ensure a two-way flow of information?

Extend Find out how your setting forms links with healthcare practitioners.

Although babies and young children are regularly checked and monitored by healthcare professionals, issues might not be picked up straight away, for example, any problems in hearing. It is important to look out for signs that indicate that young children may need additional support. For this reason, assessment in the early years needs to be ongoing (formative), as well as summative.

Assessment requirements and how information about assessment is shared

Progress check at 2 years

Children's progress is assessed at the age of 2 years. At this check, children's progress in the prime areas of learning (personal, social and emotional development, physical development, and communication and language) is reviewed by practitioners. Parents and carers are given a short summary of their child's development in these areas. They are asked to share this with other professionals, for example, health visitors or teachers if they are moving to a school-based nursery, as it will coincide with the child's health and development review.

The summary includes observations about a child's progress, as well as any concerns. If there are any areas in which a child is not making expected progress, the provider should set out a plan showing how the child's future learning and development will be addressed by the setting, and showing how professionals will work together to share information. Parents and carers are also advised on how to support their child's learning at home.

⏸ PAUSE POINT How does your setting carry out the progress check at 2 years?

Hint Speak to your early years manager and parents/carers about how each of them are involved.

Extend What is the procedure for reporting back to parents and carers and involving other professionals if necessary?

Assessment at the end of the EYFS

Until Summer 2015, all children were assessed at the end of the EYFS and their progress recorded in line with the EYFSP assessment and the 17 early learning goals. Early years settings had to state whether children had met, were exceeding or had not yet reached the expected level of learning and development, and this had to be shared with, and explained to, parents and carers, and the child's Year 1 teacher. From 2016, schools may continue to use these profiles if they wish, but they will no longer be a statutory requirement.

From September 2016, there will be revised assessment when children start school, known as baseline assessment. This was introduced in September 2015 as a pilot and should be available to all schools in September 2016. It will not be mandatory, but it is likely that most schools will use it to measure progress to the end of Key Stage 2.

Assessment practice 11.2   B.P3 B.P4 B.M2

- Write a report on the seven areas of learning in the EYFS and the scope of each one. How do they influence the development of educational programmes and assessment, and provide opportunities across the areas of learning?
- Assess the extent to which the learning and development and assessment requirements of the EYFS prepare children for school at the age of 5 years.

Plan
- How will I set out my report? What are the success criteria for this task?
- What do I need to ensure that I include in the report?

Do
- Am I confident in what I need to do?
- Can I ask the opinions of others and seek the support available to me?

Review
- Can I explain which aspects of this task I found easiest/hardest?
- Do I realise where I still have knowledge gaps and can I resolve them?

 **C**

Examine the safeguarding and welfare requirements of the Early Years Foundation Stage

C1 Safeguarding and welfare requirements

The safeguarding and welfare requirements form the third section of the statutory EYFS framework. These requirements focus on the safety and well-being of children. They set out in detail what settings must do to make sure children are able to learn in a safe and welcoming environment, and the range of policies they will need to have in place to do this.

Discussion

In groups, discuss what you already know about safeguarding and the protection of children.

How do you know that children in your setting are being cared for and supervised appropriately? What kinds of measures do you think a setting should have in place to ensure the safety and well-being of each child?

The safeguarding and welfare requirements

Children are more likely to learn and do well when they are in a healthy, safe and secure environment, and are cared for by adults with whom they have a positive relationship. A number of areas are covered under the safeguarding and welfare requirements in the EYFS, and practitioners are required to show how they make sure all children are cared for appropriately.

All settings need to show they meet the requirements and practical implications for:

▶ child protection, including a safeguarding policy

▶ suitable people, to include disclosures about staff

▶ staff qualifications, training, support and skills

▶ providing a key person for each child

▶ staff : child ratios

▶ health and safety

▶ managing behaviour

▶ safety and suitability of premises, including risk assessment

▶ equal opportunities

▶ special educational needs

▶ information and record keeping.

The requirement for a safeguarding policy

Child protection

The requirements for child protection are set out in the statutory guidance and list a number of measures that settings must have in place to ensure the safeguarding of children in their care.

These must include the following measures.

▶ **A designated safeguarding officer in the setting** – this person must be responsible for safeguarding in the setting, liaising with the local children's agencies and the Local Safeguarding Children Board (LSCB), and providing ongoing support and training to staff, as well as attending a specific safeguarding course themselves.

▶ **A policy for safeguarding** – this means that all staff must be aware of the setting's policy for dealing with any safeguarding issues that arise. They will need to know how to be alert for any issues that arise in a child's life and what kinds of signs might be indicators of abuse. Policies must be in line with guidance from the LSCB and include an explanation of what will happen if there are any allegations made against members of staff. They should also include the setting's policy on the use of mobile phones and cameras.

▶ **'Working together to safeguard children 2015'** – all settings must use this statutory guidance when addressing any safeguarding issues within the setting, and should notify agencies who have statutory responsibilities as soon as possible in this instance (local children's social care services or the police).

▶ **Staff training** – all staff must be trained to understand the policies and procedures of the setting with regard to children's protection, including the importance of recognising and recording any changes in children's behaviour. They must also have an up-to-date knowledge of safeguarding issues.

▶ **Ofsted notification** – all providers must inform Ofsted if there are any allegations of serious abuse at a setting, as well as informing them of any action taken. These notifications must be made as soon as possible, but at the latest within 14 days.

The importance of safeguarding children

Josh is working as a teaching assistant in a reception class. It is the autumn term. He has noticed that Akrim often comes to school in dirty clothes and is always hungry, taking fruit from the fruit tray and asking for more food at lunchtime.

Josh knows that Akrim comes from a large family. Other children in his family are regularly absent from school, although Akrim has had full attendance so far.

Check your knowledge

1   What should Josh do?
2   How would you know when to follow up these kinds of indicators in your setting?
3   What would you do in Josh's situation?

Requirements for staff recruitment

In recent years there have been several high-profile cases in which people working with children and young people have been found to be unsuitable, and in some cases have harmed or abused children. Legal steps have been taken to ensure this does not happen in the future.

Suitable people

To make sure settings meet the requirements for suitable people, they need to:

▶ ensure they have systems in place that allow them to check the suitability of all those who come into contact with children
▶ meet Ofsted requirements (or the requirements of the relevant childminder agency) for any people living on the premises or working directly with children
▶ ensure all staff disclose any criminal convictions, cautions and court orders that may affect their suitability to work with children through a criminal records check
▶ record information about staff qualifications and identity/vetting checks
▶ inform Ofsted or the childminder agency within 14 days if any employee is convicted or disqualified from registration
▶ ensure they conform to the requirements of the Safeguarding Vulnerable Groups Act 2006, by referring to the Disclosure and Barring Service (DBS) any instance of staff dismissal related to harming a child or putting a child at risk of harm.

Requirements for training, ongoing supervision and staff appraisal

All those working with young children and their families must have appropriate qualifications, training, support and knowledge to make sure they understand their roles and responsibilities. Early years settings must provide appropriate supervision that promotes mutual support between colleagues and opportunities to discuss issues as and when they arise. This should include regular staff appraisals and opportunities for further training if necessary.

In group settings, there must be a manager who:

▶ has a full and relevant Level 3 qualification
▶ has worked in an early years setting for at least 2 years (or has at least 2 years' other suitable experience)
▶ is supported by a named deputy who is able to manage the setting in their absence.

At least half of all the other staff need to have a full and relevant Level 2 qualification. In addition, at least one person with a current paediatric first-aid certificate must be on the premises at all times and accompany children on any outings away from the setting. It is a further requirement that all staff in early years settings have a good command of English so that they are able to care for children effectively, keep records and understand policies and instructions.

Ⅱ PAUSE POINT   Find out how your setting ensures that staff are suitable to work with children.

   Hint   Look at the processes that your setting goes through when employing staff.

   Extend   Read through the statutory framework for the EYFS document from Section 3.9 (Suitable people) onwards. How are these requirements kept up to date?

The requirements of the key person role and requirements for staff : child ratios

Key person role

All settings must provide a key person for each child so that the care meets the child's individual needs. The key person should work closely with parents and/or carers during the settling-in period to make sure the child develops confidence and settles in well. They should also maintain an ongoing relationship with parents and carers so that this continues throughout the EYFS. In some settings the key person for each child is displayed with a photograph so that staff and parents are able to locate them easily if needed.

Staff : child ratios

Staff : child ratios must be appropriate to the setting and the level of qualifications held by the staff. Only those aged 17 or over may be included in staff ratios. Table 11.3 shows the staff : child ratios for different settings.

▶ **Table 11.3:** Staff : child ratios for different settings

Provider	Age of child	Staff : child ratio	Qualifications and experience
	Under 2	1 : 3	• At least one member of staff must hold a full and relevant Level 3 qualification, and must be suitably experienced in working with children under 2 • At least half of all other staff must hold a full and relevant Level 2 qualification • At least half of all staff must have received training that specifically addresses the care of babies • Head of under-2s room must have suitable experience of working with under 2s
	2 years	1 : 4	• At least one member of staff must hold a full and relevant Level 3 qualification • At least half of all other staff must hold a full and relevant Level 2 qualification
Early years setting	3 years +	1 : 13	Where a person with Qualified Teacher Status, Early Years Professional Status, Early Years Teacher Status or another suitable Level 6 qualification is working directly with the children, at least one other member of staff must hold a full and relevant Level 3 qualification

▶ **Table 11.3:** Staff : child ratios for different settings – *continued*

Provider	Age of child	Staff : child ratio	Qualifications and experience
Early years setting	3 years +	1 : 8	Where a person with Qualified Teacher Status, Early Years Professional Status, Early Years Teacher Status or another suitable Level 6 qualification is not working directly with the children: <ul><li>at least one member of staff must hold a full and relevant Level 3 qualification</li><li>at least half of all other staff must hold a full and relevant Level 2 qualification.</li></ul>
Independent school	3 years +	1 : 30 if majority of children will reach 5 that school year 1 : 13 in all other classes	Where a person with Qualified Teacher Status, Early Years Professional Status, Early Years Teacher Status or another suitable Level 6 qualification, an instructor, or another suitably qualified overseas trained teacher is working directly with the children, at least one other member of staff must hold a full and relevant Level 3 qualification
Independent school	3 years +	1 : 8	Where there is no person with Qualified Teacher Status, Early Years Professional Status, Early Years Teacher Status or another suitable Level 6 qualification, no instructor, and no suitably qualified overseas trained teacher working directly with the children: <ul><li>at least one member of staff must hold a full and relevant Level 3 qualification</li><li>at least half of all other staff must have a full and relevant Level 2 qualification.</li></ul>
Maintained nursery schools and nursery classes in maintained schools (not reception)	3 years +	1 : 13	<ul><li>At least one member of staff must be a school teacher</li><li>At least one other member of staff must hold a full and relevant Level 3 qualification</li></ul>

Source: Adapted from the Statutory Framework for the Early Years Foundation Stage (2014) pp22–24 © Crown copyright 2014

In reception classes, there must be no more than 30 children per school teacher. In the case of childminders, the total number of children under the age of 8 must not be more than six.

The requirements for the health, safety and security of children

All settings need to ensure they take steps to promote good health in children, as well as ensuring their safety at all times. This includes the following.

▶ **Administering medicines** – settings need to have a policy for administering medicines and gain written permission from parents and carers for doing so. The setting should have a written record of any medicines that have been given to children and these should only be given if they have been prescribed by a healthcare professional. Training must be given to staff if the administration of medicine requires specific knowledge.

▶ **Provision of food or drink** – settings need to ensure that any meals or snacks are healthy. Drinking water should be available to children at all times. Staff need to be made aware of any dietary needs that children have.

▶ **Accident and injury** – settings are responsible for ensuring a first-aid box is accessible at all times. The box should contain contents suitable for use with children, with a written record of accidents, injuries and any first aid given. Settings are also responsible for informing Ofsted and local child protection agencies of any serious accident, illness or injury to a child while in the care of the setting, as well as the action taken, within 14 days of the incident.

▶ **Risk assessment** – settings need to ensure that they manage risks by checking the environment regularly and training staff appropriately.

▶ **Outings** – settings must ensure that children are kept safe when on outings and undertake a risk assessment prior to the visit so they can assess any hazards. Vehicles need to be insured and adult : child ratios checked.

▶ Adult administering first aid to young child in setting

The requirements for managing behaviour

Children need to be supported by clear and appropriate behaviour management in the setting.

The statutory guidance states that no member of staff or anyone who is in regular contact with a child in a setting where care is provided should give or threaten corporal punishment. Physical intervention should only be used if there is a possibility of danger to the child or another person. In this instance, a record must be kept and parents should be informed.

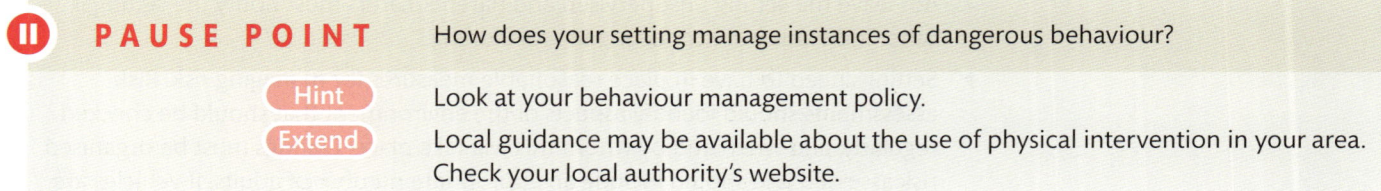

❙❙ PAUSE POINT   How does your setting manage instances of dangerous behaviour?

Hint   Look at your behaviour management policy.

Extend   Local guidance may be available about the use of physical intervention in your area. Check your local authority's website.

The requirements for the safety and suitability of premises, environment and equipment

All early years settings must comply with requirements for keeping their premises safe for all who use them. Health and safety requirements are such that settings should have in place policies and procedures that ensure the environment is kept safe and free from hazards.

Settings must make sure the premises – both indoor and outdoor – as well as all equipment and furniture are safe for use by children and suitable for the ages of children and the types of activities provided for them. Specific space requirements are given in the statutory guidance. These requirements are shown in Table 11.4.

Link

Unit 5 looks at this topic in more detail.

▶ **Table 11.4:** Specific space requirements

Age of child	Space requirement
Under 2 years	3.5 m² per child
2 years	2.5 m² per child
3–5 years	2.3 m² per child

Source: Adapted from the Statutory Framework for the Early Years Foundation Stage (2014) pp27–28
© Crown copyright 2014

The learning environment must be safe and secure and kept clean. Settings should have a health and safety policy that outlines procedures that will be followed when identifying, reporting and dealing with accidents, hazards and any faulty equipment. Settings must show that they have procedures in place for managing safety and have appropriate equipment such as smoke detectors, fire extinguishers and fire alarms, all of which must be regularly tested.

Ⅱ PAUSE POINT   Suggest three potential health and safety issues relating to the EYFS.

(**Hint**)   Re-read this section; also look at the headings in the statutory guidance.

(**Extend**)   How does your setting's health and safety policy map to the statutory guidance?

Other specific requirements

▸ In settings where there are children under the age of 2, there needs to be a separate baby room (except in childminding settings), although children attending a baby room should be moved into a room with an older age group when it is appropriate to do so.

▸ There should be adequate toilets and hand basins available for the number of children (usually one toilet and one hand basin for every ten children over the age of 2 years). Except in childminding settings, separate toilet facilities should usually be provided for adults.

▸ Settings need to provide an area for any confidential meetings or discussions.

▸ Settings must ensure that anyone entering the premises is identified. Children may not leave the setting unsupervised and parents/carers must notify the setting if other individuals are collecting their children.

▸ Settings need to have in place reasonable measures for managing risk. Risk assessments should identify aspects of the environment that should be checked regularly, and when and by whom this will take place. Outings must be organised, risk assessed and should include an appropriate number of adults. If vehicles are used to transport the children, the vehicles and the drivers must be insured.

▸ Settings must not allow smoking in or on the premises when children are present or about to be present.

▸ Settings must have public liability insurance.

The requirements for equal opportunities

All forms of prejudice and discrimination have a negative effect on children's lives. Childcare workers have a duty to protect children from discrimination and to promote respect for others. It is important that settings have a policy, procedure and practices in place to promote equality and diversity. These should help everyone to engage in inclusive practice within the setting and provide a framework for discriminatory practices to be challenged should these practices be observed.

All settings must show they support children with special educational needs and disabilities. Settings that are funded by the local authority for the provision of early education need to comply with the Special Educational Needs and Disability (SEND) Code of Practice, which came into effect in September 2014. The code of practice is statutory guidance from the Department for Education that provides practical advice on how to carry out duties to identify, assess and make provision for children and young people with special educational needs. In addition, preschools are expected to identify a member of staff who will act as Special Educational Needs coordinator (SENCO).

Staff should be aware that they need to follow their legal responsibilities under the Equality Act 2010, which states all children should have equal access to facilities and activities. They should also always challenge inappropriate attitudes and practices among other children and adults, whether they are other staff or parents and/or carers.

Assessment practice 11.3   C.P5   C.M3

You are a mentor for two new members of staff in your setting.

As part of their induction, you have been asked to explain the safeguarding and welfare requirements of the EYFS and assess the importance of meeting these for children's learning and development.

Plan
- What is the clearest way of explaining the safeguarding and welfare requirements?
- How much time do I need to complete the task?

Do
- Can I identify the important information in the statutory document and use all the support available to me from other staff members?

Review
- What did the other staff members find most useful about this experience?
- What would I do differently next time in order to enhance the experiences of new staff members?

The requirements in relation to information and records

As in any organisation, records need to be kept by settings and information shared with others in order for them to run smoothly. Settings need to show how they keep the required records and how and when information is collected, stored and shared. It is important that all staff are aware of the confidentiality of the information and the requirements of the Data Protection Act 1998, which states that information must only be used for the purpose for which it was gathered.

Confidentiality of information

Settings need to keep basic information about the child, which they will need to gather from parents or carers before the child starts at the setting. This should include the child's full name, address and date of birth as well as the name, address and contact details of all parents or carers who have parental responsibility. This information should be updated regularly in case of emergency.

Discussion

Talk in your group about how your setting gathers basic information about children. How do you ensure that it is updated when necessary and remind parents and carers to do this?

Provision of information for parents and carers

Your setting needs to make certain information available to parents and carers. This should include:

▶ staffing and the name of their child's key person

▶ information about the EYFS and how it is delivered in the setting, including where they can access more information

▶ the types of activities and experiences that are provided and how they can support their child's learning

▶ how children with special educational needs and disabilities are supported

▶ policies and procedures of the setting

▶ information about food and drink.

All of this information needs to be easily accessible to parents and carers through different means, for example, via a website, emails, letters, noticeboards and/or regular newsletters.

❚❚ PAUSE POINT   In what ways does your setting make information available to parents and carers?

Hint   Speak to others in your setting.

Extend   Talk to parents about how they access information. Which method is best for them?

Information about the provider

As well as having a certificate of registration, the setting must keep records of the names, addresses and phone numbers of all staff working with children, as well as anyone else who will be in contact with them. They also need to keep a register detailing when children have attended and the name of each child's key person.

Information about complaints

There must be a written procedure for dealing with any complaints, as well as records kept of the outcome. All settings must investigate written complaints within 28 days and the record of complaints must be made available to Ofsted.

As well as any direct complaints, information must be made available to parents and carers about how to contact Ofsted if they believe the setting is not meeting its obligations under the EYFS. They also need to be given a copy of the report following an Ofsted inspection.

Circumstances when Ofsted must be notified

All settings need to inform Ofsted about:

▶ a change of address of the premises or any changes in the premises itself that may affect the space available

▶ a change of the name or address of the provider, or changes in management

▶ any event that may affect the suitability of the provider or any person caring for children on the premises

▶ any proposal to change the hours of childcare

▶ any changes to the organisation that runs the provision, whether this is a company, charity or partnership.

Assessment practice 11.4

As part of a local early years cluster group, you have been asked to evaluate the impact of the EYFS. The findings will be fed back to early years national groups. This includes the requirements for learning and development, assessment, and safeguarding and welfare on practice in local early years settings.

You will be presenting your findings alongside others at a local cluster group meeting.

Set out how you will prepare for your presentation.

BC.D2

Plan

- Do I need clarification about anything regarding my presentation?
- Do I have sufficient knowledge or should I speak to others? If so, who, and how will I do this?

Do

- Can I make connections between what I am reading/researching and the task, and identify the important information?
- Am I recording my own observations and thoughts?

Review

- Can I explain how I would approach the harder elements of the task differently next time?
- Can I identify how this learning experience relates to future experiences (e.g. in the workplace)?

D Apply skills to support children's progress towards early learning goals and to meet safeguarding and welfare requirements of the Early Years Foundation Stage

D1 Support children's learning and development towards early learning goals

How to plan play and activities to support children's progress

As an early years worker you need to know how to plan play and activities to support children's progress towards the EYFS outcomes, creating a balance of activities that are adult-led with those that are child-initiated.

Your plans should show how you provide activities for each of the seven areas of learning and development within the EYFS, and include opportunities for both child-initiated and adult-directed play. These activities need to reflect the needs of individual children as well as showing that they are being given opportunities to develop in each area. You need to have long-, medium- and short-term plans to demonstrate that what you are doing fits together with what the children have done previously and will do in the future. However, you must also remember that plans should be flexible. You constantly need to evaluate and think about what is working or not working with children, and what will meet the needs and interests of individual children.

Although settings all plan in different ways, they need to include in their plans the same key information and be clear about how children are making progress towards the early learning goals of the EYFS.

Planning should show:

- how children's individual needs and interests are being met and that plans are built on regular observations by staff and parents/carers
- how the seven areas of learning are being included, as well as indoor and outdoor provision

Link

To remind yourself of the seven areas of learning and development, see Figure 11.1 in Section A1.

- that there is a balance of adult-led and child-initiated activities
- what children will be learning and how it will build on what they already know
- how children are progressing towards the early learning goals
- how observations and assessment tie in with the process
- how to plan for children's progress through working with others.

How to plan for purposeful and playful activities

One of the key things you need to consider when planning is that the EYFS is based around play. Children should have opportunities to play together, with little adult direction or involvement (child-initiated play), as well as access to the kinds of activities where adults give more direction or join in. It is useful to look at the different ways in which settings plan, as this can be a good way of sharing ideas to get inspiration and cutting down on paperwork.

Play should be purposeful. In other words, it should make sense to children. When planning an activity or a problem-solving task for children, remember it will be more meaningful if the context is clear to them. For example, children could carry out a sorting activity such as matching a large pile of socks and putting them together when they have become muddled up, or they could make a home for an animal during an animal topic, using junk modelling.

As mentioned above, your planning must include the seven areas of learning in the EYFS and you need to show that children have opportunities for both indoor and outdoor play activities. If outdoor play needs to be timetabled for practical reasons, this should be shown in your plans.

Discussion

In small groups, talk about the different ways in which you plan in your settings.

If possible, bring examples so that you can share ideas and feed back to the larger group.

How to identify children's needs and interests

Your setting needs to show how it plans for children's individual needs. This may be the way in which it implements a programme for a child who has special educational needs, or through work that is carried out with parents and carers to support a child or group of children who have English as an additional language.

Discussions with key persons

Children's needs change over time – for example, a child might be particularly sensitive if a family pet has just died, or if there are some issues at home due to the birth of a new sibling. All staff should be aware of these kinds of issues and in some settings a book is kept in which key workers are able to note down any issues or changes, which staff check daily.

Observations

In order to meet children's interests in your planning, you need to use different methods. This is done over time but may include formal or informal observations carried out by staff and key people, as well as conversations with the child and discussions with other staff. Planning may be based on items of special interest that the child has brought in to the setting, or things that they often like to talk about. You could note down what children have said and then act on it, or develop a particular area that has caught their imagination. In some cases, whole topics can be built on children's ideas and interests.

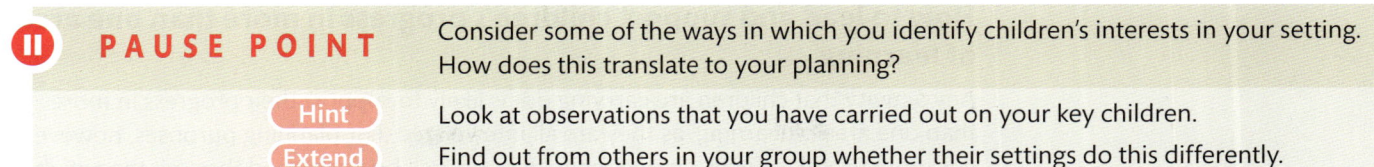

PAUSE POINT   Consider some of the ways in which you identify children's interests in your setting. How does this translate to your planning?

Hint   Look at observations that you have carried out on your key children.

Extend   Find out from others in your group whether their settings do this differently.

How to balance adult-led and child-initiated activities

Plans should be clear about which activities are adult-led and what kinds of activities are available for children to self-select or initiate themselves. You can do this through highlighting or amending them, as they are a working document.

Your plans need to show how you balance adult-led and child-initiated activities, while allowing equal opportunities for each child to participate fully and be included. In some settings, daily plans only show adult-directed activities – there may be a few of these each day depending on staffing – whereas those that are child-initiated will be detailed on a separate, overarching plan for the whole week. Children should be free to self-select what they are going to do within the structure of the day – for example, if they are in the role play area, they should be able to take resources from other areas of the room to support their play. However, it is important that all of the children in the setting have access to all of the resources; for example, if one group of children always heads for the bikes and outdoor toys, make sure that this is not preventing other children from using them. In some settings, there may be a 'wheel of activities' to prevent this from happening, so that children move to a new activity after a set amount of time. However, some practitioners do not like using this system as it interrupts the free flow of activities.

PAUSE POINT   How does your setting plan for each area of learning and maintain a balance of adult-led and child-initiated activities?

Hint   Check through your planning and highlight adult-led and child-initiated activities in different colours.

Extend   Compare your planning ideas with others.

How to support and extend children's learning and thinking

When planning and setting up activities for children, it is important to consider how, as an early years professional, you can support their learning and thinking as well as their development.

Sustained shared thinking

One way of supporting children's learning and thinking is to engage in sustained shared thinking. This is when practitioners support and challenge children's critical thinking skills by getting involved in their thinking process and working with them to develop and clarify their ideas and build upon their interests. Sustained shared thinking can be done on a one-to-one basis between a child and adult, or between groups of children.

A major part of supporting and extending children's learning and thinking comes in the form of talking to them about what they are doing as they are doing it. This is because children need to be able to make sense of what they are doing and relate it to their world. You will find that some children do this more easily and are more able to discuss and extend their ideas, whereas others may need you to question them further to stimulate more ideas.

How to lead and support children's progress in more than one area of learning

Any activity that children are carrying out is likely to support their progress in more than one area of learning, as they are all interrelated. For planning purposes, however, it is more useful to focus on one main area that will be developed through the activity.

For example, singing counting songs with children will mainly support their mathematical development, but the activity will also develop their musical skills as well as their phonemic awareness through rhyme. (If they are action rhymes they may also support children's physical development.)

Reflect

What activities have you recently carried out in your setting? How might they support more than one area of learning?

▶ What is the main area of learning that this activity is supporting?

How to carry out observational assessment and record children's progress

As already discussed, you and your colleagues need to carry out regular observations of children in all contexts so you are aware of their progress towards early learning goals. Observations may take the form of sticky notes, annotated photographs, notes on a tablet or more detailed observations, as well as information on home or school achievements.

The format is less important than what is being recorded; for example, a couple of lines on a sticky note observing that a child has been able to fasten their own coat for the first time is sufficient. You should regularly check your records to ensure you are recording observations consistently for all children and all areas of learning, as you may find some areas of learning come up more regularly than others.

II PAUSE POINT   Explain to someone from another setting how you carry out and record observations and assessments.

> Hint   How are observations consistent between members of staff?

> Extend   Evaluate what is the most effective method of storing observations and assessments. Say why.

How to promote diversity, equality and inclusion

Settings need to show they promote diversity, equality and inclusion in all areas of learning when they are planning, leading and assessing play and education programmes. Your setting may be in a catchment area that is diverse, or you may be working in a setting in which children are mainly from one ethnic group. In either case, your curriculum should reflect a wide range of cultures, beliefs and ethnicities, to make sure children are exposed to a true reflection of society.

So that all children are included equally in the setting, you need to make sure activities are available to all children. This can sometimes be challenging; for example, if a group of children always go to the same types of activities. You need to be aware that this can happen and encourage all children to participate equally.

Assessment practice 11.5   D.P6   D.M4

Plan, lead and record a series of purposeful play and educational activities with colleagues, using observations and assessments of children's progress towards early learning goals.

Include a balance of:

- adult-led activities
- child-initiated activities.

Give examples of ways in which you have demonstrated confidence and independence to plan, lead and record these activities across all areas of learning.

Plan

- How will I approach this task? What experience do I have and how can I use this to help me when planning?
- What resources do I need to plan educational activities and how will I get access to them?

Do

- Have I spent some time planning out my approach to this task?
- How will I ensure that there is an equal balance of adult-led and child-initiated activities?

Review

- Can I explain what skills I employed and which new ones I have developed?
- Do I realise where I still have learning gaps and can I resolve them?

D2 Support the safeguarding and welfare requirements of the EYFS

How to act on own responsibilities in relation to safeguarding and promoting health and safety

It is important to remember that the areas of safeguarding and health and safety are not the same – these are sometimes confused in early years settings. Safeguarding relates to the welfare and protection of children from abuse and neglect. Health and safety issues relate to the general safety of all those in the setting.

You will have a safeguarding policy in your setting and will need to be aware of health and safety procedures –these should outline your responsibilities and how you should act on them. It is important that all staff are responsible in each of these areas and recognise that this is the case. If you see any hazards, or are at all concerned about a child in your care, it is vital that you take action and report it to the appropriate person.

How to act on own responsibilities in relation to safety and security

Your responsibilities in relation to safety and security in an early years setting are around ensuring children are kept safe and secure while they are in your care. This means following the correct procedures for health and safety at all times and making sure you act on them. All visitors need to enter the premises through the main entrance and sign in/be given identification badges. Any issues with security should be reported straight away.

Case study

Taking responsibility

Ella has recently started work in a nursery. She regularly works in a portable building that is separate from the main building and during the winter months she is there in the dark. She feels vulnerable as the caretaker often does not lock the side gate straight after children have gone home, but waits for half an hour until after he has had his tea break and all the parents/carers should have left.

Ella does not want to make a fuss as she is fairly new in her position. However, she knows that the situation has safeguarding and health and safety implications. One day she notices an unfamiliar adult hanging around outside the building and begins to feel uneasy.

Check your knowledge

1 What would you do in Ella's situation?

2 Do you think Ella should have said something earlier?

How to assess risk

Early years workers should take 'reasonable steps' to ensure that others in the setting are not exposed to unnecessary risks. The guidance applies within and outside the setting, in the outside area and when on educational visits, including transport, staff : child ratios and any hazards that may arise.

You should be able to make written risk assessments where needed, and to demonstrate how you manage risks on a day-to-day basis. Your setting should give you some training and guidance about how to identify risk in different areas, as well as providing any pro-forma paperwork where necessary.

Outline what you would do in the situations below. What are your responsibilities?

1 You find a broken item of furniture that has a sharp edge.

2 You are aware that there has not been any kind of fire practice for over a year in your setting.

3 You find a number of children's coats have not been put on pegs and are lying on the floor in a narrow part of the corridor.

How to identify and provide for children's physical welfare needs

As well as keeping children safe and secure, you have a responsibility to make sure they are well looked after and that all their needs are met. This includes making sure they have enough sleep and rest, and that they have appropriate amounts of food and drink. Very young children will not always be able to identify when they have needs in these areas and you should make sure you know the signs to look for, ensuring they have access to toilets, rest, or food and drink when necessary. As you get to know children, you will also be able to look out for signs that they are unwell and may need to support them if they are unaware of this themselves.

The importance of recognising and recording changes in children's behaviour

As you get to know children in your care, it is likely that you will be aware of any changes in their overall behaviour. This may take different forms, such as withdrawal, an unwillingness to join in with others, tiredness, or erratic, attention-seeking behaviour.

If you notice this, it is important that you record it and report it to another member of staff. This is because changes in children's behaviour are usually an indication that something is wrong. Behavioural changes should be discussed with the SENCO or the setting's safeguarding officer.

❚❚ PAUSE POINT   What would you do if you noticed a difference in a child's behaviour?

> **Hint**   Consider whether you would need to record this change and how you would report it.

> **Extend**   Who is responsible for safeguarding in your setting? What can they tell you about recognising changes in behaviour and when you should be concerned?

How to value diversity and promote equality of opportunity and anti-discriminatory practice

You need to show that you value diversity and promote equality of opportunity and anti-discriminatory practice in your setting, in ways other than through the curriculum. Make sure you are aware of the importance of valuing and respecting others in all of your actions within the setting and that you model this to children.

Discrimination should always be challenged. If you ignore it, it could be assumed that you condone discriminatory language or behaviour. To be able to challenge discrimination it is essential that you have a good understanding of legislation and the policy, procedures and practice in your own setting. You should feel confident that you know what good practice is. You should also be prepared to challenge your own prejudices as these can lead to discriminatory practice. Prejudice can be overcome by undertaking training and becoming more aware of the diverse groups of people that exist in society.

How to record and manage accurate and coherent information about children, and how to pass information to those who need to know

You should show you have an awareness of the importance of maintaining confidentiality when managing information about children, and that your records are accessible only to those who need to see them. Be aware that staff may work different shifts or times of day, and ensure you pass information to others if they are not present at meetings.

Make sure any information you record about children is accurate and coherent – in other words that it is based on facts and what you have seen or observed yourself. You should not include anything that is speculation or that has been heard from others.

You may need to suggest additional ways of passing on information so that all staff are included, for example, through confidential emails or by ensuring that you meet with them at an alternative time. If information is stored in filing cabinets or on computers, ensure that these are locked or password protected.

Ⅱ PAUSE POINT How does your setting ensure the promotion of equality and diversity, and of anti-discriminatory practice?

Hint Think about the inclusion of all groups, including those from different cultures and those with disabilities.

Extend What government legislation does this relate to?

Assessment practice 11.6 | D.P7 | D.M5 | D.D3 |

Examine the safeguarding and welfare requirements of the EYFS.

- How do you and your colleagues show that you adhere to your responsibilities consistently under these requirements?
- Outline ways in which your self-management and professional conduct consistently support your adherence to the safeguarding and welfare requirements.

Plan
- How will I set out the safeguarding and welfare requirements?
- How confident do I feel in my own abilities to complete the task?

Do
- How can I demonstrate that I am consistent in my practice?
- How can I work with others and use the support available to me?

Review
- Can I explain what skills I have and the new ones I have developed?
- Do I realise where I still have learning/knowledge gaps and can I resolve them?

Further reading and resources

Department for Education publications

Department for Education (2003) *Every Child Matters*, London: The Stationery Office.

Department for Education (2007) *Letters and Sounds* (DFES-00281-2007), London: DfE – this is a government document, produced through the Primary National Strategy, which starts in the Foundation Stage and builds up through different stages. Although it is no longer used, it features valuable suggestions for progression, including focused activities. Many still refer to it for ideas.

Books

Department for Education (2014) *Statutory Framework for the Early Years Foundation Stage*, London: DfE.

Langston, A. and Doherty, J. (2012) *The Revised EYFS in Practice. Thinking, Reflecting and Doing!* London: Featherstone Education.

Moylett, H. and Stewart, N. (2013) *Emerging, Expected and Exceeding: Understanding the Revised Early Years Foundation Stage Profile*, London: The British Association for Early Childhood Education.

Shurville Publishing (2014) *EYFS Statutory Framework, Outcomes & Development Matters*, London: Shurville Publishing and Early Education.

Tassoni, P. (2012) *Penny Tassoni's Practical EYFS Handbook,* 2nd edition, Harlow: Pearson.

Websites

www.foundationyears.org.uk/eyfs-statutory-framework – EYFS documentation: information and guidance on using the EYFS.

http://eyfs.info – EYFS forum: a useful site for resources, information and support for early years practitioners.

www.nurseryworld.magazine.co.uk – Nursery World magazine: useful articles, information and jobs – there is a subscription fee.

www.ofsted.gov.uk – Ofsted: information about EYFS Ofsted requirements.

THINK ▶FUTURE

Fi McCarthy
nursery worker
on being a key
worker

Fi has been working at Tadpoles Nursery for 2 years and she is a key worker to twenty children, who come to nursery at different times. The children are all different ages and some of them are siblings – this helps Fi as she only needs to get to know one set of parents or carers in order to develop her relationship with the family.

Fi finds that the key worker system at her nursery really works. The system starts as soon as children come into the setting. The nursery holds 'Getting to know you' events so that parents and carers can come in with their children the term before they start. This means that they are introduced to their key worker and the setting before the first day, which helps to make the transition less difficult for the children.

Staff are asked to work closely with their key families so that they are aware of any changes in circumstances that may affect the child. They are also asked to look carefully for any significant changes in behaviour or at any concerns that parents have, and report these to the nursery manager.

In order to help parents understand what is happening in the nursery, there are information evenings about the EYFS. Staff members take it in turns to speak about the seven areas of learning and discuss the way in which the nursery assesses children's development. Fi has a particular interest in communication and language so she talks about the importance of adults spending time doing things with children and talking with them about what they are doing. Staff members also talk about the importance of parents and professionals sharing knowledge about children's interests and what they have been doing outside the setting. It is also a good opportunity to ask for parental support with assessing children's development by informing the nursery about children's achievements at home. Although this may be verbal, the nursery also has a noticeboard with a 'Proud Cloud' in the entrance hall, and all parents are invited to contribute to it; this then feeds into assessments.

Focusing your skills

- Remember that the EYFS is about the whole child.
- Consider the role of the key worker and how you work with parents/carers in your own setting, such as the different ways in which the setting ensures regular contact.
- Think about the skills you need to have in order to work in this way, and how you ensure that you meet the statutory requirements, both in learning and development and safeguarding and welfare.

- Take opportunities to discuss the children's day with parents or carers and show how you promote the importance of working in partnership with parents.
- Demonstrate how you use the policies and procedures in your setting to ensure that you fulfil the requirements of the EYFS.

Glossary

Adolescence – a period of time over which children's bodies develop into sexually mature adult bodies.

Adult-directed play – where an adult takes a role in planning, organising or leading play.

Adult-initiated play – play in which an adult provides resources or sets up an activity with a specific learning intention in mind.

Advocate – a person who represents the views of the child.

Alliteration – words that start with the same sound, e.g. Maisy's mother.

Apprenticeship learning – when a child learns by watching an adult complete an activity.

Asthma – a long-term lung condition that inflames and narrows the airways causing difficulty in breathing.

Attachment – a special relationship or bond between a child and someone who is emotionally involved with them.

Attitudes – views or opinions about an issue or topic; these views may be positive or negative.

Attribute – a particular quality that is characteristic of an individual.

Atypical development – where the pattern and rate of a child's development falls outside the expected range for the child's age group.

Audiology test – a hearing test carried out with a machine called an audiometer.

Auditory discrimination – the ability to hear and pick out particular sounds amid others.

Axon – the part of the neuron through which electricity travels.

Axon terminal – a part of the neuron involved in making a connection with another neuron.

Behaviourist – behaviourist theories state that development is shaped by the environment.

Behaviourist theory – a theory of learning that states development and behaviour can be conditioned and shaped by the environment.

Bias – a tendency to allow factors, such as prejudice or discrimination for or against individuals or groups of people, to influence research and how this is carried out. This could also affect the validity of the results obtained.

Bibliography – a list of all the sources you have used or referred to in your work.

Block play – play using wooden bricks of different shapes and sizes.

Causal relationships – relationships where something happens (the cause) and produces a reaction (the effect). Causal relationships may occur between events, properties, behaviours or other variables.

Child-directed speech (CDS) – speech patterns used by parents speaking to their children, usually involving slow and simplified vocabulary, a high-pitched voice and the use of repetition and questions.

Child-initiated play – where children choose the resources, the location and how to play.

Chronic illness – a long-term medical condition.

Cohesive society – a society or group whose members identify with the same values and beliefs and who work together to ensure the well-being of all members.

Conditioning – learning to act in a certain way because past experiences have taught us to do, or not do, certain things.

Conductive hearing loss – a hearing loss often caused by glue ear.

Constructivist approach – a model to explain children's cognitive development, which considers that children develop their own ideas based on experiences and interactions.

Conventions – a set of agreed characteristics used in a particular situation, e.g. in writing we use full stops, capital letters, commas and sentences.

Cooperative – working together with other people or groups to achieve something.

Cooperative friendships – when children negotiate, play or agree what to do with each other.

Cooperative play – when children play well with each other.

Cooperative working – working with a family, but taking responsibility for different tasks.

Correlation – a relationship or connection between two things.

Cursive script – form of writing in which the letters are joined together in a flowing manner.

Data – the information produced by your research methods, for example, facts, statistics, measurements, or perceptions. Data has to be interpreted.

Debriefing – a conversation between a researcher and participant following an experiment to inform the participant about their experience and allow them to talk about it.

Defecate – excrete faeces (solid waste) from the body.

Delayed global development – where a child's rate of progress across all areas of development is lower than the expected range for their age group.

Dendrite – a part of the neuron involved in making a connection with another neuron.

Detergent – a cleaning product that is water soluble. Unlike soap, it doesn't form a scum.

Development – the acquisition of skills, knowledge or physical or mental abilities, in a set order (or sequence).

Developmental milestones – typical skills that most children have acquired at given ages.

Disclosure – when someone tells you, or makes it known in another way, that something (for instance, abuse) has happened.

Discrimination – not giving equality of opportunity to groups or individuals because they belong to a particular group.

Disposition – a person's temperament or nature.

Emollients – special moisturisers designed to prevent skin from drying.

Emotionally available – able to respond, support and deal with the emotions of others.

Emotionally labile – having emotions that change rapidly and may be stronger than usual.

Empathetic – showing empathy (the ability to feel or understand the emotions of others).

Empathy – the ability to feel or understand the emotions of others.

Encoding – the process by which ideas or experiences are converted to memories by the brain.

Ethics – the values and principles that govern the way a society operates.

Ethologist – a person who studies patterns of animal behaviour.

Ethos – the philosophy or approach used by a setting, which will affect the setting's practice.

European Union Directive – a legislative act that countries in the European Union are required to implement in their home country.

Expressive language – the ability of a child to communicate actively using sounds and, over time, words.

Fine motor skills – control of the smaller muscles, such as those in the fingers, to carry out activities such as threading beads onto a necklace, using a knife and fork, or holding a pencil.

Formative assessment – assessment that takes place during the learning process on an ongoing basis, or 'assessment for learning'.

Foster care – temporary care in foster families for looked-after children who are not with their parents.

Gestation – the period of time between conception and birth.

Gifted – with the potential to develop cognitive abilities significantly ahead of other children in the same age group.

Gloop – a mixture of cornflour and water used as a resource for sensory play.

Glue ear – a condition in which fluid builds up in the auditory (Eustachian) tube in the ear, preventing sounds from being heard properly.

Graphemes – individual written symbols.

Gross motor skills – control of the larger muscles, such as those in the arms and legs, to carry out activities such as running, throwing or kicking a ball.

Growth – an increase in physical size, beginning with muscular control and development of coordination and balance.

Guided participation – when a child learns by working with an adult to complete a task or solve a problem.

Hand–eye coordination – the ability to use the eyes to direct the muscles towards completing a task.

Hazard – something in the environment that could cause harm.

Health and Safety Executive – an independent national body that regulates health, safety and illness in the workplace.

Heuristic play – provision of natural and man-made everyday objects that give babies and children opportunities for exploration and open-ended play.

Hypoglycaemia – a lack of sugar (glucose) in the bloodstream, which may cause shakiness, sweating, hunger, difficulty seeing, lack of concentration, headaches, changes in temperament, pallor and drowsiness.

Hypothesis – an unproven idea or assumption that can be tested by research.

Hypothesise – to speculate or propose an idea or theory.

Immunisation – the process by which someone is protected against an infectious disease.

In need – refers to children who are unlikely to maintain, or be given the opportunity to maintain, a reasonable standard of health or development, or children whose health could be impaired without the support of local authority services. It includes children who are disabled.

Indiscriminate attachments – when babies and children respond equally to anyone who interacts with them, and do not seem to have formed a special relationship with anyone in particular.

Infant mortality – the rate of death in the first year of life.

Infection control – the process of minimising the spread of infection.

Informal care – childcare provided by friends or family members who are not registered childcare practitioners.

Ingestion – swallowing.

Inhalation – breathing in.

Innate – inborn. An innate characteristic is one a child is born with.

Innate theory – a theory of learning that states children are able to complete certain behaviours or actions instinctively.

Interpersonal skills – the skills required for building relationships.

Intrinsically motivated – if an activity is intrinsically motivated, the interest or the drive towards action comes from within the child.

Key person – an early years professional designated to take responsibility for a child's emotional well-being by having a strong attachment with them and a good relationship with their parents/carers.

Learning journey/learning story – a way of assessing and planning for children's development using a narrative approach that can easily be constructed and shared with parents and children.

Linguistic phase – the second stage of language acquisition when children begin to use words that have meaning.

Literature review – an assessment of existing research around a particular issue or area of study.

Longitudinal observations – observations of individual children that take place over a number of months or years.

Looked-after children – children whose care is the responsibility of the local authority.

Makaton – a language programme used to help children with specific difficulties understand the spoken word.

Malleable – soft and able to be moulded and shaped.

Malnourished – having a lack of proper nutrients.

Mean length of utterance (MLU) – the average length of children's sentences.

Mentee – the person who is being mentored.

Mentor – someone who guides and supports a less experienced person and gives feedback on their work.

Microorganisms – living organisms, including viruses and bacteria, that are too small to be seen with the naked eye.

Modelling – demonstrating an action, gesture or behaviour so that a child can observe and later imitate.

Modes of cognitive representation – ways in which a child learns to makes sense of the world, or develops problem-solving skills.

Morbidity – the rate of incidence of ill health within a population.

Mouthing – exploring items by putting them in the mouth.

Multi-agency – involving staff from different agencies working together.

Multidisciplinary teams – teams involving professionals from a range of services who work in close association with each other, and plan services and interventions together.

Multiple attachments – when babies and children have many specific attachments to other people.

Myelin – the substance that coats the axon of a neuron.

Myelination – the process by which the myelin coating of an axon is formed.

Named person – a person who is the main point of contact.

Nativist – nativist theories state that children's skills and personalities are predetermined and not affected by the environment.

Need-to-know policy – a way of making sure that personal information is only provided to those people who genuinely 'need to know'.

Neural growth – when neuron cells increase in size and complexity.

Neural pathway – an established route for signals within the brain.

Neurological development – the growth and development of the brain, including the formation of new neurological connections.

Neuron – a brain cell.

Neuroscience – the study of how the brain grows and works.

Non-contemporaneous – in the context of observing children, this refers to events that are recorded or reported after they have occurred.

Norovirus – a common stomach bug that causes severe diarrhoea and vomiting.

Notifiable disease – a disease that has to be reported to the authorities.

Object permanence – recognition that when objects are out of sight, they have not disappeared.

Onlooker play – when young children watch other children play and copy their actions from a distance.

Operant conditioning – a theory that suggests that the environment 'operates' on and thus influences a child's learning. Skinner's theory of operant conditioning suggests that learning occurs through behaviour being rewarded or punished.

Palmar grip – holding an object with the palm of the hand.

Parallel play – when young children play next to each other using similar actions and materials. They are aware of each other but are not playing with each other.

Parentese (originally motherese) – the language patterns of parents speaking to their children, which are often simplified and repetitive. The term was originally used to refer to mothers.

Participant bias – where an observer is subconsciously recording information in a subjective way.

Partnership working – combining expertise to work jointly with a family.

Phonemes – the smallest units of sound in a language that help to distinguish one word from another. In the English language, for example, 'p' and 'b' are separate phonemes because they distinguish words such as 'pit' and 'bit'.

Phonemic awareness – the ability to hear individual sounds (phonemes) in words.

Phonic awareness – being aware of different sounds within words.

Phonics – a method used to teach reading that breaks down different letter patterns into their individual sounds.

Physiological effects – effects that change or influence normal bodily functions.

Policy – states the aims of the setting in relation to an aspect of early years provision.

Pre-linguistic phase – the early stage of language learning when babies start to understand words and babble, but are not producing intelligible words.

Predisposition – an increased likelihood of showing a particular skill or trait, or of developing a condition, as a result of genetic inheritance.

Preventer inhaler – an inhaler that is used to control the symptoms of asthma with the aim of preventing or reducing attacks.

Primary research – research compiled directly from original sources, for example, by observing children directly. It usually provides new information.

Procedures – detail the steps and actions that must be taken in given situations.

Professional indemnity – insurance which protects professionals from being sued for mistakes.

Psychological effects – effects that change the pattern of behaviour or thinking.

Purposeful play – play which allows children to investigate and experience things, and 'have a go'.

Qualitative – relating to opinions or feelings rather than facts, for instance, how someone feels about something.

Qualitative research – research that is based on thoughts, feelings and opinions. This type of research produces descriptive information that is more difficult to analyse than quantitative data. Common research methods include interviews and observations.

Quantitative research – research that is based on facts and figures and uses statistics to analyse results.

Raw data – data as it is collected, before it has been organised, analysed or interpreted in any way.

Receptive language – the ability to listen to, and understand, what is being communicated.

Reciprocal friendships – when children take equal or similar pleasure in being in each other's company.

Reflective practice – thinking about the way you work in order to make changes, build on strengths and stay up to date with developments.

Reflexes – automatic movements that occur without conscious thought.

Regress – to move backwards to a previous stage.

Regression – moving backwards developmentally to a previous stage.

Reinforcers – positive or negative experiences that strengthen children's behavioural responses.

Reliever inhaler – an inhaler that is used during an asthma attack. It works by enlarging the airways, so helping to facilitate breathing.

Resilient – able to recover quickly from different or difficult situations.

Respiratory disease – a condition that affects the lungs or a person's ability to breathe.

Respite care – short-term care with the assistance of professional carers.

Retrieval – the process by which memories are 'activated' or recalled, i.e. remembering.

Rickets – a bone disease caused by lack of vitamin D.

Risk – the probability that someone could be harmed by a hazard.

Risk assessment – the process of identifying and minimising dangers and hazards.

Scaffolding – a term used to describe a style of working with children in which an adult helps a child to acquire information.

Schema – a repeated action, way of doing something or way of thinking/reasoning that can be specific or generalised.

Secondary research – research based on an analysis of published research reports and data, rather than on data that has been collected first-hand.

Selective mutism – where a child does not talk although they have the ability to do so.

Self-efficacy – the understanding that you are able to do things for yourself.

Self-evaluation form – a form that settings fill out on a regular basis showing how they intend to review and improve their provision.

Separation anxiety – a set of behaviours and actions that occur when a child is distressed as a result of being separated from the person or people to whom they are attached.

Serious case review – a review carried out when a child has died or has been seriously injured as a result of neglect.

Signposting – giving guidance about how to access additional services or information.

Small-world play – a type of imaginative play that involves children using toys to re-create scenarios on a small scale, e.g. a farm, a railway track.

Social constructivist – a model that explains children's cognitive development by suggesting that their logic and reasoning is developed through experiences, but also by interactions with, and questions from, adults and older children.

Social interactionist theory – a theory of learning that states children learn behaviours/actions as a result of gaining information and feedback during interaction with adults and other children.

Sociogram – a recording method whereby children indicate their friendship preferences.

Specific attachments – when babies and children show a particular preference for a single person, or a few people.

Spurt – a short period of intense growth.

Statute laws – written laws which are usually enacted as legislation.

Statutory – required by law (statute).

Statutory guidance – advice that settings or individuals are legally obliged to follow or pay regard to.

Stratum – the level or class to which people are assigned according to their social status, education or income.

Summative assessment – assessment of what a child knows and can do at the end of a period of learning, or 'assessment of learning'.

Sustained shared thinking – opportunities for children to interact with adults in ways that will extend their thinking and develop their thoughts about a topic or concept.

Synapse – the gap between two neurons; electrical impulses pass across this gap from the dendrite of one neuron to the axon terminal of the other neuron.

Taboo – a custom that prevents discussion of a particular practice or association with a person, place or thing.

Talented – demonstrating higher than average skills in a practical area, such as creative, musical or sporting achievements.

Theory of mind – children recognising their own conscious mind and understanding that other people will have different thoughts to them.

Topical corticosteroids – prescribed creams that are used in the treatment of eczema.

Transitions – changes in children's lives, especially in relation to adults who may be looking after them.

Triangulation – a process whereby a researcher uses at least three different sources of information in order to verify results.

Tripod grip – a way of holding a pencil or pen. The pencil is gripped between the thumb and first (index) finger, and rests against the side of the middle finger.

Undernourished – having insufficient food/nutrients.

Vaccine – a very weak dose of an infectious organism that is injected into someone in order to prevent a disease.

Values – principles or personal rules or standards that allow people to make decisions and choose between alternatives; what a person considers to be important in life.

Variable – an element, feature or factor in an experiment or research project.

Variables – factors that may be involved in development.

Vigilance – keeping a careful watch on children and being alert to signs that show they may be at risk of harm or abuse.

Virtuous errors – mistakes in children's expressive language that are logical.

Visual perceptual skills – the ability to understand and interpret what you see, for instance, being able to recognise an object when seen from different angles.

Vocalisations – sounds that are made by babies either for communication or as a way of exploring. Sounds may include words.

Welfare – holistic needs, including health and well-being.

Whistleblowing – raising concerns about the actions of an individual, group or organisation.

Zone of proximal development – the gap between what a child is currently able to do and what they may be able to achieve if an adult provides some support.

Index